Scott Foresman SCIENCE

Series Authors

Dr. Timothy Cooney
Professor of Earth Science and Science Education
Earth Science Department
University of Northern Iowa
Cedar Falls, Iowa

Michael Anthony DiSpezio
Science Education Specialist
Cape Cod Children's Museum
Falmouth, Massachusetts

Barbara K. Foots
Science Education Consultant
Houston, Texas

Dr. Angie L. Matamoros
Science Curriculum Specialist
Broward County Schools
Ft. Lauderdale, Florida

Kate Boehm Nyquist
Science Writer and Curriculum Specialist
Mount Pleasant, South Carolina

Dr. Karen L. Ostlund
Professor
Science Education Center
The University of Texas at Austin
Austin, Texas

Contributing Authors

Dr. Anna Uhl Chamot
Associate Professor and ESL Faculty Advisor
Department of Teacher Preparation and Special Education
Graduate School of Education and Human Development
The George Washington University
Washington, D.C.

Dr. Jim Cummins
Professor
Modern Language Centre and Curriculum Department
Ontario Institute for Studies in Education
Toronto, Canada

Gale Philips Kahn
Lecturer, Science and Math Education
Elementary Education Department
California State University, Fullerton
Fullerton, California

Vincent Sipkovich
Teacher
Irvine Unified School District
Irvine, California

Steve Weinberg
Science Consultant
Connecticut State Department of Education
Hartford, Connecticut

Scott Foresman

Editorial Offices: Glenview, Illinois • Parsippany, New Jersey • New York, New York
Sales Offices: Parsippany, New Jersey • Duluth, Georgia • Glenview, Illinois
Carrollton, Texas • Ontario, California
www.sfscience.com

Content Consultants

Dr. J. Scott Cairns
National Institutes of Health
Bethesda, Maryland

Jackie Cleveland
Elementary Resource Specialist
Mesa Public School District
Mesa, Arizona

Robert L. Kolenda
Science Lead Teacher, K-12
Neshaminy School District
Langhorne, Pennsylvania

David P. Lopath
Teacher
The Consolidated School District of New Britain
New Britain, Connecticut

Sammantha Lane Magsino
Science Coordinator
Institute of Geophysics
University of Texas at Austin
Austin, Texas

Kathleen Middleton
Director, Health Education
ToucanEd
Soquel, California

Irwin Slesnick
Professor of Biology
Western Washington University
Bellingham, Washington

Dr. James C. Walters
Professor of Geology
University of Northern Iowa
Cedar Falls, Iowa

Multicultural Consultants

Dr. Shirley Gholston Key
Assistant Professor
University of Houston-Downtown
Houston, Texas

Damon L. Mitchell
Quality Auditor
Louisiana-Pacific Corporation
Conroe, Texas

Classroom Reviewers

Kathleen Avery
Teacher
Kellogg Science/Technology Magnet
Wichita, Kansas

Margaret S. Brown
Teacher
Cedar Grove Primary
Williamston, South Carolina

Deborah Browne
Teacher
Whitesville Elementary School
Moncks Corner, South Carolina

Wendy Capron
Teacher
Corlears School
New York, New York

Jiwon Choi
Teacher
Corlears School
New York, New York

John Cirrincione
Teacher
West Seneca Central Schools
West Seneca, New York

Jacqueline Colander
Teacher
Norfolk Public Schools
Norfolk, Virginia

Dr. Terry Contant
Teacher
Conroe Independent School District
The Woodlands, Texas

Susan Crowley-Walsh
Teacher
Meadowbrook Elementary School
Gladstone, Missouri

Charlene K. Dindo
Teacher
Fairhope K-1 Center/Pelican's Nest Science Lab
Fairhope, Alabama

Laurie Duffee
Teacher
Barnard Elementary
Tulsa, Oklahoma

Beth Anne Ebler
Teacher
Newark Public Schools
Newark, New Jersey

Karen P. Farrell
Teacher
Rondout Elementary School District 72
Lake Forest, Illinois

Anna M. Gaiter
Teacher
Los Angeles Unified School District Los Angeles Systemic Initiative
Los Angeles, California

Federica M. Gallegos
Teacher
Highland Park Elementary
Salt Lake School District
Salt Lake City, Utah

Janet E. Gray
Teacher
Anderson Elementary - Conroe ISD
Conroe, Texas

Karen Guinn
Teacher
Ehrhardt Elementary School - KISD
Spring, Texas

Denis John Hagerty
Teacher
Al Ittihad Private Schools
Dubai, United Arab Emirates

Judith Halpern
Teacher
Bannockburn School
Deerfield, Illinois

Debra D. Harper
Teacher
Community School District 9
Bronx, New York

Gretchen Harr
Teacher
Denver Public Schools - Doull School
Denver, Colorado

Bonnie L. Hawthorne
Teacher
Jim Darcy School
School District 1
Helena, Montana

Marselle Heywood-Julian
Teacher
Community School District 6
New York, New York

Scott Klene
Teacher
Bannockburn School 106
Bannockburn, Illinois

Thomas Kranz
Teacher
Livonia Primary School
Livonia, New York

Tom Leahy
Teacher
Coos Bay School District
Coos Bay, Oregon

Mary Littig
Teacher
Kellogg Science/Technology Magnet
Wichita, Kansas

Patricia Marin
Teacher
Corlears School
New York, New York

Susan Maki
Teacher
Cotton Creek CUSD 118
Island Lake, Illinois

Efraín Meléndez
Teacher
East LA Mathematics Science Center LAUSD
Los Angeles, California

Becky Mojalid
Teacher
Manarat Jeddah Girls' School
Jeddah, Saudi Arabia

Susan Nations
Teacher
Sulphur Springs Elementary
Tampa, Florida

Brooke Palmer
Teacher
Whitesville Elementary
Moncks Corner, South Carolina

Jayne Pedersen
Teacher
Laura B. Sprague School District 103
Lincolnshire, Illinois

Shirley Pfingston
Teacher
Orland School District 135
Orland Park, Illinois

Teresa Gayle Rountree
Teacher
Box Elder School District
Brigham City, Utah

Helen C. Smith
Teacher
Schultz Elementary
Klein Independent School District
Tomball, Texas

Denette Smith-Gibson
Teacher
Mitchell Intermediate, CISD
The Woodlands, Texas

Mary Jean Syrek
Teacher
Dr. Charles R. Drew Science Magnet
Buffalo, New York

Rosemary Troxel
Teacher
Libertyville School District 70
Libertyville, Illinois

Susan D. Vani
Teacher
Laura B. Sprague School
School District 103
Lincolnshire, Illinois

Debra Worman
Teacher
Bryant Elementary
Tulsa, Oklahoma

Dr. Gayla Wright
Teacher
Edmond Public School
Edmond, Oklahoma

ISBN: 0-328-03426-6

6 7 8 9 10 V063 06 05 04 03

Activity and Safety Consultants

Laura Adams
Teacher
Holley-Navarre Intermediate
Navarre, Florida

Dr. Charlie Ashman
Teacher
Carl Sandburg Middle School
Mundelein District #75
Mundelein, Illinois

Christopher Atlee
Teacher
Horace Mann Elementary
Wichita Public Schools
Wichita, Kansas

David Bachman
Consultant
Chicago, Illinois

Sherry Baldwin
Teacher
Shady Brook
Bedford ISD
Euless, Texas

Pam Bazis
Teacher
Richardson ISD
Classical Magnet School
Richardson, Texas

Angela Boese
Teacher
McCollom Elementary
Wichita Public Schools USD #259
Wichita, Kansas

Jan Buckelew
Teacher
Taylor Ranch Elementary
Venice, Florida

Shonie Castaneda
Teacher
Carman Elementary, PSJA
Pharr, Texas

Donna Coffey
Teacher
Melrose Elementary - Pinellas
St. Petersburg, Florida

Diamantina Contreras
Teacher
J.T. Brackenridge Elementary
San Antonio ISD
San Antonio, Texas

Susanna Curtis
Teacher
Lake Bluff Middle School
Lake Bluff, Illinois

Karen Farrell
Teacher
Rondout Elementary School, Dist. #72
Lake Forest, Illinois

Paul Gannon
Teacher
El Paso ISD
El Paso, Texas

Nancy Garman
Teacher
Jefferson Elementary School
Charleston, Illinois

Susan Graves
Teacher
Beech Elementary
Wichita Public Schools USD #259
Wichita, Kansas

Jo Anna Harrison
Teacher
Cornelius Elementary
Houston ISD
Houston, Texas

Monica Hartman
Teacher
Richard Elementary
Detroit Public Schools
Detroit, Michigan

Kelly Howard
Teacher
Sarasota, Florida

Kelly Kimborough
Teacher
Richardson ISD
Classical Magnet School
Richardson, Texas

Mary Leveron
Teacher
Velasco Elementary
Brazosport ISD
Freeport, Texas

Becky McClendon
Teacher
A.P. Beutel Elementary
Brazosport ISD
Freeport, Texas

Suzanne Milstead
Teacher
Liestman Elementary
Alief ISD
Houston, Texas

Debbie Oliver
Teacher
School Board of Broward County
Ft. Lauderdale, Florida

Sharon Pearthree
Teacher
School Board of Broward County
Ft. Lauderdale, Florida

Jayne Pedersen
Teacher
Laura B. Sprague School
District 103
Lincolnshire, Illinois

Sharon Pedroja
Teacher
Riverside Cultural Arts/History Magnet
Wichita Public Schools USD #259
Wichita, Kansas

Marcia Percell
Teacher
Pharr, San Juan, Alamo ISD
Pharr, Texas

Shirley Pfingston
Teacher
Orland School Dist #135
Orland Park, Illinois

Sharon S. Placko
Teacher
District 26, Mt. Prospect
Mt. Prospect, IL

Glenda Rall
Teacher
Seltzer Elementary
USD #259
Wichita, Kansas

Nelda Requenez
Teacher
Canterbury Elementary
Edinburg, Texas

Dr. Beth Rice
Teacher
Loxahatchee Groves Elementary School
Loxahatchee, Florida

Martha Salom Romero
Teacher
El Paso ISD
El Paso, Texas

Paula Sanders
Teacher
Welleby Elementary School
Sunrise, Florida

Lynn Setchell
Teacher
Sigsbee Elementary School
Key West, Florida

Rhonda Shook
Teacher
Mueller Elementary
Wichita Public Schools USD #259
Wichita, Kansas

Anna Marie Smith
Teacher
Orland School Dist. #135
Orland Park, Illinois

Nancy Ann Varneke
Teacher
Seltzer Elementary
Wichita Public Schools USD #259
Wichita, Kansas

Aimee Walsh
Teacher
Rolling Meadows, Illinois

Ilene Wagner
Teacher
O.A. Thorp Scholastic Acacemy
Chicago Public Schools
Chicago, Illinois

Brian Warren
Teacher
Riley Community Consolidated School District 18
Marengo, Illinois

Tammie White
Teacher
Holley-Navarre Intermediate School
Navarre, Florida

Dr. Mychael Willon
Principal
Horace Mann Elementary
Wichita Public Schools
Wichita, Kansas

Inclusion Consultants

Dr. Eric J. Pyle, Ph.D.
Assistant Professor, Science Education
Department of Educational Theory and Practice
West Virginia University
Morgantown, West Virginia

Dr. Gretchen Butera, Ph.D.
Associate Professor, Special Education
Department of Education Theory and Practice
West Virginia University
Morgantown, West Virginia

Bilingual Consultant

Irma Gomez-Torres
Dalindo Elementary
Austin ISD
Austin, Texas

Bilingual Reviewers

Mary E. Morales
E.A. Jones Elementary
Fort Bend ISD
Missouri City, Texas

Gabriela T. Nolasco
Pebble Hills Elementary
Ysleta ISD
El Paso, Texas

Maribel B. Tanguma
Reed and Mock Elementary
San Juan, Texas

Yesenia Garza
Reed and Mock Elementary
San Juan, Texas

Teri Gallegos
St. Andrew's School
Austin, Texas

Unit A

Life Science

Unit B
Physical Science

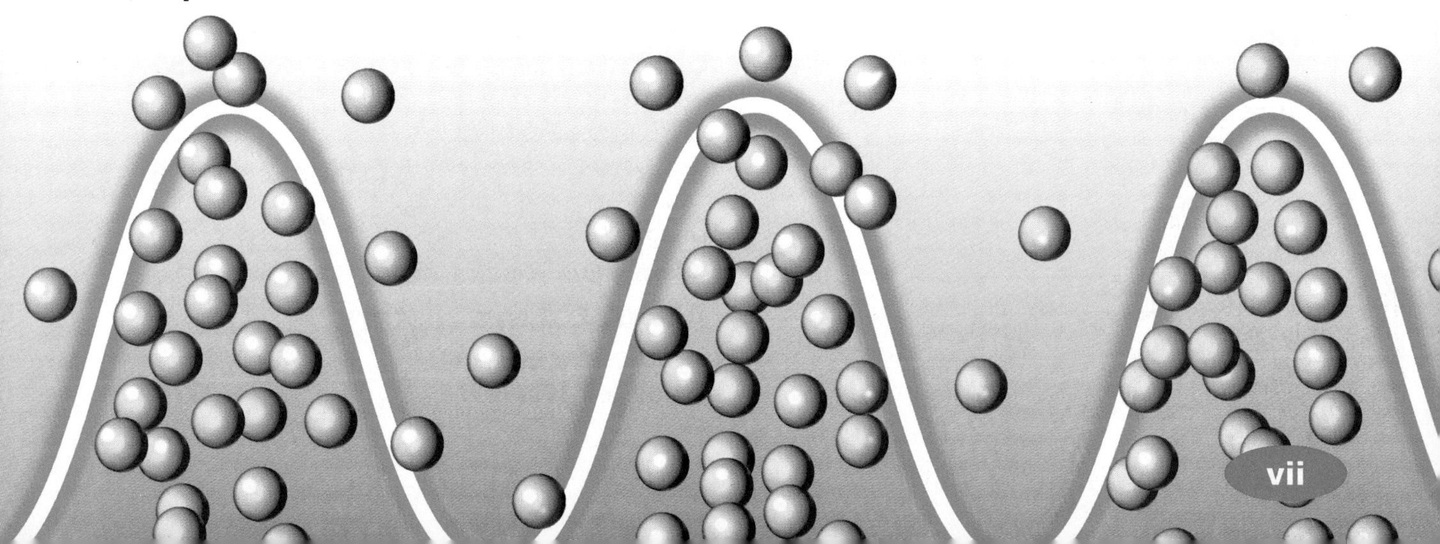

Unit C

Earth Science

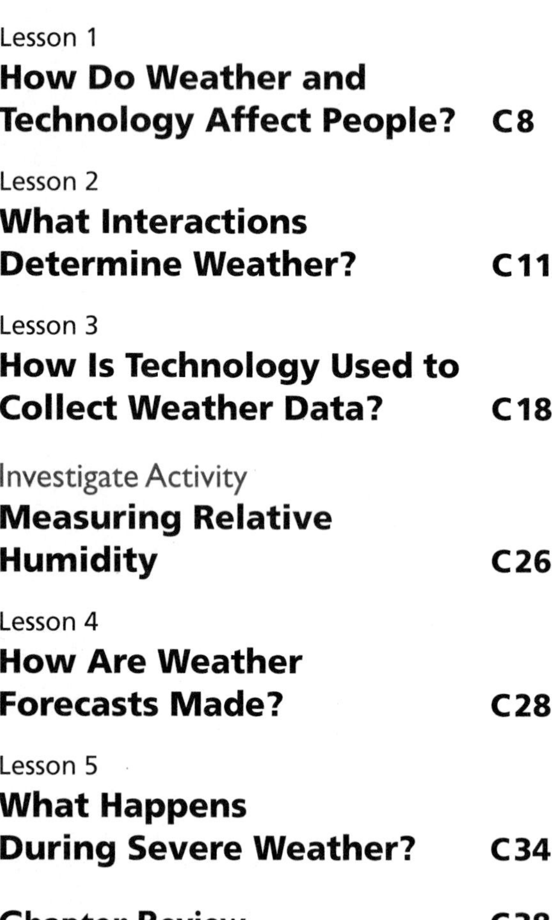

Unit D

Human Body

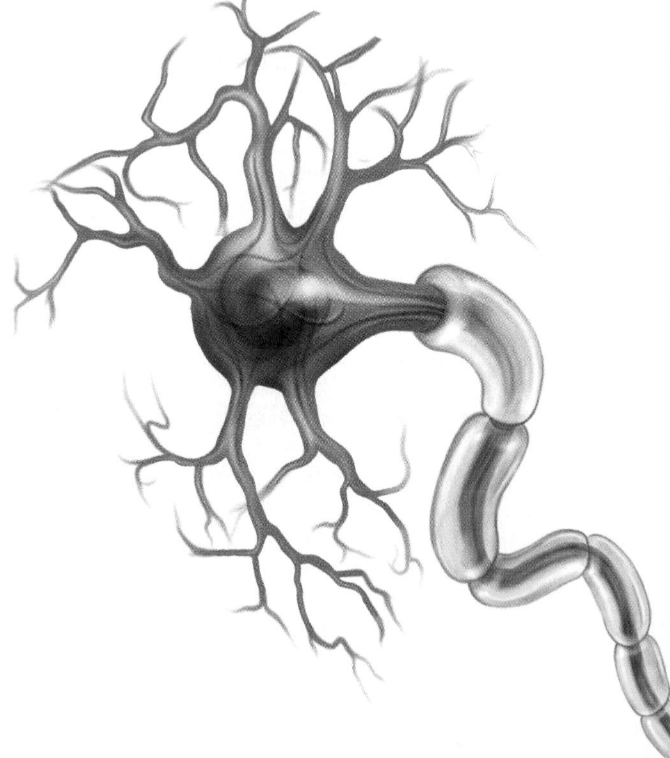

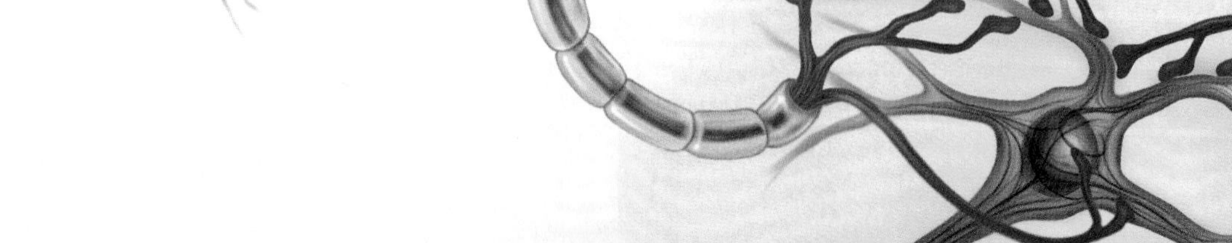

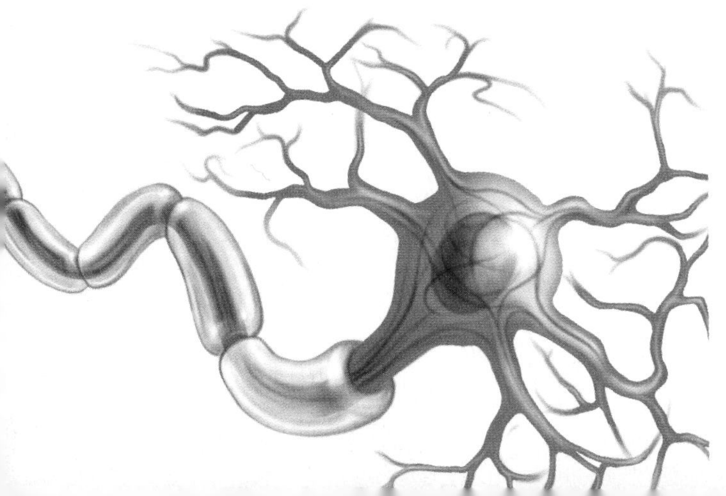

Your Science Handbook

Using Scientific Methods for Science Inquiry

Scientists try to solve many problems. Scientists study problems in different ways, but they all use scientific methods to guide their work. Scientific methods are organized ways of finding answers and solving problems. Scientific methods include the steps shown on these pages. The order of the steps or the number of steps used may change. You can use these steps to organize your own scientific inquiries.

State the Problem

The problem is the question you want to answer. Curiosity and inquiry have resulted in many scientific discoveries. State your problem in the form of a question.

Which sail design makes a boat move faster?

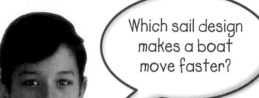

Formulate Your Hypothesis

Your hypothesis is a possible answer to your problem. Make sure your hypothesis can be tested. Your hypothesis should take the form of a statement.

◀ *A square sail will make a boat move faster.*

Identify and Control the Variables

For a fair test, you must select which variable to change and which variables to control. Choose one variable to change when you test your hypothesis. Control the other variables so they do not change.

▲ *Make one sail square and the other sail triangular. The other parts of the boat should be the same.*

Test Your Hypothesis

Do experiments to test your hypothesis. You may need to repeat experiments to make sure your results remain consistent. Sometimes you conduct a scientific survey to test a hypothesis.

◀ *Place the boat in the water. Use a straw to blow air onto the sail for 10 seconds. Measure how far the boat goes. Repeat with the other boat.*

Collect Your Data

As you test your hypothesis, you will collect data about the problem you want to solve. You may need to record measurements. You might make drawings or diagrams. Or you may write lists or descriptions. Collect as much data as you can while testing your hypothesis.

Distance boat moved	
Square sail	43 cm
Triangular sail	26 cm

Interpret Your Data

By organizing your data into charts, tables, diagrams, and graphs, you may see patterns in the data. Then you can decide what the information from your data means.

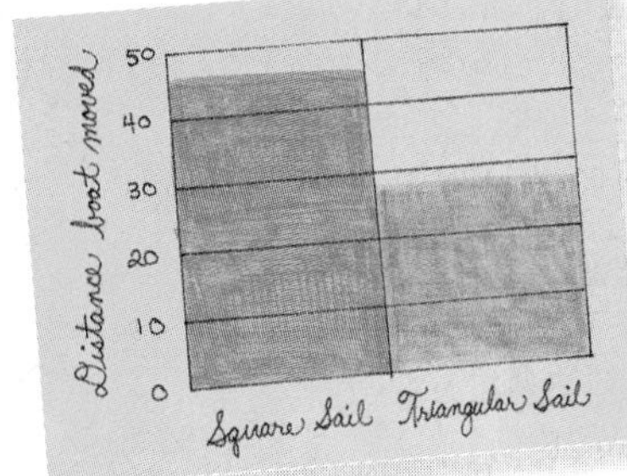

State Your Conclusion

Your conclusion is a decision you make based on evidence. Compare your results with your hypothesis. Based on whether or not your data supports your hypothesis, decide if your hypothesis is correct or incorrect. Then communicate your conclusion by stating or presenting your decision.

The square sail moves the boat faster.

Inquire Further

Use what you learn to solve other problems or to answer other questions that you might have. You may decide to repeat your experiment, or to change it based on what you learned.

◀ *Does the shape of the boat affect its speed?*

Using Process Skills for Science Inquiry

These 12 process skills are used by scientists when they do their research. You also use many of these skills every day. For example, when you think of a statement that you can test, you are using process skills. When you gather data to make a chart or graph, you are using process skills. As you do the activities in your book, you will use these same process skills.

I see..., I smell...,
I hear..., It feels like...,
I never taste
without permission!

Observing

Use one or more of your senses—seeing, hearing, smelling, touching, or tasting—to gather information about objects or events.

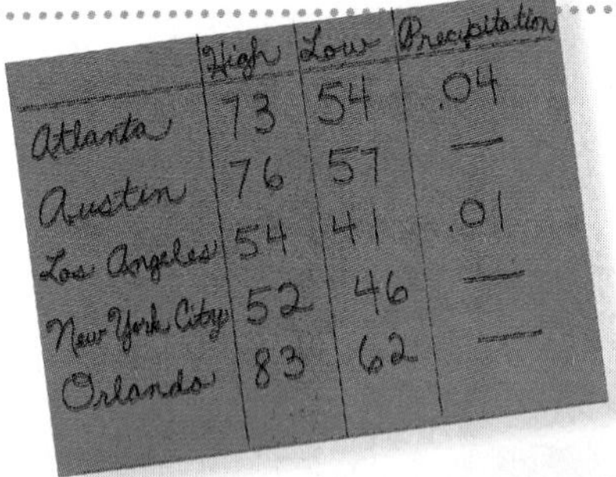

	High	Low	Precipitation
Atlanta	73	54	.04
Austin	76	57	—
Los Angeles	54	41	.01
New York City	52	46	—
Orlando	83	62	—

Communicating

Share information about what you learn using words, pictures, charts, graphs, and diagrams.

Classifying

Arrange or group objects according to their common properties.

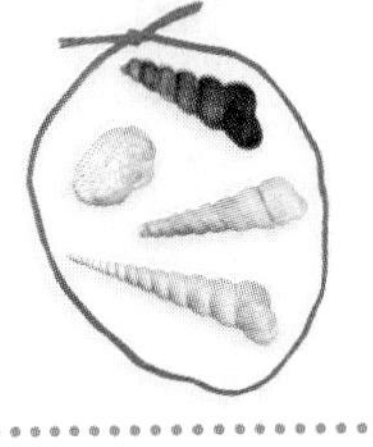

◀ *Shells with one color in Group 1.*

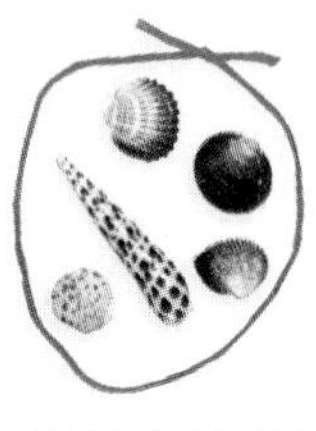

Shells with two or more colors in Group 2. ▶

Estimating and Measuring

Make an estimate about an object's properties, then measure and describe the object in units.

Inferring

Draw a conclusion or make a reasonable guess based on what you observe, or from your past experiences.

I think
what's in here
is shaped like . . .

Predicting

Form an idea about what will happen based on evidence.

◀ Predict what type of sail will work best.

An acid is a substance that changes blue litmus paper to... ▶

Making Operational Definitions

Define or describe an object or event based on your experiences with it.

Making and Using Models

Make real or mental representations to explain ideas, objects, or events.

◀ My model mouth is like a real mouth because...

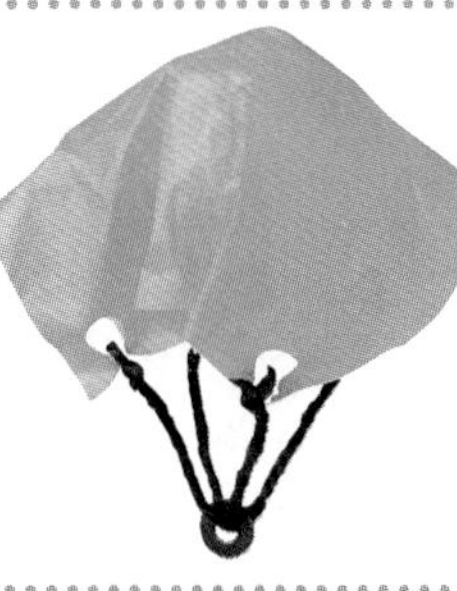

If I add another washer... ▶

Formulating Questions and Hypotheses

Think of a statement that you can test to solve a problem or to answer a question about how something works.

Collecting and Interpreting Data

Gather observations and measurements into graphs, tables, charts, or diagrams. Then use the information to solve problems or answer questions.

Adding salt to water raises the boiling point of the water.

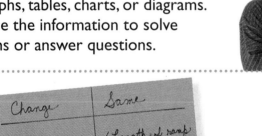

Change	Same
✓ Height of ramp	✓ Length of ramp
	✓ Ramp surface
	✓ car

Identifying and Controlling Variables

Change one factor that may affect the outcome of an event while holding other factors constant.

I'll write a clear procedure so that other students could repeat the experiment.

Experimenting

Design an investigation to test a hypothesis or to solve a problem. Then form a conclusion.

Science Inquiry

Throughout your science book, you will ask questions, do investigations, answer your questions, and tell others what you have learned. Use the descriptions below to help you during your scientific inquiries.

1. **Ask questions that can be answered by scientific investigations.**
   Direct your questions and inquiries toward objects and events that can be described, explained, or predicted by scientific investigations.

2. **Design and conduct a scientific investigation.**
   Investigations can include using scientific methods to carry out science inquiry. As you conduct your investigations, you will relate your ideas to current scientific knowledge, suggest alternate explanations, and evaluate explanations and procedures.

3. **Use appropriate tools, and methods to gather, analyze, and interpret data.**
   The tools and methods you use will depend on the questions you ask and the investigations you design. A computer can be a useful tool for collecting, summarizing, and displaying your data.

4. **Use data to develop descriptions, suggest explanations, make predictions, and construct models.**
   Base your explanations and descriptions on the information that you have gathered. In addition, understanding scientific subject matter will help you develop explanations, identify causes, and recognize relationships of events you observe with science content.

5. **Use logic to make relationships between data and explanations.**
   Review and summarize the data you have gathered in your investigation. Use logic to determine the cause and effect relationships in the events and variables you observe.

6. **Analyze alternative explanations and predictions.**
   Listen to, consider, and evaluate explanations offered by others. Asking questions and querying and evaluating explanations is part of scientific inquiry.

7. **Communicate procedures and explanations.**
   Share your investigations with others by describing your methods, observations, results, and explanations.

8. **Use mathematics to analyze data and construct explanations.**
   Use mathematics in your investigations to gather, organize, and collect data and to present explanations and results in a meaningful manner.

Unit A

Life Science

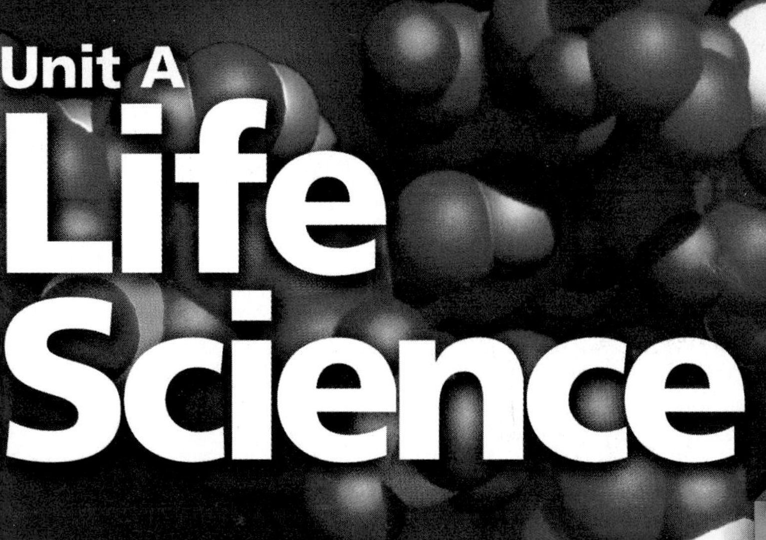

Your Science Handbook

Science and Technology In Your World!

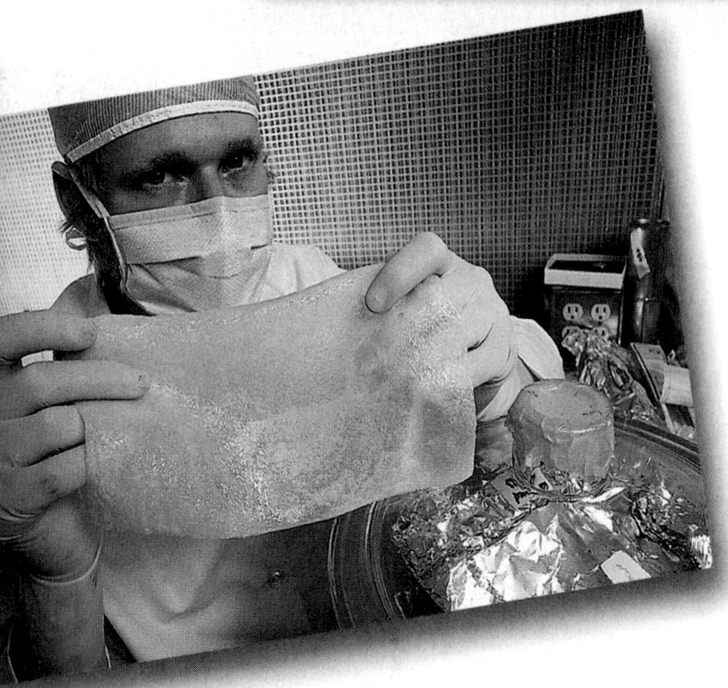

Artificial Skin Has Burn Injuries Covered

Scientists make artificial skin using molecules from body parts from cows. When the artificial skin is placed over the injured skin, natural skin cells grow back with little scarring. Learn about cells that make up living things in **Chapter 1 Structure and Function of Cells.**

Making Plants that Insects Hate

In the never-ending battle against insects and diseases that destroy corn, potatoes, apples, and many other food crops, scientists have a powerful weapon—genes. Changing a plant's genes can make it tasty to us, but untasty to bugs. Learn more about genes and traits in **Chapter 2 Reproduction and Heredity.**

Satellites Spot Fossils from Space

How can satellites "see" fossils from space? Devices that detect heat and moisture content point scientists to rocks where fossils are likely to be found. Learn more about fossils in **Chapter 3 Changing and Adapting.**

A Glimpse of Tomorrow

What will happen to plants as pollution increases? To find out, scientists pump carbon dioxide and other gases onto test fields. By mimicking air as it might be in the future, they hope to discover pollution's effect on plant life. Learn more about the environment in **Chapter 4 Ecosystems and Biomes.**

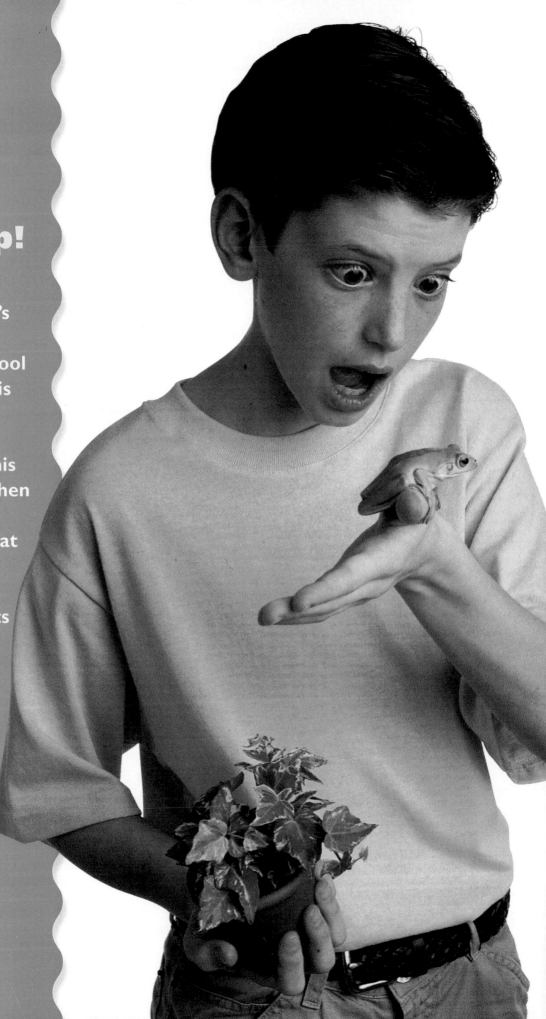

IT'S ALIVE! It's green, shiny, smooth, and cool to touch! Say, is it a plant—or an animal? **WHOOPS!** This one jumps! When you get right down to it, what **ARE** the differences between plants and animals?

Chapter 1

Structure and Function of Cells

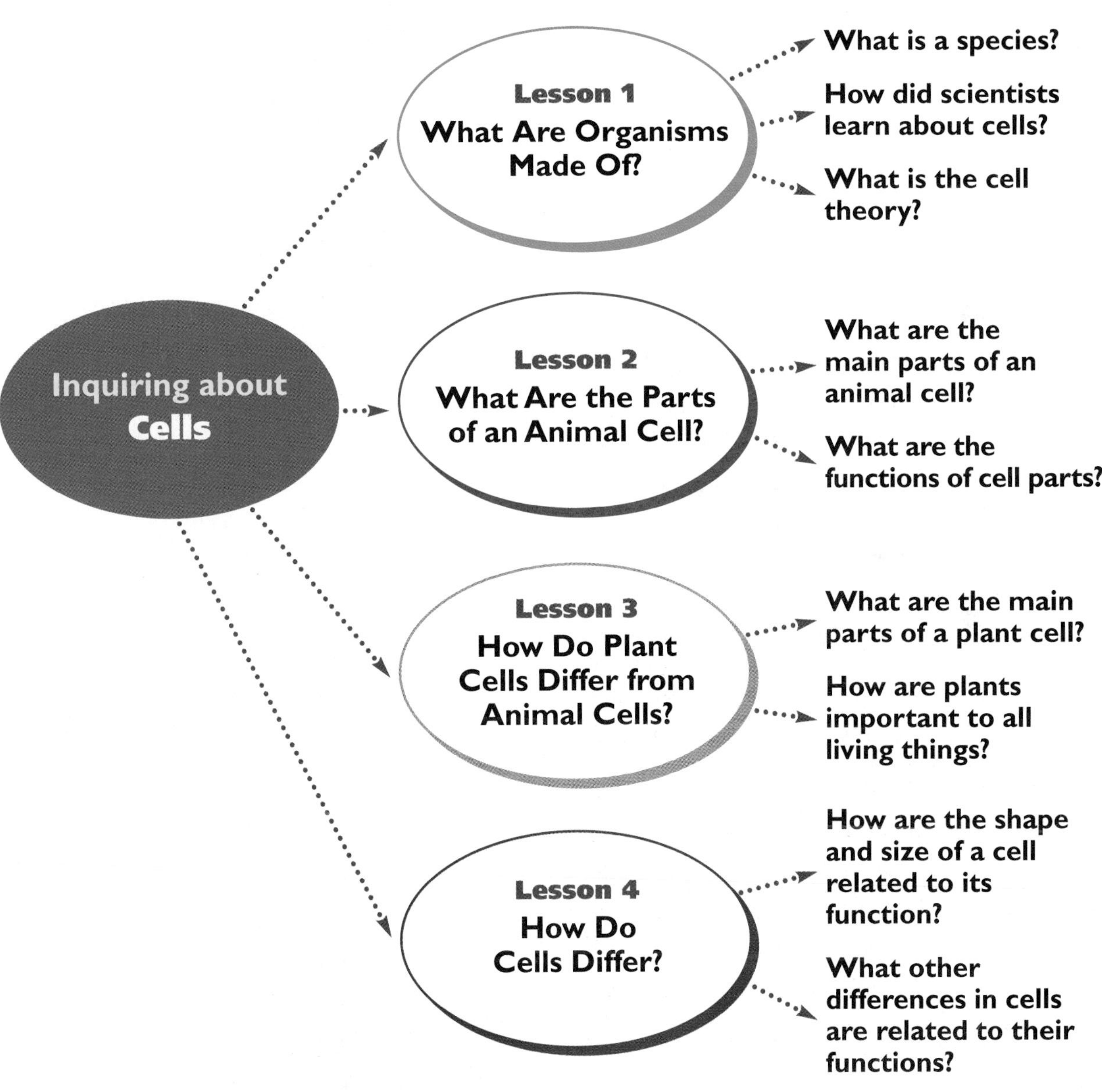

Inquiring about Cells
Lesson 1
What Are Organisms Made Of?
What is a species?
How did scientists learn about cells?
What is the cell theory?
Lesson 2
What Are the Parts of an Animal Cell?
What are the main parts of an animal cell?
What are the functions of cell parts?
Lesson 3
How Do Plant Cells Differ from Animal Cells?
What are the main parts of a plant cell?
How are plants important to all living things?
Lesson 4
How Do Cells Differ?
How are the shape and size of a cell related to its function?
What other differences in cells are related to their functions?

__Copy the chapter graphic organizer__ onto your own paper. This organizer shows you what the whole chapter is all about. As you read the lessons and do the activities, look for answers to the questions and write them on your organizer.

Explore Activity

Exploring Magnification

Process Skills

Process Skills

- predicting
- observing
- inferring
- communicating

Materials

- safety goggles
- wire
- sharpened pencil
- newspaper
- cup of water

Explore

1. Put on your safety goggles.
2. Straighten a 10 cm piece of thin wire. Make a loop in the end of the wire by winding it around the sharpened end of a pencil. Your loop should be 5 mm across.
3. Place the loop into a cup of water. Slowly pull the loop out of the water. There should be a water drop in the loop. If not, dip the loop into the water again.
4. What will happen if you view newspaper through the water-filled loop? Record your **prediction.** Explain a past experience that led you to make your prediction.
5. Test your prediction by holding the water drop over a section of newspaper. Move the loop toward and away from the newspaper until you can see the print clearly. Record what you **observe** through the loop.
6. Move the loop away from the newsprint and blow out the water drop. Place the empty loop over the same letters in the newsprint as in step 5. Record what you see through the loop.

Reflect

What can you **infer** from your prediction and observations? **Communicate** your ideas with others in the group. Make a list of the ways that magnification can help you study living things.

Inquire Further

What would the newsprint look like if you viewed it through another substance, such as oil? Develop a plan to answer this or other questions you may have.

Bar Graphs

The adult human body is made up of trillions of cells, such as blood cells, brain cells, and skin cells. Each type of cell has different characteristics and a different function.

You can use **bar graphs** to organize and compare data about cells or other topics.

Math Vocabulary

bar graph, a graph using horizontal or vertical bars to display numerical information

Example

This bar graph shows approximately how long different kinds of blood cells live. How much longer than a platelet does a red blood cell live?

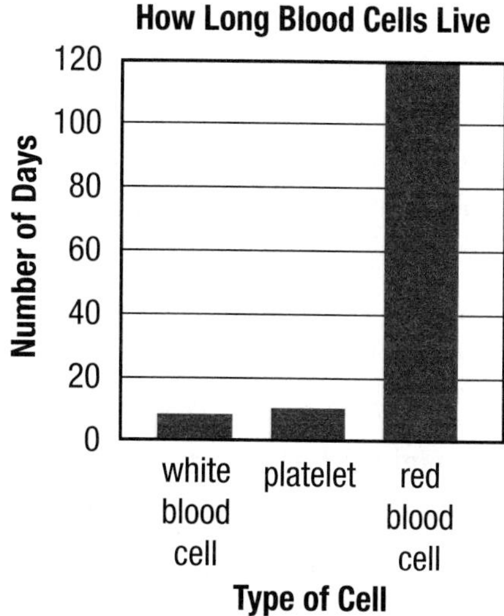

Look at the bar for the platelet. It represents 10 days. The red blood cell bar represents 120 days. So, since 120 - 10 = 110, red blood cells live 110 days longer than platelets.

Did you know?

The color of blood varies among animals. All vertebrates have red blood. Segmented worms have blood that is green or red. Some crustaceans, which includes shrimp and lobsters, have blue blood!

Talk About It!

How does a bar graph show the value of a data item?

You will learn:
- what a species is.
- how scientists learned about cells.
- what the cell theory is.

Glossary

Glossary

species (spē′shēz), a group of organisms that have the same characteristics and are able to produce offspring that can reproduce

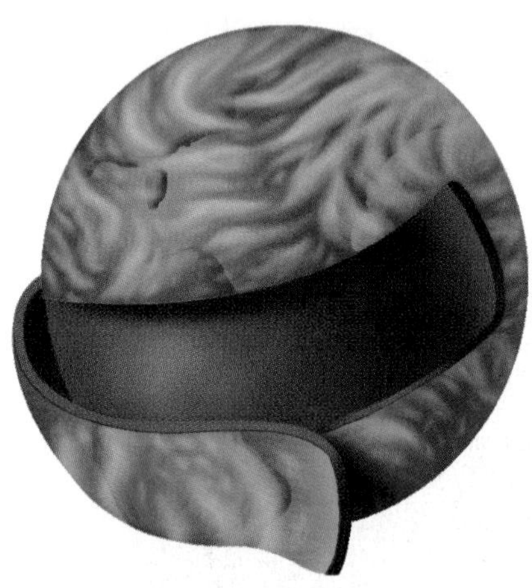

▲ *Life exists in a small area above and below the surface of the earth. Some microscopic organisms live in the almost freezing cold of the upper atmosphere. Some of the many different kinds of organisms can be seen on the next page.*

Lesson 1

What Are Organisms Made Of?

It's big and green—and it's moving! Should you be afraid of this living creature? Not unless you have a fear of pine trees blowing in the wind! Organisms come in many sizes, shapes, and colors. How else do living creatures differ? How are they the same?

Earth's Species

All the organisms you see pictured on the next page live on Earth. Some live on land or underground. Others live in the air. Still others live in water. Organisms can live only where they can get the things they need.

Most life is found only in a small layer of the earth, from just below the surface to the lower part of the atmosphere. Imagine that you could shrink the earth so that it was the size of an apple. As you can see at the left, the layer where living things are found would be thin like the peel of that apple. Yet within that thin layer, numerous kinds of life exist. In fact, more than 30 million different kinds of living things live on Earth. Each different kind of organism is a **species**. What's so special about species? Just how do scientists tell them apart?

Individuals in a species share certain characteristics. For example, all humans belong to a single species. What characteristics do they share?

Only members of the same species can mate and produce offspring that, in turn, can mate and produce offspring. That is, monarch butterflies produce monarch butterflies that can produce more monarch butterflies.

Not only is there an amazing number of species on Earth, but there is an amazing variety among them. Yet no matter how different organisms are from one another, they all have one thing in common. All organisms are made of cells.

Variations Among Living Things

Just one look at the species pictured here shows you how they can differ in size and complexity.

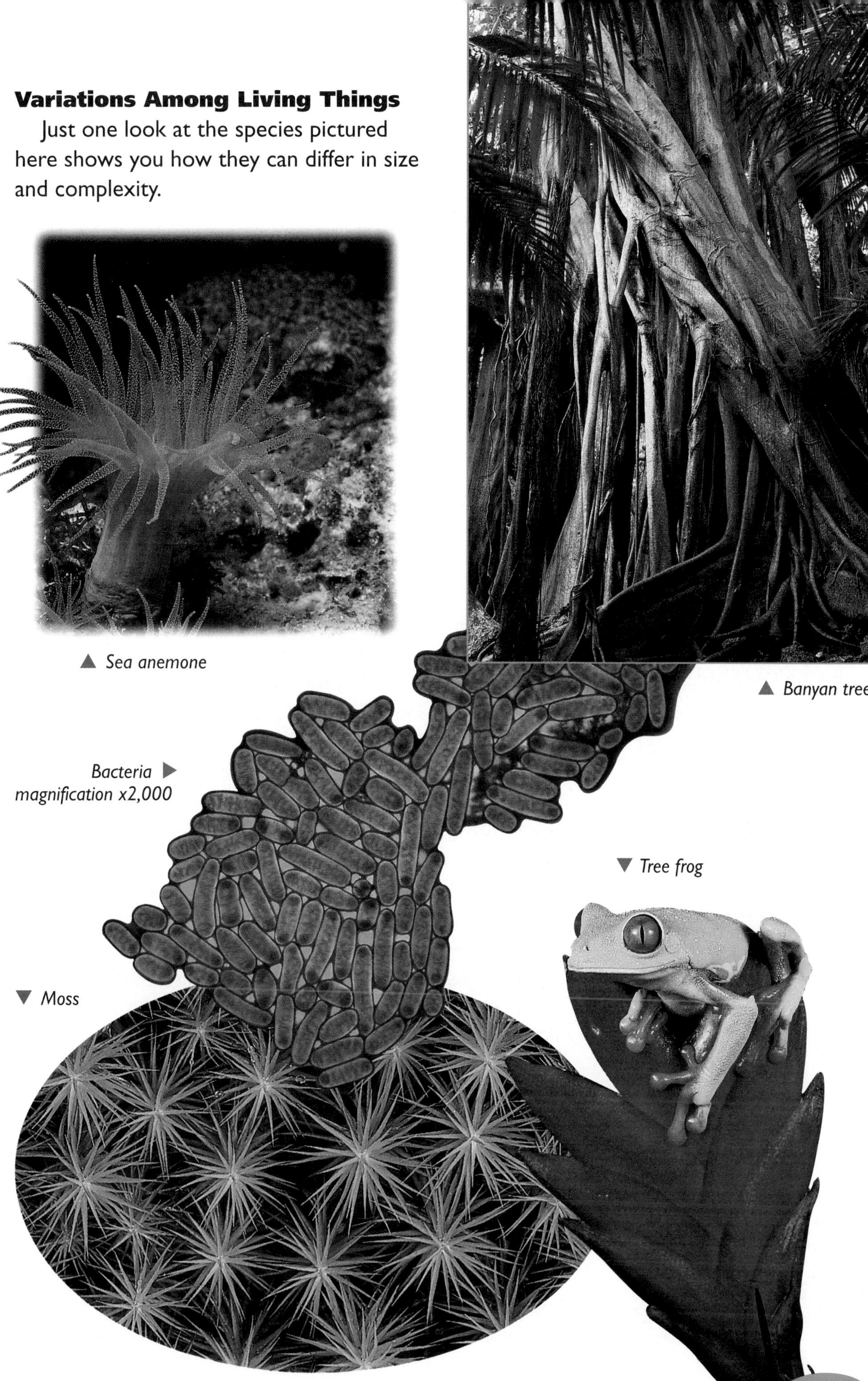

▲ *Sea anemone*

▲ *Banyan tree*

Bacteria ▶
magnification x2,000

▼ *Tree frog*

▼ *Moss*

Glossary

Glossary

compound microscope (kom′pound mī′krə skōp), microscope having more than one lens

Robert Hooke's microscope allowed him to see the tiny compartments, or cells, in a piece of cork. He made detailed sketches, such as this one, to record what he saw. ▼

Discovery of Cells

If you hold your arm out and look at the palm and fingers of your hand, you can see patterns of lines. Move your hand closer, and you can see even more details. However, if you bring your hand too close to your face, your eyes can no longer focus. Your hand appears blurred. The cells that make up the skin on your hand are simply too small for your eyes to see.

For thousands of years, scientists wondered what living things were made of. However, like you trying to see your hand, they were limited by their eyes and could not see tiny details.

If you have ever used a hand lens, you know that the lens magnifies, or makes larger, what you see. People have known about lenses for almost two thousand years. About A.D. 50, they were using lenses—as toys! Around 1300, lenses were made to correct vision problems—the first eyeglasses. By the mid-1400s, scientists were using lenses to study extremely small things. However, a single lens just couldn't magnify a very tiny object enough for scientists to learn much.

Finally, around 1590, a Dutch eyeglass maker, Hans Janssen, and his son, Zacharias, put two lenses together at the opposite ends of a tube. They had invented the first **compound microscope**.

In the mid-1600s, the English scientist Robert Hooke used the compound microscope you see in the picture to peer at a thin slice of cork. He saw "a great many little boxes" separated by walls. Hooke called these little boxes "cells." Today we still use the term *cells* to refer to the microscopic building blocks of all living things.

Above the microscope, you can see what Hooke saw when he looked under the microscope. The cork that he looked at did not contain living cells. Rather, Hooke saw the cell walls that had surrounded cork cells when they were living. The other important materials that were the basis of life were missing.

Living organisms were studied by Dutch lens grinder, Anton van Leeuwenhoek. Around 1673, he used a simple microscope to look at a drop of water. He called the tiny organisms he observed "wee beasties." Leeuwenhoek also used a microscope to study teeth scrapings and blood cells.

Although these early scientists saw things that no one had ever seen before, their microscopes actually did not provide very good images. Their lenses were made of poor-quality glass. Today's microscopes are very different from those used by Hooke and Leeuwenhoek. For example, Hooke's microscope was able to magnify objects only 30 times. Today's best compound microscopes can magnify objects more than 1,500 times. You can see the parts of a compound microscope below.

Typical Compound Microscope

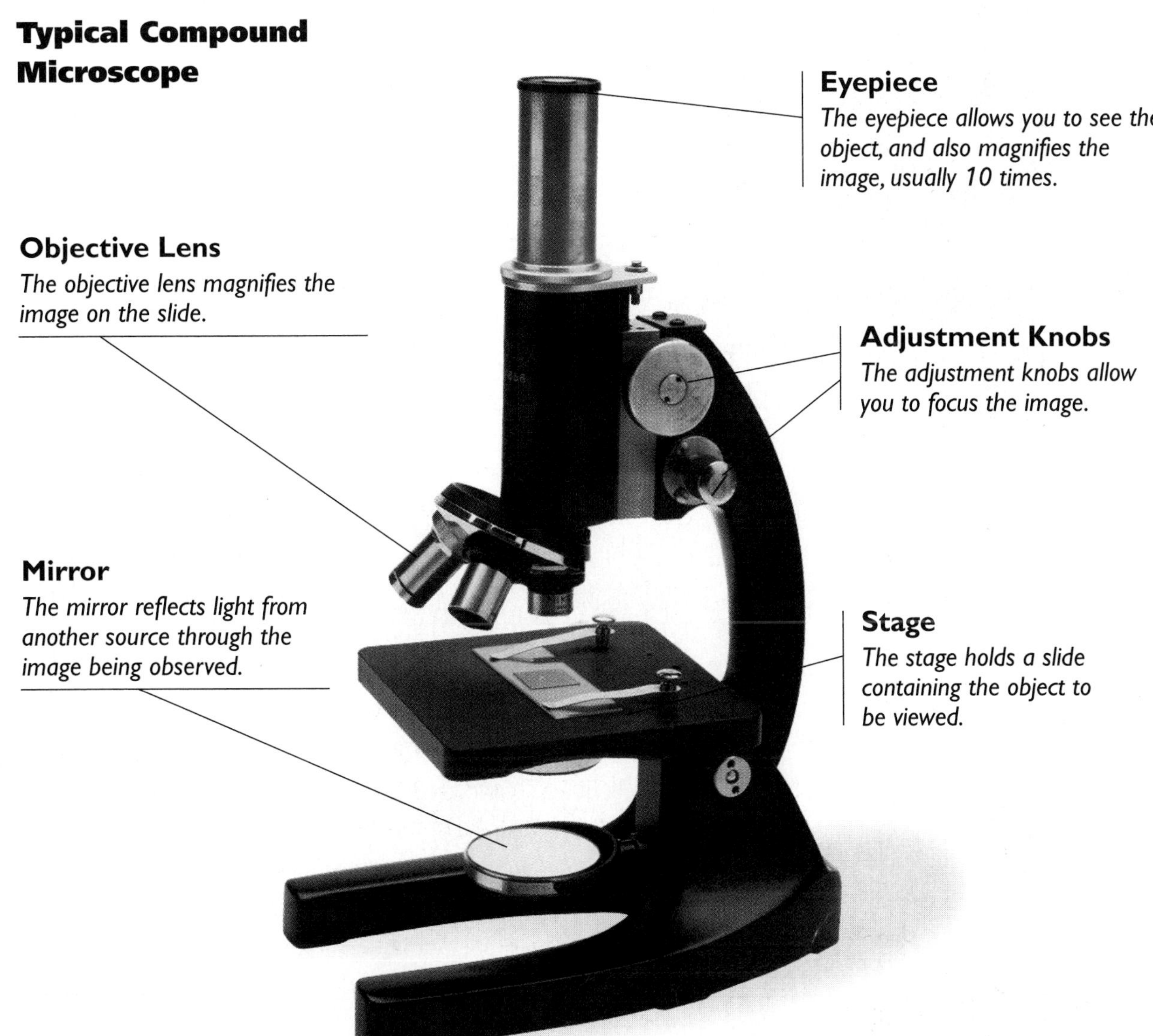
Eyepiece
The eyepiece allows you to see the object, and also magnifies the image, usually 10 times.
Objective Lens
The objective lens magnifies the image on the slide.
Adjustment Knobs
The adjustment knobs allow you to focus the image.
Mirror
The mirror reflects light from another source through the image being observed.
Stage
The stage holds a slide containing the object to be viewed.

A compound microscope is a light microscope. You place the object to be viewed on a glass slide and position the slide on the microscope stage over a small opening. This stage opening allows light from a mirror or lamp to shine through the object to be viewed. The light then passes through magnifying lenses.

Light microscopes can magnify objects many times their actual size. However, at times this magnification is not enough. Very tiny structures that are close together appear blurred.

Physical Science

Today, scientists can use electron microscopes, similar to the one below, to study "wee beasties" and to look directly into cells. Instead of light, an electron microscope uses beams of atomic particles called electrons to produce an image. You can then see the magnified image on a screen or photographic plate.

Electron microscopes produce sharper pictures than do light microscopes. They can clearly magnify objects up to one million times. Look how different feathers appear when they are viewed with a light microscope and an electron microscope.

Light Microscope

If you looked at a feather under a compound microscope, you might see something like this. ▼

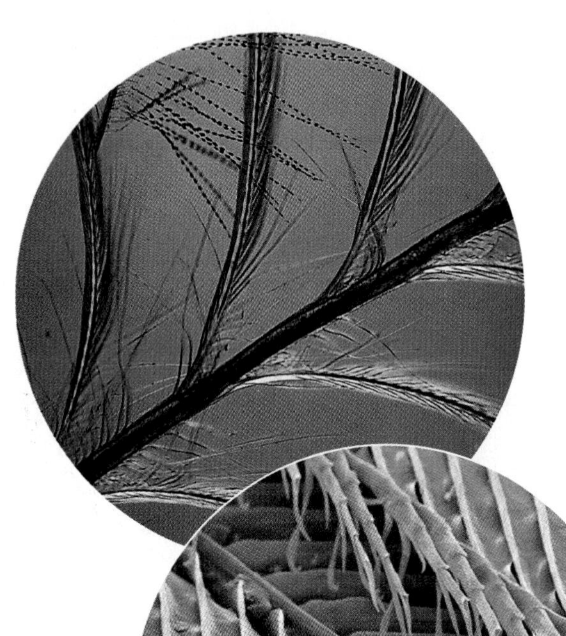

Electron Microscope

▲ *Magnified 270 times under an electron microscope, a feather appears like this.*

Electron microscopes use electrons to make things look up to one million times bigger. They allow scientists to study cells in great detail. ▶

Cell Theory

History of Science Although Robert Hooke discovered cells in the mid-1600s, it took nearly 200 years for scientists to understand just what they were. Even after Hooke's discovery, many scientists thought that life could develop from nonliving matter. For example, around 1600, a Belgian doctor placed wheat grains in a sweaty shirt. He placed the shirt on the floor in the corner of a room. When he returned several weeks later, he found mice. The doctor concluded that human sweat changed wheat grains to mice. Later scientists conducted experiments that proved this idea wrong.

As the years went by, scientists made more and more observations of microscopic organisms. They began to realize that cells are the building blocks of all living things. In the 1800s, three German biologists—Theodor Schwann, Matthias Schleiden, and Rudolph Virchow—developed the **cell theory**. This theory states the following:

- The cell is the basic unit of all living organisms.
- Only living cells can produce new living cells.

The cell theory points out the basic similarity among very different organisms—they are all made of cells. You can see by the pictures on this page that some organisms, such as the meerkat, are made of many cells, while others, like the green alga, are made of only one.

Glossary

cell theory
(sel thē′ər ē), theory stating that the cell is the basic unit of all living organisms, and only living cells can produce new living cells

Some organisms, such as this green alga, are made of a single cell. Green algae produce their own food. ▼

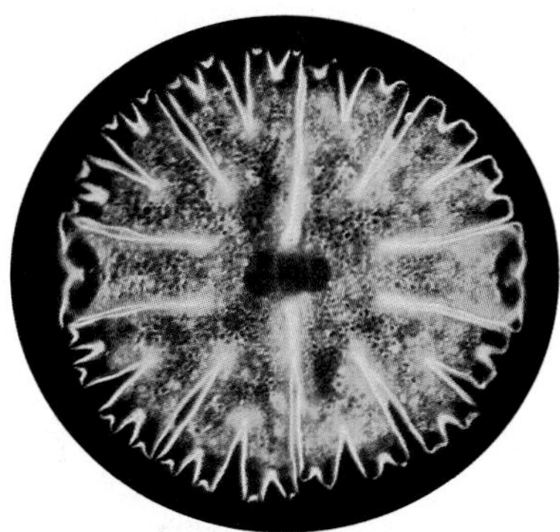

magnification x170

Meerkats are many-celled animals that live in parts of Africa. ▶

Lesson 1 Review

1. What is a species?
2. How did scientists learn about cells?
3. What is the cell theory?
4. **Bar Graphs**
   Species vary in life span. Make a bar graph, in years, of the maximum life spans of these animals: goldfish, 41; giant panda, 26; platypus, 17; cat, 34.

Investigate Activity

Investigating Cells

Process Skills

Process Skills

- observing
- communicating
- classifying

Materials

- microscope
- prepared slide of animal cells
- scissors
- elodea plant
- forceps
- microscope slide with coverslip
- dropper
- cup of water

Getting Ready

In this activity you'll find out how plant and animal cells are alike and how they are different.

Follow This Procedure

1. Make a chart like the one shown. Use your chart to record your observations.

Animal Cells	Elodea

2. Place a microscope on the table in front of you (Photo A). Study each part of the microscope to find out what it does. Find the light source, the eyepiece, and the objective lens.

3. Locate the adjustment knob that moves the stage closer or farther from the objective lens. Turn the adjustment knob so that the lens is almost touching the stage.

4. Place a prepared microscope slide of animal cells on the stage of the microscope. Look through the eyepiece. Use the adjustment knob to move the lens away from the microscope slide until you can clearly see the animal cells. Fine-tune your adjustment.

5. **Observe** the animal cells. Find the cytoplasm, cell membrane, and nucleus. Make a drawing to **communicate** what you see.

Self-Monitoring

Have I drawn all the cell parts that I can see?

Photo A

Photo B

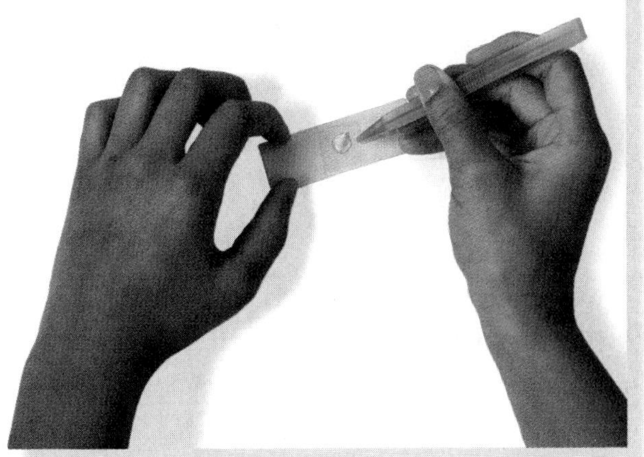

Photo C

6 Use the scissors to remove a leaf tip from an elodea plant (Photo B).

7 Use forceps to place the leaf tip on a microscope slide. Use a dropper to add a drop of water to the slide. Then use the forceps to carefully cover the leaf with a coverslip (Photo C).

8 Place the slide on the microscope stage. Observe the leaf through the microscope. Draw what you see.

Interpret Your Results

1. Look at your drawings of the plant and animal cells. Explain how the plant and animal cells that you observed are alike and different.

2. Tell what characteristics you could use to **classify** a cell as either a plant or an animal cell.

Inquire Further

Do all plant cells have the same parts? Develop a plan to answer this or other questions you may have.

Self-Assessment

- I followed instructions to **observe** plant and animal cells.
- I identified the parts of plant and animal cells.
- I **communicated** by drawing my observations.
- I compared and contrasted plant and animal cells.
- I used cell characteristics as a way to **classify** plant and animal cells.

You will learn:

- what the main parts of an animal cell are.
- what the functions are of some cell parts.

Lesson 2

What Are the Parts of an Animal Cell?

Walls, a ceiling, and a floor surround your school. What inside parts make up your school? You might answer, "The classrooms, a library, and a gym." Would the space be a school without these parts?

Glossary

Glossary

nucleus (nü′klē əs), part of the cell that controls activities of other cell parts

chromosome (kro′mə sōm), stringlike structure in a cell nucleus that carries information controlling all the cell's activities

Animal Cells

Just as your school wouldn't be a school without the parts inside it, neither would a cell. All cells have important parts that have certain functions.

A cell is like a school with many rooms. A school usually has offices, a gym, a cafeteria, a boiler room, a library, and classrooms. Having separate rooms allows different activities to be carried out in particular places.

Most cells have the same basic structure. The photo to the left shows part of an animal cell as it might be seen under an electron microscope. The first thing you probably notice is the **nucleus**. The nucleus is the control center of the cell. It is like the main office in a school.

In this electron microscopic image of a liver cell, you can easily see the nucleus. ▼

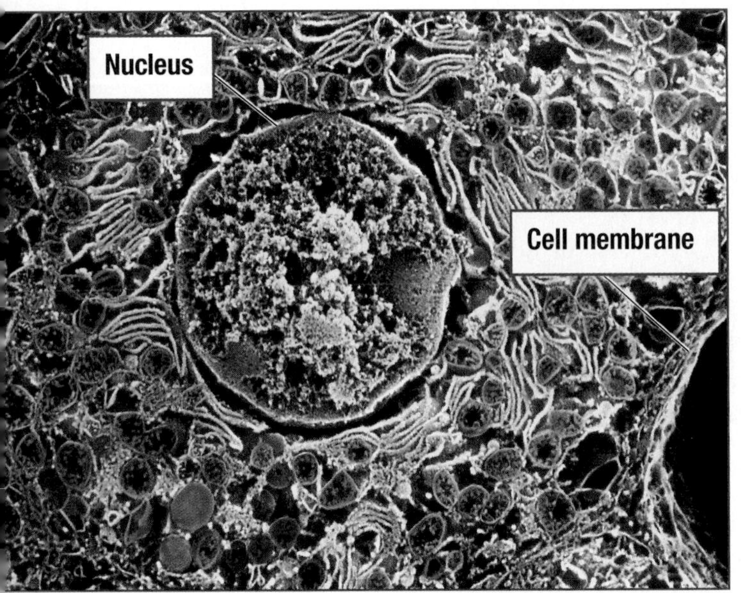

Inside the nucleus is a stringlike structure called a **chromosome**. Chromosomes store directions that the cell uses to carry on activities. They control processes such as how fast a cell grows or when it reproduces.

Not all organisms have the same number of chromosomes in their cells. You—and all other normal humans—have 46 chromosomes in each body cell. A housefly has 12 chromosomes in each of its body cells, a cat has 38, a dog has 78, and a crayfish has 200.

Just as walls, ceilings, and floors hold a school building together, a **cell membrane** holds the contents of a cell together. It gives support and shape to the cell. This thin, flexible covering helps the cell by allowing only certain substances to enter or leave it.

Think of people who stand by the doors of a school to control who enters or leaves the building. Like the monitors, the cell membrane controls what comes into and goes out of the cell. You can see in the picture below that the cell membrane allows materials such as oxygen to enter the cell. These substances are needed by the cell for energy and growth. The cell membrane also allows wastes such as carbon dioxide to leave the cell. The membrane also protects the cell by keeping substances that could harm the cell outside.

Cytoplasm fills the space inside the cell between the cell membrane and the nucleus. **Cytoplasm** is a clear, jellylike material similar to the white of a raw egg. It is made mostly of water. Cells depend on water for their survival. Without water, cells could not carry out all their necessary activities. Your body cells are more than two-thirds water. That's why you could not survive more than about four days without water.

Glossary

cell membrane
(sel mem′brān), thin outer covering that holds a cell together

cytoplasm
(sī′tə plaz′əm), clear, jellylike material that fills the space between the cell membrane and the nucleus

Glossary

Oxygen and carbon dioxide can move through the cell membrane. ▼

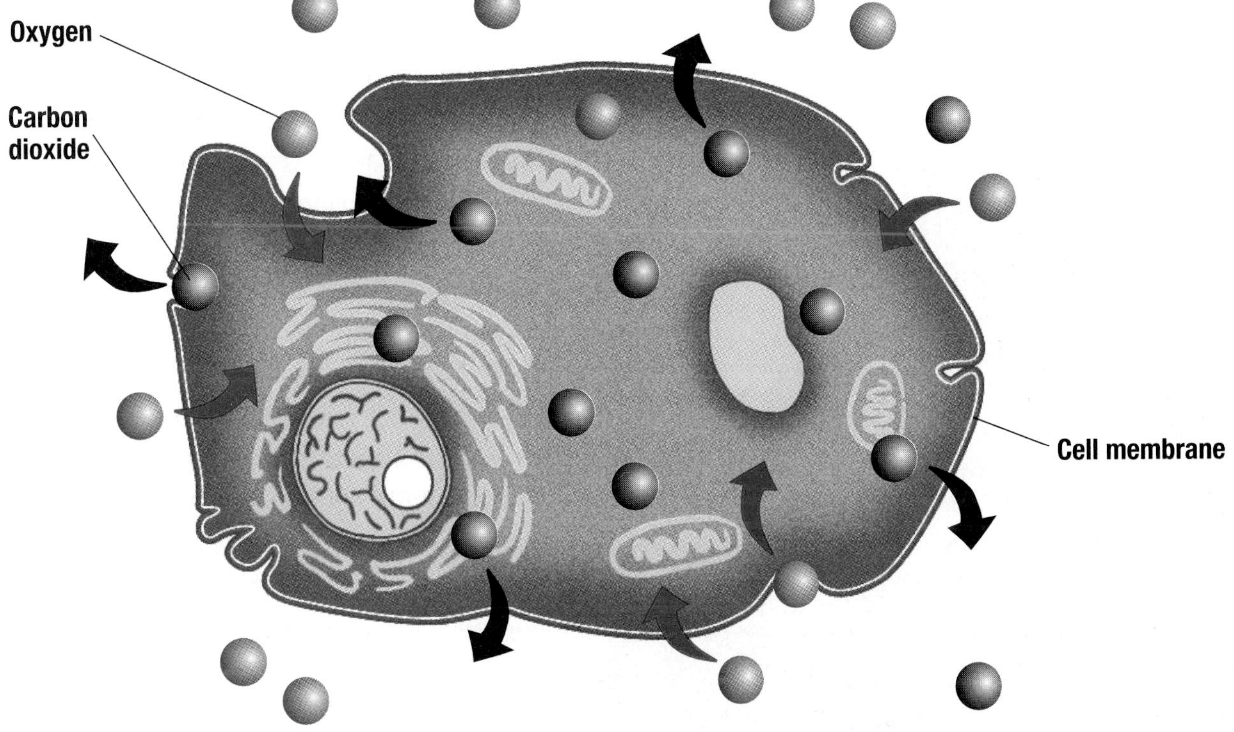

Glossary

Glossary

organelle (ôr′gə nel′), tiny structure in the cytoplasm of a cell that performs a special job

mitochondria (mī′tə kon′drē ə), organelles where food and oxygen react to release energy

vacuole (vak′yü ōl), saclike organelle used for storing materials

endoplasmic reticulum (en′dō plaz′mik ri tik′yə ləm), organelle that transports materials inside the cell

ribosome (rī′bə sōm), organelle that puts together proteins for the cell

Functions of Cell Parts

Inside the cytoplasm of all cells, including the fat cells below, are tiny parts that have special jobs. Each of these structures is an **organelle.** Just as each kind of room in a school has a different function, so does each organelle in a cell. You can see some of these organelles in the diagram on the next page.

Think about what happens in a school boiler room. Fuel is burned to make heat energy. Likewise, scattered throughout a cell's cytoplasm are **mitochondria.** Food and oxygen react in these bean-shaped organelles to release energy. This energy is needed to run the cells. Mitochondria are the "powerhouses" of cells. A cell can have as few as one mitochondrion or as many as 10,000 mitochondria or more. The number depends on the cell's level of activity. The more active a cell is, the more energy it needs and the more mitochondria it has.

Where does a school store the supplies it needs? Many schools store these materials in closets and storage rooms. Where do they store wastepaper and other trash until it can be disposed of? A school stores them in wastebaskets and dumpsters, of course.

Cells also need storage spaces. A **vacuole** is an organelle that stores nutrients and water, as well as waste products. Materials pass into and out of vacuoles through a thin membrane. Some vacuoles can expand and contract as needed. Animal cells contain many small vacuoles.

You and your fellow students need to be able to move from one classroom to another in a school. Books and supplies also need to be moved around. In a school, the hallways serve this purpose.

Cells also need to move materials from one part to another. The organelle that handles this function looks like a series of channels. It is called the **endoplasmic reticulum,** or ER for short. Some parts of the endoplasmic reticulum are covered by tiny structures called **ribosomes.** Ribosomes put together proteins for the cell.

These ball-shaped cells store fats. Fats not used in the body are carried to these cells through tiny blood vessels, which you can see in blue. ▼

magnification x1038

Look at the typical animal cell below. Nearly all animal cells have a cell membrane, cytoplasm, and a nucleus with chromosomes, but the number of chromosomes in the nucleus varies from species to species. (That's what helps make each species unique.) Also, the number of each kind of organelle varies among the cells of different kinds of organisms. The number also varies among different cells in the same organism.

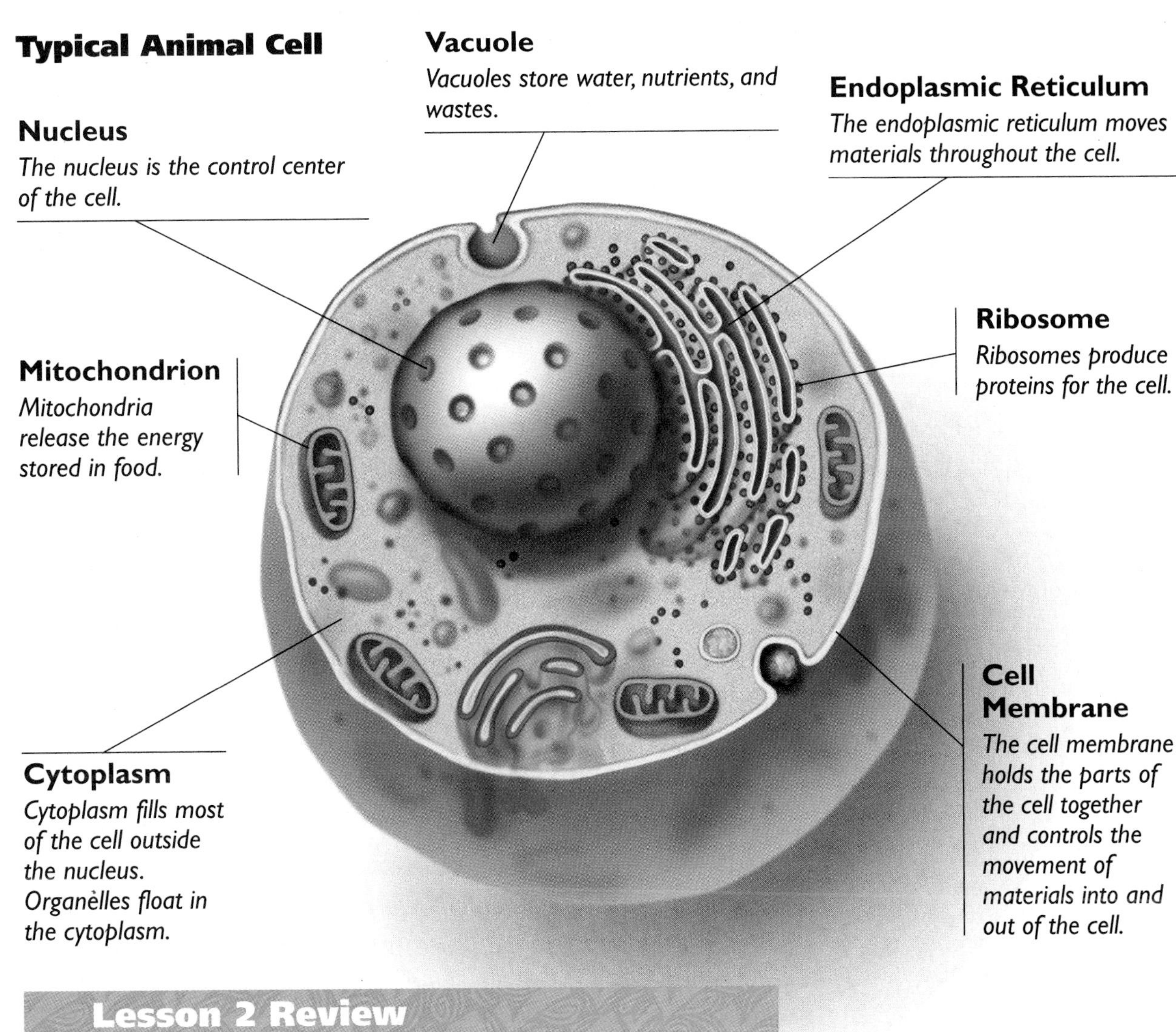

Typical Animal Cell
Vacuole
Vacuoles store water, nutrients, and wastes.
Endoplasmic Reticulum
The endoplasmic reticulum moves materials throughout the cell.
Nucleus
The nucleus is the control center of the cell.
Ribosome
Ribosomes produce proteins for the cell.
Mitochondrion
Mitochondria release the energy stored in food.
Cell Membrane
The cell membrane holds the parts of the cell together and controls the movement of materials into and out of the cell.
Cytoplasm
Cytoplasm fills most of the cell outside the nucleus. Organelles float in the cytoplasm.

Lesson 2 Review

1. What are the main parts of an animal cell?
2. Name three organelles in an animal cell and tell what each does.
3. **Bar Graphs**
   Make a bar graph showing the number of chromosomes in the cells of humans, dogs, houseflies, and crayfish.

You will learn:

- what the parts of a plant cell are.
- how plants are important to all living things.

Lesson 3

How Do Plant Cells Differ from Animal Cells?

Ahh! Sit outside in the sunlight all day. Take in some air, water, and minerals. What if that's all you needed to do to survive? Sound hard to believe? You can't do it, but a plant can. That's because its cells have special parts that your cells don't.

Glossary

Glossary

chloroplast (klôr′ə plast), organelle that makes sugars, using carbon dioxide, water, and the energy from sunlight

chlorophyll (klôr′ə fil), green substance in the chloroplasts that traps energy from sunlight

The chloroplasts in these moss cells contain chlorophyll. The chloroplasts enable the plant to make glucose. ▼

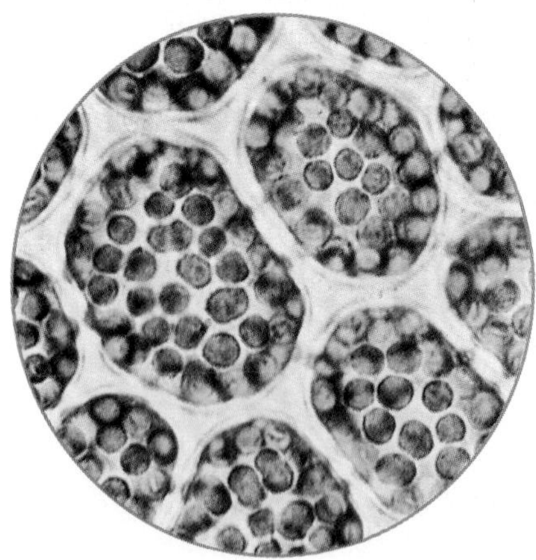

magnification x1100

Plant Cells

Nearly all animal and plant cells contain cell membranes, nuclei, cytoplasm, and other organelles, but they differ in some ways too. First, plant cells are usually much larger than animal cells. Second, plant cells usually have only one large vacuole. Animal cells often have many smaller ones.

Look at the diagram of the plant cell on the next page. The large vacuole of a plant cell is located near the center of the cell. It fills with water and pushes the cytoplasm against the cell membrane. That pressure helps to keep the cell firm.

If you have ever noticed a wilting plant, you have seen a plant whose cells are low in water. The vacuoles have shrunk, so the plant's cells have become less stiff. Give the plant water, and the vacuoles in its cells will fill with water and make the plant firm again. Animal cells shrink too when there isn't enough water, but not as much as plant cells do.

Perhaps the most important way that plant cells and animal cells differ is that many plant cells have organelles called **chloroplasts**. You can see these green, egg-shaped organelles scattered in the cytoplasm of the plant cells at the left. Inside each chloroplast is a green substance called **chlorophyll**. Chlorophyll traps energy from the sun to make sugars. Animal cells can't do that.

If you live in a region where leaves change color in the fall, you have seen the presence—and disappearance—of chlorophyll in chloroplasts. Chloroplasts belong to a group of organelles called plastids. Plastids store plants' colors—green, red, orange, yellow, or blue. Normally, the green of chlorophyll hides the other colors in the chloroplasts. In fall, when temperatures drop, chlorophyll breaks down, and other colors in the leaf show through.

A plant cell has a **cell wall** in addition to a cell membrane. The tough, nonliving material of the wall acts like an outer skeleton for each cell. It gives the cell support, strength, and shape. In Lesson 1, you read about Robert Hooke and his famous discovery. It was the cell walls of cork that Hooke saw under the microscope. The living material that had been inside the walls of the cork tree cells was no longer there.

Glossary

cell wall (sel wôl), tough, nonliving material that acts like an outside skeleton for each plant cell

Typical Plant Cell

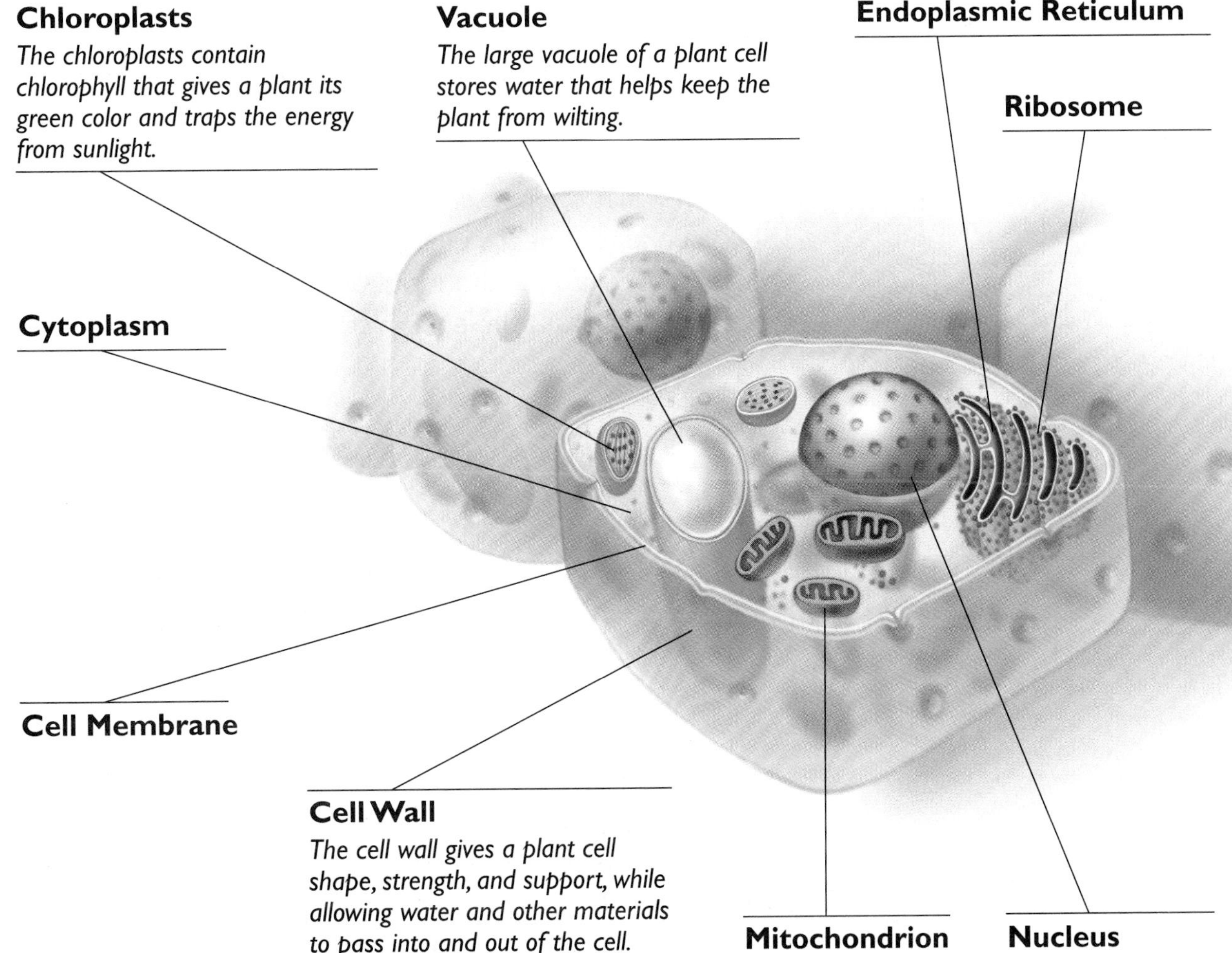
Chloroplasts
The chloroplasts contain chlorophyll that gives a plant its green color and traps the energy from sunlight.
Vacuole
The large vacuole of a plant cell stores water that helps keep the plant from wilting.
Endoplasmic Reticulum
Ribosome
Cytoplasm
Cell Membrane
Cell Wall
The cell wall gives a plant cell shape, strength, and support, while allowing water and other materials to pass into and out of the cell.
Mitochondrion
Nucleus

Importance of Plants

The sun showers Earth with huge amounts of energy in the form of sunlight. Most of this energy is absorbed by the land or the oceans, or it is reflected back into space. However, a small percentage of this energy is absorbed by green plants, such as the bean plant below.

Then a complex and important process takes place. In fact, it is a process on which you and almost all life on Earth depend. The chlorophyll in green plant cells traps the energy from the sun. The chloroplast also uses carbon dioxide that the plant takes in from the air and water that is transported through plant roots and stems. With these three ingredients, the chloroplast makes glucose, a simple sugar, during a process called photosynthesis. *Photo* means "light," and *synthesis* means "putting together." So *photosynthesis* means "putting together with light." During photosynthesis, oxygen is also formed and released by the plant into the atmosphere.

What a plant can do, then, is change light energy into chemical energy, which is stored in glucose. This chemical energy is stored until the plant needs it to grow, transport materials, or perform some other process.

What happens when a plant needs some of this energy? Remember that the mitochondria are the powerhouses of a cell. When a plant needs energy, a process called respiration occurs in its cells' mitochondria. Oxygen is used in a process that releases the energy stored in the glucose.

The energy for photosynthesis comes from sunlight. Green plants use it to combine carbon dioxide and water to make simple sugars. Oxygen is given off during photosynthesis. ▼

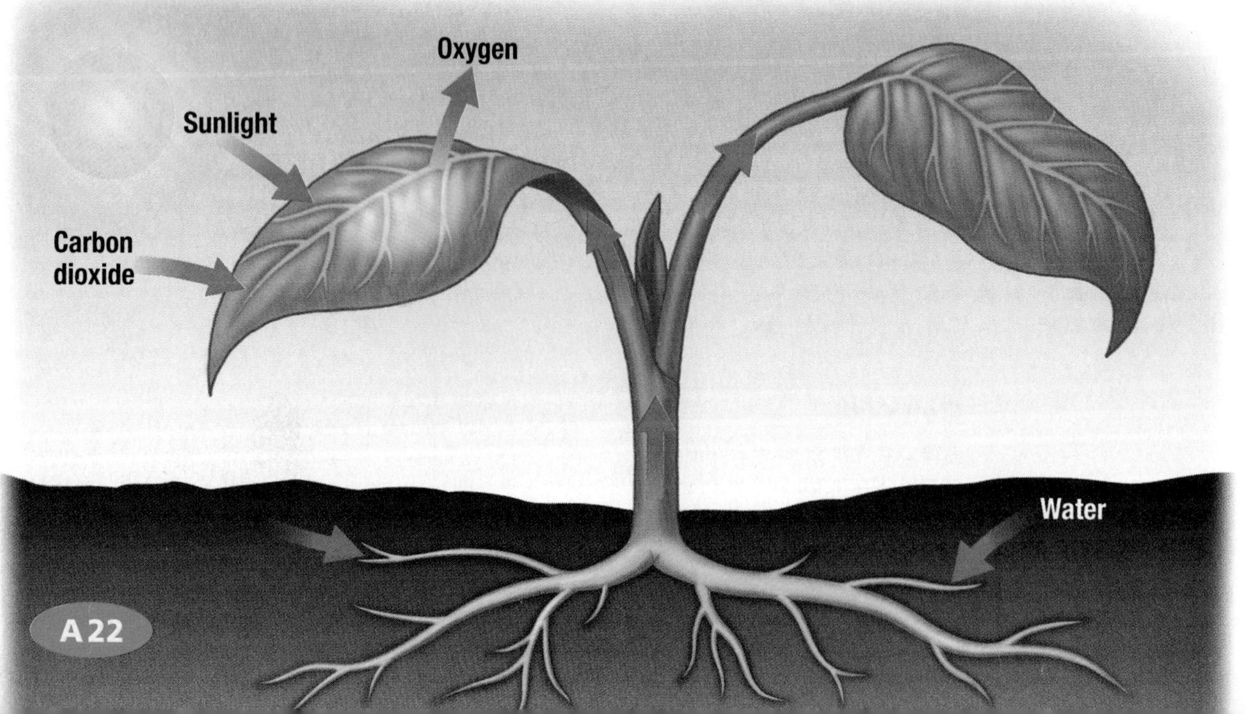

Carbon dioxide and water are produced during this process. How is respiration different from photosynthesis?

If you need food, you can't just sit in the sun for a few hours while drinking water and taking in carbon dioxide. Neither can any other animal. The reason is simple. Neither you nor other animals have cells that contain chlorophyll. Animals, unlike plants, can't make their own food. Then how do animals get the energy they need? They get it from eating food. They get food energy when they eat plants or when they eat other organisms that have eaten plants.

▲ *How is this leaf a source of energy for these caterpillars?*

For example, the caterpillar in the picture is munching hungrily on a leaf. Some of the energy it gets from the leaf will be stored in its body. Then along comes the bird pictured below, who likes a fat, juicy caterpillar for a meal. That bird gets its food energy when it eats and digests the caterpillar that has eaten the plant.

What about the peanut-butter-and-jelly sandwich and glass of milk you have after school? Where did this food come from? The peanut butter is made from seeds of the peanut plant. Grape jelly is made from grapes—the fruit of another plant. The bread is made with flour from wheat seeds—still another plant. The milk comes from a cow. However, before the cow could produce milk, it needed the energy it got from eating grass.

Some animals get energy from eating other animals. This bird gets energy from eating the caterpillar. ▼

Lesson 3 Review

1. How do plant cells differ from animal cells?
2. How are plants important to all living things?
3. **Bar Graphs**
   Using the diagrams on pages A19 and A21, make a bar graph comparing the parts of a plant cell and an animal cell.

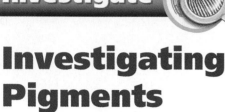

Investigating Pigments

Process Skills

Process Skills

- observing
- predicting
- communicating
- making operational definitions

Materials

- safety goggles
- parsley
- 6 plastic cups
- scissors
- dropper
- rubbing alcohol
- 3 spoons
- 3 flat toothpicks
- 3 filter paper strips
- tape
- 3 pencils
- mushrooms
- beet leaves
- paper towel

Getting Ready

How do the pigments in parsley, beet leaves, and mushrooms differ? In this activity you will separate the pigments in these organisms.

Follow This Procedure

1. Make a chart like the one shown. Use your chart to record your predictions and observations.

Test material	Color of liquid	Predictions	Observations
Parsley			
Mushrooms			
Beet leaves			

2. Put on your safety goggles. Place several parsley leaves in a plastic cup. Use scissors to cut the leaves into very small pieces. Add 2–3 droppersful of rubbing alcohol. Crush the leaves in the alcohol with the back of a spoon. **Observe** and record the color of the alcohol solution.

3. Use a toothpick to place a small drop of the parsley liquid about 0.5 cm from the bottom of a filter paper strip (Photo A). When the drop is dry, place a second drop of the parsley liquid on top of the first. Do the same for two more drops.

4. Label the strip with the letter *P*. Tape it to a pencil.

5. Repeat steps 2–4 with the mushrooms and with the beet leaves, labeling the strips *M* and *B*.

6. Fill 3 plastic cups with about 1 cm of rubbing alcohol.

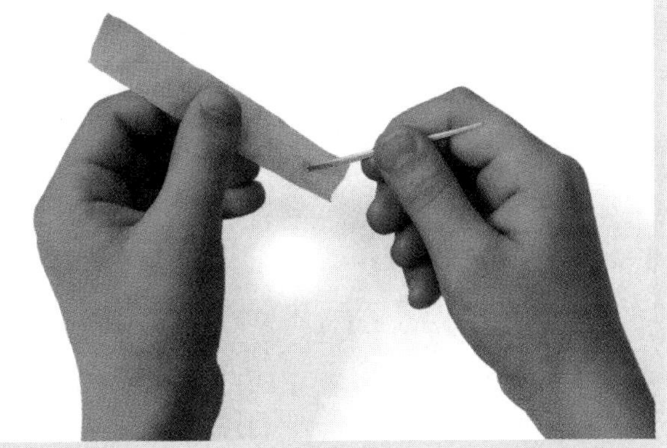

Photo A

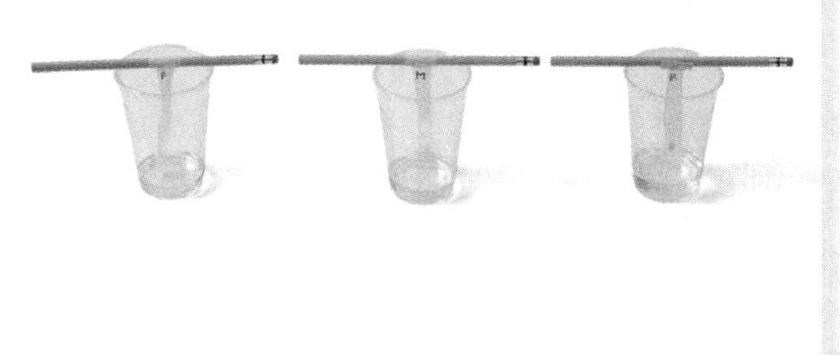

Photo B

7 Place one pencil across the top of each cup of alcohol so that the bottom of the paper strip is just touching the alcohol (Photo B). Be sure that the drops you placed on the strip are not touching the alcohol.

8 As the alcohol rises up the strip, you will be able to see the different pigments that give the test item its color. **Predict** what colors you will see. On what information did you base your predictions?

9 Allow the alcohol to rise up the paper to a height of 7 cm. Remove the strips from the alcohol and lay them on a paper towel to dry. Observe the filter strips. Record your observations in your chart.

Interpret Your Results

1. Did the color of the alcohol solutions always match the color shown on the filter paper? Based on the results of this activity, which test items can you conclude contain more than one pigment?

2. How is the mushroom strip different?

3. How could you use this activity to tell whether a test item was a plant? **Communicate** your ideas to the group.

4. An **operational definition** describes what an object does, or what you can observe about the object. Write an operational definition of a green plant leaf.

Inquire Further

What pigments might you find in the leaves, roots, and stems of a carrot plant? Develop a plan to answer this or other questions you may have.

Self-Assessment

- I followed instructions to separate pigments in test organisms.
- I **predicted** what pigments would be present in each test item.
- I recorded my **observations** about the colors that appeared on the filter paper.
- I **communicated** how to tell whether a test item was a plant.
- I wrote an **operational definition** of a plant.

You will learn:

- **how the shape and size of a cell are related to its function.**
- **how other differences in structure are related to a cell's function.**

Lesson 4

How Do Cells Differ?

How do you think the cells in the body of a dog compare with the cells in the body of the flea that sits on it? Are the dog's body cells bigger than those of the flea? Or are there just more cells in the dog's body?

Cell Shape and Size

You've learned that all cells have similar parts and that plant cells have some parts that animal cells do not. There are many other differences among the cells of different kinds of organisms. In fact, there are even differences among the cells of the same many-celled organism.

These Wandering Jew leaves are made of several different kinds of tissues. Each tissue is made of groups of similar cells that perform a similar function. The photo shows cells that cover the leaf of the plant. ▼

magnification x60

Look at the pictures to the left. The cells you see in the top picture cover the outer part of the leaf on the plant. These cells protect the leaf. The shapes of these cells help them fit together tightly so that they cover the other cells inside the leaf completely.

Now look at the photo of the leaf cells again. Do you see the bean-shaped cells that occur in pairs? These cells are called guard cells. They allow gases such as oxygen and carbon dioxide to enter and exit the leaf. How does the shape of these cells help them do this job?

As you can see, the shape of a cell helps it perform a specific function within an organism. On the next page, you can see the shapes of some of the 100 different cells within the human body.

Human Body Cells

Skin

Skin cells cover and protect your body. They keep harmful organisms from entering your body. The lifespan of a skin cell is 19-34 days.

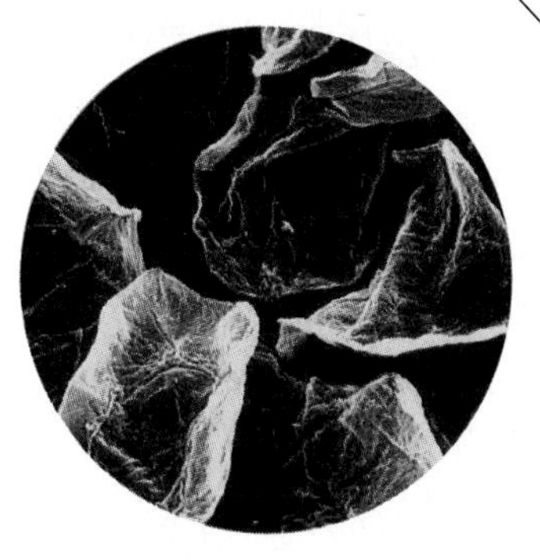

magnification x4,800

Blood

Notice the difference in shape between these red blood cells and white blood cells. Red blood cells live about 120 days. They carry oxygen to your body cells and carry wastes away. White blood cells, which live from several hours to several years, protect you from disease.

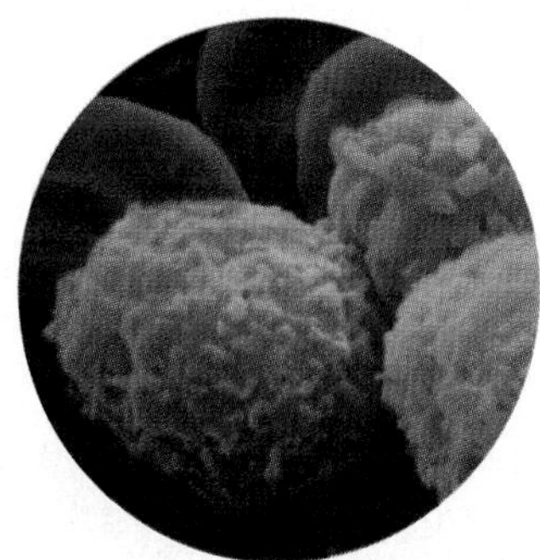

magnification x4,800

Nerve

Long, narrow nerve cells carry messages—from one cell to the next—throughout your body. Nerve cells live for the lifetime of the individual. How does the shape of this nerve cell enable it to carry on its functions?

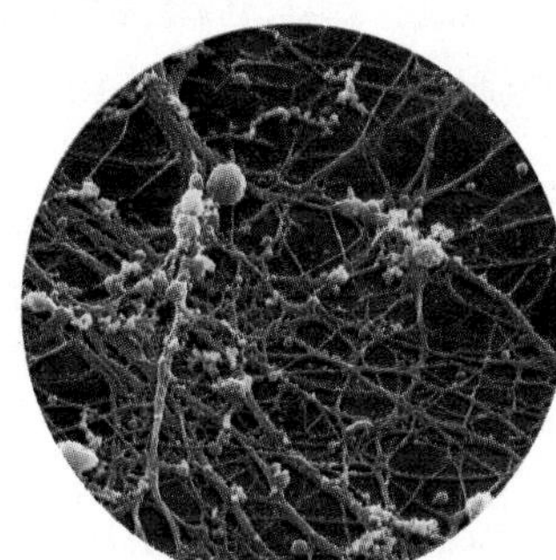

magnification x5,920

Muscle

Muscle cells work together to help you move, to push food through your digestive system, and to keep your heart beating. The long, thin shape of these cells allows them to contract to move parts of your body. Their lifespan can be as long as the lifespan of the organism.

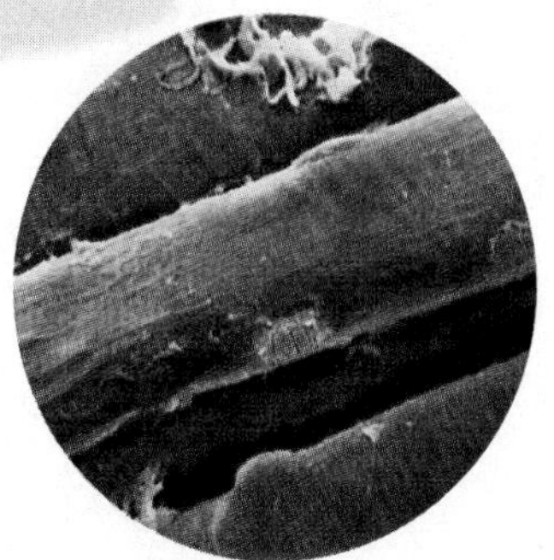

magnification x560

Here's one example of how the shape of cells in your body helps them do their job. When bacteria invade your body, the white blood cells take action. Their job is to find and destroy the invaders. White blood cells are irregularly shaped. Their shape allows them to slip through the thin walls of blood vessels and move among your muscle cells and other tissues. Do you see how this would help them find the invaders in your body?

You might think that one-celled organisms are similar to each other, but they too have a large variety of shapes. A single cell must carry out the same jobs that are carried out by all the cells of many-celled organisms like you. Notice how the one-celled organisms pictured below have different cell shapes that allow them to survive in their environment.

Vorticella lives in ponds attached to solid objects, such as twigs. Notice the special funnel shape of this one-celled organism. The small hair-like structures, called cilia, around the top of the funnel in vorticella beat, creating a whirlpool. Microscopic food particles are swept into the funnel and drawn into the vorticella.

The shape of the vorticella helps it feed and, therefore, survive in its environment. ▼

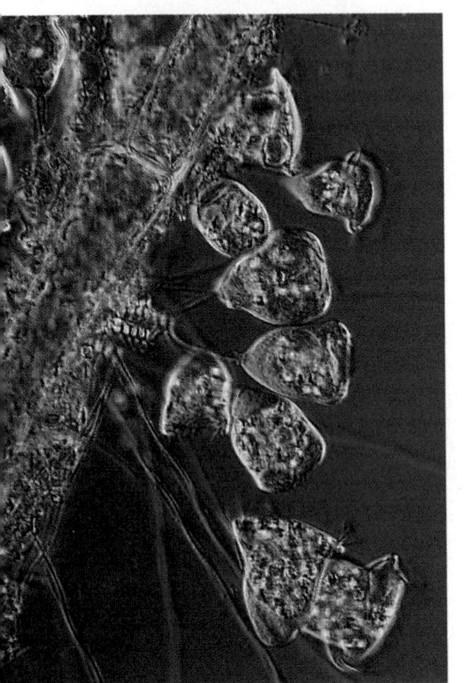

magnification x151

Thousands of volvox cells group together to form a hollow sphere filled with water. Inside these spheres, new colonies are forming. ▼

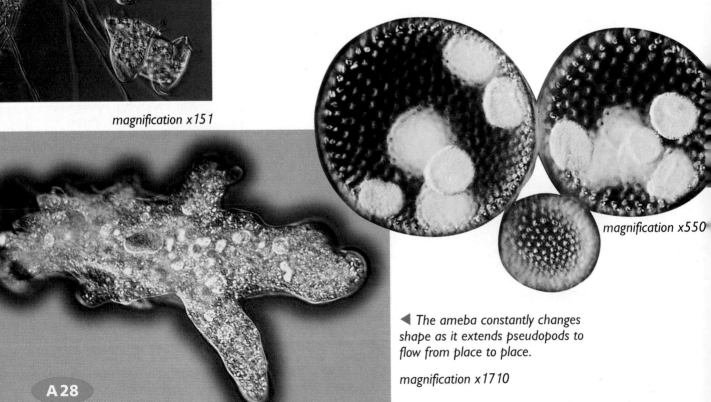

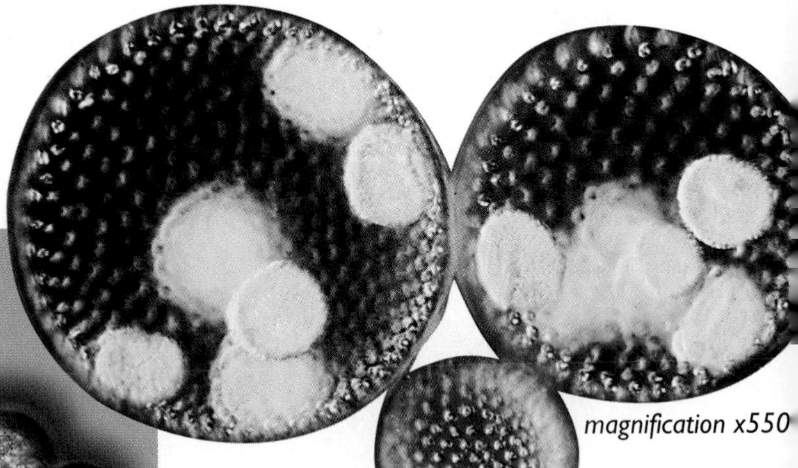

magnification x550

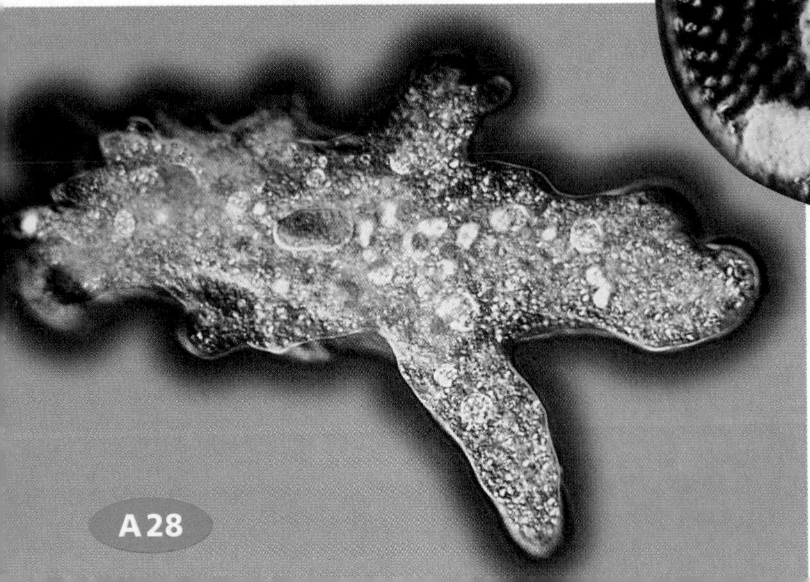

◀ *The ameba constantly changes shape as it extends pseudopods to flow from place to place.*

magnification x1710

Amebas live on the bottom of bodies of water. An ameba has no definite shape. It moves by pushing out its cytoplasm into thin pouches in the cell membrane. These pouches are called pseudopods, which means "false feet." An ameba feeds on small organisms by flowing around them. Once a pseudopod surrounds the food, the ameba digests it.

Volvox live in fresh water and form hollow balls. Each ball contains from 500 to 50,000 cells. Although the cells of Volvox group together, they do not form a tissue. Each of the green cells makes its own sugars. Each of the cells has a pair of whiplike structures called flagella. When all the cells in the group move their flagella together, the ball of cells moves by rolling over and over.

Cells vary in size as well as shape. Does that mean that large organisms have large cells? Not always. Think of yourself as a baby. You were made of many cells of different tissues. However, you didn't grow bigger because your cells got bigger. Instead, your bone cells produced more bone cells to make longer, bigger bones. Your skin cells produced more skin cells to make your skin cover more area. The number of cells in your body increased, not the size. In fact, an adult human body has about 100 trillion cells.

Cells within your body differ in size, and cells in different organisms differ in size. As the picture shows, bacteria are among the smallest cells. A nerve cell in the giraffe is one of the longest cells. The cell with the largest volume of all is so large that you don't even need a microscope to see it—the yolk of an ostrich egg.

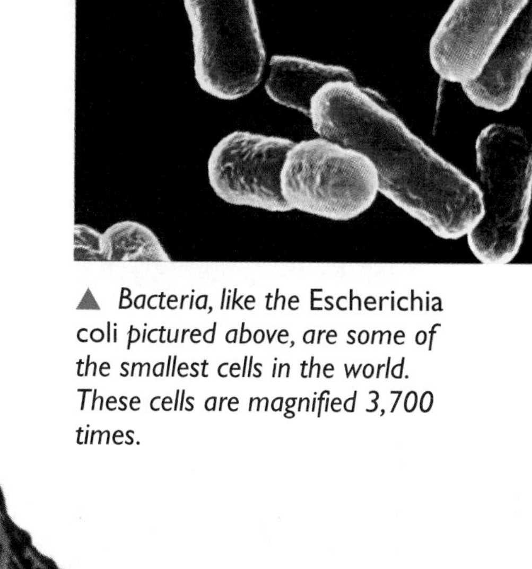

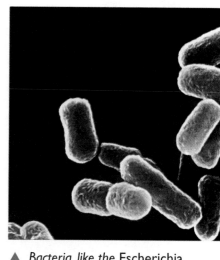

▲ *Bacteria, like the* Escherichia coli *pictured above, are some of the smallest cells in the world. These cells are magnified 3,700 times.*

6 m

Cells vary greatly in size. The nerve cell that runs from the giraffe's hip to its toe is almost 6 meters long! ▶

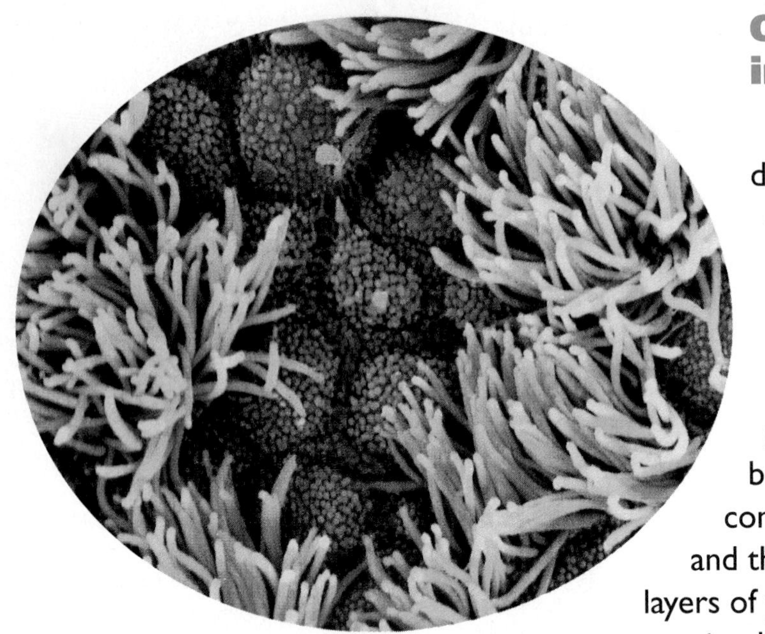

▲ *Cilia that line your windpipe carry mucus and trapped dust upward toward your throat. These cilia have been magnified 4,170 times.*

Other Differences in Structure

The function that a cell performs determines the kinds and number of organelles it has. For example, a muscle cell in your leg has to contract quickly as you stand, walk, and run. It contains a greater number of energy-producing mitochondria than a bone cell does. Think about the constantly active cells in your heart and the cells that make up the growing layers of your skin. Which would have more mitochondria?

Some cells have special outgrowths from their membranes. Flagella extend from volvox and help them move. The vorticella has hairlike structures called cilia on top of its funnel. The cilia move rapidly to create the whirlpool that helps the vorticella feed. The pictures on this page also show other cells with cilia. The cells that line your breathing passages, lungs, and nose have hundreds of cilia. Their motion helps keep your air passages clean. On a single-celled paramecium, the cilia beat rhythmically, moving the paramecium through the water in which it lives.

magnification x4500

▲ *Cilia on a slipper-shaped paramecium allow it to move from place to place and help it feed.*

Lesson 4 Review

1. How is the shape and size of a cell related to its function?
2. What other differences in a cell are related to its function?
3. **Bar Graphs**
   How do the lifespans of different cells vary? Use the information on page A27 to make a bar graph that answers this question.

Experimenting with Membranes

Materials

- safety goggles
- 6 plastic graduated cups
- water
- sugar test strips with key
- clock
- dropper
- iodine solution
- sugar solution
- starch solution
- masking tape
- marker
- scissors
- dialysis tubing
- metric ruler
- 6 pieces of string
- funnel
- paper towel

Process Skills

- formulating questions and hypotheses
- identifying and controlling variables
- making and using models
- experimenting
- estimating and measuring
- observing
- collecting and interpreting data
- communicating

State the Problem

What dissolved materials pass through a membrane?

Formulate Your Hypothesis

If cell models containing starch and sugar solutions are placed in plain water, which substances will pass through the membrane into the water? Write your **hypothesis.**

Identify and Control the Variables

To see which materials will pass through a membrane, you must control the variables. The dissolved substance is the **variable** that changes in this experiment. You will use three cell **models.** One cell will contain only water. A second cell will contain starch solution, and the third will contain sugar solution. Remember to keep all other variables the same.

Test Your Hypothesis

Follow these steps to perform an **experiment.**

1. Put on your safety goggles. Make a chart like the one on page A33. Use your chart to record your observations.

Photo A

Continued →

2 **Measure** 30 mL of water in a plastic graduated cup. Place a sugar test strip in the water for about 15 seconds. Remove the strip and wait 1 minute. Compare the color of the tip of the test strip with the key (Photo A). Record your **observations.** Add 3 drops of iodine solution to the same cup of water. Record your observations.

Safety Note *Handle iodine solution carefully. Do not get iodine on skin or clothing.*

3 Repeat step 2 with the sugar solution. Repeat step 2 with the starch solution.

4 Use tape and a marker to label 3 plastic cups *Control, Starch,* and *Sugar.* Fill the cups with water until each is about two-thirds full. Each cup should contain the same amount of water.

5 Use scissors to cut 3 pieces of dialysis tubing, each about 12 cm in length. Soak the tubing in a cup of water for 1 minute. Remove the tubing from the water and tie one end of each piece with a string. Be sure to tie the string tightly.

6 Use a funnel to add water to the open end of one tied tube. Then tightly tie the tube with string (Photo B). Place the tube in the cup of water marked *Control.*

7 Fill a second tube with starch solution. Tie the other end of the tube with a string and rinse the outside carefully. Place it in the cup of water labeled *Starch.*

8 Clean the funnel with a paper towel. Repeat step 7 using sugar solution. Place the tube in the cup of water labeled *Sugar* (Photo C).

9 Allow the tubes to remain in the cups of water overnight. Remove the tubes from the cups. Use a sugar test strip to test the liquid in all 3 cups. **Collect data** by recording your observations. Use a dropper to place 3 drops of iodine solution in each cup. Record your observations.

Photo B

Photo C

Collect Your Data

	Sugar test strip	Iodine solution
Water (step 2)		
Starch solution (step 3)		
Sugar solution (step 3)		
Liquid in *Control* cup		
Liquid in *Starch* cup		
Liquid in *Sugar* cup		

Interpret Your Data

Use your data. How can you tell if a solution contains starch? How can you tell if it contains sugar? Which cups in step 9 contained solutions with sugar? Which contained solutions with starch?

State Your Conclusion

Study your data. How do your results compare with your hypothesis? **Communicate** your results. Tell which materials, if any, can pass through a membrane.

Inquire Further

Does the amount of sugar or starch dissolved in the water in the cell affect the experiment results? Develop a plan to answer this or other questions you may have.

Self-Assessment

- I formulated a **hypothesis.**
- I **experimented** to see which materials will pass through a membrane.
- I **controlled variables.**
- I **collected** and **interpreted data.**
- I **communicated** my results.

Chapter 1 Review

Chapter Main Ideas

Lesson 1

- A species is a group of organisms that have the same characteristics and can produce similar offspring that can also reproduce.
- The invention of the compound and electron microscopes enabled scientists to learn about cells.
- The cell theory states that the cell is the basic unit of all living organisms, and only living cells can produce new living cells.

Lesson 2

- The main parts of an animal cell are the nucleus, cell membrane, and cytoplasm.
- Structures called organelles inside the cytoplasm carry on different functions for the cell.

Lesson 3

- Parts of a plant cell include the cell membrane, nucleus, cytoplasm, and organelles, including chloroplasts, and a tough outer support called a cell wall.
- Through photosynthesis plants give off oxygen and make sugars that store energy. Other organisms need these materials to survive.

Lesson 4

- The shape and size of a cell is related to its specific function within an organism.
- The function of a cell is related to the kinds and number of organelles it has.

Reviewing Science Words and Concepts

Write the letter of the word or phrase that best completes each sentence.

a. cell membrane
b. cell theory
c. cell wall
d. chlorophyll
e. chloroplast
f. chromosome
g. compound microscope
h. cytoplasm
i. endoplasmic reticulum
j. mitochondria
k. nucleus
l. organelle
m. ribosome
n. species
o. vacuole

1. All dogs are members of the same ___.
2. An instrument using two lenses for magnifying objects is a(n) ___.
3. According to the ___, all organisms are made of one or more cells.
4. The control center of a living cell is the ___.
5. A structure in the nucleus that carries information that controls cell activities is the ___.
6. A thin, flexible protective cell covering is the ___.
7. The jellylike material filling the space between the cell membrane and the nucleus is ___.
8. Ribosomes, mitochondria, and vacuoles are examples of a(n) ___.

9. Organelles in the cytoplasm where energy is released are ___.
10. A saclike organelle where a cell's food and water are stored is a(n) ___.
11. An organelle for transporting materials inside the cell is the ___.
12. Part of a cell that puts together proteins for the cell is the ___.
13. Green substance in plant cells is ___.
14. An organelle that makes sugar is the ___.
15. The tough outer support of a plant cell is the ___.

Explaining Science

Create a comparison chart or write a paragraph that explains these questions.

1. How do various species differ?

2. How do the parts of an animal cell function?

3. How do plant and animal cells differ?

4. What are the differences in the cells within an organism?

Using Skills

1. The actual number of species on Earth is unknown because scientists continue to identify new species. The table shows the total number of bird species that were known in three different years. Convert this information to a **bar graph**.

Year	Number of known species
1758	360
1845	4500
1990	9000

2. Make a list of at least 10 different species you are familiar with. **Classify** the species into groups according to their characteristics. Identify the characteristics of each group.

3. On page A13, you read about the experiment of a Belgian doctor in the 1600s to show that mice develop from wheat. Describe an experiment to prove the doctor's theory wrong. **Identify** the **variables.**

Critical Thinking

1. **Compare** and **contrast** the similarities and differences in the characteristics among species of pets owned by classmates.

2. Imagine looking at an unknown cell through an electron microscope. How might you apply what you know about cell structure to **infer** whether the cell is from a plant or animal?

3. **Compare** and **contrast** the human body cells pictured on page A27. **Draw a conclusion** about how the shape of each cell makes it well suited to its function.

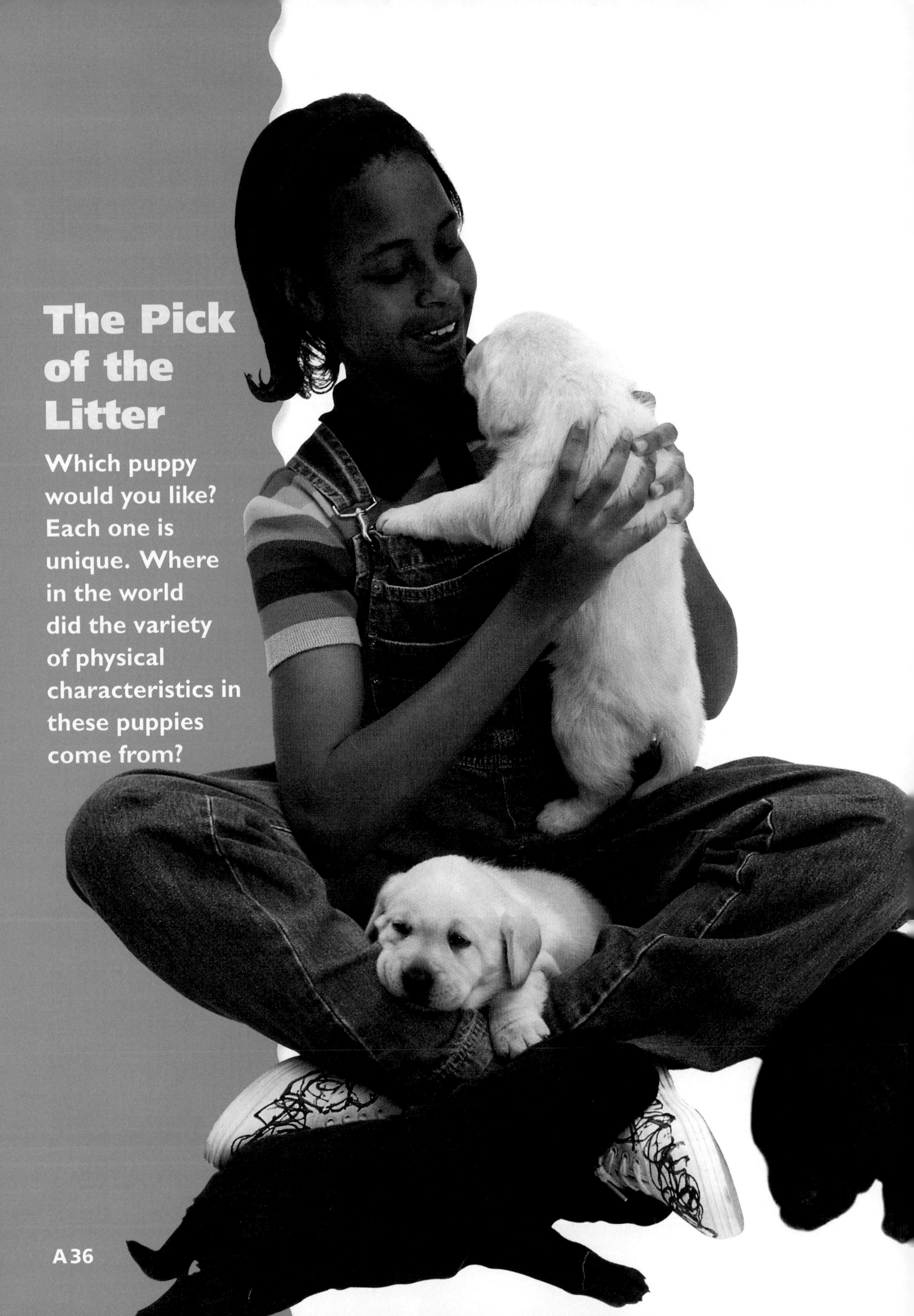

The Pick of the Litter

Which puppy would you like? Each one is unique. Where in the world did the variety of physical characteristics in these puppies come from?

Chapter 2

Reproduction and Heredity

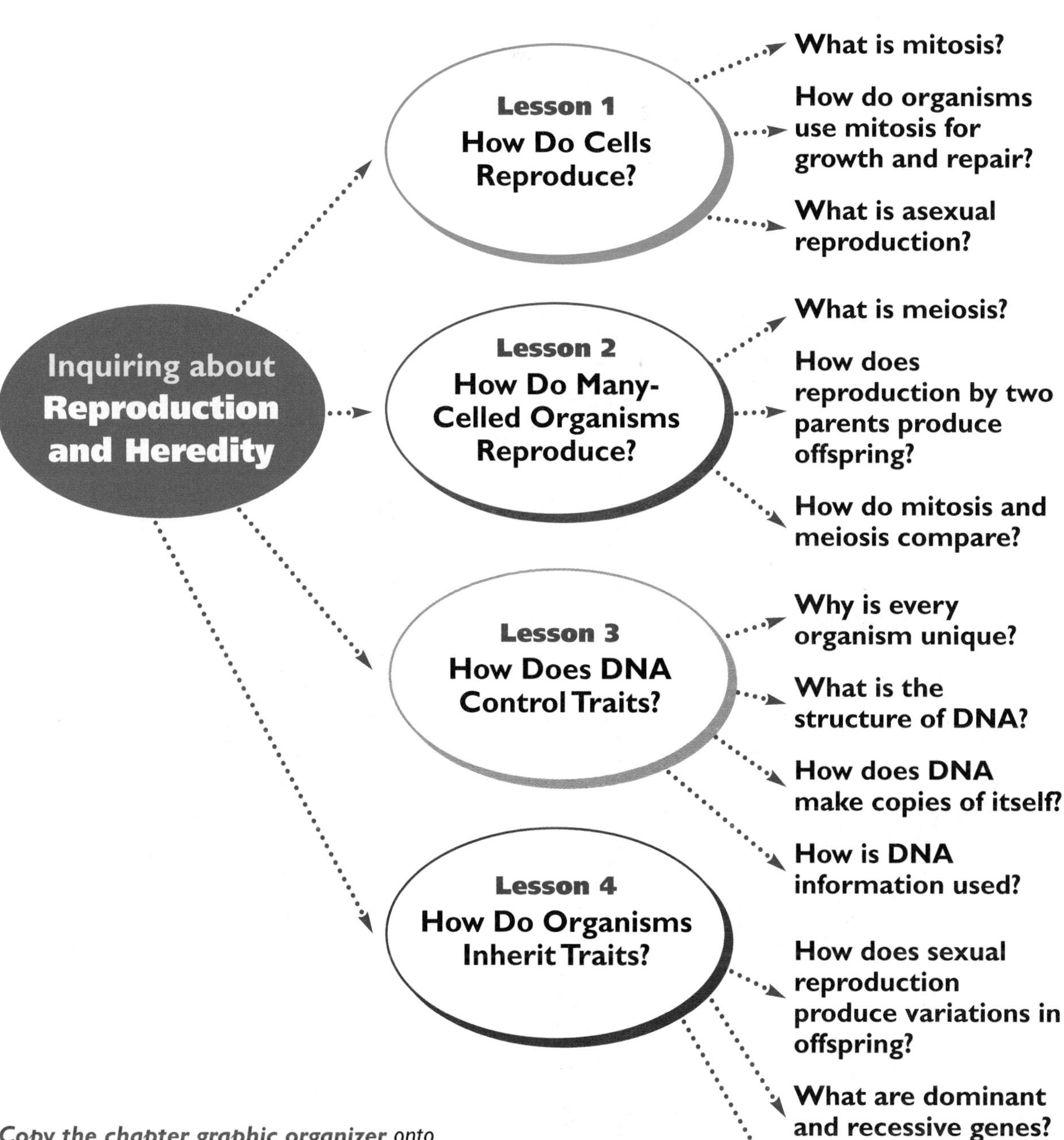

Copy the chapter graphic organizer *onto your own paper. This organizer shows you what the whole chapter is all about. As you read the lessons and do the activities, look for answers to the questions and write them on your organizer.*

Explore Activity

Exploring Variation in Species

Process Skills

Process Skills

- observing
- estimating and measuring
- communicating
- inferring

Materials

- 10 peanuts in the shell
- metric ruler
- graph paper

Explore

1 Make a chart like the one shown. Use your chart to record your observations.

Peanut	Observations	Length
1		
2		
3		

2 **Observe** 10 peanut shells closely. Record your observations. What differences do you notice?

3 **Measure** the length of the 10 peanut shells to the nearest millimeter. Record your measurements.

4 Combine your data with the data of the other groups.

5 Make a bar graph that shows the data collected by your group and a bar graph that shows the combined class data. Label the graphs as shown.

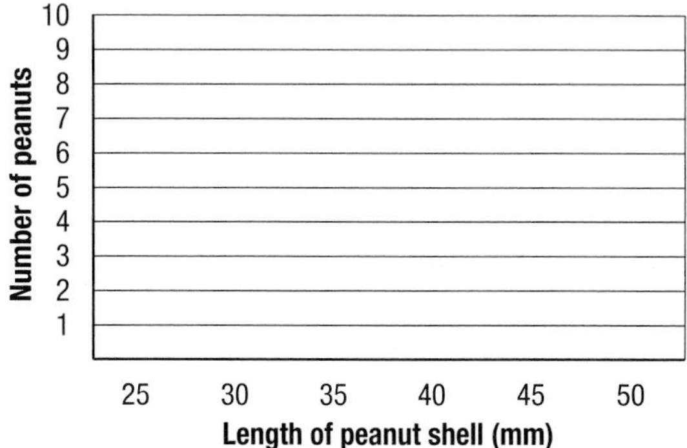

Reflect

1. What can you **infer** about the variation within a species on the basis of your observations?

2. Compare your group's graph with the class data. Which graph shows a greater variation? Why do you think this is so? **Communicate** your ideas to the class.

Inquire Further

Do other species show similar variation? Develop a plan to answer this or other questions you may have.

Metric Conversions

Height is one trait that you inherit from your parents. You can use the metric system to measure height.

The base unit for measuring height (length) in the metric system is the **meter.** You can convert the meter to different units to describe amounts that are longer or shorter.

Math Vocabulary

meter, the basic unit of length in the metric system

Example

Name	Abbreviation	Number of Base Units	Approximate Comparison
Kilometer	km	1,000	9 football fields
Meter	m	1	Half the height of a door
Centimeter	cm	$\frac{1}{100}$	Length of a raisin
Millimeter	mm	$\frac{1}{1000}$	Width of a period at the end of a sentence

Look at the chart. Notice that to convert a unit, you multiply or divide by a power of 10. For example, to convert from a kilometer to a meter, you multiply by 1,000 $\frac{\text{m}}{\text{km}}$.

1 km x 1,000 $\frac{\text{m}}{\text{km}}$ = 1,000 m

To convert from centimeters to meters, you divide by 100 $\frac{\text{cm}}{\text{m}}$.

200 cm ÷ 100 $\frac{\text{cm}}{\text{m}}$ = 2 m

Did you know?

The meter was originally defined as $\frac{1}{10,000,000}$ of the distance from the equator to the North Pole. It took the French from 1792 to 1798 to measure this distance. Today's satellites confirm that their measurements were only off by 0.2 mm.

Talk About It!

1. Can any measurement in millimeters be converted to meters? Explain.

2. Why is it more appropriate to measure your height in centimeters than in meters?

You will learn:

- what mitosis is.
- how organisms use mitosis for growth and repair.
- what asexual reproduction is.

Lesson 1

How Do Cells Reproduce?

Wow! That sunflower plant sure grew a lot since last week. It must be a meter tall already. How did it get so big so fast? Are its cells just getting fatter? Maybe it just has more cells. But where did they come from?

Mitosis

All over the world, the cells of organisms—single-celled organisms, plants, animals, even your own body—are dividing to produce new cells. How does this happen?

You learned in Chapter 1 that the nucleus of a cell contains chromosomes. Each species has a certain number of chromosomes in its body cells. Humans have 46 chromosomes in each body cell, bullfrogs have 26, chickens have 78, and an onion plant has 32.

Before one cell divides into two cells, it makes copies of all its chromosomes. What would happen if a cell didn't copy its chromosomes before dividing?

After the chromosomes are copied, the cell goes through a process called mitosis. During **mitosis**, the cell's nucleus divides to form two identical nuclei. Mitosis is a continuous process. However, to make it easier to understand, scientists often describe it as a series of steps. You can see these steps on the next page.

After mitosis, a cell divides in two in a process called **cell division**. Two new offspring cells are formed. After cell division, each of the two new cells has one of the nuclei that formed during mitosis. Therefore, each new cell has a complete set of chromosomes. The chromosomes are the same in both offspring cells, and they are the same as in the parent cell. All your body cells were formed—and some, like the red blood cell in the picture, are forming right now—by mitosis and cell division.

Glossary

Glossary

mitosis (mī tō′ sis), the process by which a cell produces two new identical nuclei

cell division (sel də vizh′ ən), the dividing of a cell following mitosis

Your body produces 32 million new red blood cells like this every day! ▼

Mitosis

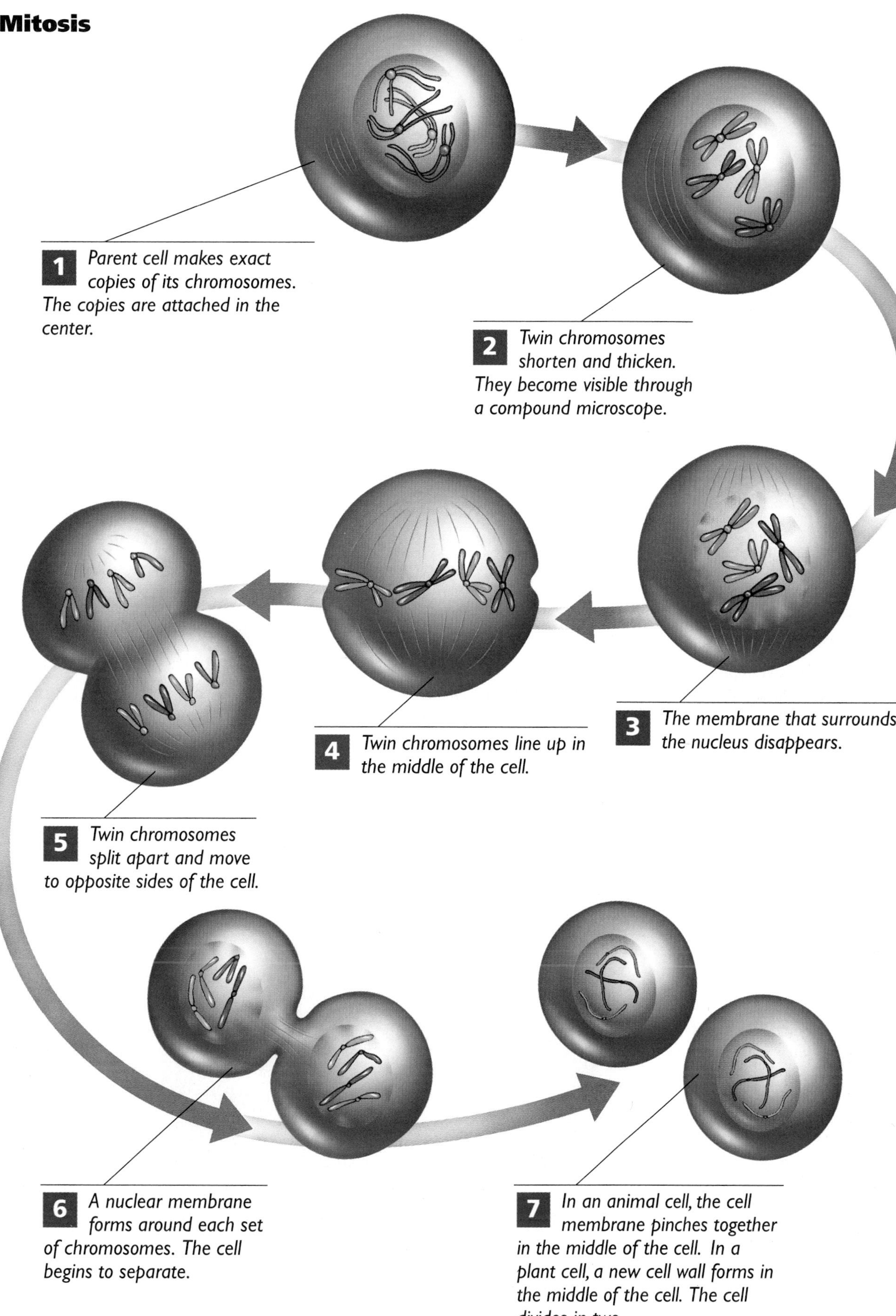

1 Parent cell makes exact copies of its chromosomes. The copies are attached in the center.
2 Twin chromosomes shorten and thicken. They become visible through a compound microscope.
3 The membrane that surrounds the nucleus disappears.
4 Twin chromosomes line up in the middle of the cell.
5 Twin chromosomes split apart and move to opposite sides of the cell.
6 A nuclear membrane forms around each set of chromosomes. The cell begins to separate.
7 In an animal cell, the cell membrane pinches together in the middle of the cell. In a plant cell, a new cell wall forms in the middle of the cell. The cell divides in two.

Growth and Repair

Your growth is just one example of what happens when cells reproduce. You are much taller now than when you were born. You grew largely because of mitosis and cell division. When you are fully grown, your body will contain about 100 trillion cells! Cell reproduction, therefore, results in the growth of organisms.

Have you ever planted a sunflower seed and watched it grow into a tall plant like the one in the picture? Each seed contains a partially developed plant called an embryo. When the embryo swells, grows, and breaks out of the seed, a young plant called a seedling forms. The seedling grows as new cells are constantly made.

The first part of the seedling to start growing is the root. Then the shoot—the part of the plant that makes the stems, leaves, and flowers—begins to grow. New cells produced at the tips of the stems make the plant grow bigger. Throughout its life, the sunflower plant grows by adding new cells at the end of its roots and shoots.

Animals grow by producing new cells too. Consider the kitten below. Throughout its body, mitosis produces new cells. Many of these cells result in the growth of the kitten into an adult cat.

▲ *Mitosis in this plant produces new cells for growth.*

This kitten could live more than 20 years. During that time, mitosis produces new cells for growth and repair of the cat's body cells. ▶

Mitosis and cell division also result in the replacement of old cells that have died and in the repair of cell tissue. For example, the outer layer of your skin is made up of dead cells that continually flake off. Below these dead cells are cube-shaped cells that form new skin cells. These new cells continually move up to the surface and replace the worn-out cells. The skin covering your entire body is replaced about once every month.

If you cut your finger, new cells will eventually grow to heal the cut. ▼

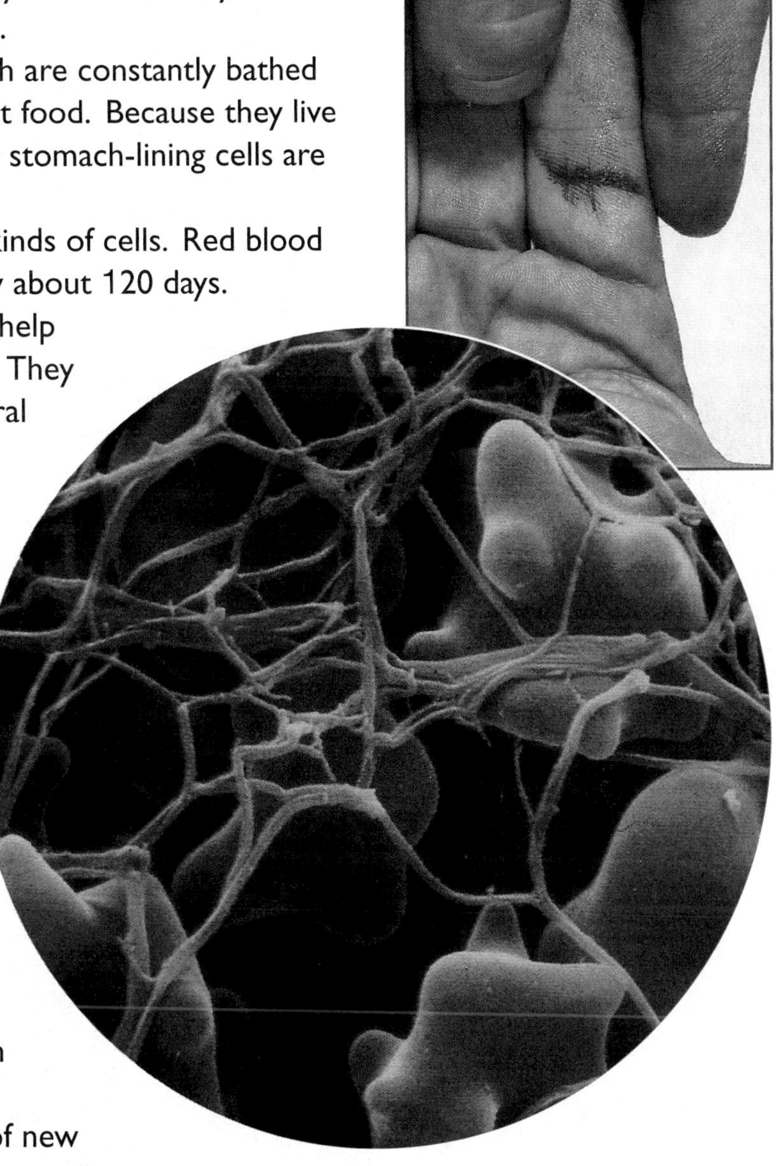

▲ *These platelets help stop bleeding in two ways. They form a plug by sticking to the tears in a blood vessel. They also release a substance that causes fibrin, the stringy material in the picture, to be produced. What do you think the function of fibrin is?*

The cells that line your stomach are constantly bathed in strong acid that helps you digest food. Because they live in such a harsh environment, your stomach-lining cells are replaced about every two days.

Your blood contains different kinds of cells. Red blood cells, which carry oxygen, live only about 120 days. Then they die. White blood cells help defend your body against disease. They can live from a few hours to several years. Your body is constantly making both red and white blood cells to replace those that die.

Platelets are a third kind of cell found in your blood. They live for about ten days. In the cut finger shown in the picture, platelets come in contact with the ends of the broken blood vessels. They swell and stick to the rough surface of the cut and to one another. In this way, platelets help a clot form to stop the bleeding. In time, the injury is repaired by the growth of new cells. These cells replace those that were damaged by the cut.

Plants also produce new cells for repair. For example, you have probably seen branches broken off from trees after a violent storm. When this damage happens, the tree makes new cells that gradually cover and repair the wound. What happens to grass after it is mowed?

Glossary

asexual reproduction
(ā sek′ shü əl rē prə duk′ shən), reproduction by one parent

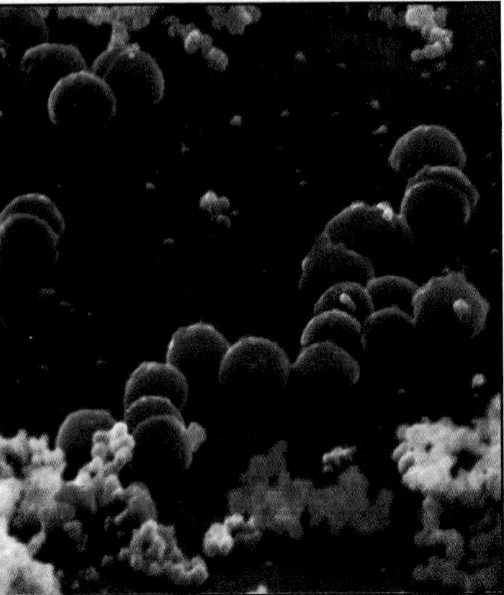

▲ *These bacteria can enter your body through injury to your skin. Once they're in your body, the bacteria can cause several diseases.*

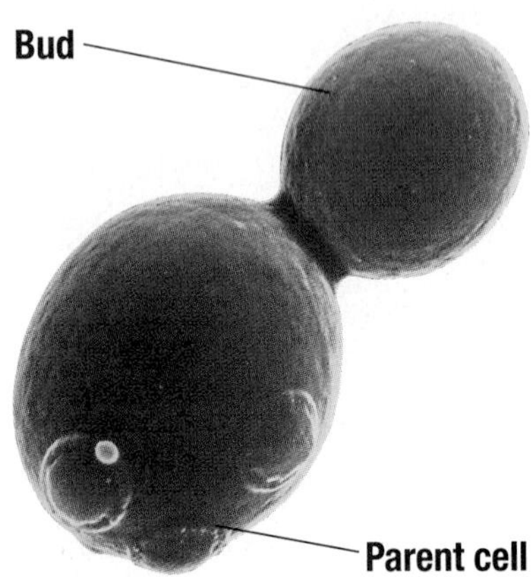

▲ *The tiny holes you see in bread result from the bubbles made by microscopic organisms like the one you see here. These organisms, called yeasts, belong to a group of organisms known as fungi. This process in which yeasts reproduce asexually is called budding.*

Asexual Reproduction

You just learned that, in many-celled organisms such as you, cell reproduction leads to new body cells. But did you know that in one-celled organisms, cell reproduction leads to new organisms? The process in which a new organism is produced by just one parent is called **asexual reproduction** .

The pictures below show a one-celled ameba reproducing. After mitosis and cell division, you can see the two new amebas that are produced. Both these amebas are identical to the parent ameba because their chromosomes are identical.

Many other single-celled organisms also reproduce asexually. Bacteria are single-celled organisms that cause many illnesses, such as strep throat and pneumonia. Bacteria are also used to make vinegar, yogurt, cheese, pickles, and other food products. Bacterial cells, like those in the picture to the left, do not have a nucleus. However, they do have a single, loop-shaped chromosome. When a bacterium reproduces, it makes a copy of its chromosome. Then the cell divides in two. As with the ameba, the two bacteria are identical to the parent.

The organism in the photo to the lower left is a yeast. Bakers add yeast to the dough that bread is made from. The yeast causes the bread to rise. Yeast cells reproduce asexually. After a yeast cell's nucleus has completed mitosis, a small part of the parent cell begins to pinch off. The cytoplasm, the clear, jellylike substance that fills the cell, divides unequally. The smaller part, called

2 *When a single-celled ameba reaches a certain size, it gets ready to divide.*

1 *An ameba reproduces by asexual reproduction.*

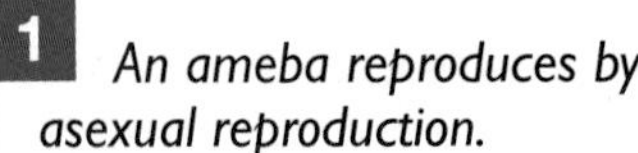

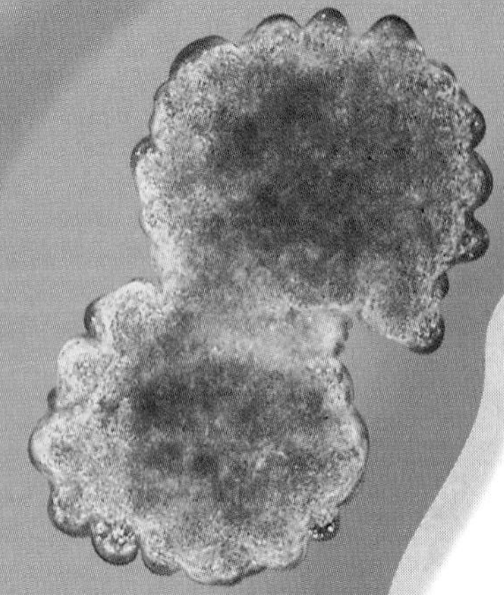

a bud, at first stays attached to the parent cell. Then it grows and eventually separates from the parent to live on its own. The parent cell and the new cell are identical because their chromosomes are identical.

At times, some many-celled organisms also reproduce asexually. For example, a ribbon worm sometimes attaches its tail to a rock or other hard surface. It then crawls in the opposite direction. Eventually, its body tears in half. Each half will grow into a complete worm by making new cells. The new individuals are identical to the original organism.

In the spring, potato farmers get ready for planting. They cut potatoes into pieces so that each piece has an "eye." After planting, each eye develops into a new plant. From one potato, a number of new plants are formed. Each plant has chromosomes that are exactly like those of the original potato.

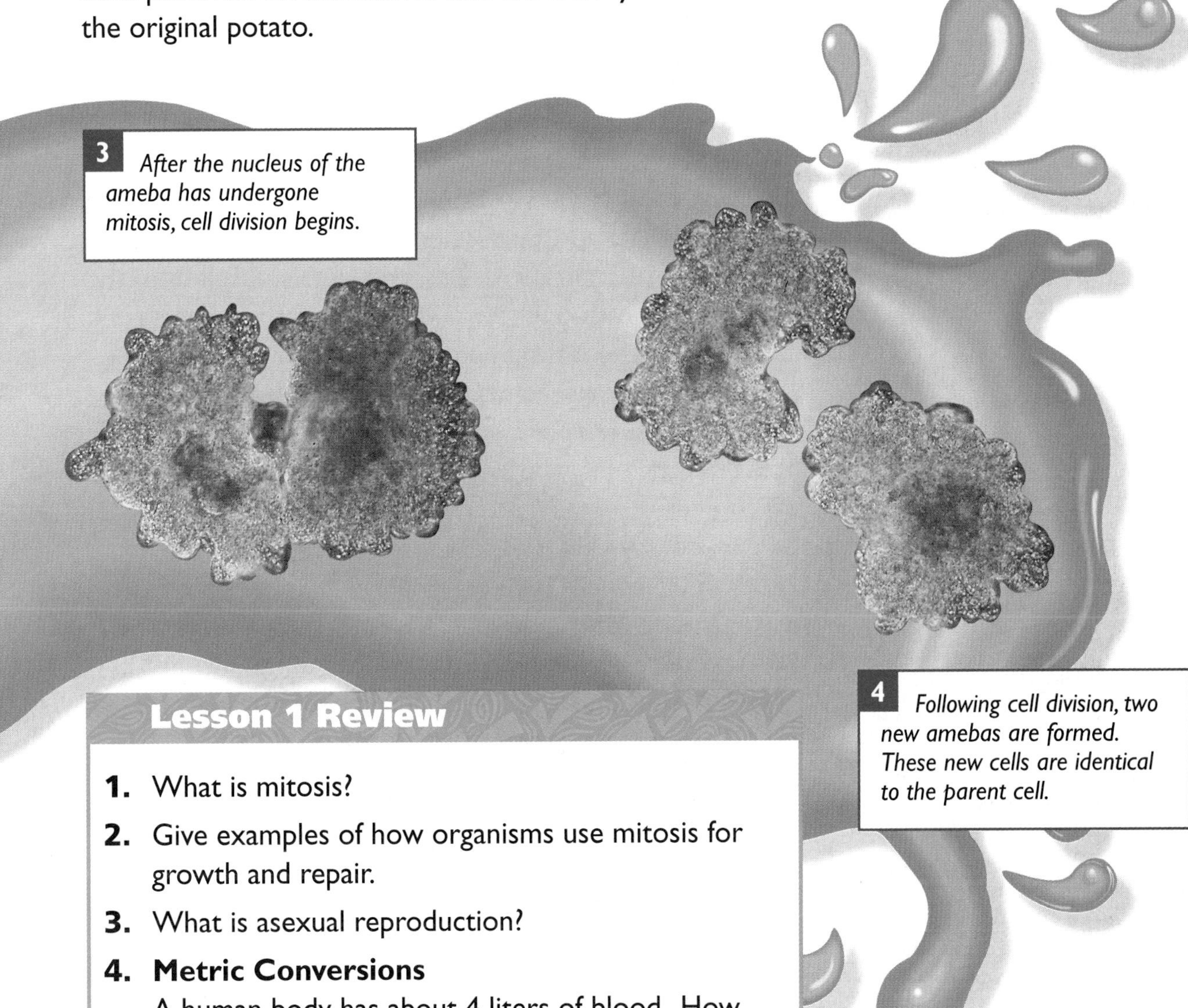

3 *After the nucleus of the ameba has undergone mitosis, cell division begins.*

4 *Following cell division, two new amebas are formed. These new cells are identical to the parent cell.*

Lesson 1 Review

1. What is mitosis?
2. Give examples of how organisms use mitosis for growth and repair.
3. What is asexual reproduction?
4. **Metric Conversions**
   A human body has about 4 liters of blood. How many milliliters of blood does a human body have?

You will learn:
- what meiosis is.
- how reproduction by two parents produces offspring.
- how mitosis and meiosis compare.

Lesson 2

How Do Many-Celled Organisms Reproduce?

They're so cute! At your friend's house is a new litter of puppies. The mother dog is a black poodle, and the father dog is a white, short-haired terrier. What do you think the puppies will look like? Will they look more like the mother or the father?

Meiosis

When a litter of puppies is born, none of the puppies will be identical to its mother or father. That is because the puppies are the result of **sexual reproduction**, or the reproduction by two parents. Dogs, and other organisms that reproduce sexually, have special cells called **sex cells**. Each puppy results when one sex cell from the mother joins with one sex cell from the father. The sex cell that comes from the female parent is an egg cell. The sex cell that comes from the male parent is a sperm cell. You can see sperm cells surrounding an egg cell in the photo. Notice that the sperm cells are much smaller than the egg cell.

Unlike body cells, sex cells form by a process called **meiosis**. Sex cells have only half the number of chromosomes as the parent cell. Follow the process on the next page as you read how this happens.

Before meiosis begins, each chromosome duplicates itself, forming twin chromosomes. Meiosis itself occurs in two stages. During the first stage of meiosis (steps 1–5), the twin chromosomes separate, and the cell divides. Two cells are the result. Each has the same number of chromosomes as the first cell.

During the second stage of meiosis (steps 6–10), the chromosomes in each cell split apart, and each cell divides. Four cells are formed. Each has half the number of chromosomes as the first cell.

Glossary

Glossary

sexual reproduction (sek′ shü əl rē prə duk′ shən), reproduction by two parents

sex cell (seks sel), a type of cell produced only by an organism that reproduces sexually

meiosis (mī ō′ sis), the process by which sex cells form

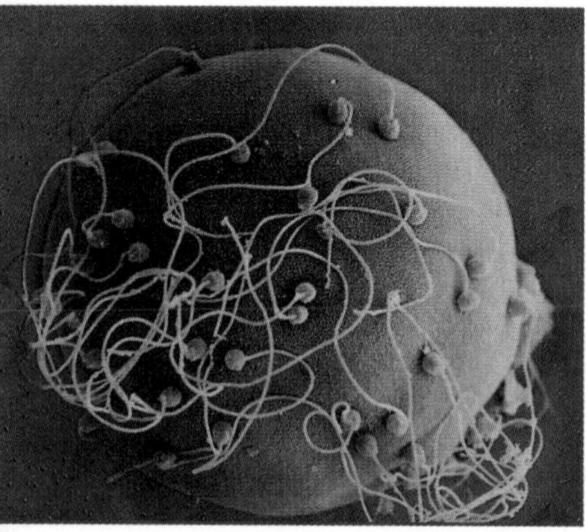

▲ *Many sperm cells surround this egg cell. However, only one sperm cell will unite with the egg cell.*

Meiosis

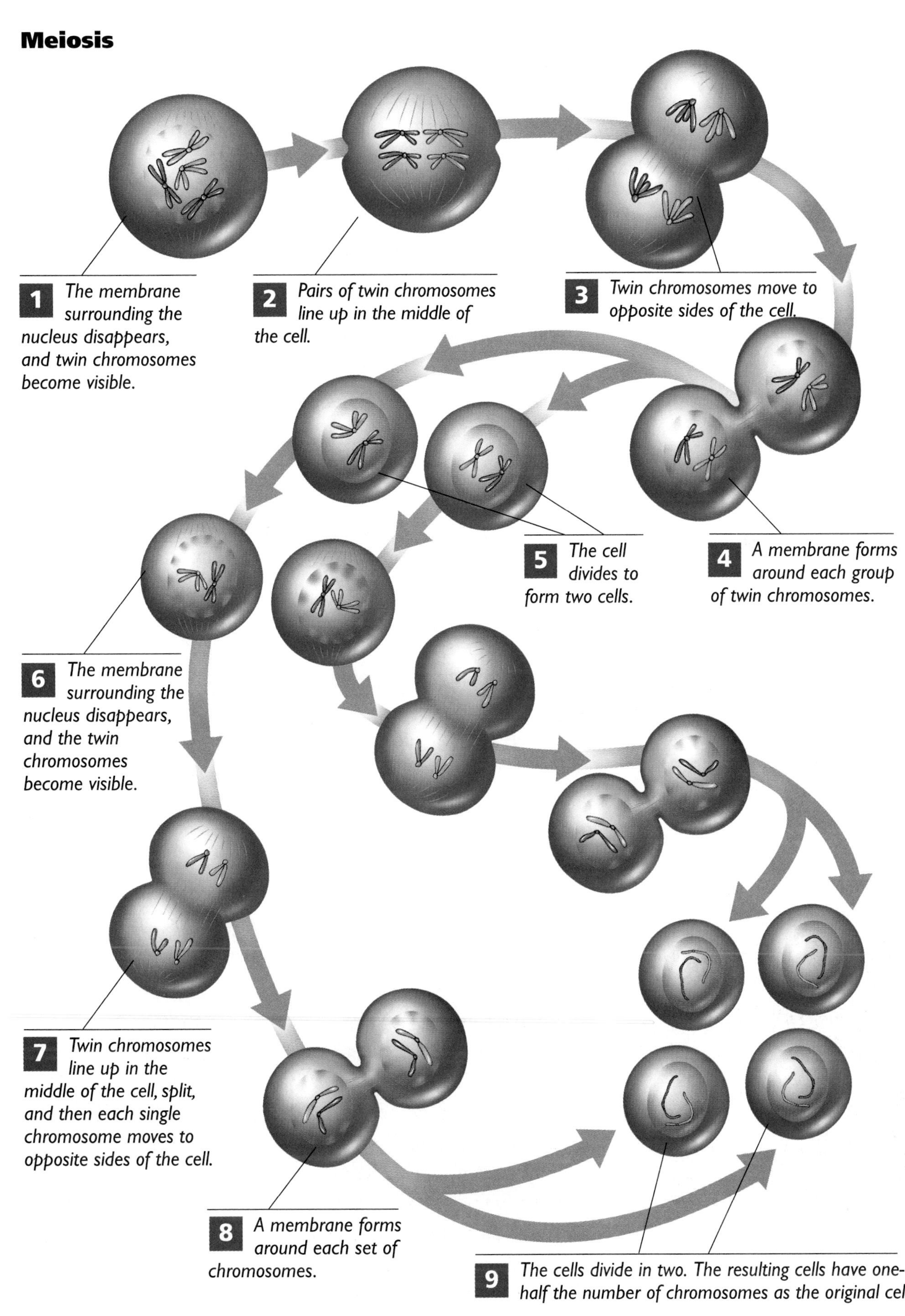

1 The membrane surrounding the nucleus disappears, and twin chromosomes become visible.
2 Pairs of twin chromosomes line up in the middle of the cell.
3 Twin chromosomes move to opposite sides of the cell.
4 A membrane forms around each group of twin chromosomes.
5 The cell divides to form two cells.
6 The membrane surrounding the nucleus disappears, and the twin chromosomes become visible.
7 Twin chromosomes line up in the middle of the cell, split, and then each single chromosome moves to opposite sides of the cell.
8 A membrane forms around each set of chromosomes.
9 The cells divide in two. The resulting cells have one-half the number of chromosomes as the original cell.

Meiosis in Dogs

This diagram shows how the number of chromosomes in each cell changes as sex cells are produced. ▼

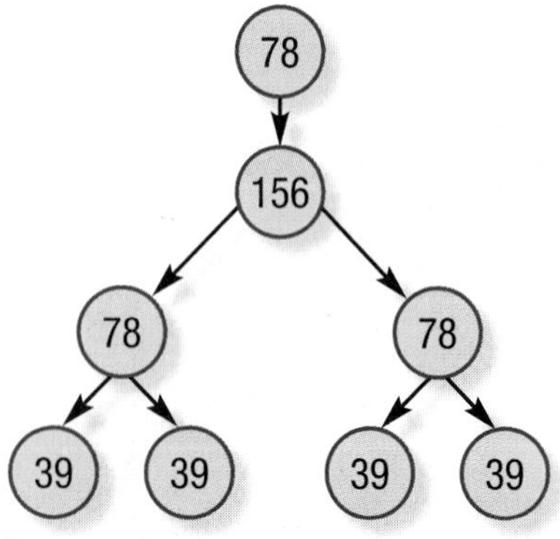

Think back to the litter of puppies. Each resulted from the joining of sex cells from two parents. A dog has 78 chromosomes in each of its body cells. Before meiosis begins, the chromosomes double in the special cell that is going to produce sex cells. At that point, this parent cell has 156 chromosomes.

During the first stage of meiosis, the cell divides in two. Each of the two new cells has 78 chromosomes.

During the second stage of meiosis, each of those cells divides again. Each of the four sex cells that are produced has 39 chromosomes. In other words, each sex cell has only half the number of chromosomes as do the other cells in the dog's body. This process is summarized in the diagram to the left.

Glossary

Glossary

fertilization (fėr′ tl ə zā′ shən), the joining of an egg cell and a sperm cell during sexual reproduction

zygote (zī′ gōt), the first cell of an offspring, formed when an egg cell and a sperm cell join

Reproduction by Two Parents

The joining of an egg cell and a sperm cell during sexual reproduction is called **fertilization.** Suppose, for example, a female frog lays a mass of eggs in water. The male frog releases a fluid containing sperm cells over the eggs. When a sperm cell enters an egg cell, fertilization results. Only the first sperm cell to enter an egg cell can fertilize that egg.

When an egg cell and a sperm cell join, the resulting cell is called a **zygote.** The first picture below shows the fertilized egg, or zygote, of a frog. The zygote undergoes mitosis and cell division to form two cells within two to three hours after fertilization.

The two cells that were produced by the zygote then divide to form four cells. The four cells divide to become

Frog Development

These microscopic photos show how a single-celled frog zygote divides to produce more cells. The cells will continue to divide many times until a multicellular tadpole is hatched. ▶

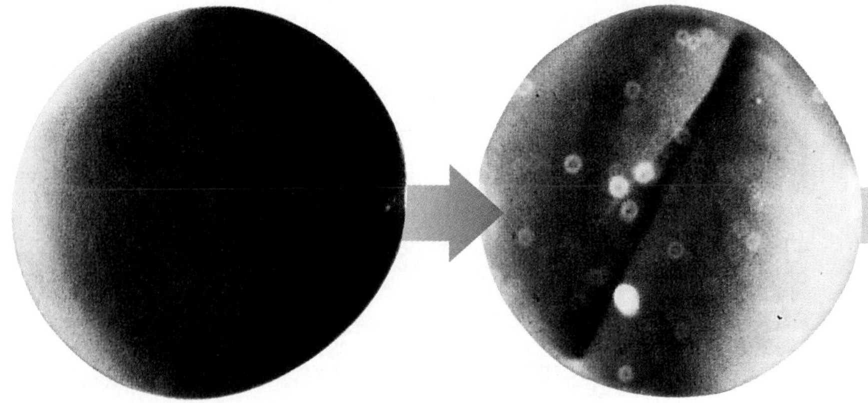

Zygote

eight cells, and so on. You can see this ongoing development of the frog in the next three pictures. Mitosis and cell division continue, with each new cell producing more cells. After a period of six to nine days, a complete tadpole has formed.

The young alligator in the picture resulted from sexual reproduction. Unlike the egg cells of frogs, alligator egg cells are fertilized by the male parent's sperm inside the female parent's body. After fertilization occurs, a leathery covering forms over each zygote. These fertilized zygotes develop into eggs, which the female lays in a large nest on the bank of a pond or river. In about 60 days, the zygote in each egg has developed into a many-celled organism, and the young alligator hatches. The newly hatched alligator is much smaller than its parents. How will the alligator grow to adult size?

In most mammals, not only does fertilization take place within the female's body, but development of the offspring does too. Like the mother dog at your friend's house, most female mammals give birth to live young.

▲ *As in all cases of sexual reproduction, this young alligator started out as a single cell.*

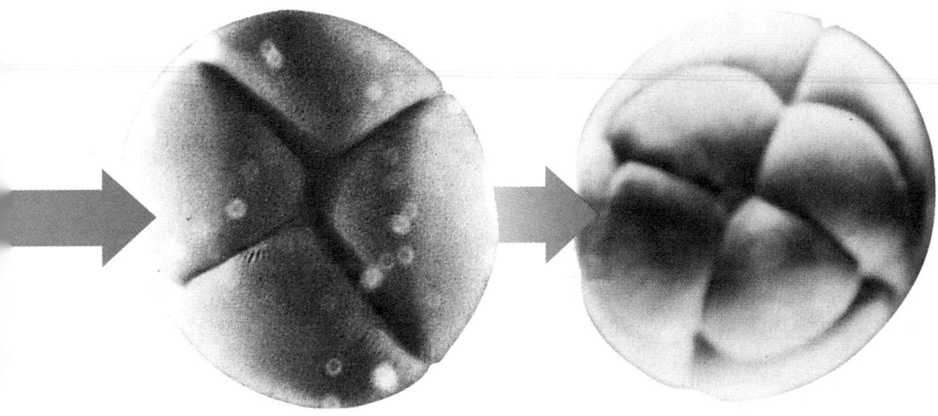

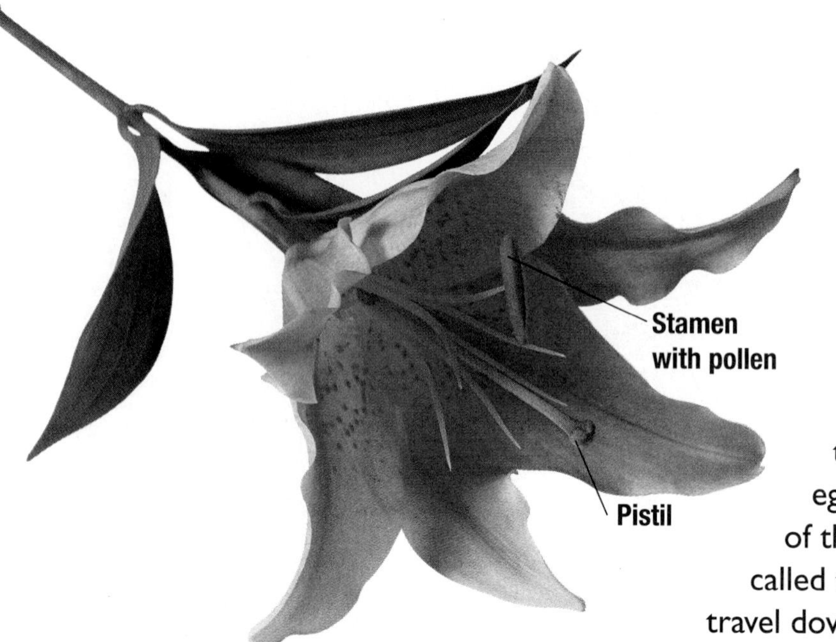

▲ *Flowers are organs of sexual reproduction. In many plants, both male and female sex cells are produced in the same flower.*

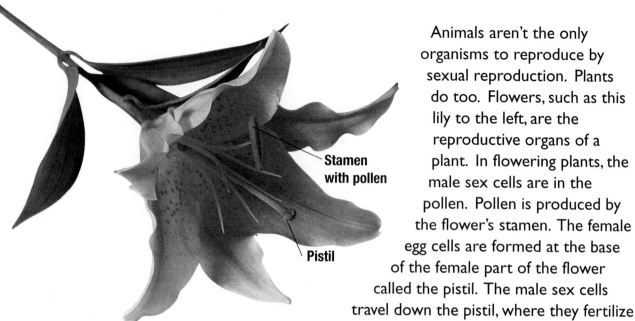

Animals aren't the only organisms to reproduce by sexual reproduction. Plants do too. Flowers, such as this lily to the left, are the reproductive organs of a plant. In flowering plants, the male sex cells are in the pollen. Pollen is produced by the flower's stamen. The female egg cells are formed at the base of the female part of the flower called the pistil. The male sex cells travel down the pistil, where they fertilize the eggs, forming zygotes. A protective covering forms around the zygote, resulting in a seed. The seed protects the developing organism.

There's an important difference between sexual and asexual reproduction. The kittens in this picture resulted from sexual reproduction. What do you notice about their appearance? Compare each kitten with its parent. You'll see that its coloring is different from that of the mother. That difference is a result of sexual reproduction. The mother's egg cell contributed half the chromosomes that the kitten has. The father's sperm cell contributed the other half. Therefore, the kittens are not exactly like either their mother or their father. How does this result differ from the offspring produced during asexual reproduction?

▲ *How do these kittens look like their parent? How do they differ from their parent and from one another?*

Comparing Mitosis and Meiosis

Important differences exist between mitosis and meiosis. The chart on the next page makes it easier to picture and compare these two processes and their results.

In many-celled organisms, mitosis occurs in body cells and leads to new body cells. Meiosis occurs in special cells to produce sex cells. The main difference between body cells and sex cells is the number of chromosomes in their nuclei. All body cells have the normal number of chromosomes for the species. For example, a human body cell has 46 chromosomes. Sex cells have half the number of normal chromosomes for the species. A human egg cell and a human sperm cell each have 23 chromosomes.

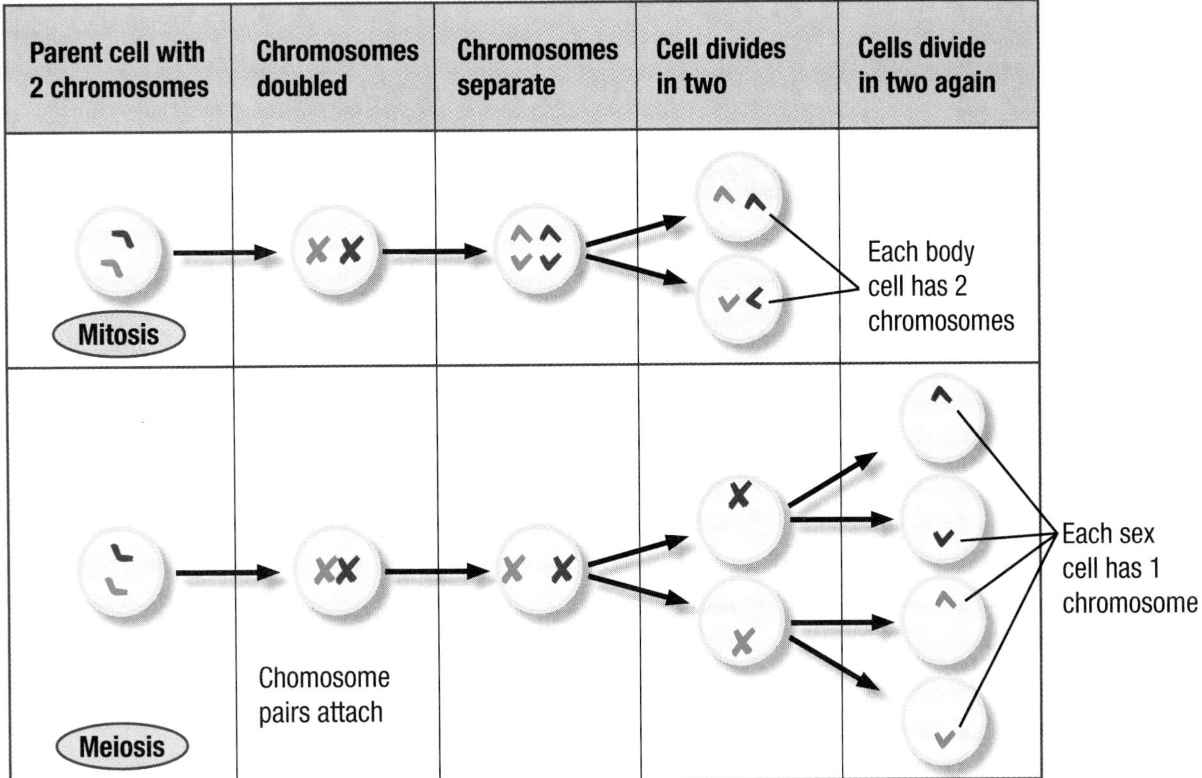

The number of chromosomes in body cells and sex cells differs because the number of divisions in mitosis and meiosis differs. In mitosis, the cell divides once. During meiosis, two divisions occur.

Finally, because the number of chromosomes differs, the offspring that result differ too. Mitosis leads to offspring that are identical to the parent because their chromosomes are identical. Meiosis leads to offspring that are not identical because their chromosomes are not identical to either parent's chromosomes.

Lesson 2 Review

1. What is meiosis?
2. How does reproduction by two parents produce offspring?
3. How do mitosis and meiosis compare?
4. **Metric Conversions**
   A human fetus grows by the process of mitosis from 0.02 cm at 6 days to about 46 cm at birth. Convert these measurements to millimeters.

You will learn:

- why every organism is unique.
- what the structure of DNA is.
- how DNA makes copies of itself.
- how DNA information is used.

Lesson 3

How Does DNA Control Traits?

Look in a mirror. WOW! Who is that you see? Did you know that the person you see is unique? That means "one of a kind," and that's what you are. Why? The answer lies within your cells.

Unique DNA

If you were asked to contrast the animals in the picture, what would you say? You might recognize that some of the animals are giraffes and some are zebras. Recall what you learned in Chapter 1 about species. The giraffes belong to a species that is different from the species that the zebras belong to. Each animal has all the physical characteristics, or **traits**, of the species to which it belongs.

How do the traits of these giraffes and zebras differ? The giraffes have longer necks and legs than those of the zebras. The colors and patterns on the body of each group are also different. Their differences, however, are more than in just the way they look.

Inside the nucleus of each giraffe cell is a set of instructions for building the giraffe's body. Those instructions are found in the giraffe's chromosomes. You've already learned that chromosomes are the parts of a cell's nucleus that carry information that controls all the cell's activities. Chromosomes contain a substance called **DNA**—deoxyribonucleic acid. The DNA determines the kind of organism that the cell belongs to—in this case, a giraffe.

Glossary

Glossary

trait (trāt), a characteristic of an organism

DNA, the molecule in each cell that directs the cell's activities

Look at these animals around a waterhole in Namibia, Africa. What characteristics do the animals share? Are they members of the same species? How do you know? ▼

The DNA of a chromosome is divided into sections called genes. Each **gene** controls how a certain trait will develop. For example, a gene might control the color of a giraffe's hair. A giraffe's body develops and works in certain ways because of the particular genes that the zygote received from the parents during fertilization.

Giraffes and zebras are more alike than giraffes and dogs. This means that giraffes and zebras share more of the same genes than do giraffes and dogs. Yet their genes are different enough that they belong to separate species.

How do the genes of the giraffes in the picture compare? Since the giraffes are all members of the same species, they share most of the same genes. However, the giraffes are not exactly alike. Each giraffe has a slightly different combination of genes that makes it a one-of-a-kind giraffe.

No two living things that are produced by sexual reproduction—except identical twins—have exactly the same genes. The cells in an organism's body carry a chemical pattern of DNA that makes it different from every other organism. What are some traits that make you unique?

Structure of DNA

More than a hundred years ago, biologists first observed chromosomes. Later, they suggested that genes were located on chromosomes. It wasn't until 1953 that two scientists, James Watson of the United States and Francis Crick of Great Britain, discovered the structure of chromosomal DNA. Their discovery helped scientists understand how the structure of DNA allows it to make copies of itself. From this discovery, scientists were able to better understand how traits can be passed from parent to offspring. In 1962, Watson and Crick received a Nobel Prize for their model of DNA.

History of Science

You can take a closer look at models of DNA molecules on this page and the following pages. Each chromosome inside the nucleus of a cell is a long, tightly coiled strand of DNA.

Glossary

gene (jēn), a section of DNA on a chromosome that controls a trait

Glossary

DNA

Long, twisted strands of DNA make up the chromosomes in a cell's nucleus. In fact, the DNA is coiled so tightly that if the DNA in a single chromosome could be stretched out, it would be up to 10,000 times longer than the chromosome itself. Follow this DNA strand on the following pages. ▼

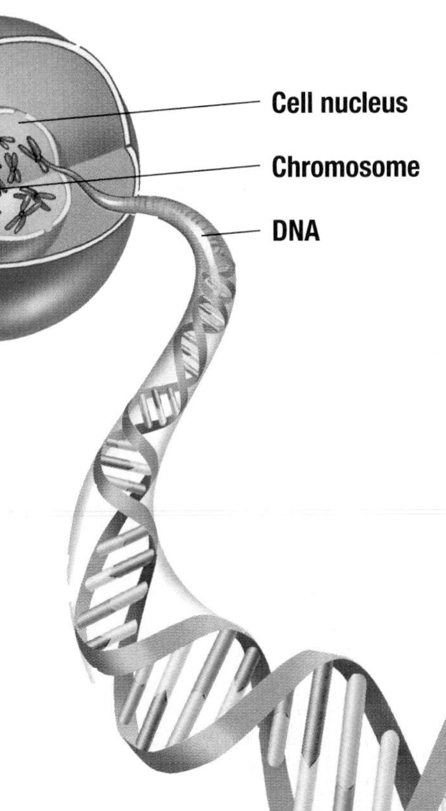

Glossary

base (bās), one kind of molecule that makes up a DNA strand

The shape of the DNA molecule looks like a long, twisted ladder. The ladder has millions of rungs made of four kinds of smaller molecules called **bases.** The four bases are represented by the letters *A, T, G,* and *C.* Bases have shapes that allow them to fit together only in certain combinations. Find the rungs in the diagram. Notice the color combinations that appear. Use the key to the left to see which bases fit together.

The bases pair up in this way to form the rungs of the ladder. The order in which the base pairs are arranged determines what instructions the cell receives. Notice that the arrangement of the base pairs varies from place to place on the chromosome. Different segments of the DNA ladder—genes—have different sequences of base pairs.

The differences in the sequences of base pairs in the genes allow the genes to give the cell an almost endless set of instructions for controlling all the characteristics of the individual. For example, an arrangement of GC-TA-CG-GC, which is shown on the DNA segment below, will give a different set of instructions to the cell than the arrangement shown on the next page, which is GC-TA-AT-GC.

DNA Bases

DNA is made of four different kinds of bases. ▼

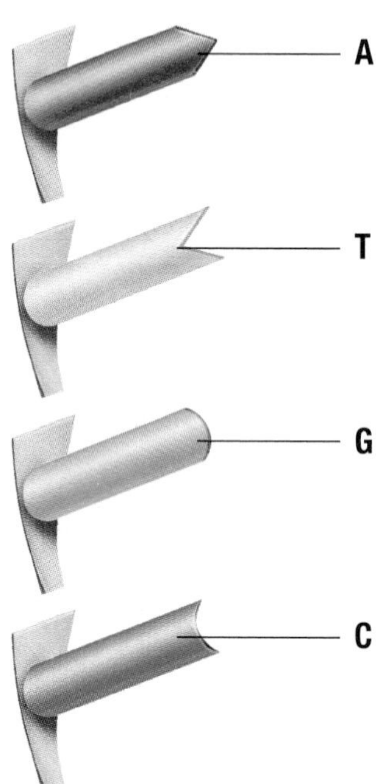

DNA Structure

A DNA molecule looks like a twisted ladder. The ladder has millions of rungs. ▼

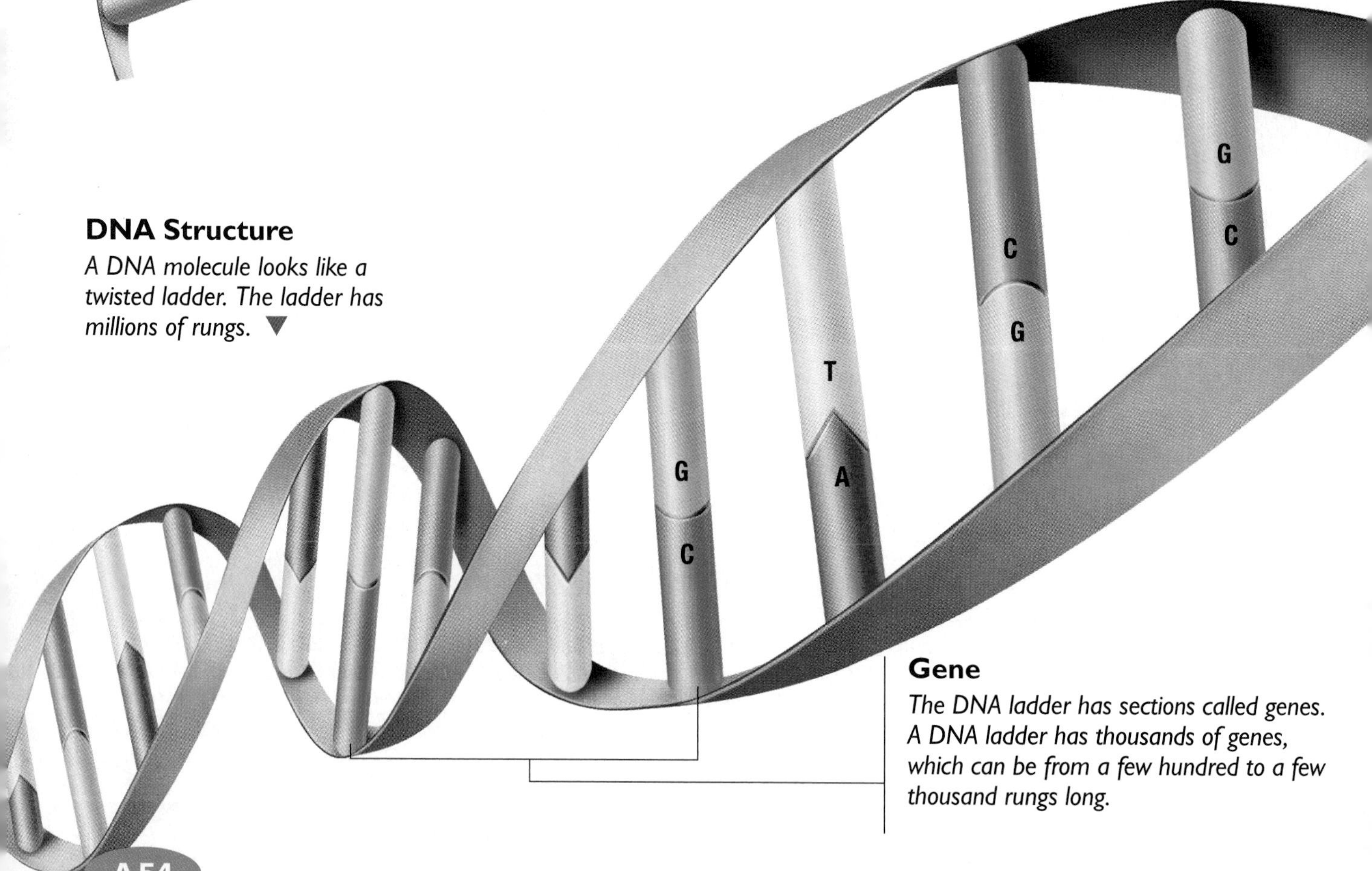

Gene

The DNA ladder has sections called genes. A DNA ladder has thousands of genes, which can be from a few hundred to a few thousand rungs long.

The DNA on all the chromosomes of an organism carries all the information about that organism's traits. For example, certain genes in your cells carry the information that determines the shape of your body. Likewise, instructions for the formation of a giraffe's body are contained in the DNA in the giraffe's cells. Every cell in the giraffe's body carries that same information.

Why is the information coded in the DNA of a giraffe so different from the information in your cells? After all, the same four bases—A, T, G, and C—make up the DNA of all living organisms. The information is different because the way in which the base pairs are arranged on the rungs of the DNA ladder is different in a giraffe than it is in your body cells. It is the unique arrangement of base pairs in DNA that is responsible for the uniqueness of each organism.

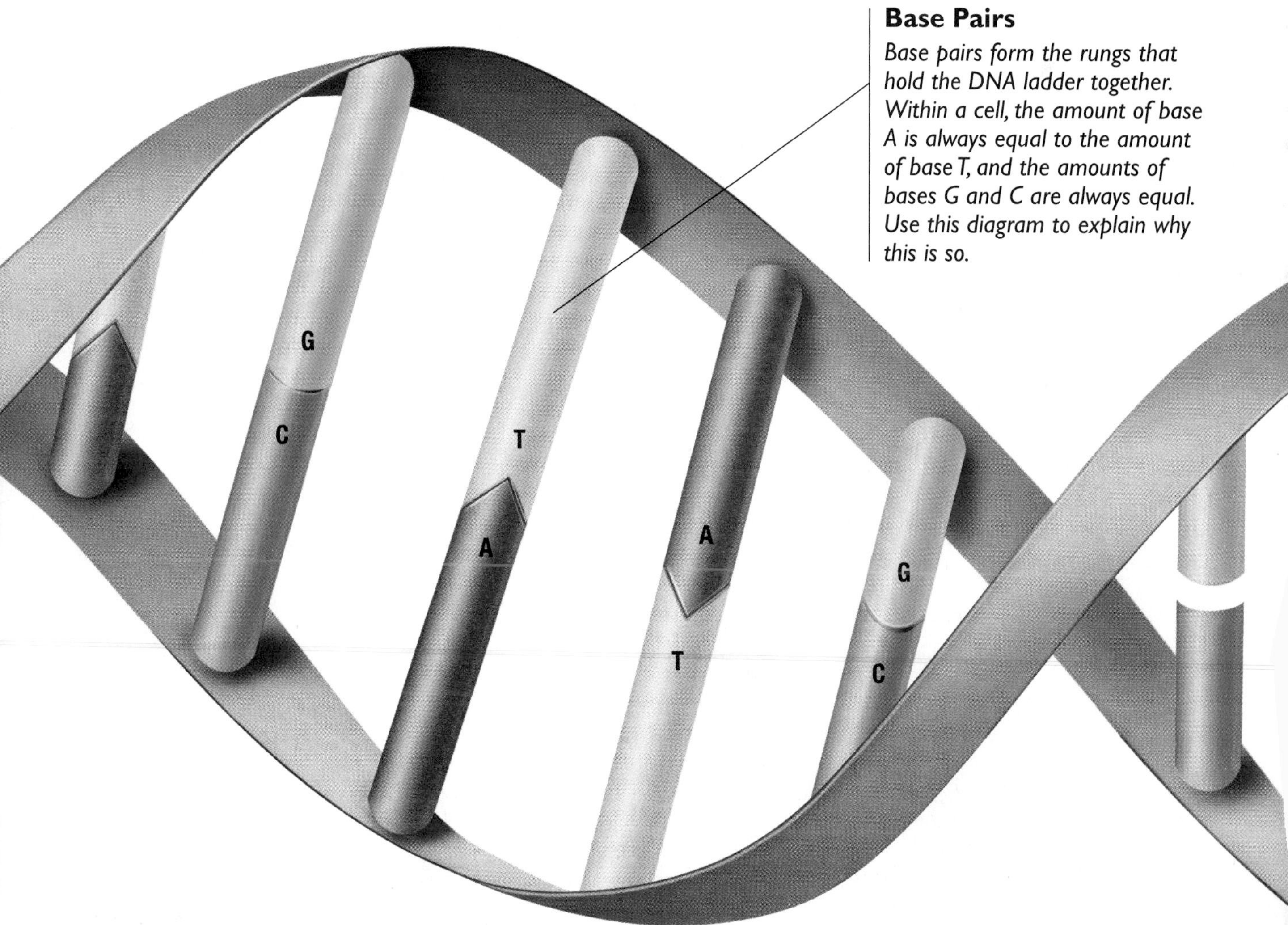

Base Pairs

Base pairs form the rungs that hold the DNA ladder together. Within a cell, the amount of base A is always equal to the amount of base T, and the amounts of bases G and C are always equal. Use this diagram to explain why this is so.

DNA Bases

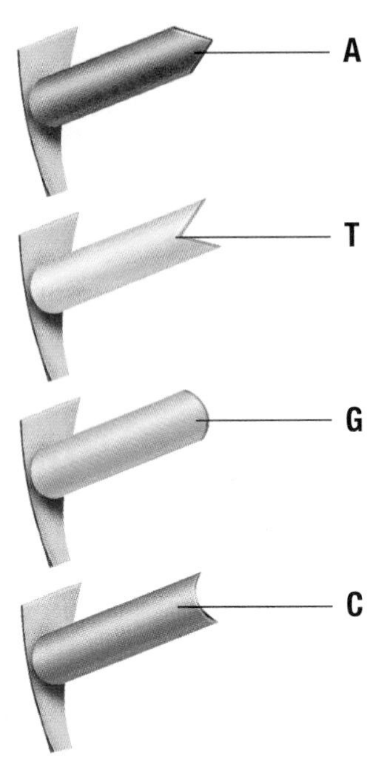

Making Copies of DNA

Think about what happens in cell reproduction before mitosis occurs. The chromosomes in the cell's nucleus double, and the DNA in the chromosomes is copied exactly. These exact copies are needed to give each new cell the same instructions that the original cell had.

How is DNA able to make an exact copy of itself? Look at the diagram as you read the following description.

Think of the DNA molecule as a zipper. When you unzip a zipper, the teeth that hold the zipper together separate, and you end up with two halves. The DNA molecule "unzips" when the long strand unwinds and the base pairs separate.

Within each cell nucleus are free-floating bases. These bases are not paired with other bases, but they are

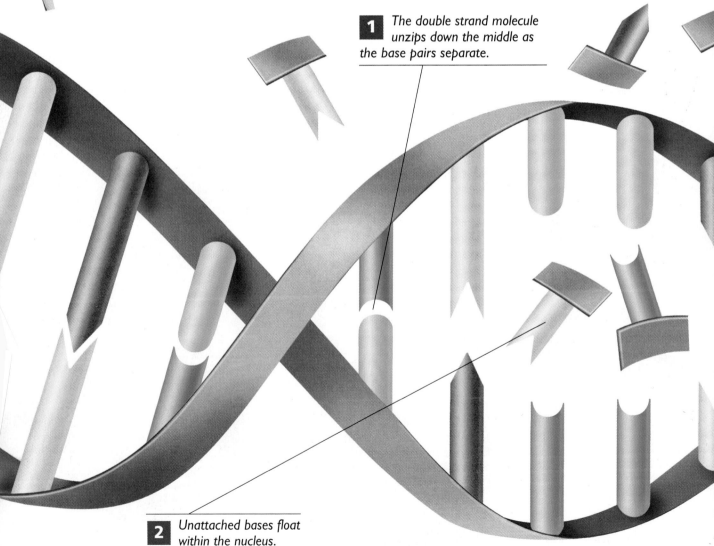

1 *The double strand molecule unzips down the middle as the base pairs separate.*

2 *Unattached bases float within the nucleus.*

attached to the same molecules that make up the side of the DNA ladder. When the DNA molecule unzips, these bases attach themselves to other bases on the DNA molecule. Remember that bases A and T can fasten only to each other, and G and C can fasten only to each other. This process continues until the two halves of the DNA molecule become two complete double-stranded molecules of DNA. Notice below how each of the two new DNA molecules is identical to the original DNA molecule.

Sections of DNA molecules—genes—direct the building of molecules called proteins. The different cells in your body are largely built from proteins. Your DNA code stores information about what proteins must be made. It also carries instructions that tell the cell when to start or stop building proteins.

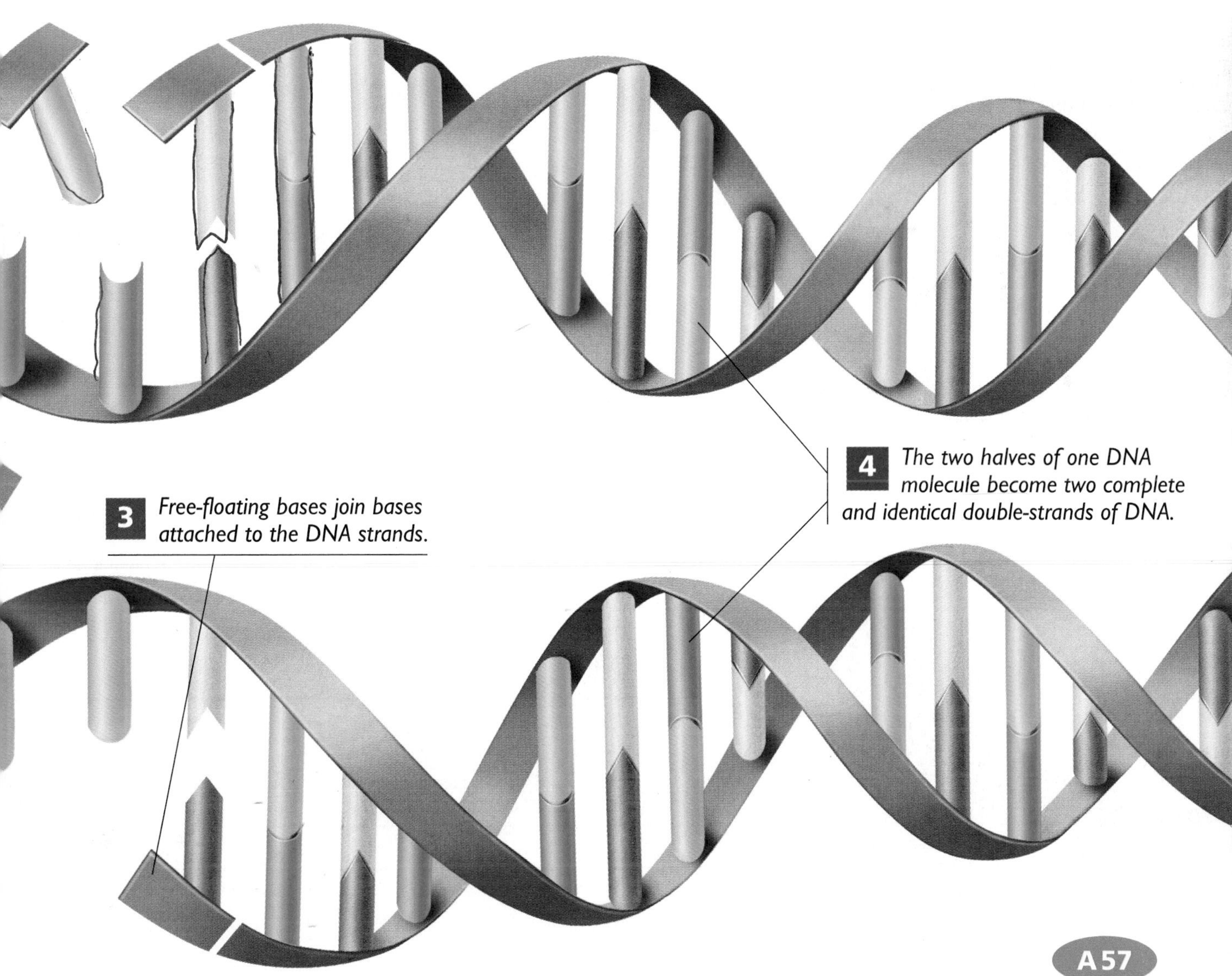
3 *Free-floating bases join bases attached to the DNA strands.*

4 *The two halves of one DNA molecule become two complete and identical double-strands of DNA.*

High blood pressure

Brown hair color

Green/blue eye color

▲ *Scientists have been able to find the exact location of many traits on the 46 human chromosomes. This drawing of one human chromosome shows just a few.*

Using DNA Information

Knowledge of DNA has come a long way since Watson and Crick first identified its structure. In 1990, scientists started working on the Human Genome Project. The goal of the project is to locate all the genes on the 46 human chromosomes, as well as to map the sequence of all the base pairs in DNA. The particular order of the bases on the rungs of the DNA ladder is called the DNA sequence. The sequence of DNA in an organism's cells holds the exact genetic instructions needed to make that organism. This complete set of instructions for making an organism is called that organism's genome.

The human genome contains at least 100,000 genes organized into 46 chromosomes. You can see the location of some genes on the chromosome shown to the left.

Since the human genome contains about 3 billion base pairs, the Genome Project is a huge undertaking. Scientists around the world hope to complete the project by the year 2003.

Information from the Human Genome Project and other DNA research may help doctors detect and treat disorders. Scientists have already identified genes that are associated with diseases such as cystic fibrosis and muscular dystrophy. They have also identified genes that seem to make a person more likely to have heart disease, diabetes, and certain cancers.

The fingerprint below is unique to the person who made it. Likewise, each individual has a unique set of

Each person has a set of fingerprints that is unlike that of any other person. The pattern of bands in the DNA "fingerprint" to the right is also unique for each individual. ▼

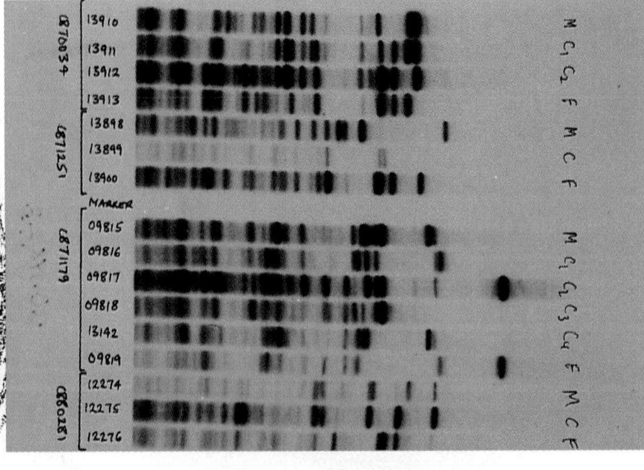

DNA, which can be used to identify a person. Samples of DNA can be taken from blood, hair, or skin. A special machine analyzes the DNA and produces a characteristic pattern of bands, or a genetic "fingerprint." Why do you think scientists call these patterns a fingerprint?

Police and other law-enforcement workers can use DNA fingerprints to determine whether a suspect was at a crime scene. For example, suppose someone broke into a store and stole some money. While breaking a window, the burglar cut his or her hand on the glass. Blood on the broken window would be an important clue for the police. White blood cells carry a person's DNA. Scientists could analyze the blood and make a DNA fingerprint of the person who broke the window. This fingerprint would be part of the crime evidence gathered.

Suppose the police had three possible suspects in the burglary. They could make a genetic fingerprint of each suspect's DNA. They could then compare the DNA fingerprints of the suspects with the DNA fingerprint collected from the broken, bloody glass at the crime scene. If the bands were to match, the police could be confident they had the right suspect.

The DNA fingerprint to the bottom right is a portion of the fingerprint made from the blood on the store window. Compare it with the DNA fingerprints of the three suspects. Which suspect do you think broke into the store?

Suspect A

Suspect B

Suspect C

Lesson 3 Review

1. Why is every organism unique?
2. Describe the structure of DNA.
3. How does DNA make copies of itself?
4. How is DNA information used?
5. **Metric Conversions**
   A trait of hummingbirds is that they are fast fliers. A hummingbird can fly 80 kilometers per hour. How many centimeters per hour can it fly?

Evidence

▲ *The bottom picture represents the DNA fingerprint collected from evidence at the site of the crime. Compare it to the DNA fingerprints above of the three suspects.*

Investigating DNA

Process Skills

- estimating and measuring
- observing
- communicating
- inferring

Materials

- safety goggles
- funnel
- graduated plastic cup
- coffee filter
- cup with onion cell mixture
- toothpick with flat end
- meat tenderizer
- rubbing alcohol
- sheet of dark construction paper

Getting Ready

In this activity you will be using an onion cell mixture so that you can see the DNA in an onion cell.

It is easier to see the DNA separate from the onion mixture when the mixture is held against the dark construction paper.

Follow This Procedure

1. Make a chart like the one shown. Use your chart to record your observations.

	Observations
Filtered liquid (step 3)	
Alcohol layer (step 6)	
End of toothpick (step 7)	

2. Put on your safety goggles. Place a funnel in a graduated cup. Fold a coffee filter as shown below. Place the folded filter in the funnel.

3. Pour the cell mixture into the filter paper (Photo A). Allow the liquid portion of the mixture to drip through the filter into the plastic cup until you have collected 60 mL of liquid. Remove the filter and remaining liquid. **Observe** the filtered liquid carefully. Record your observations.

Folding Coffee Filters

1.

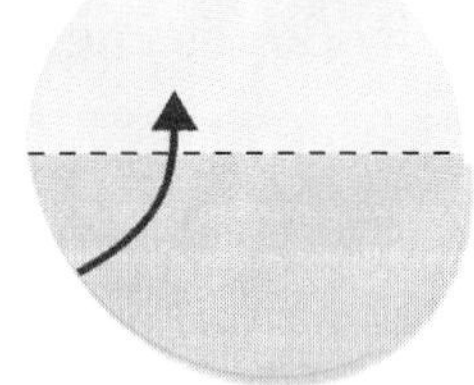

2.

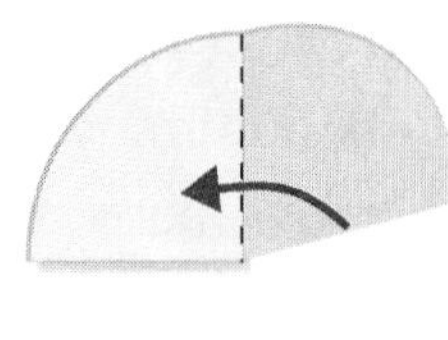

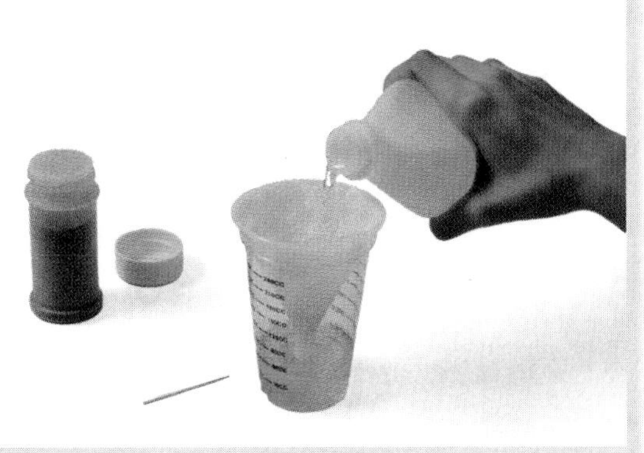

Photo A

4 Using the large end of a flat toothpick, add a few grains of meat tenderizer to the filtered liquid in the cup. Use the toothpick to gently stir the mixture.

5 Slowly add rubbing alcohol up to the 120 mL line on the cup. The alcohol will form a layer on top of the onion mixture.

6 Place a sheet of dark construction paper behind the cup. Observe the alcohol layer from the side of the cup for several minutes. Record your observations.

7 Use a toothpick to slowly stir the alcohol layer. Do not stir the bottom layer. What happens at the end of the toothpick? Record your observations.

Interpret Your Results

1. How did the observations in step 3 compare with those in step 7?

2. The material you collected on the toothpick in step 7 is DNA. Why do you think you were able to see the DNA in step 7 but not in step 3? **Communicate** your ideas to the group.

3. What can you **infer** about the shape of DNA molecules from this activity? Give reasons for your answer.

Inquire Further

How does the DNA of the onion cells you observed compare with the DNA in other organisms? Develop a plan to answer this or other questions you may have.

Self-Assessment

- I followed instructions to isolate DNA from plant cells.
- I recorded my **observations** about what happened as I stirred the alcohol layer.
- I compared the onion cells with the DNA material I collected.
- I **communicated** my ideas about the DNA in step 3 and step 7.
- I made an **inference** about the structure of DNA.

You will learn:

- how sexual reproduction produces variation in offspring.
- what dominant and recessive genes are.
- how mutations can affect an organism.

Lesson 4

How Do Organisms Inherit Traits?

You're looking through an old family photo album. Who's that? He looks just like you! What you're looking at is a picture of your father when he was your age. It's almost eerie how much he looks like you. How can that be?

Variation

The members of the family in the picture below look different enough so that you can tell them apart. On the other hand, the children, parents, and grandparents are certainly alike in many ways. For one thing, they all have the traits that you recognize as human traits—two eyes, a nose, a mouth, and two arms, to name just a few.

If you look even more closely at the family, you see that some members share the same shape of nose or the same shape and size of mouth. Children in a family often share

What traits do the children have in common? What traits were passed on to each child from the mother? from the father? from each grandparent? ▶

certain traits with one or both parents. In some cases, children may look more like a grandparent than a parent.

How does a child get his or her mother's eyes or father's nose? The process by which traits are passed from parents to offspring—from generation to generation—is called **heredity.** Remember that genes control how traits develop. When you remember that genes make up chromosomes and that chromosomes are passed on during sexual reproduction, you can begin to see how heredity works.

Recall that DNA in the egg cell combines with DNA in the sperm cell during fertilization. Then a single cell—the zygote—forms. You can see how this happens in the picture to the right.

Find the chromosomes in the sex cells that are alike in size and shape. Each contains genes for similar characteristics. After fertilization, the resulting zygote has a pair of chromosomes that act together to produce traits.

Organisms that are produced as a result of sexual reproduction receive, or **inherit,** at least two genes for every trait. One gene is inherited from the mother. The other gene is inherited from the father.

The children in the picture on page A62 resemble both parents because they inherited chromosomes, and thus genes, from both parents. They each inherited 23 pairs of chromosomes, or a total of 46 chromosomes. One set of 23 chromosomes was inherited from the father. The other set of 23 chromosomes was inherited from the mother.

Not every child in a family receives the same set of genes from the mother and father. Each egg cell of the mother contains a different combination of genes. Each sperm cell of the father also contains a different combination of genes. The appearance of each child in the family results from the particular combinations he or she received during fertilization. So, the children may show differences, or variations, in the same trait. What differences do you see in the children in the family?

Glossary

heredity (hə red′ ə tē), the process by which traits are passed from parents to offspring

inherit (in her′ it), to receive from one's mother or father

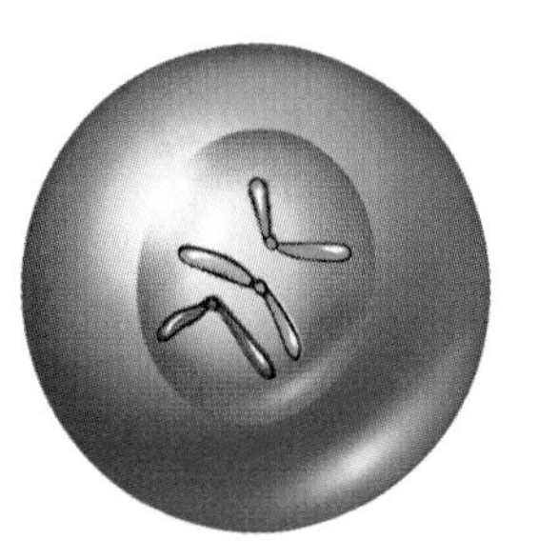

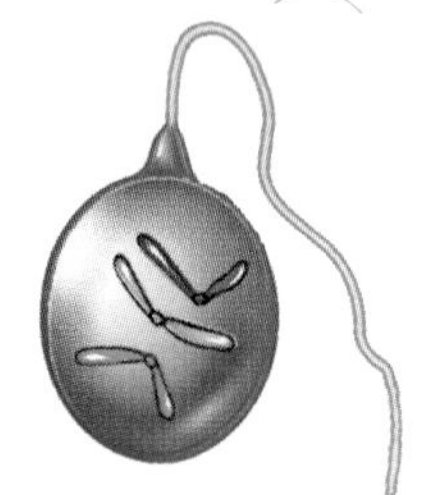

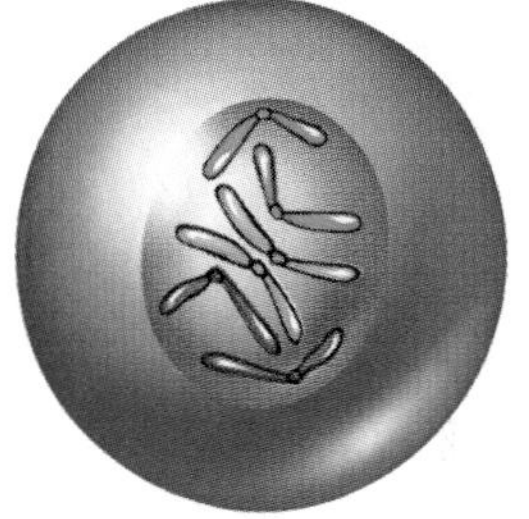

▲ *Look closely at the chromosomes in this diagram to see how they form pairs during fertilization.*

Glossary

Glossary

dominant gene
(dom′ə nənt jēn), a gene that prevents the expression of another gene

Dominant and Recessive Genes

If you mixed red paint and white paint together, you would expect them to blend to form pink paint. A similar thing happens in some flowers. Plant growers often mix the traits of the same kind of flowers in order to make variations of traits.

For example, a grower can gather pollen from a red flower on a snapdragon plant. The pollen carries genes for red flowers. Then, the grower can brush the pollen onto the pistil of a white flower on a different snapdragon plant. This pistil holds egg cells that carry genes for white flowers. Each new seed that is produced when the pollen fertilizes the eggs will inherit a gene for red flower color and a gene for white flower color. When the seeds are planted, they will grow into new snapdragon plants.

In the new snapdragon plants, the effects of the genes for flower color are blended. Therefore, when the new plants bloom, the flowers will be pink. The diagram shows how this blending occurs. Notice how each flower has a pair of genes that determine its color. The offspring plant received one gene from each parent.

Blending also occurs in some animals. In shorthorn cattle, when a red bull is mated with a white cow, their offspring are roan. Roan calves have a mixture of red and white hairs on their bodies. The same blending occurs when a white bull is mated to a red cow.

The blending effect of the snapdragon genes is only one way genes act together. Many times, two genes do not produce a blended effect. Instead, one trait appears while the other trait stays hidden. In such cases, a **dominant gene** is completely hiding the effect of another gene.

The diagram on the next page shows how flower color is inherited in pea plants. Notice that the offspring pea plant inherited a gene for red flowers from one parent and a gene for white flowers from the other parent. In pea plants, the gene for red flowers is a dominant gene. It is represented by a capital *R*. All dominant traits are represented by capital letters.

Blending of Traits

Compare the offspring produced in this picture with the offspring produced in the picture on the next page. How do they differ? ▼

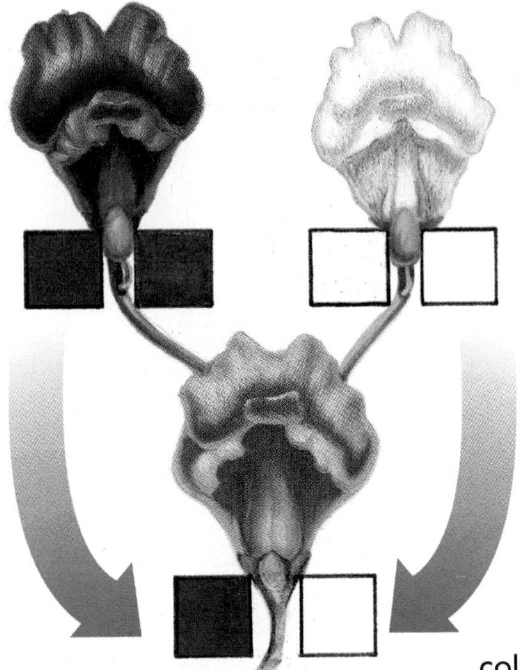

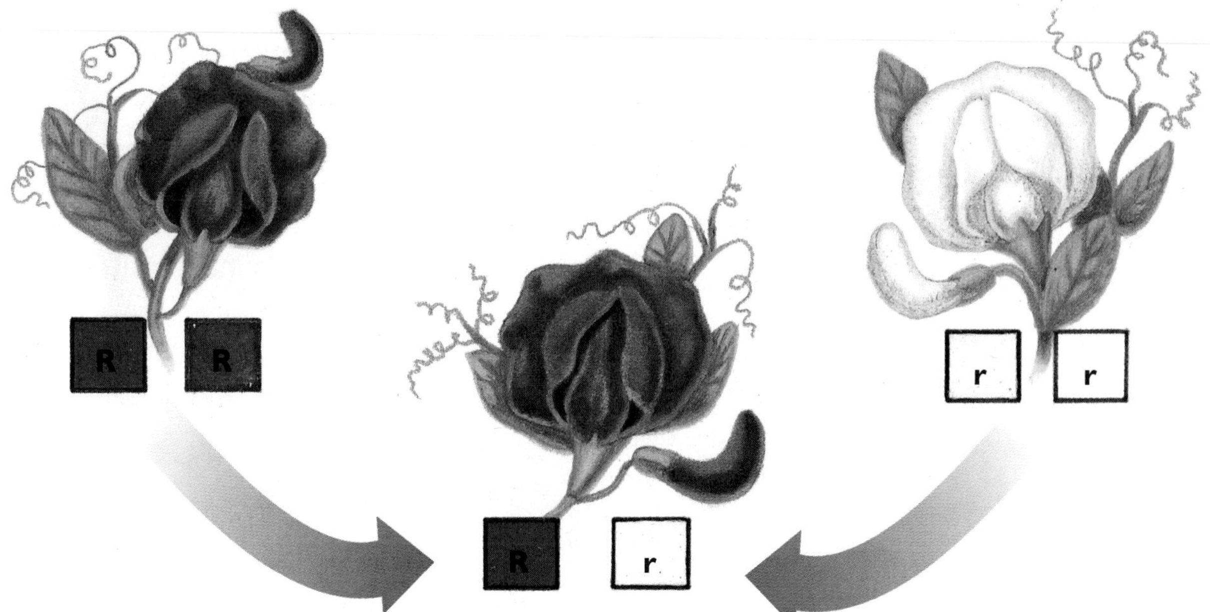

Dominant and Recessive Traits

▲ *These parent pea plants are purebreds. The offspring is a hybrid.*

The gene for red flowers hides the effect of the gene for white flowers. The gene whose effect is hidden is called a **recessive gene.** In this case, the gene for white flowers is recessive. It, like all recessive genes, is represented by a small letter.

You might wonder how a pea plant can have white flowers if the gene for red flowers is always dominant. To answer this question, you need to look at the genes of the parents and the offspring. Notice that the parent plant with red flowers has two genes for red flower color. The offspring plant has one gene for red and one gene for white. Because the gene for red flowers is dominant, that plant also has red flowers.

Now look at the parent plant that has white flowers. It has two recessive genes for white flower color. A recessive gene for a trait is expressed only when an organism has two recessive genes for that trait. It must receive a recessive gene from each parent.

An organism with two dominant or two recessive genes for a trait is called **purebred.** Both of the parent pea plants in the diagram are purebred for flower color.

An organism with one dominant and one recessive gene for a trait is a **hybrid.** The offspring pea plant in the diagram is hybrid for flower color. Suppose two pea plants that are hybrid for flower color are bred. What color flowers could their offspring have? The diagram on the right shows you the possible combination of genes for any offspring.

Glossary

recessive gene (ri ses′ iv jēn), a gene whose expression is prevented by a dominant gene

purebred (pyůr′ bred′), an organism with two dominant or two recessive genes for a trait

hybrid (hī′ brid), an organism with one dominant and one recessive gene for a trait

Offspring of Hybrid Plants

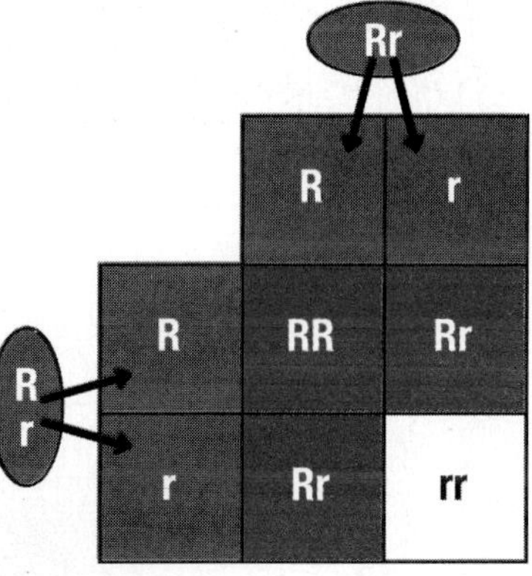

Many traits that you observe in yourself are the result of dominant or recessive traits. Can you roll your tongue like the girl to the left below? If you can, then you have at least one dominant gene for this trait. If you can't, then you must have two recessive genes for the trait. Tongue rolling is only one of the common dominant traits found in humans. Let's look at some others.

Notice the hairline of the girl on the right. Her hairline is straight. Many people have a hairline with a point in the middle of the forehead. This pattern of hair growth is called a widow's peak. This trait is also caused by a dominant gene. If you don't have a widow's peak, you inherited two recessive genes for this trait. If you do, then either your mother or your father—if not both parents—also has a widow's peak.

The boy in the middle has freckles. Freckles are a human trait caused by two recessive genes. How many of your classmates inherited recessive genes for freckles? How many inherited a dominant gene, and thus have no freckles? What about you?

These students are showing some traits. Which of these traits do you have? ▼

Mutations

You learned in Lesson 3 that before a cell divides, each DNA molecule in the cell makes an exact copy of itself. Sometimes during the copying process, mistakes happen. For example, a whole section of the DNA strand might be rearranged so that the base pairs are in a different order. More often, the error is as small as a single base ending up out of place. Any change that occurs when DNA copies itself is a **mutation**.

When a mutation occurs in a sex cell, a different DNA instruction is passed along to the offspring. Some changes in DNA might not change the instructions very much. In such a case, the change might not even be noticed in the offspring. However, other changes can result in the appearance of a new trait.

The bullfrogs to the right blend in well with their environment because of their coloring. They are able to hide from predators. However, the bullfrog below would have a hard time hiding from its enemies. That bullfrog is an albino. The albino bullfrog resulted from a mutation in a gene that causes normal coloring. Its body is not able to make a pigment. Because pigment gives color to skin, the bullfrog is colorless.

Glossary

mutation
(myü tā′ shən), a permanent change in DNA that occurs when DNA copies itself

A bullfrog with normal coloring can easily hide along the edge of a pond and snatch up insects. ▼

▲ *The mutation that produced this albino frog could have been caused by chemicals or radiation in the environment.*

Lesson 4 Review

1. How does sexual reproduction produce variations in offspring?
2. What are dominant and recessive genes?
3. Give an example of how a mutation can affect an organism.
4. **Bar Graphs**
   Survey your class for the trait of eye color. Make a bar graph to show your results.

Investigate Activity

Investigating Variation in Seedlings

Process Skills

Process Skills

- observing
- predicting
- collecting and interpreting data
- inferring

Materials

- 15 corn seeds
- hand lens
- marker
- masking tape
- aluminum pan
- metric ruler
- seed starter mix
- cup of water
- plastic wrap
- source of light

Getting Ready

In this activity, you'll germinate corn seeds to see if they produce plants that are alike.

Look at the self-assessment section at the end of the activity. This tells you what your teacher will expect of you.

Follow This Procedure

1. Make a chart like the one shown. Use your chart to record your observations and predictions.

Prediction:

Date	Seeds germinated	Plants with green leaves	Plants with white leaves

2. **Observe** some corn seeds with a hand lens. Do you observe any differences? Make a **prediction.** Do you think all the plants grown from these seeds will look alike? Explain why you made the prediction.

3. Use a marker and masking tape to label an aluminum pan with your group's name. Place about 2 cm of seed starter mix in the bottom of the pan.

4. Place 15 corn seeds, one by one, in the pan. The seeds should be evenly spaced about 1.5 cm apart (Photo A).

5. Cover the seeds with a 1 cm layer of starter mix. Gently sprinkle water over the starter mix to make it moist. Cover the pan with plastic wrap and place it in a lighted area (Photo B).

Photo A

Photo B

6 Check the seeds each day. If the starter mix starts to dry out, add water to keep it moist.

7 Observe when the first seeds begin to germinate. Record the date and the number of seeds germinated. Also record the number of plants with white leaves and the number of plants with green leaves.

8 Continue to observe the seeds every other day for 4 more days. Record your observations.

Interpret Your Results

1. What differences did you observe in the dry corn seeds? What differences did you observe in the leaves of the germinated seeds?

2. How does your prediction compare with your results?

3. What **inference** can you make about the presence of chlorophyll and the different colored corn leaves that you observed?

4. What can you infer about the genes of the corn plants you observed?

Inquire Further

Which plants will live longer—the plants with the white leaves or the plants with green leaves? Develop a plan to answer this or other questions you may have.

Self-Assessment

- I followed instructions to germinate corn seedlings.
- I made a **prediction** about how the plants would look.
- I explained why I made the prediction.
- I **collected and interpreted data** about the germinating seeds.
- I made an **inference** about the genes of the corn plants in this activity.

Chapter 2 Review

Chapter Main Ideas

Lesson 1

- Through mitosis and cell division, a cell copies its nucleus to produce two new cells with identical chromosomes.
- Mitosis results in growth and repair.
- In asexual reproduction, two new organisms are produced by just one parent.

Lesson 2

- In meiosis, a cell divides to produce four sex cells, each with half the number of chromosomes as the parent cell.
- In sexual reproduction, an egg cell and a sperm cell join to produce a zygote.
- In mitosis, cells divide once and develop identical offspring. During meiosis, cells divide twice to produce sex cells with half the number of chromosomes as the parent.

Lesson 3

- Organisms are unique because their cells have unique DNA.
- DNA is a coiled strand of base pairs that looks much like a spiraling ladder.
- DNA copies itself when base pairs split and connect with free-floating bases.
- DNA information can be used to treat and identify certain diseases and to identify individuals through their genetic "fingerprint."

Lesson 4

- In sexual reproduction, genes for all traits are inherited from each parent.
- Dominant genes for a trait hide the effect of recessive genes.
- Mutations occur when DNA does not make an exact copy of itself.

Reviewing Science Words and Concepts

Write the letter of the word or phrase that best completes each sentence.

a. asexual reproduction
b. base
c. cell division
d. DNA
e. dominant gene
f. fertilization
g. gene
h. heredity
i. hybrid
j. inherit
k. meiosis
l. mitosis
m. mutation
n. purebred
o. recessive gene
p. sex cell
q. sexual reproduction
r. trait
s. zygote

1. An organism with one dominant and one recessive gene for a trait is a(n) ___.
2. A characteristic of an organism is also called a(n) ___.
3. A(n) ___ hides the effect of a recessive gene.
4. The process that produces cells with half the number of chromosomes as the parent is ___.
5. A molecule that appears in pairs on a DNA strand is a(n) ___.
6. An organism with two dominant or two recessive genes for a trait is a(n) ___.
7. An egg is one kind of ___.
8. Production of new organisms from one parent is ___.

9. A change that occurs in DNA is a(n) ___.
10. The offspring cell formed after fertilization is a(n) ___.
11. The process by which two cells form from one cell is ___.
12. Production of a new organism by two parents is ___.
13. During ___ an egg and sperm cell join.
14. The process that produces new identical nuclei is ___.
15. A substance in chromosomes that directs the cell's activities is ___.
16. The process in which traits pass from parents to offspring is ___.
17. You ___ traits from a parent.
18. A gene whose effect is hidden is a(n) ___.
19. A section of DNA that controls a trait is a(n) ___.

Explaining Science

Use a diagram or write a paragraph to answer these questions.

1. What happens during asexual reproduction of single-cell organisms?

2. What is the role of meiosis and mitosis in sexual reproduction?

3. How does DNA of a chromosome determine an organism's traits?

4. How do offspring inherit traits in sexual reproduction?

Using Skills

1. Make a chart showing the height of each classmate. Show each person's height in millimeters, centimeters, and meters. Decide which **metric** unit is easiest to use to describe height.

2. Suppose you meet a set of identical twins. What can you **infer** about their genes? Give reasons for your inference.

3. Predict the possible offspring if two plants are crossed. One plant is purebred with both genes dominant for red flowers. The other is hybrid with genes for red and white flowers.

Critical Thinking

1. Draw and label two diagrams showing the sequence of steps in mitosis and meiosis. Identify the steps in each where a mutation could occur.

2. Suppose you want to breed some plants. You want all the offspring to be the dominant color. Apply what you learned about the way traits are inherited to decide whether the parent plants should be purebred, hybrid, or both.

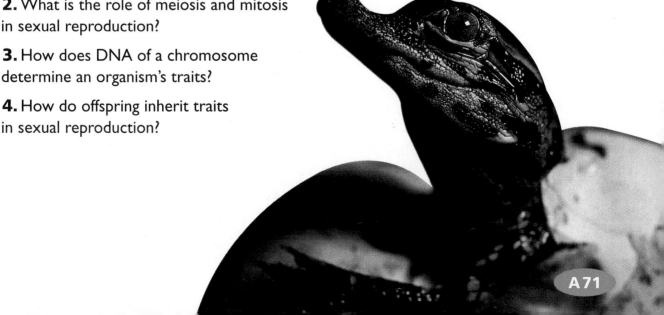

Don't Mess With Me!

Ouch! Those spines sure are sharp. Wouldn't you want to protect yourself and the water inside your body if you lived outdoors in the harsh conditions of the desert?

Chapter 3

Changing and Adapting

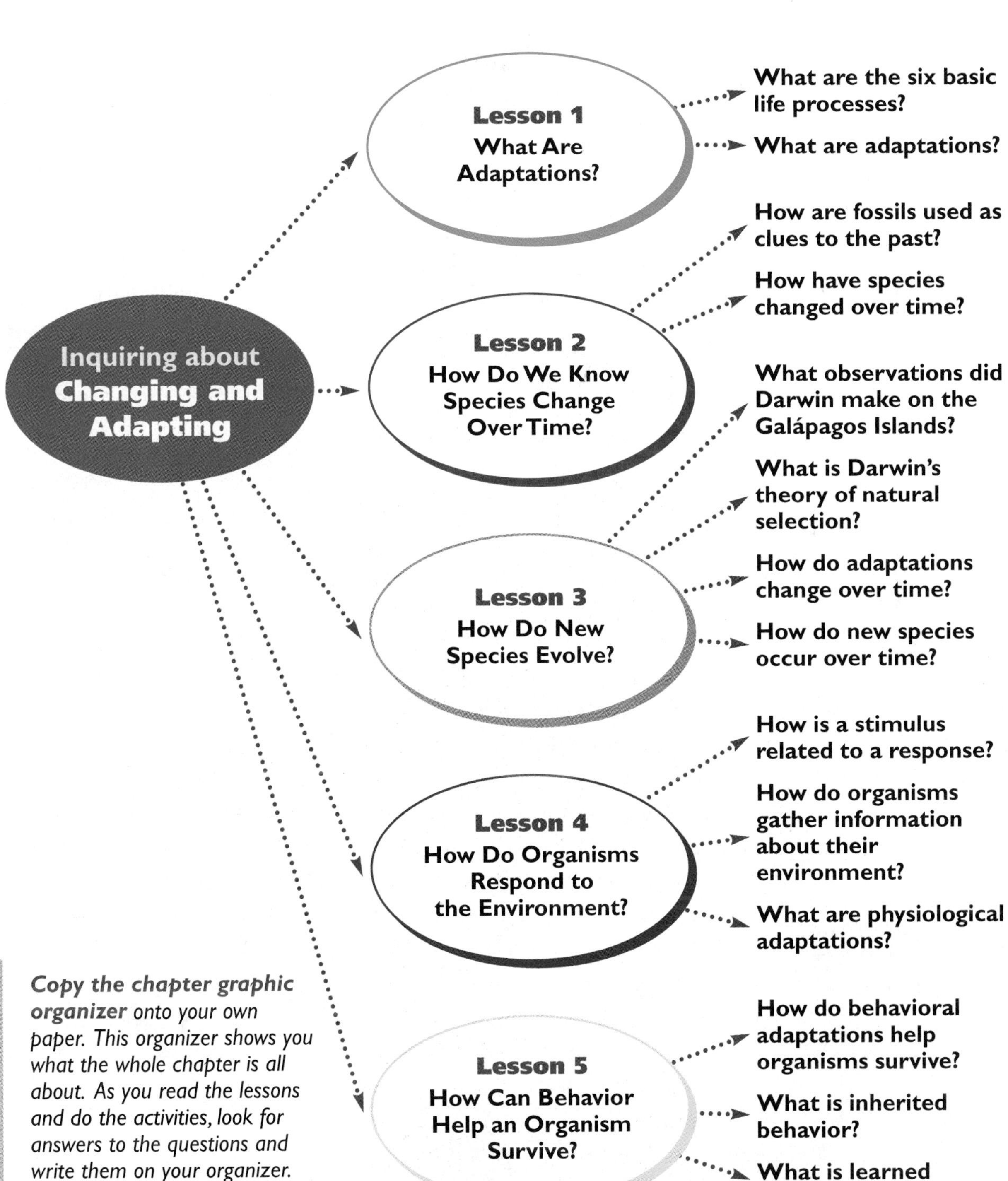

__Copy the chapter graphic organizer__ onto your own paper. This organizer shows you what the whole chapter is all about. As you read the lessons and do the activities, look for answers to the questions and write them on your organizer.

Explore Activity

Exploring Feeding Adaptations

Process Skills

Process Skills

- making a model
- inferring
- communicating

Materials

- envelopes
- model feeding stations
- assorted feeding tools

Explore

1 **Make a model** mouth by placing your hand inside an envelope. Place your thumb at one end of the envelope and your fingers at the other end. Bring the corners of the envelope together to form a beaklike mouth.

2 Look at the model animal feeding stations. You will "adapt" your paper mouth to eat the food at one of the stations. Decide if your model mouth will scoop worms from the ground, grab fish in the sea, or catch bugs in the air.

3 Look at the feeding tools. How could you use them to make a better mouth for catching and eating the food you chose in step 2? Choose a tool—or a combination of tools—and add it to your paper mouth.

4 Go to the feeding station you chose in step 2. Try to catch and eat the food at the station. Can you make your model mouth work better? If so, make changes and try again.

Reflect

1. Communicate your results to your classmates. Based on class results, what can you **infer** about variation in mouth structure and the food an animal eats?

2. Make a list of some other mouth "adaptations" you would like to test.

Inquire Further

Look at the variety of model mouths your classmates made. Could any of them eat efficiently at all three places? Develop a plan to answer this or other questions you may have.

Drawing Conclusions

Drawing a **conclusion** means using your past experience, previous knowledge, and current information to make a decision or form an opinion. In Lesson 1, *What Are Adaptations?,* you will be drawing conclusions about how adaptations help species survive.

Reading Vocabulary

conclusion, a decision reached by examining all the facts

Example

One way to draw conclusions is to think about past experiences. Make a list of what you already know about the topic. Then think about reasonable explanations for the facts.

When you look at the pictures of the birds and read the text on page A79, think about birds you have observed eating. Use what you already know about the way birds eat to help you draw a conclusion about what each bird eats. For each bird, make a chart of what you already know that might help you draw a conclusion about the bird.

▲ *You can draw conclusions about what each bird eats.*

Talk About It!

1. What have you observed on your own about the way birds eat that might help you to understand what you are reading?

2. What do you observe about each bird's beak that might help you draw conclusions about what kind of food it eats?

You will learn:

- what the six basic life processes are.
- what adaptations are.

Lesson 1

What Are Adaptations?

Take a look in the mirror. Wow! What human traits do you see? Now picture yourself with a nose like an elephant's trunk and a neck the length of a giraffe's. Would those new traits help or harm you? How?

Life Processes

How do you know that something is alive? You might say that something is alive because it can move. Think about that—a car can move. Does that mean a car is alive? Of course not! You might say that you know you are alive because you can think—but a plant can't think and it's alive. Just how can you tell if something is alive?

Although living things come in many shapes and sizes, like the organisms shown on these pages, they all carry on the same six basic life processes. First, all living things take in energy. They need energy to carry out life processes. An oak tree gets its energy from sunlight. You take in energy by eating food.

Basic Life Processes
Taking in energy
Releasing energy in food
Using energy for body processes
Producing and excreting wastes
Responding to the environment
Reproducing

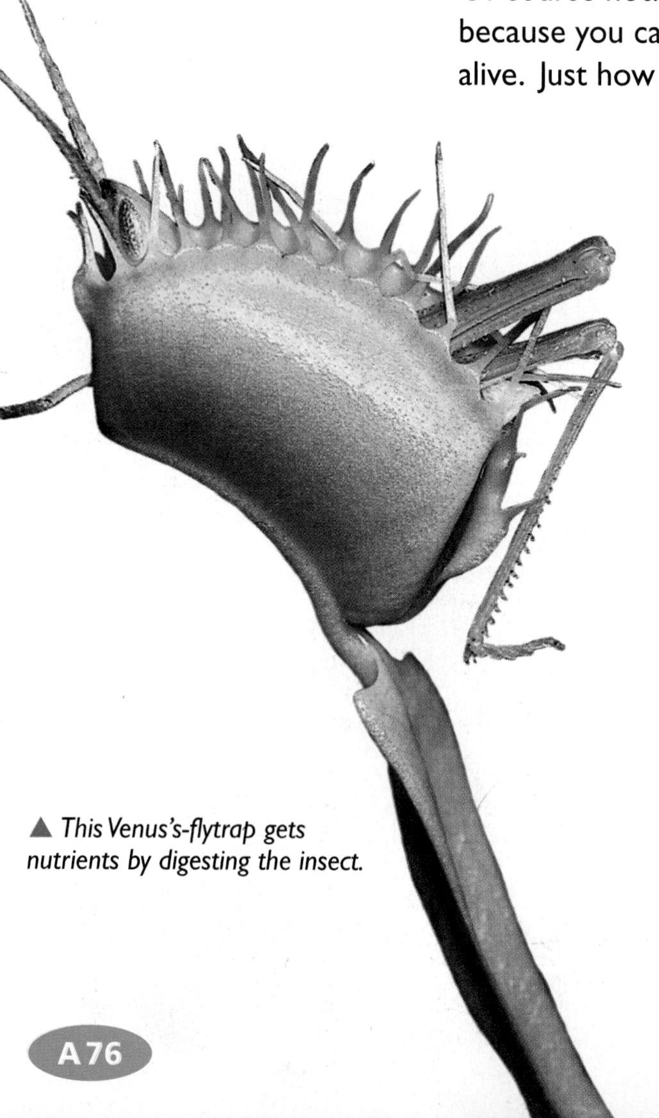

▲ *This Venus's-flytrap gets nutrients by digesting the insect.*

All living things must release the energy in food in order to use it. To release energy, an organism combines it with oxygen in a process is called respiration. An oak tree, the anteater to the right—and you—all carry on respiration.

Living organisms use the energy that is released from food for growth, movement, repair, and other body processes. A huge oak tree uses energy when it grows from a tiny acorn. The tree also needs energy to repair a wound when a branch is cut off. You, too, use energy for growth and repair. If you cut your finger, your body is able to repair the injury by making new cells. This process uses energy.

Living things must get rid of wastes that are produced during respiration. This process, called excretion, keeps organisms from poisoning themselves with built-up wastes.

Another life process of all living things is reproduction. You learned in Chapter 2 that offspring can be produced from one or two parents. During an oak tree's life, it might produce millions of acorns. Think of the amount of energy that would take! Some of those acorns will grow into oak trees, which produce more acorns.

The beetle in the pictures below is carrying on another life process. The Namib Desert in Africa, where this type of beetle lives, is hot and dry during the day. To escape the heat, the beetles burrow into the sand. In the desert, the beetles don't have any water to drink. However, at night the desert turns misty. Then hundreds of these beetles stand on their heads in long lines along the tops of sand dunes. In the cool air, water collects on the beetles' bodies. As the water collects, it runs down the beetles' bodies into their mouths. The beetles, like all living things, are responding to changes in their environment. If the beetles didn't respond in this way, they couldn't survive in the desert. In what ways do you respond to your environment?

▲ *This anteater ingests food, releases the food energy during respiration, and secretes the wastes produced.*

Notice the large drop of water at the mouth of this beetle in the top photo. In the bottom photo, you can see how the water collects on the beetle's back. It then runs down the beetle's body to its mouth. ▼

Glossary

Glossary

adaptation
(ad′ap tā′shən), an inherited trait that helps a species survive in its environment

Adaptations

Think of two different species of organisms you are familiar with—perhaps a lion and a tiger. How do they differ from each other? Do you know why they are different? Variations among species are related to survival.

Let's look at some traits of one animal—the beaver—to see how they help it survive. The teeth of a beaver are long and sharp. This trait allows the beaver to chew through tree trunks. With its large, webbed hind feet, a beaver can swim at speeds of 8 kilometers an hour. Its broad, scaly tail helps the beaver steer itself right, left, up, or down. Transparent eyelids cover and protect the beaver's eyes underwater. Long hairs protect its thick undercoat and help it stay warm, even in icy water. A beaver can even close its mouth by pressing flaps of skin behind its front teeth. Then it can chew on wood underwater, without getting water or wood down its throat. These traits help the beavers live successfully in rivers, lakes, and streams.

Where do beavers get these traits? Young beavers inherit all these traits from their parents. An inherited trait that helps a species survive in its environment is an **adaptation.** An adaptation can aid survival in many ways. It might help an organism get food, attract a mate, build a shelter, avoid enemies, or live in a harsh environment.

A beaver has many adaptations that help it survive in its environment. For example, it can hold its breath for 20 minutes or more. How does this adaptation help the beaver survive? ▼

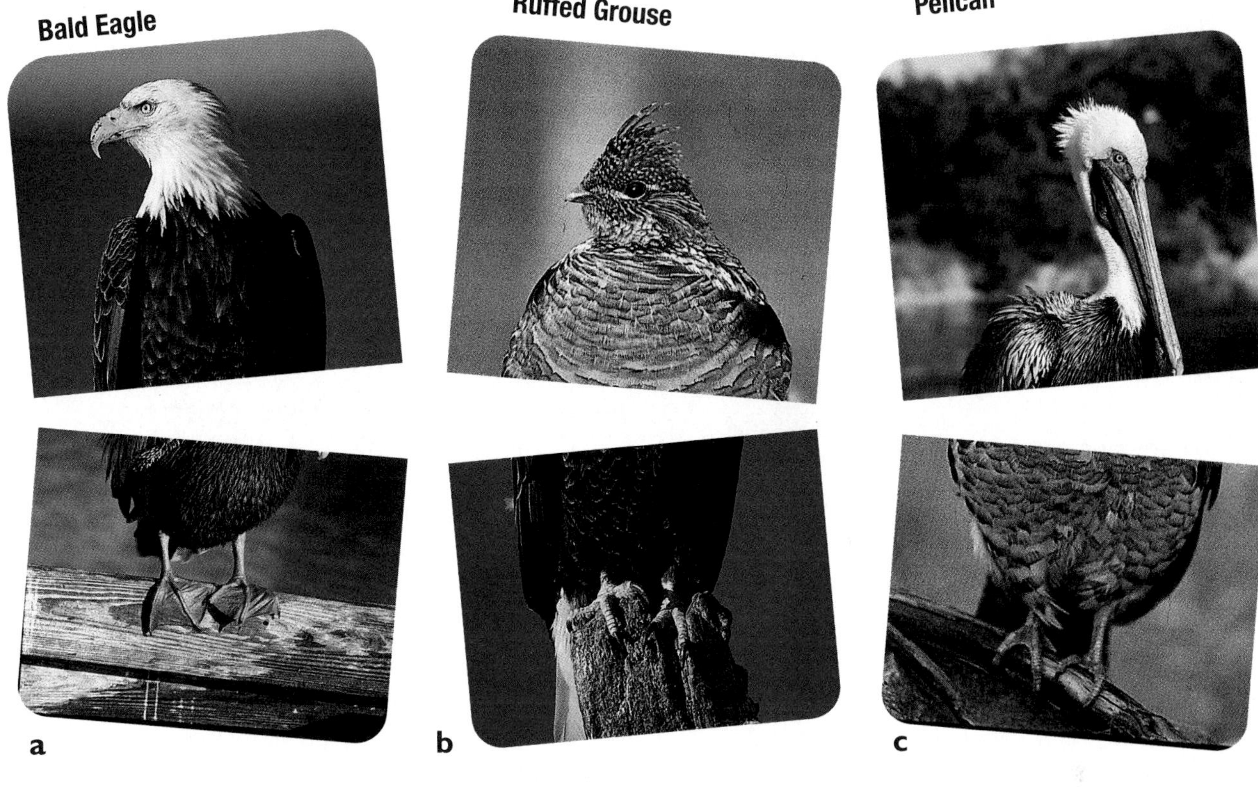

▲ *Can you match each bird's head to the correct feet? Each of these birds eats a different kind of food. Which pair of feet would help each bird with its task of catching food?*

Species do not adapt quickly. Adaptations like those of the beaver take a very long time to develop. Generation after generation reproduces before a trait becomes an adaptation of the entire species.

To get a better understanding of how adaptations help a species survive, look at the pictures on this page. The heads and feet of these birds are mixed up. The head of the bird at the left belongs to a bald eagle. Bald eagles are predators that eat small prey. Which feet might help it catch its prey? The ruffed grouse in the middle lives on the ground. Which feet are best suited for scratching and running? The brown pelican on the right lives on and near the ocean. Which feet might help it swim? How would each bird's survival be affected if it had the mixed-up feet as shown?

Lesson 1 Review

1. What are the six basic life processes?
2. What are adaptations?
3. **Draw Conclusions**
   Suppose a friend shows you an interesting object under a microscope and tells you it is a living organism. What conclusions can you draw about the organism?

You will learn:
- how fossils are used as clues to the past.
- how species have changed over time.

Lesson 2

How Do We Know Species Change Over Time?

Zap! You're in a time machine that has taken you back 65 million years. What do you see? You might watch a tiny dinosaur hatching from an egg. You'd better take photos. How else will people know what life was like so long ago?

Some of the most common fossils are molds of the shells of ammonites. The soft body parts of these organisms were not fossilized. The shells range in size from 13 centimeters to 2 meters. ▼

Fossils—Clues to the Past

You know that time machines don't exist, so how do scientists know what life was like on Earth long, long ago? One way that scientists learn about the different kinds of organisms that have lived on Earth is by studying fossils. Fossils are the remains or traces of organisms that once lived. They are a record of past life on Earth. Look at the pictures on these two pages to see some different kinds of fossils.

Many fossils form when organisms die and sink to the bottom of a stream, ocean, or swamp. There, the organisms are covered by sediment—mud, sand, or clay that settles to the bottom of the water. Over millions of years, the sediment changes to rock. The remains of the organisms in the rock layers are fossils. Even the burrows of worms and other animals, termite nests, and animal droppings have been found as fossils.

Most often, an organism's hard parts, such as its shell, bones, or teeth, are the only body parts that become fossils. Soft body parts usually decay without leaving a trace.

However, in the 1980s, an Italian fossil hunter found an unusual specimen. He thought that the fossil was a bird. Later in the 1990s, paleontologists—scientists who study fossils—examined the fossil. They realized that it belonged to a 110-million-year-old baby dinosaur. The unusual thing about the fossil was that some of the dinosaur's soft tissue also fossilized along with the bones. Scientists were able to see parts of a dinosaur that they had never seen before—most of its intestines and muscles, the windpipe, and perhaps the liver.

The lungs of the dinosaur were not fossilized. However, by studying the position of the intestines, researchers might be able to figure out the size and the shape of the lungs. With this information they can come closer to answering an important question—Were dinosaurs more closely related to reptiles or to birds?

Scientists have found nearly complete fossils of other kinds of organisms. The insects below were trapped when the sticky resin of an ancient pine tree flowed over it. Later, the tree resin hardened into what we call amber, and the insect was fossilized. Plant seeds, feathers, and even frogs have been found preserved in amber.

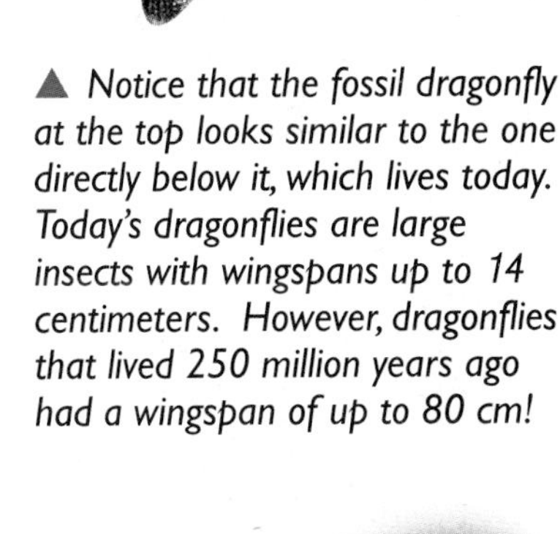

▲ *Notice that the fossil dragonfly at the top looks similar to the one directly below it, which lives today. Today's dragonflies are large insects with wingspans up to 14 centimeters. However, dragonflies that lived 250 million years ago had a wingspan of up to 80 cm!*

When scientists find fossils, they combine new information from the fossils with what they already know to draw conclusions about life long, long ago. New evidence can help support what scientists believe to be true, or at times the new evidence will prove scientists wrong. Each new piece of information helps scientists form a better picture of life that no one has seen.

Much amber, like what you see here, is found in Europe along the shores of the Baltic Sea, where it formed 40 to 60 million years ago. Organisms like these insects were often trapped in the amber. ▶

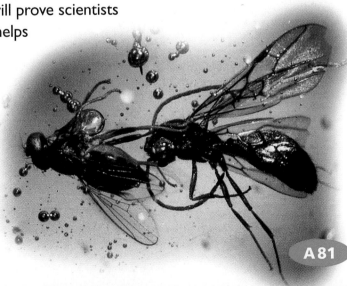

Glossary

Glossary

evolution (ev/ə lü shən), process that results in changes in the genetic makeup of a species over very long periods

Change Over Time

Recall from Chapter 2 that mutations are changes in an organism's DNA. Some mutations lead to traits that harm an individual—like the albino frog you learned about in Chapter 2. Other mutations lead to traits that are helpful. Harmful mutations could cause an organism to die, but organisms with helpful mutations may produce offspring with similar traits. These traits, in turn, can be passed from generation to generation for many years.

When helpful mutations are passed along to future generations, a species' chances of survival improve. Genetic change that occurs within a species over long periods, from generation to generation, is called **evolution**. What evidence do scientists have that organisms evolve?

You've learned that fossils give scientists clues to past life on Earth. Usually, the fossil record is incomplete. Working with an incomplete fossil record is like working with a jigsaw puzzle that has some missing pieces. You can still figure out the whole puzzle picture when only a few pieces are missing. Likewise, scientists can use fossil "puzzle pieces" to determine what the whole picture is. Often, fossil puzzle pieces indicate to scientists how certain species evolved over time.

Evolution of the Camel

By studying fossil bones, scientists have been able to put the pieces together to show the evolution of the common camel. ▼

Scientists have used fossil puzzle pieces to conclude how today's camel evolved over millions of years. The pictures at the bottom of these pages show some of the steps in the camel's evolution. Scientists have studied the fossil leg bones, skulls, and teeth of different camel species that have lived over a period of 65 million years. These fossils indicate that the first camels were small animals the size of a rabbit. What evidence do you think scientists used to form this conclusion?

Fossils indicate that by 37 million years ago, camels still had a small body size, feet with four toes, and teeth with low crowns. Crowns are the part of the teeth that show above the gums. Over time, camels appear to have evolved into larger animals.

By 26 million years ago, the larger camel species had feet with only two toes and teeth with high crowns. Its hump began to appear. What other difference do you notice in the camel during this 65-million-year period?

Lesson 2 Review

1. How are fossils used as clues to the past?
2. Give an example of how species have changed over time.
3. **Draw Conclusions**
   Look at the insects trapped in the amber on page A81. What conclusion can you draw about these insects?

You will learn:

- what observations Charles Darwin made on the Galápagos Islands.
- what Darwin's theory of natural selection is.
- how adaptations change over time.
- how new species occur over time.

Lesson 3

How Do New Species Evolve?

Hey! Look at that weird insect. What does it do with those strange pinchers on its body? And those eyes. They look so huge! Why does an insect need these strange looking body parts? How did it get them in the first place?

Charles Darwin

History of Science

On December 27, 1831, the ship HMS *Beagle* sailed from England to study the coast of South America. It was on this ship that some important ideas about how species evolve began to develop. You can follow the course of the *Beagle* on the map.

The HMS Beagle *traveled around the world. Its most important stop was at the Galápagos Islands, where Darwin made observations that led to an understanding of how species evolve.* ▼

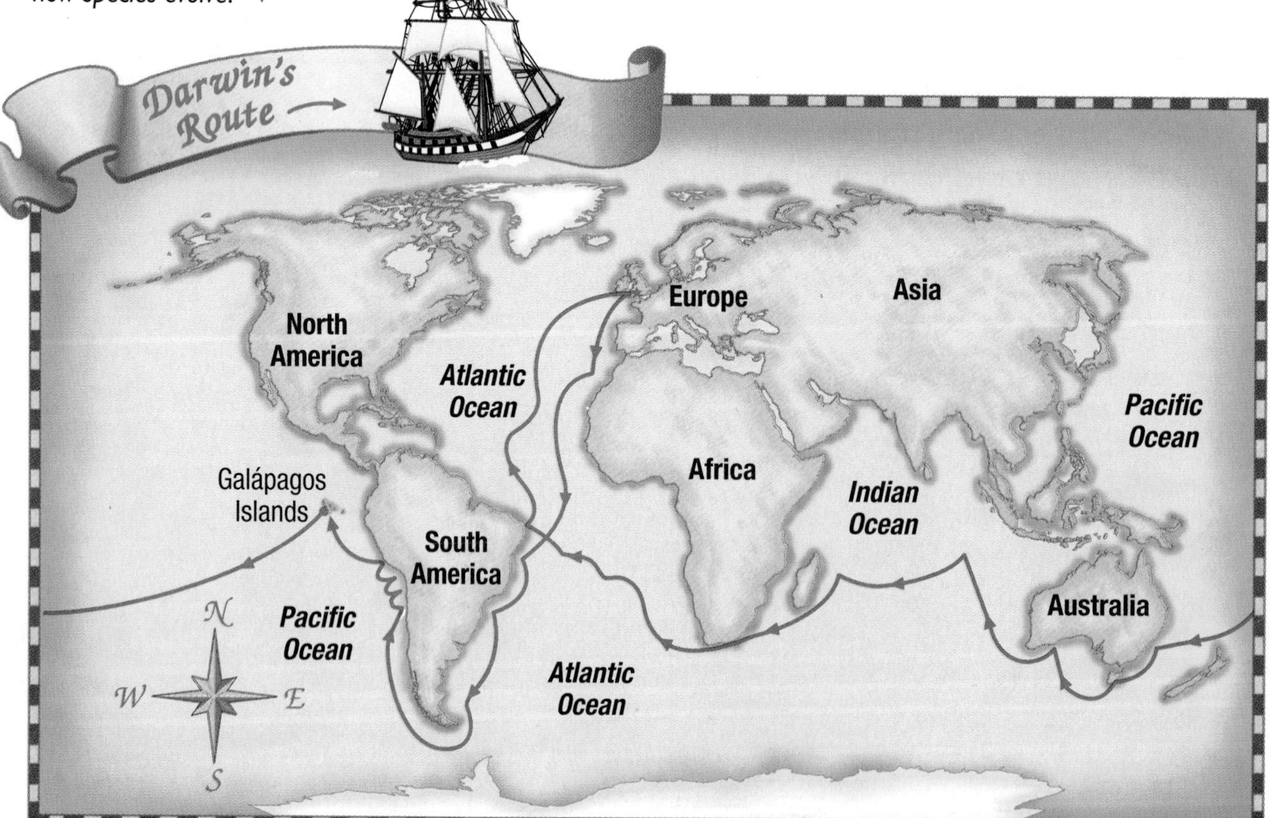

On board the *Beagle* was 22-year-old Charles Darwin. As the ship's naturalist, Darwin's job was to collect and describe the many different species he observed at the places the ship visited. When Darwin left for the trip, he was convinced that species didn't change. In 1835, the *Beagle* reached the Galápagos Islands after making stops on the continent of South America. The Galápagos Islands were named after the Spanish word for *tortoise* because of the giant land tortoises found living on them. Find these islands on the map.

▲ *The differences in shape of the shells of these two tortoises give clues to the kind of environment in which they live. What other differences can you observe?*

For five weeks, Darwin roamed the Galápagos Islands. He made many observations and collected many specimens. The observations that Darwin made on the islands later changed his view about species.

Darwin found many unusual species living on the islands. Many of these species weren't found anywhere else in the world. Although many resembled species that Darwin had seen in other places, each species was different from every other species in some way.

For example, Darwin discovered that island inhabitants could tell what island a tortoise came from just by looking at it. One clue was the color of the tortoise's shell. Another clue was its shape. The two main shapes of shells depended on the kind of island where the tortoise lived. On the one hand, one island had humid, green highlands with many short plants. Tortoises on this and similar islands had dome-shaped shells, short necks, and short front legs, as in the upper picture. These tortoises were adapted to eating ground plants.

Tortoises from low, dry islands looked more like the tortoise in the lower picture. They were smaller and had long necks and slender legs. The front parts of the tortoises' shells were bent upward in the shape of a saddle. This shell shape made it possible for the tortoise to reach high into the dry shrubs to feed.

Glossary

natural selection (nach′ər əl si lek′shən), the idea that those organisms best adapted to their environment will be the ones most likely to survive and reproduce

Darwin noticed that tortoises weren't the only animals that differed from island to island. He observed at least 13 different species of finches. The finches resembled those he had seen on the continent. Darwin thought that perhaps finches from the continent had landed on the island and produced offspring. Then Darwin noticed that the species on each island had different kinds of beaks that seemed to match the kinds of food they ate. For example, some finches had long beaks for removing insects hidden deep within a tree's bark. Others had short, thick beaks for cracking nuts. Darwin recorded his thoughts about these differences by writing that "one might really fancy that one species had been modified for different ends."

Natural Selection

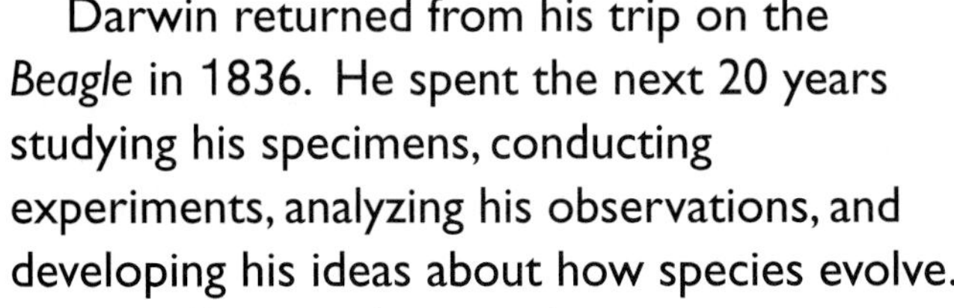

Darwin returned from his trip on the *Beagle* in 1836. He spent the next 20 years studying his specimens, conducting experiments, analyzing his observations, and developing his ideas about how species evolve.

During that time, Darwin thought about a common practice used by farmers. The process, called selective breeding, involves breeding only plants or animals that have desired traits. For example, sheep farmers often kept only the sheep with the best wool to be parents of their future flocks. After several generations, the offspring would have much thicker wool than even the original parents. Darwin wondered if some type of selective breeding occurred in nature. In other words, did nature select certain traits over others?

After nearly 20 years of study, Darwin theorized that, indeed, nature did select certain traits over others. He proposed the theory of evolution by **natural selection**. Darwin's ideas are summarized on the next page.

Charles Darwin is the founder of the modern theory of evolution. ▼

Main Points of Darwin's Theory

1 Organisms usually produce more offspring than can survive.

Female frogs lay large clusters of eggs in the water of a pond. Individual egg clusters range from a few eggs to hundreds of eggs. A female bullfrog may lay as many as 20,000 eggs. Only a few eggs will survive to become adult frogs.

2 Competition exists among organisms. Those organisms that survive the competition are the only ones to reproduce and pass on their traits to offspring.

Adult male elephants often fight to test their strength. Only the strongest bulls mate with females to produce offspring.

3 Organisms best adapted to their environments are the ones most likely to survive long enough to reproduce.

Desert plants compete for a limited amount of water. Having a waxy skin and spines rather than leaves reduces the amount of water a cactus loses. These adaptations allow cacti to survive in the desert.

4 Parent organisms pass traits on to their offspring. Offspring usually look like their parents, but variations may occur.

These tree snails are members of the same species, but they have shells that vary in color. The color variations of these snails will be passed on to their offspring.

Glossary

Glossary

structural adaptation (struk′chər əl ad′ap tā′ shən), adaptation that involves body parts or color

Adaptations Over Time

You've seen how some traits help a particular organism survive in its environment better than other organisms of the same species without the traits. These traits that enable an organism to survive are passed from generation to generation. Over time, more and more members of the species share these traits. Eventually, these traits may become adaptations of the species.

The mole rat shown on the next page is a good example of how adaptations evolve. Today mole rats live underground. They use their long front teeth and claws to help dig tunnels. Their tiny eyes don't see well. They don't need to—it's dark where they live! Mole rats feel their way around in their dark tunnels with sensitive hairs on their heads. These traits that make mole rats well suited to live in their environment are examples of structural adaptations. **Structural adaptations** are any coloring or body parts that help an organism survive.

How did these structural adaptations evolve in mole rats? The pictures below give you one explanation that scientists have developed.

Evolution of the Mole Rat

▲ *The ancestors of mole rats lived aboveground and had different traits from those of today's mole rats.*

▲ *Over time, variation in structural adaptations occurred. For example, larger teeth and claws helped some individuals dig underground. They were safer from predators. These variations were passed on to offspring.*

Often structural adaptations take thousands or even millions of years to evolve. However, sometimes they occur in a population more quickly. The peppered moths shown to the right are a good example of rapid evolution.

Until the 1850s, almost all peppered moths in England were pale speckled gray. Dark gray peppered moths were so rare that they were prized by moth collectors.

Around 1850, dark moths started to become more common, especially near cities where factories were located. The increase in dark moths occurred at the same time that more and more factories were being built. Light tree trunks in those areas became darkened with soot from the factory smokestacks. Dark moths sitting on soot-darkened trees blended in and were harder for birds to see than light moths. Thus, they were more likely to escape being eaten by birds. They survived and passed on genes for dark color to their offspring.

However, in the countryside, the situation didn't change. There, the trees were not darkened by pollution from factories. On the light-barked trees, dark moths were easier for hungry birds to spot. Most of the peppered moths continued to be light colored.

▲ *Peppered moths exist in two varieties—dark and light. Which moth blends in better with this light tree bark? Which moth would more likely be noticed by a hungry bird and eaten?*

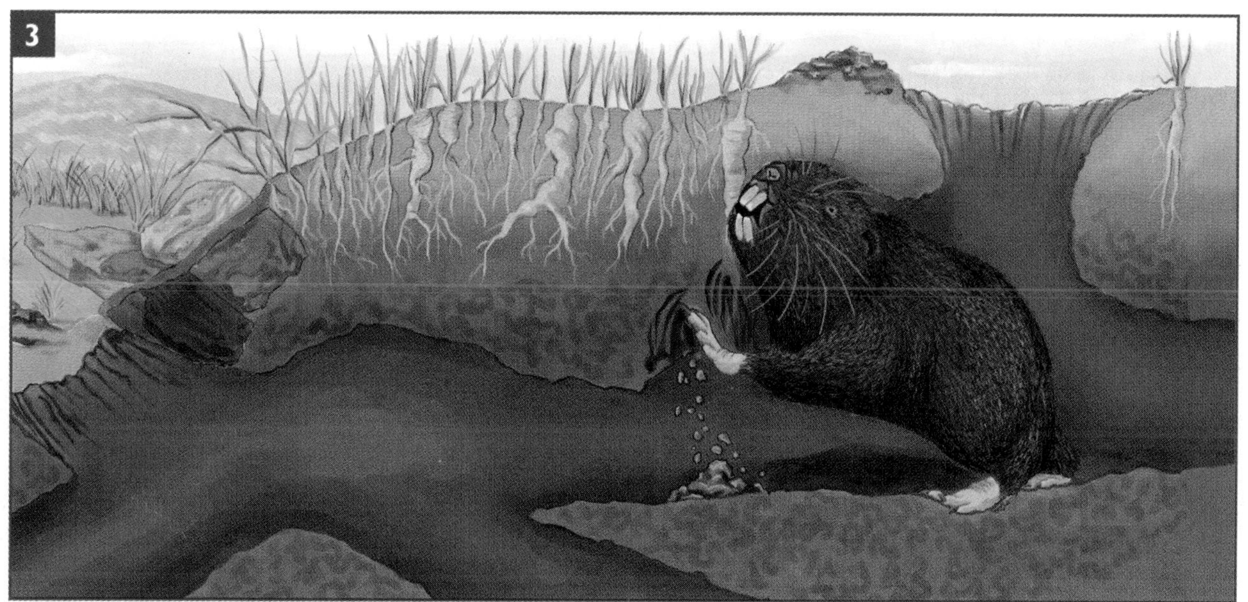

▲ *Over many generations, evolution resulted in the adaptations of today's mole rats.*

Glossary

Glossary

population
(pop′ yə lā′ shən), all the organisms of one species that live in a certain place

New Species over Time

You've seen how adaptations evolve within a species, but how do new species evolve? Look at the drawings on these two pages. Suppose a group of frogs of the same species—a **population**—lives near a small stream as in picture 1. This population of frogs has slight variations in color. Some are dark and some are light. At first, the stream is small enough that the frogs can cross the stream to mate. The offspring that are produced by these frogs share the same traits as the parents share.

What would happen if, as in pictures 2 and 3, the stream became wider and flowed more rapidly over time? A large canyon might form. The frog population on one side of the canyon would become isolated from the population on the other side because they wouldn't be able to cross the canyon. Frogs from one side would no longer be able to mate with frogs from the other side.

What might result from this isolation? At first, the frogs from each population would share the same traits. But the conditions on each side of the canyon might vary in some ways. For example, the vegetation on the two sides might vary. Each population of frogs would adapt to the environment it lives in through the process of natural selection. In time, the frogs from one side of the canyon

When a population is divided and one group becomes isolated from the other in a different environment, a new species may evolve. ▼

▲ *How do these two species of frogs differ? How is each species adapted to its environment?*

would become different enough from the population of frogs on the other side to form two different species. Each species would be adapted to a slightly different environment.

Sometimes isolation occurs because animals migrate. This is what happened on the Galápagos Islands. Animals from Central and South America flew, swam, or were carried on clumps of dirt or plants to the islands. When these populations were cut off from one another, they adapted to their new environment and evolved into separate species.

Lesson 3 Review

1. What observations did Darwin make on the Galápagos Islands?
2. What is Darwin's theory of natural selection?
3. How do adaptations change over time?
4. How do new species occur over time?
5. **Draw Conclusions**
   What conclusions did Darwin draw about the differences in the beaks of different species of finches on the Galápagos Islands?

You will learn:

- how a stimulus is related to a response.
- how organisms gather information about their environment.
- what physiological adaptations are.

Lesson 4

How Do Organisms Respond to the Environment?

You're outside, shooting hoops. Suddenly the wind starts to blow, and the temperature drops. Brrr! You start to shiver. You grab a jacket. You are reacting to a change in your environment.

Glossary

Glossary

stimulus (stim′yə ləs), a change in the environment of an organism that causes a response

response (ri spons′), a reaction of an organism to a change in the environment

Stimulus and Response

You've read about how evolution produces species that are adapted to their environment. An important adaptation for any organism is the way it reacts to changes within its environment. Look at the ptarmigan in the photos. What kind of change in its environment causes the change you see?

The change in environment that causes the reaction is called a **stimulus**. The reaction—a change in color—is called a **response**. All organisms have stimulus-and-response reactions. The response of the ptarmigan is so extreme that you may think you are seeing two different birds. In far northern Canada and Alaska where ptarmigans live, summers are short and cool. The bird's feathers are flecked brown. This coloring allows it to blend well with its brown and green surroundings.

Ptarmigan in Winter

Ptarmigan in Summer

▲ *The color change of the ptarmigan is an inherited trait that improves its chances of survival in its environment.* ▶

However, when early snows start to cover the ground, the white feathers of the ptarmigan gradually replace the brown ones. By the time the environment is completely snow covered, the ptarmigan is totally white. The new color helps the bird survive in its winter environment.

Have you ever played basketball like the girls in the pictures? The girl on the right is responding to an external stimulus—a stimulus from outside the body. What is this external stimulus? When you eat pizza because you are hungry or drink lemonade because you are thirsty, you are responding to internal stimuli—stimuli from inside the body—hunger and thirst.

Plants, too, respond to stimuli. You may have noticed how the stems and leaves of a houseplant on a window ledge curve toward sunlight. This response happens because plants respond to light by growing toward it. Some plants open or close their flowers in response to changes in light or temperature. The leaves of the Venus's-flytrap on page A76 respond to the touch of an insect by snapping shut.

Remember that response is a basic life process. Even single-celled organisms respond to their environment. For example, some bacteria respond to a lack of water by forming a new, thick membrane inside the old one. The cell material outside the new membrane dies. The organism is then called a bacterial spore. The spore can remain inactive until water is in the bacteria's environment again.

▲ *Stimulus-and-response reactions play an important role in this basketball game.*

Gathering Information About the Environment

In order for an organism to respond successfully to changes in its environment, it first must get information about those changes. Compare the different ways the organisms on these two pages gather this information.

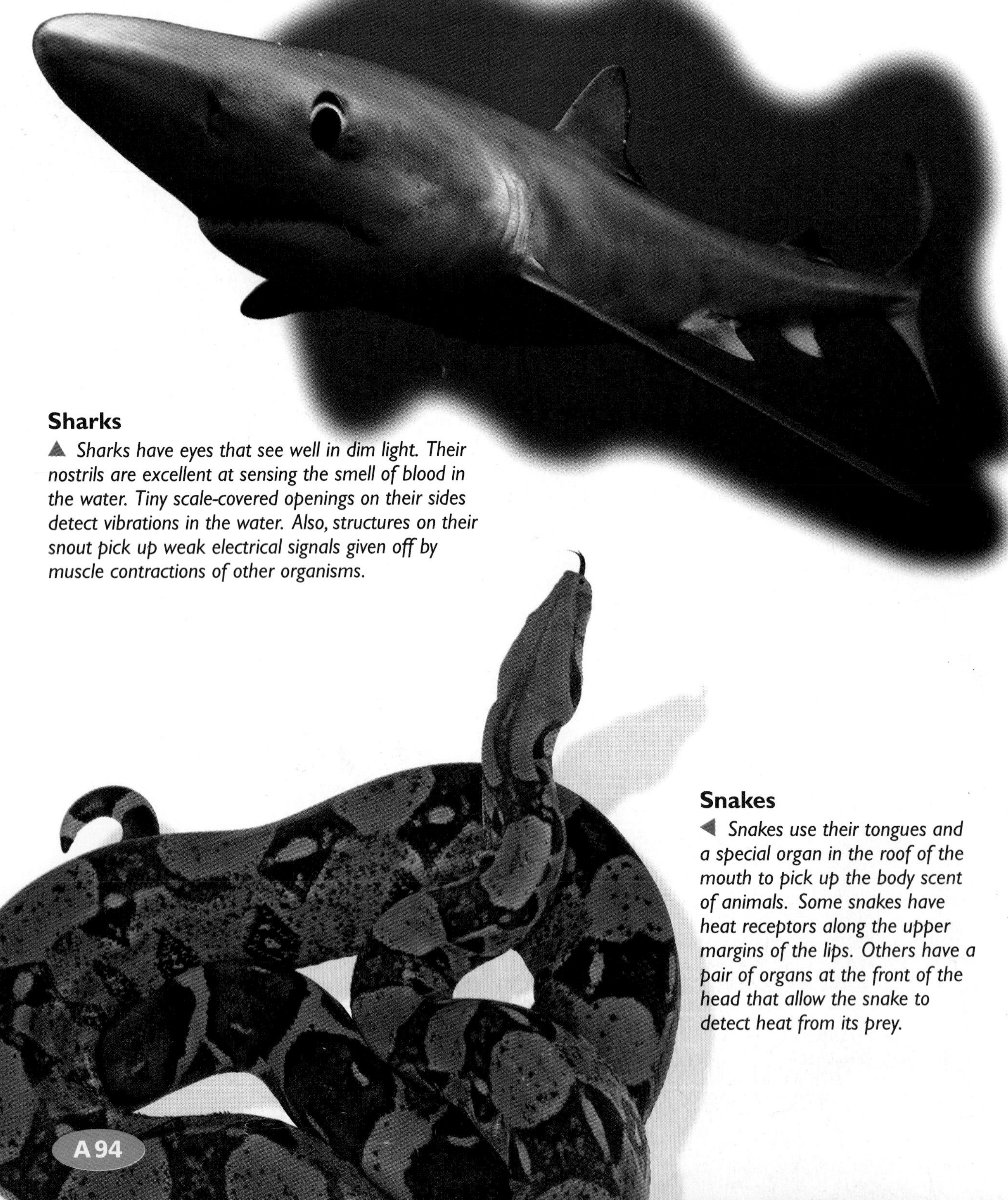

Sharks

▲ *Sharks have eyes that see well in dim light. Their nostrils are excellent at sensing the smell of blood in the water. Tiny scale-covered openings on their sides detect vibrations in the water. Also, structures on their snout pick up weak electrical signals given off by muscle contractions of other organisms.*

Snakes

◀ *Snakes use their tongues and a special organ in the roof of the mouth to pick up the body scent of animals. Some snakes have heat receptors along the upper margins of the lips. Others have a pair of organs at the front of the head that allow the snake to detect heat from its prey.*

Flies

◀ *Flies taste with hairs around their mouths. They also taste with their feet. That's why you might see a fly walking across your food. It's testing the taste! Flies also have sensors for touch and temperature on their legs. The eyes of a fly don't form clear images, but they can easily detect movement.*

Moths

▲ *Male moths use sensory hairs on their feathery antennae to detect chemicals produced by female moths. These detectors enable them to find females during mating season. Some moth species can detect these chemicals more than a kilometer away.*

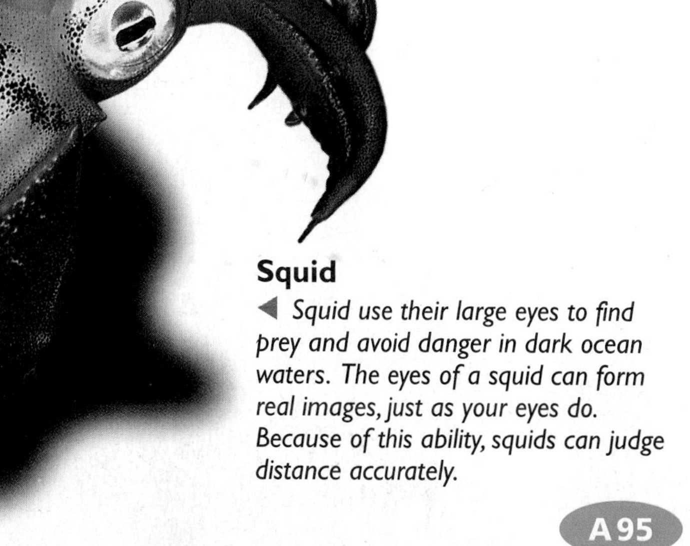

Squid

◀ *Squid use their large eyes to find prey and avoid danger in dark ocean waters. The eyes of a squid can form real images, just as your eyes do. Because of this ability, squids can judge distance accurately.*

Glossary

Glossary

physiological adaptation
(fiz′ē ə loj′ə kəl ad′ap tā′shən), adaptation that involves a body part's job of controlling a life process

Plant Leaf

This photo shows a magnified image of the outer layer of a leaf. Notice the pores that allow important gases to enter and leave the cell. The guard cells control the opening and closing of the pores. ▼

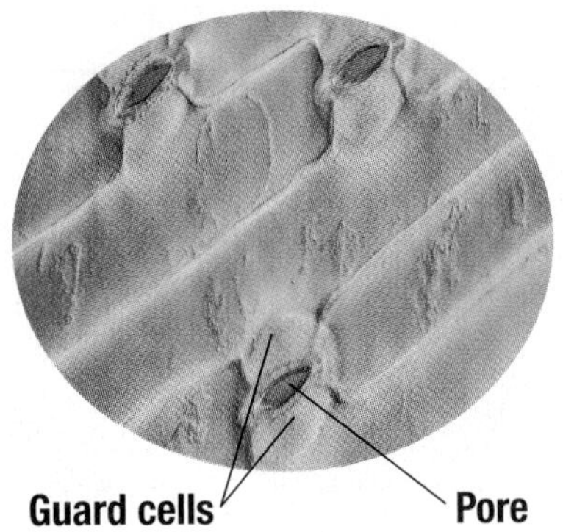

Physiological Adaptations

For plants to survive, carbon dioxide must enter the leaves, and water vapor and oxygen must exit. The tiny pores you see in the leaf cells to the left below open and close to control the flow of these and other gases. Each pore is surrounded by two special guard cells. During the day, water moves into the guard cells, causing them to swell and bend. The pore opens. At night the guard cells lose water into surrounding cells, causing them to straighten, and the pore closes. The guard cells are able to do this because of a **physiological adaptation**—an adaptation in which an organism's body part does its job in response to a stimulus.

Like all sea mammals, the seal shown below must swim to the surface of the water to breathe. It holds its breath while underwater, searching for food. In fact, some seals can hold their breath for as long as an hour.

In the case of the seal, the stimulus is the lower amount of oxygen that gets into its blood when it hold its breath. What is the seal's response? The seal's response is to "shut off" the blood circulation in the outer layers of its body and limbs. This response conserves oxygen, so the seal doesn't have to breathe as often. A physiological adaptation enables the seal to respond in this way.

◀ *This seal feeds on fish, squid, krill, and seabirds that it catches while swimming. Holding its breath while swimming underwater is one response of the seal to its environment. What others can you think of?*

Sweaty socks are just one result of some physiological adaptations you have. When you are very active, such as during a basketball game, your muscles produce a lot of heat energy. To keep from overheating, your body reacts in several ways. For one thing, blood vessels in your skin enlarge. As more blood flows through the vessels, more heat is carried to your body's surface. The heat escapes through your skin. Also, your sweat glands become more active. When the sweat evaporates from your skin, it cools your body. In other words, your body senses a change in internal temperature and responds to it.

▲ *Single-celled organisms like this ameba respond to changes in their environments.*

The ameba at the top of the page has physiological adaptations that allow it to respond to light and certain materials that are found in the water surrounding its body. The mimosa plant shown here has adaptations that allow it to respond to the external stimulus of the person's touch. Its leaves close and droop. The plant's response is due to the quick loss of water from special cells at the base of each leaf. What other responses do organisms have to their external environment?

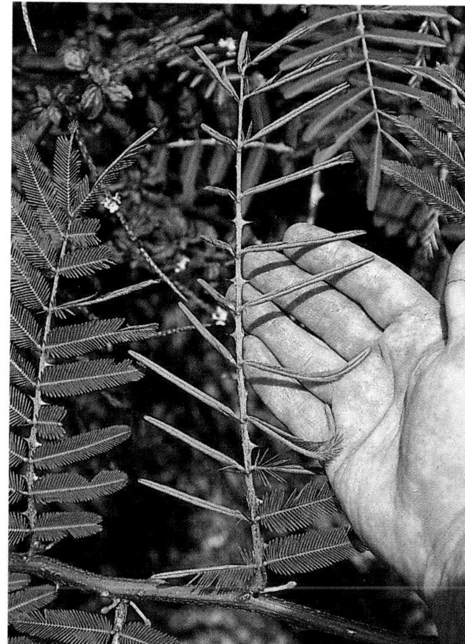

▲ *The response of the mimosa plant to touch is to close its leaves. Scientists think this response protects the plant by conserving water and by making it look less tasty to insects and other animals.*

Lesson 4 Review

1. How is a stimulus related to a response?
2. What are two ways that organisms gather information about their environment?
3. What are physiological adaptations?
4. **Draw Conclusions**
   Look at the photo of the plant leaf on page A96. Was the photo most likely taken during the day or at night? Give the reasons for your conclusion.

Investigate Activity

Observing the Effects of Salt Water on Cells

Process Skills

Process Skills

- observing
- communicating
- inferring

Materials

- piece of red onion
- forceps
- microscope slide with coverslip
- dropper
- water
- microscope
- salt solution
- paper towel

Getting Ready

Fresh water plants can't survive in salt water. Do this activity to find out why.

You might want to practice tearing small pieces of onion until you can get a piece with a thin red layer.

Review the proper use of a microscope.

Follow This Procedure

1. Make a chart like the one shown. Use your chart to record your observations.

Cells in water	Cells in salt water

2. Gently and slowly bend a small piece of red onion until it breaks in half. Look for a thin layer of red tissue at the edge of the tear (Photo A). Remove this thin layer, being careful not to wrinkle it.

3. Use forceps to place the thin piece of onion on a microscope slide. Use the dropper to add one or two drops of water to the slide. Place a coverslip over the onion skin.

4. Place the slide on the microscope stage. Carefully turn the adjustment knob of the microscope to focus on several onion cells. **Observe** the cells. Draw what you see.

Self-Monitoring

Was I careful to focus the lens away from the microscope slide?

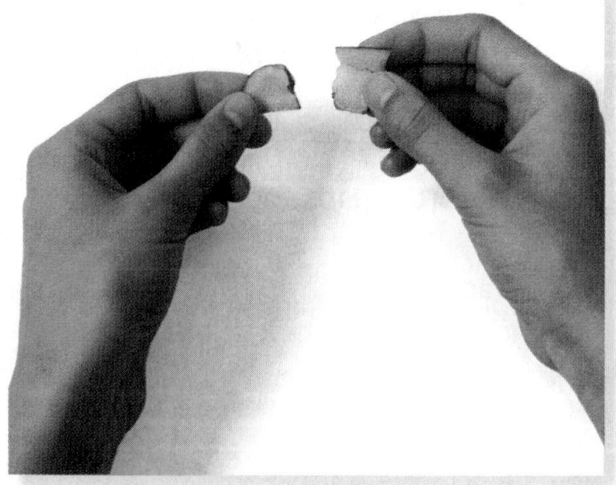

Photo A

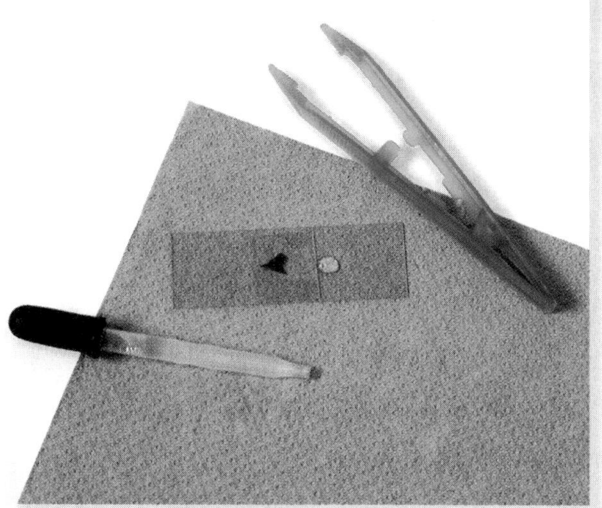

Photo B

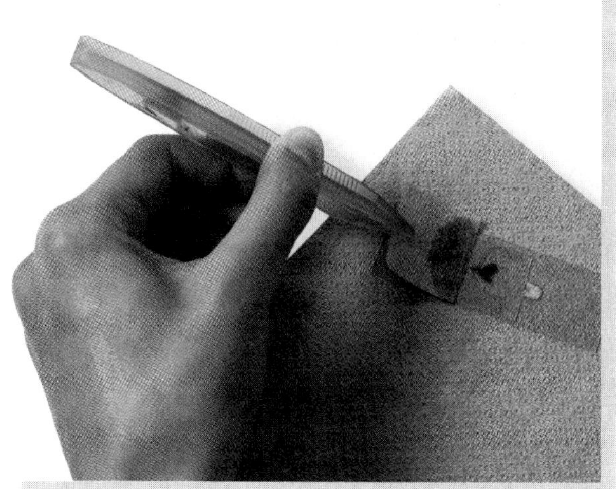

Photo C

5 Remove the slide from the microscope stage. Using a dropper, place a drop of the salt solution along the right edge of the coverslip (Photo B).

6 Place a small piece of paper towel in the forceps. Touch the paper towel along the left edge of the coverslip. This will draw the salt solution under the coverslip. Repeat this step so that there are two drops of salt water under the coverslip (Photo C).

7 Place the slide back on the microscope stage. Observe the cells for about 3 minutes. Make a sketch of what you see.

Interpret Your Results

1. Look at your drawings of the onion cells before and after the salt water was added. **Communicate** how the cells are alike and how they are different.

2. Draw a conclusion. Are onion cells adapted to salt water? What observations support your conclusion?

3. Make an **inference.** What would happen if you introduced a salt water solution to animal cells?

Inquire Further

How do animal cells react in the presence of salt water? Develop a plan to answer this or other questions you may have.

Self-Assessment

- I followed instructions to test the effects of salt water on plant cells.
- I made **observations** of the plant cells in water and in the salt water solution.
- I **communicated** by drawing what I saw when I looked at the onion cells through the microscope.
- I drew a conclusion about onion cells and salt water.
- I made an **inference** about how salt water might affect animal cells.

You will learn:

- how behavioral responses help organisms survive.
- what inherited behavior is.
- what learned behavior is.

Glossary

Glossary

behavioral adaptation (bi hā′vyər əl ad′ap tā′ shən), an action that aids survival

Lesson 5

How Can Behavior Help an Organism Survive?

Zzzz! Have you ever pretended to be asleep when you really weren't? If so, you might say you "played possum." The act gets its name from the way an opossum sometimes behaves. Playing possum can save an opossum's life.

Behavioral Adaptations

Behavior is one kind of response an organism can make to a stimulus. An organism's behavior includes all the actions of that organism. What are some of your behaviors?

Some behaviors help animals escape danger. Other behaviors help adults protect their young. The Ringed plover in the picture is protecting its young by pretending to have a broken wing. Although it risks its own life, the adult's display may draw the attention of the predator away from the young in the nest. In this way, the young have a better chance of survival. When the danger is gone, the plover returns to its nest. This unusual response of the plover is a **behavioral adaptation**.

This Ringed plover is pretending to be injured in order to distract a predator from its nest. This is a behavioral adaptation. ▼

The behavioral adaptations of the plover help individual organisms survive. Sometimes, behavioral adaptations help an entire population survive. Termites are an example. Look at the termite colony to the right.

Four different kinds of termites within the same species share a termite mound. Each kind of termite has different behaviors that aid the survival of the colony. Worker termites gather food, care for offspring, and build the tunnels and chambers of the mound. Soldier termites guard the tunnels and covered trails that extend out from the nest. A single queen termite lays all the eggs, and a king termite fertilizes all the eggs.

Behavioral adaptations also help organisms get food. A spider spins a web in which to capture flying insects.

Still other behavioral adaptations help animals, such as the crocodile, find mates. A male crocodile swims to a female and strokes her with his head and front legs. After mating, the female builds a mounded nest on land and protects her eggs. After the eggs hatch, she continues to care for her young. She may even carry them through the water in her mouth, as you see in the picture. A female cares for her young for up to a year.

▲ *Few reptiles show as much gentle care for their young as a mother crocodile. Young crocodiles are often killed by predators. To protect them, the mother carries them to safety!*

How do crocodiles get these behaviors? An organism's behavior can result from the species's adaptations or from learning. The crocodile's behaviors probably are the result of adaptations that it inherited from its parents.

◀ *A termite mound can house up to 5 million insects, but only one queen. The large termite in the center is the queen.*

Glossary

Glossary

instinct (in′stingkt), an inherited behavior

Inherited Behavior

A behavior that an organism is born with is an inherited behavior. Inherited behavior is a way of responding to a stimulus that doesn't require learning.

One type of inherited behavior is an **instinct.** All young are born with instincts. For example, the behavior of the newly hatched kittiwakes in the photo results from instincts. Notice that the birds nest on high cliffs. When young kittiwakes hatch, they instinctively remain still in the nest. If they moved around, they could fall off the cliff. The young of ground-nesting birds do not show this same instinctive behavior. Their young move around soon after they hatch.

Not all instinctive behavior is simple. Some instinctive behavior may involve several steps and take several weeks to complete. For example, brown-headed cowbirds don't build nests. When the female is ready to lay eggs, she scouts the area to locate the nests of other birds. She finds the nest of another species where the female is laying eggs. She waits quietly until the other female flies off to feed. Then the cowbird moves in and quickly lays a single egg among the other eggs in the nest. Every morning for four or five days, the cowbird lays an egg in a different nest. Then she leaves. The female birds who laid the other eggs in the nests incubate the cowbird's egg along with their own.

Large colonies of kittiwakes nest high on cliffs.

Another example of instinctive behavior is web spinning. Have you ever watched a spider spin a web like the one in the picture? It's a complex process. Yet spiders spin webs correctly the very first time. The kind of web a spider spins is an inherited behavior. For example, an orb weaver spider does not spin the same kind of web as a cobweb weaver spider.

The simplest inherited behavior is a **reflex.** A reflex is a quick automatic response to a stimulus. In a reflex, a signal passes from a sense organ, such as your eye, along nerves to your spinal cord and right back to your muscles. The message doesn't have to travel to the brain for a reaction to occur. A reflex occurs very quickly—in less than a second. It happens without an organism's thinking about it. For example, if something is thrown toward your face, you blink your eyes as shown below. If you touch a hot stove or a sharp thorn, you jerk your hand away. Or, if something irritates your nose, you sneeze.

All animals have reflexes. The fur on a cat's back stands on end when it is frightened. An octopus changes color when it senses danger. When a light is turned on, a cockroach runs from it. If you swat at a fly, it flies away. Reflexes allow an animal to act quickly, especially in times of danger.

Glossary

reflex (rē′fleks), quick, automatic response to a stimulus

▲ *This garden spider is born with instincts that enable it to spin this web. What instincts were you born with?*

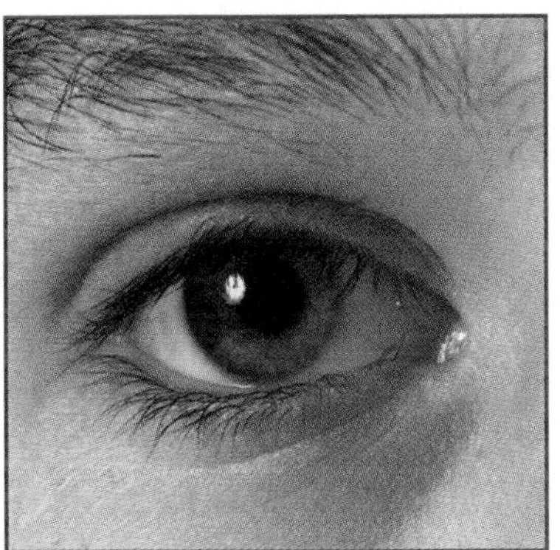

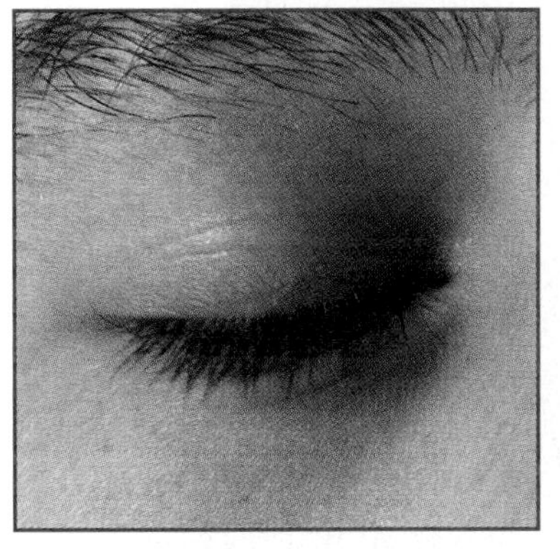

Blinking Reflex

◀ *Your eye blinks reflexively whenever an object quickly approaches your face. How does this reflex help protect you?*

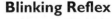

Learned Behavior

Can you remember when you learned to ride a bicycle, roller-skate, or hit a softball? You probably fell several times while trying to balance on a bike or skates. You probably missed hitting the ball a lot at first. But eventually you learned to do these things without having to think about them.

Many animal behaviors are learned. Think about very young leopard cubs. They are quite helpless when they are first born. Their mother cares for them and nurses them. When the cubs are older, the mother will lead them to an animal she has killed. They start eating solid food. The young leopards spend about two years with their mother learning to hunt. At first, they mostly watch what their mother does. Later, they begin to hunt with her. Finally, when they are fully grown and can hunt well enough, the cubs go off on their own.

A trained guide dog helps a blind person get around without danger. What might a dog trained to help a deaf person need to learn? ▼

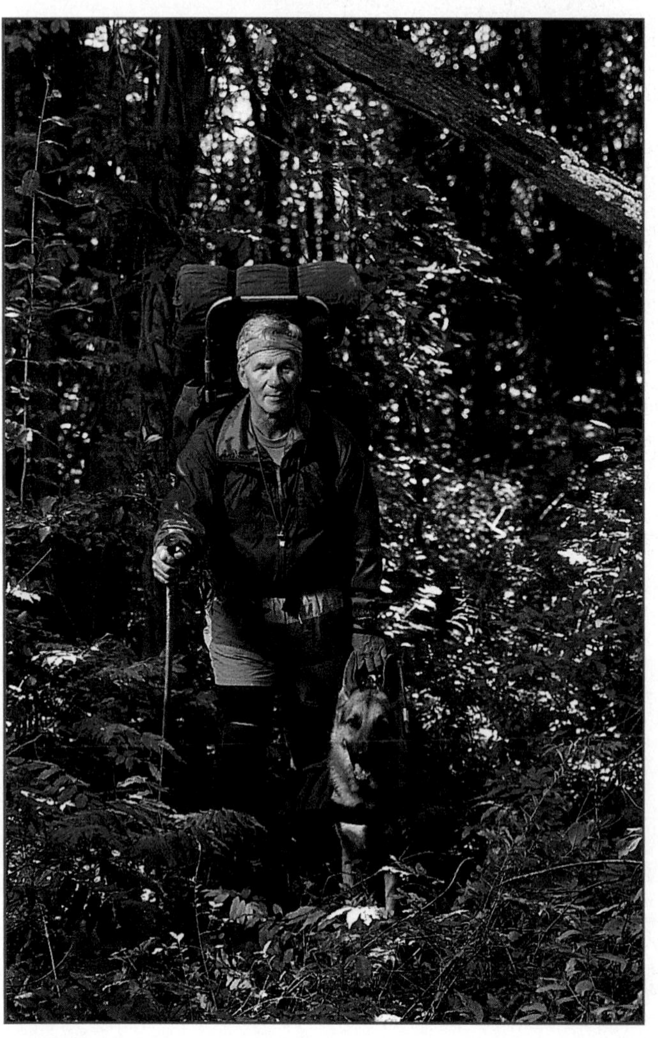

If you have a dog, you may have observed some learned behavior. A dog usually learns to come when its name is called. It may have learned to sit or stay when told. Some animals come running when they hear the sound of an electric can opener. They have learned that the sound may mean dinner is about to be served. Goldfish who are fed by people learn to come to the surface of a pond. They come when people stand by the pond, even if there's no food.

The dog in the photo was trained as a guide dog. When the dog was about a year old, it began its training. It had to learn to obey commands and to take a person safely through crowds, traffic, and other hazards, such as this forest. The dog had to learn to disobey commands that might put its owner in danger. Finally, when the dog is fully trained, it begins work as a guide dog.

You may have seen young ducklings like the ones below following their mother. Within a short time after hatching, ducklings follow the first moving object they see. If that object is the mother duck, they follow her. This behavior is important because they then learn to watch her and do what she does. They learn to find food and escape predators.

However, ducklings hatched in an incubator may see a human as the first moving object. They follow the human. In this case, the human must teach the ducklings how to behave in order to survive. They must learn to go to water to swim and get food. Fortunately for ducklings, swimming is not a learned behavior.

Imprinting

▲ *These baby mallard ducks will follow the first moving object they see when they hatch. This behavior is called imprinting.*

Lesson 5 Review

1. How do behavioral adaptations help an organism survive?
2. What is inherited behavior?
3. What is learned behavior?
4. **Draw Conclusions**
   A human infant learns to walk at about one year. Is this behavior learned or inherited? Give reasons for your conclusion.

Investigating How Plants React to Light

Process Skills

Process Skills

- predicting
- observing
- communicating
- inferring

Materials

- large shoe box with lid
- small bean plant
- marker
- scissors
- pieces of cardboard
- masking tape
- light source

Getting Ready

In this activity, you will find out how light can affect a plant's growth.

As part of this activity, you will create a maze. It might be helpful to first look up or study some simple mazes—perhaps in a puzzle book.

Follow This Procedure

1. Make a chart like the one shown. Use your chart to record your observations.

Day	Observations
2	
4	
6	
8	
10	

2. Stand a shoe box on one of its ends. Place a small bean plant inside the shoe box. Use a marker to make a line inside the box to show the height of the plant (Photo A).

3. Remove the plant from the box.

4. Cut an opening about 4 cm wide at the end of the box opposite where the plant will be placed. This hole will be the light source for the plant (Photo A).

5. Draw a maze inside the shoe box. You might use a design like the one shown in Photo A, or make one of your own. Be sure to allow room at the bottom of the box for the plant. Secure a piece of cardboard to the shoe box with masking tape to make the first wall of the maze (Photo B).

Photo A

Photo B

6 Mark one side of the plant pot with an X. Place your plant inside the box with the X facing the back of the box.

7 Place the lid on the box. Place the box under a light source. **Predict** how the plant will grow. Give reasons for your prediction.

8 **Observe** the plant every 2 days and record what you observe about its growth. As the plant grows above the first wall, add the next wall to your maze. Be sure to water the plant when necessary. If you take the plant out of the box, use the X to make sure you place the plant back in the same position.

9 Repeat step 8 for all of the walls that you have.

Interpret Your Results

1. Use your observations to **communicate** to the class how the barriers in the box affected the plant's growth.

2. Why do you think the plant grew the way it did?

3. Make an **inference.** What would happen if you added more walls to your maze? How might the plant's growth be affected?

Inquire Further

How would the plant's growth be affected if you added more walls to your maze? Develop a plan to answer this or other questions you may have.

Self-Assessment

- I followed instructions to test how a plant reacts to light.
- I **predicted** how the plant would grow.
- I recorded my **observations** about the plant's growth.
- I used my observations to **communicate** about why the plant grew as it did.
- I made an **inference** about how the height of the barriers might affect the plant's growth.

Chapter 3 Review

Chapter Main Ideas

Lesson 1

• All living things take in energy, release energy in food, use energy, excrete wastes, reproduce, and respond to the environment.

• Adaptations are inherited traits that help a species survive.

Lesson 2

• Fossils give clues about the organisms that lived long ago.

• Species have changed as a result of evolution.

Lesson 3

• Darwin discovered that species are adapted to their different environments.

• Darwin's theory of natural selection states that certain traits are selected over others and organisms best suited to their environment will survive.

• Adaptations that enable an organism to survive are passed on to offspring.

• Sometimes new species evolve when populations are isolated.

Lesson 4

• A stimulus is a change in environment that causes a response or reaction.

• Organisms use sensory organs to gather information about their environment.

• Physiological adaptations are the work of body parts in response to stimuli.

Lesson 5

• Behavior adaptations cause actions that enable organisms to survive.

• Inherited behavior is a way of responding that does not require learning.

• Learned behavior is an action that is not inherited from the parents.

Reviewing Science Words and Concepts

Choose the letter of the answer that best matches each description.

a. adaptation
b. behavioral adaptation
c. evolution
d. instinct
e. natural selection
f. physiological adaptation
g. population
h. reflex
i. response
j. stimulus
k. structural adaptation

1. Nest-building in birds is a(n) ___, or inherited behavior.
2. An action that aids survival is a(n) ___.
3. Responding to bright light by blinking is an example of ___.
4. A change that causes a reaction is a(n) ___.
5. A quick, automatic response to a stimulus is a(n) ___.
6. The process by which organisms best adapted to an environment survive is ___.
7. The sharp teeth of a tiger is an example of a(n) ___.
8. An inherited trait that helps a species survive in its environment is a(n) ___.
9. A reaction to a stimulus is a(n) ___.

10. Genetic changes in species over time is ___.

11. All the organisms of a species that live in a certain place is a(n) ___.

Explaining Science

Write a paragraph or create an outline to explain these questions.

1. Describe three adaptations that help organisms survive.

2. What evidence do scientists have to support evolution?

3. Give an example of how populations that become isolated might evolve.

4. How are sensory organs important to organisms?

5. List four ways you are responding to your environment right now. What is the stimulus and response in each example?

Using Skills

1. Suppose you discovered a fossil of a new species. The fossil is of an organism with two large webbed feet, two winglike structures, and two large ears. What **conclusions** can you **draw** about the organism?

2. Predict what might happen to the peppered moth population in the cities of England if pollution from smokestacks is reduced. Give reasons for your predictions.

3. Observe the frog on page A87. What adaptations can you identify? Tell how each might help the frog survive.

Critical Thinking

1. Think about ways you respond to stimuli that help you survive. **Classify** each behavior as an instinct, reflex, or learned behavior.

2. Suppose you have found a fossil. Describe your imaginary fossil and **infer** about past life based on what you know about a similar organism that is alive today.

3. Apply Darwin's theory of natural selection to explain why the ptarmigan on page A92 changes color.

A World in Her Hands!

Imagine having a tiny world of your own to observe! The world in this girl's hands has a balanced supply of everything it needs. What can you do to help create, protect, and keep the natural balance in your world?

Chapter 4

Ecosystems and Biomes

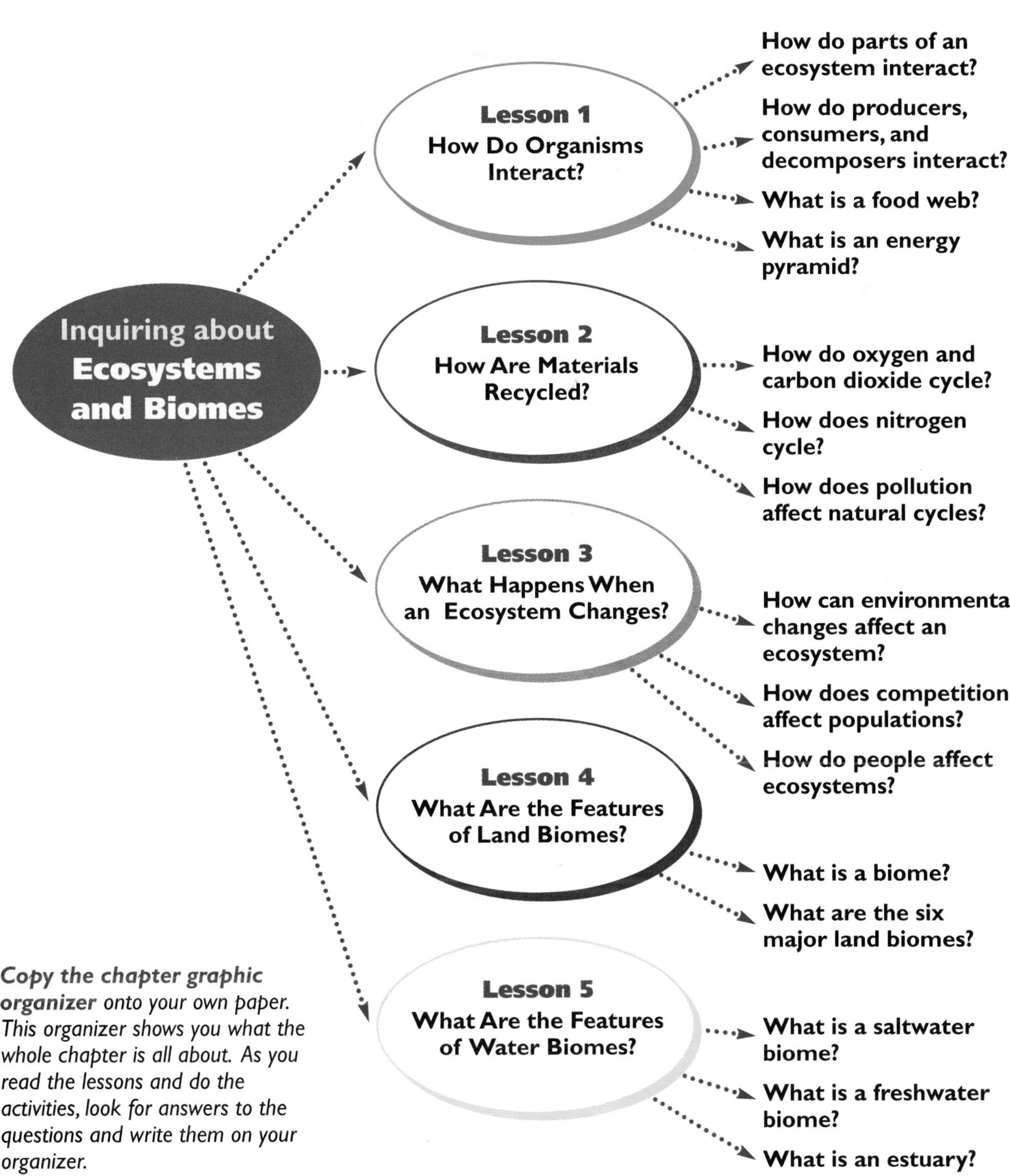

Inquiring about Ecosystems and Biomes
Lesson 1
How Do Organisms Interact?
How do parts of an ecosystem interact?
How do producers, consumers, and decomposers interact?
What is a food web?
What is an energy pyramid?
Lesson 2
How Are Materials Recycled?
How do oxygen and carbon dioxide cycle?
How does nitrogen cycle?
How does pollution affect natural cycles?
Lesson 3
What Happens When an Ecosystem Changes?
How can environmental changes affect an ecosystem?
How does competition affect populations?
How do people affect ecosystems?
Lesson 4
What Are the Features of Land Biomes?
What is a biome?
What are the six major land biomes?
Lesson 5
What Are the Features of Water Biomes?
What is a saltwater biome?
What is a freshwater biome?
What is an estuary?

Copy the chapter graphic organizer *onto your own paper. This organizer shows you what the whole chapter is all about. As you read the lessons and do the activities, look for answers to the questions and write them on your organizer.*

Explore Activity

Exploring a Water Ecosystem

Process Skills

- predicting
- observing
- inferring
- communicating

Materials

- masking tape
- plastic bottle with top portion removed
- metric ruler
- small pebbles
- aquarium water
- elodea plant
- marker

Explore

1. Use masking tape to cover the cut edge of a plastic bottle from which the top portion has been removed.

   Safety Note *Handle the cut bottle carefully. The edges may be sharp.*

2. Place about 1 cm of pebbles in the bottom of the plastic bottle. Add water to a depth of about 8 cm.
3. Add an elodea plant to your water ecosystem. Be sure the roots of the plant are anchored in the pebbles.
4. With a marker, mark the water level of your ecosystem on the side of the bottle.
5. **Predict** what will happen to the water level after several days. Record your prediction.
6. **Observe** your ecosystem for at least 3 days. Record your observations.

Reflect

What can you **infer** from your predictions and observations? **Communicate** your observations to your classmates. Make a list of possible explanations for what you observed.

Inquire Further

What might happen if you placed a land ecosystem above the water ecosystem? How might this affect the water level in the water ecosystem? Develop a plan to answer these or other questions you may have.

Making Predictions

As you read Lesson 1, *How Do Organisms Interact?*, you'll be **making predictions**. A prediction is an educated guess about what may happen in the future. When making a prediction, rely on the information provided, as well as what you already know about similar events. Assume that what happened in the past could happen again.

Reading Vocabulary

prediction, an educated guess about what may happen in the future

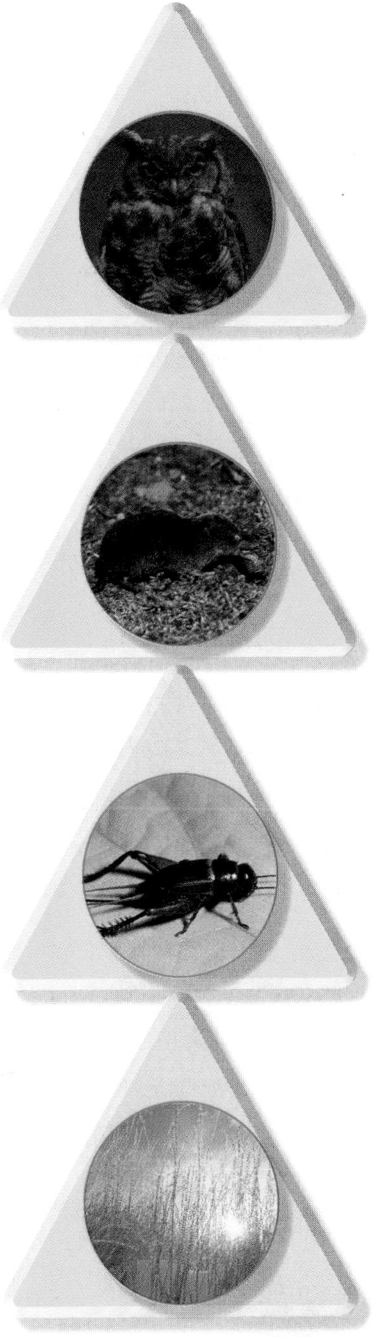

Example

Look at the food chain to the right. To make a prediction about how this food chain would change if all the grass died, follow these steps:

1. Identify the events or actions provided in the picture.
2. Think about how the events and actions might be related.
3. Identify a similar situation. Recall what happened there.
4. Use the information from the picture and the past situation to make a prediction.

Talk About It!

1. What information can you gain from analyzing the food chain?

2. Predict what would happen to the number of owls if the number of crickets decreased.

You will learn:

- how parts of an ecosystem interact.
- how producers, consumers, and decomposers interact.
- what a food web is.
- what an energy pyramid is.

Lesson 1

How Do Organisms Interact?

Shhh! What could THAT be? It's the end of a long day on your camping trip. Your campfire is just glowing embers. You get the feeling you're being watched. You wonder what animal might be rustling around out there in the dark.

Interactions Within Ecosystems

You could spend hours looking through field guides before you figure out what might be lurking in a forest. A forest is full of different kinds of living things, including animals, plants, mushrooms, molds, algae, and microscopic one-celled organisms. All the living things in a forest interact with each other. They also interact with nonliving parts of the forest.

The city park shown on these pages is also made up of different living and nonliving things that interact. A park and a forest are both examples of ecosystems. Each ecosystem includes the living and nonliving parts that affect the organisms living there. An ecosystem can be small like a puddle or vast like the ocean.

People, dogs, grass, shrubs, trees, flowers, birds, squirrels, insects, spiders, and worms—these are some of the living things you might find in this park ecosystem. What are some of the nonliving things you might find in a park?

Like other ecosystems on Earth, this park has both living and nonliving parts. ▼

Air, water in a pond or puddle, soil, rocks, concrete sidewalks, and park benches are a few of the nonliving parts of a park ecosystem. What other living or nonliving parts can you think of?

To survive in a park ecosystem, organisms must be adapted to the environmental conditions of the park—the kind of soil, the temperature of the air, and the amount of light and water. In fact, the nonliving parts of an ecosystem often determine what organisms live there. For example, cactus plants don't normally live in a park like this one. Cactuses live in hotter, dryer ecosystems that have sandier soil than this park does.

Each organism in an ecosystem is also affected by the other organisms living there. Look at the grass growing on the ground in the park. The grass has a thick root system that is able to spread new grass tufts through the field. The grass roots hold moisture in the soil. When grass blades die and decay, they make the soil rich. The moisture and nutrients in the soil enable other plants to grow. Other plants you might see in the park include dandelions and clovers, as well as garden flowers.

Insects are attracted by the grasses and other plants in the park. If you look closely near ground level, you might see grasshoppers, crickets, honeybees, butterflies, or fireflies. Animals are attracted by the insects and plants. If you look underground, you might find burrowing animals, such as ground squirrels, earthworms, or garter snakes.

Now, think about what's above the ground. Birds, such as cardinals, fly through the air and land on the ground, looking for seeds. Other birds, such as robins, seek out worms for their meals. All these parts make up a healthy park ecosystem. A healthy ecosystem is one in which the living and nonliving parts are balanced.

Glossary

Glossary

herbivore (hėr′bə vôr), a consumer that eats only plants or other producers

carnivore (kär′nə vôr), a consumer that eats only animals

omnivore (om′ni vôr), a consumer that eats both producers and consumers

Producers, Consumers, and Decomposers

When you read about life processes in Chapter 3, you learned that living things are alike in that they all must get the energy they need to carry on other life processes. However, organisms vary in how they get energy. How do you get energy?

Green plants are different from you and most other organisms. They get energy from food that they make during photosynthesis. During this process, a green plant uses sunlight to change carbon dioxide and water into glucose, a type of sugar. The sugar is stored by the plant until the plant needs energy. Then the plant releases the stored energy. Because green plants produce their own food, they are called producers.

Most other organisms can't use sunlight to make their own food as plants can. Instead, they get energy by eating, or consuming, food. These organisms are called consumers. What's the food that consumers eat? It's other organisms.

Some consumers, like the insects in the picture, feed directly on plants. They get the energy they need to carry on life processes from the stored energy in the plant leaves. Other consumers eat animals. A bird, for example, may come along and snatch one of the insects shown. It gets its energy from the energy in the insect.

These caterpillars are consumers because they feed on plants. ▼

One type of consumer, called an **herbivore**, eats only plants. Beavers are herbivores because they feed on the bark of aspen, birch, willow, and other trees. Caterpillars, deer, rabbits, ducks, and elephants are other examples of herbivores. Other consumers, called **carnivores**, eat only other animals. The brown bat is a carnivore because it feeds only on insects. Tigers, hawks, weasels, frogs, pelicans, and killer whales are other examples of carnivores.

Still other consumers, called **omnivores**, eat both plants and animals. A skunk is an omnivore because it eats plants, insects, and worms.

What are you—an herbivore, a carnivore, or an omnivore? You probably answered that humans are omnivores because they eat both plants and animals. In fact, humans eat plants, animals, fungi, and even certain bacteria.

Did you ever think about what happens to all the leaves that fall off trees in autumn? Do you know what happens to the body of an animal that dies in the forest? Eventually, the bodies of dead organisms disappear. Every ecosystem contains consumers called **decomposers**. These organisms get nutrients and energy from dead bodies and the wastes of living organisms. Decomposers break down the wastes and complex chemicals in dead organisms into simple chemicals. These simple chemicals can then be used again by plants.

Fungi, such as molds and mushrooms, are decomposers. You've probably seen molds growing on food, or perhaps you've noticed mushrooms like the one shown here growing on the ground or on trees. Some species of bacteria are also decomposers. Without decomposers, all ecosystems on the earth would soon be piled high with dead organisms and their wastes!

In general, plants are producers, and animals are consumers. However, one special producer is not a plant. In fact, this producer, a type of bacteria, does not even depend on sunlight to make its own food!

Sunlight can't reach the deep ocean floor, so no photosynthesis can occur. In these places, hot plumes of water rise from small vents on the ocean floor. Sulfur-containing compounds, called sulfides, are dissolved in the water. Unusual bacteria around the vents use oxygen and sulfides from the water to release energy. With this energy, they convert carbon dioxide and water into sugars. Therefore, in this ecosystem, bacteria are the producers. The tube worms, giant clams, and other organisms seen in the picture are consumers.

Glossary

decomposer (dē′kəm pō′zər), an organism that obtains energy by consuming dead organisms and the wastes of living organisms

▲ *Decomposers like this scarlet waxy cap mushroom break down dead organisms and return nutrients to the soil.*

Sulfides from within the earth are the original energy source for organisms of the deep-ocean vent ecosystem. These tubeworms eat the bacteria that convert these sulfur-containing compounds to chemical energy. ▶

Food Webs

The pictures show some organisms you might find in a field. The grass plants in the bottom picture convert light energy from the sun, water, and carbon dioxide into sugar that has stored energy. The cricket eats the grass plant, transferring the plant's energy and nutrients to itself. Later, the cricket is eaten by a shrew. The shrew lives on energy and nutrients it gets from eating the cricket. Even later, the shrew is eaten by the owl. The owl lives on energy and nutrients from the shrew's body.

As you can see from this diagram, energy and nutrients move through organisms within an ecosystem. Arrows in the diagram show the direction in which energy and nutrients are transferred from one organism to the next. Producers, such as grass plants, are eaten by consumers. Those consumers are eaten by other consumers. A model such as this that shows how energy moves in an ecosystem is called a food chain. The grass, the cricket, the shrew, and the owl are all links in this food chain.

When the owl dies, decomposers will get energy by breaking down the owl's body. The minerals and gases that are released in this process become nutrients that can be used again by plants. Decomposers make up the final link in any food chain.

You probably know that crickets in a field are not the only animals that eat grass plants. A rabbit also eats grass. A snake might eat the rabbit, and an owl might eat the snake. In this food chain, the grass, the rabbit, the snake, and the owl are the links. Notice that the grass and the owl are links in both this food chain and the one shown to the left. Most organisms in an ecosystem are part of more than one food chain.

◀ *This is only one of the food chains you might find in a field ecosystem.*

Different food chains in an ecosystem are linked together in a food web. Study the food web below. In this food web, algae, water lilies, cattails, arrowheads, and duckweed are all producers. Notice the variety of consumers that eat these producers. Tadpoles, worms, and waterfleas eat the algae. Crayfish eat duckweed, but also eat worms. Perch and sunfish eat crayfish. In turn, the sunfish may be eaten by a bullfrog.

The arrows in this pond food web show the flow of energy and nutrients in each individual food chain. ▼

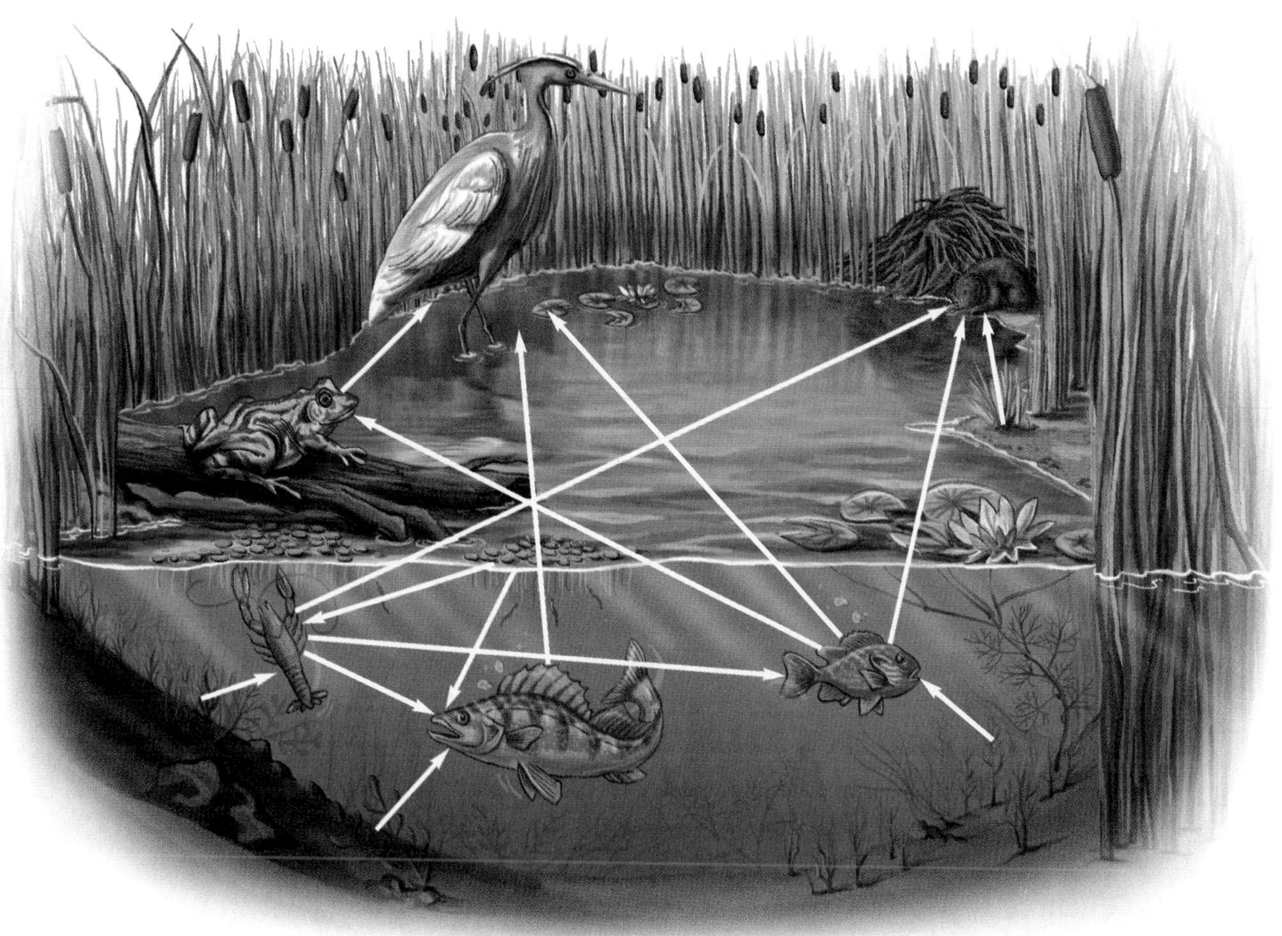

Notice, too, that all the organisms shown in this food web don't actually live in the water of the pond. Muskrats spend much of their time in the water, but also spend time on land. Look at the food web to find out what muskrats eat. A heron nests and sleeps on land. However, in early morning or evening, the heron flies to the pond to hunt for food. It stands quietly in shallow water, waiting to grab a fish or frog with its long, pointed beak. See how many food chains you can find that end with the heron.

Glossary

Glossary

energy pyramid
(en′ər jē pir′ə mid), a model that shows how energy is used in a food chain or an ecosystem

Energy Pyramids

A food chain shows how energy moves from one organism to another. However, the same amount of energy does not move between organisms. Why not?

Remember that each organism needs energy for its life processes. Each organism uses some of the energy it gets from its food before it, in turn, becomes food for another organism. An **energy pyramid** is a model that can be used to show how energy is used in a particular food chain or ecosystem. The energy pyramid below shows the use and availability of energy in a grassy field.

The amount of energy available to a certain group of organisms depends on its feeding order in a food chain. In other words, it depends on which level of the pyramid it is on. Some energy is used at each link of a food chain to carry out life processes. That means less energy is available at any level in the pyramid than in the level below it. At which level is the least amount of energy available?

Most food chains have no more than five links. The reason is that the amount of energy left by the fifth link is only a small percentage of what was available at the first link.

Less and less energy is available as you near the top of an energy pyramid. ▼

The two energy pyramids below show how energy is transferred through organisms in the Arctic Ocean. The energy pyramid on the left shows a food chain with six links. The energy pyramid on the right shows a food chain with only three links. Notice that both food chains begin with algae and end with killer whales.

In the first food chain, energy is first transferred from algae to protists and zooplankton. Energy from these organisms is then transferred to squid. However, as the second pyramid shows, squid will also eat algae. When they do so, squid are at a lower level on the pyramid, and thus have more energy available to them. How does the amount of energy available to the killer whale differ in the two pyramids? If the killer whale feeds directly on squid, as shown in the second pyramid, much more energy is transferred to it. In any energy pyramid, the fewer the links in the food chain, the more energy that is available to the organisms at the top of the pyramid.

If the middle layers of consumers are eliminated, the same amount of producers can provide energy for more top consumers. ▼

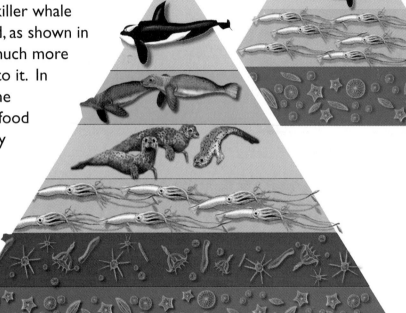

Lesson 1 Review

1. How do parts of an ecosystem interact?
2. How do producers, consumers, and decomposers interact?
3. What are food webs?
4. What are energy pyramids?
5. **Predict**
   What might happen to the fish population in the food web shown on page A119 if the heron population disappeared?

Observing a Bottle Ecosystem

Process Skills

Process Skills

- predicting
- observing
- inferring

Materials

- gauze
- cup of water
- plastic bottle assembly
- water ecosystem from Explore Activity, page A112
- metric ruler
- pebbles
- graduated cup
- soil
- grass seed
- plastic wrap

Getting Ready

How do ecosystems interact? Do this activity to observe the interaction between a water ecosystem and a land ecosystem.

Use the water ecosystem that you made in the Explore Activity to complete this activity.

Follow This Procedure

1. Make a chart like the one shown. Use your chart to record your observations.

Day	Observation
2	
4	
6	

2. Place a piece of cotton gauze in a cup of water. Remove the gauze from the cup and squeeze out the excess water. Then thread the gauze through a hole in a plastic bottle cap. Screw the bottle cap onto the top part of the bottle.

3. Assemble the bottle top and midsection as shown in Photo A.

4. Place the assembly over the water ecosystem you made in the Explore Activity on page A112. Adjust the cotton gauze so that it is just above the bottom of your water ecosystem (Photo B).

Photo A

Photo B

Photo C

5 Make a land ecosystem by placing 2 cm of pebbles in the empty bottle top. Add about 240 mL of soil. Make sure the cotton gauze is in the soil—not stuck to the side of the bottle.

6 Sprinkle some grass seed evenly over the soil. Sprinkle water on the soil to make it moist but not soggy. Place plastic wrap over the top of the bottle (Photo C).

7 Think about how the two ecosystems will interact over several days. **Predict** what will happen to both the land and water ecosystem. Tell what information you used to make your prediction.

8 **Observe** your land and water ecosystems for several days. Record observations.

Interpret Your Results

1. Review your observations of the land and water ecosystems. What interactions did you observe between the two ecosystems?

2. Make an **inference.** What do you think would happen to the ecosystems if you added more plants?

Inquire Further

Would doubling the number of plants affect the ecosystem? Develop a plan to answer this or other questions you may have.

Self-Assessment

- I followed instructions to make a combination land and water ecosystem.
- I **predicted** what would happen to the land and water ecosystems over time.
- I tested my prediction.
- I recorded my **observations** about the ecosystems for several days.
- I made an **inference** about how the two ecosystems are related.

You will learn:

- how oxygen and carbon dioxide cycle.
- how nitrogen cycles.
- how pollution affects natural cycles.

Lesson 2

How Are Materials Recycled?

Hey! Look at that tiny leaf! Did you know that it not only traps the sun's energy to make food for other living organisms, but it also helps you breathe? Do you know how?

Oxygen-Carbon Dioxide Cycle

Oxygen and carbon dioxide cycle through the living parts of an ecosystem. ▼

You've seen how energy available to organisms lessens as it flows through a food chain. As long as the sun shines, however, energy on Earth can be replenished. Yet organisms also require certain materials in order to survive. Like energy, these materials move through the food chain. Unlike energy, they are not less available as they do so. These materials are naturally recycled.

Water is one of the most important materials required by organisms. You are probably familiar with how water is recycled through precipitation and evaporation. Like water, carbon dioxide and oxygen are essential materials that also cycle within ecosystems. Recall that during photosynthesis green plants use energy from sunlight to combine carbon dioxide and water. Sugars and oxygen are produced. The first equation below shows this process.

Photosynthesis
carbon dioxide + water + energy → sugar + oxygen
Respiration
sugar + oxygen → carbon dioxide + water + energy

Now look at the bottom equation on the previous page. It shows the process of **respiration,** through which energy is released in cells. During respiration, sugar and oxygen combine, and carbon dioxide and water are produced. How do the equations for photosynthesis and respiration compare?

Much of the oxygen released by plants during photosynthesis is used by organisms during respiration. The carbon dioxide produced during respiration is exhaled by animals and may later be used by plants. This exchange is called the oxygen-carbon dioxide cycle. Follow the cycle in the diagram below.

Glossary

respiration
(res′pə rā′shən), energy-producing process in which a cell combines oxygen with sugars and gives off carbon dioxide and water

Nitrogen Cycle

Nitrogen is another material that cycles through an ecosystem. Its pathway is called the nitrogen cycle.

All living things need nitrogen in order to make the proteins they need to survive. Almost 80 percent of the earth's air is nitrogen gas, so it might seem like getting enough nitrogen wouldn't be a problem. However, most organisms can't use nitrogen gas directly from the air. The nitrogen gas must first be changed into nitrogen compounds. This change happens in two ways in the environment.

The first way nitrogen is changed into nitrogen compounds is by special bacteria and other microscopic organisms that live in the soil. The bacteria, known as nitrogen-fixing bacteria, grow in nodules on the roots of certain plants, such as peas, soybeans, and clover. You can see the nodules on the clover roots on the next page. These bacteria can change nitrogen in the air into nitrogen compounds. The nitrogen compounds dissolve in water. Plants are then able to take them up when they take in water through their roots. Animals are able to get the nitrogen they need when they eat plants.

Do you see the lightning in the diagram? It shows the second way in which nitrogen gas can be changed. When lightning flashes through the air, nitrogen combines with the oxygen in the air to form nitrogen compounds. These compounds combine with rainwater to form nitrogen compounds that plants can use.

Without the nitrogen that these bacteria produce during decomposition, nitrogen could not cycle through the environment. ▶

Getting nitrogen into the ground is only half the cycle. To complete the cycle, nitrogen must be returned to the air. Once nitrogen compounds are made into proteins by plants, they pass through food webs. Bacteria in food webs decompose waste products or dead organisms. During decomposition, nitrogen compounds may be changed to nitrogen gas. The nitrogen gas returns to the air, completing the nitrogen cycle.

◀ *The nodules on the roots of clover plants contain bacteria that change nitrogen into nitrogen compounds the plants can use.*

Glossary

Glossary

pollution (pə lü′shən), anything produced that harms the environment

Pollution Affects the Cycles

People are part of many different ecosystems. Unfortunately, they also often cause **pollution** that harms these ecosystems. Some pollution occurs naturally, such as when a volcano erupts and sends dust and poison gases into the air. However, most pollution is caused by people.

Some pollution disturbs the natural recycling of materials in the environment. For example, humans have disturbed the oxygen-carbon dioxide cycle by burning fossil fuels. Coal, oil, and natural gas are fossil fuels that are burned to run cars and factories, to heat buildings, and to make electricity. When these fossil fuels are burned, carbon dioxide is released into the air. Carbon dioxide prevents heat from escaping back into space from Earth.

Scientists have drilled into the core of glaciers and found evidence that carbon dioxide in the air has increased greatly since the 1700s. Some scientists think that this increase might be causing Earth's temperatures to rise. This effect is called global warming. Global warming may result in some of the polar ice melting. This melting might result in rising sea levels and flooding of low-lying coastal areas of land.

People have also disturbed the nitrogen cycle by using fertilizers that contain nitrogen compounds. In some places, fertilizer from farms seeps into the soil and

Through certain activities, humans pollute the air, water, soil, and groundwater. ▼

groundwater. Decomposers can't break down these nitrogen compounds fast enough, and they build up. Groundwater polluted by nitrogen compounds can be harmful to health, especially that of very young children.

To help control pollution, many laws have been passed by the U.S. government, as well as by states and local communities. Laws now require communities to treat sewage and to prevent factories from dumping chemicals.

Like the boy in the picture, you can do your part to reduce pollution by recycling newspapers, aluminum cans, glass bottles and jars, and plastics. You can also help by building a compost pile. Yard wastes, such as grass and leaves, and other plant matter, such as fruit and vegetable peels, can be mixed with soil. If the pile is kept moist, decomposers will recycle the materials, and you will have nutrient-rich soil to use on your garden or lawn.

Lesson 2 Review

1. Describe how oxygen and carbon dioxide cycle through the environment.
2. How does nitrogen cycle through the environment?
3. How does pollution affect the natural recycling of materials in an ecosystem?
4. **Predict**
   How might the oxygen–carbon dioxide cycle be affected if most of the trees in an ecosystem were destroyed?

When materials are recycled, they can be reused. That makes manufacturing new materials, which can cause pollution, less necessary. ▼

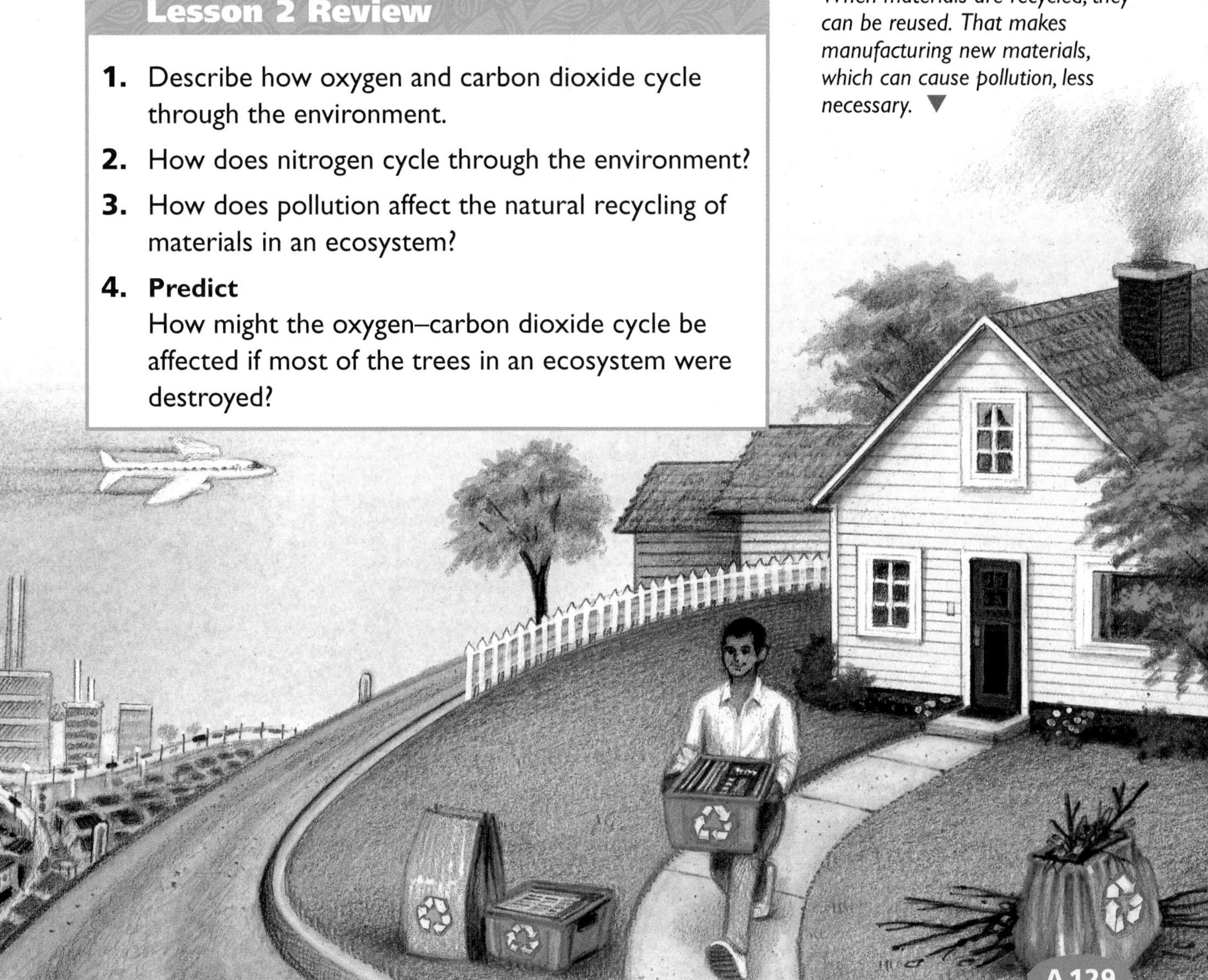

You will learn:

- how environmental changes can affect an ecosystem.
- how competition affects populations.
- how people affect ecosystems.

Lesson 3

What Happens When an Ecosystem Changes?

C-R-A-C-K! Lightning strikes a tree in the forest, setting it ablaze. A lack of rain has left the forest dry. The fire spreads rapidly from tree to tree and through the underbrush. How will such a fire change the forest ecosystem?

Environmental Changes

Changes are a natural part of the history of any ecosystem. Fires, droughts, floods, or shifts in temperature can and do change ecosystems.

As conditions in an ecosystem change, populations in the ecosystem might also change. All organisms have a certain range of conditions in which they can survive. Think about temperature, for example. As you see below, one species of fish may be able to tolerate only a narrow range of temperatures in cooler water. Another species, however, can tolerate a much wider range of temperatures. What do you think would happen if the water in which these fish lived became warmer?

This picture shows an example of how different species of fish can tolerate different ranges of temperature. ▼

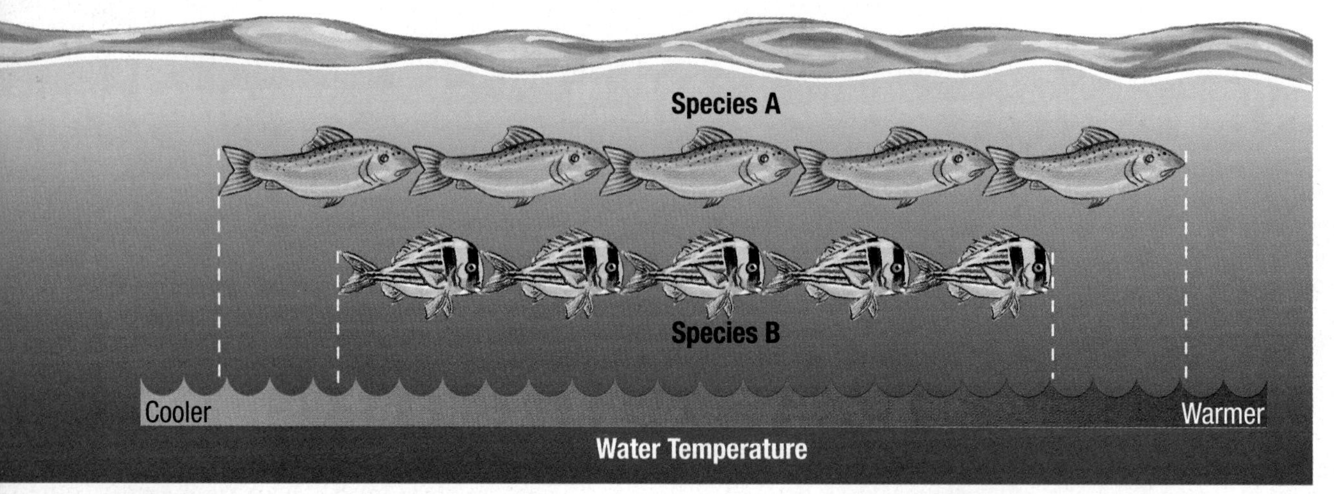

The amount of light an ecosystem gets is also a condition that affects its populations. Coral polyps are small marine animals that build limestone shells. These shells build up to form colorful coral reefs, like the one shown below. Coral reefs can grow only in ocean waters that are warmer than 25°C and less than 10 meters deep. A change in world climates could cause a rise in sea levels. As a result, less light would reach the coral reefs. If the amount of light dipped under the range necessary for coral polyps to survive, the corals would die, and the entire ecosystem might be destroyed.

You have probably read or seen stories about an event called El Niño. Every few years, the westward-blowing trade winds in the Pacific Ocean reverse direction, and a mass of warm water flows eastward along the equator. El Niño causes environmental changes worldwide, from floods in California to droughts in Australia. Ecosystems change as a result. For example, off the coast of South America, higher water temperatures kill plankton and fish. Birds that feed on fish may starve, or they abandon their nests.

In any ecosystem, populations change as conditions change. New populations that can tolerate the new conditions move in. A new community of organisms is established, creating a new and different ecosystem.

▲ *These soft corals are one of the many species you might find around a coral reef.*

You can find a large variety of species around most coral reefs. ▼

Glossary

Glossary

competition
(kom′pə tish′ən), a situation in which two or more organisms attempt to use the same resource

Competition

Within an ecosystem, populations of different species live together and interact. You've already learned that one way organisms in an ecosystem interact is as consumers and producers in food webs.

Another way organisms in an ecosystem interact is by **competition.** Organisms can live only in ecosystems where their needs are met. These needs include food, water, space, shelter, light, minerals, and gases. These resources, however, are in limited supply in an ecosystem. When two or more organisms try to use the same resource, competition results. Members of different species may compete for food, water, and space. Members of the same species may also compete for these resources and for mates.

Think about the prairie ecosystem shown below. Populations of grasses, grasshoppers, mice, bison, and hawks all live together in the prairie ecosystem. Grasshoppers, mice, and bison compete for food because all three species eat plants. All organisms in the prairie ecosystem compete for water.

The mice that live in the prairie ecosystem compete with each other too—for space, food, water, and mates. As the population of mice becomes larger, competition among the mice increases. Not all the mice will survive. Competition is one way that the size of a population is controlled naturally.

Suppose that one year the prairie did not receive as much rain as usual. The lack of rain would limit the growth of the grasses and thistles. The reduced amount of these plants, in turn, would affect the populations of other

Organisms within an ecosystem compete for resources. How do the plants in the prairie compete? ▼

organisms. Less grass to eat would increase competition among grass-eaters. Fewer mice and grasshoppers would survive. In turn, the hawks that feed on the mice, like the one to the right, would be affected. Competition for food would also increase among hawks. How might this increase in competition affect the hawk population?

Whenever resources are limited, the organisms that survive will be those that are best adapted to the new conditions. These organisms are the ones that can best compete. For example, the grasslands of the African savannah have only two seasons, rainy and dry. When the dry season arrives, grass blades on the savannah turn brown, curl, and die. Acacia trees shed their leaves. However, both the acacias and the underground parts of the grasses live off stored food until the rains return. Both species are adapted to survive the dry conditions. In the meantime, most of the plant-eating animals, such as zebras and wildebeests, leave and move to new feeding grounds. Some of the weaker members of these migrating herds—especially the very young and the very old—may not survive the move.

▲ *Hawks soar and circle over the prairie for long periods of time, competing to find mice or other small mammals for their next meal.*

What happens to the organisms of the savannah that don't migrate? Frogs, toads, and hedgehogs bury themselves in the ground, where they sleep until the rains return. As waterholes dry up, elephants often use their tusks to dig into the ground in search of water. As the grasses die off, elephants peel bark from trees to get moisture and food. When they can no longer find enough water and food, they move to areas where they can.

Lions change their diets during the dry season. With no zebras or wildebeests to eat, they compete to feed on warthogs and other small animals. Some lions may die during the dry season, but those that are the best hunters will probably survive.

People Affect Ecosystems

▲ *How have people changed this ecosystem? What effect will this have on the ecosystem?*

Ecosystems change naturally, but they may also be changed by humans. All the materials that people use and the food that people eat come from the environment. As people use these resources, such as the trees to the left, they change the ecosystems from which the resources come.

People have cut or burned forests, drained wetlands, and dammed or altered the courses of rivers. They have made these changes to make room for farms, roads, and houses, or to provide water, electricity, and other materials. As forests and wetlands disappear, animals and other organisms lose their homes and territories. They are less able to find food. Some populations of organisms—even entire species—may disappear forever.

People also change ecosystems when they introduce new species to areas. For example, the purple loosestrife pictured below did not naturally grow in the United States. It was introduced from Europe. With no natural predators or diseases, the plant crowded out other wetland plants. It spread rapidly and uncontrollably.

Ten thousand years ago, when people first developed farming, there were about 10 million people on Earth. By 1997, there were almost 6 billion people—about 600 times more. More than a quarter of a million people are added to the world's population every day. As the human population grows, its effect on the environment increases.

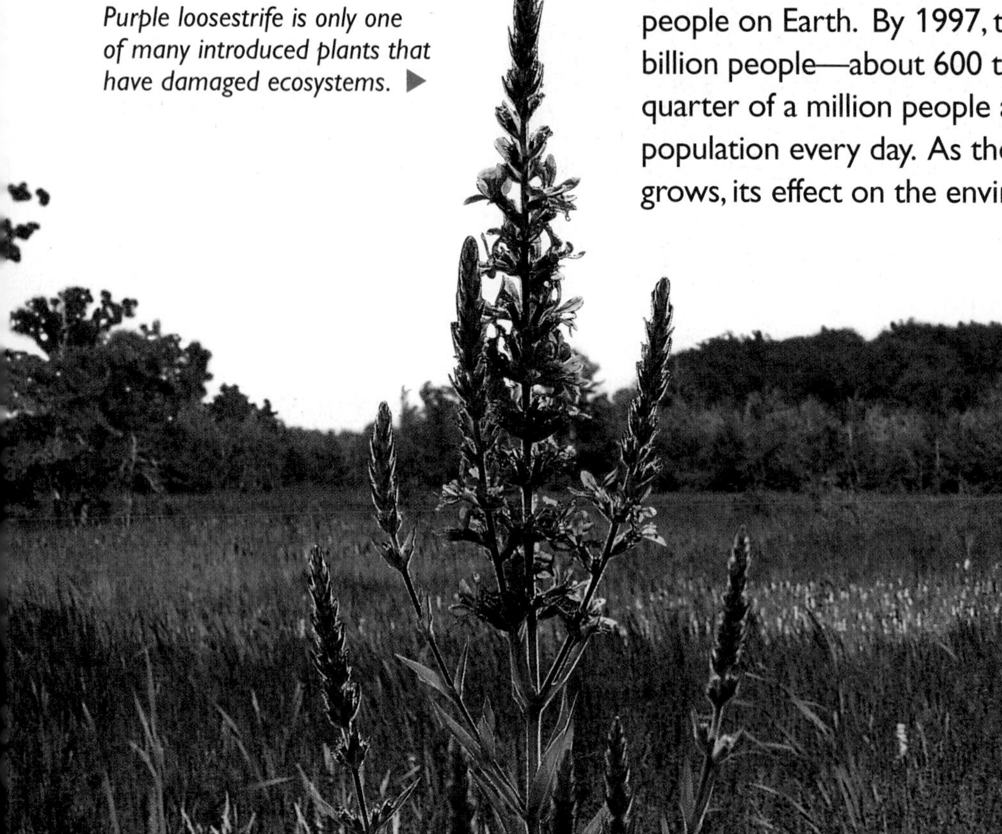

Purple loosestrife is only one of many introduced plants that have damaged ecosystems. ▶

Mining coal, oil, and natural gas from the earth damages or causes risks to many ecosystems. However, people all over the world are taking steps to protect the environment. Through conservation methods, less fuel is needed. More energy-efficient cars, such as this electric car, also help. Recycling paper saves forest ecosystems, and using less water helps preserve wetland, river, and lake ecosystems. How are the people below acting to protect the environment?

▲ *Electric cars help protect the environment because they don't use fossil fuels, which can harm the environment.*

◀ *Many groups work to restore ecosystems that have been damaged by people. These people are restoring a prairie by replanting natural species.*

Lesson 3 Review

1. How can environmental changes affect an ecosystem?
2. How does competition affect populations?
3. Describe two ways that people affect ecosystems.
4. **Predict**
   What might happen to the ecosystem shown in the picture at the bottom of these pages if an insect that ate purple loosestrife were introduced into the environment?

You will learn:

- **what a biome is.**
- **what the six major land biomes are.**

Lesson 4

What Are the Features of Land Biomes?

The sun is HOT—beating down on you. The air is so dry that your throat is parched. The few plants you can see are covered with spines. Not many animals seem to be around. Do you know where you are?

Glossary

Glossary

biome (bī′ōm), large geographic region with a particular kind of climate and community

Biomes

If the place that you are standing is hot and very dry with few plants and animals, you could probably guess that you are in a desert. The hot, dry air is your first clue. The spiny plants and lack of animals is your second.

On land, a number of major types of ecosystems are described by their climates and the communities of organisms that live there. Similar ecosystems with similar climates and communities are called **biomes.** These large geographic regions are found in many locations around the earth. For example, desert biomes are found on almost every continent.

Climate is one of the most important factors that determines the kinds of organisms found in a biome. For example, some plants need more water than other plants. Plants such as large broadleaf trees can't live in biomes that receive little yearly precipitation, as cactus plants can. Some animals require cooler yearly temperatures than others do. Do you think a polar bear could survive in a desert? Why?

The kinds of plants that live in a biome determine the kinds of animals that live there. For example, grasslands support large populations of grass-eating animals, such as gazelles, as well as large predators that feed on them, such as lions. You won't find either in a desert biome, where little grass can grow.

▲ *The climates in these two biomes are very different. As a result, the kinds of organisms in each are also different.*

Biomes change as latitude—or distance from the equator—changes because climate changes with latitude. At latitudes near the equator, the sun appears at the highest angle in the sky. Therefore, regions near the equator have the warmest climates. At latitudes near the poles, the sun is never very high in the sky. These places have the coldest climates. In the middle latitudes, the sun is rather high in the sky in summer and rather low in winter. These places have climates with seasonal changes.

Climate is also affected by altitude. As you hike up a mountain or travel closer to the poles, temperatures drop and climates change. Notice in the diagram how biomes change on a mountain.

The map on the next two pages shows the locations of the six major land biomes of the earth. Refer to this map as you read the rest of the chapter.

If you travel up a mountain in North America, you see biomes change in the same way as they do if you travel northward toward the North Pole. ▼

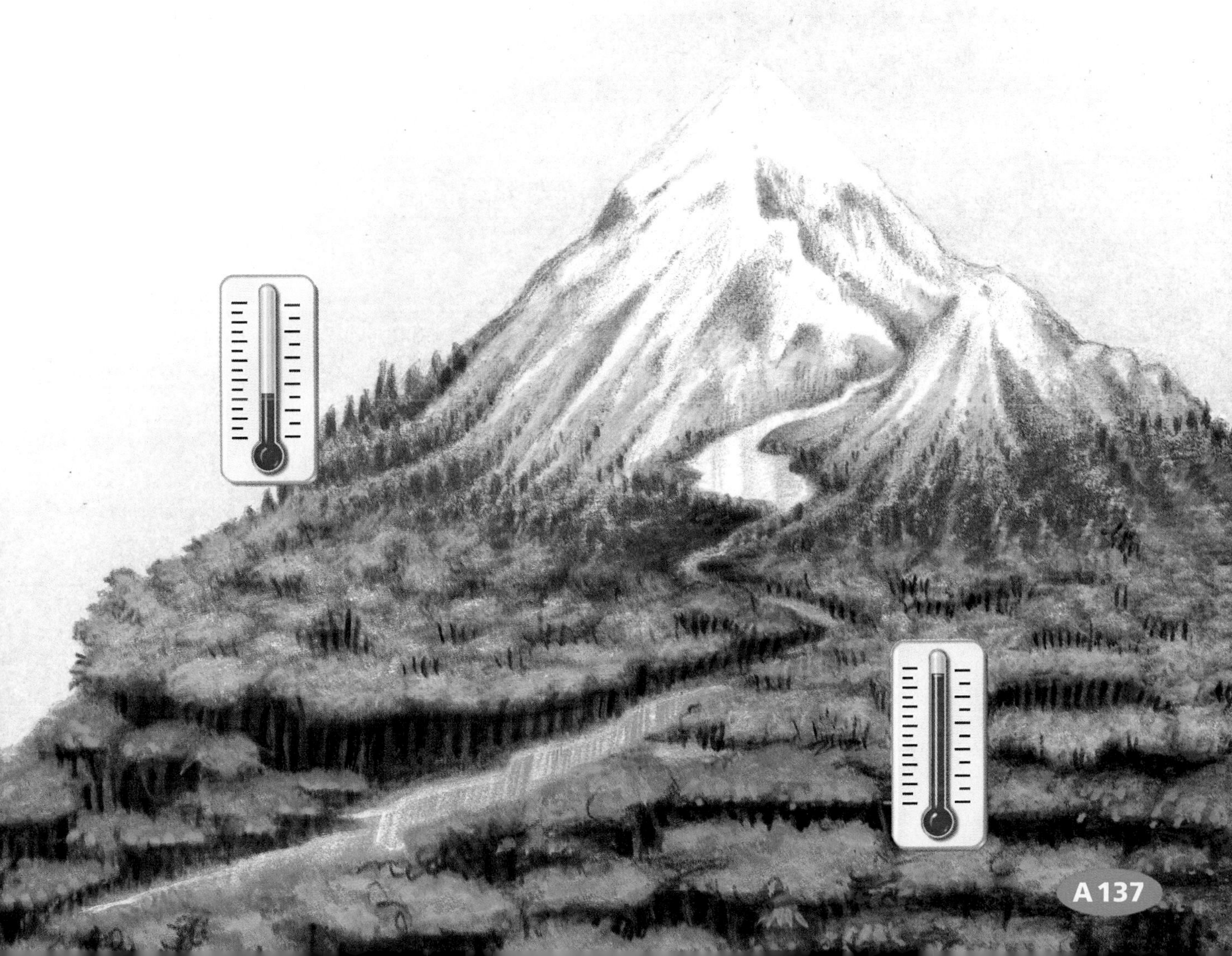

World Biomes

The type of climate of each biome is indicated by the yearly temperatures and precipitation. Look at the map and find the biome in which you live. What other biomes have you traveled to?

Tundra	Taiga	Temperate Deciduous Forest
Yearly temperatures: –57°C to 10°C *Average precipitation: 20 cm*	*Yearly temperatures: –29°C to 22°C* *Average precipitation: 50 cm*	*Yearly temperatures: –20°C to 35°C* *Average precipitation: 125 cm*

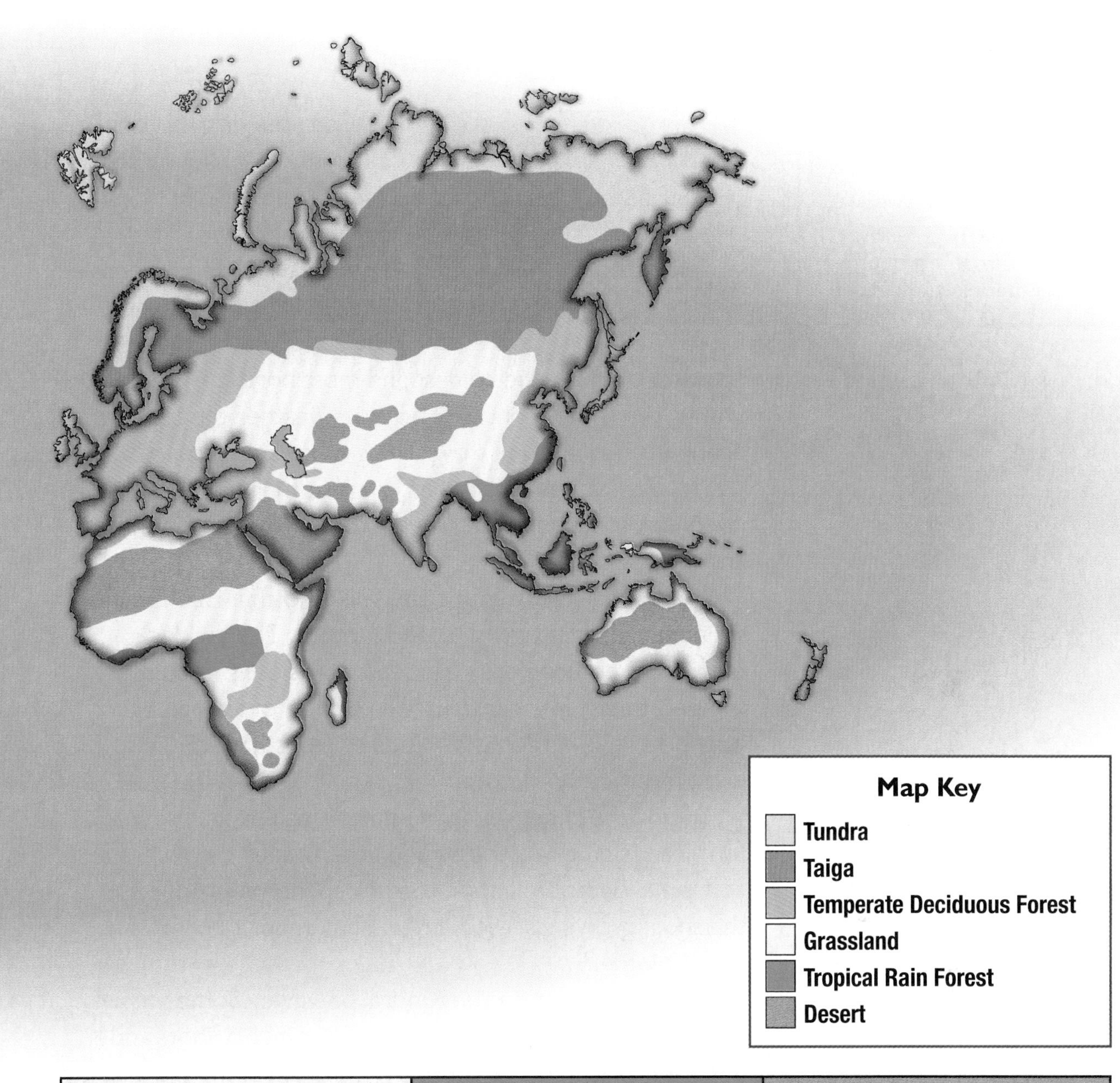

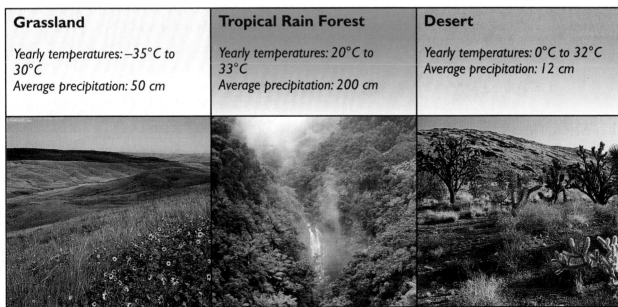

Grassland	Tropical Rain Forest	Desert
Yearly temperatures: –35°C to 30°C *Average precipitation: 50 cm*	*Yearly temperatures: 20°C to 33°C* *Average precipitation: 200 cm*	*Yearly temperatures: 0°C to 32°C* *Average precipitation: 12 cm*

Glossary

Glossary

tundra (tun′drə), the northernmost and coldest biome

permafrost (pėr′mə frôst′), ground that is permanently frozen

Land Biomes

Tundra

Can you imagine living in a biome that has very cold, harsh weather about nine months of the year and completely frozen ground during that time? These are the conditions in the **tundra** biome—the coldest and most northern biome. During the three months of warmer weather, the top few centimeters of ground thaw. The ground below, called **permafrost**, remains frozen. Ice that melts in the top layers can't seep into the ground, so it forms lakes, ponds, and marshy areas.

In most areas of tundra, the soil is so thin that it can support only plants with shallow roots. The soil lacks nutrients because decay happens very slowly in cold temperatures. In fact, the frozen bodies of animals that have been extinct for thousands of years have been discovered in the tundra.

During the short tundra summer, small plants grow and form seeds quickly. Mosses and lichens, seen below, are also common. Because all food chains depend on producers, the short growing season limits the number of organisms in this biome.

Animals do live on the tundra, however. Some animals you might find include polar bears, wolves, caribou, and mice. Birds include geese, ptarmigans, and snowy owls like the one below. Insects, especially flies and mosquitoes, are plentiful during the short summer.

The snowy owl feeds on small mammals, especially lemmings, and ptarmigan in the tundra. ▼

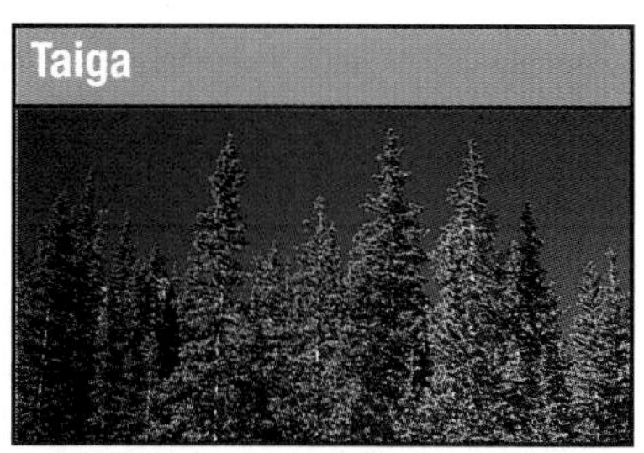

Just south of the tundra in the Northern Hemisphere is the **taiga**, or coniferous forest biome. In the United States, you can find taiga in parts of Alaska, Maine, and Michigan and in the mountains of western states. Have you ever visited Yellowstone National Park in Wyoming or Yosemite and Sequoia National Parks in California? If so, you've visited the taiga. Look back at the map. Where else in the world can you find the taiga biome?

The taiga has cold winters, but its summers are longer and warmer than those of the tundra. Longer, warmer summers allow the ground to thaw completely, so there is no permafrost.

The most common plants in the taiga are conifers—trees such as pines, firs, spruces, cedars, and redwoods. Conifer trees, like those you see to the right, bear seeds in cones and do not lose all their leaves at one time. The plentiful trees of the taiga provide food and shelter for animals. However, they also shade the forest floor, so many low-lying shrubs and flowering plants can't grow. The needles and branches that fall to the forest floor take a long time to decay. Can you guess why? Most decomposers in the taiga are fungi.

Common mammals of the taiga include black bears, elk, moose, wolves, porcupines, mice, and squirrels. Birds include hawks, owls, geese, gray jays, and black-capped chickadees.

Glossary

taiga (tī′gə), forest biome just south of the tundra, characterized by conifers

The needles on these trees in this conifer forest are adapted to help the plants survive the cold, windy conditions of the taiga. ▼

Glossary

Glossary

temperate deciduous forest
(tem′pər it di sij′ü es fôr′ist), forest biome characterized by trees that lose their leaves each year

If you live in or near woods in the eastern United States, you probably live in the **temperate deciduous forest** biome. This biome gets its name from the trees that grow there. Trees that shed their leaves each autumn are deciduous trees. Maples, beeches, willows, and oaks, whose leaves you see here, are examples.

▲ *The leaves of deciduous trees such as oaks change color in autumn, before they fall from the trees. New green leaves bud in the spring.*

The annual fall of leaves in the forest provides food for worms, fungi, and bacteria. These organisms break down the leaves and recycle the nutrients from the leaves into the forest soil. Under the rich top layer of soil is usually a deeper layer of clay.

The temperate deciduous forest has four seasons. You probably know what they are. Winters are cold, summers are hot, and spring and autumn are mild.

Because of the rich soil, relatively short winters, and much precipitation, many kinds of plants grow in the deciduous forest. In addition to trees, you'll find shrubs, mosses, and small flowering plants. The plant life supports a variety of animal life, including eagles and owls, deer, chipmunks, raccoons, quail, snakes, and salamanders. The animals live in different layers of the forest—in the trees, in the shrubs, on and under the ground.

The picture shows forestland being cleared. When European settlers arrived in North America, they cut down large areas of the forests for farming. Much of the forest today is second-growth forest.

◀ *Settlers cut trees to make room for growing crops. The temperate deciduous forest is not as extensive as it once was.*

Did you eat any of the foods in the picture today? These foods come from another biome—the **grassland**. In grasslands, the temperatures and seasons are similar to those in temperate deciduous forests. However, the precipitation is less, and dry periods occur often. That difference is important. It results in a different major form of plant life. Because grasslands get less rain, few trees grow there. As you can guess, grasses do. Grasses can survive the dry periods because they have root systems that spread out over large areas. When rains come, new plants sprout from the roots.

On the world biome map, you'll notice that grasslands are found in many places. Different species of grasses grow in different grasslands.

The soil of grasslands is very fertile. Each winter, the tops of many grasses die off. Decomposers act on the dead grass and return nutrients to the soil. Bacteria, fungi, worms, and burrowing animals live on or in the soil. On the grasslands of North America, bison, pronghorns, rabbits, prairie dogs, and mice feed. Coyotes, bobcats, badgers, and snakes eat the grass-eaters. Grassland birds include meadowlarks, plovers, and prairie chickens.

Grasslands have been called the "breadbaskets" of the world because, as you can see below, they are ideal for growing grass cereal grains. Wheat, corn, rice, oats, rye, barley, sorghum, millet, and sugarcane are all grasses used in food products. Grasses also provide most of the food for farm animals, such as cattle and sheep.

Glossary

grassland (gras′land), biome characterized by few trees and many grasses

Glossary

▲ *Grass seeds, or grains, provide food for people and animals around the world.*

The wheat this tractor is harvesting is just one of the many food products that are grown in grasslands. ▼

Glossary

tropical rain forest (trop′ə kəl rān fôr′ist), biome that has much rainfall and high temperatures all year

Picture a biome where trees grow tall—50 meters or more. Beneath the tall trees are shorter trees that can grow in shade. In most areas, the trees form such a thick canopy that little sunlight reaches the forest floor. Only a few plants, such as ferns and mosses, grow there. However, vines hang from the trees, and orchids and other plants live on the branches of the trees.

Most animals in this biome live in the trees too. Parrots, monkeys, sloths, snakes, frogs, and butterflies all have adaptations for living in trees. Overripe fruits and dead leaves drop from trees, providing food for some organisms that live on the ground. Insects, molds, and bacteria quickly consume this food.

Can you guess which biome you're in? You're right—the **tropical rain forest**. This biome is located near the equator. Because of this location, the tropical rain forest has no seasons. Rainfall is heavy and temperatures are high all year round. More species of organisms live in the tropical rain forest than in all the other land biomes combined.

In the warm, moist conditions of the tropical rain forest, nutrients that are released into the soil are quickly taken up by the plants. As a result, the soil is thin and not very rich. The trees of the rain forest are the main storage place of nutrients. If the trees are removed, the entire ecosystem is disturbed. Yet much of the rain forest is being cleared for farmland. Crops use up soil nutrients quickly, and the sun bakes the soil into a hard claylike material.

Rain forests are important because many of the things you use come from them. Fruits, nuts, and spices come from the rain forest. Other rain forest plants are used to make medicines, perfumes and cosmetics, and latex for rubber.

The cacao tree grows in tropical rain forests. Its seeds are used to make chocolate. Some cacao tree farmers now plant their trees beneath the canopy of the rain forest instead of cutting it down. ▼

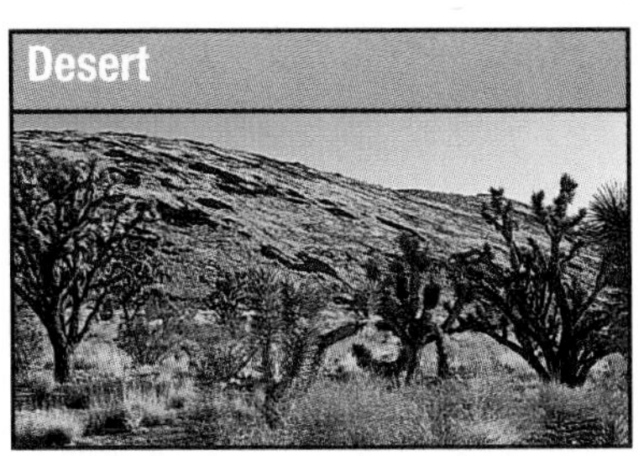

You may think of **deserts** as dry, hot places. It's true—all deserts are dry. The desert biome gets less than 25 centimeters of rain each year. The Atacama Desert in Chile is the driest place in the world, with an average annual rainfall of zero. Also, most deserts do have high temperatures during the day. But did you know that they can be cold at night? Temperatures might even drop to freezing. Some deserts, such as the Gobi Desert in Asia and the Patagonian Desert in South America, are cold for several months of the year.

Most people think of deserts as being covered with sand. Some deserts, like the Namib Desert in the top right photo, are sandy, but others, like the Creosote Bush Desert shown in the bottom photo, are covered in gravel and boulders.

Desert soils are usually low in nutrients. The dry conditions don't provide good environments for the decomposers that return nutrients to soil through decay.

Organisms that live in the desert have special adaptations that allow them to survive dry climate, poor soil, and wide temperature changes. Many animals spend the hottest part of the day underground. Some don't need to drink water very often because they can store a lot of water in their tissues. Cactus and other desert plants store water in their stems. What other adaptations make cactuses suited for the hot, dry environment they live in?

In some areas, grasslands that once bordered deserts have become part of the desert through overgrazing and drought. People are trying to restore these areas by replanting trees and other plants.

Lesson 4 Review

1. What is a biome?
2. What are the six major land biomes?
3. **Predict**
   What do you think might happen to an orchid plant from the taiga if you moved it to a grassland? Explain.

Glossary

desert (dez′ərt), biome with little rainfall and usually high daytime temperatures

▲ *The Namib Desert in Namibia (top), is sandy, unlike the rocky desert in the Creosote Bush Desert in Death Valley, California (below).*

Investigating Soils

Process Skills

Process Skills

- observing
- classifying
- communicating
- making operational definitions

Materials

- soil sample
- plastic cup
- distilled water
- spoon
- litmus paper
- clock with second hand

Getting Ready

The characteristics of the soil in a biome determine the kind of plants that will grow there. In this activity, you'll test your local soil for one important characteristic—acidity.

Follow This Procedure

1. Make a chart like the one shown. Use your chart to record your observations.

	Color of litmus paper
10 sec	
5 min	
15 min	

2. Collect a soil sample from your home or school yard in a plastic cup.

3. Slowly add distilled water to the soil as you stir it with a spoon. Keep adding water until the soil is muddy and about as thick as applesauce.

4. You will be using litmus paper to test how acidic the soil sample is. The litmus paper will change from blue to red if the soil is acidic.

5. Insert 3 strips of litmus paper halfway into the muddy soil (Photo A). Wait 10 seconds.

Photo A

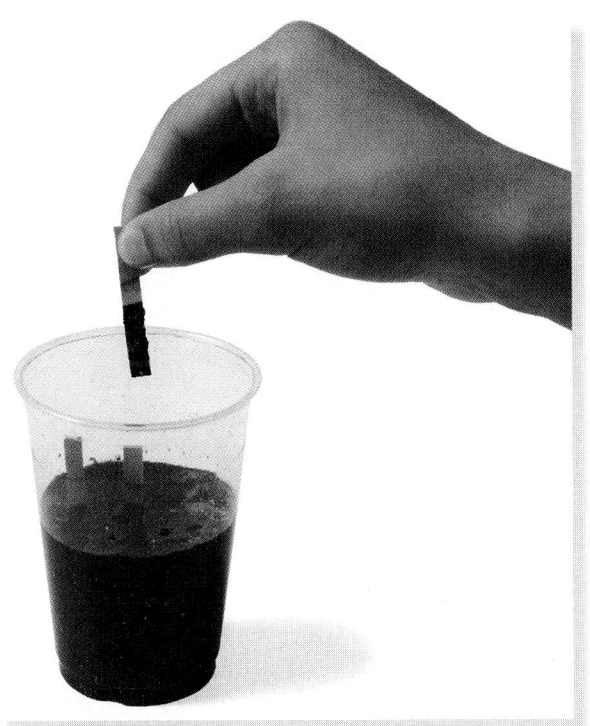

Photo B

6 Remove one piece of litmus paper (Photo B). Dip it into a cup of distilled water to rinse off the soil. **Observe** the color of the litmus paper. Record this color in your chart.

7 If the litmus paper is blue, wait another 5 minutes. Then remove another piece of litmus paper from the soil. Repeat step 6.

8 If the second piece of litmus is blue, wait another 10 minutes and repeat step 6.

Interpret Your Results

1. Blue litmus paper turns red or pink in acid. Based on your observations, how would you **classify** your soil—acidic or not acidic?

2. Why do you think some acidic soils take longer than others to turn the litmus paper red? **Communicate** your ideas to your group.

3. An **operational definition** describes what an object does or what you can observe about it. Write an operational definition for an acidic soil.

Inquire Further

How do you think changing the acidity of soil would affect the plants that grow there? Develop a plan to answer this or other questions you may have.

Self-Assessment

- I followed instructions to test the acidity of a soil sample.
- I made and recorded **observations** of the color of the litmus paper.
- I **classified** the soil sample as an acid or a non-acid.
- I **communicated** activity results to my group.
- I wrote an **operational definition** of an acidic soil.

You will learn:

- what a saltwater biome is.
- what a freshwater biome is.
- what an estuary is.

Lesson 5

What Are the Features of Water Biomes?

You're at the beach, running into the water. The waves are splashing up your legs. Suddenly, a huge wave comes crashing in. You yell as it drenches you. Yuk! The water tastes awful. It's salty. You must be at the ocean!

Glossary

Glossary

saltwater biome (sôlt′wô′tər bī′ōm), water biome that has a high salt content

plankton (plangk′tən), microscopic, free-floating organisms that serve as food for larger organisms

Saltwater Biomes

About three-quarters of Earth's surface is covered by water. Like the land that covers Earth, the water areas, too, have biomes characterized by certain conditions and communities of organisms. A water biome that has a high salt content is called a **saltwater biome**. As you can see from the picture on the left, this biome is Earth's largest.

This saltwater biome can be divided into three different regions. The three zones differ in their physical characteristics and in the organisms that live there. As you read about each zone, find it in the picture on the next page.

The shallow ocean zone makes up only a small part of the saltwater biome. If you've ever been to the ocean, it's this zone that you're probably most familiar with. It occurs along the coasts of continents and islands. The water in this area is shallow enough for sunlight to reach the bottom. Water temperature changes little from day to night or from season to season.

The area of ocean away from the coast is divided into two zones—the ocean surface zone and the deep ocean zone. Sunlight can reach the top areas of the surface zone, but no light reaches the deep ocean. Also, as you go farther down into the ocean water, the temperature gets colder. How will the differences in temperature and light in these two zones affect the organisms that live there?

▲ *Almost three-fourths of the earth's surface is covered by the saltwater biome.*

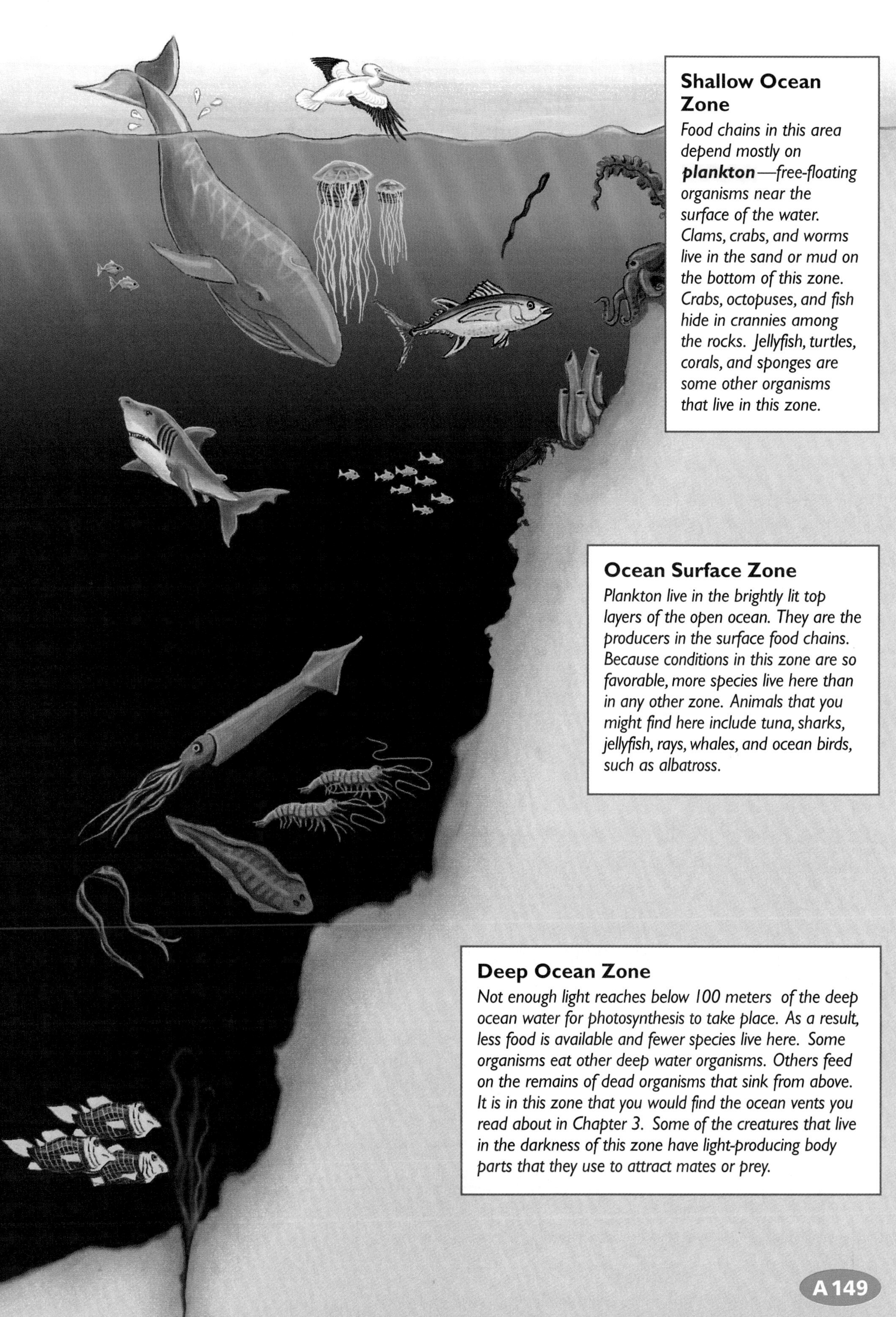

Shallow Ocean Zone

*Food chains in this area depend mostly on **plankton**—free-floating organisms near the surface of the water. Clams, crabs, and worms live in the sand or mud on the bottom of this zone. Crabs, octopuses, and fish hide in crannies among the rocks. Jellyfish, turtles, corals, and sponges are some other organisms that live in this zone.*

Ocean Surface Zone

Plankton live in the brightly lit top layers of the open ocean. They are the producers in the surface food chains. Because conditions in this zone are so favorable, more species live here than in any other zone. Animals that you might find here include tuna, sharks, jellyfish, rays, whales, and ocean birds, such as albatross.

Deep Ocean Zone

Not enough light reaches below 100 meters of the deep ocean water for photosynthesis to take place. As a result, less food is available and fewer species live here. Some organisms eat other deep water organisms. Others feed on the remains of dead organisms that sink from above. It is in this zone that you would find the ocean vents you read about in Chapter 3. Some of the creatures that live in the darkness of this zone have light-producing body parts that they use to attract mates or prey.

Glossary

Glossary

freshwater biome (fresh/wô/tər bī/ōm), water biome that has a low salt content

Freshwater Biomes

Most bodies of water other than the ocean, such as lakes, ponds, rivers, and streams, contain very little salt. Each of these bodies is a **freshwater biome**. Freshwater biomes can be divided into two types. Those that have standing water include lakes and ponds. Those that have running water include rivers and streams.

Lakes, like the one shown on this page, are larger and usually deeper than ponds. Most lakes are deep enough to have a colder, lower layer of water that receives little or no sunlight. Temperature and available sunlight determine the kinds of organisms that live in each area of a lake.

When you consider what you know about producers and food chains, you can probably guess that most organisms live near the upper, sunnier part of a lake. Floating duckweed plants and plants that grow in shallow water around the lake's edges form the basis of food chains. These food chains include fish, insects, frogs, turtles, beavers, and a variety of birds, including herons and grebes.

Few animals live in the deep part of a lake. Those that do live there include bacteria, worms, and other decomposers. They feed on the remains of dead organisms that settle to the lake bottom.

Mountain lakes like this one were formed when melting valley glaciers dumped a ridge of sand, gravel, and rocks across a river. Other lakes form in a variety of ways. ▼

The main difference between lakes and rivers or streams is the movement of water. Like the one shown here, the water in streams moves quickly. As a result, air is mixed with the water. This mixing adds oxygen to the water, which allows certain organisms, such as trout, frogs, and many insects, to live there. Do you notice anything about the shape of the fish that live in rapidly moving water? Can you guess how this shape allows them to travel in the river?

Mountain streams are made up of a series of fast, shallow, rocky stretches, called rapids, followed by pools of deeper, quieter water. While flowing through the rapids, the water picks up particles of sand, silt, and even gravel and carries them downstream. The result is that these areas are left as bare rock. Here insect larvae, algae, and some worms attach themselves to the rocky beds. In some areas, black fly larvae form such dense groups that they look like a carpet of black moss on the rocks.

As water flows through the rapids, it also sweeps food downstream to the quieter pools. There, water plants can root and not be washed away. Animals find plenty of food here. The pools also provide breeding areas for frogs.

Because stream water is constantly moving and mixing, a small stream will have a more constant temperature than would a pond. Daphnia and many other microscopic organisms are part of the food chain in this stream. ▼

Glossary

estuary (es′chü er′ē), place where fresh water from rivers or streams mixes with saltwater from the ocean

Estuaries

Many rivers and streams empty into the ocean. Where fresh water from a river or stream mixes with saltwater from the ocean, an **estuary** forms.

Pieces of rock, soil, and other materials are washed into an estuary by both the river and the ocean tides. There they settle to form a muddy or sandy floor. Water in an estuary is usually warmer than ocean water and contains less salt. However, the salt content of the water changes with the tides. With high tide, more salty ocean water flows in. At low tide, when ocean water moves out, the water of the estuary becomes less salty.

Salt content is not the only thing that changes daily in an estuary. For part of the day, the entire area is under water. However, when the tide goes out, some of the sand or mud flats may be exposed to the sun. The remains of algae and other organisms begin to decay, returning nutrients to the estuary floor. There, plants such as cordgrasses, sea lavender, and spike grass provide food and shelter for many organisms.

Species that live in the estuary have adapted to the changing rhythm of the tides. For example, the air-breathing coffee bean snail climbs the stems of cordgrass twice a day as the tides come in. Nonflying insects also climb up plants to avoid high water. These insects provide insect-eating birds, such as marsh wrens and seaside sparrows, with an easy meal during high tide.

Many microscopic organisms like this Hyperia *provide food for estuary species.* ▼

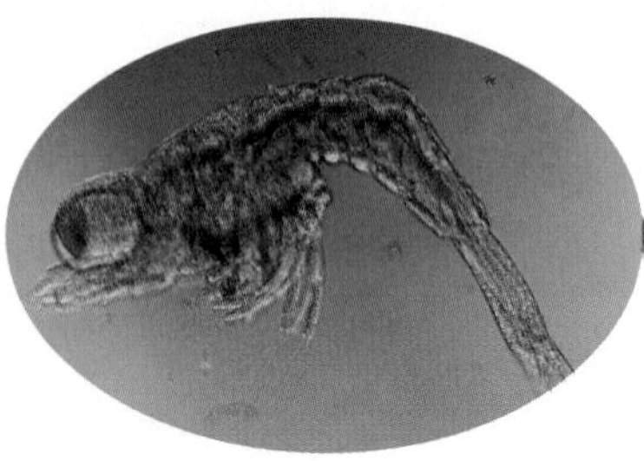

An estuary is constantly changing, and the organisms that populate it must be adapted to living with daily changes in water level and salt content. ▼

Estuaries are important as breeding grounds for many birds and ocean organisms. Many fish lay their eggs in estuaries. When they hatch, young fish feed on the plentiful plankton. More than three-fourths of all the shellfish and seafood harvested in the United States spend their early lives in estuaries, including the crab shown here. These crabs, shrimp, and mussels provide food for diamondback terrapins and wading birds, such as the snowy egret and clapper rail.

Many migrating birds stop to rest and feed in estuaries. Snow geese, Canada geese, dabbling ducks, black ducks, and blue-winged teals all feed on estuary plants. Northern harriers and short-eared owls feed on mice and other small mammals in the estuary.

Have you ever eaten the meat from a crab? Chances are that crab began its life in an estuary. ▼

Lesson 5 Review

1. What is a saltwater biome?
2. What is a freshwater biome?
3. What is an estuary?
4. **Predict**
   Suppose a manufacturing company dumped harmful wastes into the river that empties into the estuary below. What changes might you see in the estuary over time?

Chapter 4 Review

Chapter Main Ideas

Lesson 1

• Living and nonliving parts of an ecosystem enable organisms to survive.
• The energy needed for life processes is trapped by producers and used by consumers and decomposers.
• Different food chains in an ecosystem are linked together in a food web.
• An energy pyramid is a model that shows how much energy is available at each level of a food chain or ecosystem.

Lesson 2

• Green plants use carbon dioxide and give off oxygen during photosynthesis. Plants and other organisms use oxygen and release carbon dioxide during respiration.
• Nitrogen cycles through an ecosystem in the nitrogen cycle.
• Pollution disturbs the natural recycling of materials in an ecosystem.

Lesson 3

• Environmental changes can change the populations in an ecosystem.
• Species often adapt or die off when populations compete for resources.
• People can change ecosystems by using resources or introducing new species.

Lesson 4

• Biomes are large geographic regions with a particular climate and community.
• The six major land biomes are the tundra, taiga, deciduous forest, tropical rain forest, grassland, and the desert.

Lesson 5

• A saltwater biome is a water biome that has a high salt content.
• A freshwater biome is a body of water such as a lake, pond, river, or stream that does not have a high salt content.
• An estuary is a water biome where fresh water mixes with salt water.

Reviewing Science Words and Concepts

Write the letter of the word or phrase that best completes each sentence.

a. biome	**g.** omnivore
b. carnivore	**h.** permafrost
c. competition	**i.** plankton
d. energy pyramid	**j.** respiration
e. estuary	**k.** taiga
f. herbivore	**l.** tundra

1. Ground that is always frozen is ___.

2. A region with a particular climate and community is called a(n) ___.

3. The process that releases energy in cells is known as ___.

4. A name for an animal-eating consumer is a(n) ___.

5. A coniferous forest biome is called a(n) ___.

6. A place where saltwater and fresh water mix is called a(n) ___.

7. A consumer that eats plants and animals is called a(n) ___.

8. The coldest and most northern biome is a region called the ___.

9. A microscopic food source found floating in oceans is called ___.

10. Organisms interact as they try to use the same resources when ___ occurs.

11. A plant-eating consumer is called a(n) ___.

12. A model of energy use in a food chain is represented as a(n) ___.

Explaining Science

Write a paragraph or create a dialogue for a radio show that explains these questions.

1. Why is the amount of available energy different for each type of organism in a food chain?

2. Give two examples of what can happen if natural cycles are disrupted by people.

3. How are populations affected by environmental changes?

4. How do climate, altitude, and latitude affect biomes?

5. What determines the amount and kinds of organisms that live in each area or zone of a water biome?

Using Skills

1. Predict what will happen next if you remove all the crickets from a field ecosystem.

2. Choose an ecosystem such as your schoolyard or a park. Make a list of six interactions that you **observe** in the ecosystem.

3. Identify three foods you ate today. Make a **model** of a food chain showing the path of energy in the food you ate.

Critical Thinking

1. Create a poster that will **compare** and **contrast** the six major land biomes.

2. Suppose you have a fish tank with several fish. A friend wants to give you two new fish for your tank. What information should you **evaluate** before you **make a decision** about whether or not to add the new fish?

3. Make a **model** of a water biome using a shoe box. Draw a scene and place three-dimensional items inside the box to represent organisms. Then cover the opening with plastic wrap instead of a lid.

Unit A Review

Reviewing Words and Concepts

Choose at least three words from the Chapter 1 list below. Use the words to write a paragraph about how these concepts are related. Do the same for each of the other chapters.

Chapter 1
cell theory
chromosome
cytoplasm
mitochondria
organelles
species

Chapter 2
DNA
genes
inherit
meiosis
sex cells
sexual reproduction

Chapter 3
adaptation
evolution
inherited behavior
instinct
natural selection
reflex

Chapter 4
biome
competition
energy pyramid
grassland
pollution
taiga

Reviewing Main Ideas

Each of the statements below is false. Change the underlined word or words to make each statement true.

1. The <u>vacuole</u> is an organelle that puts together proteins for the cell.
2. Chloroplasts in plant cells contain <u>chromosomes</u> which use sunlight to make sugars.
3. Long, narrow <u>body</u> cells carry messages throughout your body.
4. In <u>meiosis</u>, body cells divide producing two new cells with identical nuclei.
5. A <u>gene</u> is the cell that results when an egg cell and a sperm cell join.
6. Organisms that form during <u>asexual</u> reproduction inherit traits from both parents.
7. An <u>evolution</u> is an inherited trait that helps an organism to survive in its environment.
8. A <u>learned behavior</u> is a quick reaction to a stimulus.
9. <u>Food webs</u> are models that show how energy is used in an ecosystem.
10. A <u>desert</u> is a biome with high yearly temperatures and about 200 cm of rainfall.

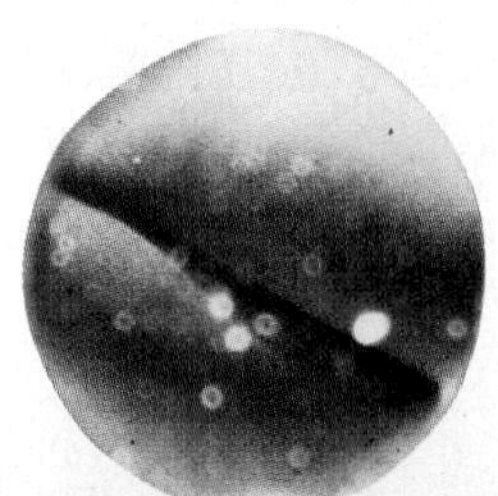
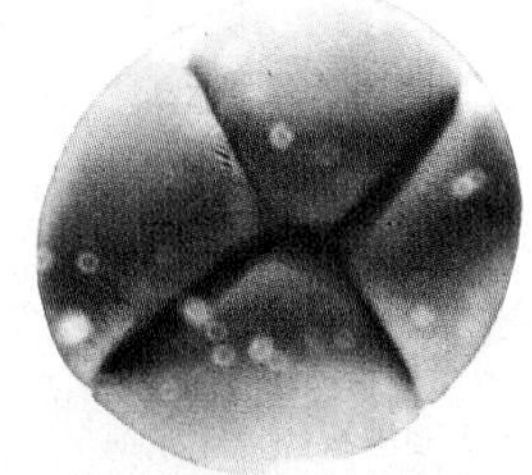
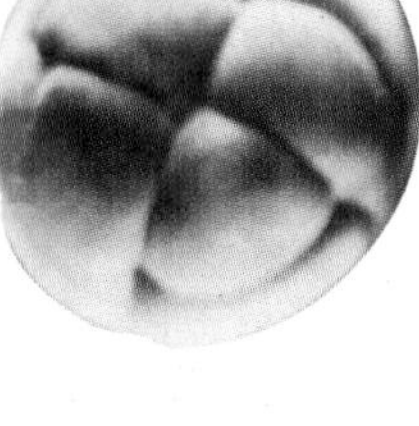

Interpreting Data

The following chart shows the number of chromosomes found in the nucleus of a body cell of different species.

Animal	No. of chromosomes in nucleus of body cells
Housefly	12
Bullfrog	26
Rabbit	44
Human	46
Chicken	78
Crayfish	200

1. How many chromosomes are contained in the sperm or egg cell of a chicken?

2. How many chromosomes would the body cells of an unborn rabbit have?

3. What relationship appears to exist between the size or complexity of an animal and the number of chromosomes contained in its body cells?

Communicating Science

1. Draw and label a diagram comparing the major parts of plant and animal cells.

2. Write a paragraph explaining when and with what result cells undergo mitosis and meiosis.

3. Make a table showing several examples of physiological adaptations, structural adaptations, and behavioral adaptations.

4. Draw and label a diagram showing how pollution can affect the carbon dioxide-oxygen and nitrogen cycles.

Applying Science

1. Write a paragraph explaining why members of a family have some characteristics that are similar and some that are different.

2. Write copy for a brochure explaining why antibiotics shouldn't be overused. Explain how bacteria can become resistant to the antibiotics through natural selection.

Unit A
Performance Review

Life Science Convention

Using what you learned in this unit, help prepare exhibits and presentations for a Life Science Convention to be held at your school. Complete one or more of the following activities. You may work by yourself or in a group.

Art

Using common materials, build a model that shows the relationship among DNA, chromosomes, and genes. Be sure to label the parts of your model. Show how DNA is responsible for traits being passed from one generation to another.

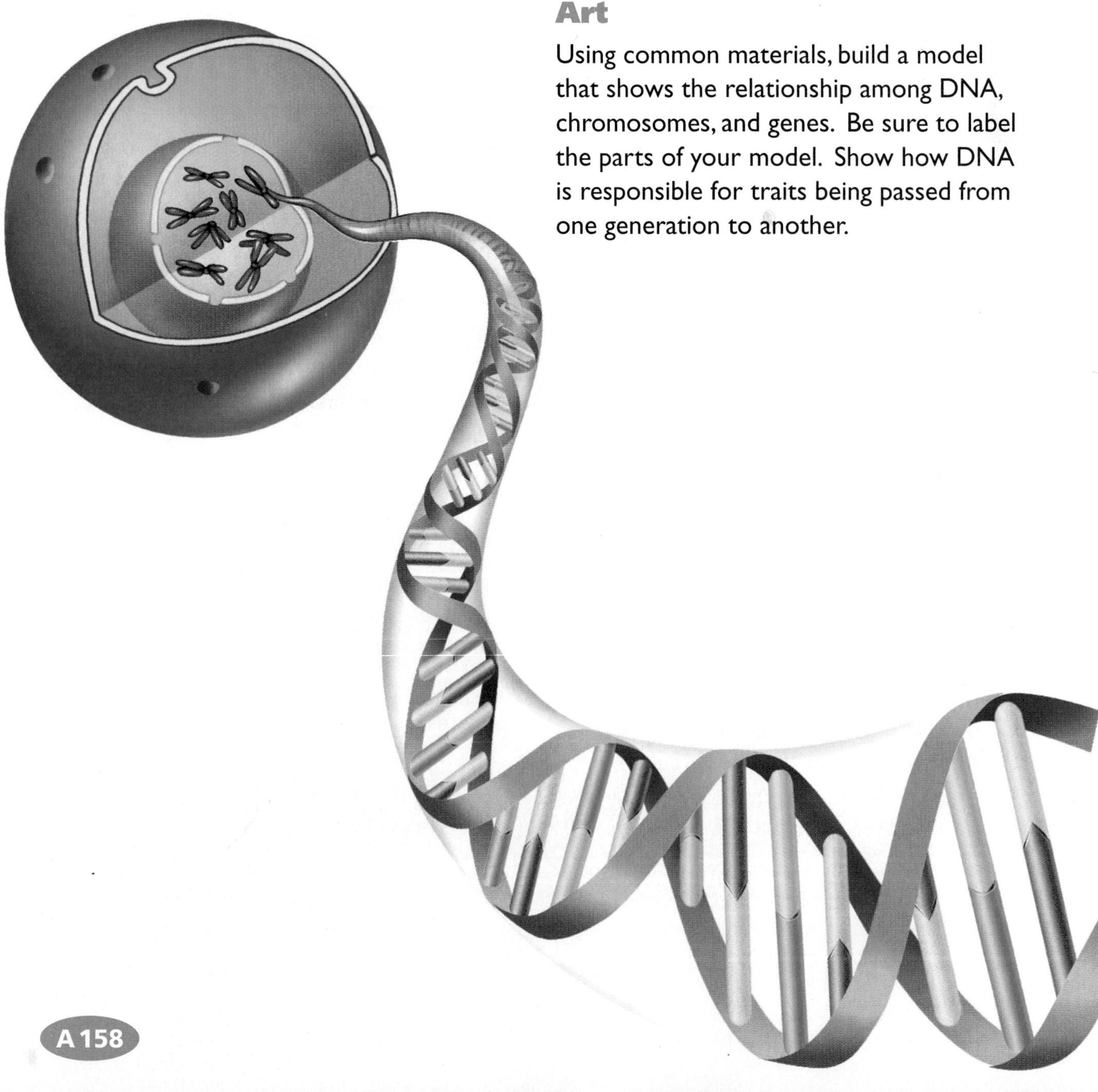

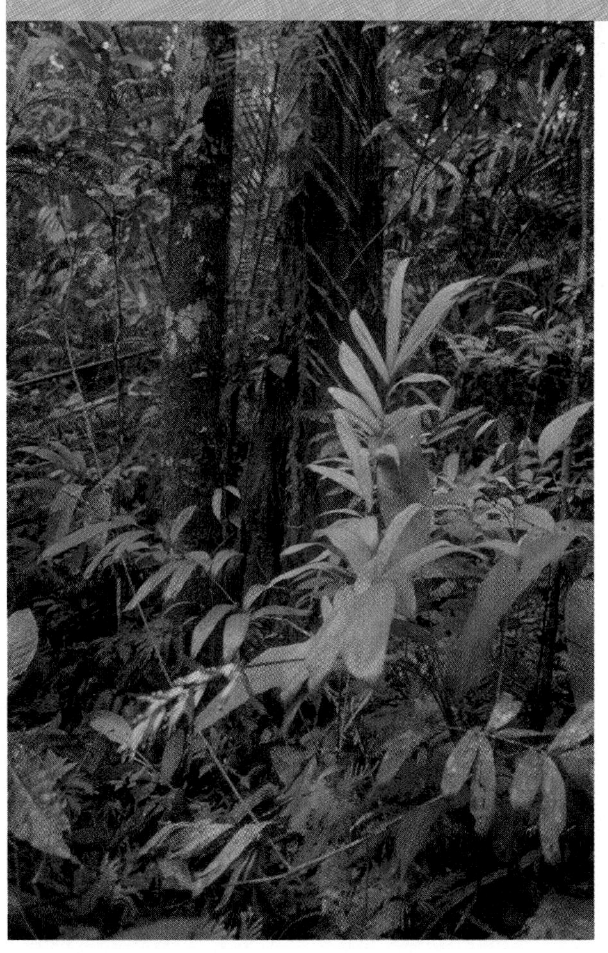

Variety of Life

Prepare a display showing the variety of species of organisms. Include a microscopic display with prepared slides of different microscopic organisms. If possible, include different types of microscopes. Be prepared to explain to visitors what they are seeing.

Mathematics

Prepare a display board on sickle cell anemia, showing how you can predict the chances of children inheriting sickled cells from their parents. Include tables showing what happens when one parent has genes for normal and sickled cells and when both parents have genes for normal and sickled cells.

Environment

Work with other students to present a panel describing why the rainforests are disappearing and how this affects the environment, both locally and globally. Have each student on the panel talk about a different topic. Allow time for questions after the presentation.

Drama

In 1962, James Watson, Maurice Wilkins, and Francis Crick shared the Nobel prize for their work explaining the structure of DNA. Plan a skit of the presentation ceremony. Have a presenter from the Nobel committee speak first, and then have Watson, Wilkins, and Crick explain their model and give their acceptance speeches.

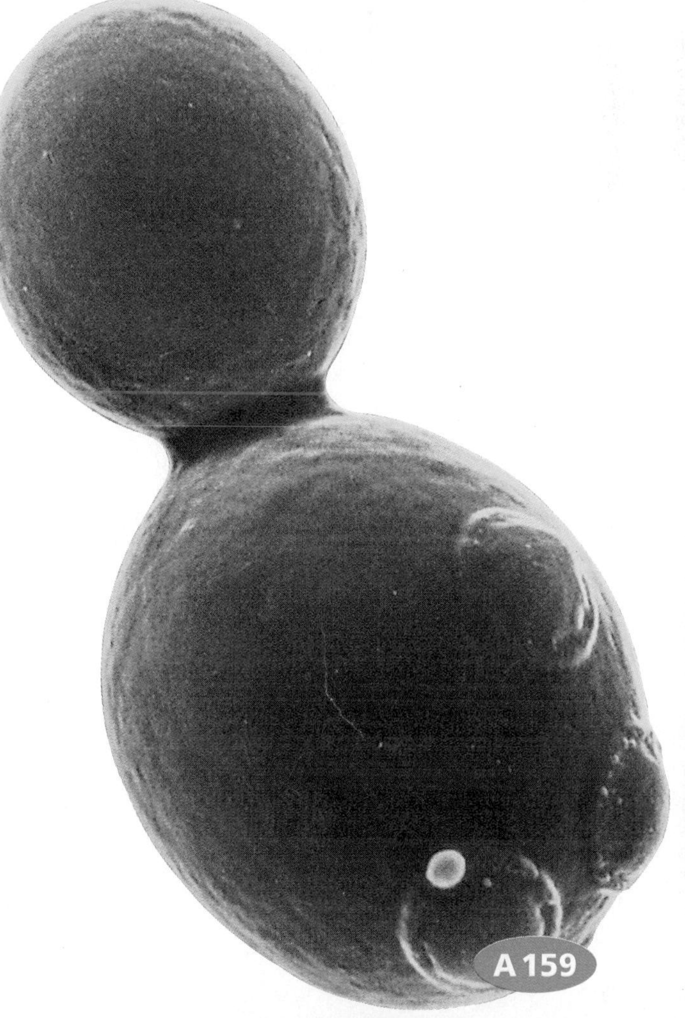

Using Graphic Organizers

A graphic organizer is a visual device that shows how ideas and concepts are related. There are many different kinds of graphic organizers. Word webs, flowcharts, and tables are a few examples.

Make a Graphic Organizer

In Chapter 1, you learned about the parts of cells. Use this information to make a graphic organizer. Your graphic organizer should show how cell parts can be used to classify plant and animal cells. Use the graphic organizer below to get you started.

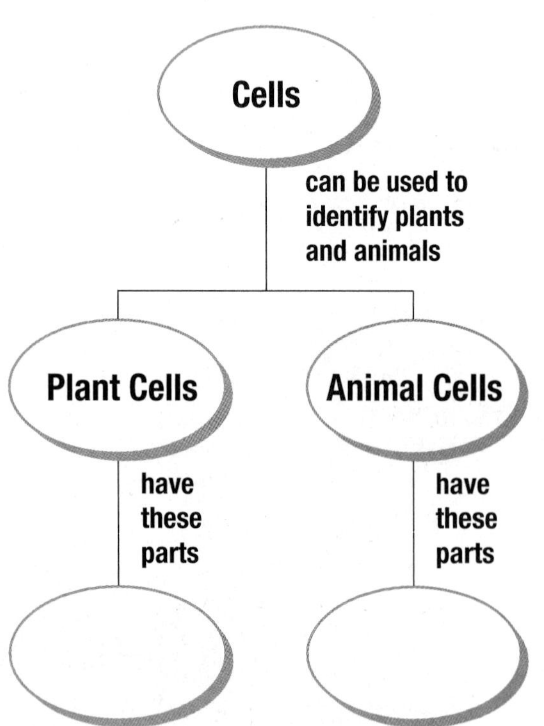

Write Descriptive Paragraphs

Use your completed graphic organizer to write a three-paragraph description of cells and their parts. Your first paragraph should include an introduction and discuss parts that are present in all cells. Your second paragraph should discuss parts found only in plant cells. Your third paragraph should include a description of parts found only in animal cells and a summary of your writing.

Remember to:

1. **Prewrite** Organize your thoughts before you write.
2. **Draft** Write your description.
3. **Revise** Share your work and then make changes.
4. **Edit** Proofread for mistakes and fix them.
5. **Publish** Share your description with your class.

Physical Science

Science and Technology In Your World!

How Hot Is Your Ear?

Now "ear this!" The new way to take your temperature measures heat from your eardrum. A tiny electronic device accurately reads the temperature and displays it on a little screen in 21 seconds or less. Learn more about heat and thermometers in **Chapter 1 Heat and Matter.**

Metal with a Memory

Eyeglass frames and teeth braces may get out of shape—but not for long if they are made from a new metal alloy called Nitinol. It "remembers" to return to its original shape after it's bent. Learn more about alloys in **Chapter 2 Changes In Matter.**

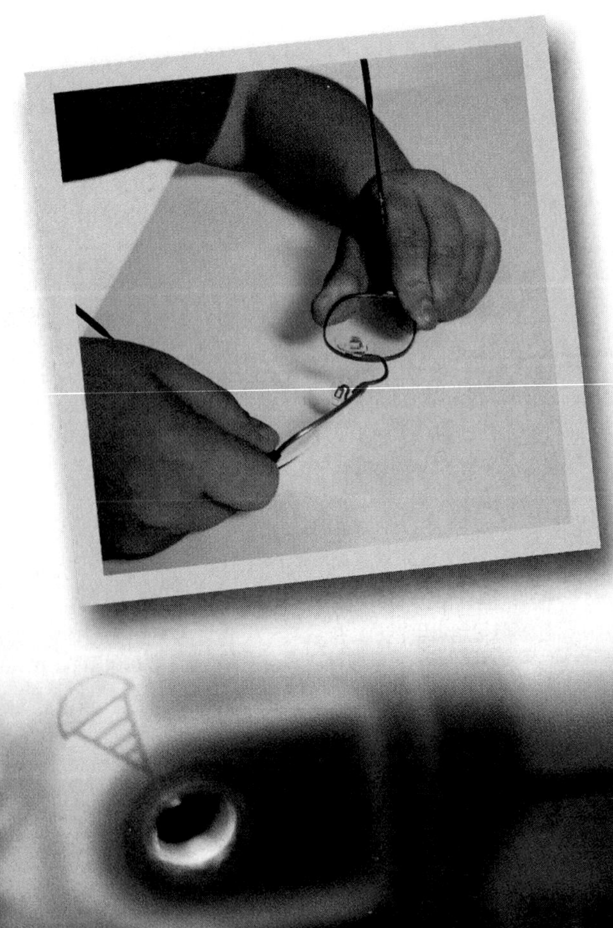

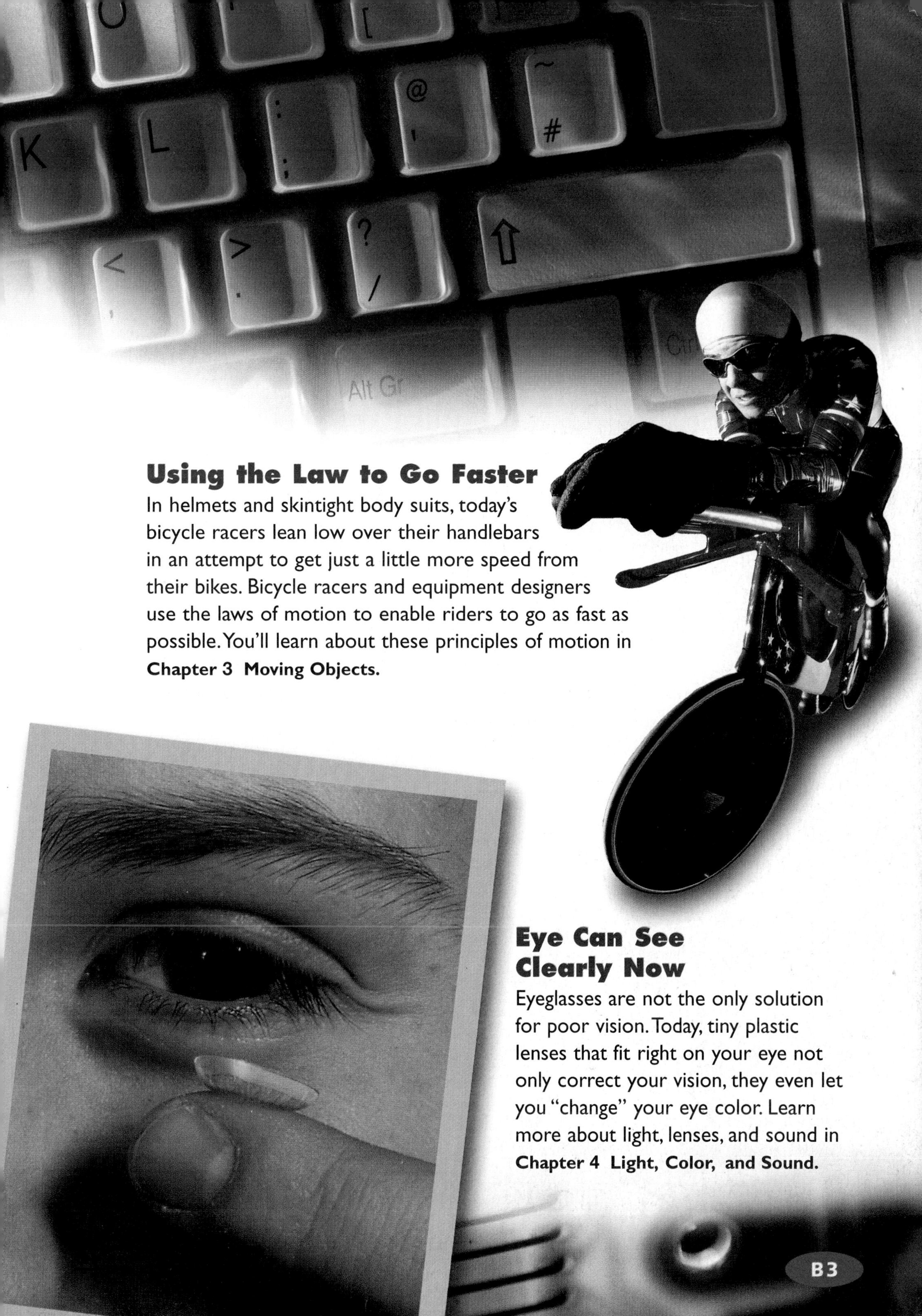

Using the Law to Go Faster

In helmets and skintight body suits, today's bicycle racers lean low over their handlebars in an attempt to get just a little more speed from their bikes. Bicycle racers and equipment designers use the laws of motion to enable riders to go as fast as possible. You'll learn about these principles of motion in **Chapter 3 Moving Objects.**

Eye Can See Clearly Now

Eyeglasses are not the only solution for poor vision. Today, tiny plastic lenses that fit right on your eye not only correct your vision, they even let you "change" your eye color. Learn more about light, lenses, and sound in **Chapter 4 Light, Color, and Sound.**

I'm Radiant!

How many things in this picture give off heat? The blow dryer, right? But what about the girl? Did you know that humans give off heat too!

Chapter 1

Heat and Matter

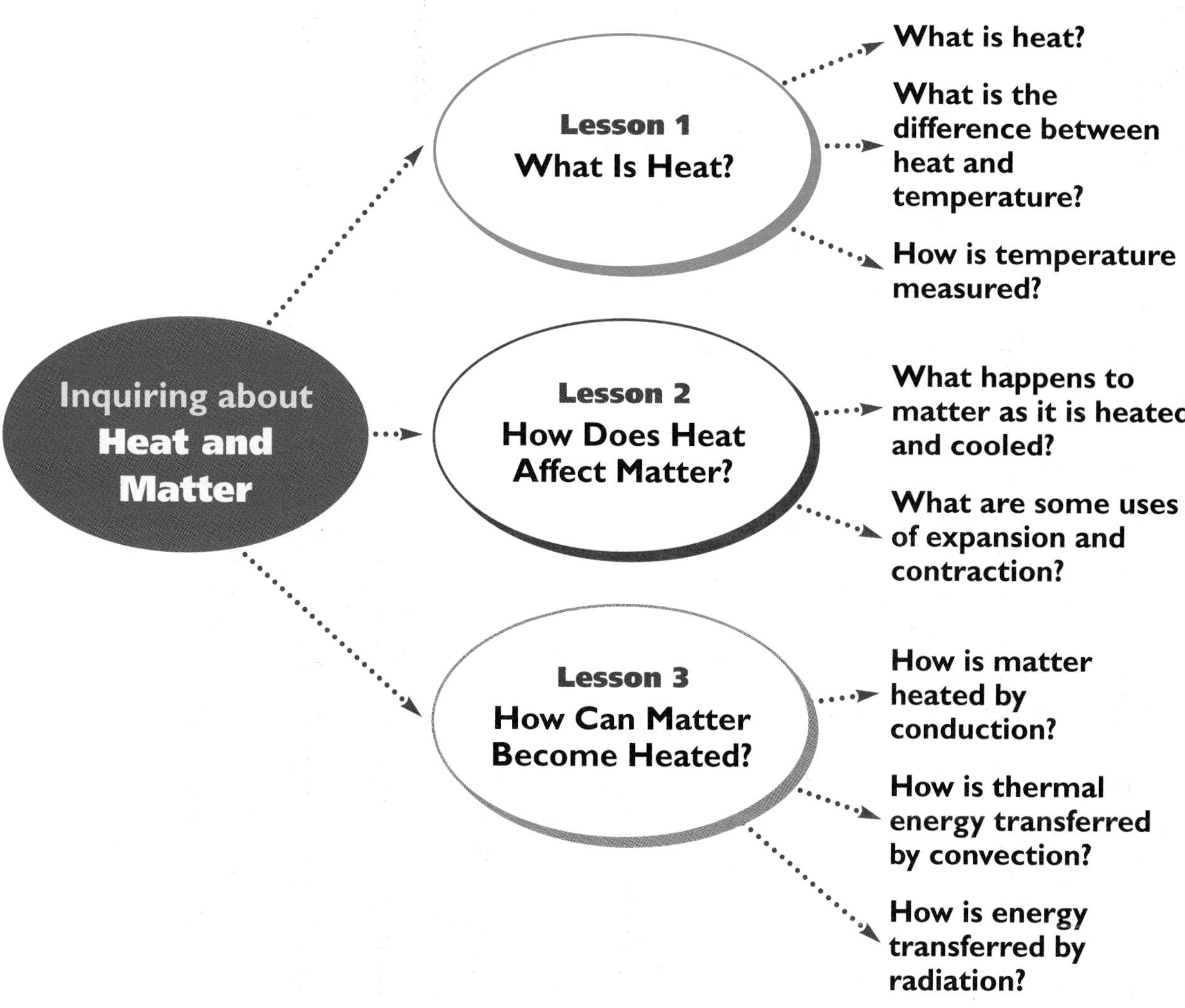

Inquiring about
Heat and
Matter
Lesson 1
What Is Heat?
What is heat?
What is the difference between heat and temperature?
How is temperature measured?
Lesson 2
How Does Heat Affect Matter?
What happens to matter as it is heated and cooled?
What are some uses of expansion and contraction?
Lesson 3
How Can Matter Become Heated?
How is matter heated by conduction?
How is thermal energy transferred by convection?
How is energy transferred by radiation?

Copy the chapter graphic organizer *onto your own paper. This organizer shows you what the whole chapter is all about. As you read the lessons and do the activities, look for answers to the questions and write them on your organizer.*

Explore Activity

Exploring Temperature Scales

Process Skills

Process Skills

- estimating and measuring
- predicting
- communicating

Materials

- 3 plastic cups
- thermometer
- ice water
- room-temperature water
- warm water

Explore

1. Fill a cup with ice water. Place a thermometer in the cup. Wait 1 minute and read the temperature on both the Fahrenheit and the Celsius scales. Record your **measurements.**
2. Fill another cup with room-temperature water. Place the thermometer in the cup.
3. **Predict** which temperature scale, Fahrenheit or Celsius, will show a higher number for the temperature of the water. Give a reason for your prediction.
4. After 1 minute, record the temperatures shown on both scales.
5. Fill a third cup with warm water. Place the thermometer in the cup. Repeat steps 3 and 4.

Reflect

1. How are the Fahrenheit and Celsius temperature scales alike? How are they different? **Communicate** your ideas to your classmates.

2. Will the temperature at which water boils be higher on the Celsius or the Fahrenheit scale? How do you know?

Inquire Further

Both temperature scales use degrees. Is a Fahrenheit degree the same size as a Celsius degree? Develop a plan to answer this or other questions you may have.

Positive and Negative Numbers

Zero degrees (0°) is the freezing point of water on the Celsius scale. Temperatures below this point use **negative numbers** and have a minus (–) sign. Temperatures above this point use **positive numbers** and usually have no sign.

The boiling point of water on the Celsius scale is 100°. Is this temperature a positive or a negative number?

Math Vocabulary

positive number, number greater than zero

negative number, number less than zero

Example

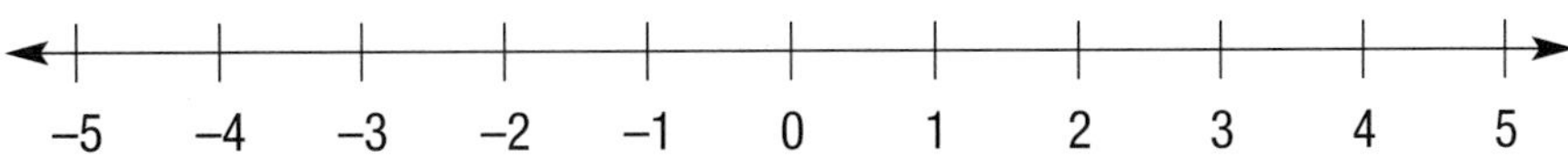

This number line shows positive and negative numbers. The further to the right a number is, the greater it is. The further to the left it is, the less it is.

Order these integers from least to greatest: 1, –2, 4, –5, 0.

First, locate the numbers on the number line.

$-5 < -2$ $-2 < 0$ $0 < 1$ $1 < 4$

So, the integers from least to greatest are –5, –2, 0, 1, 4.

Talk About It!

1. Is a negative number always less than a positive number? Explain.

2. Which temperature is higher, 2°C or –5°C?

Did you know?

The highest temperature in the world was recorded as 58°C (136°F) at Al Aziziyah, Libya, on September 13, 1922. The lowest temperature was –89.6°C (–128.6°F) at Vostok Station in Antarctica on July 21, 1983.

You will learn:

- what heat is.
- the difference between heat and temperature.
- how temperature is measured.

Lesson 1

What Is Heat?

"Ouch! That's hot!" "Brrr! That's cold!" "Things are heating up." "That was cool!" "Let's warm up those leftovers." We talk about it, cook with it, complain about it, dress for it, and try to control it. What is this thing called heat?

Heat

People were using heat long before anyone knew what it was. Early civilizations huddled around fires to keep warm and to cook their food. These ancient people may not have known what heat was, but they knew that when the air was cool, the fire made them feel better. The ancient Greeks noticed that heat was everywhere. They believed that all matter was made of only four basic elements—fire, air, earth, and water.

For centuries, people tried to explain what heat was. In the 1700s, many people thought that heat was matter, which they called caloric fluid. They thought that as caloric fluid flowed into or out of objects, their temperatures changed. Today, even though scientists no longer think of heat as matter, they talk about particles of matter to explain heat.

When the girl in the picture picks up the glass of cold water, why do her fingers get cold? Think particles! All matter—the girl, the glass, the food you eat, your clothes, and the air you breathe—is made of tiny particles. These particles are always moving. Particles in matter move because they have energy.

Energy flows from the girl's hand into the glass, making her fingers feel cool. ▼

Not all the particles in a substance have the same amount of energy, so some particles move faster and some move slower. The total energy of the particles that make up any matter is **thermal energy**.

Think about this example. If you and your classmates were to walk around in a small room, you'd occasionally bump into one another. If you collided with a person moving slower than you, some of your energy would be transferred to that person. The other person would move a little faster, while you'd move a little slower.

The same thing happens to the particles in matter. As faster-moving particles collide with slower-moving particles, the faster ones lose energy and the slower ones gain energy. However, the total amount of energy always stays the same.

When we touch matter that has faster-moving particles, we say that it is warmer. By comparison, matter with slower-moving particles feels cooler.

Remember—your skin is also made of moving particles. When the girl on the previous page picks up the glass of cold liquid, the particles in her skin collide with the slower-moving particles in the glass. Because the girl's skin particles are moving faster, they transfer some of their energy to the glass particles. The result is that the skin particles move more slowly. With slower-moving particles, the girl's fingers feel cold. The girl might say that the glass is cold, but what she really senses is the temperature change in her fingers.

When particles collide, energy is always transferred from faster-moving particles to slower-moving particles. This flow of energy from warmer matter to cooler matter is called **heat**. The warmer substance cools, and the cooler substance warms—until both objects are equally warm. What is happening to the particles of matter as the boy on the right holds the cup of warm soup?

Glossary

thermal energy (thėr′məl en′ər jē), the total energy of the particles that make up any matter

heat (hēt), a flow of energy from warmer matter to cooler matter

Energy is transferred from this hot cup of soup to the boy's hand. ▼

▲ *The heat that is produced when the particles in your skin rub together causes your hands to feel warm.*

Where do particles of matter get their energy? On Earth, most thermal energy comes from the sun. You can feel your skin get warmer when the sun's rays strike it. On a sunny day, the sun's energy reaches cars or sidewalks, and they feel hot.

Not all thermal energy on Earth comes directly from the sun. Rub your hands together quickly as shown to the left. Feel the heat? The same thing happens when parts of a car engine rub together as the engine runs. As objects move against one another, heat is produced.

You've probably felt the heat that comes from your stove. Where does this heat come from? On electric stoves, the heat comes from electricity. The stove converts electrical energy to heat energy. On gas stoves, heat is produced during the chemical change that happens when natural gas burns. The sun, chemical changes, objects rubbing, and electricity are only some of the sources of heat. Can you think of others?

Comparing Heat and Temperature

As the pans of water on the burners to the right are heated, the hot burners transfer energy to the particles that make up the pans. Those particles, in turn, collide with water particles near the bottom of the pans. As these water particles gain energy and move faster, they bump into other water particles, transferring their energy from one particle to another. **Temperature** is a measure of the average motion of the particles in a substance or object. As more water particles gain energy and move faster, the temperature of the water in both pans rises. Can you guess which pan will boil first?

Glossary

Glossary

temperature
(tem′pər ə chər), a measurement of the average motion of the particles in a substance or object

The more water you have in a pan, the longer it takes for the water to boil. Why? More water means more particles! You have to add more energy to get all of those particles up to speed. The smaller pan will boil first—it takes less energy.

Once the water in both pans has reached the boiling point, the water particles in both pans will have the same temperature. Although the water in the two pans is at the same temperature, the water in the larger pan has more thermal energy because it contains more particles. More heat was added to bring all of its particles up to the boiling point. Look at the picture to the right. Which has more thermal energy—the pail of ocean water or the ocean?

As you can see, temperature and heat are different. The temperature of a substance depends on the average speed of its particles. The amount of thermal energy in the substance, and therefore the amount of heat that can flow out of it, depends on the number of particles as well as their speed. Temperature measures the motion of particles, while heat describes the energy flow that produces the motion.

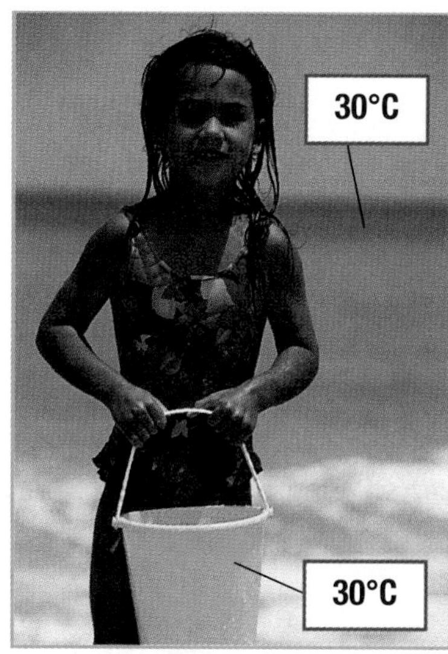

▲ *The water in this girl's pail has a certain amount of energy. How does it compare with the amount of energy in the ocean water?*

How would adding more water to these pans affect the time it takes for the water to boil? ▼

Water boils

°F

212°

200°

180°

160°

140°

120°

100°

80°

60°

40°

32°

20°

0°

°C

100°

90°

80°

70°

60°

50°

40°

30°

20°

10°

0°

-10°

Water freezes

▲ *Compare these two temperature scales. What is the outside temperature today in both Fahrenheit and Celsius?*

Measuring Temperature

Not everyone senses heat in the same way. For example, suppose you and a friend go swimming in a lake. You think the water is just right. Your friend thinks the water is too cold. In describing the temperature of the lake to another friend, who would be correct? In this case, you are both right. You are both describing how the water feels, not the actual temperature. For this reason, it is important to have a device that measures temperature accurately.

Remember that temperature is the measurement of the average motion of the particles in an object. You can't easily measure particle motion directly in the same way you measure length or weight. Instead, scientists have developed a different system of measuring temperature. This system is based on the way common substances, such as water, behave at different temperatures. Although this system may sound complicated, it's quite simple—use a thermometer!

History of Science

In the early 1700s, Gabriel Fahrenheit, a German scientist, developed the first standard scale for measuring temperature. He put some mercury in a sealed tube and placed this device—a thermometer—in a mixture of ice, salt, and ammonia. The mixture offered the coldest temperature he could get. Fahrenheit marked the level of the mercury in the tube at this temperature and called this point 0 degrees, or 0°. Then Fahrenheit measured the level of the mercury at the temperature of the human body and labeled this point 96°. He also marked the temperature at which plain water freezes, calling it 32°.

Fahrenheit's scale became the first standard measure of temperature. It is still the most commonly used temperature scale in the United States. A temperature of 38°F means "38 degrees on the Fahrenheit scale."

In 1742, Anders Celsius, a Swedish astronomer, developed another scale for measuring temperature. He experimented with measuring the melting point of snow and the boiling point of water. Celsius called these points 0° and 100°. He divided the distance between these points into 100 equal degrees. This system became known as the Celsius scale. Today scientists use the Celsius scale, which is part of the metric system. Use the thermometers in the picture to compare the Fahrenheit and Celsius scales.

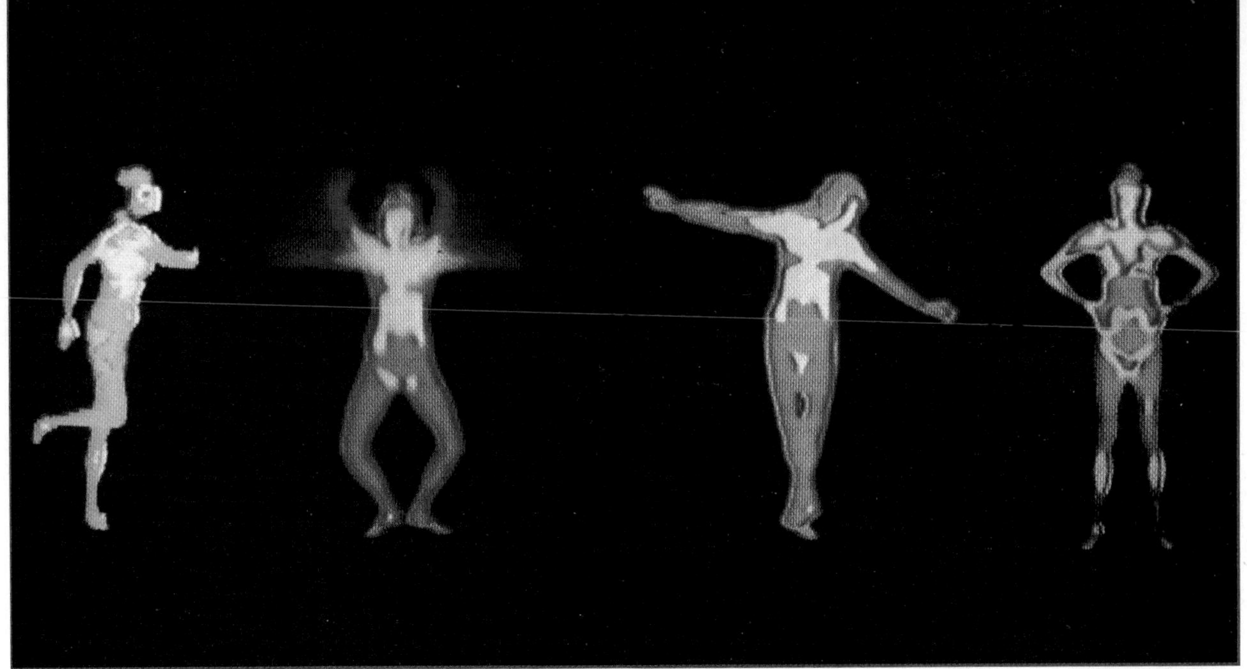

▲ *In this thermogram of four people exercising, blues and greens show cold areas while reds and yellows are hotter areas. Using what you know about exercise, which person do you think has been exercising the longest? Which one has just begun to exercise?*

Not all temperatures on Earth fall between 0°C and 100°C. If you wanted to measure the lava in a volcano, your thermometer would have to reach more than 1000°C. In some laboratories, scientists have created temperatures so cold that particles nearly stop moving. That would happen at –273°C. In space, temperatures range from about –270°C up to millions of degrees in the sun. Many different types of thermometers and other devices have been developed to measure these extremes.

Sometimes, scientists aren't interested in exact temperatures of objects. The picture above, called a thermogram, shows different ranges of temperatures as different colors. Thermograms can be used to spot weaknesses in solids, to detect heat loss in buildings, and to locate some diseases in the body, such as cancers.

Lesson 1 Review

1. What is heat?
2. What is the difference between heat and temperature?
3. How is temperature measured?
4. **Positive and Negative Numbers**
   Water boils at 100°C, hydrogen at –252°C, and oxygen at –184°C. Which substance boils at the highest temperature? Which boils at the lowest?

You will learn:

- what happens to matter as it is heated and cooled.
- some uses of expansion and contraction.

Lesson 2

How Does Heat Affect Matter?

Bif! Pow! "Hey—quit being so rough!" If you were a particle of matter, you'd spend all your time getting bounced around by other particles. How do you think particles react to a change in temperature?

Glossary

expand (ek spand′), to take up more space; to get larger

contract (kən trakt′), to take up less space; to get smaller

Heating and Cooling Matter

Suppose you were a gas particle inside a balloon. You'd fly around, bouncing off the sides of the balloon like a trampoline gymnast. Occasionally, you'd bump into another particle that sends you off in a new direction.

Someone takes the balloon outside into the bright sunlight. The sun's rays beat down on you and the other particles, giving you more energy and making you move faster. You and the other particles hit one another and the sides of the balloon harder and more often. As a result, the balloon stretches, or expands. To **expand** means to "take up more space."

Now someone takes the balloon inside and puts it in the freezer. Brrrr! Heat flows out of the balloon and into the cooler air in the freezer. The balloon contracts. To **contract** means to "take up less space." Why does this

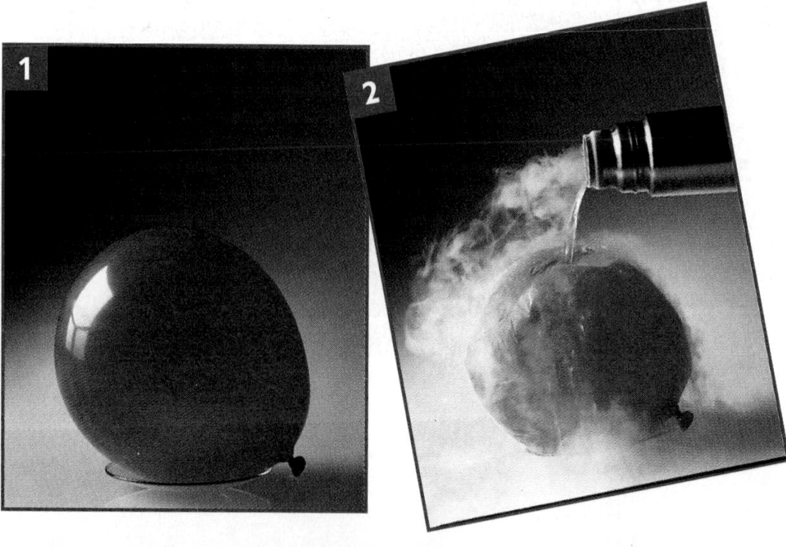

Expanding and Contracting

At normal temperatures, nitrogen is a gas. At very low temperatures—about –200°C—it changes to a liquid. In pictures 2 and 3 you can see how the balloon contracts as the cold liquid nitrogen is poured over it. In pictures 4 and 5, when the liquid nitrogen is removed, the balloon expands. ▶

happen? Each time you bang into the wall of the balloon, you lose more energy to it. With less energy, you and the other gas particles move slower. You don't have the energy to travel very far or hit the walls very hard. What is happening to the particles of matter as liquid nitrogen cools the balloon in the pictures below?

All matter expands when it is heated and contracts when it cools. Not all matter expands and contracts the same amount. For every degree rise in temperature, gases expand the most, liquids expand less, and solids expand the least.

Have you noticed pieces of rubber from blown-out tires on the road when the highways get hot in summer? Sometimes this happens because the heat from the road causes the air in the tire to expand, and the tire blows up like a balloon. The rubber of the tire doesn't expand as much as the air. When the air expands too much, the tire can tear and cause a blowout.

Because ice is a solid, you might think that it is heavier than water. If this were true, ice would sink. Water behaves differently from other liquids. As water cools, it contracts like most other liquids—until the temperature reaches 4°C. At this point, the particles in the water are packed together as tightly as they can get. However, water changes to ice at 0°C. As the water cools from 4°C to 0°C, the water particles form little rings, like those in the picture to the right, as they become ice. Because water particles in rings take up more space, an ice cube is actually larger than the water from which it formed.

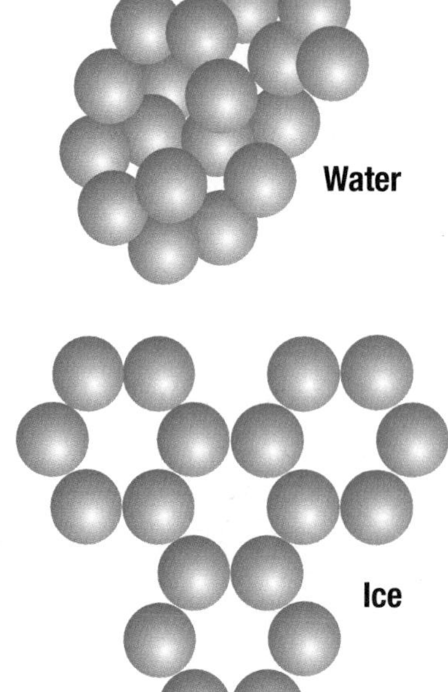

▲ *The particles that make up water are more tightly packed together than ice particles.*

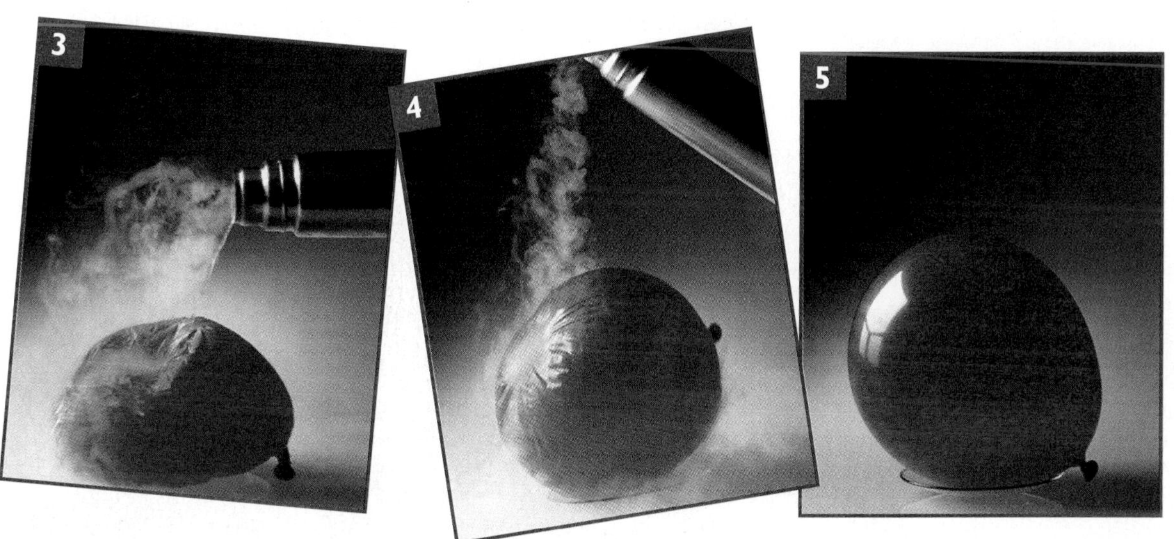

Using Expansion and Contraction

Kadunk. Kadunk. Kadunk. You might hear that sound when a train passes by. The sound occurs when the train wheels pass over the spaces between the tracks. But why are there spaces? From the cold of winter to the heat of summer, the track constantly expands and contracts. A mile of track can change its length by more than half a meter. Without room to expand, the track could twist.

Concrete expands too. In the building of long bridges, such as the one below, metal joints are placed between sections of concrete roadway. As the concrete expands, it pushes the metal in these joints into the spaces between the metal. This action prevents the concrete from breaking or buckling.

Scientists use the expansion and contraction of mercury, a heavy liquid metal, to produce an important tool that is used not only in the laboratory but in your home too. Can you guess what that tool is? In the temperature range between 0°C and 100°C, liquid mercury expands almost the same amount for every degree of temperature rise. A puddle of mercury would expand equally in all directions, but if you put the mercury in a thin tube, it can expand only in one direction. When you heat it, the column of mercury gets longer as the mercury particles move away from each other. When you cool it, the column gets shorter. Sound familiar? It should. This is how a thermometer works.

Joints like this one are built into bridges and roadways to allow for the expansion and contraction of the concrete. ▼

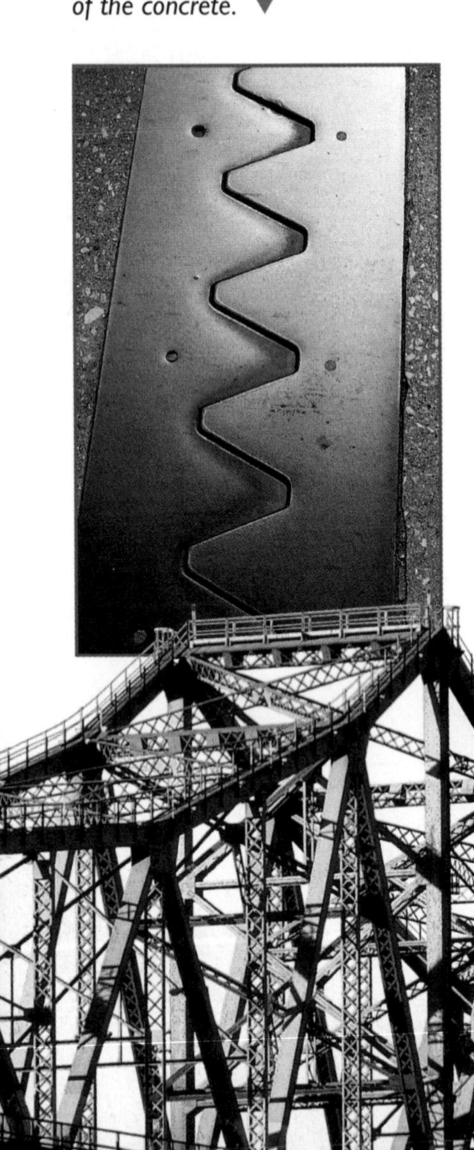

You can see the effects of expansion in your own home. Electric lines sag in summer and can contract so much in winter that they snap. The water pipes in your home expand and contract. Sometimes, this expansion and contraction causes the water pipes to creak or make other noises.

When you adjust the thermostat in your home, you might be using expansion and contraction. Many thermostats use a bimetallic strip, like the ones to the right. A bimetallic strip is made of two different metals, such as brass and iron. As temperature changes, the brass expands and contracts more than the iron. When you cool the strip, the brass contracts more than the iron and the strip bends toward the brass. When heated, the brass expands more and the strip bends toward the iron.

You can see in the picture how a bimetallic strip works in a thermostat. As the temperature in the room rises, the bimetallic strip straightens a bit. The switch opens, and the furnace shuts off. As the room cools, the strip bends back and once again closes the switch. The furnace turns on. What other examples of expansion or contraction can you think of?

The bimetallic strip bends up at cold temperatures because the brass contracts more than the iron. The strip bends down at warmer temperatures because the brass expands more than the iron. ▼

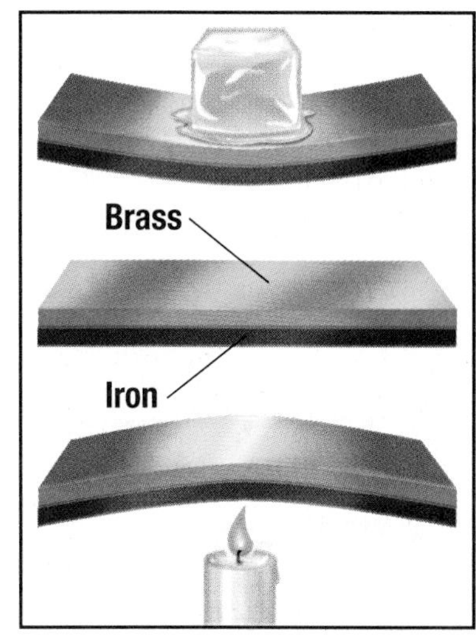

Switch off

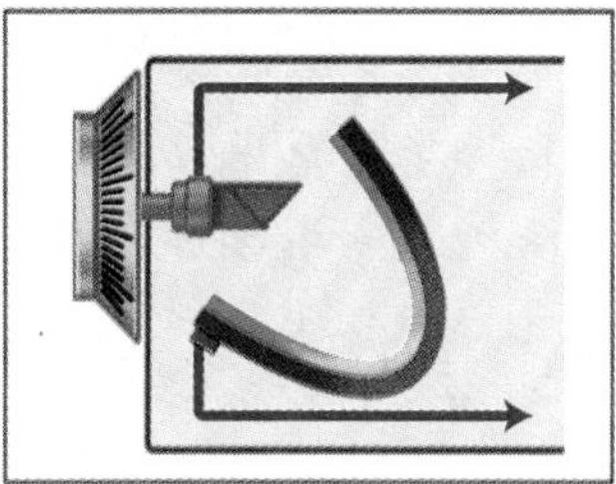

Switch on

Lesson 2 Review

1. Explain what happens to matter as it is heated and cooled.
2. Give two examples of uses of the expansion and contraction of materials.
3. **Positive and Negative Numbers**
   Mercury is a metal that contracts as it cools. Would it contract more at –2°C or at –20°C?

Thermostat

A thermostat uses a bimetallic strip to control a furnace. As the air temperature changes, the strip opens and closes the switch to turn the furnace off and on. ▶

Comparing Expansion and Contraction

Process Skills

Process Skills

- observing
- predicting
- inferring

Materials

- safety goggles
- balloon
- plastic bottle
- rubber band
- bucket of warm water
- bucket of ice water

Getting Ready

Think about the words *expand* and *contract*. Write a definition for each in your own words. Then do this activity to find out how expansion and contraction are related to temperature.

Follow This Procedure

1. Make a chart like the one shown. Use your chart to record your predictions and observations.

Temperature	Predict: What will happen to the balloon?	Description of balloon
Room temperature	x	
Warm water		
Cold water		

2. Put on your safety goggles. Stretch the opening of the balloon over the neck of the bottle. Use a rubber band to make sure the balloon is secure and no air can get in or out.

3. **Observe** the balloon and the bottle. Record your observations.

4. What do you think will happen to the balloon if you place the bottle in the bucket of warm water? Record your **prediction** in your chart. Tell what information you used to make your predictions.

5. Place the bottle and balloon assembly in the bucket of warm water, as shown in the photo. Hold the bottle upright in the water until the bottle becomes warm—about 10–15 seconds.

6 Observe the balloon again and record your observations. In your chart, record any changes you see in the balloon.

7 What will happen if you remove the bottle from the warm water and place it in the bucket of ice water? Record your prediction in your chart. Tell what information you used to make your prediction.

8 Remove the bottle and balloon from the warm water and quickly place it in the bucket of ice water. Hold the bottle in the water until the bottle cools. Then repeat step 6.

Interpret Your Results

1. What happened to the balloon when the bottle was warmed?

2. Describe what you observed as the bottle cooled.

3. **Infer** what happened to the air in the bottle when it was warmed. What observation supports your inference?

Inquire Further

Suppose you cooled the bottle before you attached the balloon. What changes might you have observed when you warmed the bottle? Develop a plan to answer this or other questions you may have.

Self-Assessment

- I followed instructions to heat and cool a gas (air).
- I made **predictions** about how a temperature change would affect the balloon.
- I made **observations** about changes in the balloon.
- I recorded my observations about the balloon.
- I made an **inference** about what happens to the air in the bottle when it is heated and cooled.

You will learn:

- how matter is heated by conduction.
- how thermal energy is transferred by convection.
- how energy is transferred by radiation.

Lesson 3

How Can Matter Become Heated?

"Phew! It's so hot that you could cook an egg on the sidewalk!" How many times have you heard that expression? Is it true? Can heat from the sidewalk really fry an egg? If so, how?

Conduction

You could cook an egg on a hot sidewalk—if the temperature were high enough. The egg would be heated by conduction. **Conduction** is the flow of heat from one object to another by direct contact between the objects. The particles in the sidewalk are hotter and have more energy than the particles in the egg. When the particles of both objects come in contact, heat flows from the sidewalk to the egg, causing the egg to cook.

All over the world, people use conduction to do much of their cooking. Some people place their food in direct contact with hot surfaces, such as rocks. Other people use pans to cook their food. How do you think energy is transferred to cook the food in the picture?

Have you ever felt a metal spoon get hot as you stirred a hot liquid? The spoon can get so hot that you have to put it down. Heat travels by conduction from the hot pan, through the spoon, and into your fingers. The metal that the spoon is made of is a conductor. A **conductor** is a substance through which energy travels easily. Most metals are good conductors. They are used to transfer heat quickly, such as in cooking pans or in an iron. Conductors are used to carry heat away from electrical parts in computers and other electronic devices.

Glossary

Glossary

conduction (kən duk′shən), the flow of heat from one object to another by direct contact between the objects

conductor (kən duk′tər), a substance through which energy travels easily

This woman is using conduction to cook. How else can you use conduction to cook? ▼

Handles of cooking pans are often made of wood or plastic. These substances are called insulators. An **insulator** slows down the transfer of heat. Particles in insulators don't pass along their energy as quickly as those in conductors.

You can feel the difference between an insulator and a conductor if you place your hand on a bicycle that has been sitting in the sun. Why do the metal parts of the bike feel hotter than the tires, even though they are at the same temperature? Metal is a conductor. It transfers heat to your fingers faster than the rubber, which is an insulator.

Buildings are made with insulating materials to prevent heat from leaving or entering through the walls or roof. In Tunisia, some homes are built into the sides of hills, where the soil acts as insulation. In Japan, China, and Korea, clay is used for walls because it is a good insulator.

Animals use insulation too. How does the fur of the polar bear in the picture keep the bear warm? Air, which is an insulator, is trapped in the fur. Each strand of fur contains pockets of air that insulate the bear against the cold water and air, in which it lives. The boy in the picture below is wearing layered clothing. He is using the air that is trapped between the layers to insulate his body from the cold. How do you think the feathers of birds help to keep them warm?

Glossary

insulator (in′sə lā tər), a substance that slows down the transfer of heat

Glossary

Air trapped in each hair of this polar bear's fur keeps the animal from losing body heat to the air and water. ▼

◀ *Air trapped between layers of clothing helps keep this boy warm.*

Glossary

Glossary

convection
(kən vek′shən), the flow of thermal energy that occurs when a warm liquid or gas moves from one place to another

◀ *Convection currents may be seen as bubbles of liquid move up and down in this lamp.*

Convection

When you heat a pan of water, particles of water at the bottom of the pan gain energy by conduction and move faster. The particles of heated water spread out more than the particles in the cooler water around it. The water that is not yet heated is more tightly packed. It sinks to the bottom of the pan while the hotter and lighter water moves toward the top.

When the hotter water particles reach the top, they lose some energy to the particles of air. The water particles cool off, become denser, and sink. At the same time, the water particles at the bottom are being heated, and they rise. Thermal energy is carried through the liquid in a circular up-and-down motion called a convection current. **Convection** is the flow of thermal energy that occurs when a warm liquid or gas moves from one place to another.

You can see the results of convection currents in the lamp. The lamp contains two liquids of different colors that don't mix. Each liquid has properties that are different from the other. For example, the liquids do not expand and contract at the same rate when they are heated and cooled.

When the lamp is cool, the blue bubbles are denser than the clear liquid that surrounds them, and they sink. When the lamp is turned on, the light bulb in the base of the lamp warms the bubbles and the liquid around them. The bubbles expand more than the surrounding liquid. The expansion of the bubbles causes them to rise. As they rise, the bubbles cool, contract, and eventually sink. Bubbles rise and sink as they warm and cool. Energy is carried throughout the lamp by the movement of the liquid particles in the lamp.

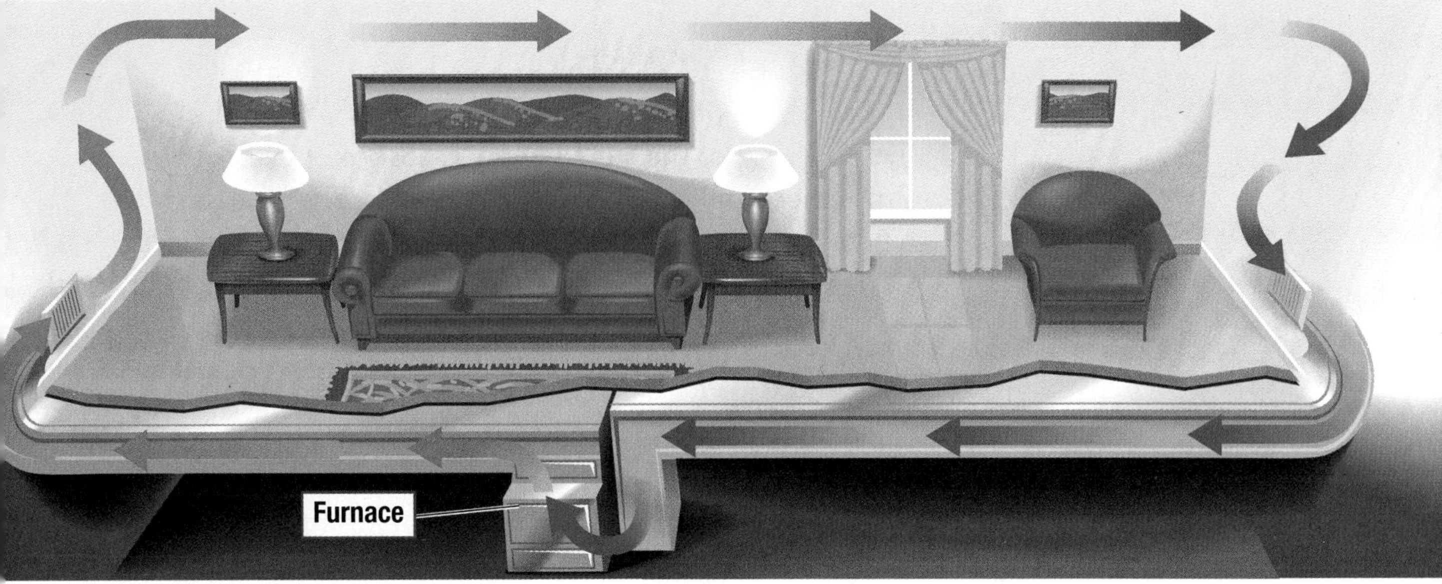

▲ *Convection currents carry heat through this room. What is the source of heat?*

Many homes are heated by convection. Follow the flow of air in the picture above to see how this happens. Air is warmed in the furnace. The warm air enters the room through vents. Once in the room, the warm air rises toward the ceiling, carrying energy through the room. Cooler air sinks to the floor. This cool air returns through vents to the furnace, where it is heated again.

Radiation

When you stand in the sun, you feel warm. The sun's rays reach you and give energy to the particles in your skin. Yet the few particles that exist in the space between Earth and the sun are too far apart to transfer energy by conduction. There is no flow of particles for convection to take place. Energy from the sun reaches us without the help of matter. This form of energy transfer from one place to another without the use of matter is called **radiation.** The energy that travels in this way is called radiant energy.

You experience radiant energy when you stand near a fire and feel the heat. The energy travels through the air to reach you, but it doesn't use the air to help it travel.

More energy usually reaches you through radiation than through conduction or convection. Materials with dark, dull surfaces take in a lot of radiation. Other materials reflect radiation. Air, glass, and other clear materials allow radiant energy to pass through them. That's why you feel warm when you sit by a window on a sunny day.

Glossary

radiation (rā′dē ā′shən), the transfer of energy from one place to another without the use of matter

Glossary

Heating the Earth

The earth is naturally heated by radiation from the sun, but most of the sun's energy is absorbed by the atmosphere and the surface of the earth. The rest is reflected back into space or scattered by the atmosphere. Convection and conduction help transfer heat throughout the earth. Study the information on these pages to see how conduction, convection, and radiation heat the earth.

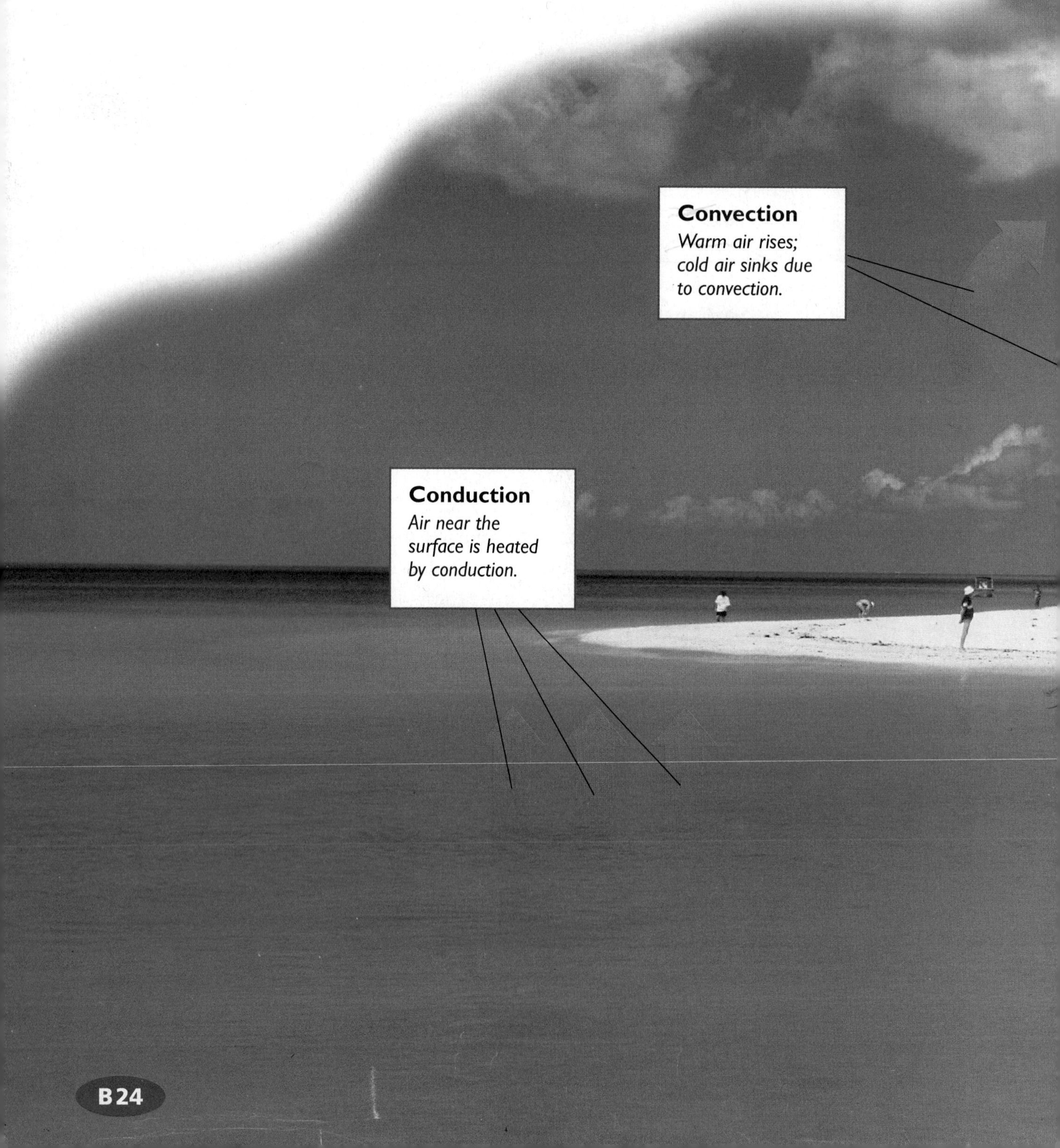

Convection

Warm air rises; cold air sinks due to convection.

Conduction

Air near the surface is heated by conduction.

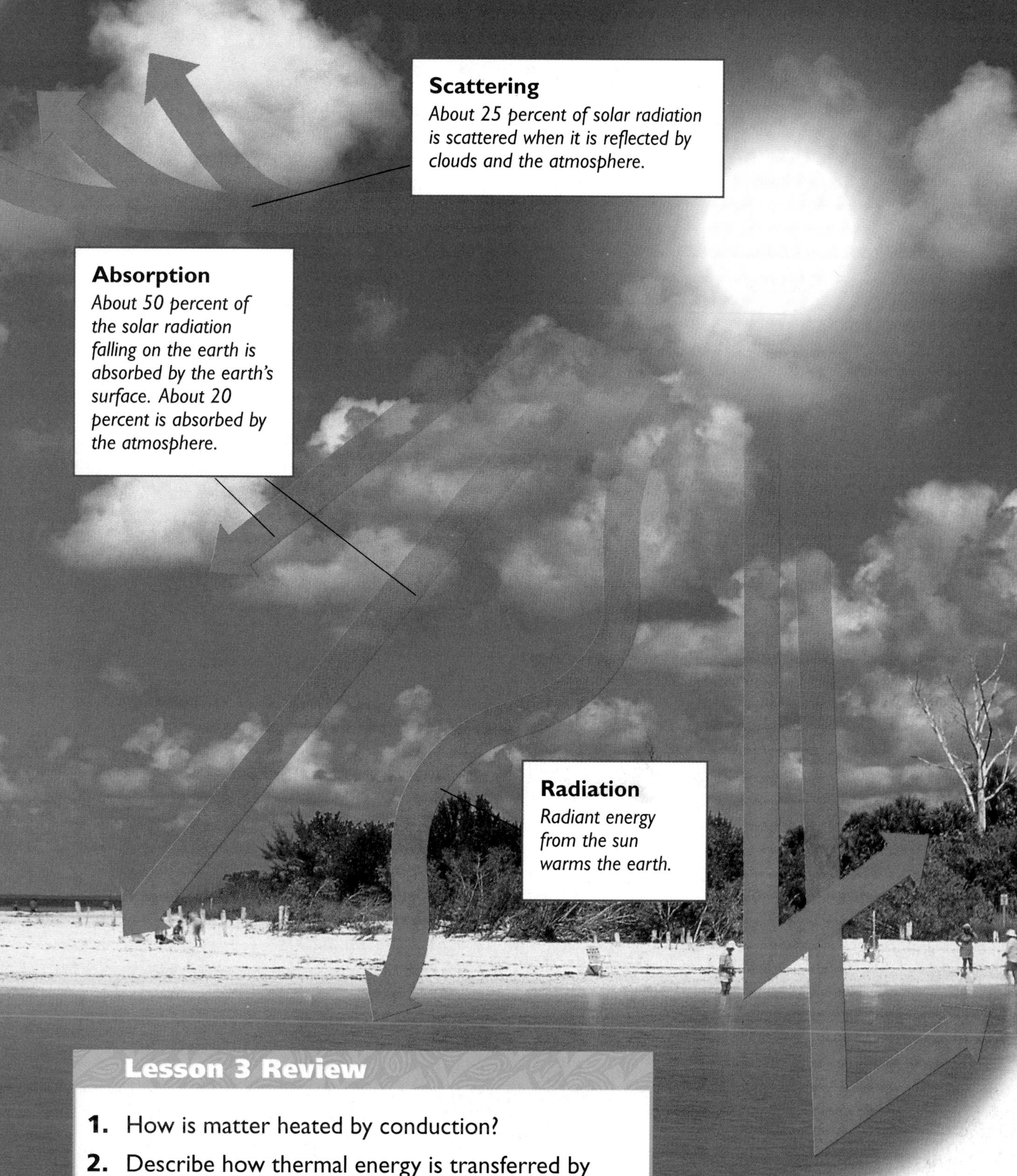

Scattering
About 25 percent of solar radiation is scattered when it is reflected by clouds and the atmosphere.
Absorption
About 50 percent of the solar radiation falling on the earth is absorbed by the earth's surface. About 20 percent is absorbed by the atmosphere.
Radiation
Radiant energy from the sun warms the earth.
Reflection
About 5 percent of solar radiation is reflected back into space.

Lesson 3 Review

1. How is matter heated by conduction?
2. Describe how thermal energy is transferred by convection.
3. How is radiation different from conduction and convection?
4. **Predict**
   Using the picture on these two pages, predict what would happen if the sky became very cloudy.

Investigate Activity

Keeping Ice Frozen

Process Skills

Process Skills

- communicating
- predicting
- observing
- inferring

Materials

- 2 ice cubes
- 2 resealable plastic bags
- assorted insulating and packaging materials
- clock

Getting Ready

In this activity, you will design and test a package that will keep an ice cube frozen.

Recall that heat is transferred by conduction, convection, and radiation. Consider the kinds of materials that might best limit heat transfer.

Follow This Procedure

1. Make a chart like the one shown. Use your chart to record your predictions and observations.

	After 30 minutes	
	Predictions	Observations
Uninsulated ice cube		
Insulated ice cube		

2. **Communicate.** Discuss with your partners ways in which you can package an ice cube to keep it frozen. Use one of the insulating materials provided by your teacher (Photo A). Choose the packaging method that you think will work best.

3. Place an ice cube in a plastic bag. Remove as much air as possible from the bag, and then seal it (Photo B). This ice cube will be your control. It shows how fast ice melts without insulated packaging.

Self-Monitoring

Did I seal the bag tightly?

Photo A

4 Place another ice cube in a sealable plastic bag. Remove as much air from the bag as possible, and then seal the bag.

5 Construct your insulated package. Place the plastic bag with the ice cube in the package you designed.

6 **Predict** what will happen after 30 minutes to both your ice cube and the control ice cube. Record your predictions. They should be as detailed as possible.

7 After 30 minutes, open or unwrap your package. **Observe** how much of your ice cube has melted. Compare your ice cube with the control ice cube. Record your observations in the chart.

Interpret Your Results

1. Describe your package. Did you design it to stop conduction of heat? heat convection? heat radiation?

2. How well did your package work? Was your ice cube completely frozen, partially melted, mostly melted, or completely melted?

Photo B

3. Infer how heat reached your ice cube. What evidence do you have to support your inference?

4. Compare your results with those of your classmates. Describe the packaging method that seemed to work best. How did it stop heat from reaching the ice cube?

Inquire Further

How could you package an ice cube to keep it frozen for 24 hours? Develop a plan to answer this or other questions you may have.

Self-Assessment

- I followed instructions to design a package that would keep an ice cube frozen.
- I **communicated** my ideas about the packaging design.
- I **predicted** how well my design would work and what would happen to the control ice cube.
- I tested my design, and recorded my **observations** of the results.
- I **inferred** how heat reached the ice cube in my package.

Chapter 1 Review

Chapter Main Ideas

Lesson 1

• Heat is a flow of energy from warmer areas to cooler areas.

• Temperature is a measure of the average motion of the particles in a substance or object.

• To measure temperature, scientists use thermometers with scales that are based on the temperatures at which water boils and freezes.

Lesson 2

• Most substances expand when heated and contract when cooled.

• Expansion and contraction can be used to make useful devices but can also cause problems as temperature changes.

Lesson 3

• In conduction, heat flows from one object to another by direct contact between the objects.

• In convection, particles in a fluid carry heat from one place to another.

• Thermal energy can travel by radiation, the transfer of energy without the use of matter.

Reviewing Science Words and Concepts

Write the letter of the word or phrase that best completes each sentence.

a. conduction
b. conductor
c. contract
d. convection
e. expand
f. heat
g. insulator
h. radiation
i. temperature
j. thermal energy

1. As the particles that make up a substance gain energy and move faster, the ___ of the substance rises.
2. Wood makes good handles for cooking pans because it is a(n) ___.
3. As a substance gets smaller or takes up less space, it is said to ___.
4. The total energy of the particles that make up any matter is its ___.
5. Energy from the sun reaches Earth by the process of ___.
6. The flow of energy from warmer matter to cooler matter is called ___.
7. Thermal energy passes from particle to particle in the process of ___.
8. When substances ___, they get larger or take up more space.
9. The flow of thermal energy that occurs when a warm liquid moves from one place to another is ___.
10. Heat travels through metal easily because metal is a good ___.

Explaining Science

Draw and label a diagram or write a paragraph to explain these questions.

1. What is the difference between heat and temperature?

2. How do particles of matter react to an increase in temperature?

3. Why is the motion of particles important to the transfer of energy by conduction?

4. What happens to particles during the process of convection?

Using Skills

1. Are the temperatures below the freezing point of water on the Celsius scale **positive** or **negative numbers?**

2. **Classify** each of the following methods of cooking as conduction, convection, or radiation.

a. broiling chicken under an electric grill

b. cooking an egg in a frying pan

c. steaming rice in a closed pan

3. How does insulated clothing help keep you warm on cold days? **Communicate** your ideas by drawing a picture.

Critical Thinking

1. Suppose the fireplace you use in cold weather is in the same room as the thermostat that controls the furnace. **Predict** what effect this arrangement will have on the temperature in other rooms of the house when the fireplace and furnace are both in use. Give reasons for your predictions.

2. After a very cold night, you find that a clay flowerpot full of wet dirt has broken on your porch. Which of the following would you **infer** happened?

a. Someone accidentally kicked it.

b. The clay contracted in the cold.

c. The water in the dirt expanded as it froze.

3. Clare places a marshmallow at the end of a branch taken from a nearby tree, while Ben puts his marshmallow at the end of an unbent coat hanger of the same length as the branch. **Hypothesize** what will happen when Clare and Ben hold their marshmallows over the campfire.

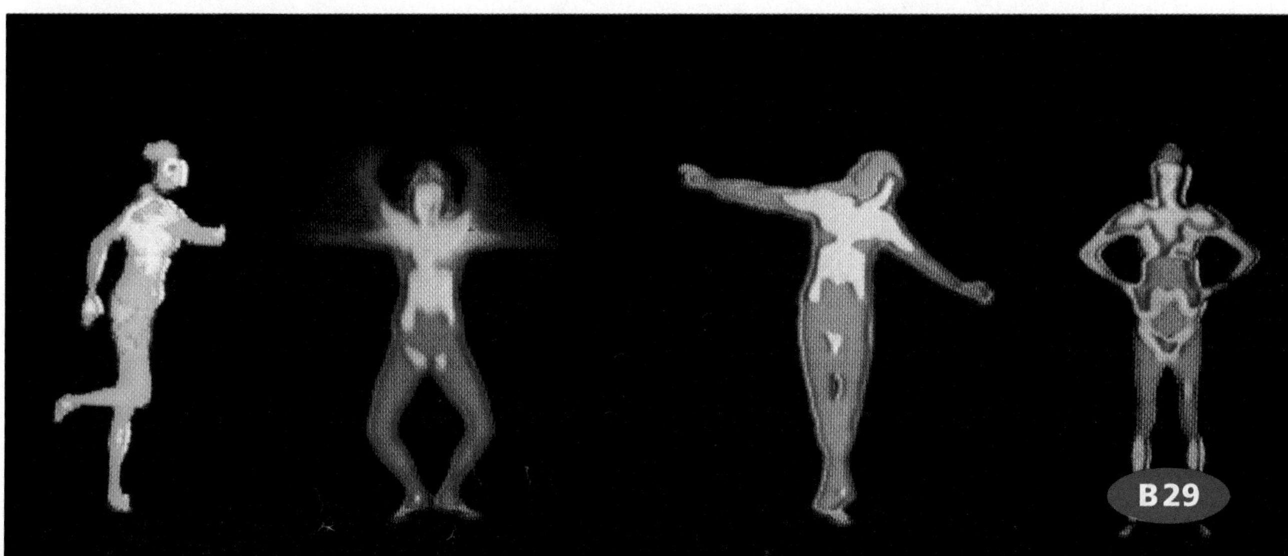

Get a Reaction!

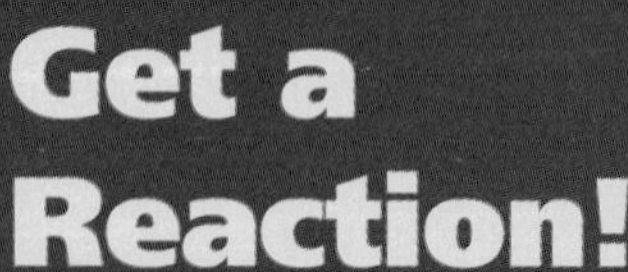

Let's see. If we mix this yellow liquid with this white powdery solid, what will happen? Uh, oh! Maybe the powder will react chemically and change into an entirely different substance. What do you think will happen?

Chapter 2

Changes in Matter

Inquiring about Changes in Matter

Lesson 1
How Does Matter Change State?

- How is temperature related to the states of matter?
- What happens during melting and freezing?
- What is the difference between boiling and evaporation?

Lesson 2
How Do Solutions Form?

- What happens when solutions form?
- What are some types of solutions?
- How can materials dissolve faster?

Lesson 3
How Are Chemical Reactions Described?

- What happens during a chemical reaction?
- What are four major types of chemical reactions?
- How is energy involved in chemical reactions?
- What is a chemical equation?

Lesson 4
What Are the Properties of Acids and Bases?

- What are acids and bases?
- What is the pH scale?
- How do changes in pH affect the environment?
- What is neutralization?

Copy the chapter graphic organizer *onto your own paper. This organizer shows you what the whole chapter is all about. As you read the lessons and do the activities, look for answers to the questions and write them on your organizer.*

Explore Activity

Exploring Dissolving

Process Skills

Process Skills

- predicting
- observing
- inferring
- communicating

Materials

- masking tape
- 3 clear plastic cups
- ice water, room temperature water, very warm water
- 3 sugar cubes
- timer or watch with second hand

Explore

1. Label three plastic cups as follows: *I*, *R*, and *W*. Pour ice water into the plastic cup marked *I*. Pour room temperature water into the cup marked *R*, and pour very warm water into the cup marked *W*. Each cup should be about half full.

Safety Note *Very warm water can cause burns.*

2. If you place a sugar cube in each of the cups, will the sugar dissolve at the same rate in each cup? Write down your **prediction.**

3. **Observe** the sugar in each cup every 30 seconds for 3 minutes. Observe which sugar cube dissolves fastest.

Reflect

1. In which cup did the sugar cube dissolve fastest? slowest?

2. What can you **infer** about the effect of temperature on the rate that a solid dissolves?

3. Form a possible explanation for what you observed. **Communicate.** Discuss your explanation with your classmates.

Inquire Further

What could you do to make the sugar cube dissolve more quickly in water? Develop a plan to answer this or other questions you may have.

Using Context Clues

As you read Lesson 1, *How Does Matter Change State?* you can use context clues to help you understand words that are unfamiliar to you. **Context clues** are the familiar words or ideas that surround a new word. Context clues help you to picture or understand unfamiliar words.

Reading Vocabulary

context clues, familiar words or ideas surrounding a new word

Example

As you read these sentences on page B39, look for clues to the meaning of the word humidity. Write the clues in a chart like the one below.

> Water vapor, a gas, is always present in the air. We call it humidity. When the fast-moving water vapor particles in the air collide with a cool surface, such as the window glass, the gas particles lose energy.

Context Clues	Word Meaning
water vapor a gas always present in the air	

Talk About It!

1. What are context clues?

2. What did you learn about the meaning of the word *humidity* from using context clues?

▼ *Have you ever wondered where the water on a window comes from?*

You will learn:

- how temperature is related to the states of matter.
- what happens during melting and freezing.
- what the difference between boiling and evaporation is.

Lesson 1

How Does Matter Change State?

"Hey! The water in this water bottle changes shape as it pours out! I'm glad my bicycle doesn't!" Did you ever wonder why some substances change shape easily and others don't? Let's find out.

States of Matter

Look at all the matter around you. How many different kinds do you see? If you were asked to place all matter into three groups, how would you group it?

One way you could group all matter is by its three forms, or states. The three states of matter are solid, liquid, and gas. Everything you see on Earth can be grouped into one of these three categories. You can tell the difference between materials in these states by observing their shape and their volume. Volume is the space that a certain amount of matter takes up.

The bike in the picture is made of different solids. The solids in the bike have definite shapes and definite volumes. That means that if you move the bike from one place to another, its shape or volume doesn't change. This fact is true of all solids.

States of Matter

◀ *In different states of matter, particles move differently. Particles in a solid, such as this metal bicycle frame, are close together and can only vibrate. In a liquid such as water, they are farther apart and move more freely. In a gas, such as the air in tires, particles are far apart and free to move in every direction.*

The water in the girl's bottle is a liquid. If you pour a liquid from one container to another, it takes the shape of the container, but its volume stays the same.

The air in the bicycle tires is a gas. A gas has no definite shape and no definite volume. If the tire gets a hole in it, the air inside will mix with the outside air. Both the air's shape and the space it takes up will change.

Why are some things solids, while others at the same temperature are liquids or gases? The particles that make up matter always have an attraction among them. Some attractions are strong and some are weak.

In a solid, a strong attraction holds the particles close together. Each particle can only vibrate. In a liquid, the particles aren't held together as strongly. They can move past one another, so the liquid can flow into different shapes. In a gas, the attraction between the particles is so weak that they move quickly and freely in all directions. As a result, a gas takes both the shape and the volume of the container it is in.

You now know that the amount of attraction between particles determines whether something is a solid, liquid, or gas. If so, how does a substance such as ice change from a solid to a liquid? Think about what happens to cause ice to melt.

To keep ice from melting, you place it in the freezer, where it is cold. If you remove the ice from the freezer, heat flows from the warmer air to the particles of ice. As you heat ice—or any solid or liquid—the particles in it gain energy and move faster. Eventually, the particles have enough energy to escape the pull between them. When this happens, the matter changes state.

Within the range of normal temperatures usually found on Earth, very few substances can naturally exist in all three states. Water is an exception. In the picture to the right, water is present in all three states at the same time. The particles in the water vapor, which is a gas, are moving the fastest, and those in the ice are moving the slowest.

These macaque live in troops of varying size, mostly in Asia. What states of water are found around this troop? ▼

Melting and Freezing

All materials can exist as solids, liquids, or gases—if the temperature is right. On Earth we are used to seeing the metal lead as a solid, mercury as a liquid, and oxygen as a gas. What do you think would happen to these materials on other planets with different temperatures?

On the hot surface of Venus, which can have temperatures up to 425°C, lead would be a liquid, and both mercury and oxygen would be gases. On Neptune, which has a surface temperature of –210°C, lead and mercury would be solids and oxygen would be a liquid. Can you imagine breathing a liquid?

▲ *Temperatures on the planet Venus are much hotter than those on Earth. As a result, substances that are solids on Earth are liquids or gases on Venus.*

The state of a substance depends on both its temperature and the amount of attraction between its particles. If you heat the particles in a solid, such as the ice cube pictured below, they vibrate faster. Finally, the particles gain enough energy to break free from the attraction that holds them together in the shape of a cube. They move freely around each other. The solid ice undergoes a change of state and becomes liquid water.

This process in which a substance changes from a solid into a liquid is called melting. The temperature at which a solid melts is called its melting point. The melting point of ice is 0°C. The melting point of lead is 327°C. Because the temperature on the surface of Venus is over 400°C, solid lead would melt to a liquid.

Melting happens because particles gain heat. What happens if particles lose heat? Did you ever touch an ice cube with wet fingers? Did the ice stick to your fingers? When you touch the ice cube, heat flows from the water on your fingers to the ice. The water on your fingers gets so cold that it freezes and sticks to the particles of ice in the ice cube.

Melting

As the particles in the solid ice cube gain energy and vibrate faster, they break apart and become liquid water. ▶

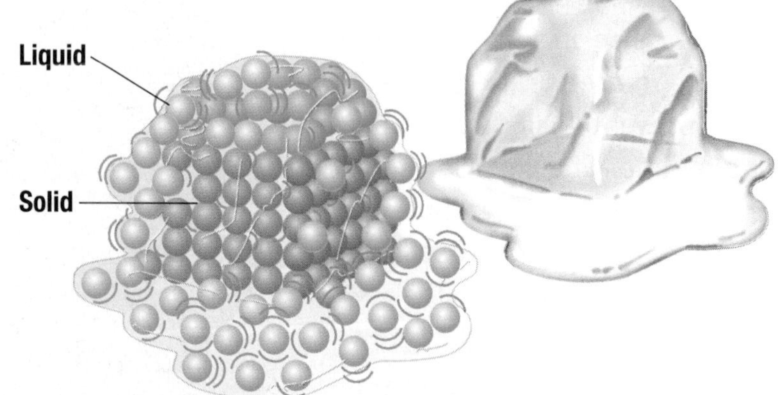

Freezing occurs when a substance changes from a liquid to a solid. The temperature at which a liquid freezes is called its freezing point. How do you think the melting point and freezing point of a substance compare?

To answer this question, think about water. As liquid water cools, its particles move more slowly. The water contracts because the particles move closer together. At 0°C, the particles slow down enough that the attraction between them pulls them together. The particles form a solid—ice.

It might seem that the temperature at which solid particles can break free from one another (the melting point) might be higher than the temperature at which liquid particles attract to form a solid (the freezing point). In pure substances, melting and freezing happen at the same temperature. You can see both ice and liquid water in the picture below.

This river in the Sawtooth National Forest, Idaho, has both liquid water and ice. In many places along the edge of the water, melting and freezing are happening at the same time. ▼

Glossary

Glossary

evaporation
(i vap′ə rā′shən), the change of state from liquid to gas at the surface of a liquid

Boiling and Evaporation

Have you ever heard someone say that the weather is "boiling hot"? If it were really that hot, all the water in the oceans and rivers would change from a liquid to a gas.

When a liquid changes to a gas, we say that it is boiling. The temperature at which this happens is called the boiling point. Water boils at 100°C, but some substances boil at much colder temperatures and some at hotter temperatures. Oxygen boils at about –183°C. Oxygen is a gas at temperatures found on Earth.

The particles of water in the pan below speed up as they become heated and the temperature increases. The water stays in liquid form because the water particles have enough attraction to keep pulling one another back into the liquid when one tries to escape. At the boiling point, the particles in the water can gain enough energy to break free and become a gas.

If you continue heating the water as it boils, the particles of water don't speed up any more. Instead, the energy moves the water particles farther apart. How will this movement affect the attraction between particles? The water's temperature stays the same until all of the water has changed to a gas—water vapor.

Recall that temperature is a measure of the average motion of particles. Not all particles in a container of water move at the same rate. Even at room temperature, a few of the particles in a glass of water are moving fast enough to break free at the surface and become a gas. This process is called **evaporation** .

The difference between boiling and evaporation is that at the boiling point, particles throughout the liquid have enough energy to escape. With evaporation, only those particles at the surface with enough energy to break free can change to a gas. Evaporation can take place at just about any temperature. However, the closer the liquid is to its boiling point, the more particles can evaporate.

Boiling

At the boiling point, all the particles in the water have enough energy to break free and change to a gas. ▼

Have you ever noticed that you feel cold right after you climb out of a swimming pool? Heat flows from your warm body to the water on your skin. As your skin particles move more slowly, you feel cold. The water particles eventually gain enough energy to evaporate. Before long, you're dry! Because evaporation removes the faster-moving particles in a liquid, it always produces a temperature drop. Where else might you notice this cooling effect?

Look at the water on the window glass in the picture. How did the water get there? Water vapor, a gas, is always present in the air. We call it humidity. When the fast-moving water vapor particles in the air collide with a cool surface, such as the window glass, the gas particles lose energy. The particles slow down and move closer together. When they are close enough, attraction takes over. The water vapor becomes liquid water drops, which stick to the glass. The water comes from the air. This change of state from gas to liquid is called **condensation**.

Glossary

condensation
(kon′den sā′shən), the change of state from a gas to a liquid

Glossary

You can't see these flowers clearly through the glass because water from the air has condensed on the cool glass. ▼

Lesson 1 Review

1. How is temperature related to the states of matter?
2. Describe what happens during melting and freezing.
3. What is the difference between boiling and evaporation?
4. **Context Clues**
   What is the meaning of the word *contracts* on page B37? What context clues did you use?

You will learn:

- what happens when solutions form.
- what some types of solutions are.
- how materials can dissolve faster.

Lesson 2

How Do Solutions Form?

Plop! You drop a sugar cube into a glass of water. Five minutes later—it's gone! What happened to the sugar? Is it really gone? Do you think you could get it back?

Forming Solutions

When you mix sugar with sand, the sand and sugar form a mixture. In this mixture, you can still see the individual sugar and sand particles. However, when you place sugar—and many other substances—in water, the sugar seems to disappear. As the sugar mixes with the water, it dissolves. When a substance dissolves, it breaks down into individual particles. When sugar dissolves in water, the sugar particles mix with the particles of water. The sugar and water form a solution. In a solution, the particles are evenly distributed. How does this happen?

Look at the picture below. When you put a sugar cube into water, water particles are attracted to the solid sugar

Dissolving

Sugar dissolves as water particles are attracted to sugar particles in the crystal and pull them free. The sugar particles spread throughout the water and are too tiny for you to see. ▼

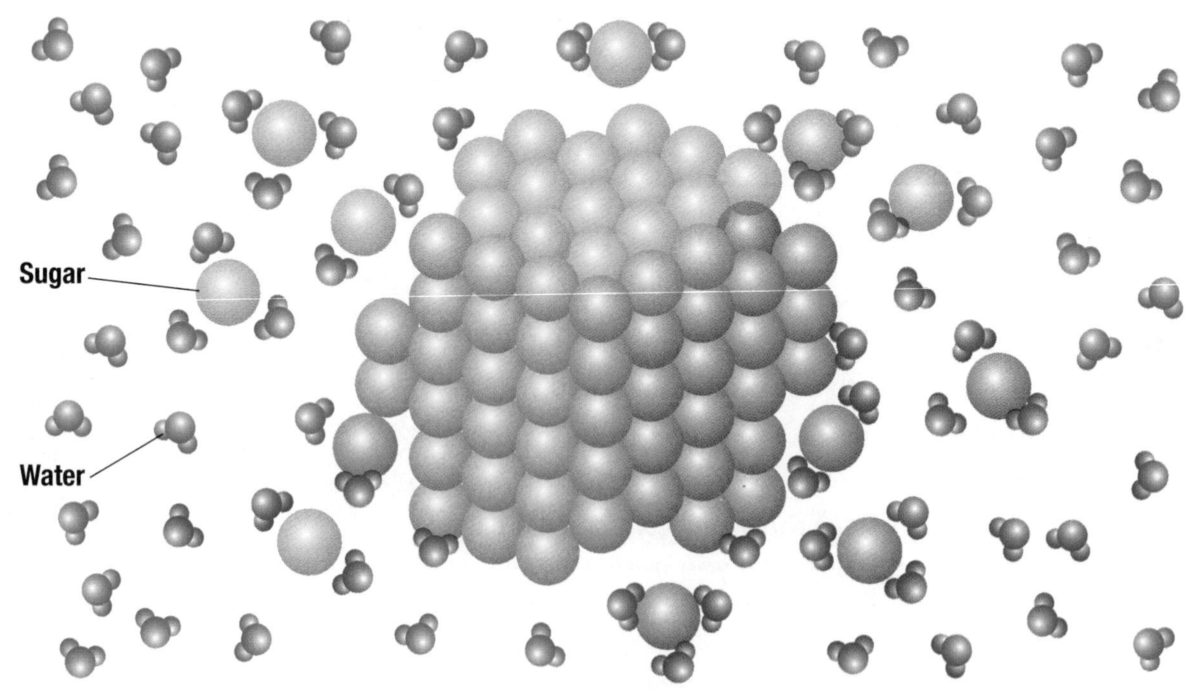

particles. Sugar particles at the surface of the cube pull free. They move about the water particles and fill the spaces between them. After a while, all the particles of sugar and water are evenly mixed. When all the sugar has dissolved in this way, you have a solution of sugar water.

How do you know that the sugar is still there in a sugar-water solution? If you've ever tasted sugar water, you know the sugar is still there because of the solution's sweet taste. You just can't see the sugar because its individual particles are too small to be seen. They are so tiny that they can even pass through a piece of filter paper. This is why the solution looks like a single substance.

The water in the sugar-water solution is a solvent. A **solvent** is a substance that dissolves other materials. The sugar is a **solute**, a substance that is dissolved. All solutions have solvents and solutes. Many common solutions, like the sugar-water solution, are solid solutes dissolved in liquid solvents.

Solutions also can be made using liquids as both the solvent and the solute. In the picture, liquid food coloring (the solute) dissolves in water (the solvent). The particles of the two liquids mix. At first, you can see where the food coloring is, but after a while, the whole solution is the same color. The particles of water and food coloring are evenly mixed.

You can easily decide which of the two substances in a solution is the solvent and which is the solute. When the substances are in two different states, such as sugar and water, the substance that appears to change is the solute. The sugar seems to disappear, so it is the solute.

Glossary

solvent (sol′vənt), a substance that dissolves other materials

solute (sol′yüt), a substance that is dissolved

When water and food coloring are mixed, the particles of food coloring spread out evenly in the water. ▼

▲ *Many perfumes are solutions of substances dissolved in alcohol.*

Solutions have many uses. For example, solvents can remove oils from flowers, such as roses. They also remove oils from peppermint, cloves, and vanilla beans. These oils contain the scent and flavors of the plant they came from. Then some of the solvent is allowed to evaporate so that the flavor or scent gets stronger in the solution that remains. The solutions have many uses in cooking and baking. You can see another use of a solution to the left.

History of Science

Solutions have long been of interest to scientists. Long before the modern scientific era, people called alchemists, shown in the picture below, experimented with common substances. They wanted to understand what matter was. Much of their time was spent trying to turn common metals into gold. Imagine what would have happened had they been successful!

One of the most famous alchemists, Phillipus Paracelsus, lived in the 1500s. He thought that there was a substance from which all other substances came. Paracelsus believed that once this substance was found, it would dissolve anything. He called this substance alkahest.

Do you think a solvent that would dissolve anything would be useful? If you discovered such a substance, what kind of container would you keep it in? Although some of what the alchemists did seems strange to us today, their equipment and methods formed the beginning of the modern science of chemistry.

Alchemists were early chemists who tried to understand more about matter. They invented some of the lab equipment used by chemists today. ▶

Types of Solutions

The air you breathe, the gasoline that powers the family car, and the nickel coins you put into a drink machine—all of these substances are solutions. Although you probably think of solutions as liquids, the solvent or solute in a solution can be a solid, a liquid, or a gas. That means that there are many different types of solutions. You can see examples of some of these types in the chart.

Solution	Solute	Solvent
Carbonated beverage	Carbon dioxide (gas)	Water (liquid)
Brass	Copper (solid)	Zinc (solid)
Dental fillings	Mercury (liquid)	Silver (solid)

▲ *It is possible to make nine different types of solutions. The table shows three of them. Can you name the others?*

Did you know that the air you breathe is a solution formed by a gas dissolving in another gas? Because there is more nitrogen than oxygen in the air, nitrogen gas is the solvent and oxygen is the solute. Other gases, such as water vapor and carbon dioxide, are also solutes dissolved in the nitrogen.

The gasoline people use in their cars is a solution too. It is made of several different liquids. The liquids are called hydrocarbons because they contain hydrogen and carbon. All of these liquids burn to produce energy.

A nickel coin is a solution of two solids—nickel and copper. Even though it is called a nickel, the coin you see to the right actually contains more copper than nickel. Therefore, copper is the solvent and nickel is the solute. To make this kind of solution, you have to melt the solids, mix them together, and then let them cool.

This nickel coin is just one of the many solutions you use every day. ▼

Solid-in-solid solutions, like the nickel coin, are sometimes called alloys. Other common alloys are steel (carbon in iron), sterling silver (copper in silver), and bronze (tin and zinc in copper). In automatic sprinkler systems, an alloy is used that melts from the heat of a fire. When the alloy melts, the water can flow through the pipes to the sprinkler.

Some tooth fillings are solutions of liquid mercury in a solid, such as silver. Other fillings are made of a solution of plastic and other solids.

One solution you might be very familiar with is a carbonated drink. It is a solution of a gas in a liquid. While the bottle is sealed, the substance inside appears to be a plain liquid. But when the cap is removed, the bubbles of carbon dioxide gas that were dissolved in the liquid are able to escape from the solution.

Glossary

Glossary

dilute (dī lüt′), describes a solution with a small amount of solute compared to the amount of solvent

concentrated (kon′sən trā′tid), describes a solution with a large amount of solute compared to the amount of solvent

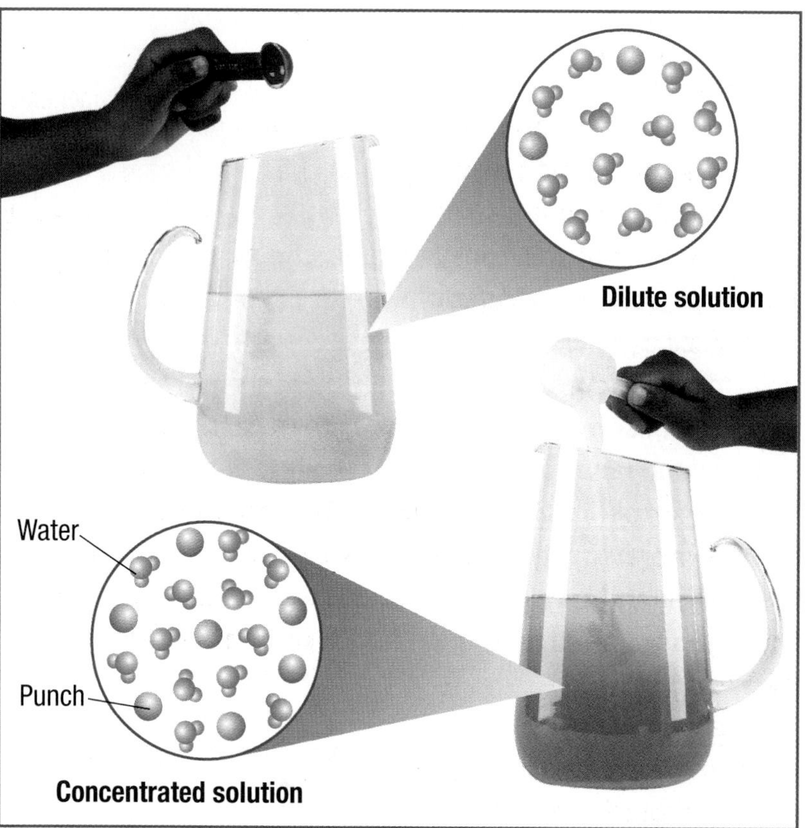

Although both pitchers contain the same substances, water and punch mix, the amount of mix in each pitcher is different. ▶

Another beverage that is a solution is fruit punch. If you make fruit punch, do you like to add a lot of sugar or just a little? When you make a solution, you can add a little or a lot of solute to the solvent.

Compare the two pitchers of punch in the picture. If you add a large scoop of powdered punch mix to a pitcher of water, the solution will taste strong. Each sip will contain many particles of the drink mix. If you add only a spoonful of mix to the water, very few particles of mix will be present in each sip. The drink will taste much too watery.

A solution that has a small amount of solute compared to the amount of solvent is called a **dilute** solution. In a dilute solution, solute particles are spread far apart in the solvent. Some people might say that a dilute solution is weak.

In a **concentrated** solution, particles of solute are much closer together than in a dilute solution. In this type of solution, there is a large amount of solute compared to the amount of solvent. If someone says that a punch is "strong," the person means that it is concentrated. It contains a lot of punch particles in a cup of water.

Dissolving Faster

How can you make a solid dissolve faster in a liquid? To answer this question, review how dissolving takes place.

When a solute such as sugar is added to a solvent such as water, the solvent particles must collide with the solute in order to knock particles of solute free. Molecules of the solute and solvent have an attraction for one another. They must be near one another for that attraction to have an effect. Anything that increases the chances for solvent and solute molecules to collide should speed up the dissolving process. Can you think of any ways to do this?

Think about a large group of classmates sitting at their desks. Are these classmates likely to bump into one another? Now suppose these same classmates started moving around the room. Are collisions more likely between classmates? How would the chance of collisions change if your classmates moved faster?

Similarly, stirring a solution makes the particles of both the solvent and solute move around more. Increased movement means increased collisions. It also means that particles of solute can move away from a solid faster so that the solvent can contact more undissolved solute. You can see in the flask to the right that the blue copper sulfate crystals are resting on the bottom of the unstirred flask. Only the particles of water that are directly in contact with the crystals are causing them to dissolve.

Water particles are always moving. Therefore, if you wait long enough, the crystals in the flask will eventually dissolve. You can make that happen much faster by stirring the mixture. Stirring increases collisions between the particles of copper sulfate and the water particles, spreading the copper sulfate more quickly.

Stirring

Stirring makes the water and copper sulfate particles collide more often, so the rate of dissolving increases. ▼

Increasing Surface Area

▲ *Squeezing the lemons and crushing the sugar make the solutes dissolve faster.*

The photo to the left shows some ingredients you might use to make lemonade. Would you throw the lemons in whole or would you cut them up? Would you use sugar cubes or sugar grains?

To make lemonade, you'd probably cut up or even squeeze the lemons. Experience has taught you that the smaller you make the pieces, the faster they will dissolve. To understand why this works, consider how dissolving takes place. The pictures below will help.

Recall that dissolving can only take place at the surface. How many surfaces does the whole sugar cube have? By breaking the cube in half, you increase the number of surfaces to 12. Notice in the drawing that each time you break the cubes into smaller pieces you increase the number of surfaces and, therefore, the surface area. The surface area of an object is the sum of the areas of all its surfaces.

Particles of solute can only escape into the solvent at a surface. When you increase the surface area of a sugar cube, more sugar particles are able to make contact with the water and then escape. The more particles that escape, the faster the solute dissolves.

It's not always possible to stir or crush a solute. How else could you speed up the time it takes to dissolve a substance? Consider the two ways to make tea shown in the pictures on the next page. Is it easier to make tea by using hot water or cold water? Why?

The color and flavor of tea come from substances found in tea leaves. In order to form the solution you know as tea, water has to dissolve these substances and carry them out of the tea leaves. The more contact the water has with the leaves, the more collisions will occur between the water molecules and the solute.

Surface Area

This sugar cube has been cut into smaller and smaller pieces. Notice how the number of surfaces also increases. ▼

Cold water

Hot water

Heating a substance makes its particles move faster and bounce around more. This increased movement affects a dissolving solute in several ways. First, particles of hot water collide with the leaves in the tea bag harder and more often than do particles in cold water. Second, heat from the water causes the tea particles to move faster and spread farther apart. Therefore, it doesn't take as much energy to break them loose. Third, because of the motion of the water, the dissolved tea particles move away from the bag more quickly. This movement leaves new surfaces for the water to contact.

Many solids and liquids dissolve better in a heated solvent. Heating a solvent not only increases the rate of dissolving, but it also increases the amount of solute that will dissolve in it. Because particles of hot water are farther apart than in cold water, there's more space between them for solute particles. In this way, a more concentrated solution can form.

Heating

▲ *Fast-moving molecules in the boiling water will collide harder and more often with the leaves in a tea bag than the slow-moving molecules in cold water will.*

Lesson 2 Review

1. Describe what happens to particles when solutions form.
2. Describe several different types of solutions.
3. How can you make materials dissolve faster?
4. **Context Clues**
   Use context clues on page B43 to write a definition for the word *hydrocarbon*.

Investigate Activity

Investigating Solutions

Process Skills

Process Skills

- predicting
- observing
- communicating
- inferring
- classifying

Materials

- funnel
- vegetable oil
- clear plastic bottle with lid
- water
- blue or green food coloring

Getting Ready

In this activity, you will mix several materials to see which are solvents and which are solutes.

Review the terms *solvent, solute,* and *solution.*

Follow This Procedure

1. Make a chart like the one shown. Use your chart to record your predictions and observations.

In the bottle	Predictions	Observations
Oil and water		
Oil, water, and food coloring		

2. Use a funnel to pour oil into the plastic bottle until it is about half full.

3. What will happen if you add water to the bottle of oil? Record your **prediction.**

4. Add water to the bottle until it is almost full, as shown in the photo. Tightly cap the bottle and mix the contents by gently tipping the bottle upside down three or four times. Record your **observations.**

5 What will happen if you add food coloring to the bottle of oil and water? Record your prediction.

6 Add 3 drops of food coloring to the bottle. Tightly cap the bottle and mix the contents by gently tipping the bottle upside down 10 times. Record your observations.

Safety Note *Handle the food coloring carefully. It will stain skin and clothing.*

Interpret Your Results

1. Communicate. Tell what you observed when you mixed the water and the oil. What explanation can you give for these results?

2. What can you **infer** from the results of this activity about the solubility of food coloring in water and in oil? What evidence do you have to support your inferences?

3. Classify the materials in the bottle as solvents or solutes.

Inquire Further

How does temperature affect the solubility of the materials in the bottle? Develop a plan to answer this or other questions you may have.

Self-Assessment

- I followed instructions to test the solubility of substances in a bottle.
- I made **predictions** about the interactions of oil, water, and food coloring.
- I recorded my **observations** of the behavior of solutions as they were mixed together.
- I made **inferences** about the solubility of materials in the bottle.
- I **classified** the materials as solvents or solutes.

You will learn:

- what happens during a chemical reaction.
- what four types of chemical reactions are.
- how energy is involved in chemical reactions.
- what a chemical equation is.

Lesson 3

How Are Chemical Reactions Described?

Pour a little clear liquid into the jar. Add a little of the yellow liquid. Bam! Suddenly, there's a red substance in the jar. The yellow liquid is gone. What happened?

Chemical Reactions

Look at the objects at the bottom of this page. What do they have in common? The necklace is made of silver and the jaguar is made of gold. Silver and gold are elements—the simplest forms of matter. These elements are metals. Nonmetallic elements include the oxygen and nitrogen in the air, carbon in coal, and neon found in some electric signs.

Each element contains only one kind of particle, called an atom. The atoms from one element are different from the atoms of every other element. Because the atoms in each element are different, each element has its own set of properties. Gold is yellow and shiny and can be formed into different shapes. Carbon is black and cracks easily. Oxygen is a colorless gas.

The number of different elements is more than 100, but many of them are not very common. What elements can you name?

These two objects were made from elements that are metals. Compare the metal as it appears in its natural form to its finished form. ▼

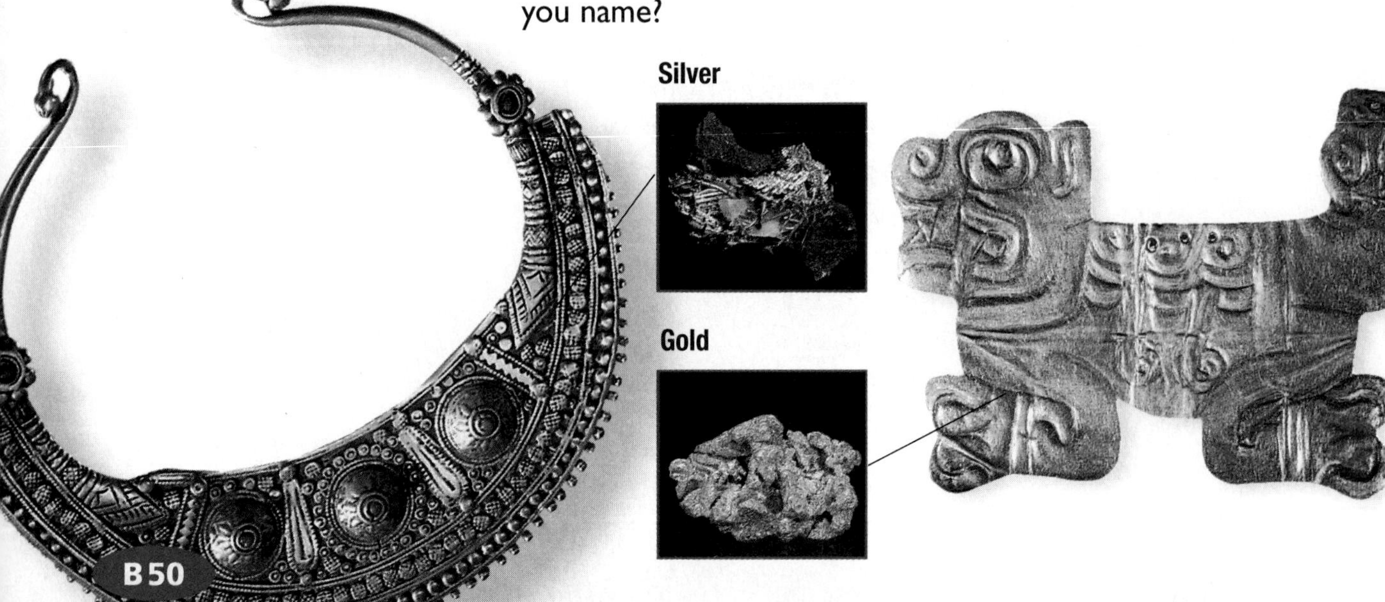

All matter is made up of combinations of elements. You might wonder how so few elements can make up all the matter on Earth. Think about this example. When you mix butter, flour, sugar, eggs, milk, and flavorings together and bake them, the ingredients seem to disappear. The product is a cake. The substances really didn't disappear, but they combined into something that has properties entirely different from those of any of the ingredients.

The same thing happens when elements combine. Look at the diagram of the water molecule. It is made of hydrogen and oxygen atoms. Hydrogen and oxygen are both colorless gases. Hydrogen explodes if you light it. Oxygen is the gas that must be present in order for things to burn. However, when two atoms of hydrogen combine with one atom of oxygen, they make a very different substance—a molecule of water. Water doesn't burn or explode. In fact, it puts out fires!

Water is a compound—a substance in which two or more elements are held together by a chemical bond. This chemical bond is an attraction between the atoms in the compound. Sugar, salt, and rust are all compounds. Sugar is made of the elements carbon, hydrogen, and oxygen. Salt is made of sodium and chlorine. Rust is made of iron and oxygen.

The properties of a compound always differ from the properties of the elements in it. Properties of a substance include its color, hardness, state, and whether or not it will dissolve in water.

Compounds can be separated into their elements or combined with another compound to form new substances. The process by which new substances with new properties form is called a chemical reaction. In a chemical reaction, each substance that undergoes the chemical reaction is a **reactant.** It's the substance that you begin with. Any new substance that is formed during the chemical reaction is a **product.**

Glossary

reactant (rē ak′tənt), a substance that undergoes a chemical reaction, often by combining with another substance

product (prod′əkt), a substance that is formed in a chemical reaction

This flowing water is made of tiny molecules made of two hydrogen atoms and one oxygen atom. A chemical bond holds the atoms together. ▼

Sometimes it's difficult to tell whether a chemical reaction is actually taking place. For example, if you open a bottle of carbonated water, you see bubbles in the liquid that you couldn't see before. Has a new substance formed? No, carbonated water is a solution of a gas, carbon dioxide, dissolved in a liquid, water. When you remove the cap from the bottle, you release the pressure on the solution, and bubbles of carbon dioxide gas form. The carbon dioxide isn't a product because it was there before you removed the cap. Therefore, no chemical reaction took place.

In the picture to the left, you also can see bubbles forming. Is this a chemical reaction? In this case, it is. If you drop an antacid tablet into a glass of water, bubbles form so quickly that they can even splash liquid out of the glass. These bubbles are made of the same gas as in the carbonated water—carbon dioxide. However, this carbon dioxide wasn't present in the tablet. It formed when the compounds in the tablet and the water chemically reacted. The antacid tablet is a reactant. The bubbles of carbon dioxide are products.

▲ *The bubbles forming in the glass are one of the products of the reaction between the tablet and the water.*

Chemical reactions take place all around you. Whenever wood burns, a chemical reaction takes place. Wood is made from a mixture of compounds. When wood burns, some of these compounds react with oxygen that is present in the air. During the reaction, the compounds that make up the wood change, and new products form. These products are gases and ashes, which are mostly carbon.

When food cooks, grass grows, cars rust, or a cut on your finger heals, chemical reactions are taking place. Even thinking is the result of chemical reactions. What other chemical reactions are you familiar with? (Remember—a new product must form if a reaction takes place.)

Some reactions happen quickly. The reaction in which an antacid tablet combines with water to produce carbon dioxide is one example. Other examples are matches burning, dynamite exploding, and lightning bugs flashing.

Other reactions happen very slowly, such as when rust forms from the iron on this can. You don't notice anything happening, but eventually you see something that wasn't there before—the rust.

Remember that if a process is a chemical reaction, one or more new substances must form. The new substances have different properties from those of the reactants.

▲ *The rust on this can is the product of the chemical reaction of iron with the oxygen in the air.*

Types of Chemical Reactions

What a breakfast! You burned your breakfast toast, and the bananas were brown. These are just two of the thousands of different chemical reactions that go on all around you every day. In most cases, you've gotten so used to them that you don't notice. Chemical changes are even going on inside you as you digest your breakfast!

Do all these changes around you have anything in common? As you learned earlier in the chapter, there are only about 100 different elements, and only about half of them are very common. The same few elements are involved in most of the reactions around you. However, these few elements can create thousands of compounds. How can this happen?

Think about the word *rate*. It contains only four letters, but many other words can be made from those same four letters. The picture shows some of those words. What others can you think of?

Likewise, elements can combine in different ways to form the compounds around you. Those compounds can react to form thousands of products.

With so many different chemical reactions going on, it might be confusing to understand how chemical reactions form new products. Luckily, elements react in only a few different ways. You can read about four kinds of chemical reactions on the following two pages.

Like the letters in these words, elements combine in different ways to make many different compounds. ▼

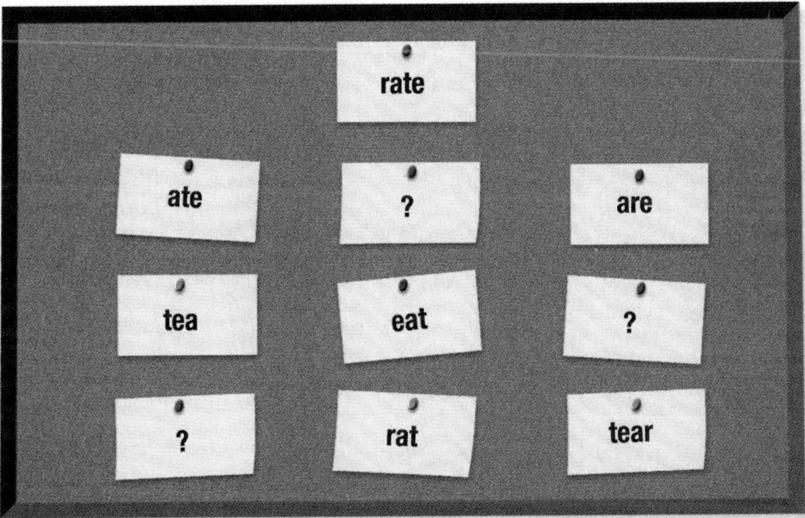

The pictures on these pages show the four main types of chemical reactions. For each picture, a diagram shows what happens to the elements and compounds during the reaction. Each colored ball stands for one substance. A substance can be either an element or a group of elements that stay together. Two balls together represent a compound. Follow the bouncing balls!

Substances Combine

In the first type of chemical reaction, two substances combine to form a single new substance. In 1937, the hydrogen gas that made the airship Hindenburg *float combined with oxygen in the air to produce water. The reaction gave off so much heat that the airship exploded and burned.* ▶

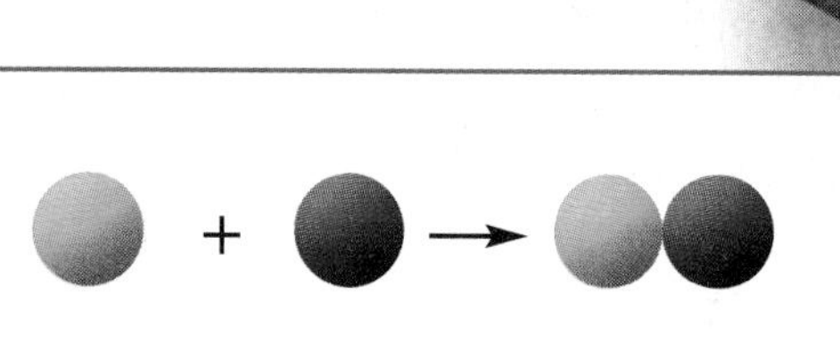

A Substance Breaks Apart

◀ *In the second type of reaction, a single substance breaks apart into two new substances. When sugar burns, it breaks apart into carbon and water. The carbon is the black substance in the pan, and the water moves into the air as a gas.*

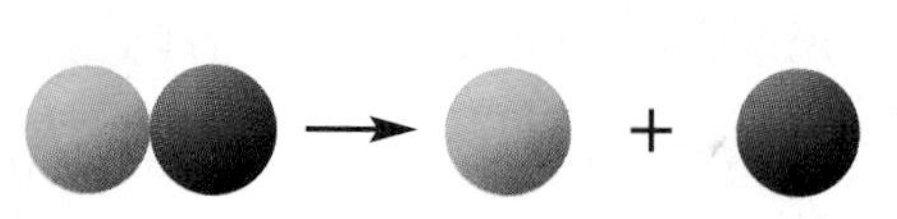

One Element Replaces Another

In the third type of chemical reaction, one element takes the place of another element in a compound. The girl's bracelet is made of the element copper. Her skin contains many compounds. When the copper switches places with an element from one of the compounds, it forms the new green-colored compound on her skin. ▶

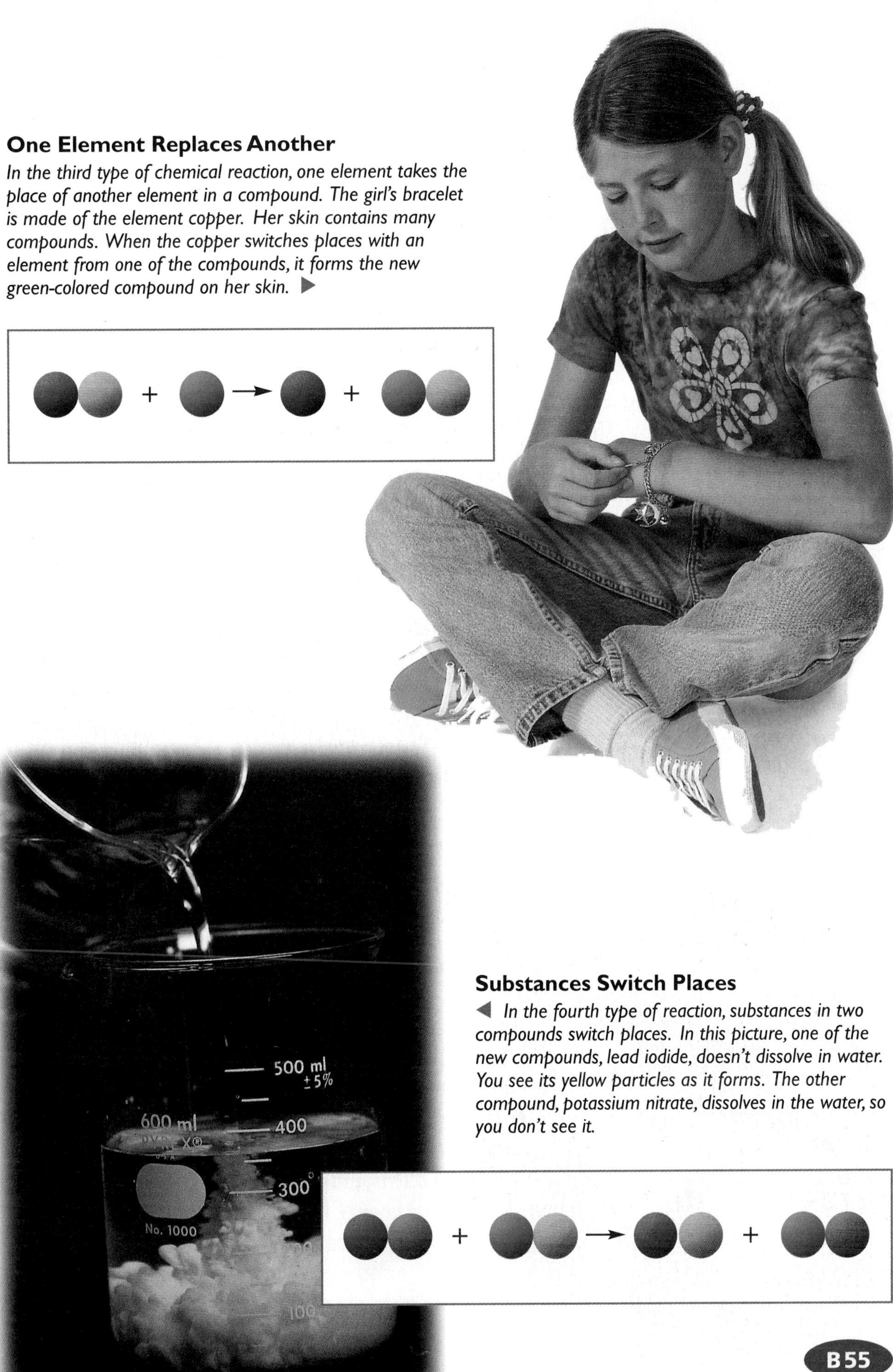

Substances Switch Places

◀ *In the fourth type of reaction, substances in two compounds switch places. In this picture, one of the new compounds, lead iodide, doesn't dissolve in water. You see its yellow particles as it forms. The other compound, potassium nitrate, dissolves in the water, so you don't see it.*

▲ *Chemical reactions inside the firefly produce light.*

Energy in Chemical Reactions

Why do we eat food, burn gasoline in our cars, and use gas, oil, wood, or coal to heat our homes? Energy! It takes energy to do work, to make things move, and to allow our bodies and machines to work the way they're supposed to. The firefly shown to the left also needs energy from the food it eats to produce its light. How is the energy from the food released?

Suppose you have two magnets that are held fast together. To separate the magnets you have to use energy to overcome the attraction between them and pull them apart. If you add enough energy, you can pull the magnets so far apart that they won't draw together again. In a similar way, during a chemical reaction you have to add energy to break the bonds holding the atoms in the reactants together.

Now suppose you move the separated magnets around on the table top. At some point, the two magnets get close enough together that they attract each other. Snap! They quickly move together. If you had your finger between them when it happened, you'd feel the energy that is released when they come together. Particles of matter also move around. As atoms of elements come together to form compounds, energy is released too.

▲ *The burning of wood is an exothermic reaction that not only keeps itself going but produces extra energy for cooking.*

In order to start the fire in the picture to the left, someone had to light it. Doing so added enough energy to break some bonds that hold together the atoms in the compounds that make up the wood. As a result, chemical reactions take place to form new products. When the products form, energy is released. This released energy causes more atoms in the compounds to break apart and form more of the products. In this way, the reaction keeps going until all the reactants are used up.

When wood burns, the reaction is an **exothermic reaction** —more energy is given off than is taken in. Some exothermic reactions, such as in explosions, give off heat very quickly. In others, such as the rusting of iron, heat is given off so slowly that you don't notice it.

Glossary

Glossary

exothermic reaction (ek/sō thėr/mik rē ak/ shən), a chemical reaction in which more energy is given off than is taken in

Not all energy given off in exothermic reactions is heat. The firefly produces light as a result of an exothermic reaction. This reaction occurs when the food the firefly eats is slowly changed in its body.

People use exothermic reactions to heat their homes and run their cars. People are always looking for more sources of energy to keep things running. A fuel is a substance used as a source of chemical energy. Many of the fuels we use, such as food, gasoline, oil, and natural gas, come from once-living things. Remains of ancient plants and animals were buried under tons of rock. Over millions of years, heat and pressure broke these remains down to create the compounds we use as fuels. These fuels are called carbon fuels. What things can you think of that use carbon fuels?

Not all reactions give off energy. For example, water can be taken apart to form hydrogen and oxygen. This reaction does not give off energy—it needs energy.

A very strong attraction exists between the hydrogen and oxygen atoms in a water molecule. In order to pull hydrogen and oxygen atoms away from each other, you have to add enough energy to overcome that attraction. However, very little energy is given off as hydrogen and oxygen—the products—form. This type of reaction is an **endothermic reaction**—a reaction that takes in more energy than it gives off.

Endothermic reactions don't keep going on their own. To take water apart, you add electrical energy to the water. Bubbles of hydrogen and oxygen form. If you turn off the electricity, the reaction stops. No more bubbles!

The boy in the picture is using an endothermic reaction to treat his wounded knee. When the boy squeezes the pack, he breaks a seal between the reactants, allowing them to mix. As the reactants mix, they use energy from the surrounding air and the boy's body to keep the reaction going. The pack feels cold because heat flows away from the boy's body.

Glossary

endothermic reaction (en′dō thėr′mik rē ak′shən), a chemical reaction in which more energy is taken in than is given off

The endothermic reaction that takes place in this cold pack keeps the boy's knee from swelling. ▼

Glossary

Glossary

formula (fôr′myə lə), arrangement of symbols that shows both the kinds and number of atoms in a compound

chemical equation (kem′ə kəl i kwā′zhən), an arrangement of symbols and formulas used to show what happens during a chemical reaction

You use symbols to represent the names of the elements neon (Ne), argon (Ar) and silicon (Si). ▼

Chemical Equations

What state do you live in? When you write the name of your state, you probably use an abbreviation, such as NC for North Carolina or NJ for New Jersey. It's much faster than writing out the whole name.

Scientists use abbreviations for the names of elements. The abbreviation for an element is called a symbol. For example, the pictures show the symbols for three common elements. Can you tell what element each symbol stands for? What other symbols do you know?

A **formula** is an abbreviation for a compound. The formula groups the symbols of the elements that make up the compound. The arrangement of symbols shows both the kind and number of atoms in a compound. For example, the formula for water, H_2O, tells you that water contains hydrogen and oxygen. It also tells you that a molecule of water contains two hydrogen atoms and one oxygen atom. Compare the formula with the picture of the water molecule on page B51.

Scientists use symbols and formulas to show what happens during a chemical reaction. This arrangement of symbols, formulas, and numbers is called a **chemical equation.** Look at the chemical equation below.

reactants			→	products
Fe	**+**	**S**	**→**	**FeS**
iron	(combines with)	sulfur	(to produce)	iron sulfide

This equation tells you that one atom of Fe (iron) combines with one atom of S (sulfur) to produce one molecule of FeS (iron sulfide). The arrow in a chemical equation means "produces." The reactants are written to the left of the arrow and the products are written to the right.

Now study the equation for the formation of water.

$$2H_2 + O_2 \rightarrow 2H_2O$$

Notice that hydrogen and oxygen are written H_2 and O_2. That means that molecules of oxygen gas and hydrogen gas each contain two atoms joined by a chemical bond. The air you breathe contains H_2 and O_2 molecules.

Find the number 2 written before each of the H symbols in the equation. These numbers refer to the number of molecules of each substance. When no number is present, you know that there is only one molecule of the substance. In this equation, two molecules of hydrogen gas combine with one molecule of oxygen gas to produce two molecules of water.

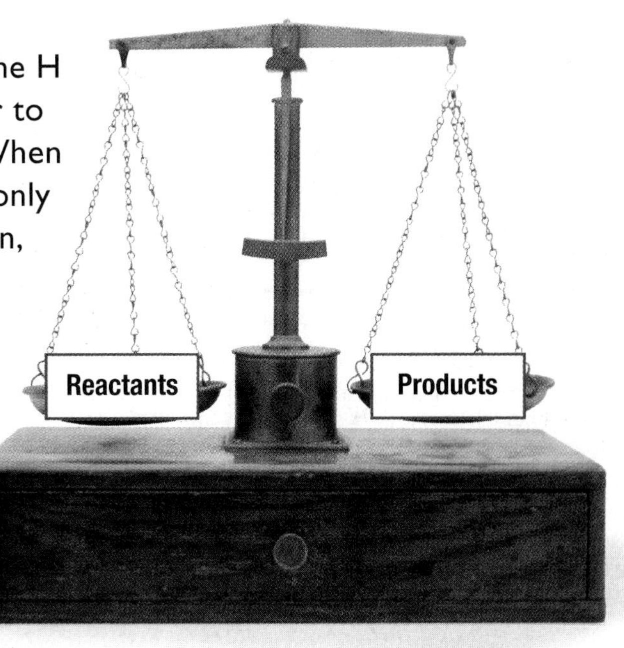

Conservation of Mass

▲ *The Law of Conservation of Mass states that in a chemical reaction, no mass is lost. The mass of the reactants equals the mass of the products.*

Notice that the number of oxygen and hydrogen atoms is equal on both sides of the equation. Every time matter goes through a chemical change, the same amount of matter is present afterward as before. That is, the number of atoms of each element always stays the same. No atoms are destroyed and no new atoms are made. Instead, atoms change how they are arranged or connected with one another.

If you write a chemical equation correctly, the number of atoms on the left of the equation will equal the number on the right side. This balance shows that no atoms have been created or destroyed. A scientific law, known as the Law of Conservation of Mass, states that atoms are saved—or conserved—during a chemical reaction. Study the equation for the formation of water. Does the number of atoms in the reactants equal the number of atoms in the products?

Even when something seems to be smaller after a reaction, such as when a piece of wood burns into a tiny pile of ashes, no atoms were lost. In burning, most of the atoms in the products go into the air as gases. You can't see them, but they're still there!

Lesson 3 Review

1. What happens during a chemical reaction?
2. Describe four types of chemical reactions.
3. How is energy involved in chemical reactions?
4. What is a chemical equation?
5. **Context Clues**
   What does the phrase *chemical bond* in the third paragraph on page B51 mean?

Investigate Activity

Investigating Temperature Change in a Reaction

Process Skills

Process Skills

- estimating and measuring
- predicting
- observing
- inferring

Materials

- safety goggles
- thermometer
- graduated plastic cup
- vinegar
- plastic spoon
- baking soda
- clock or watch with second hand
- paper towels

Getting Ready

In this activity, you will observe a chemical reaction that involves a temperature change.

Mix the ingredients slowly to prevent them from overflowing. Have paper towels on hand.

Follow This Procedure

1. Make a chart like the one shown. Use your chart to record your prediction and observations.

Predict: Will the temperature increase or decrease?

Time	Temperature
Before reaction	
30 seconds	
60 seconds	
2 minutes	
3 minutes	
5 minutes	
10 minutes	

2. Put on your safety goggles. Place a thermometer in the cup. Pour just enough vinegar into the cup to cover the bulb of the thermometer, about 30 mL. **Measure** the temperature of the vinegar, and record it in your chart in the row labeled "Before reaction."

3. When you add baking soda to the vinegar, a chemical reaction and a temperature change will occur. Before you add the baking soda, **predict** whether the temperature of the materials after the reaction will be higher or lower than the starting temperature. Record your prediction in your chart.

4. Add about one-half spoonful of baking soda to the vinegar. Stir the materials. Then add one more half spoonful of baking soda as shown in the photo.

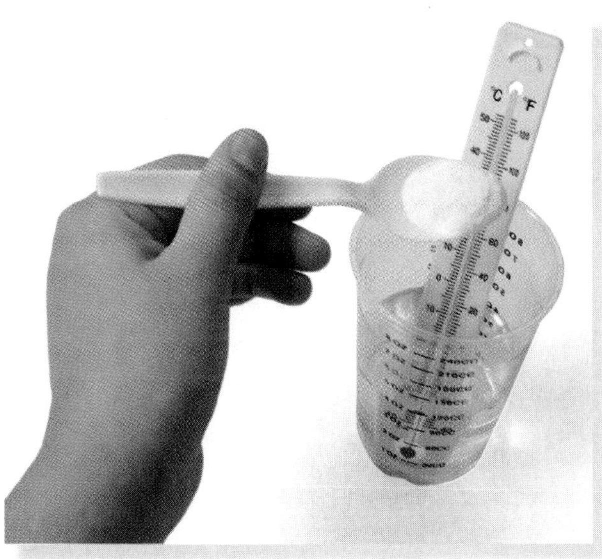

❺ Read and record the temperature of the materials after 30 seconds.

Self-Monitoring

Have I read the thermometer and recorded the temperature correctly?

❻ Continue to record the temperature for 10 minutes at the time intervals shown in the chart or until the reaction has stopped.

Interpret Your Results

1. What happened when you added the baking soda to the vinegar? Describe at least two **observations** that show that a chemical reaction occurred.

2. List the reactants in the chemical reaction. What do you know about the products of the chemical reaction?

3. Look at your measurements. What happened to the temperature of the ingredients when you combined them?

4. Make an **inference.** Was the chemical reaction exothermic, giving off heat? Or was it endothermic, taking in heat? Use your measurements to support your inference.

Inquire Further

Is the melting of ice an exothermic or endothermic change? Develop a plan to answer this or other questions you may have.

Self-Assessment

- I followed instructions to produce a chemical reaction.
- I made and recorded **predictions** about the temperature change that would occur when the materials were combined.
- I recorded my **measurements** of the temperature of the mixture as the chemical reaction progressed.
- I used my **observations** to determine whether a chemical reaction was occurring.
- I used my measurements to make an **inference** about whether the chemical reaction was exothermic or endothermic.

You will learn:

- what acids and bases are.
- what the pH scale is.
- how changes in pH affect the environment.
- what neutralization is.

Lesson 4

What Are the Properties of Acids and Bases?

"Here! Eat this acid!" Would you do it? Believe it or not, you probably already have! Yuk! Whenever you eat grapefruit, drink lemonade, or use vinegar in salad dressing, there's acid in your food. Luckily, it's not very strong.

Glossary

Glossary

acid (a′sid), a compound that releases hydrogen ions in water

Acids and Bases

When you think of an acid, you might picture a scary, smoking liquid eating away at a piece of metal. Some acids do react that way, but many acids are much more common and safer. Grapefruit, lemons, and vinegar taste sour because they contain acids. The word *acid* comes from the Latin word *acidus,* which means "sour." All **acids**, such as the ones in the picture, taste sour. They also have some other properties in common.

All acids contain hydrogen atoms. Hydrogen atoms are neutral—that is, they have equal numbers of positive and negative charges. When some elements combine, atoms of one element can lose negative charges to atoms of the other element. That leaves the atoms of one element with more negative charges and atoms of the other element with more positive charges. These charged atoms are called ions.

Common Acids

Many common substances contain acids. Which of these acids are unsafe to handle? ▼

When an acid compound is added to water, the acid dissolves in the water to form an acid solution that contains hydrogen ions. A hydrogen ion has a positive charge and is written H^+.

The more hydrogen ions the acid releases when it dissolves in water, the stronger the acid is. Strong acids burn your skin and are poisonous. They react quickly with many metals, releasing hydrogen gas. That's where the popular image of smoking acids comes from. Weak acids give foods the sour, sharp taste that you find in vinegar, soda water, spinach, and the apple, lime, and lemon in the picture.

Your stomach contains an acid that dissolves your food. If you eat too many pickles or other sour foods, the acid can become too strong, giving you a "sour" stomach.

The products in the picture below contain **bases**. Bases release hydroxide ions in water. A hydroxide ion is written OH^-. It's made of oxygen and hydrogen atoms and has a negative charge.

Just as with acids and hydrogen ions, the more hydroxide ions that are released into the water as a base dissolves, the stronger the base is. Bases taste bitter and feel slippery. Soap is made from a base. Weak bases are found in baking soda and some antacids. Strong bases are often found in cleaning products, such as ammonia.

It's important to remember that strong bases such as lye, which is used to unclog drains, are as dangerous and poisonous as strong acids. They can burn your skin just as badly.

Glossary

base (bās), a compound that releases hydroxide ions when dissolved in water

▲ *This lime, lemon, and apple contain citric acid. This same acid is used as a medicine and in making dyes.*

Common Bases

◀ *All of these common household bases contain OH in their formulas. When they dissolve in water, they release hydroxide ions (OH^-).*

Glossary

pH scale (pē′āch skāl), a set of numbers between 0 and 14 used to measure the strength of acids and bases

The pH Scale

Because acids and bases can be very dangerous, you shouldn't touch them or taste them. So how do you know if something is an acid or a base?

A simple test using litmus paper can tell you if a substance is an acid or a base. Litmus paper is a paper that changes color when it contacts acids or bases. If you place a strip of blue litmus paper into an acid, the paper changes to a pink or red color. In a base, pink litmus paper changes to blue.

Litmus paper shows whether you have an acid or a base but doesn't show how strong the acid or base is. How strong should your stomach acid be? How much base can laundry soap contain before it burns holes in your clothes?

The strength of an acid or base is measured using a set of numbers from 0 to 14. This set of numbers is called the **pH scale.** As you can see below, the strongest acids are found at the low end of the pH scale. For example, if a compound has a pH of 1, it is a very strong acid.

As the pH number increases, the strength of the acid becomes weaker. An acid with a pH of 3 is weaker than an acid with a pH of 1. A solution with a pH of 7—halfway between 0 and 14—is neutral. It is neither an acid nor a base. Pure water is neutral. What is its pH?

Substances with pHs beyond 7 are bases. The pH scale on the next page shows that the higher the number, the stronger the base.

pH Scale

Substances with very low numbers are strong acids. Those with very high numbers are strong bases. Substances in the middle, such as water, are neutral—neither acid nor base. ▼

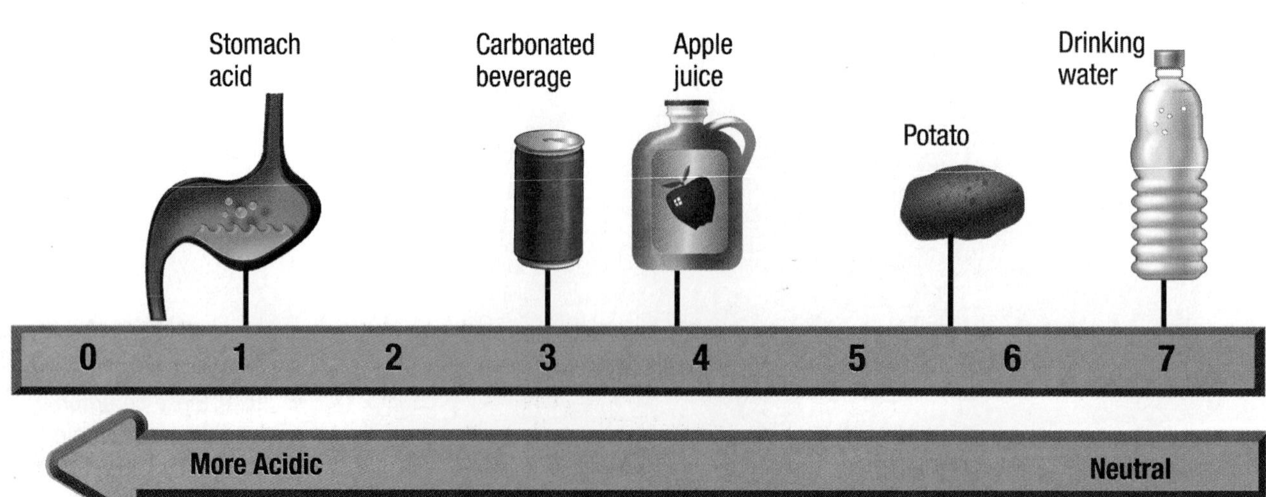

You might be surprised to find out which substances are acids and bases. An egg is slightly basic. Sea water is also. Look at the pH of stomach acid. That's pretty strong, isn't it? The walls of your stomach are made to stand up to strong acid, but if the acid gets stronger, it can irritate your stomach walls. Why could drinking too much carbonated beverage cause this to happen?

Some animals use acid substances to protect themselves. When the ants in the photo sting, they inject formic acid into the victim. The acid causes a burning sensation. Formic acid is a strong acid. At which end of the scale would you find its pH?

Litmus paper can't tell you how strong an acid or a base is, but certain other substances, called indicators, can. **Indicators** are substances that change color at a certain range of the pH scale. Some indicators change color many times as the pH of the solution changes.

A number of common substances act as good indicators. For example, red cabbage juice can change from red to green to greenish yellow as the pH changes. Blueberries and grape juice also contain natural indicators. If you use soap, which is basic, to clean leftover blueberries from a bowl, the blueberries change from reddish-purple to greenish-purple. The next time you're washing dishes and you see the dishwater turn colors, it may be an indicator at work. Try to figure out what it indicates.

Glossary

indicator
(in′də kā′tər), a substance that changes color at a certain range of pH values

▲ *The sting of the stinging ant contains formic acid. Early people boiled stinging ants to produce acid.*

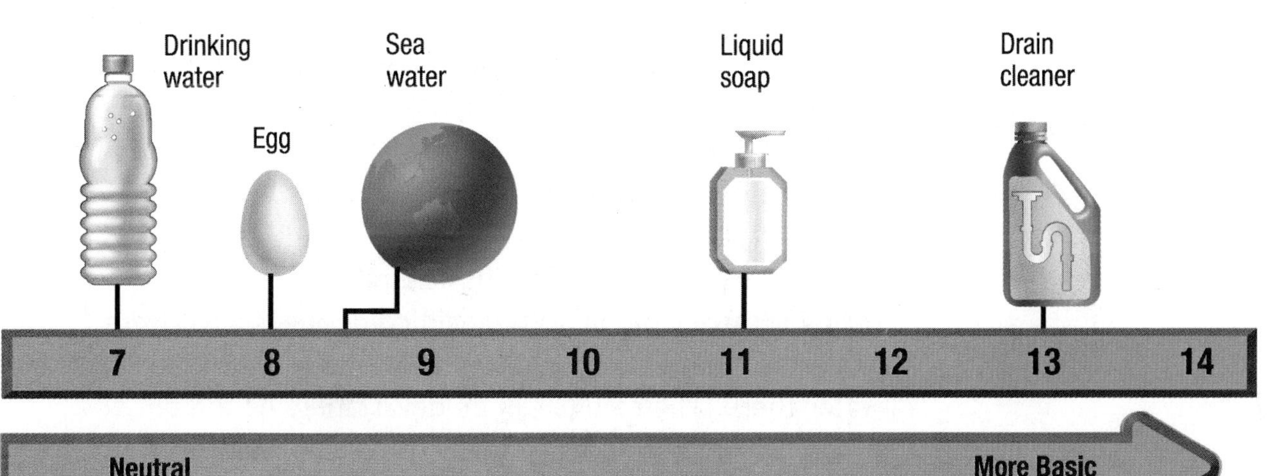

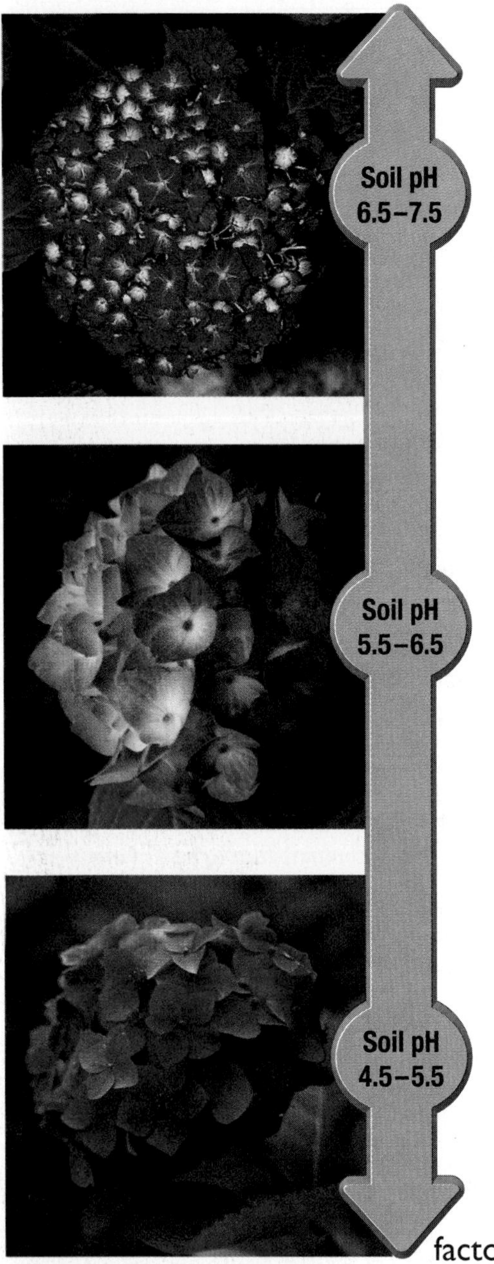

▲ *A gardener can change the color of these hydrangea flowers by adding an acid or base to the soil. Hydrangeas are a natural indicator.*

Effects of pH Changes

The pH of soil, rivers, lakes, and even rain is very important to life on Earth. Many of the plant foods that you eat grow well in soil with a pH range between 5 and 7, which is slightly acidic. Some of the acid gets into the soil as plants decay and acid forms. Rain washes the acid into the soil. This process keeps the soil slightly acid. Farmers also add materials to the soil to keep its pH in the correct range. In dry areas, the soil tends to be basic, and very few plants grow.

The pH of the soil has a very visible effect on the hydrangea plant. As you can see in the pictures, the color of the hydrangea flower varies. When hydrangea plants grow in acidic soil with a pH of 4.5 to 5.5, hydrangea flowers are blue. In soil with a pH of 6.5 to 7.5, the flowers are pink. Between 5.5 and 6.5, they have a color somewhere between blue and pink. Other plants have similar color changes as the pH of the soil changes.

Many lakes have a natural pH between 6 and 7, which is slightly acidic. A large number of species survive well in this range. If the pH isn't kept within this range, most organisms—and species—that live there won't survive.

What might cause a change in pH? Smoke from factories and exhaust from cars contain acid compounds. Sometimes when you're outside, you can feel the effects of these compounds. These acid compounds dissolve in the moisture of your eyes or nose and make them burn. Once these compounds are in the air, they can fall to the ground or dissolve in water that eventually falls as precipitation. This type of precipitation is called acid rain.

Acid rain can have serious effects on living things. For example, as snow that contains acid rain melts in the spring, it carries the dissolved acid compounds into rivers and lakes. These acid compounds lower the pH of the water there. The results can be devastating. As the pH drops, fish stop laying eggs. Many plants and animals die.

Some animals, such as frogs, might not die from the increase in acid, but they are left with nothing to eat. Lowering the pH of the water affects the whole ecosystem of the lake.

The damage caused by acid rain is not limited to lakes and rivers. Acid rain affects organisms that live on land too. Look at the photo to see how acid rain affected trees in one area.

▲ *Acid rain damaged the leaves of this tree. With so much leaf damage, this tree and others in the area died.*

Acid rain can affect buildings and statues too. Acid rain reacts with the compounds in the buildings or statues to produce new compounds. These new compounds dissolve in water and wash away. Little by little, the objects break up. The result can be similar to the damage on the statue in the picture.

To help prevent more acid rain from falling, national and local governments have passed laws. Some control the amount and kinds of smoke that factories can release into the air. Others control emissions on automobiles.

Neutralization

You might wonder what can be done to change substances that are too acidic or basic. Recall that plain water is a neutral substance. When an acid reacts with a base, water is always one of the products. The other product depends on which acid and base you combine.

For instance, study the equation below.

NaOH	+	HCl	→	NaCl	+	H_2O
base	+	acid	→	salt	+	water

▲ *The acid in acid rain can react with and eat away the stone or metal in statues and buildings.*

Sodium hydroxide (NaOH) is the base found in some drain cleaners. Hydrochloric acid (HCl) is an acid used in cleaning concrete. When hydrochloric acid and sodium hydroxide react, the products are table salt (NaCl) and water (H_2O). Mixing the right amount of this strong acid and strong base produces salt water, which is neutral.

Neutralization is a process in which an acid and a base react to produce a salt and water. The kind of salt produced depends on the acid and base that reacted with each other. Sodium chloride is only one of the salts that can be formed during neutralization.

Glossary

neutralization (nü′trə li zā′shən), a process in which an acid and a base react to produce a salt and water

Some people take antacids to ease their excess stomach acid. *Anti* means "against." The word *antacid* is like *anti-acid.* The acid in your stomach is HCl—the same as the one in the neutralization example on page B67. Many antacids are bases that neutralize some of the acid in your stomach. If the antacid were calcium hydroxide, the salt produced in the reaction would be calcium chloride, not sodium chloride.

Salts have many different uses. Look below at the salt found in the Great Salt Lake. This kind of salt is table salt, and it is used by farmers, meat packers, glass makers, and leather processors, as well as in the foods you eat. Baking soda is a salt used in cooking, and another salt, calcium chloride, is used to melt ice on roads and sidewalks. Silver bromide is an important salt used in developing film. Calcium sulfate salt is found in the plasterboard walls of many homes. All of these salts can be produced by reacting an acid with a base.

Far away from any salty ocean, the Great Salt Lake in Utah is a concentrated saltwater solution. The salt comes from deposits in the ground. ▼

Lesson 4 Review

1. What are acids and bases?
2. What is pH?
3. How do changes in pH affect the environment?
4. What is neutralization?
5. **Context Clues**
   The last paragraph on page B66 says that the results of acid rain can be devastating. List the context clues on pages B66 and B67 that help you understand the meaning of *devastating.*

Experimenting with Acids and Bases

Materials

- marker
- masking tape
- 10 small graduated cups
- safety goggles
- baking soda solution
- white vinegar
- red cabbage juice
- distilled water
- dropper
- 9 plastic stirrers
- lemon juice
- carbonated water
- milk of magnesia
- Epsom salt solution
- tap water
- clear cleaning solution

Process Skills

- formulating questions and hypotheses
- identifying and controlling variables
- experimenting
- observing
- collecting and interpreting data
- communicating

State the Problem

Which household substances are acids and which are bases?

Formulate Your Hypothesis

Red cabbage juice is an indicator that changes color when it is added to acids and bases. If you add red cabbage juice to different household substances, which substances will change the cabbage juice to a color that indicates an acid? Which will change to a color that indicates a base? Write your **hypothesis.**

Identify and Control the Variables

For a fair test, you must control the **variables.** The distilled water is your control. It is not acidic or basic. The kind of substance you test is the variable you can change.

Test Your Hypothesis

Follow these steps to perform an **experiment.**

1. Make a chart like the one shown on the next page. Use your chart to record your **observations.**

2. Use a marker and masking tape to label 4 graduated cups: *Indicator (red cabbage juice), Base (baking soda solution), Acid (vinegar),* and *Control (distilled water).*

3. Put on your safety goggles. Pour 15 mL of baking soda solution into the cup labeled *Base.* Pour 15 mL of vinegar into the cup labeled *Acid.* Pour 15 mL of distilled water into the cup labeled *Control.* Pour 15 mL of red cabbage juice in the cup labeled *Indicator.* **Observe** the color of the indicator (Photo A).

Continued →

Photo A

Photo B

4. Use a dropper to add 10 drops of the cabbage juice indicator to the cup labeled *Base*. Stir gently with a clean stirrer. In your chart, record any color changes you **observe** (Photo B).

5. Now add 10 drops of the indicator to the cup labeled *Acid*, and stir with a clean stirrer. Record any color changes you observe in your chart.

6. Add 10 drops of cabbage juice indicator to the distilled water in the control cup. Stir gently with a clean stirrer. Record your observations.

7. Make masking tape labels for the remaining items in the chart. Place each label on a cup.

8. Pour 15 mL of each of the test substances into their respective cups.

 ***Safety Note*** *Do not taste any of the substances.*

9. Add 10 drops of the cabbage juice to each substance, and stir each with a clean stirrer. Record any color changes.

Collect Your Data

Test substance	Color after adding indicator	Acid or base?
Baking soda solution		base
Vinegar		acid
Distilled water		neutral
Lemon juice		
Carbonated water		
Milk of magnesia		
Epsom salt solution		
Cleaning solution		
Tap water		

Interpret Your Data

Complete your chart by filling in the last column. Use your observations of the indicator's color change to help you determine whether each substance is an acid or a base.

Compare Your Results and Hypothesis

Look at the last column of your chart. Describe how you were able to tell which substances were acids and which were bases. How do your results compare with your hypothesis for each substance?

State Your Conclusion

Communicate your results. Explain how you used the color change of the indicator in a known acid (vinegar), base (baking soda solution), and a neutral substance (distilled water) to determine whether other substances were acids or bases. Tell which variables you controlled during the experiment. How would you change the experiment if you were going to repeat it?

Inquire Further

How can you use cabbage juice to develop a pH scale? Develop a plan to answer this or other questions you may have.

Self-Assessment

- I made a **hypothesis** about using an indicator to identify acids and bases.
- I followed instructions to find out which substances are acids and which are bases.
- I identified and controlled **variables.**
- I **collected** my **data** in a chart and **interpreted** the results to determine which substances were acids and which were bases.
- I **communicated** by stating my conclusion.

Chapter 2 Review

Chapter Main Ideas

Lesson 1

- The state in which a substance exists depends on the amount of energy in the particles of the substance.
- Particles of matter gain heat during melting and lose heat during freezing.
- During boiling, particles throughout the liquid have enough energy to escape. With evaporation, only surface particles escape.

Lesson 2

- In a solution, substances mix so that they look like a single substance.
- Both solvents and solutes can be solids, liquids, or gases.
- Crushing, stirring, and heating are three ways to make a solid dissolve faster.

Lesson 3

- During every chemical reaction, one or more new substances are formed.
- There are four major types of chemical reactions.
- Energy is given off or absorbed in chemical reactions.
- Chemical equations show the number and kind of atoms in the reactants and the products.

Lesson 4

- Acids and bases are found in many common substances.
- pH is a measure of the strength of acids and bases.
- Changes in the pH of materials in the environment can have positive and negative effects.
- In a neutralization reaction, an acid and a base react to form water and a salt.

Reviewing Science Words and Concepts

Write the letter of the word or phrase that best completes each sentence.

a. acid
b. base
c. chemical equation
d. concentrated
e. condensation
f. dilute
g. endothermic reaction
h. evaporation
i. exothermic reaction
j. formula
k. indicator
l. neutralization
m. pH scale
n. product
o. reactant
p. solute
q. solvent

1. Water droplets appear on the side of a cold glass by the process of ___.
2. A substance that dissolves other materials is a(n) ___.
3. If you dissolve two cups of sugar in a cup of water, you have made a(n) ___ solution.
4. A(n) ___ is used to determine the pH of an acid or base.
5. A(n) ___ describes what happens when reactants reorganize to form products.
6. A substance that forms during a chemical reaction is a(n) ___.
7. A substance, such as HCl, that releases hydrogen ions in solution is a(n) ___.
8. When water is broken into hydrogen and oxygen, the water is the ___.

9. A teaspoon of lemon juice dissolved in a gallon of water is a ___ solution.

10. The ___ describes the strength of acids and bases.

11. The process in which an acid and a base react to produce a salt and water is ___.

12. The change of state from liquid to gas at the surface of a liquid is ___.

13. When paper burns, heat and light are given off in a(n) ___.

14. The arrangement of symbols showing the number and types of atoms in a compound is a(n) ___.

15. A substance such as NaOH that releases hydroxide ions in solution is a(n) ___.

16. A cold pack used on an injury becomes cold through a(n) ___.

17. Carbon dioxide gas is a(n) ___ in a carbonated beverage.

Explaining Science

Write a paragraph to answer these questions, or discuss them with a classmate.

1. How does a substance change from a solid to a liquid?

2. Give examples of three different types of solutions.

3. How are the four types of chemical reactions alike and different?

4. How can you test a substance to see if it's an acid or a base?

Using Skills

1. Write a short paragraph about indicators. Provide **context clues** that help explain the meaning of the word *indicator.*

2. When electricity is passed through liquid water (H_2O), hydrogen gas (H_2) and oxygen gas (O_2) form. **Classify** this reaction as one of the four major types.

3. Suppose you place a container of water outside on a cold day. In an hour it freezes. What can you **infer** about the air temperature surrounding the container of water?

Critical Thinking

1. Brittany mixed some vinegar and some liquid antacid together to see what would happen. After a lot of bubbles formed, the liquid turned clear. Brittany came back several days later to find the liquid gone and a white solid at the bottom of the cup. Help Brittany **draw a conclusion** about what happened.

2. Suppose that you add some crystals to a glass of liquid at room temperature. As you stir the crystals, the glass gets colder. What can you **infer** about the reaction?

3. You and a friend are considering which beverages to buy at the grocery store. Your friend reads the label on the one you want to buy and notices that one of the ingredients is carbonic acid. She says that because the drink contains acid, it isn't safe to drink. **Make a decision.** Would you buy the drink? Explain your reasoning.

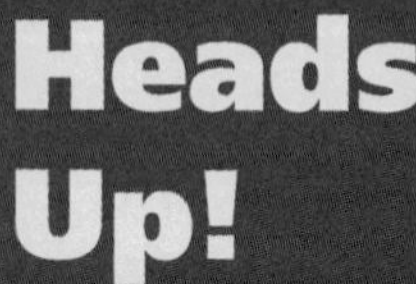

Heads Up!

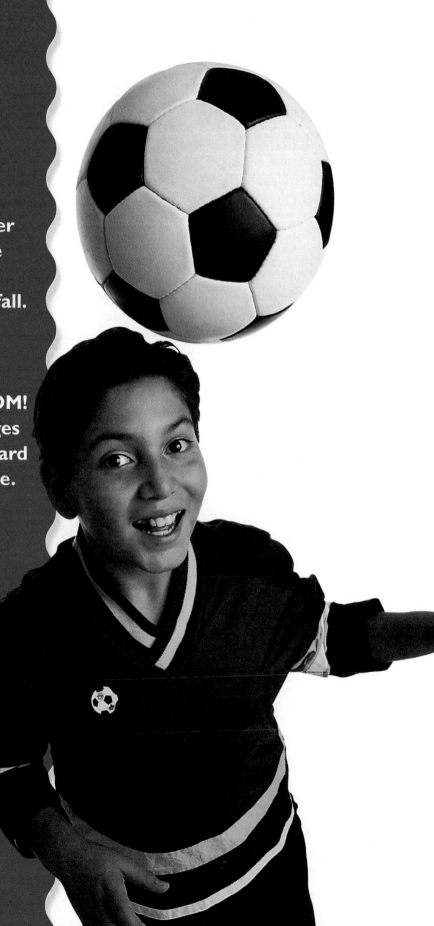

BAM! The other team kicks the ball. It flies up and begins to fall. YES! You get right under it and aim your forehead. BOOM! The ball changes directions toward your teammate. How do forces work together to put you, your team, or the ball in motion?

Chapter 3

Moving Objects

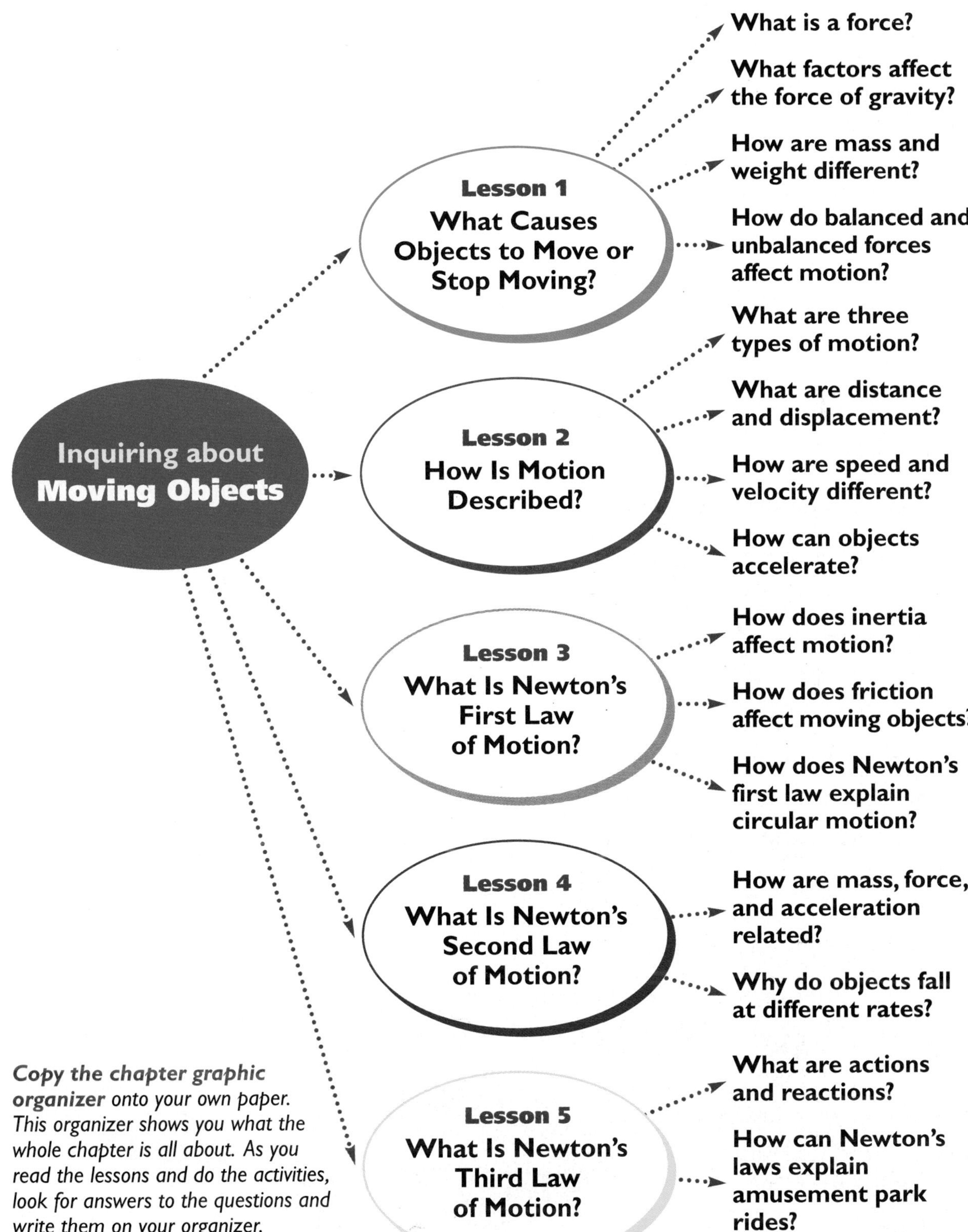

Inquiring about Moving Objects
Lesson 1
What Causes Objects to Move or Stop Moving?
What is a force?
What factors affect the force of gravity?
How are mass and weight different?
How do balanced and unbalanced forces affect motion?
Lesson 2
How Is Motion Described?
What are three types of motion?
What are distance and displacement?
How are speed and velocity different?
How can objects accelerate?
Lesson 3
What Is Newton's First Law of Motion?
How does inertia affect motion?
How does friction affect moving objects?
How does Newton's first law explain circular motion?
Lesson 4
What Is Newton's Second Law of Motion?
How are mass, force, and acceleration related?
Why do objects fall at different rates?
Lesson 5
What Is Newton's Third Law of Motion?
What are actions and reactions?
How can Newton's laws explain amusement park rides?

***Copy the chapter graphic organizer** onto your own paper. This organizer shows you what the whole chapter is all about. As you read the lessons and do the activities, look for answers to the questions and write them on your organizer.*

Explore Activity

Exploring Acceleration

Process Skills

Process Skills

- observing
- predicting
- communicating
- inferring

Materials

- safety goggles
- 10 pennies
- 2 plastic cups
- plastic wrap
- 2 rubber bands
- 10 paper clips
- ruler

Explore

1. Put on your safety goggles. Place 10 pennies in a cup. Cover the cup with plastic wrap and secure the wrap with a rubber band.
2. Repeat step 1 using 10 paper clips.
3. Pick up the cups, one in each hand. **Observe** how their masses compare.
4. Place both cups along the edge of a table. Place a ruler behind the cups, as shown in the photo.
5. Make a **prediction.** What will happen if you push both cups off the table at the same time? Will they fall at the same rate? If not, which will fall faster? **Communicate** the reasons for your prediction to your classmates.
6. Use the ruler to push the cups off the table at the same time. Observe the cups as they fall.
7. Repeat step 6 four more times. Record your observations.

Reflect

1. How did the activity results compare with your prediction?

2. What **inferences** about mass and falling objects can you make from your predictions and observations?

Inquire Further

What would happen if you dropped a table tennis ball and a soccer ball from the same height at the same time? Develop a plan to answer this or other questions you may have.

Identifying Cause and Effect

Throughout this chapter, be aware of ideas that show a **cause**-and-**effect** relationship. When you talk about cause and effect, you are telling why something happens. If you remember that a cause creates a result, or effect, it may help you to better understand what you are reading.

Reading Vocabulary

cause, a person, place, or thing that makes something happen

effect, something that is produced by a cause; a result

Example

When you read Lesson 1, *What Causes Objects to Move or Stop Moving?* look for causes and effects in the photo of the ball and racket on page B78 and below. For example, ask yourself, "What caused the ball to flatten?" Using a chart like the one below can help you identify causes and effects.

Causes	Effects
	ball flattens
	racket indents

Talk About It!

1. How can you find a cause and effect?
2. What causes and effects did you find in the photo?

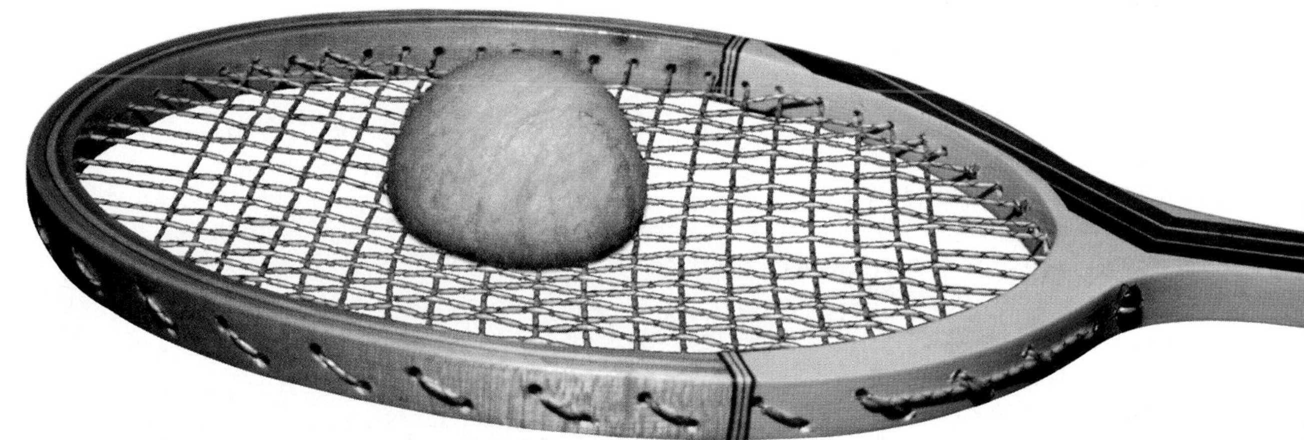

You will learn:

- what a force is.
- what factors affect the force of gravity.
- the difference between mass and weight.
- how balanced and unbalanced forces affect motion.

Lesson 1

What Causes Objects to Move or Stop Moving?

Wham! You hit the ball with your racket. Off it goes—right out of the court! Your swing must have packed a lot of force! Up and up it goes—and then it starts to fall. No matter how hard you hit it, the ball always comes back down. Why is that?

Forces: Pushes and Pulls

When you hit a tennis ball with a racket, you apply a **force**—a push or a pull—to the ball. But did you know that the ball also exerts a force on the racket? Look at the picture. What evidence do you have that these two objects are exerting forces on each other?

The pictures on the next page show other examples of the many types of forces around you. In each picture, is the force a push or a pull? What is the source of each force? What is the result of each force?

It's easy to identify a force when you can see one thing pushing or pulling another. When a tennis player hits a tennis ball, you can see the racket push the ball. Other times, you can't actually see a force acting, but you know it must be there because something moves.

Glossary

Glossary

force (fôrs), a push or a pull

What exerts the force that makes this racket move toward the ball? ▼

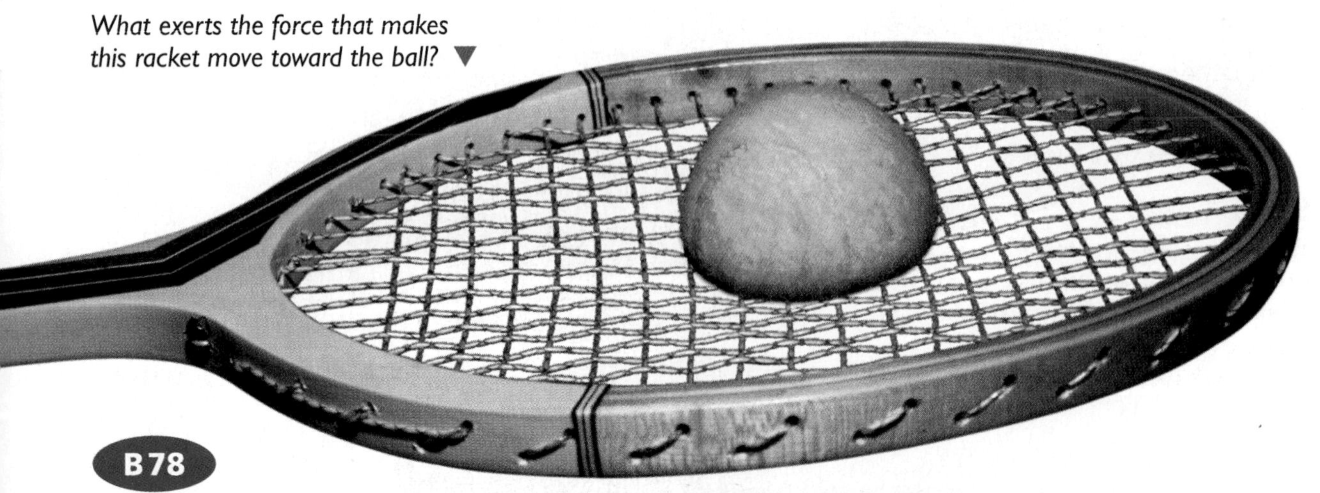

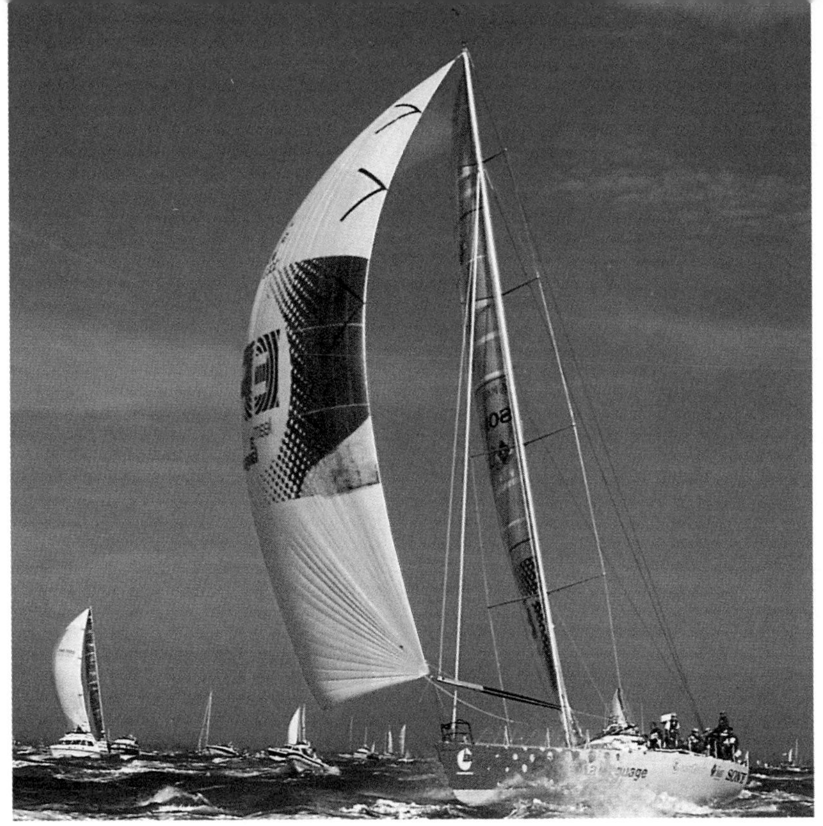

◀ *Sailors can turn the sails on these boats. To go faster, the sailors turn the sails so that they get the greatest push from the wind.*

The sailboats in the picture move because the wind pushes on the sails. You can't see the wind. You can only see the result of its force—the moving boats.

You also can't see the magnetic force that pulls objects toward a magnet, but you can see the objects move as the magnet attracts them. If you place two like poles of a magnet close enough, you can feel the push.

Look at the girl with the balloon. What force is causing her hair to stand out like it is? The girl probably rubbed the balloon against her clothing. Rubbing the balloon against clothing transfers electric charges from the girl's clothing to the balloon. The charges on the balloon attract opposite charges in the girl's hair. These opposite charges pull the girl's hair and the balloon toward each other.

Static Changes

The unlike charges of the balloon and the girl's hair exert a pulling force on each other. These charges are called static charges. What other examples of static charges are you familiar with? ▶

▲ *What would happen to this ball if there weren't gravity between it and Earth?*

Gravity

Earth Science

"What goes up must come down!" You've probably heard someone say that. No matter how hard a person hits the ball in the picture, it will always fall back to Earth. Why? The answer is **gravity.**

Many people think of gravity as the pull of Earth on an object. In reality, just as Earth exerts a pull on the ball, the ball also exerts a pull on Earth. In fact, a force of attraction exists between any two objects. This force is gravity.

You might know that Earth pulls on the moon. Without Earth's pull, the moon would fly off into space. As the moon orbits Earth, it pulls on everything in and on Earth. This pull causes the ocean water to pile up on the side of Earth facing the moon. This bulge of water is a high tide. As high tides form on one area of Earth, water levels drop in other places. This drop produces low tides, like the one below.

Glossary

Glossary

gravity (grav′ə tē), the force of attraction that exists between any two objects

▲ *The force of gravity between Earth and the moon keeps the moon in orbit and pulls ocean water into tides on Earth. People who live near an ocean see its water levels rise and fall twice each day.* ▶

The penguin in the picture is being pulled toward the earth as a result of gravity. Earth pulls on the penguin, but the penguin also pulls on Earth. The pull of gravity between any two objects depends on the amount of matter, or **mass**, each object has. The greater the masses of the objects, the greater the force of gravity between them. Gravity acts equally on both objects. If this is true, then why doesn't the earth jump up to meet the penguin when it leaps from the ice above the ocean?

To answer this question, imagine pulling on a penguin and Earth with the same amount of force. Which would move more? Because Earth has so much mass, the pull of gravity between it and the penguin causes Earth to barely move upward. This same amount of force pulls the penguin, which has much less mass, down toward Earth's center.

Mass isn't the only thing that affects the force of gravity between two objects. Think about this question: How far does an object have to get from Earth before gravity disappears? Did you guess millions of kilometers or more? Even then, a very tiny force acts between the object and Earth. The closer the centers of two objects are, the greater the force of gravity between them. Thinking about another kind of force—magnetic force—might help you understand this. If you hold the unlike poles of two magnets near each other, they quickly snap together. As you move the poles farther apart, the force between them finally gets so weak that it can't pull them together.

Gravity works in a similar way. The force of gravity decreases as you get farther from the center of Earth. When rockets are sent to the moon, Earth's pull decreases as the distance of the rocket from Earth increases. At a certain distance, the moon's pull on the rocket is greater than Earth's pull, and the rocket falls toward the moon. Understanding how gravity works allows scientists to know how fast and in what direction to send rockets so that they can circle Earth or escape its gravity.

Glossary

mass (mas), the amount of matter in an object

The force of gravity between Earth and the penguin is the same. Because the penguin has much less mass, the force moves the penguin much more than it moves Earth. ▼

Glossary

Glossary

weight (wāt), a measure of the pull of gravity on an object's mass

newton (nüt′n), in the metric system, the unit used to measure force or weight

Mass and Weight

Want to lose weight quickly? Go to the moon! Look at the picture below and compare the boy's weight on Earth and on the moon. Why does the boy weigh less on the moon than on Earth?

To answer that question, you need to know about gravity, weight, and mass. Remember that mass is the amount of matter an object has. In the metric system, mass is measured in grams or kilograms. If you walk across the room, travel from home to school, or even fly to the moon, the amount of matter in your body—your mass—doesn't change.

You learned that gravity is the force acting between two objects. Because the mass of any object on Earth is so much less than the mass of Earth itself, everything is pulled toward Earth's center. When you stand on a scale, the scale is actually measuring your **weight**—the force with which Earth is pulling you down. An apple has less mass than you do and, as a result, is not pulled toward Earth's center with as much force. That's why its weight is less than yours.

You probably measure your weight in pounds. Notice that the picture shows the boy's weight in pounds and newtons. In the metric system, the **newton** is the unit used to measure this attraction between an object and Earth. The pineapple on the next page weighs about 10 newtons. Its mass is about 1 kilogram.

People can "lose weight" by going to the moon. Will their clothes feel any looser? ▼

100 lbs
450 N

Earth

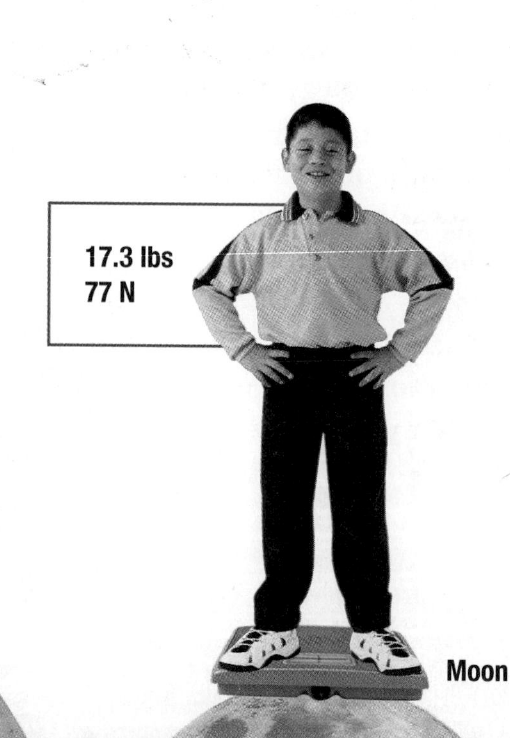

So let's put what you just learned about mass, weight, and gravity together to see why the boy weighs less on the moon than on Earth. The moon has less mass than Earth, and it is smaller in size. Because of this difference, the force with which the moon pulls on an object is only about one-sixth as strong as the pull of Earth. The person weighing 450 newtons on Earth would weigh about 77 newtons on the moon. On the huge planet Jupiter where gravity is stronger, that same person would weigh a whopping 1143 newtons! As an object travels in space, its weight can change from nearly zero to many times its weight on Earth, but its mass is always the same.

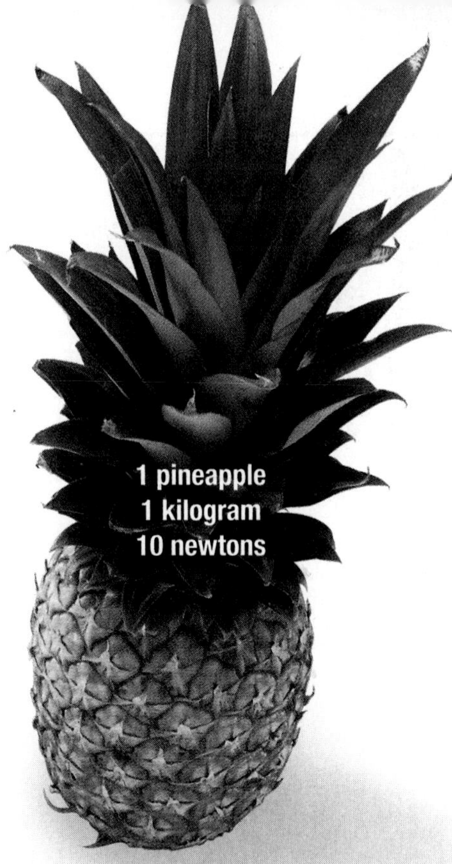

▲ *If another smaller pineapple had a mass that was half as much as the one in the picture, what would it weigh?*

Balanced and Unbalanced Forces

When you're riding a bike, many forces may be acting on you at the same time. Gravity is pulling you down, the wind might be pushing you toward one side or the other, and the forces between the bike's tires and the road are pushing you forward. Most objects have many forces acting on them at all times. When many pushes and pulls are acting on an object at the same time, which way does it move?

Look at the dumbbells below. The dumbbells aren't moving but forces are acting on them. What are these forces? In science, forces are represented by arrows. The length of an arrow shows the strength of the force. The direction of the arrow shows the force's direction. For example, you can show the forces acting on the dumbbells by using two arrows. Because the forces acting on the dumbbells are equal in strength, the arrows are of the same length. Notice how the arrows point in opposite directions.

What do the arrows show about the forces acting on the dumbbell? ▶

Glossary

Glossary

net force (net fôrs), the combination of all the forces acting on an object

balanced forces (bal′ənst fôrs′əs), equal forces acting in opposite directions

The combination of forces acting on an object is called the **net force.** In the case of the dumbbells on page B83, the two forces balance each other out. The net force is zero. You would say that the forces are balanced. **Balanced forces** are equal forces acting in opposite directions.

How would the net force on the dumbbells change if someone picked them up? The girl on the right is lifting two dumbbells. The force of gravity is still acting downward on the dumbbells, but the girl is also exerting an upward force on them.

Let's look at the situation using arrows. Notice that the arrow pointing downward is smaller than the arrow pointing upward because the force exerted by the girl on each dumbbell is greater than the force exerted by gravity. When two forces are exerted in opposite directions, the net force is the difference between the two forces. The result is that each dumbbell moves upward.

Now look at the girl holding the dumbbells over her head. What forces are acting on each dumbbell? How do you know that the forces acting on each dumbbell are balanced?

The girl on the right is lifting the dumbbells. She exerts force on the dumbbells that is opposite and greater than the force of gravity. ▼

▲ *If the train started going uphill, what would have to happen to keep it moving? Why?*

The forces acting on each dumbbell are acting in opposite directions. What happens to the net force when the forces acting on an object are in the same direction?

Because of its great mass, the train in the picture needs two engines to pull it forward. Each engine produces a forward-moving force. How will these forces affect the motion of the train?

When two or more forces act in the same direction, the net force is the combination of all the forces. The net force on the train is the sum of the forces of both engines. This net force causes the train to move forward.

Lesson 1 Review

1. What is a force? Give three examples.
2. What are the two factors that affect the force of gravity between two objects?
3. What is the difference between mass and weight?
4. How do balanced and unbalanced force affect motion?
5. **Cause and Effect**
   When you hit a baseball with a bat, the bat causes the ball to fly off in the opposite direction. What other cause-and-effect relationship happens at the same time?

You will learn:

- what three types of motion are.
- what distance and displacement are.
- how speed and velocity differ.
- how objects can accelerate.

Lesson 2

How Is Motion Described?

"Hey! Slow down! Stand still for a minute, will you?" It's not likely that you'll ever get your wish. Everything in the universe is always moving. Even things that seem to be standing still are in some kind of motion. But what's motion?

Types of Motion

Are you sitting in a chair as you read this lesson? What would you say if someone asked you if you and the chair were moving? You might be surprised to know that both you and the chair are moving at about 1600 kilometers per hour! You and the chair are sitting on the surface of Earth, which rotates once every 24 hours. That's nearly 40,000 kilometers every day! You don't feel that motion because the surface on which you are standing—Earth—is moving too.

How you see an object's motion depends on its **relative motion**, or the position of one object compared to the position of another object. If you compare your position to Earth's surface as you sit on the chair, you sense no motion. However, if you compare your position to the sun's, you would observe motion.

Study the pictures below. In which of the three pictures is the boy moving? The answer depends on what

Glossary

Glossary

relative motion (rel′ə tiv mō′shən), the change in position of one object compared to the position of another

One frame of reference for this series of pictures is the traffic light. What other references could you use to determine if something is moving? ▼

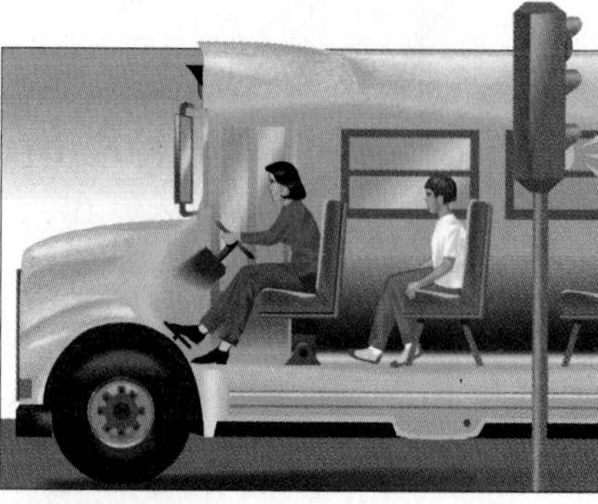

frame of reference you choose. In the first picture, the frame of reference might be the traffic light. If so, then neither the bus, the driver, nor the boy are moving. If you use the same frame of reference—the traffic light—in the next two pictures, what is moving?

Motion is going on all around you. Leaves rustle on the trees, birds dart through the sky, and boats glide over waves. Although many motions seem complicated, they are usually combinations of three types—vibrational, circular, and straight-line.

How are the metal cymbal and the drumhead moving in the picture? They can't move very far because they are attached to other objects. The cymbal and drumhead can only move in a tiny but very rapid back-and-forth motion. This type of motion is called vibration. The vibration of parts of musical instruments creates sound waves in air that carry music to our ears. As vibrations speed up or slow down, you hear different notes. What other things have you seen that move in a vibrating motion?

Have you ever seen a yo yo, such as the one in the picture? As the yo yo moves up and down the string, it moves in a circle around the center of the yo yo. Circular motion is motion around a central position. It is seen in the motion of planets around the sun, a rotating bicycle wheel, and many amusement park rides.

Glossary

frame of reference (frām ov ref′ər əns), the object an observer uses to detect motion

▲ *What force produces the vibrations of the drumhead and cymbal?*

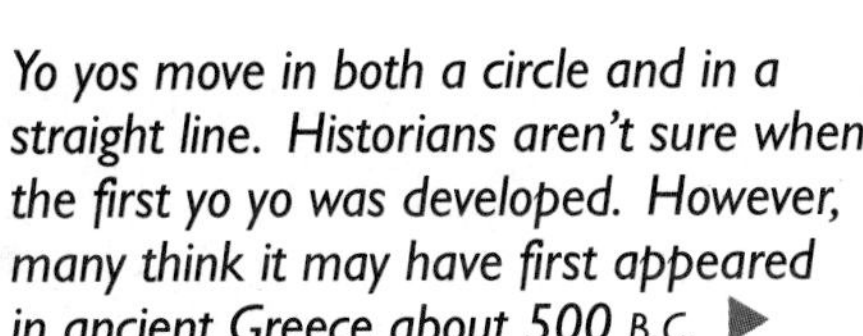

Yo yos move in both a circle and in a straight line. Historians aren't sure when the first yo yo was developed. However, many think it may have first appeared in ancient Greece about 500 B.C. ▶

The photo of the jet shows another type of motion—motion in a straight line. You can tell from the cloud trail following the jet airplane that the pilot flew the plane in a straight line. Many types of motion are straight-line motion. You often walk in a straight line, and bicycles, trains, and cars travel in straight lines.

Think about the types of motion going on with some moving objects around you. What kinds of motion do you see?

The straight line formed by the cloud trail behind the jet shows the direction in which the plane flew. The trail forms when water vapor from the engine exhaust condenses on cold particles in the air. ▼

Distance and Displacement

Have you ever heard the saying, "The shortest distance between two points is a straight line"? The same idea is expressed when you say you are traveling somewhere "as the crow flies" or "in a beeline."

If you were going to a friend's house from your own home, would you be able to go there by traveling in a straight line? Or would you have to make several turns because there are buildings or other structures in the way? You might take a side trip to another friend's house or stop at the store first. When you finally get to the friend's house, the total distance you traveled might be much farther than if you were able to travel in a straight line.

Consider the school in the picture on the next page. The school is 50 meters directly north of the student's home. But the actual path the student takes goes first to the south for 10 meters, west for 150 meters, north for 200 meters, east for another 150 meters, and 10 meters south before she reaches the school. The distance of the path that the girl travels is much longer than the actual distance between the school and her house. To get the total distance traveled, you'd have to add the lengths of all five paths.

10 m + 150 m + 200 m + 150 m + 10 m = 520 m

Distance includes only the sum of the lengths of the paths. The direction of the paths doesn't matter.

When the student reaches the school, how far and in what direction is she from her home? The yellow arrow shows this measurement. The arrow shows that the student's displacement is 50 meters north. Displacement is the direction and shortest distance traveled during a change of position. Displacement must include both the shortest distance between the points and the direction of travel. If the girl traveled from her house to the next house, what would her distance and displacement be?

Now, think about this question: If a race car travels once around a circular track, it may have traveled a distance of a mile. But what is its displacement?

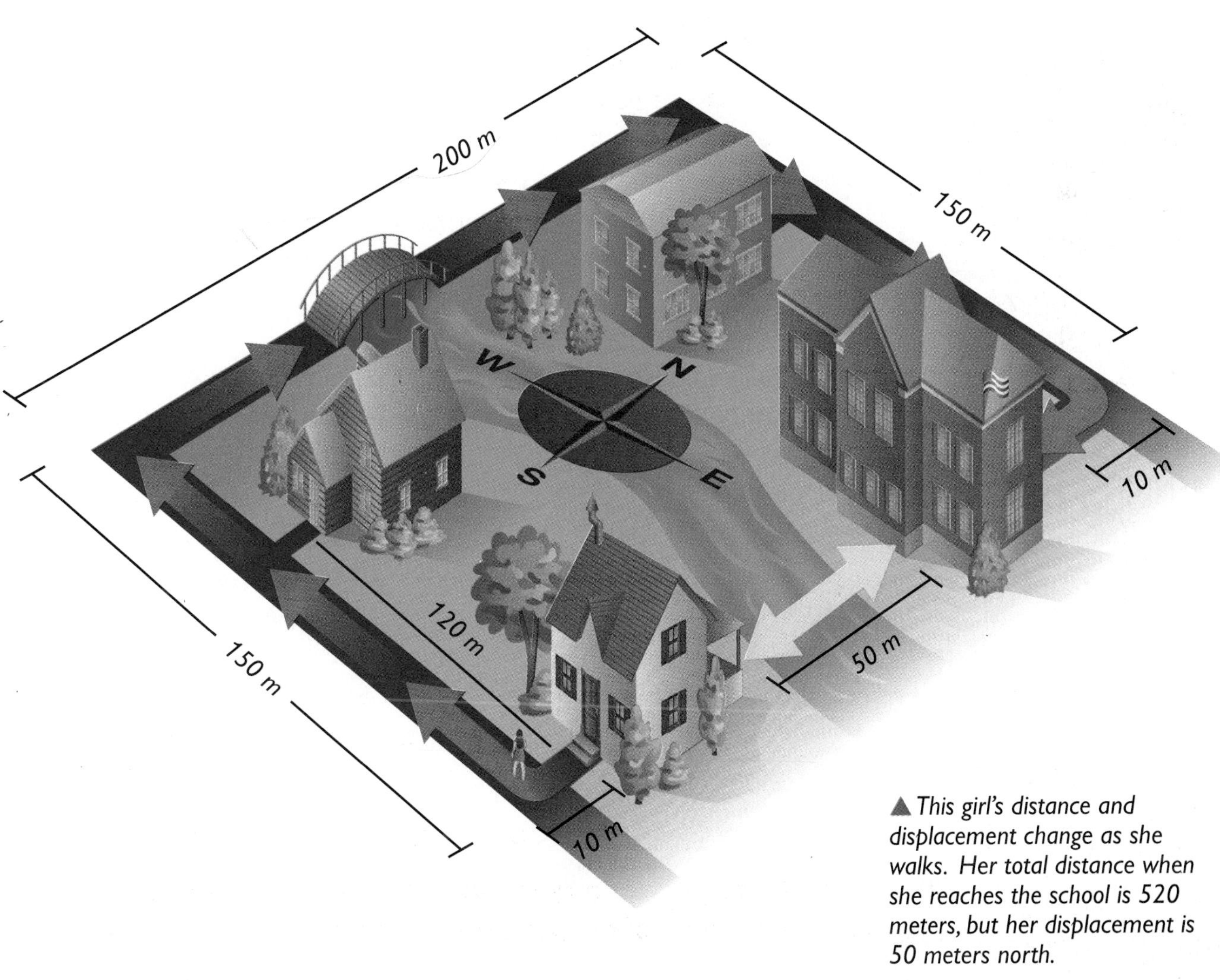

▲ *This girl's distance and displacement change as she walks. Her total distance when she reaches the school is 520 meters, but her displacement is 50 meters north.*

Glossary

speed (spēd), the distance an object moves in a certain period of time

Speed and Velocity

Speed—It tells how fast an object is moving. What's your speed? Are you "speedy," a "slowpoke," or somewhere in between?

The African cheetah in the picture is definitely speedy. The cheetah is the fastest moving animal on Earth. At full speed, it can travel at 110 kilometers—that's 70 miles—an hour. At that speed, the cheetah could keep up with traffic on the fastest highway. Even faster is a rocket that has to overcome Earth's gravity. Its speed is about 10.6 kilometers—about 6 and a half miles—every second. That's fast! Even a snail has speed. It creeps along so slowly that it might appear to be standing still. However, it has speed—0.05 kilometers per hour.

The speed of the cheetah can be written as 110 kilometers per hour, 110 kilometers/hour, or 110 km/hr. Speed always contains a distance unit divided by a time unit. ▼

You can figure out an object's speed if you know the distance it traveled and how long it took. Just use this equation:

speed = distance ÷ time

Here's an example. In the picture below, point A is 8 kilometers from point B. Suppose the runner travels that distance on the running path in one hour. His speed is:

8 kilometers ÷ 1 hour = 8 kilometers/hour

The runner's speed is 8 kilometers per hour.

The runner's speed probably isn't the same over the entire length of the path. He most likely travels slower going uphill than down. His speed is probably faster near the beginning of his run than at the end. His **instantaneous speed** —his speed at any given point along the course—might be 250 meters per minute at his fastest point and only 100 meters per minute at his slowest point.

You can check your instantaneous speed when traveling in a car by looking at the **speedometer.** If you are walking or running, you probably don't know how fast you're moving every moment. When people say that they run at a speed of 10 kilometers an hour, they aren't referring to instantaneous speed. Instead, they are talking about average speed.

For example, suppose that the total jogging path is 12 kilometers in length. It takes the jogger one hour to run its length. What is his average speed?

Speed measures how fast you're moving over a certain distance, but not the direction in which you're moving. If you want to describe both the speed and direction of travel, you refer to a moving object's **velocity.** A change in speed or direction causes a change in velocity. Even if the runner travels at the same speed on the entire track, he isn't always traveling in the same direction. If you add his direction to his instantaneous speed at any point, you find his velocity. Velocity is written as a speed and direction, such as 10 meters per second north.

Glossary

instantaneous speed (in′stən tā′nē əs spēd), the speed at any given point

speedometer (spē dom′ tər), a device that shows instantaneous speed

velocity (və los′ə tē), a measure of both the speed and direction of a moving object

Where, on the course, would the jogger probably have the slowest instantaneous speed? The fastest instantaneous speed? ▼

Glossary

acceleration
(ak sel′ə rā′shən), the change in velocity during a particular time period

Acceleration

The racers in this wheelchair racing event all start with a velocity of 0—in other words, they aren't moving. Once the starting gun goes off, they begin pushing their wheels and increasing their speed. After the first second, their instantaneous speed might be 1 meter per second. After 2 seconds, it's 2 meters per second. After 3 seconds, it might be 3 meters per second. Each second, their speed increases 1 meter per second. As the racers increase their speed, they also increase their velocity.

The velocity of the racers changes slowly as they leave the starting line. But as they move away from the line, their velocity increases more quickly. **Acceleration** tells the rate at which velocity is changing. The racers changed their velocity 1 meter per second every second. If the racers want to accelerate at a greater rate, they will have to push the wheel of the wheelchair faster.

Acceleration means more than just speeding up. Acceleration also happens when an object slows down or when it changes direction. When the racers turn a curve, they accelerate because they change direction.

These racers must have great strength and coordination to accelerate from the starting line, go as fast as possible, and keep their wheelchairs moving on the course. ▼

The airplane to the right is traveling at a constant velocity. As it moves through the sky, the people inside also travel at a constant velocity. The plane and the people inside have no acceleration. However, at a certain point the parachutist jumps from the plane. How does this affect her acceleration?

At first, the parachutist changes direction as she falls downward. She also speeds up because a falling object—including the parachutist—goes about 10 meters per second faster every second it falls. After a few seconds, the parachutist is falling much faster than a car moves! The parachutist is accelerating in a downward direction.

At some point, the parachutist opens the parachute. It catches the wind, which causes an upward force on the parachute. The force partially overcomes the pull of gravity, and the parachutist slows down. The parachutist might change direction. These changes cause changes in the parachutist's velocity and in her acceleration.

This parachute keeps the parachutist safe as it changes her acceleration. Leonardo DaVinci sketched a parachute around 1495, but it took nearly 300 years before someone actually used one to jump from a tower safely. ▼

Lesson 2 Review

1. What are three types of motion?
2. What is distance and displacement?
3. What is the difference between speed and velocity?
4. What are three ways that an object can accelerate?
5. **Cause and Effect**
   Suppose the path of the racers on page B92 goes uphill at some point. What effect will that most likely have on their velocity?

You will learn:
- how inertia affects motion.
- how friction affects moving objects.
- how Newton's first law explains circular motion.

Glossary

law (lȯ), a statement that describes events or relationships that exist in nature

▲ *Stonehenge is a massive stone circle that may have been used by ancient astronomers to track the sun's motion.*

Lesson 3

What Is Newton's First Law of Motion?

"You had a tough time getting moving this morning. Not me! Once I got rolling, I couldn't stop!" These might seem like opposite ideas, but they can both be explained by the same law.

Inertia and Motion

History of Science

Long ago people were interested in understanding motion. For example, you may have seen pictures of the large stones in the photo below. This arrangement of stones, called Stonehenge, was built around 2200 B.C. in England. Historians and scientists think they were probably built so people could track the motion of objects in the sky.

Later in the 1500s and 1600s, scientists did many experiments to try to understand motion. The Italian scientist Galileo Galilei studied falling bodies and the idea of gravity. His ideas were carried on by Sir Isaac Newton, an English scientist. In the 1660s, Newton suggested three laws of motion that describe how all things move. In science, a **law** is a statement that describes events or relationships that exist in nature.

Newton combined observations from experiments with thoughts about how things would move in ideal conditions. Newton's laws still apply to most motion on Earth, and they help us understand how and why things act as they do.

The first of Newton's three laws states that all objects resist changes in motion. In other words, an object at rest stays at rest unless some unbalanced force acts on it from outside. If an object is in motion, it continues moving in a straight line. It doesn't speed up, slow down, or change direction unless, once again, some unbalanced force acts on it.

Inertia is the tendency of an object to resist any change in its state of motion. The more mass an object has, the greater its inertia. Newton's first law is sometimes called the law of inertia.

The first part of the law is easy for most people to understand. You'd be pretty surprised if a rock laying on a flat surface starting rolling on its own. Experience tells you that it takes some effort—an outside force—to move things when they are at rest.

The second part of the law isn't quite as easy. You're used to seeing things that are in motion slow down, fall, or seem to "run out of energy." Look at the baseball player in the picture at the right. Once the player starts running around the bases, it's pretty tough to stop. Because his body has a lot of inertia, it tends to keep moving. To stop, he really has to "put on the brakes." He has to lean back and put more force on the ground beneath his feet. That's the outside force.

Newton was thinking about motion under ideal conditions. Outer space comes close to those conditions. Once a rocket is launched into space toward the moon and is going fast enough to overcome the force of gravity, the engines shut down. Earth's gravity slows the rocket down some, but because of its distance from Earth, the rocket doesn't slow nearly as much as it would closer to Earth's surface. It continues moving toward the moon.

Glossary

inertia (in ėr′shə), the resistance of an object to change in its state of motion

Newton's First Law of Motion

All objects resist changes in motion.

Inertia helps to keep Sammy Sosa moving forward. ▶

Have you seen pictures of astronauts in the space shuttle? Did you notice that when they let go of an object, the object just floats around the shuttle? The object changes direction only when it hits a wall or some other surface. It doesn't fall and it doesn't slow down. This is Newton's first law in action.

You can experience Newton's first law here on Earth when you're riding in a car. When the car first starts moving forward, you feel like you are pushed back into your seat. Actually, it's just the opposite. Because your body is at rest, it resists moving and tries to remain back where the car started! As the car moves forward, the seat pushes forward on your body.

According to Newton's first law, once the car is moving, both you and the car tend to keep moving at the same velocity. Suddenly, the driver stops the motion of the car by using an outside force—the brakes! However, the brakes don't have any effect on you. Because you are an object in motion, you stay in motion! You keep moving forward. Depending on the speed you were traveling before the car stopped, you could keep going all the way through the windshield! You need an outside force that can stop your motion too. That outside force might be a seatbelt and shoulder harness. Because they're attached to the car, when the car stops, the seatbelt and harness stop. When they stop, you stop too. Notice how the car in the photo is damaged, but the test dummies are unharmed. Part of the reason for this is the seatbelt and harness. The airbags also play an important role.

▲ The seatbelt, shoulder harness, and airbag in this car all act as outside forces to keep the test dummy from moving forward. ▶

Friction

According to Newton's first law, once an object moves, it should keep going. So if you push off on your skateboard on a level surface, why don't you keep moving?

The first law also says that an object will continue moving UNLESS some force acts on it from outside. On Earth, many outside forces act on moving objects. One is the force of gravity pulling the object toward the center of Earth. Another is a force that you experience all the time—friction.

Friction is a force between surfaces that resists the movement of one surface past the other surface. Try rubbing your hands together. Do they feel warmer? You used energy to move your hands. Friction converted that energy into thermal energy. Likewise, friction occurs when the blades of the ice skates in the photo rub against the ice. This friction produces heat that melts some of the ice.

Friction between a car's tires and the road turns the car's energy into thermal energy. This thermal energy is lost to the air, and the car slows down. When all the energy is gone, the car stops. That's why you have to keep adding energy by burning gasoline if you want to keep the car moving.

If you used a powerful microscope to look at the surface of a road, it would look like a mountain range! Even surfaces that look smooth, like the rubber in the tires, have bumps and ridges. Imagine trying to rub two pieces of sandpaper together! The rougher the surface, the greater the friction.

Friction affects you when you ride your bike, too. You can feel the air you ride through pushing against your skin. This is another form of friction. Recall from Chapter 1 that colliding particles transfer energy between them. As you and your bike collide with particles in the air, you lose energy to them. If you don't keep pedaling, the friction from the air and the surface of the road will convert all the bike's energy to thermal energy and you'll stop.

Air resistance is the friction from air particles hitting an object as the object moves through the air. The faster the object goes, the more air particles it collides with and the greater the air resistance.

Glossary

friction (frik′shən), a force between surfaces that resists the movement of one surface past the other surface

air resistance (er ri zis′təns), the friction from air molecules hitting an object as the object moves through the air

Friction occurs between this girl's skates and the ice. What other friction does she experience? ▼

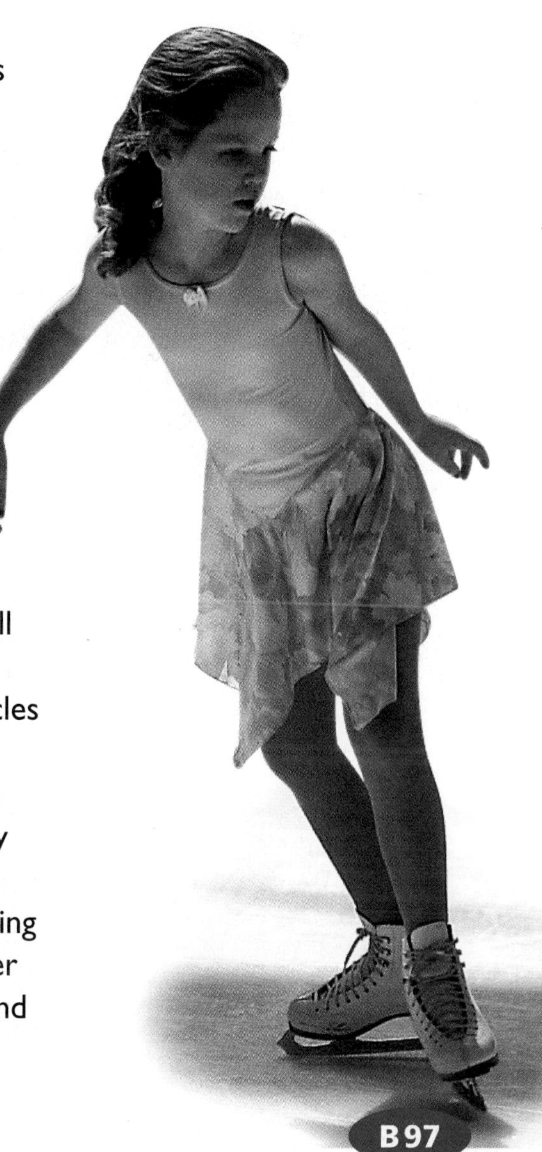

The effects of friction can be helpful. Think about riding your bike on an icy road. You may just spin your wheels without going anywhere. Normally, your bike moves forward because, as the wheels turn, your tires push against the road surface. However, there is much less friction between your tire and ice. The push turns into a slide and you don't go anywhere!

Imagine what would happen if friction disappeared! You wouldn't be able to walk, and if you pushed something, you'd slide away from it. You couldn't slow down. The picture of the skateboarder shows how friction can have both good and bad effects on motion.

Useful Friction

If there were no friction between the wheels and the road, the wheels would just spin and slide over the surface. The skateboarder wouldn't be able to get started or move forward. If he were moving, he wouldn't be able to stop.

Air Resistance

As the skateboarder collides with particles in the air, friction from collisions with air molecules takes away some of his energy. To keep moving, the boy has to keep pushing forward with his feet.

Rolling Friction

Wheels reduce friction because tires and road surfaces "peel" apart rather than scrape across each other. Ball bearings reduce friction inside the wheels, allowing the wheels to turn easily.

Circular Motion

According to Newton's first law of motion, an object moves in a straight line unless some outside force acts on it. If this is true, how can we explain objects moving in a circle, such as a satellite orbiting Earth?

Imagine holding a softball and swinging your arm in a circle. When your hand reaches the bottom of the circle, you let go of the ball. What happens? The ball flies away in a straight line. That's what the first law predicts. When you hold the ball as your arm circles, your hand is always at the outside of the circle. Your hand exerts a pulling force on the ball, keeping it moving in a circle rather than in a straight line. Once you remove that force, inertia kicks in and the ball flies away in a straight line.

You can see the same thing happen when mud or water flies off a spinning car wheel. It's also the reason you're strapped into many amusement park rides that move in circles. If you weren't, you'd fly off in a straight line!

A rocket, such as the space shuttle, takes off in a straight line. Why doesn't it just fly off into space? The shuttle pilots want to circle Earth. To do so, they adjust their speed so that the force of gravity keeps pulling them back into the circle, as you can see in the picture. The pilots balance inertia—the tendency to keep moving in a straight line—and the force of gravity that keeps pulling them toward Earth.

The force that holds an object in circular motion doesn't have to be a pull. It can be a push. Bobsled courses have sides that are banked, or tilted inward. When the bobsled goes around a corner and tries to keep going straight, the wall pushes it back toward the curve.

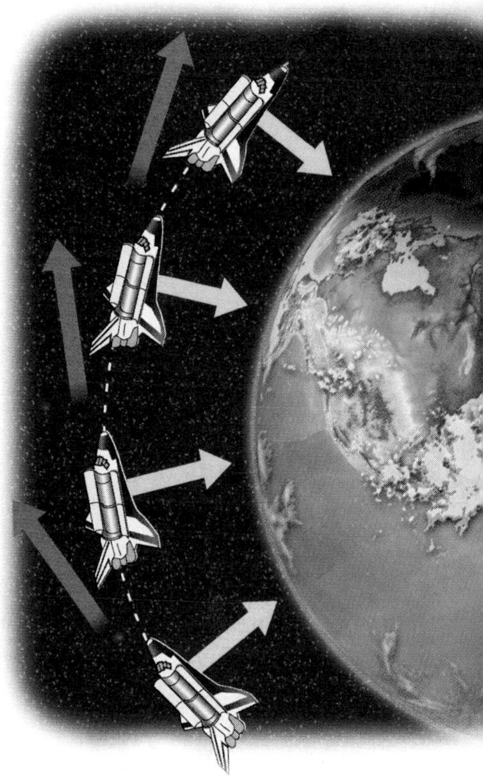

▲ *The yellow arrows show that gravity is the outside force that keeps the shuttle from moving in a straight line. The red arrows show the direction in which the space shuttle would move if the force of gravity disappeared at that point.*

Lesson 3 Review

1. How does inertia affect motion?
2. How does friction affect moving objects?
3. How does Newton's first law explain circular motion?
4. **Cause and Effect**
   You can hold a pencil because of friction. Use cause and effect to explain how this happens.

Investigating Friction and Motion

Process Skills

Process Skills

- observing
- estimating and measuring
- predicting
- inferring

Materials

- safety goggles
- balloon
- shoe box with hole in one end
- tape
- metric ruler
- 5 wooden dowels

Getting Ready

Do this activity to find out how friction affects the motion of an object.

Find a slick surface on which to do this experiment. Do not try to do it on carpet.

If in step 5 your balloon flies away, you may have to repeat the procedure.

Follow This Procedure

1. Make a chart like the one shown. Use your chart to record your predictions and data.

	Prediction	Distance
Box on table	x	
Box on rollers		

2. Put on your safety goggles. Place the balloon inside the box. Pull the neck of the balloon through the hole in the end of the box.

3. Blow up the balloon. Use your fingers to pinch the neck of the balloon closed. Do not tie it.

4. Hold on to the neck of the balloon, and place the box with the inflated balloon on a table top or other slick surface. Place a small piece of tape on the table to mark the position of the back end of the box (Photo A).

Photo A

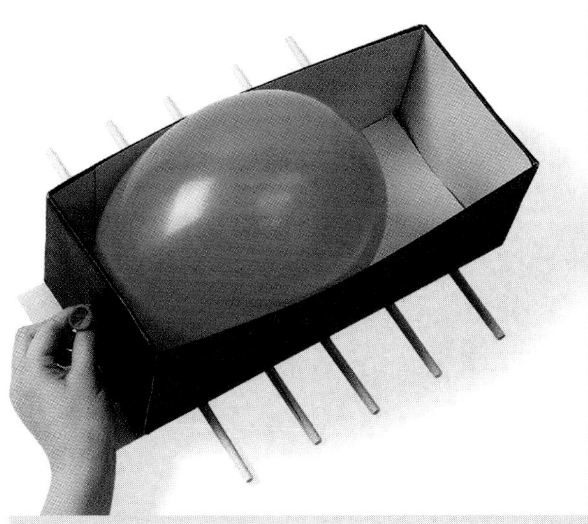

Photo B

5 Release the balloon. **Observe** what happens to the box. Then **measure** the distance from the piece of tape to the end of the box. Record your measurement in your chart.

6 How far do you think your box will move if it is placed on wooden dowels? Record your **prediction.**

7 Repeat steps 3–5, but this time place 5 wooden dowels side by side beneath the box. Be sure you blow the balloon up to the same size as in the previous trial (Photo B).

Self-Monitoring

Have I recorded my measurements in my chart?

Interpret Your Results

1. In which trial did the box move farther?

2. In trial 1, what forces did the box have to overcome in order to move? In trial 2?

3. Make an **inference.** In which trial was the friction greater between the box and the surface on which it sat? What effect did this have on the distance the box moved?

4. Why did the box eventually stop moving in both trials?

Inquire Further

What other methods could you use to decrease the friction between the box and the table? Develop a plan to answer this or other questions you may have.

Self-Assessment

- I followed the directions to **observe** how friction can affect the motion of an object.
- I **predicted** how far the box would move before the second trial.
- I **measured** the distance that the box moved each time.
- I recorded the measurements in my chart.
- I **inferred** how friction affected the box in each trial.

You will learn:

- how mass, force, and acceleration are related.
- why objects fall at different rates.

Lesson 4

What Is Newton's Second Law of Motion?

"Wow! She hit that ball out of the park! All I got was a pop-up." How can one person make a ball go farther than another? What do you have to do to hit the ball harder?

Mass, Force, and Acceleration

Is it easier for the boy in the picture to move the empty recycling bin or the one filled with newspapers? Silly question, isn't it? You know that you have to push or pull harder to move an object with a greater mass than one with less mass. The greater the mass of an object, the greater its inertia and the more force you need to move it.

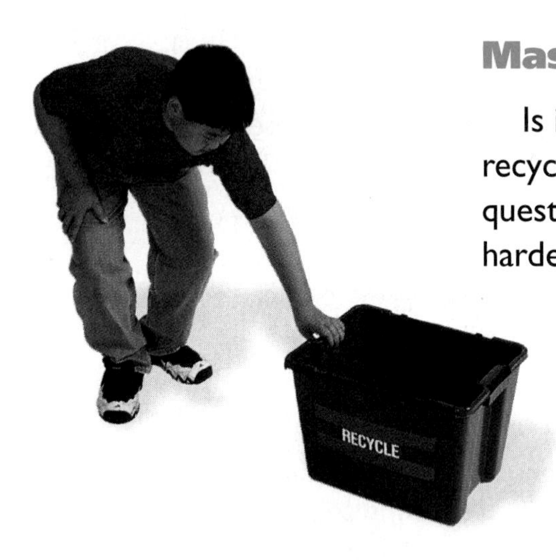

▲ *The recycling bin filled with newspapers has more mass than the empty one. Because more mass means more inertia, the boy must exert a greater force to make it move.*

Newton put this idea in his second law of motion, which shows how force, mass, and acceleration are related. The second law of motion can be written as in this equation.

force = mass x acceleration

In the equation, *force* refers to the overall force applied to the object, *mass* to the mass of the object, and *acceleration* to the object's acceleration. The equation tells you that the force you need to move any object equals the mass of the object multiplied by the acceleration you want.

Newton's second law also explains that objects accelerate in the direction of the force that acts on them. As you can easily see in the photos, both bins move in the direction of the boy's push.

Look at the pictures above. The empty truck at the top is traveling on a flat road from a building site to a lumberyard. At the lumberyard, the truck picks up a full load of lumber. Then the truck driver leaves the lumberyard and drives back to the building site on the same road. On the return trip, the driver notices that he isn't able to reach the same speed as quickly as he could with the empty truck. The engine supplies the same force on both trips. However, the loaded truck accelerates more slowly because it has more mass. It's Newton's second law in action!

The second law of motion also explains that when the acceleration of an object changes, the amount of force acting on it also must be changing. If on his way back from the lumberyard, the truck driver must stop for a red light, he puts on his brakes and the truck slows down. What new force is acting on the truck to slow it down?

▲ *Use Newton's second law to explain how air resistance affects the acceleration of this truck.*

Newton's Second Law of Motion

An object's acceleration depends on the mass of the object and the size and direction of the force acting on it.

Falling Objects

History of Science

Aristotle, a Greek philosopher from the fourth century B.C., claimed that the rate at which an object would fall depended on its mass. Because that idea seemed reasonable, no one tested it until many centuries later.

You might have heard the story about Galileo Galilei, who in the late 1500s is said to have dropped two cannon balls from the Leaning Tower of Pisa. One ball had ten times the mass of the other. Just as Galileo suspected, both balls hit the ground at the same time.

You've learned that the greater the mass of an object, the greater the pull of gravity on it. You might think that the cannonball with the greater mass would fall faster. How could they land at the same time?

The girl's picture shows that the balls are of different sizes. However, they fall at the same rate. ▼

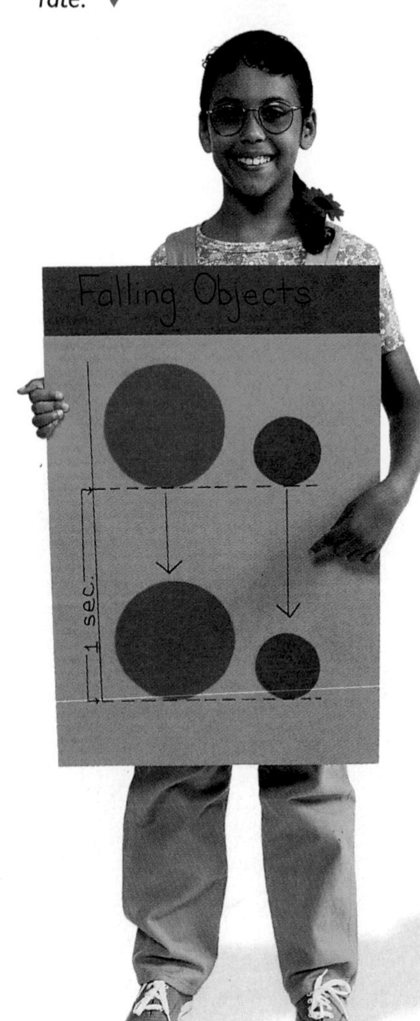

Galileo didn't use the word *inertia*, but he suspected that the more mass an object had, the harder it would be to move. Gravity does pull harder on the object with more mass. However, because the object also has more inertia, it doesn't move as easily. As a result, all falling objects have the same acceleration. This is true unless air resistance affects them in some way.

In the picture on the next page, you can see a simple demonstration of Galileo's experiment. Two sheets of paper of the same size and weight were used. One sheet was crumpled into a ball. The other sheet remained flat. Two students dropped the sheets from the same height at the same time. As you can see in the photo, the crumpled sheet is falling faster. Why?

Unlike Galileo's cannonballs, the two sheets of paper have different amounts of air resistance. As an object falls, air resistance acts as a force in the opposite direction from the downward pull of gravity. If the object has enough surface area and falls for a long enough time, enough air can pile up beneath it to stop it from accelerating. The flat sheet of paper has more surface area than the balled-up piece of paper. As a result, it experiences more air resistance. It falls slower.

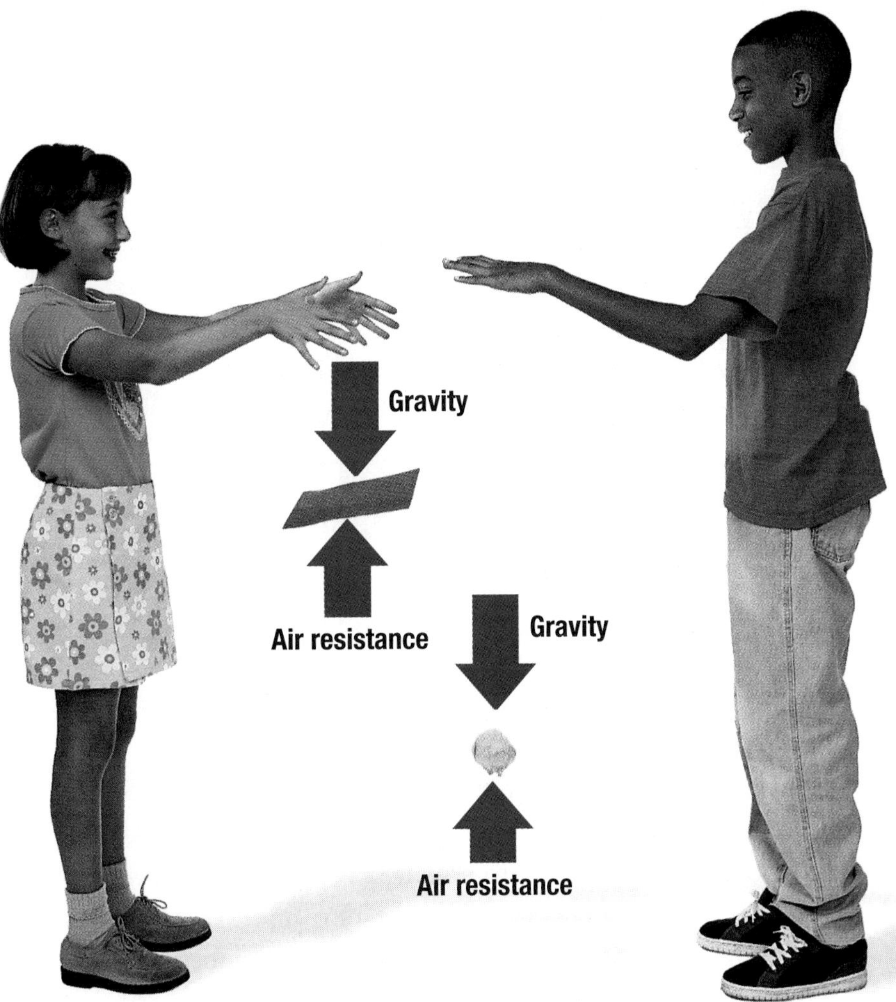

◀ Air Resistance

These two sheets of paper are falling at different rates because more air resistance acts on the open sheet. What would happen if you crumpled two sheets of paper together and dropped them at the same time you drop one crumpled sheet?

Skydivers use air resistance to control the rate at which they fall. When skydivers spread their body so that it catches a lot of air, the divers slow down. When divers tuck their arms and legs and point their heads downward, they increase their acceleration. This process is called streamlining. When you streamline an object, you give it the smallest possible surface area. Usually a streamlined object also has rounded edges so that air can flow around it instead of piling up underneath it.

This skydiver spread his body out to cause more air resistance. This causes the diver to fall slower. ▼

Lesson 4 Review

1. How are mass, force, and acceleration related?
2. Why do objects fall at different rates?
3. **Cause and Effect**
   Identify the cause-and-effect relationships in the paragraph above.

You will learn:

- what actions and reactions are.
- how Newton's laws can explain amusement park rides.

Lesson 5

What Is Newton's Third Law of Motion?

Suppose you're an astronaut making a spacewalk outside the shuttle. You fire your jetpack to go back to the shuttle. Oh, no! It's run out of fuel. How can you get back? There is nothing to push against!

Action and Reaction

An astronaut who finds himself or herself in the above situation would know just what to do—take off the jetpack and give it a hard push AWAY from the shuttle. As the jetpack moves away, the astronaut moves TOWARD the shuttle. The astronaut is using Newton's third law.

Newton's third law states that when one object exerts a force upon a second object, the second object exerts an equal and opposite force upon the first object. As the astronaut pushes the jetpack, the jetpack pushes back. This push moves the astronaut toward the shuttle.

▲ *You can see from the arrows that this boy is pushing on the wall and the wall pushes back. What other pair of forces can you identify?*

All forces come in pairs. Push downward on your desk with your hand. The desk is pushing back with equal force. Likewise, when the boy in the picture leans against the wall, the wall also pushes on the boy.

How can a desk and the wall exert a force? It might be easier to answer this question if you think about what would happen if these objects didn't push back with an equal force. Your hand would push the desk through the floor, and the boy would fall over! Forces must be balanced whenever an object is at rest.

Notice the frog in the drawing on the next page. When the frog sits still on the lily pad, the pad pushes up with the same force as the frog pushes down. But when the frog jumps from the pad, it exerts a force to the left on the pad. As a result, the pad moves away from the frog. At the same time, the pad pushes with an equal but opposite force on the frog. The frog moves to the right.

Once the frog is in the water, it uses the third law of motion to swim. Its legs push backward against the water. This force is known as the action. At the same time, the water pushes forward on the frog's legs with the same force. This force is the reaction. This push from the water makes the frog move through the water. The webbed feet of the frog help it move through the water more easily.

People who design rockets also use Newton's third law—also called the law of action and reaction. You might think that a rocket takes off when the gases from its engines push against the ground. If that's true, how does it work in space? There's nothing in space to push against.

As the gases that are produced in a rocket's engine are pushed backward, an equal but opposite force pushes the rocket forward. A rocket actually works better in space because the gases can be pushed backward more easily. The reason? Space doesn't have air particles to slow down the gases.

Even the simple act of walking is an example of action and reaction. As your foot pushes on the ground, the ground pushes back. Because you push at a slightly backward angle, the ground pushes you forward.

Newton's Third Law of Motion

When one object exerts a force upon a second object, the second object exerts an equal and opposite force upon the first object.

What force causes the frog to move forward? ▼

Newton's Laws at the Amusement Park

Motion, gravity, mass, forces, acceleration, friction, inertia, action, and reaction—all are important parts of the rides at an amusement park. This is one of the best places to see all three of Newton's laws of motion in action. After you read the examples, see if you can figure out other parts of the rides where each law is at work.

Newton's First Law

◀ *At the top of the hill, you and the car are nearly at rest. Your inertia tends to keep you there. If you weren't strapped into the car, it would fall out from under you as it heads downhill.*

Circular Motion

Newton's first law also tells us that, if these people didn't have support behind them, they'd fly off in a straight line. ▼

Newton's Second Law

How can you hit the target with enough force to ring the bell? You could use a hammer with a large mass, but you might not be able to move it very fast. Instead, you could use a lighter hammer and swing it as fast as possible. A really strong person could swing a heavy hammer very fast—that would produce the greatest force. ▶

Newton's Third Law

Part of the fun of bumper cars is bouncing off other cars. When two cars hit, both of them bounce back because when one car pushes the second, the second pushes back with equal force. ▼

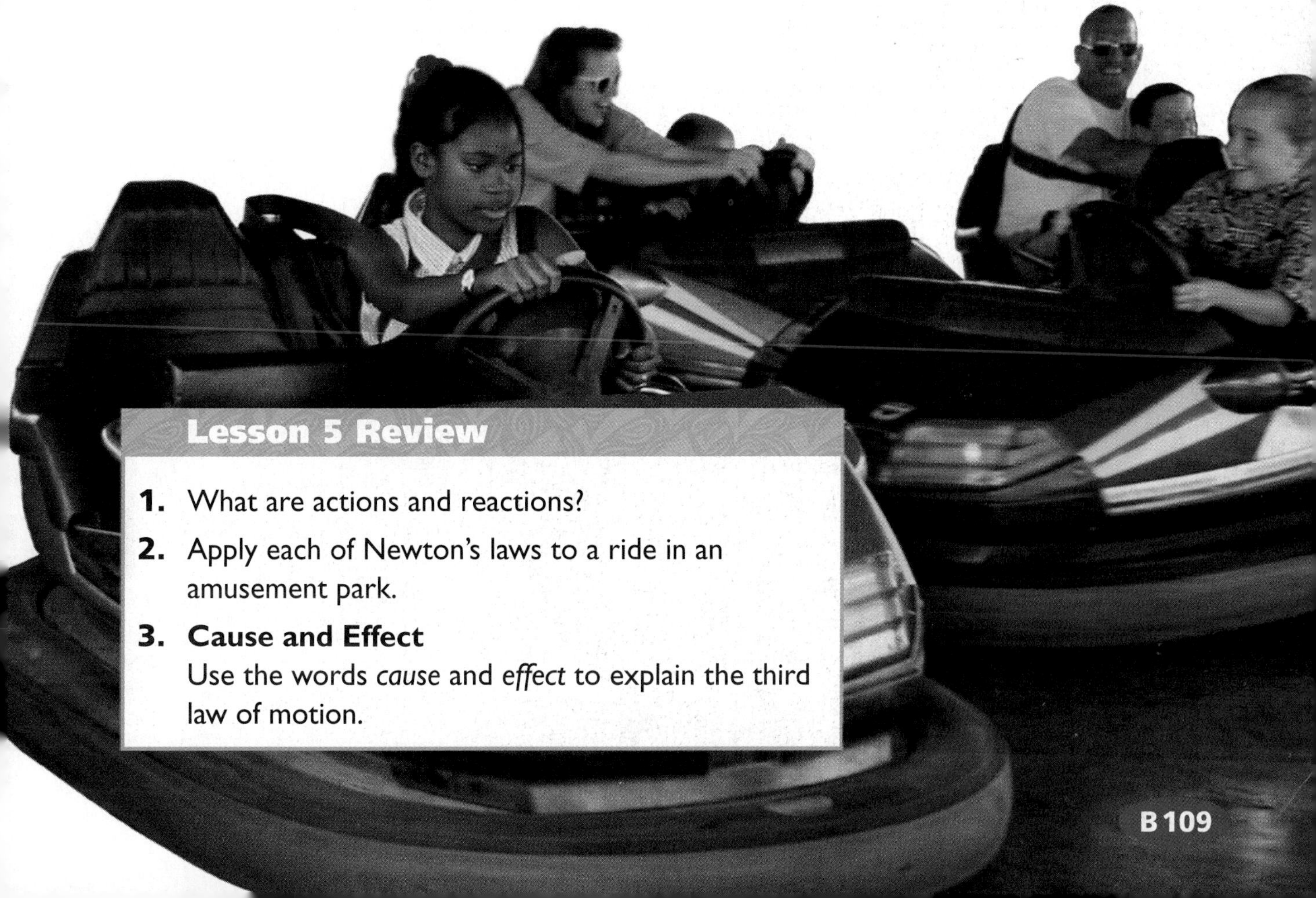

Lesson 5 Review

1. What are actions and reactions?
2. Apply each of Newton's laws to a ride in an amusement park.
3. **Cause and Effect**
   Use the words *cause* and *effect* to explain the third law of motion.

Investigate Activity

Investigating Action and Reaction

Process Skills

- estimating and measuring
- predicting
- observing
- communicating

Materials

- 10 cm square of thick cardboard
- scissors
- metric ruler
- rubber band
- shallow pan of water
- paper towels

Getting Ready

In this activity, you will build a paddle boat to observe Newton's law of action and reaction.

Follow This Procedure

1. Make a chart like the one shown. Use your chart to record your predictions and observations.

Direction paddle wound	Direction paddle moved when released	Direction boat was moved

2. Make a cardboard square into a boat shape by using scissors to cut one end to form a point. On the opposite end, cut out a 5-cm square notch from the middle.

3. **Measure** and cut a 4 cm square from the scrap of cardboard from the notch you've just cut. This will become the paddle for your boat.

4. Stretch the rubber band around the sides of the boat and position it so that it crosses the notch at the back of the boat. Insert the paddle between the strands of the rubber band (Photo A).

Photo A

5 Wind the rubber band by turning the paddle toward the front of the boat 4–5 times and hold it in place.

6 You will place the boat in the water and release the paddle. In which direction will the paddle move? In which direction will the boat move? Record your **predictions.**

Safety Note *Use paper towels to clean up any spills immediately.*

7 Place the boat in the pan of water and release the paddle (Photo B). **Observe** the direction in which the boat moves. Record your observations.

Self-Monitoring

Do I need to repeat any steps to be sure of my observations?

8 Repeat steps 5–7, but this time, wind the rubber band by turning the paddle toward the back of the boat. Predict in which directions the paddle and the boat will move. Record your predictions and observations.

Photo B

Interpret Your Results

1. When you wound the paddle toward the front of the boat, in which direction did the paddle turn when you let the paddle go? In which direction did the boat move?

2. Make a drawing that shows two sets of action-reaction forces that caused the boat to move forward.

3. Communicate. Use Newton's law of action and reaction to explain to classmates why the paddle and the boat moved as they did.

Inquire Further

How can action and reaction forces be used to lift a rocket into space? Develop a plan to answer this or other questions you may have.

Self-Assessment

- I followed instructions to build a paddle boat.
- I made **predictions** about the directions in which the boat and paddle would move.
- I recorded my **observations.**
- I made a drawing showing two sets of action and reaction forces that acted on the paddle boat.
- I **communicated** why the paddle wheel and the boat moved as they did.

Chapter 3 Review

Chapter Main Ideas

Lesson 1

• A force is a push or a pull.

• The force of gravity depends on the masses of the objects and the distance between them.

• Mass is the amount of matter an object has. Weight is the pull of gravity on an object's mass.

• Objects move when the forces acting on them are unbalanced.

Lesson 2

• The three types of motion are straight line, circular, and vibrational motion.

• Distance and displacement are two ways of measuring how far you have traveled.

• Velocity is speed in a given direction.

• An object accelerates when it speeds up, slows down, or changes direction.

Lesson 3

• Inertia is an object's tendency to remain in motion or at rest.

• Friction is a force that resists motion.

• An object moves in a circle when an outside force acts to push or pull it toward the center of the circle.

Lesson 4

• The force needed to move an object equals the mass of the object multiplied by the acceleration you want.

• Objects fall at different rates because of air resistance.

Lesson 5

• For every action, there is an equal but opposite reaction.

• Many of the actions of amusement park rides are explained by Newton's Laws.

Reviewing Science Words and Concepts

Write the letter of the word or phrase that best completes each sentence.

a. acceleration
b. air resistance
c. balanced forces
d. force
e. frame of reference
f. friction
g. gravity
h. inertia
i. instantaneous speed
j. mass
k. net force
l. newton
m. relative motion
n. speed
o. speedometer
p. velocity
q. weight

1. The rate at which the position of an object changes is its ____.
2. The unit used to measure force or weight in the metric system is the ____.
3. How a person sees an object's motion depends on the ____ the person chooses.
4. The friction from air molecules hitting an object as it moves through air is ____.
5. The force of attraction that exists between any two objects is called ____.
6. A device that displays instantaneous speed is a(n) ____.
7. When a car stops suddenly, the passenger continues moving forward because of his ____.

8. The amount of matter making up an object is its ___.
9. The rate at which an object changes its velocity is called ___.
10. Another name for a push or a pull is a(n) ___.
11. Equal forces acting in opposite directions are ___.
12. A measure of the pull of gravity on an object's mass is the object's ___.
13. The combination of all the forces acting on an object is the ___.
14. A force that resists the movement of one surface past another is ___.
15. An object's ___ depends on the observer's motion and the motion of other objects.
16. The rate at which an object is moving at any point in time is its ___.
17. To say that an object is traveling at 10 m/sec toward the north is to give its ___.

Explaining Science

Draw and label a diagram or write a paragraph to answer these questions.

1. What two factors determine the force of gravity between two objects?

2. Why is the idea of relative motion important in the study of motion?

3. How does Newton's First Law explain why seat belts are a good idea?

4. What forces are acting on a book that is lying on a table?

Using Skills

1. Make a **cause-and-effect** chart to show how objects can move in a circle despite inertia.

2. Draw a map of your classroom. On your map show the route you would take to walk from your desk to your teacher's desk. **Estimate** and **measure** the distance and displacement for your route.

3. How does friction help you do your school work? **Communicate** your ideas by writing a few paragraphs.

Critical Thinking

1. Tomás wanted to be able to hit the baseball farther for his Little League team. He tried using a heavier bat, but the ball traveled even less distance. What other **experiment** would you suggest that Tomás try in order to hit the ball farther?

2. List the **sequence** of events that occur as you get ready for school in the morning. Identify action and reaction forces in each event.

3. You are riding as a passenger on a snowmobile that is moving in a straight line at a constant speed. If you throw a baseball straight up into the air, where would you **predict** that it would land?

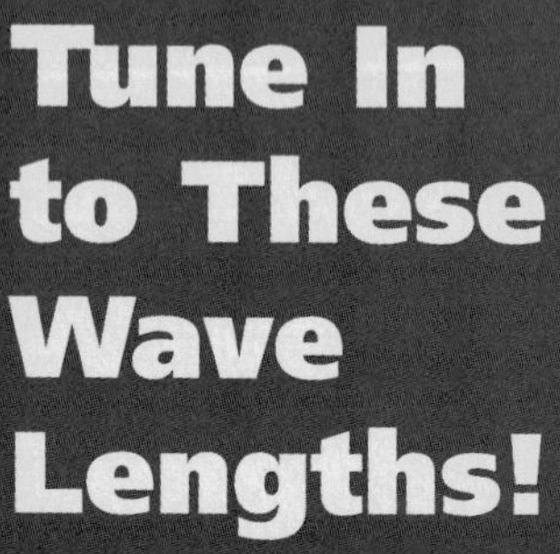

Tune In to These Wave Lengths!

This wave machine makes waves of different lengths. But what makes waves without a wave machine? What about your vocal chords?

Chapter 4

Light, Color, and Sound

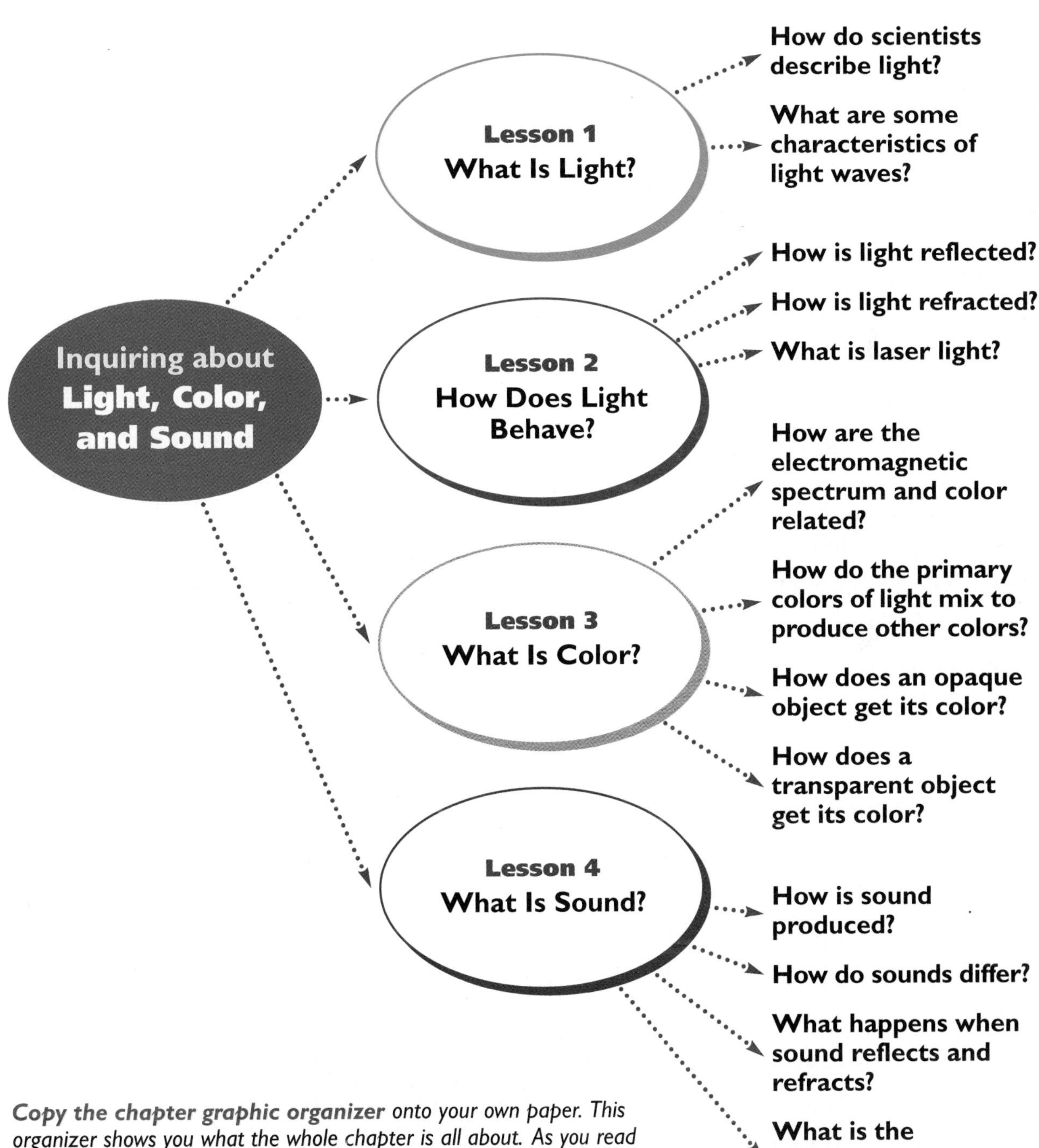

Inquiring about Light, Color, and Sound
Lesson 1
What Is Light?
How do scientists describe light?
What are some characteristics of light waves?
Lesson 2
How Does Light Behave?
How is light reflected?
How is light refracted?
What is laser light?
Lesson 3
What Is Color?
How are the electromagnetic spectrum and color related?
How do the primary colors of light mix to produce other colors?
How does an opaque object get its color?
How does a transparent object get its color?
Lesson 4
What Is Sound?
How is sound produced?
How do sounds differ?
What happens when sound reflects and refracts?
What is the difference between music and noise?

Copy the chapter graphic organizer *onto your own paper. This organizer shows you what the whole chapter is all about. As you read the lessons and do the activities, look for answers to the questions and write them on your organizer.*

Explore Activity

Exploring Light Rays

Process Skills

Process Skills

- observing
- estimating and measuring
- communicating

Materials

- small mirror
- white, unlined paper
- pencil
- flashlight
- metric ruler
- comb
- semicircular protractor

Explore

1. Place a mirror up on its side on a sheet of paper. Draw a line on the paper along the bottom edge of the mirror.

2. Place the lighted flashlight 30 cm directly in front of the mirror.

3. Place the comb, teeth down, between the flashlight and the mirror. A partner should tilt the mirror forward about 10°. Move the flashlight and the comb until you **observe** a pattern of light rays going to and being reflected away from the mirror. They will look like many side-by-side *V*s.

4. On the paper, trace one ray of light as it leaves the comb, reaches the mirror, and is reflected away. Set the mirror aside.

5. Place the protractor along the penciled mirror line, positioning the center over the point where the two lines that you just drew meet. **Measure** the angle each line makes with the penciled mirror line. Record your measurements.

6. Repeat steps 2–5 two more times, choosing rays with different angles to draw and measure.

Reflect

1. How do the measures of the angles of each ray of light and its reflection compare for each trial? **Communicate** your findings to your classmates.

2. Form a general statement about the angles of a light ray going to and being reflected by a mirror.

Inquire Further

Can the angles of light rays going to and being reflected by a mirror ever be greater than 90°? Develop a plan to answer this or other questions you may have.

Measuring Angles

Light strikes a mirror at an angle and bounces off it at an angle. If you were to measure these two angles, you would discover that they are the same size.

You can measure angles with a tool called a protractor. Angles are measured in units called **degrees**. The symbol ° indicates degrees. A complete circle measures 360°. A 1° angle is $\frac{1}{360}$ of a circle.

Math Vocabulary

degree, a unit of angle measure, $\frac{1}{360}$ of a complete circle

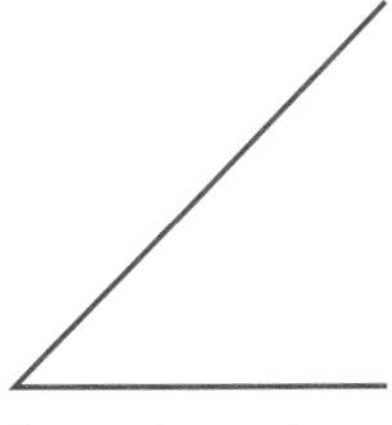

An acute angle measures more than 0° and less than 90°.

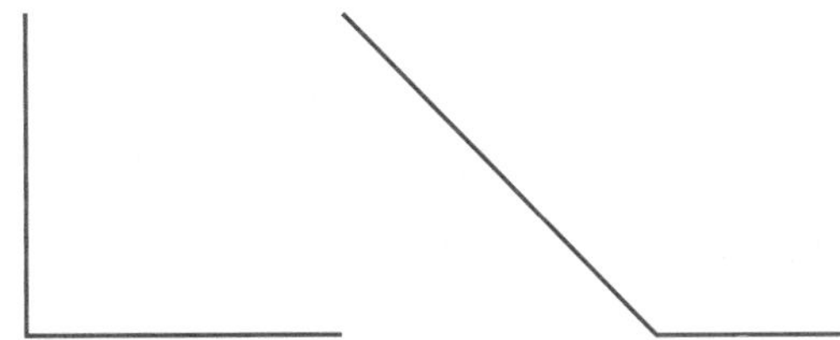

A right angle measures exactly 90°.

An obtuse angle measures more than 90° and less than 180°.

Example

Here is how to measure and classify ∠DAE. Place the protractor so that the middle of its bottom edge is over A. Read the pair of numbers where AD passes through the protractor. If the angle is an acute angle, use the smaller number in the pair. If the angle is obtuse, use the larger number.

The angle is acute. So, ∠DAE measures 60°.

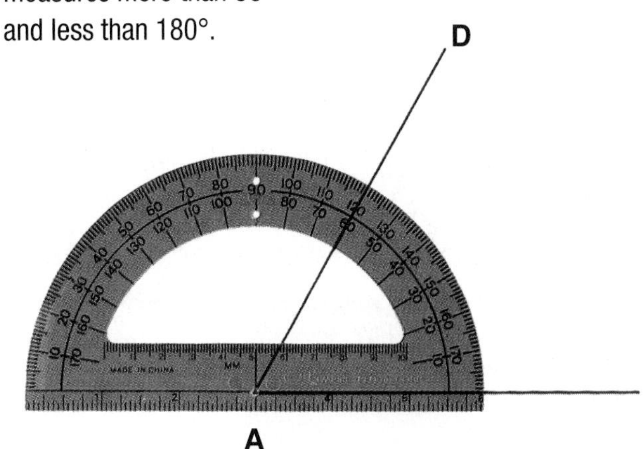

Talk About It!

How can you tell if the angle is an acute angle, a right angle, or an obtuse angle?

You will learn:

- how scientists describe light.
- what some characteristics of light waves are.

Lesson 1

What Is Light?

" Hey! Who turned off the lights? I can't see a thing!" Imagine what it would be like if all the light in the world disappeared. No sun, no stars, no candles, light bulbs, or fire. How would your life change?

Describing Light

History of Science

Few things are more familiar than light. You use light to see. Light brings you information about things around you—on Earth and in space. Without light, there would be no photosynthesis and, as a result, no food for animals.

Although light is all around you, scientists have long disagreed about exactly what it is. The ancient Greeks believed that light contained particles that somehow created vision when they entered the eye. They thought that light traveled in straight lines and at very high speeds. The Greeks didn't have the tools that scientists have today, but their ideas came pretty close to some of our present ideas.

In the 1500s, the artist Leonardo da Vinci noticed that light bounced back from some surfaces—somewhat like sound waves that bounce back to create echoes. Da Vinci thought that light might have some of the properties of waves. How do you think light might be similar to the water waves in the picture?

During the 1600s, scientists disagreed about the nature of light. Some scientists, including Sir Isaac Newton, thought that light traveled as small particles. Newton also noticed that when an object, such as a post, was in the path of light, part of the light seemed to hit the post and stop. Behind the post was a dark area where the light didn't fall—a shadow. This observation added to Newton's belief that light travels as particles.

Energy travels through water in waves. Light energy also travels as waves. ▼

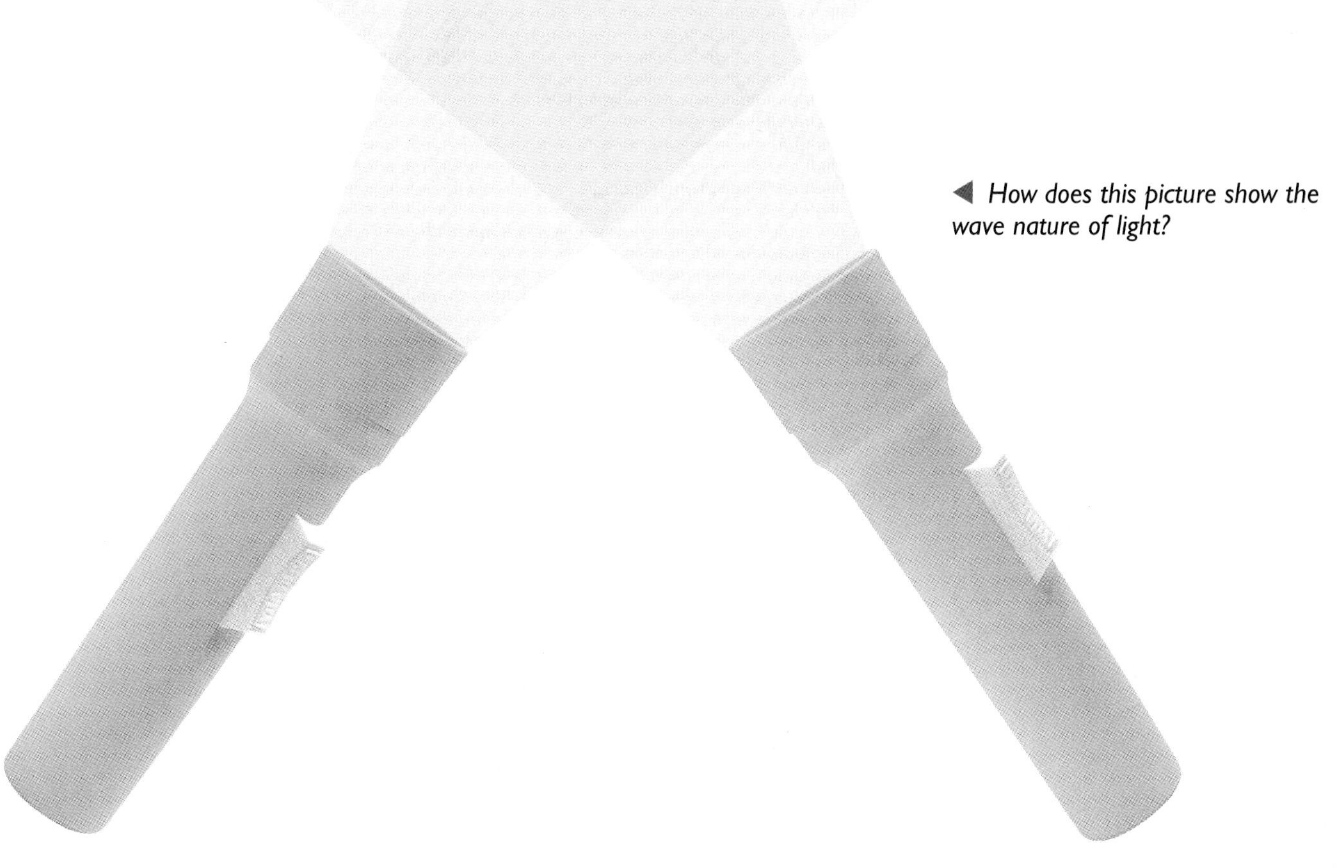

◀ *How does this picture show the wave nature of light?*

However, Dutch physicist Christian Huygens pointed out that if two beams of light cross each other, like those in the picture, the beams pass right through each other. Huygens didn't think that particles could behave that way. Instead, he thought that the behavior of light could be more easily explained if light were thought of as waves.

Today, scientists think that light has properties of both waves and particles, depending on what behaviors of light you look at. In other words, light behaves as if a particle of energy is moving in a wave pattern.

Where does light come from? Scientists think that light is produced when atoms lose energy. The extra energy is given off in packets called **photons**. Beams of light are made up of streams of photons.

Newton didn't know about photons, but he thought that light was made of different kinds of particles. Today, we would say that light is made of different kinds of photons, each of which has a different amount of energy. The wave properties of photons depend on how much energy they contain.

Glossary

photon (fō′ton), a bundle of energy that is released when an atom loses some energy

Glossary

Wave Properties

This diagram shows how some properties of a wave are measured. ▼

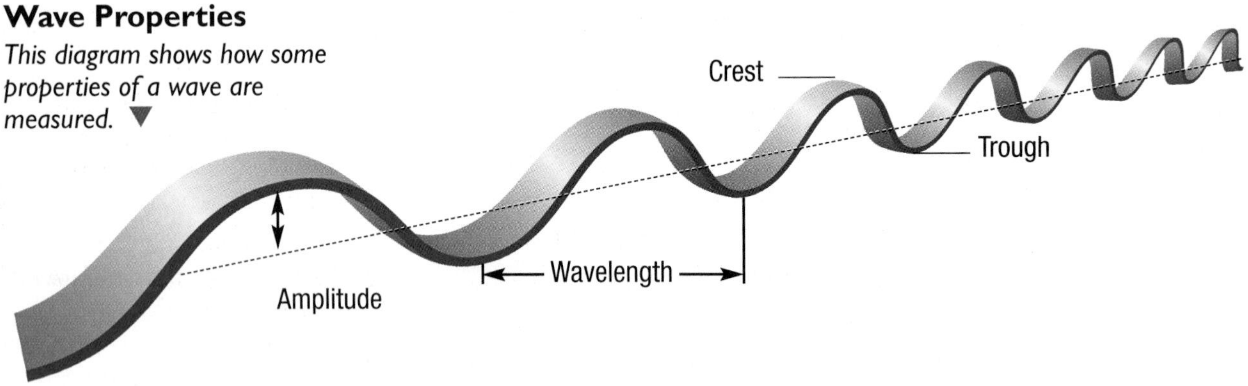

Crest

Trough

Amplitude

Wavelength

Glossary

Glossary

frequency (frē′kwən sē), the number of waves (crests or troughs) that pass a point in a given amount of time

Light Waves

You can get an idea of what light waves are like by recalling water waves that you may have seen in the ocean, lakes, ponds, or your own bathtub. Even water in a puddle will have waves if you drop a pebble into it. Waves, whether they are water waves or light waves, can be described by the same set of properties—how often the wave repeats its pattern and how much energy it has.

The picture above shows how you can measure some properties of a wave by using its up-and-down patterns. The high point on a wave is called a crest, and the low point is called a trough.

Suppose you mark two points on the wave, one at the bottom of a trough and another at the bottom of the next trough. The distance between the two points is the wavelength. The distance could also be between crests or any points in between, as long as the distance is measured between the same points on both waves. The number of waves—crests or troughs—that pass a point in a certain amount of time is called the wave's **frequency**.

All waves carry energy. The houses in the picture were damaged by the energy in the waves formed during a hurricane. To understand how waves and energy are related, imagine riding in a boat on the ocean during a hurricane.

The great energy in a hurricane's winds is transferred to the ocean's water, creating waves with huge amplitudes. ▼

A hurricane's winds carry huge amounts of energy. When the winds strike the water in the ocean, crests and troughs form. These crests can be higher than a boat. The greater the energy that produces a wave, the higher the crests and the deeper the troughs.

As a wave's energy increases, its **amplitude** also increases. You can find the amplitude of a wave by making a dotted line through the center of the wave as shown at the top of the previous page. If you measure the height of the crest or the depth of the trough from that line, you are measuring the amplitude of the wave.

Suppose you stand on a dock and watch water waves roll by toward the shore. If you dropped a ball into the waves as they passed the dock, would the ball move past the dock too? Look at the ball in the series of pictures to the right. Although the waves move to the right in the direction of the arrow, the ball just bobs up and down because the water itself moves up and down—not in the same direction as the wave. In a **transverse wave**, the crests and troughs move at right angles to the direction that the wave—and the energy—travels.

Both water and light travel in transverse waves, but there is one very important difference between the two. Water carries the energy in water waves. What carries the energy in the transverse waves of light? Nothing! Light doesn't need matter to travel, although it can pass through some kinds of matter, such as glass or air.

Lesson 1 Review

1. How do scientists describe light?
2. What are some characteristics of light waves?
3. **Cause and Effect**
   Describe the cause-and-effect relationship in the first paragraph on this page.

Glossary

Glossary

amplitude (am′plə tüd), the distance between a wave's mid-point and its crest or trough

transverse wave (trans vėrs′ wāv), a wave in which the crests and troughs move at right angles to the direction of the wave's travel

How does this ball's movement compare to the movement of the wave? ▼

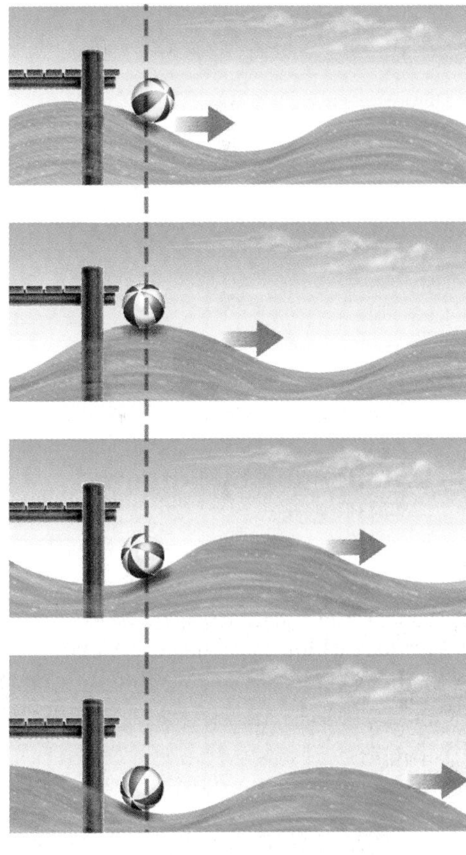

You will learn:
- how light is reflected.
- how light is refracted.
- what laser light is.

Lesson 2

How Does Light Behave?

"Mirror, mirror on the wall . . . ." Your mirror may not talk back to you, but it sure comes in handy when you want to comb your hair or check how you look. Why can you see yourself in a mirror?

Reflection of Light

History of Science

Mirrors have been around for a long time. Some of the earliest mirrors that people made were found in the tombs of women buried in Turkey about 6000 B.C. These mirrors were made of highly polished volcanic glass known as obsidian. Metal mirrors, made of polished copper or bronze, were made nearly 4000 years ago by Egyptians and by people who lived in what is now India and Pakistan. How do all these mirrors work?

Light travels in straight lines. You can observe this characteristic of light when there's dust in the air and you see "beams" of sunlight coming through the window.

When light radiates from a source, such as the sun or a flashlight, it travels in straight lines until it strikes a surface, such as the mirror to the left. The light bounces back from the smooth surface of the mirror just as a ball bounces off a wall. The reflected light strikes your eye, and you see that light as a reflection.

To understand how light bounces, consider how a ball bounces. For example, where on a wall in front of you would you aim a ball if you wanted a friend standing beside you to catch it? You'd throw it at a point on the wall between you and your friend. That way it will bounce back at an angle toward your friend. However, if you throw the ball straight at the wall, it will bounce straight back to you.

Reflection by Smooth Surfaces

Because the surface of the mirror is very smooth, all the beams of light from the flashlight bounce back at the same angle. An image is reflected. ▼

Light bounces in the same way. Look at the dotted line in the picture to the right. You can see that the beam of light strikes the mirror at the point where the dotted line meets the mirror. The beam and the dotted line form an angle. What is the angle? The light reflects, or bounces back, from a smooth surface at the same angle at which it strikes the surface but on the opposite side of this imaginary line. Notice in the picture on page B122 that all the reflected rays are parallel. These parallel rays form a reflected image that is just like the original image.

At what angle does the light bounce back? This behavior explains why you can see your reflection in a smooth surface such as a mirror. Then why can't you see your image reflected from a rough surface? Think about the bouncing ball again. If you bounce your ball on a gravel driveway, it could fly off in just about any direction. The direction in which the ball bounces back depends on how and where it hit the gravel. Light acts the same way. Notice in the picture below how beams of light that are traveling together bounce off in many directions after they strike the rough surface. Because the light reflects in all different directions when it bounces from the surface, the reflected image is scattered and you can't see it clearly.

Wouldn't it be confusing if the image of every object in a room was reflected from every surface? Walls and ceilings are often finished with rough surfaces or coated with non-reflecting paint so that they don't act like mirrors. Even a painted surface that looks smooth to the eye has lots of hills and valleys when viewed under a microscope.

Light reflects from a surface at the same angle that it strikes it. ▼

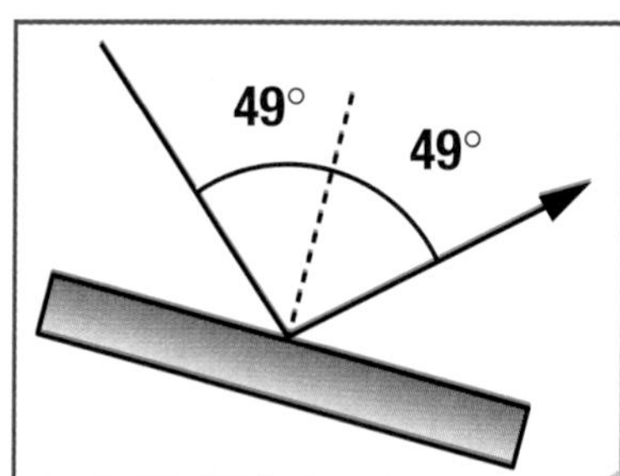

▲ *The light from this flashlight travels in straight lines.*

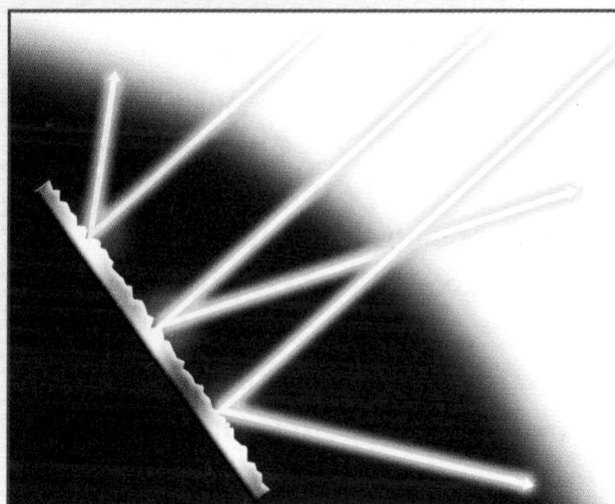

Reflection by Rough Surfaces

◀ *Imagine that every point on this rough surface is part of a tiny straight surface. Then you can figure out how each beam of light striking one of these surfaces would reflect. Because the light is scattered as it reflects from the surface, the image you see is not clear.*

Glossary

convex mirror
(con veks′ mir′ər), a mirror whose center section curves toward an object

concave mirror
(kon kāv′ mir′ər), a mirror whose center section curves away from an object

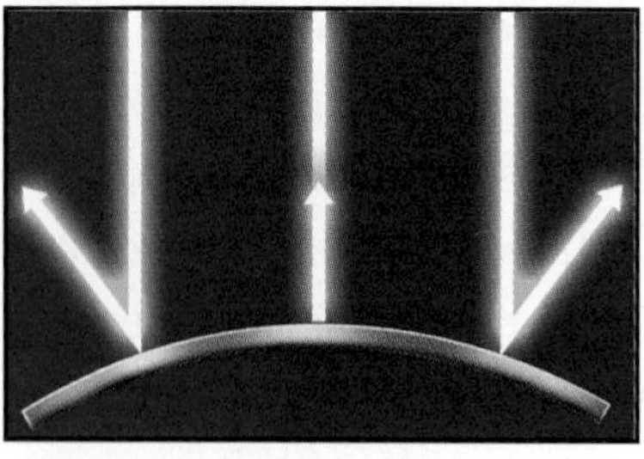

Convex Mirror

▲ *Light rays reflected from a convex mirror spread out, as shown by the arrows.*

Concave Mirror

▲ *Light rays reflected from a concave mirror come together.*

Have you ever looked at yourself in a funhouse mirror? Did you know that the strange reflection of the girl below results from the curves in the funhouse mirror? Curved mirrors are used not only in funhouses. You might be familiar with the curved mirrors mounted near the ceilings in some stores. The center of the mirror curves outward toward the center of the store. This type of mirror is a **convex mirror.** Because the mirror is curved, light coming from different corners of the store can strike the mirror's surface at the same time. You can see in the diagram that in a convex mirror the reflected beams spread out. Objects in the reflection look as if they are actually behind the mirror but smaller. Try it yourself by looking in the back of a spoon.

In contrast, a **concave mirror** is one whose center curves away from an object. As light reflects from this kind of mirror, the beams actually come together and cross, as shown in the picture above. Look at your image in the inside curve of a spoon and move the spoon in and out from your nose. You're upside down!

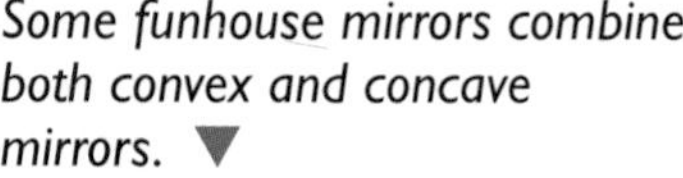

Some funhouse mirrors combine both convex and concave mirrors. ▼

Curved mirrors have many uses. For example, the reflector in a flashlight is a concave mirror. It focuses the light into a beam rather than allowing it to spread out all over as light does from a bare light bulb.

For the opposite effect, look at the reflectors on your bicycle. Most contain tiny angled convex mirrors placed at several different angles. If you're riding at night and a car's headlights strike the reflectors, the driver can see the reflection regardless of the angle between the car and bike.

Windows also reflect light like a mirror. Sometimes at night when you look out your window, instead of seeing outside, you might see a reflection of the room you're in. During the day, so much light comes in from outside that you don't notice the reflection. However, at night there's little or no light outside to pass through the window. As a result, the reflection from the window is the only light reaching your eyes.

This reflecting effect is what makes two-way mirrors work. For example, in the two-way mirror you might have seen on a TV police story, the mirror between the two rooms is really just a window. When a suspect seated in a brightly lit room looks at the glass, he sees his reflection because no light comes through the window from the dark room on the other side. If the observers—and you, as the audience—are in the dark room looking through the window, you see light coming from the suspect. Sometimes, the observer's side of the glass is coated with a very thin layer of metal. This reflects back even more light to the suspect but is not thick enough to prevent the observer from seeing through.

Another important use of reflection is in fiber optics. Light travels through a plastic or glass fiber that can be as thin as a human hair. The top picture shows that light entering one end reflects back and forth inside the fiber until it reaches the other end. Many different types of information can be converted to light energy and passed through fiber optic cables like those in the photo. Fiber optics are also used to look inside aircraft engines or other complicated machinery without taking them apart.

The ability of light to reflect enables it to travel through curved fiber optic cables. ▼

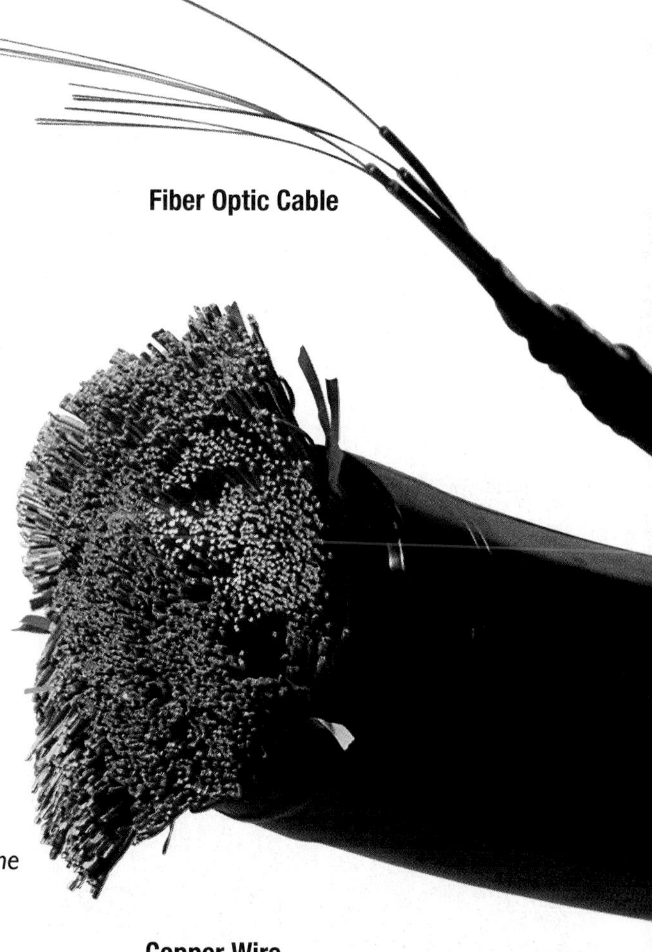

When they are used in phone lines, two fiber optic cables can carry as many as 24,000 phone calls at the same time. By contrast, regular copper wire that has traditionally been used to carry phone calls requires a much thicker cable to transmit just a single phone call. ▶

Glossary

Glossary

refraction (ri frak′ shən), the bending of a light wave as it moves from one material to another

Refraction of Light

Look at the handle of the fishnet below as it is seen from the side of the tank. Notice how it looks broken or bent. Although light travels in straight lines, when it moves from one clear substance, such as air, into another, such as water or glass, it can change direction. This happens because the wave changes speed as it travels between different types of materials.

To help you picture why this happens, imagine that you and some friends are marching arm in arm in a line across a sidewalk. Suddenly, you step off the sidewalk into a muddy patch of lawn. The thick mud makes you slow down. If you and your friends all step into the mud at the same time, you all slow down at once and your line stays straight. But if you alone step into the mud and slow down, and your friends on the sidewalk continue at the same speed, what happens? The line bends.

A light wave does the same thing. As it travels between different clear substances, the light wave bends. This bending is called **refraction**. When light passes from water into air, the light changes direction. If the girl in the picture looks down into the water as she tries to catch a fish in her net, she will probably miss the fish. The light reflecting from the fish appears to be traveling in a straight line, but the light actually bends as it comes out of the water. The fish won't be where she thinks it is!

The refraction of light waves causes the net's handle to look bent. ▼

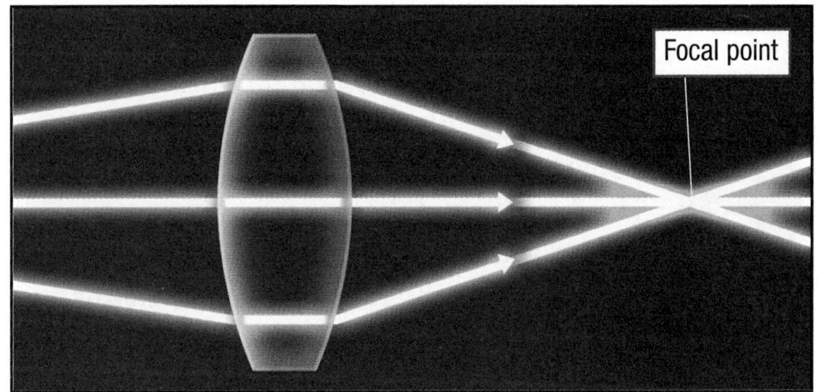

Convex Lens

◀ *Light entering a lens can change direction twice—once as it enters the lens and again when it leaves. The rays cross at the focal point of the lens. If your eye is beyond the focal point, objects will look larger and upside down.*

If you wear corrective lenses such as glasses or contacts, or know someone who does, you are already familiar with refraction. A lens is a curved piece of glass, plastic, or other clear material that refracts light that passes through it. Because lenses for different uses must bend light in different ways, not all lenses are alike.

A convex lens is a lens that is thicker in the middle than at the edges. Look at the convex lens above. You can see that light rays passing through the lens bend toward the thickest part of the lens—the middle.

The lens of your eye is a convex lens. It brings light rays together on the retina at the back of your eye. This bending allows you to see a sharp image.

In the diagram, notice that the light rays coming from the object cross each other after they leave the lens. The point at which the rays meet is called the **focal point**. If your eye is beyond the focal point, the object looks upside down. Images that fall on your retina are actually upside down. Fortunately, your brain is smart enough to flip the pictures on your retina so that the image appears to be right-side up.

The picture to the right shows a concave lens—a lens that is thicker at the edges than it is in the middle. Follow the light rays as they enter the lens. Notice that, like the light rays in a convex lens, they bend toward the thickest part of the glass. With a concave lens, that is toward the edges. A concave lens spreads out the light coming from an object.

Lenses are used in microscopes to enlarge the image of objects too small to see with the unaided eye. They are also used in eyeglasses to make words bigger and easier to read.

Glossary

focal point
(fō′kəl point), the point at which light rays meet when reflected or refracted

Concave Lens

Light rays entering and leaving a concave lens spread apart. ▼

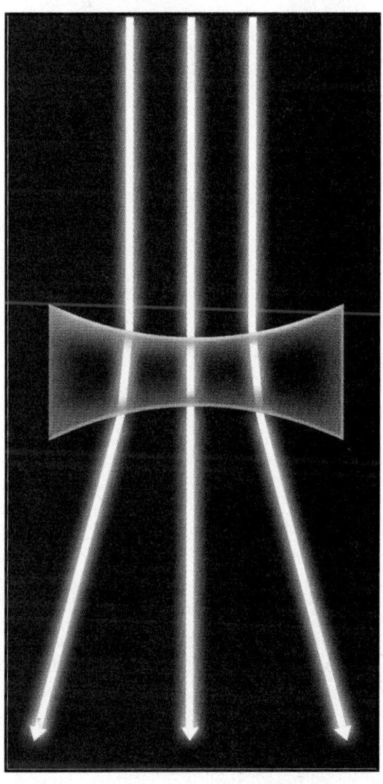

Glossary

laser light (lā′zər līt), light of a single wavelength with all the waves lined up

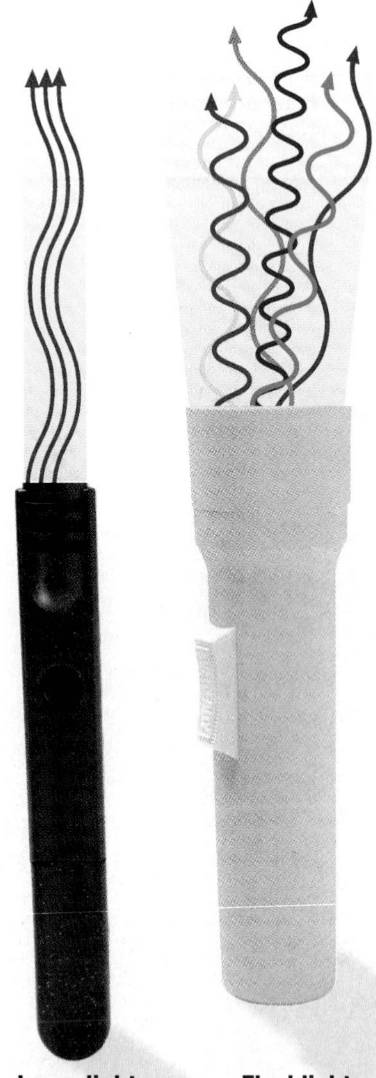

▲ *Compare the waves produced by these two light sources.*

Laser Light

Have you ever used a flashlight? Notice in the picture to the left that light travels away from the end of the flashlight in all directions. The farther the light gets from the source, the more the light spreads out and the dimmer it becomes. The light coming from a flashlight and other ordinary light sources is also made up of many different wavelengths.

In 1960, Theodore Maiman, a scientist from the United States, created a very different kind of light—the laser. Maiman built a light source that produced waves with almost the same wavelength. Even more important was the way those waves traveled.

To help you understand how a laser works, think about this example. You may have seen fans at a football game do something called "the wave." Even though many people in the wave are moving, they all move in a single pattern. The light waves in a laser work in a similar way. Instead of traveling away from the source in all different directions, the waves move together so that their crests and troughs line up. **Laser light**, therefore, is light of a single wavelength with all the waves lined up, similar to the light waves coming from the laser to the left.

Laser light has many uses. Because the laser light doesn't spread out, it can move information from one place to another at the speed of light and with very little loss of quality. This information can take many forms, such as your voice over the phone and the music that comes from your CD player.

Lasers are used in some endoscopes—tools doctors use to see inside a patient's body. A laser at the tip of the endoscope is used to burn away damaged tissue. With this treatment, a patient doesn't have to undergo major surgery and the recovery time from the surgery is much shorter.

When the checker in the grocery store passes a box or can over the glass plate in the counter, a low energy laser reads the dark and light bands in the bar code. A computer looks up the code, then prints the name of the item and its price on your receipt.

Lasers have many industrial uses too. The laser in the photo to the right is burning through metal. These kinds of lasers are used to cut out metal machine parts that have very smooth edges. Lasers can cut clothing patterns from thick stacks of material without burning the cloth.

Some lasers can do very delicate tasks such as removing dirt from works of art or mending the retina of the eye if it is torn. Laser light is used to make holograms, make and play CDs or videodisks, carry conversations by telephone, communicate with satellites, and burn away cancer cells.

▲ *Lasers, like the one here, allow people to shape tiny devices used in miniature electronics, medical tools, and sensors. Larger lasers are used in the manufacture of cars, machine tools, ships, and space vehicles.*

Lesson 2 Review

1. How is light reflected?
2. How is light refracted?
3. What is laser light?
4. **Measure Angles**
   What kind of angle is shown at the top of page B123? How do you know?

Lasers make it possible for you to listen to better-quality music recorded on CDs. ▼

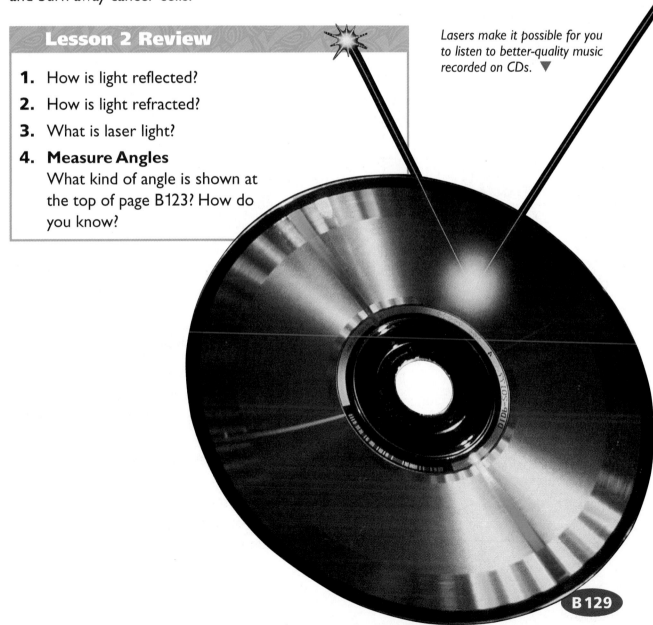

Investigate Activity

Investigating Light

Process Skills

Process Skills

- observing
- predicting
- inferring

Materials

- hole punch
- metric ruler
- black construction paper
- plastic bottle with cap
- scissors
- clear tape
- funnel
- water
- pan
- push pin
- flashlight

Getting Ready

In this activity, you can observe how light can travel in a stream of water in some conditions even though light travels in a straight line.

Follow This Procedure

1. Make a chart like the one shown. Use your chart to record your predictions and observations.

	Prediction	Observations
Bottle with cap on	x	
Bottle with cap off		
Bottle being squeezed	x	

2. Use the hole punch to punch a hole about 3 cm from the edge near the center of one side of a sheet of black construction paper.

3. Wrap the paper around the bottle, positioning the hole at the bottom of the bottle. Trim the paper with scissors as needed to leave a 3 cm wide vertical slit between the edges of the paper. The vertical slit should be directly across the bottle from the punched hole. Tape the paper to the bottle.

4. Use a funnel to fill the bottle with water. Place the cap on the bottle. Place the bottle in a shallow pan (Photo A).

Photo A

Photo B

5 Use a push pin to make a hole in the bottle, directly in the center of the hole punched in the black paper. Twist the push pin slightly to make the hole a bit larger (Photo B). Remove the push pin.

6 Dim the lights in the classroom. Shine a flashlight through the slit in the paper. **Observe** the light coming from the hole in the paper. Record your observations.

7 **Predict** what will happen to the light when you take off the bottle cap. Record your prediction.

8 Remove the bottle cap. Look at the stream of water coming from the pinhole in the bottle. Record your observations.

9 Squeeze the bottle very slightly and release it to change the angle of the stream of water. What happens to the light? Record your observations.

Interpret Your Results

1. What did you predict would happen to the light coming through the hole in the paper when you took the cap off the bottle? How did your prediction compare with your observation?

2. Make an **inference.** If light travels in a straight line, how can you explain your observations?

Inquire Further

Does the number of holes in the bottle make a difference in the way light acts? Develop a plan to answer this or other questions you may have.

Self-Assessment

- I followed instructions to make a device that would show properties of light.
- I **predicted** what would happen when the bottle cap was removed.
- I **observed** the interaction of light and water.
- I compared my prediction and observations.
- I made an **inference** to explain my observations.

You will learn:

- how color and the electromagnetic spectrum are related.
- how the primary colors of light produce other colors.
- how an opaque object gets its color.
- how a transparent object gets its color.

Lesson 3

What Is Color?

"Look! There's a rainbow! Let's see if we can find the pot of gold!" Even if there's no pot of gold at the rainbow's end, the beautiful colors in a rainbow make it something special to see. Where do the colors come from?

The Electromagnetic Spectrum and Color

History of Science

Look out the window and notice the sunlight. This sunlight is called white light. You might think of white light as having no color, but all the colors you see around you are actually contained within white light. White light is a mixture of all the different colors of light.

How do scientists know that white light is made from many different colors? In 1666, Isaac Newton first separated white light into its individual colors. He used a very simple technique that you may have already seen. Newton used a triangular piece of glass, like the prism shown here, to separate white light into all the colors of the rainbow.

How does a prism separate the colors in white light? As a beam of sunlight passes from the air into the glass prism, the light slows down and bends—it's refracted. Because each color has a different wavelength, each slows down and bends a different amount. This causes the colors to spread out into a rainbow.

Even if you haven't seen a prism separate light, you probably have seen a similar effect as light passes through other objects. For example, a rainbow results when light passes through drops of water. Even light passing through window glass will produce a rainbow effect at times.

As white light passes into a prism, waves of each color slow down and change direction. Red light waves bend the least and violet bends the most. The colors are arranged by how much each wave is refracted. ▼

Light you can see is called visible light. As you can see to the right, visible light is only a small part of all the waves that radiate from the sun. X rays, microwaves, and radio waves are also forms of the sun's radiation. All waves that radiate from the sun are called electromagnetic (EM) waves.

The different types of EM radiation, including visible light, are alike in many ways. All EM radiation travels in a wavelike pattern and at the same speed—the speed of light. How fast is that? It takes sunlight only about 8 minutes to make the trip to Earth—a distance of about 149,730,000 kilometers. That's fast! Scientists believe that the speed of light is the fastest speed that anything in the universe can go.

An important difference exists between the different types of EM radiation too. Each type of radiation differs in the amount of energy it contains and in its wavelength or frequency.

The arrangement of EM waves in order of their wavelength or frequency is called the electromagnetic spectrum. The range of wavelengths that the human eye can see is called the visible spectrum. Compared to the entire range of all EM waves, the visible spectrum is tiny. However, those few wavelengths provide you with all the color in your world.

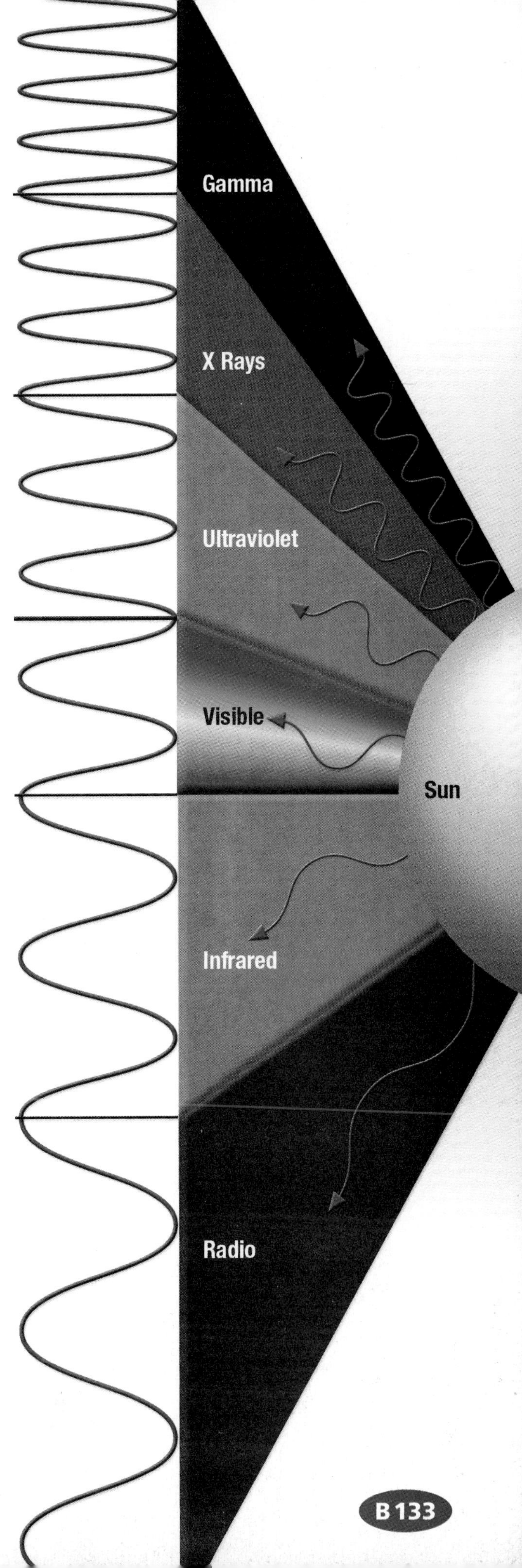

Electromagnetic Spectrum

Photons from the sun travel through space, carrying different amounts of energy. The entire range of energy waves is called the electromagnetic spectrum. ▶

You may have noticed that rainbow colors always appear in the same order—red, orange, yellow, green, blue, indigo, and violet. As you can see to the left, red light has the longest wavelength and the lowest energy of all the colors. Violet light has the most energy and the shortest wavelength in the visible spectrum.

Even though light from the sun includes all the colors, the sun looks yellow because the higher frequency colors like blue and violet get scattered away by the atmosphere. The rest of the wavelengths mix together, and when they reach your eyes, they look yellow.

▲ *Most people name only six major colors in the visible spectrum, but your eyes can actually tell the difference among many thousands of colors.*

Life Science

Not all organisms see the same range of EM wavelengths as you do. In the early part of this century, scientists thought that bees could see the same colors as humans. But in 1910, Karl von Frisch, a scientist from Germany, performed a series of experiments to test the eyesight of bees. From the results of his experiments, he concluded that bees can't see some colors you can—crimson shades of red, for example—but they can see ultraviolet light—a range of wavelengths that humans can't see.

You might wonder what advantage seeing ultraviolet light might be to bees. They use this ability to find the nectar in a flower. How? Some flowers reflect ultraviolet light in patterns that show the bees the place on the flower where they can find nectar.

Mixing Colors

Human Body

Bees may see ultraviolet light, but what do you see? Lavender. Peach. Chartreuse. People have many names to describe the wide range of colors they can see. Surprisingly, your eyes need to sense only three of the colors in the visible spectrum to be able to see all colors. These three colors—red, green, and blue—are called the primary colors of light.

Your eyes contain three types of light-sensitive cells, called cones. Each type of cone is most sensitive to wavelengths of one of the three primary colors of light. If red, blue, or green light strikes your eyes, only one type of cone responds, sending messages to your brain.

For example, if wavelengths of red light hit the cones that are sensitive to red, you will see red.

Your eyes and brain create all the colors other than the primary ones by mixing the primary colors in different amounts. You see a certain color according to the amount of signals the brain gets from each of the three types of cones. For example, what color would you see if your brain received an equal amount of signals from all three cones? Use the diagram to the right to help you answer the question.

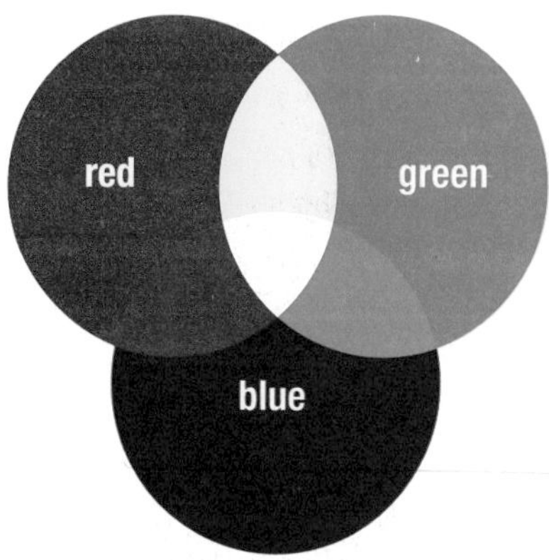

Primary Colors of Light

▲ *When beams of red, blue, and green light overlap, your eye combines each pair into yellow, blue-green (cyan), and magenta. Where all three overlap, all three types of cones in your eye receive equal signals and you see white.*

Now notice where only the red and green circles in the diagram overlap. That combination makes yellow. If yellow light enters your eye, the blue cones respond very little. However, the red and green cones react more strongly. A signal tells your brain, "red + green." Your brain knows that red and green make yellow, so that's the color you see. However, if instead of yellow light, your eye receives red and green light, you would see the same color yellow!

When you watch a television show or use a computer like the one here you probably see a wide range of colors. However, your television or computer screen is actually filled with tiny dots in only the three primary colors. When the TV camera records an image, it changes the different colors of light in the scene into electrical signals that represent red, blue, and green. When these signals reach your TV, they cause dots of the right color to light up in the right places. When the light from all the dots enters your eye, your brain interprets the amount of each signal. You see red and blue balloons and the blue and green of the people's clothing—all in their correct colors.

This computer screen combines the primary colors of light to produce the pictures you see. ▶

Glossary

Glossary

opaque (ō pāk′), does not allow light to pass through

Primary Colors of Paint

Notice that the three primary colors of paint in the top image are the same as the colors produced when two primary colors of light, shown in the bottom image are mixed. ▼

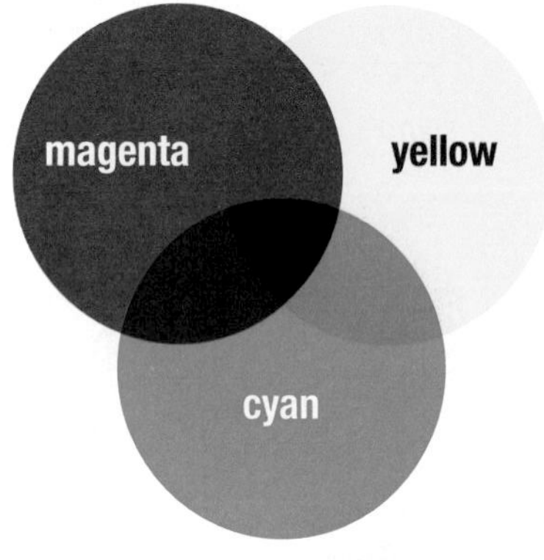

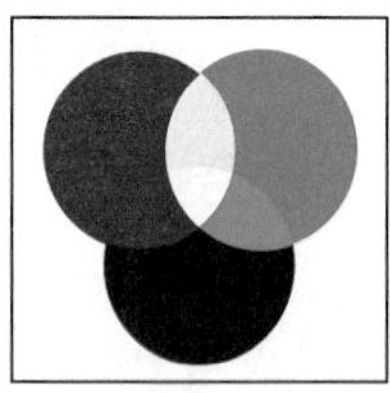

Opaque Objects

If white is a combination of all colors, what is black? In a cave, where there is no light, you don't really see black. Your eyes simply don't see anything at all because they receive no energy. Black is the sensation you get when very little light of any color enters your eye.

Opaque objects are objects that light doesn't pass through, such as the metal of a car or the bricks in a wall. Objects can absorb some of the wavelengths of the light that strikes them. Those wavelengths that aren't absorbed are reflected. Your eye can see only the wavelengths that are reflected. For example, the skin of an orange reflects orange wavelengths to your eye and absorbs the others.

If an object contains substances that absorb almost all wavelengths of visible light equally, the object reflects very little light back to the eye. As a result, the object appears to be black or dark gray.

In winter, people often wear dark clothes because the dark colors absorb most of the light energy that falls on them. The energy makes molecules in the clothing move faster. The temperature of the clothing actually rises!

People often change the color of opaque objects by painting them. You can see from the picture to the left that mixing paint is different from mixing light. What if, instead of mixing light, you mix red, blue and green paint together? It sure isn't white, is it? Red, blue, and green are the primary colors of light. The primary colors of paint are yellow, cyan, and magenta. How does mixing the primary colors of paint differ from mixing the primary colors of light?

Why do colors of light and colors of paint behave differently when they're mixed? Red paint looks red because it reflects the red wavelengths in white light and absorbs the other colors. Blue paint reflects blue, and green paint reflects green. You might think that if you mix the three colors of paint together, you'd see white. However, each of the three colors absorbs wavelengths of the other two, so those wavelengths aren't reflected. Therefore, when you mix red, blue, and green paint, few wavelengths are reflected back to your eyes. The mixture looks nearly black.

White clothing reflects most of the wavelengths of light. Because the clothing doesn't absorb much energy, you stay cooler. Black or dark clothing absorbs not only wavelengths of light, but also electromagnetic waves that aren't visible to the eye, such as infrared energy. ▶

On the other hand, white objects reflect nearly all the light that falls on them. That's why, in hot weather, people wear white or light clothing. Wearing light clothing generally keeps you cooler than wearing dark clothing—energy from the sun is reflected by your clothes rather than being absorbed by them.

Look at the picture of the leaf. You probably think of trees, grass, and other growing things as green. But these objects actually absorb and use many wavelengths of light except green, which is reflected. Artificial electric lights used to help plants grow give off wavelengths in the violet and ultraviolet range.

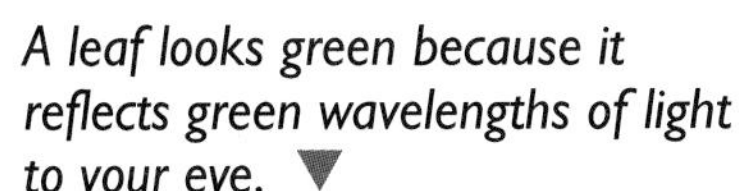

A leaf looks green because it reflects green wavelengths of light to your eye. ▼

You don't always see the color of an object the same way. For example, after the sun sets, you see much less color in objects outside. Because little light is striking Earth at that time, less light is reflected back to your eyes. Therefore, your color vision doesn't work very well. At that point, other sensors in your eyes take over. These sensors, called rods, aren't sensitive to color, but can respond to smaller amounts of light. Because of the rods, you can still see when there's not much light—you just don't see in color.

Minerals under white light

Minerals under black light

▲ *Under white light, these minerals reflect the wavelengths that produce their colors. Under black light, atoms in the minerals actually absorb invisible UV energy and produce their own visible light.*

Glossary

Glossary

transparent (tran spər′ənt), allows light to pass through so that objects on the other side can be seen

The photos show two different images of the same collection of minerals. The photo on the left was taken in natural white light. In the right photo, the minerals were lighted with a special light called a black light. Black light isn't really black. The bulb of a black light gives off wavelengths in the visible violet range and in the ultraviolet (U.V.) range of the EM spectrum.

When a high-energy ultraviolet light strikes minerals, the energy isn't simply absorbed or reflected as is visible light. Atoms in the minerals actually absorb invisible UV energy and give off their own visible light. When normal light strikes the minerals, we don't see the glow—the colors look like those of ordinary rocks. However, when you look at the minerals in black light, they seem to glow.

If you wear a white shirt near a black light, the shirt may also glow. Manufacturers add dyes to detergents that react with ultraviolet light in the same way that the minerals do. This reaction makes the clothes look "whiter and brighter."

If you've ever looked at a glow-in-the-dark poster under a black light, you've seen a similar reaction. Other substances which glow under black light include your teeth, wintergreen mints, and even scorpions!

Transparent Objects

As you probably know, light passes through many objects made of materials such as glass or plastic. An object is said to be **transparent** if light passes through it so that you can see objects on the other side. When this happens, we say that the object transmits light. What transparent objects can you see around you?

Recall that you see a color when light of a certain wavelength reaches your eye. As light passes through a colored transparent object, the object absorbs some of the wavelengths and transmits only the ones that produce the color you see. Why do some transparent objects have no color?

When you look out a regular window, such as the one shown here, you see the light that passes through it from the other side. In windows that appear to have no color, all of the wavelengths of light are transmitted. They all reach your eyes, so the scene looks the same as it would if you were on the other side.

▲ *Windows made of colorless glass allow all wavelengths of visible light to pass through them.*

On the other hand, the stained glass window below is an example of a transparent substance that transmits different wavelengths of light. Each section in the window transmits certain wavelengths of light while absorbing the rest. As the transmitted wavelengths strike your eye, they fall on the retina in the same pattern as the pattern on the window. The cones in your retina respond to those wavelengths. Then your brain converts those signals into an image of the entire colorful window.

▲ *The "stains" in a stained glass window are compounds that are mixed with the glass before it hardens or that are fused to the surface of the glass after it hardens. Specific compounds are chosen because they transmit the colors the artist wants viewers to see.*

Lesson 3 Review

1. How are the electromagnetic spectrum and color related?
2. How are the primary colors of light mixed to produce other colors?
3. How does an opaque object get its color?
4. How does a transparent object get its color?
5. **Draw Conclusions**
   A purple plum reflects and absorbs the colors of white light. Which colors are reflected and which are absorbed?

You will learn:

- how sound is produced.
- how sounds differ.
- what happens when sound reflects and refracts.
- the difference between music and noise.

Lesson 4

What Is Sound?

"Wow! Listen to the sun!" Imagine what it would be like if we could hear sounds from the sun. We get all kinds of other energy from the sun. Why don't we get any sound energy?

How Sound Is Produced

Suppose you placed a ticking clock inside a glass jar and pumped all the air out of the jar. Would you still be able to see the clock? Would you be able to hear it? In 1658, Robert Boyle, an English scientist, did an experiment to find answers to those questions.

Boyle slowly pumped air out of a glass jar containing a ticking watch. When there was very little air left in the jar, the sound of the ticking disappeared. However, Boyle could still see the watch. Light could pass through the jar even though it contained no particles of air, but sound could not. From this simple experiment, Boyle concluded that air particles must be present to carry sound to a person's ears.

Why can't sound travel through empty space when light can? Sound is produced when matter vibrates. You can feel the vibrations if you lightly touch your throat as you are speaking, like the girl to the left.

How are sound vibrations produced? As you can see on the next page, as objects vibrate, particles of air are pushed together in a particular pattern. This pattern is a sound wave.

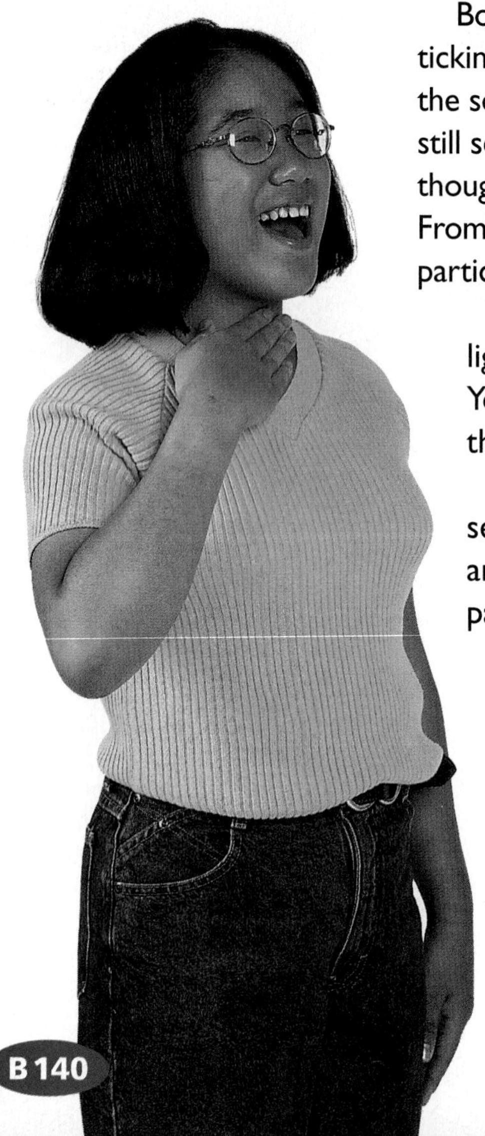

When this girl speaks, air passing over her vocal cords causes them to vibrate. These vibrations produce sound waves.

How Sound Waves Are Produced

▲ *When the clapper hits the bell, it makes the metal in the bell vibrate. This vibration causes the air to vibrate.*

▲ *As the air particles around the bell vibrate, there will be areas where the air is compressed and expanded. These areas move away from the bell.*

▲ *A sound wave is made up of these areas of compression and expansion. The areas of compression are like the crests in transverse waves. Areas of expansion are like troughs.*

Recall that light travels as a transverse wave. In a transverse wave, energy moves in one direction, while the crests and troughs move at right angles to that direction. Sound energy travels in **compressional waves**. In a compressional wave matter vibrates in the same direction as the energy waves that travel through it.

You can compare a compressional wave and a transverse wave by looking at the picture below. In a compressional wave, the areas where particles are pushed together—the compressions—are like the crests in a transverse wave. The areas where the particles are spread apart are like the troughs.

Glossary

compressional wave (kəm presh′ən əl wāv), wave in which matter vibrates in the same direction as the energy waves traveling through it

Glossary

The areas in a compressional wave where particles are pushed together and spread apart are like the crests and troughs in a transverse wave. ▼

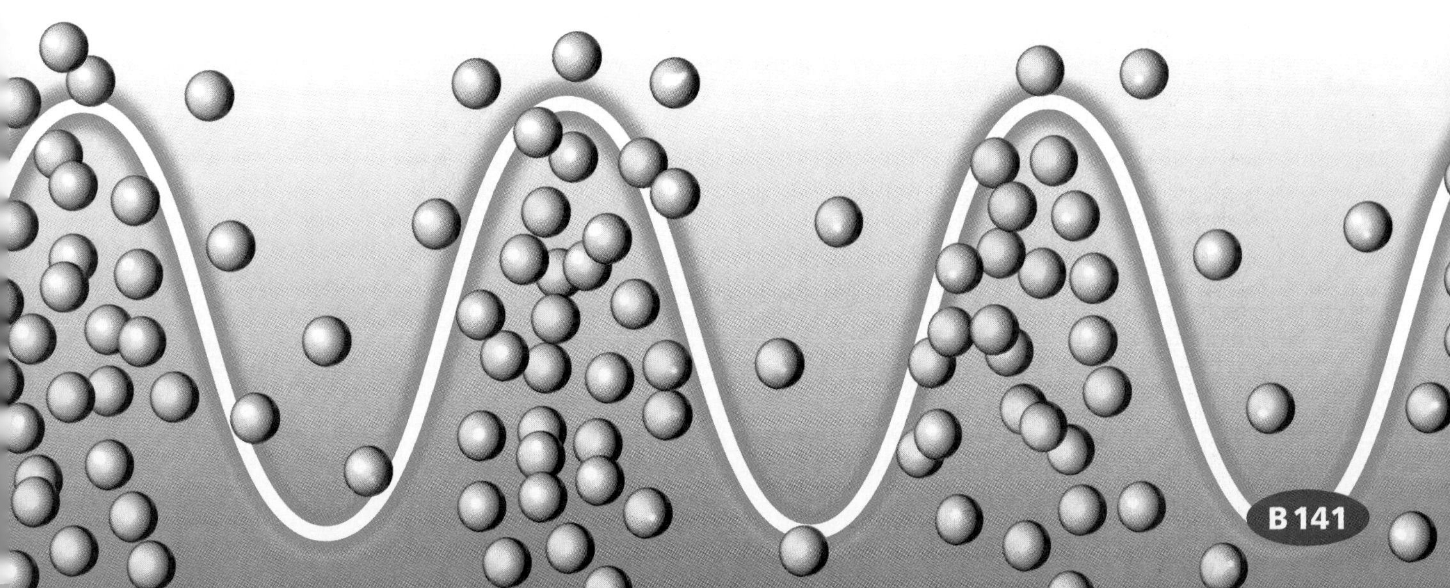

Just as you can measure the wavelength of light, you can also measure the wavelength of sound waves by measuring the distance between a wave's crests or troughs. You can measure the wavelength of sound waves by measuring the distance between the compressions. The frequency of the sound wave is the number of compressions that pass a given point in a particular amount of time.

Sound waves can only travel by passing through matter—solids, liquids, or gases. If you put your ear against the top of your desk and tap the desk lightly with your finger like the boy in the picture, you'll hear the sound through the desktop.

Because sound waves must travel through matter, they carry much less energy and move much more slowly than light waves. In fact, light travels about 870,000 times faster than sound travels in air. You can observe a dramatic example of this difference during a thunderstorm. Although storm clouds produce thunder and lightning at the exact same time, the light reaches your eyes much more quickly than the sound reaches your ears.

How Sound Differs

From the chirping of a tiny bird to the roar of a train, sounds are all around you. But how do some vibrations produce one kind of sound and other vibrations produce other kinds of sounds? You learned that the difference between one color and another is the wavelength and frequency of the light. In a similar way, different sounds are produced by sound waves with different frequencies.

Sound is carried from the boy's tapping finger to his ear by the matter that makes up the desk. ▼

As matter vibrates faster and faster, the compressions in the sound wave get closer and closer together. That is, the frequency increases. The faster the frequency of the wave, the faster it makes your eardrums vibrate when the wave reaches your ears. You sense this higher frequency as a higher tone, or pitch. Pitch is how high or low a sound seems.

The canary in the picture makes a sound that seems high to most people. The canary's vocal cords vibrate very fast, so the sound waves it makes in the air have a high frequency. The canary's song changes from one frequency to another, but most of its notes have a high pitch. The roar of a lion has a much lower pitch. Notice the long wavelength of its sound.

The frequency of sound is measured in hertz. Humans can hear sounds with frequencies from about 20 hertz to 20,000 hertz. We're most sensitive to sounds between 2,000 and 4,000 hertz. Dogs can hear frequencies up to about 30,000 hertz. That's why they perk up their ears at sounds that you don't hear.

Many birds make sounds above 20,000 hertz. Because birds can also hear frequencies much higher than humans can, they probably hear other bird sounds that you don't hear. ▼

High pitch

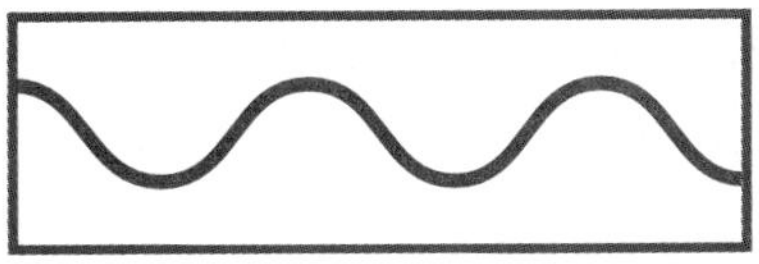

Low pitch

◀ *As the lion roars, different parts of its mouth and throat vibrate at different frequencies. The sound blends together to form a special sound unique to that lion.*

Glossary

intensity (in ten′sə tē), a measure of the amount of energy in a wave

What determines how loud a sound is? Recall that high-energy hurricane winds can produce water waves with a large amplitude—high crests and deep troughs. A wave's amplitude tells how much energy it contains. The more energy a sound wave has, the greater its **intensity** is. A very intense sound has lots of energy and a large amplitude. It seems loud. A less intense sound has less energy and a smaller amplitude. It seems soft.

Intensity can be measured in units called decibels. Below, you can see the decibel level of some common sounds. A whisper measures about 10 decibels. However, another sound may have an intensity of 20 decibels. This difference in decibels means that the sound has ten times the intensity of the whisper. This, however, does not mean it will seem ten times louder.

It's difficult to decide how loud one sound compares with another. That's because one person's ears may be more sensitive to sound than another person's ears. Some older people lose the ability to hear high or low sounds. The moving parts of the ear may not work as easily as they once did, or the eardrum may be damaged.

Remember that sounds are caused by vibrations. Have you ever watched a stereo speaker as music plays? The cardboard in the speaker vibrates back and forth. The louder the music, the farther the cardboard moves from its resting position. If the music is loud enough, the cardboard may break.

Decibel Scale

As intensity increases by ten decibels, a sound is ten times more intense and carries ten times as much energy. The sound of a power mower at 100 decibels carries 1,000 times as much energy as the sound of a vacuum cleaner at 70 decibels. (10x10x10=1,000) ▼

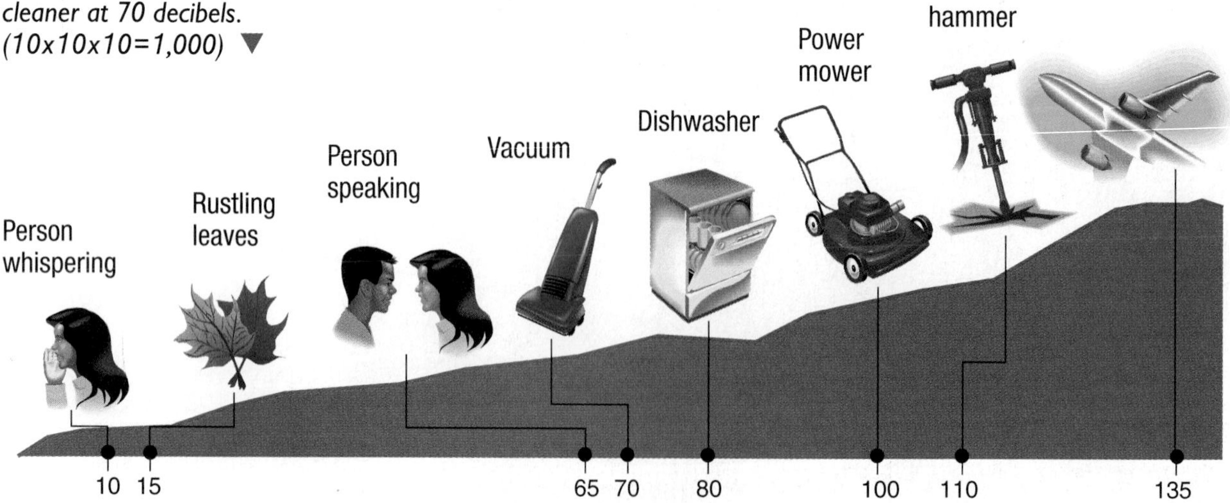

Human Body

Your eardrum is like that speaker. The louder the sounds, the harder your eardrum is forced to vibrate. Your eardrum can break like the cardboard in the speaker. Scar tissue that forms as your eardrum heals can make your eardrum thicker. If that happens, you won't be able to hear the whole range of sounds you could hear before.

Sounds from matter that vibrates above 20,000 hertz is beyond the range of hearing even for healthy human ears. Sound above this level is called ultrasound. Ultrasound waves have many uses. They can be used to weld plastic or test aircraft parts for cracks or tears.

Have you ever had an ultrasound test at the doctor's office? Doctors use ultrasonic waves to examine soft tissue in the body, often to check for injuries.

Other organisms use ultrasound waves too. Dolphins, such as those below, create ultrasonic sound waves to identify objects around them. The sounds bounce off objects and, when they return to the dolphin, the animal can figure out the distance, shape, and size of the object. Bats use sounds of up to 100,000 hertz to help them fly in the dark. By using the echo of these sounds, they can avoid objects even though they cannot see them.

The dolphin's large, bony forehead acts as a receiver when the ultrasonic signals it creates bounce back from objects in the water. ▼

Reflection and Refraction of Sound

Like light waves, sound waves can be reflected. A reflected sound wave is an echo. It's produced when sound bounces off a hard, smooth surface that is large enough to reflect sound back to your ear.

Why don't you hear echoes all the time? Why doesn't the sound of your voice always bounce off the walls of the room and return to your ears? It does! You can't hear an echo if it arrives at your ear in less than one-tenth of a second after the original sound.

A large room can produce so many echoes that people have a hard time making sense of all the sounds. Think about the noise during a basketball game in a gym. Sounds bounce all over the place. During a basketball game, individual sounds aren't as important as the action. But what about echoes in a movie theater or a concert hall like the one shown here? Echoes could drown out voices or music.

Notice the panels on the wall in the picture. You may have noticed similar panels on the walls and ceilings of a movie theater. The panels may be made of a soft material or may have tiny holes that absorb sound energy instead of reflecting it. Rough surfaces scatter the sound instead of reflecting it straight back. In addition, the seats in the theater may be covered in fabric, which absorbs sound waves. The people sitting in the theater seats also absorb sound. When you put all these sound-absorbing objects together, echoes aren't produced.

Sometimes echoes can be helpful. For example, people can use sound echoes to measure underwater distances with a device called sonar, which stands for sound navigation and ranging. French scientist Paul Langevin worked to develop this device after the *Titanic* sank in 1912. The picture on the next page shows how sonar works.

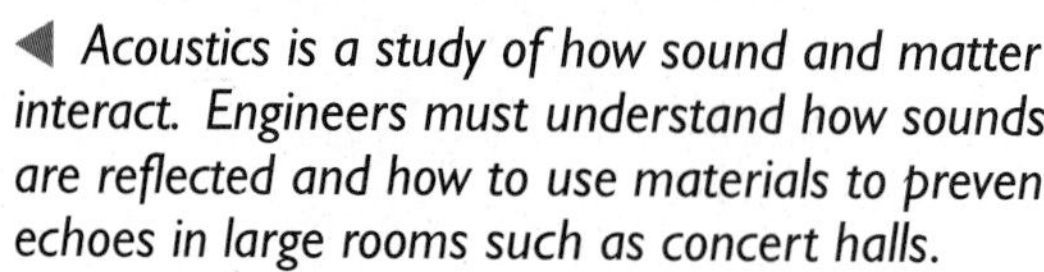
◀ *Acoustics is a study of how sound and matter interact. Engineers must understand how sounds are reflected and how to use materials to prevent echoes in large rooms such as concert halls.*

Scientists send sound waves from a ship toward the bottom of the ocean. The sound waves echo off the bottom of the ocean floor. Scientists then record the echoes of the waves as they return to the ship. Because they know how fast sound travels in water, scientists can figure out how deep the water is. Sound images let people see the shape of the lake or ocean floor. Parts of the ocean floor have been mapped in this way.

Sonar also lets people locate sunken ships, like the one in the picture, even in the deepest or cloudiest water. The *Titanic* was finally found in 1985 by using sonar.

Sound waves refract as well as reflect. Sound often refracts when it passes between states of matter, such as from air to water. Sound is also refracted when the temperature of the matter changes. If a ship is sailing on a foggy night through warm air with cooler air above it, the sound of a fog horn may bend upward. If this happens, the captain may not be able to tell where the shore is.

Glossary

sonar (sō′ när), a device which uses sound waves to measure distance

Glossary

Sonar

In the sonar image of this sunken ship, the black area is the ship's "sound shadow" on the lake bottom. If sound travels at about 1,500 meters per second in ocean water, and the signal takes 2 seconds to return to the ship, how deep is the sunken ship? ▼

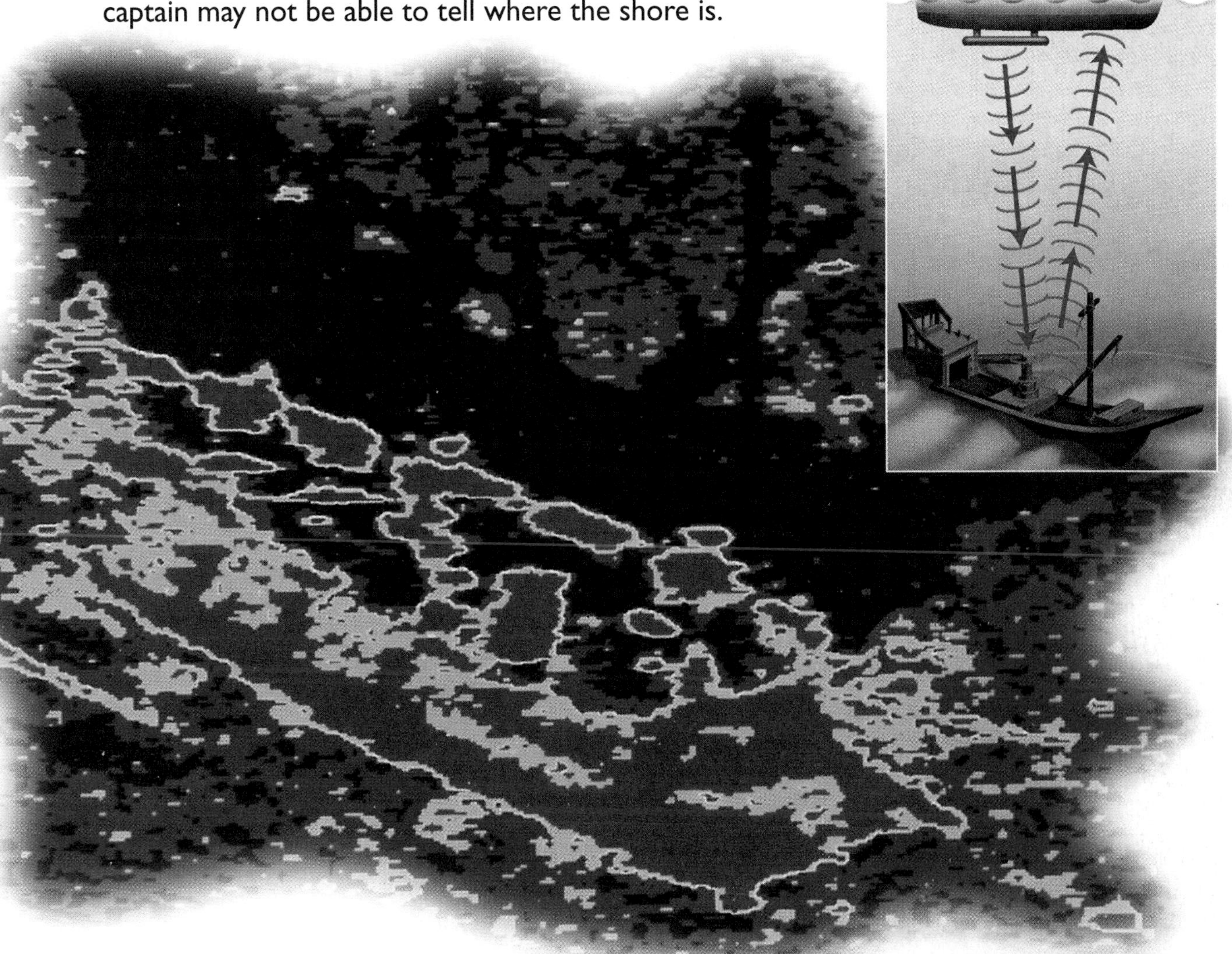

Glossary

Glossary

music (myü′zik), pleasant sound with regular wave patterns

noise (noiz), sound with no regular wave pattern

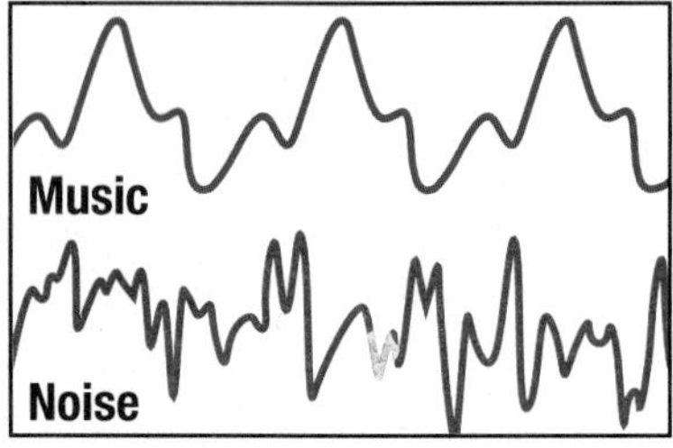

▲ *Compare the repeating pattern of the sound waves of noise to those of music.*

Music and Noise

You insist that your favorite music group plays great music, while your friend says, "That's just noise!" What's the difference? Look at the sound waves shown to the left. Notice the difference between the waves of sound and of noise. **Music** is pleasant sound with an organized and possibly a repeating pattern in its waves. **Noise** is sound with no recognizable pattern. For example, blaring car horns, banging construction work, and screeching sirens together produce sounds that have no regular wave form.

All musical instruments produce sounds by making vibrations in three different ways. Wind instruments produce sound as air vibrates inside a tube. The boy playing the wooden flute is blowing directly into the tube. In other instruments, such as a clarinet, you use your lips to start a thin reed vibrating, which in turn causes the air to vibrate.

In wind instruments, notes with higher or lower pitches are made as the musician changes the length of the air tube. You can see this clearly if you watch someone play the slide trombone.

Stringed instruments, such as a violin or a guitar, create sound waves when the musician plucks or draws a bow across the strings. This causes the strings to vibrate. Changing the length and tightness of the strings changes the frequency of the vibration.

Percussion instruments are played by striking a surface, such as a drumhead, wooden blocks, or metal plates, with a stick or with your hand. The object you strike begins to vibrate, producing sound. The size, thickness, or tightness of the instrument determines the pitch of its sounds. Some percussion instruments can't produce many different notes. They are often simply used to keep the beat of the music. However, xylophones are also percussion instruments. They have blocks of many sizes and can produce many frequencies. The woman in the picture on the next page is playing a percussion instrument.

Although all instruments work by creating vibrations, each instrument sounds different. Every vibrating object makes its own recognizable sound because the body of the instrument vibrates in several different ways. For example, when you make your vocal cords vibrate at a certain rate,

This boy changes the pitch of the sound the flute produces by covering different holes! ▼

you sing a note of a certain frequency. At the same time that the sound comes out of your mouth at that pitch, your throat, cheeks, and even the bones in your head are also vibrating at different frequencies. All those vibrations reach the listener's ear at the same time. People recognize the sound made by all those waves as your voice. Try changing the shape of your mouth as you sing a note. Hear the difference?

Although you have a distinctive voice, you can change the frequency of the notes you sing, making higher or lower sounds. *Do, re, mi, fa, sol, la, ti, do!* When one note has twice the frequency of another, the notes are said to be an **octave** apart. A musical scale like the one shown here is a series of notes in which the note at the top of the scale—the second *do*—has exactly twice the frequency of the note at the bottom—the first *do.*

Glossary

octave (ok′tiv), a musical sequence in which the top note has twice the frequency of the bottom note

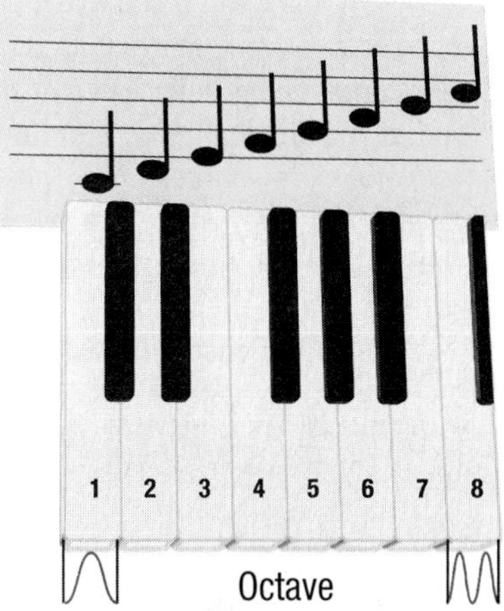

▲ *The word octave means "eight." In western music, there are eight notes in the scale. Each note increases in frequency in a natural and musically pleasing way.*

◀ *Tightening the skin of a drumhead raises the pitch in the same way that tightening a string on a stringed instrument does. The differently shaped bodies of the drums add other vibrations which give each drum its own sound quality.*

Vehicles, construction tools, machines in offices or stores, communication devices—all put sound waves into the air that create noise. Noise pollution is as serious a problem as air or water pollution. If you live in a city, you may not be able to turn all the sounds you hear into music, but you can find ways to cut down on the noise.

Air conditioning units, elevator motors, and other mechanical devices on the tops of buildings are sources of city noise. Some of the sounds they make are lower than 20 hertz. You can't hear them, but you can feel the vibrations they make in your body. These vibrations are called infrasound. ▶

The rumble of trucks, the honking of horns, and the sounds of car engines add to city noise. Intense sound vibrations can even make huge plate-glass store windows vibrate. If you have to listen to these noises all day, you can feel tired and irritable. ▼

▲ *This apartment is probably very noisy. There's nothing to keep the sound from bouncing off walls or floors. Smooth, hard surfaces of the room and the furniture reflect sound instead of absorbing it. Even footsteps sound hollow and loud in such a room.*

A building that is constructed to keep noises out has sound-absorbing insulation between the inner and outer walls and in the floors. Insulation in the walls between rooms keeps sound from traveling between apartments. Double windows can also help keep sound from entering. ▼

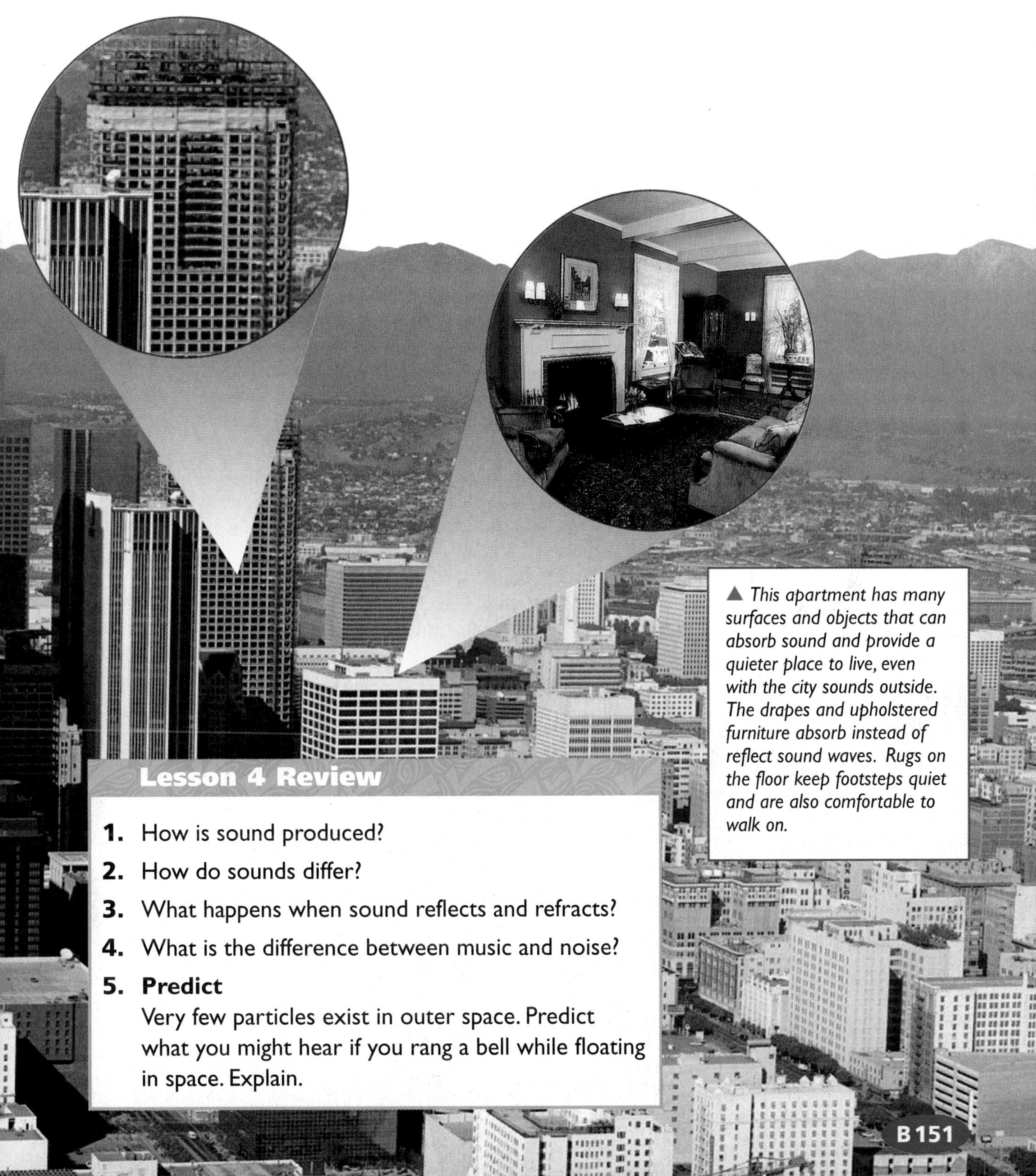

▲ *This apartment has many surfaces and objects that can absorb sound and provide a quieter place to live, even with the city sounds outside. The drapes and upholstered furniture absorb instead of reflect sound waves. Rugs on the floor keep footsteps quiet and are also comfortable to walk on.*

Lesson 4 Review

1. How is sound produced?
2. How do sounds differ?
3. What happens when sound reflects and refracts?
4. What is the difference between music and noise?
5. **Predict**
   Very few particles exist in outer space. Predict what you might hear if you rang a bell while floating in space. Explain.

Investigating Sound Insulation

Process Skills

Process Skills

- communicating
- predicting
- observing
- estimating and measuring
- inferring

Materials

- ticking clock
- assorted insulating materials such as wool, newspapers, packing "peanuts," foam rubber
- masking tape
- half-meter stick

Getting Ready

Design and test a package that will insulate the sound from a ticking clock.

Consider how you can limit the ability of sound to travel. Decide what kinds of materials you would like to test.

Follow This Procedure

1. Make a chart like the one shown. Use your chart to record your data.

Prediction: which group's design is the most soundproof?

Distance from package at which no sound is heard

Student 1:	
Student 2:	
Student 3:	
Student 4:	
Average:	

2. **Communicate.** Discuss with your group ways in which you can package a clock so that you cannot hear the clock's ticking. You may use no more than two packaging materials to insulate the sound.

3. Decide with the group on a package design. Sketch your package. Label the materials you will use to insulate sound so that it does not travel outside your package.

4. Observe the design sketches of all the groups. **Predict** which design will be the best soundproofing package.

5. Construct your package and then put the clock in it. Place the package containing the clock at one end of the classroom or hall.

6 Start by standing next to the package. Slowly walk away from the package, **observing** the ticking of the clock. Stop when you can no longer hear the ticking. Place a piece of masking tape on the floor to mark your location.

7 **Measure** the distance from the masking tape to the package. Record your measurement in the chart.

8 Repeat steps 6 and 7 for each member of the group.

9 Find the average distance for your group and record it in your chart.

Interpret Your Results

1. Describe your package. What materials did you use to stop sound from traveling?

2. Compare your group's results with those of other groups. Describe the packaging method that seemed to work best.

3. Compare your package design to the one that insulated best. What characteristics did the best package have that yours didn't?

4. Make an **inference.** How did the insulating materials stop sound from traveling?

Inquire Further

How might you make your package more soundproofed? Develop a plan to answer this or other questions you may have.

Self-Assessment

- I followed instructions to design and test a package to insulate sound.
- I **communicated** my ideas about the package design to my group.
- I recorded my **prediction** of which group's design would be the most soundproof.
- I **observed** the sound and recorded **measurements** to determine how well my package insulated sound.
- I compared my group's package with other designs and made an **inference** about insulating materials and sound.

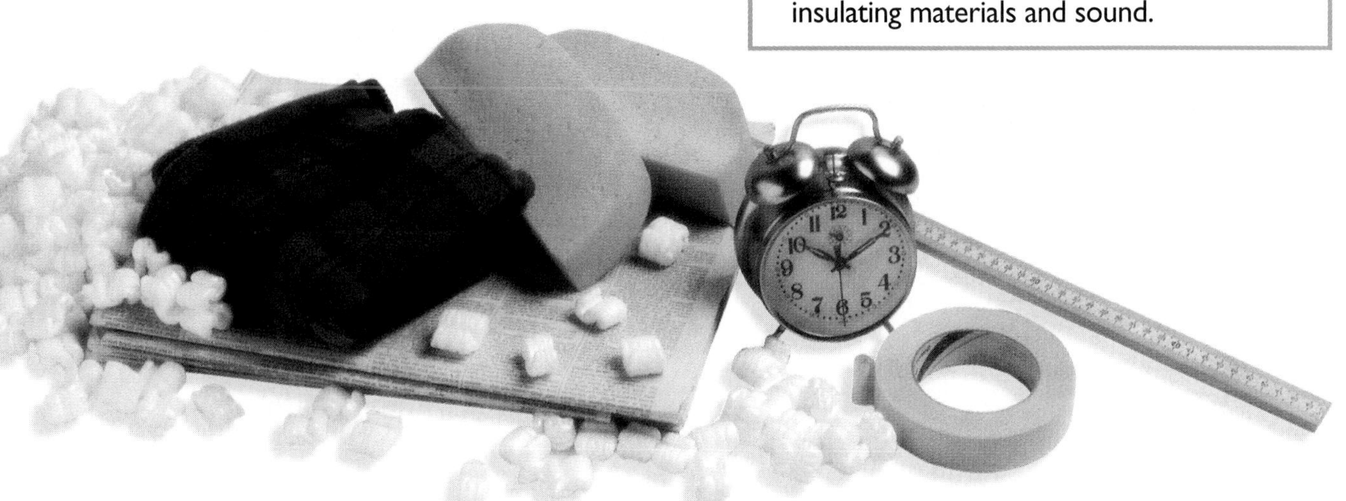

Chapter 4 Review

Chapter Main Ideas

Lesson 1

• Light has both wave and particle characteristics.

• Light waves are transverse waves with a wavelength, frequency, amplitude, and speed.

Lesson 2

• Light reflects from a surface much like a ball bounces off a wall.

• Light waves can be bent, or refracted, as they travel from one material to another.

• Laser light is light of a single wavelength with all of the waves lined up.

Lesson 3

• Visible light is only a small part of the electromagnetic spectrum.

• All colors are produced when primary colors combine in different proportions.

• An opaque object appears to be the color of light that it reflects.

• A transparent object appears to be the color of light that it transmits.

Lesson 4

• Sound is produced by the vibration of matter.

• Sounds differ because of their pitch and intensity.

• Sound can be reflected and refracted, causing echoes or distorted sounds.

• Music is an organized and repeating pattern of sound, while noise has no recognizable pattern.

Reviewing Science Words and Concepts

Write the letter of the word or phrase that best completes each sentence.

a. amplitude
b. compressional wave
c. concave mirror
d. convex mirror
e. focal point
f. frequency
g. intensity
h. laser light
i. music
j. noise
k. octave
l. opaque
m. photons
n. refraction
o. transparent
p. transverse wave

1. Light that can carry information in a beam that doesn't spread out is ___.
2. A mirror whose center section curves away from an object is a(n) ___.
3. The type of wave that carries sound is a(n) ___.
4. A pleasant sound with regular wave patterns is called ___.
5. The bending of a wave as it travels from one material to another is ___.
6. The number of waves that pass a point in a given amount of time is the wave's ___.
7. Unpleasant, irregular sound is called ___.
8. Light rays that are reflected or refracted may meet at a(n) ___.

9. A sound wave that carries a lot of energy and has a large amplitude has a lot of ___.
10. Light energy travels as a(n)___.
11. Light, X rays, and radio waves contain ___ with different amounts of energy.
12. Light rays reflected from a(n) ___ spread out.
13. This book is an example of a(n) ___ object.
14. You can see objects on the opposite side of a(n) ___ object.
15. The ___ of a transverse wave is shown by the height of the crest or trough of a wave.
16. When the frequency of a note is twice the frequency of another, the two notes are a(n) ___ apart.

Explaining Science

Draw and label a diagram or write a paragraph to answer these questions.

1. In what way does light behave as a particle? as a wave?

2. How are the types of energy in the electromagnetic spectrum alike and different?

3. How do you see black print on a white page?

4. Why can't sound travel from the sun to Earth?

Using Skills

1. Use a protractor to **measure the angles** of the light rays striking the rough surface on page B123.

2. Look at the picture of the leaf on page B137. **Predict** what would happen if only red light shined on the leaf.

3. You observe that when you blow a dog whistle, your dog comes even though you can't hear the whistle. **Infer** why you can't hear the whistle but your dog comes.

Critical Thinking

1. Lu hung a favorite picture in her room, but in the daytime she couldn't see the picture from her chair because of glare from the glass on the picture. Apply what you've learned about reflection to **solve** Lu's **problem**.

2. When Charlie wanted to read the tiny print on a map, he covered the map with clear plastic and placed a drop of water over each word. **Apply** what you have learned about lenses to explain why this works.

3. When you put on ear protectors to block sound from coming into your ears, you can still hear your own voice. **Evaluate** the following possible reasons.

a. Some of the sound waves still get into your ears.

b. The sound travels through the bones in your head.

c. Your vocal chords still vibrate.

d. The sound waves travel through the ear protectors.

Unit B Review

Reviewing Words and Concepts

Choose at least three words from the Chapter 1 list below. Use the words to write a paragraph about how these concepts are related. Do the same for each of the other chapters.

Chapter 1
conduction
expand
heat
insulator
temperature
thermal energy

Chapter 2
acid
base
concentrated
neutralization
solute
solvent

Chapter 3
force
friction
gravity
mass
newton
weight

Chapter 4
amplitude
concave mirror
frequency
photons
focal point
transverse wave

Reviewing Main Ideas

Each of the statements below is false. Change the underlined word or words to make each statement true.

1. Temperature is a flow of energy from warmer to cooler areas.
2. Heat travels from one place to another by conduction, convection, and insulation.

3. In a solution, the solute is the substance that dissolves the solvent.
4. Three ways to make a solid dissolve faster in a liquid are stirring, cooling, and heating.
5. The reactant is a substance formed in a chemical reaction.
6. In neutralization, an acid and an ion react to form water and a salt.
7. Weight is the amount of matter in an object.
8. Inertia and air resistance are two forces which resist motion.
9. Light is bent, or reflected, as it passes from one transparent substance to another.
10. The higher the frequency of a sound wave, the louder the sound.

Interpreting Data

The following graph shows the number of test problems students answered correctly while taking the test in three different sound conditions.

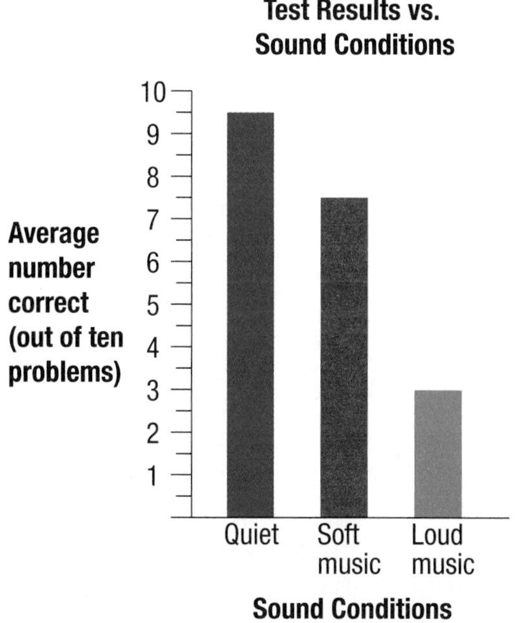

1. How does the number correct under loud conditions compare with the number correct under other conditions?

2. What conclusion might a person draw from the results?

3. What other variables might have affected the results of this experiment?

Communicating Science

1. Write a paragraph explaining what happens to the particles in a solid when the solid is heated.

2. Draw and label a diagram showing what happens to the substances in the reactants during each of the four types of chemical reactions.

3. Draw a diagram and write a paragraph explaining why a satellite stays in orbit around Earth.

4. Draw and label a diagram showing how a transparent object gets its color.

Applying Science

1. Write a paragraph describing how at least six concepts in the four chapters of this unit apply to the picture below.

2. Create a brochure selling some type of ear protection for people working in environments where the sound reaches a high decibel level. Explain why the protection should be worn and how the product protects hearing.

Unit B Performance Review

Physical Science Carnival

Using what you learned in this unit, help prepare exhibits for a carnival that demonstrates how physical science concepts apply to activities in everyday life. Wherever possible, make your exhibits interactive, so that visitors may participate. You may work by yourself or in a group.

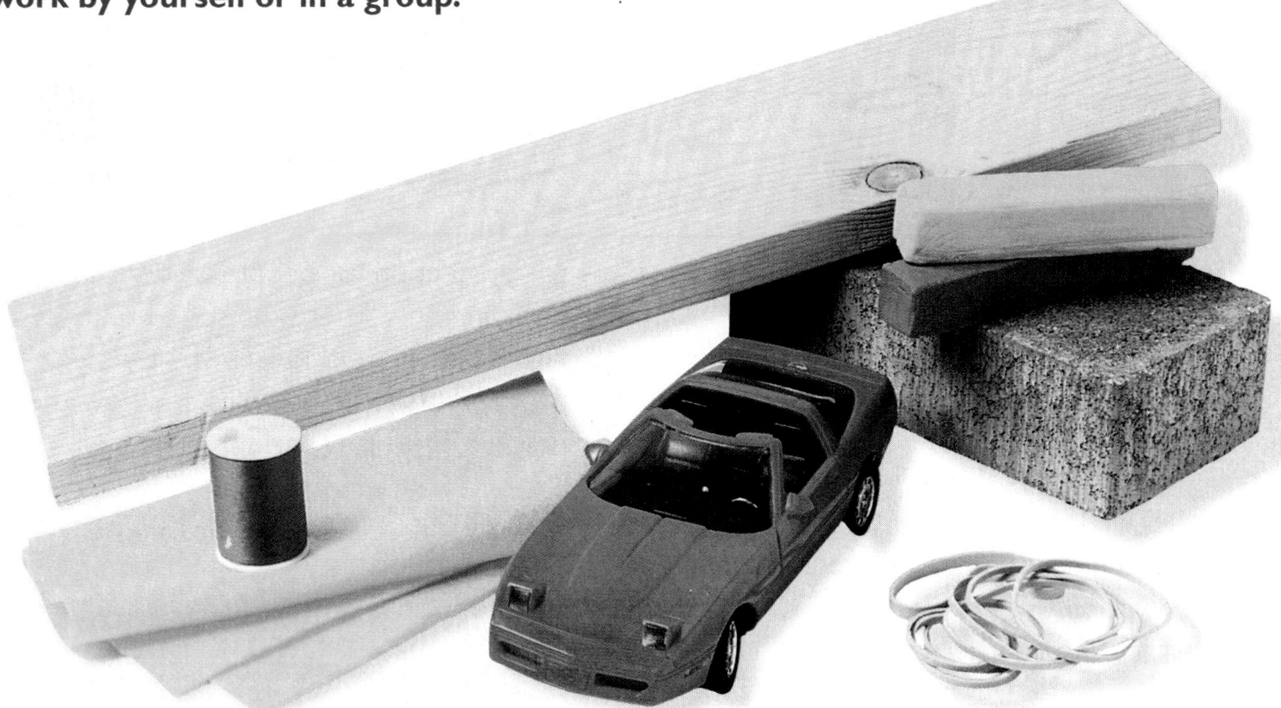

Health and Safety

Design an exhibit that will allow visitors to test the effects of using seatbelts when a car stops quickly. Use a board ramp, a toy car, a brick to stop the car, a block of clay as the person, and various materials, such as thread, rubber bands, and cloth to act as seatbelts. Visitors can investigate what happens to the clay "person" with and without a seatbelt. Be prepared to explain the results for visitors.

History

Investigate more about what arguments Newton and Huygens used to defend the particle and wave nature of light. Create a skit in which Newton and Huygens debate their beliefs and give reasons for their theories. Debaters may use visual props to demonstrate their beliefs. Present the skit at the carnival.

Music

Invent a new musical instrument which can play notes of different pitches and can play at different volumes. Learn to play several songs on your instrument for the carnival. Explain to visitors how your instrument creates sound, and how it changes pitch and volume.

Physical Education

Prepare an exhibit showing how Newton's laws of motion are demonstrated during various sporting events. Your exhibit may contain a display of pictures or actual sports equipment and explanations of which laws of motion are in effect as the equipment is used or the sport is played. Demonstrate a piece of equipment or a sports-related activity that shows each of the three laws of motion.

Biology

Prepare an exhibit which allows visitors to test the pH of common foods. You may use pH paper or the cabbage juice indicator you prepared for the activity in Chapter 3. Be sure to provide a color key so that visitors will be able to identify the pH of the foods they test. Be prepared to explain pH to visitors.

Organizing Information

Making lists is an easy way to organize information. People use lists to organize many different types of information. Some examples are grocery lists, lists of telephone numbers, and lists of the names of people invited to a party. To be useful, a list should include information about only one topic.

Make Two Lists

In Chapter 2, you learned about the properties of acids and bases. Make two lists: one titled Acids, the other titled Bases. Include brief descriptions of the properties of acids in the first list. Do the same for bases in the second list.

Write an Essay

Look at the lists you have just made. Use the information on your lists as supporting details for an essay in which you compare and contrast acids and bases. Your essay should be at least two paragraphs in length. Be sure to include a main idea sentence in each paragraph.

Remember to:

1. **Prewrite** Organize your thoughts before you write.
2. **Draft** Make an outline and write your essay.
3. **Revise** Share your work and then make changes.
4. **Edit** Proofread for mistakes and fix them.
5. **Publish** Share your essay with your class.

Unit C

Earth Science

Science and Technology In Your World!

Weather? Or Not?

Putting your hand out the window to tell if it's raining is a thing of the past. Today, TV and the Internet show radar images of approaching tornadoes or storms. You can even carry a device that tells when thunder and lightning are coming. Learn about weather forecasting in **Chapter 1 Technology and Weather.**

Exploring Earth's Deep Water

Oceans cover about 70 percent of Earth. New manned submarines that can stand up to extreme pressures are helping to solve the mysteries of the deep. Hundreds of unknown species and mineral-rich hot-water vents on the ocean floors have been discovered. Learn more about Earth's oceans in **Chapter 2 Earth Processes.**

Earthly Uses for Moon Tools

Did you know that cordless tools were first developed to help Apollo astronauts dig into the moon? And Lunar Rover controls can enable paraplegics to drive cars? Find out about space exploration and more in **Chapter 3 Exploring the Universe.**

Metal Munching Microbes

Mining metal ores and refining them has long harmed the environment. Scientists, however, have found microbes that can simply "chew up" the rock and—PRESTO! Mine wastes are gone and even more metal remains. Learn about resources and protecting the environment in **Chapter 4 Resources and Conservation.**

Grab Your Umbrella!

The radar weather map shows that heavy rains are on their way. What other technology do weather scientists use to predict the weather?

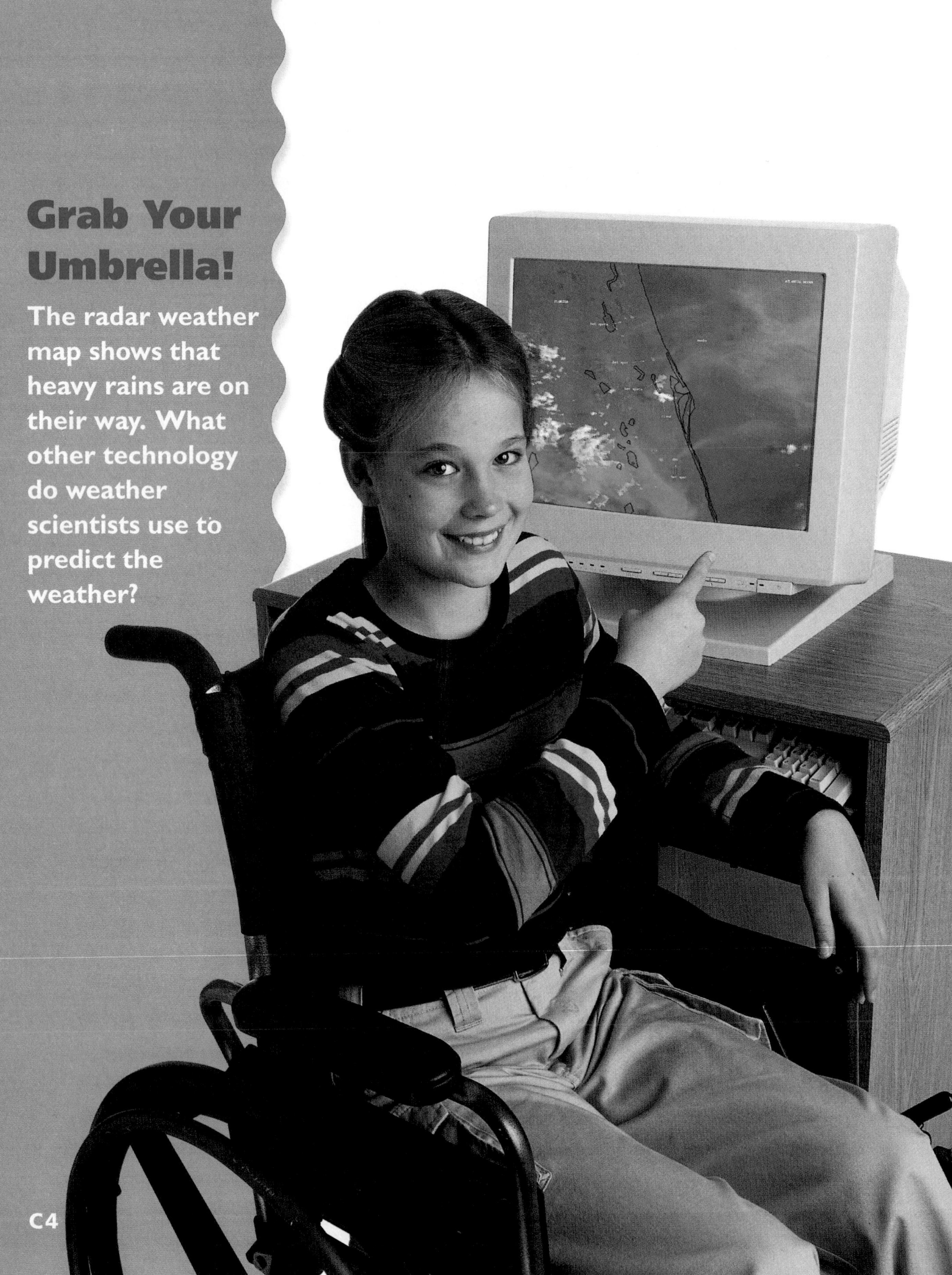

Chapter 1

Technology and Weather

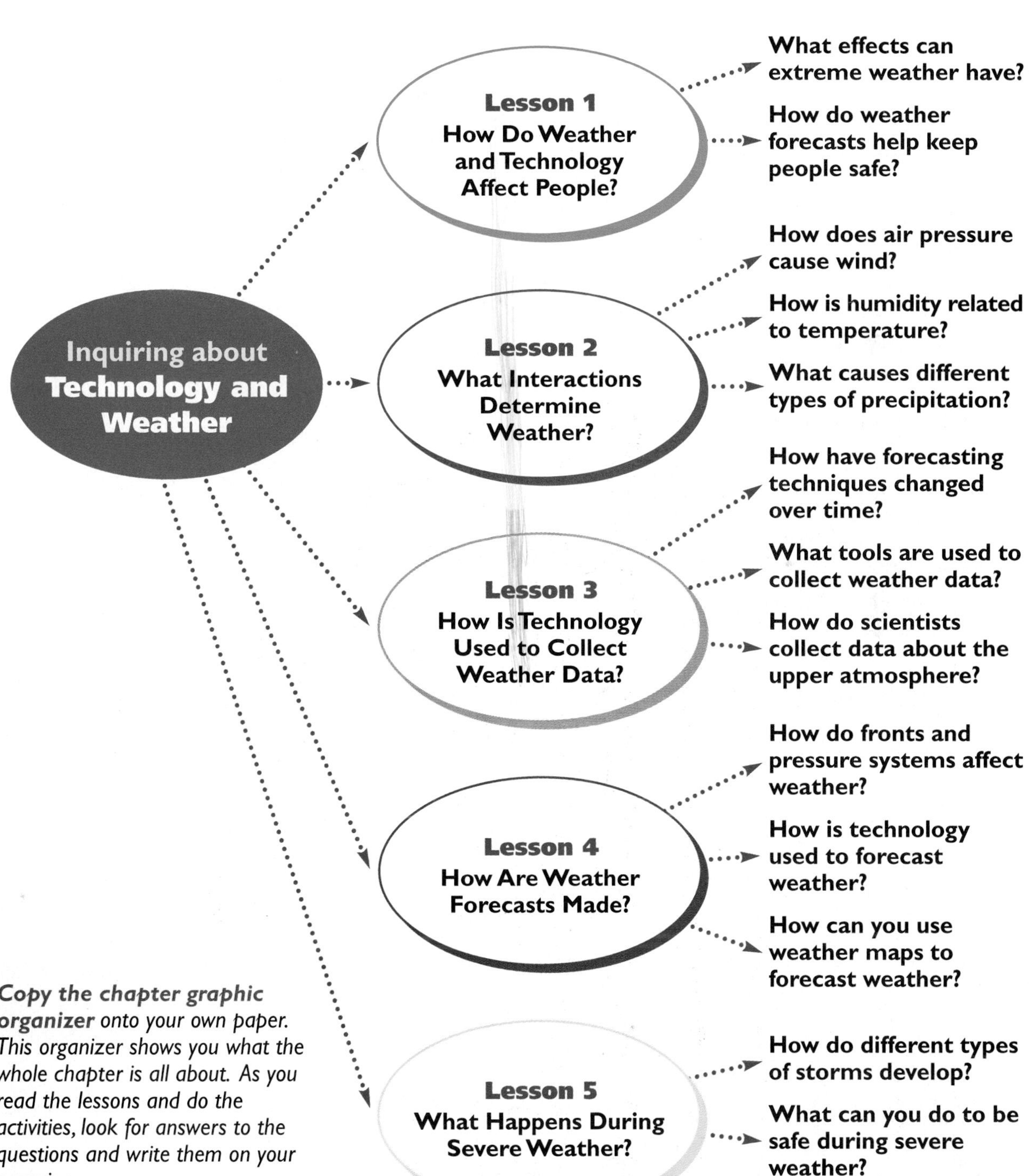

Copy the chapter graphic organizer *onto your own paper. This organizer shows you what the whole chapter is all about. As you read the lessons and do the activities, look for answers to the questions and write them on your organizer.*

Exploring Weather Patterns

Process Skills

- observing
- communicating

Materials

- weather reports

Explore

1. Obtain newspaper weather reports for one week. Arrange the reports in the order of their dates, with the earliest date first, as shown in the photo.
2. **Observe** the symbols on the map in each weather report. Look at each type of symbol you see on the maps. Notice the location of the symbols on each map. Observe how the position of the symbols on the map changes from day to day.
3. Look at the weather report for Day 1 and record the weather prediction for Day 2. Next, find out the actual weather for Day 2. This data may be in the report for Day 2 or Day 3. Record the actual weather for Day 2.
4. Repeat step 3 for a total of 5 days.

Reflect

1. What kinds of symbols did the weather reports show?

2. How did the location of the symbols change?

3. Communicate. Discuss with others in your group how you think weather forecasters use those patterns to help make predictions about the weather.

Inquire Further

What other kinds of data do you think can help predict the weather? Develop a plan to answer this or other questions you may have.

Percent

How often do you think your local weather forecaster is accurate? You can express this quantity as a **percent**. For example, you might say that your local weather forecaster is right 85% of the time.

A percent is a ratio that compares a part to a whole using the number 100. The percent is the number of hundredths that represent the part.

Math Vocabulary

percent, a ratio comparing a part to a whole using the number 100; the percent is the number of hundredths that the part is equal to

Example

Relative humidity is a ratio of the amount of water vapor in the air to how much water vapor the air can hold at that temperature. This ratio can be expressed as a percent. The grid represents the total amount of water vapor that air can hold at a given temperature. The shaded region represents the amount of water vapor that is actually present at a certain time. What is the relative humidity in the air?

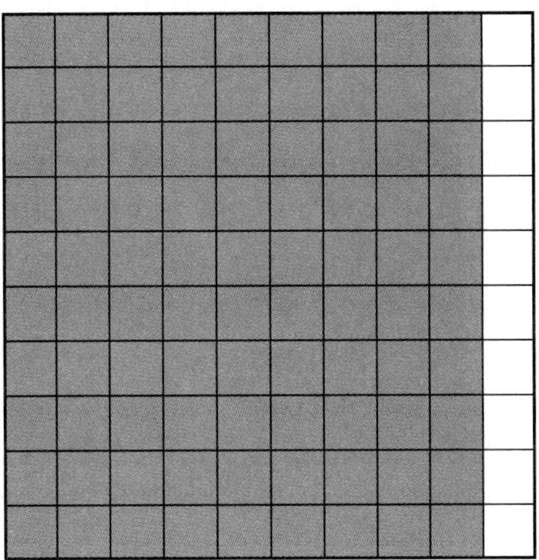

Each shaded section is $\frac{1}{100}$ of the figure. Ninety squares, or $\frac{90}{100}$, are shaded. So, because $\frac{90}{100} = 0.90$, the relative humidity is 90%.

Talk About It!

1. What is 100% of something? What is 0% of something?

2. Write 86% as a fraction.

You will learn:
- **what effects extreme weather can have.**
- **how weather forecasts help keep people safe.**

Lesson 1

How Do Weather and Technology Affect People?

Hiss! Crackle! Sizzle! The sound of fire can be pleasing when it's in a fireplace or campfire. However, when the fire is out of control, burning brush and trees in its path, and heading for your home—well, how would you feel? What would you do?

Extreme Weather

Florida, you may know, is famous for its warm, wet climate. However, in the spring of 1998, that warmth became extreme. In May, a heat wave began that stretched into June. In one Florida town, the temperature was above 35°C more than 20 days in a row. Yet while the warmth increased, the usual wetness decreased. The late-spring rains that commonly fall in the state never came. The combination of heat and drought began to affect life in the place called the Sunshine State.

At first, the effects were not too unusual. People planned fewer outdoor activities. They used more and more water. Government officials alerted them to the health threat posed by extreme heat.

Then, over the Memorial Day weekend, an even greater threat flared up—wildfire! The drought had made the Florida pine forests and brush dry and easy to burn. Lightning from brief storms started wildfires that quickly raged across the state. The map and photo on the next page show how many wildfires there were and how widely the fires spread.

This map shows that thousands of wildfires burned in Florida in early summer, 1998. Most occurred in the northeastern part of the state. ▼

Weather Forecasts Keep People Safe

Why couldn't firefighters stop the fires? Wildfires in Florida happen every year. However, tropical storms usually help put them out. In June and early July of 1998, the people of Florida waited for those storms, but the storms didn't come. Instead, dry northwest winds blew the fires from treetop to treetop and over highways and firebreaks made by firefighters. The fires continued to burn.

While wind can help spread a fire, rain can help put it out. Therefore, as the Florida fires burned, weather data became extremely important. Firefighters, like the one in the photo, especially needed accurate information about wind direction and speed. Their lives—and the lives of people in the fire's path—depended on it.

That's where **meteorologists**—scientists who study the weather—came in. Meteorologists use weather instruments to collect data about the weather. Such data include temperature, wind speed, wind direction, precipitation, and air pressure. Then meteorologists use the data and their knowledge of weather patterns to **forecast**, or predict, what the weather will be.

Meteorologists from the National Weather Service work closely with firefighters when wildfires break out. Incident Meteorologists (IMETs) go directly to the site of the fire. They take with them movable forecasting equipment and laptop computers. With this technology, the IMETs prepare up-to-date "microscale" forecasts—weather predictions for the exact spot where the fire is burning. They look for weather conditions that may endanger firefighters. Then the IMETs inform fire-control management teams so that they know where firefighting crews can safely go.

Glossary

meteorologist (mē′tē ə rol′ə jist), scientist who studies the weather

forecast (fôr′kast′), a prediction of what the weather will be like in the near future

Firefighters risked their lives but could not stop the Florida fires. This weather satellite image shows smoke rising from the Florida fires. ▼

Forecasts aren't always correct. When your local weather forecaster is wrong, what might happen to you? Perhaps you'll get caught in the rain without an umbrella. When the weather forecast for a fire-management team is wrong, people can lose their lives. Property such as homes and stores can be destroyed. Valuable natural resources such as forests can burn. Improving the science of weather forecasting is an important ongoing goal.

The IMETs who came to Florida worked to predict where the fires would be blown by the wind. People in neighborhoods, in towns, even in whole counties were ordered to evacuate when fires were predicted to move into their area. Emergency relief workers helped.

By the middle of July, scattered showers and east winds off the ocean began to stop the spread of the wildfires. Firefighters were able to get most fires under control. At least 350 homes had been damaged or destroyed. You can see one of them below. However, because of the work of meteorologists, firefighters, and others, not one person had been killed or seriously hurt.

The owner of this house was evacuated safely but lost his home in a Florida wildfire. ▼

Lesson 1 Review

1. What are some effects that extreme weather can have?
2. How do weather forecasts help keep people safe?
3. **Cause and Effect**
   What were two causes of the fires in Florida in the Spring of 1998?

Lesson 2

What Interactions Determine Weather?

SWOOSH! Hold on to your hat! That breeze is brisk, and it may be signaling a change in the weather. Wind is a funny thing. You can't see it, or draw it, or take a photograph of it—but you sure can feel it.

You will learn:

- **how air pressure causes wind.**
- **how temperature and humidity are related.**
- **what causes different types of precipitation.**

Air Pressure and Wind

Where does weather happen? It happens in the air around you. What's going on in that air to cause weather? Plenty. Gas particles in the air are in constant motion. They are pushing against each other and against the ground. Right now the air around you has a certain temperature and some amount of moisture. The air might contain clouds, or rain, or snow. All of these conditions of the air are interacting with each other to make the weather you're experiencing.

Physical Science

One of the air conditions that affects weather is air pressure. Gas particles in the air are matter and have mass. The force of gravity pulls on this mass, which causes the gases to push against Earth's surface. This push is called **air pressure.** You can think of air pressure as the weight of air. You usually don't feel air pressure because the air inside you pushes out with the same force as the air outside you pushes in.

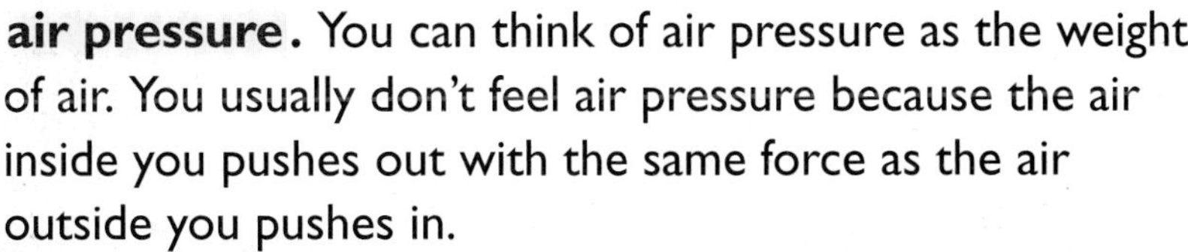

So, what does air pressure have to do with weather? The picture to the right gives you a clue. When air is heated, its molecules move faster and farther apart. The air becomes less dense, and, therefore, the air pressure lowers. A region with low pressure is called a low. As air cools, the molecules slow down and move closer together. The air becomes denser and pushes with greater pressure. A region of high pressure is a high.

Glossary

air pressure
(er presh′ər), the force of air against Earth's surface

Glossary

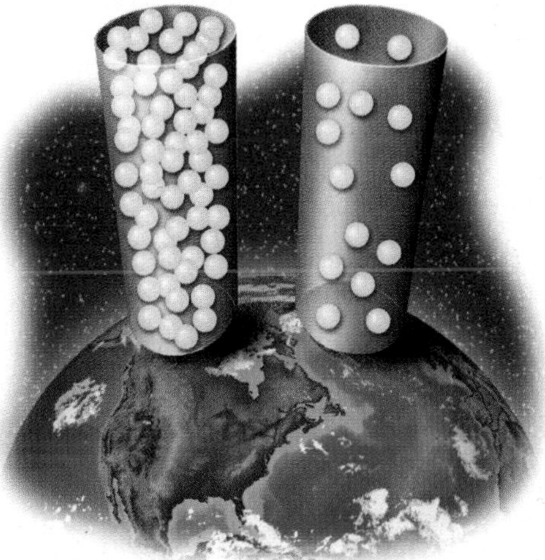

▲ *Which of these columns of air represents colder air? What do you think happens between the region of high pressure and the region of low pressure?*

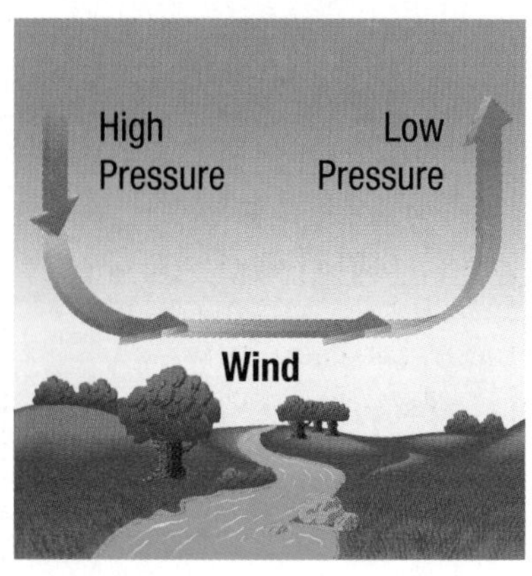

▲ *Wind results when air moves from regions of high pressure to regions of low pressure.*

Are you still wondering how air pressure affects the weather? Remember that molecules in the warm air of a low are farther apart than in the surrounding air. This means that warm air is less dense than an equal volume of cooler air. Because warm air is less dense, it tends to rise from the earth's surface.

Like other gases, air moves from a region of higher density to a region of lower density. As shown in the picture to the left, the cold, high-pressure air moves in to replace the rising air. You can't see this process, but you have felt it many times. This air moving from high- to low-pressure areas is called wind. When the differences in air pressure are great, watch out! You can expect strong winds. When the differences in air pressure are small, you can enjoy gentle breezes.

Temperature and Humidity

When you step outside in the afternoon, the air temperature may be the first weather condition you notice. If the sun has warmed the air to 32°C, you might feel uncomfortably hot. A cloudy day might be a bit cooler because the clouds block some of the sun's energy. At higher altitudes, such as in the mountains, it might be cooler too. Here, the air is less dense and there are fewer air molecules to absorb the sun's energy.

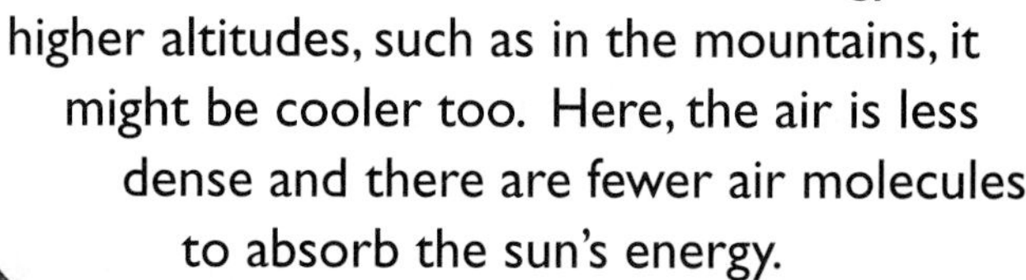

The girl in the picture is certainly noticing the air temperature. She's noticing another weather condition too. Can you guess what it is? At times the weather feels hot and sticky. Perspiration drips down your face even if you're not running or working hard. That's when people say, "It's not the heat. It's the humidity."

Water evaporates when it changes from a liquid to a gas. As sweat evaporates, it uses some of your body's energy and you feel cooler. However, evaporation occurs slowly when humid air already holds all the water vapor it can possibly hold. ▼

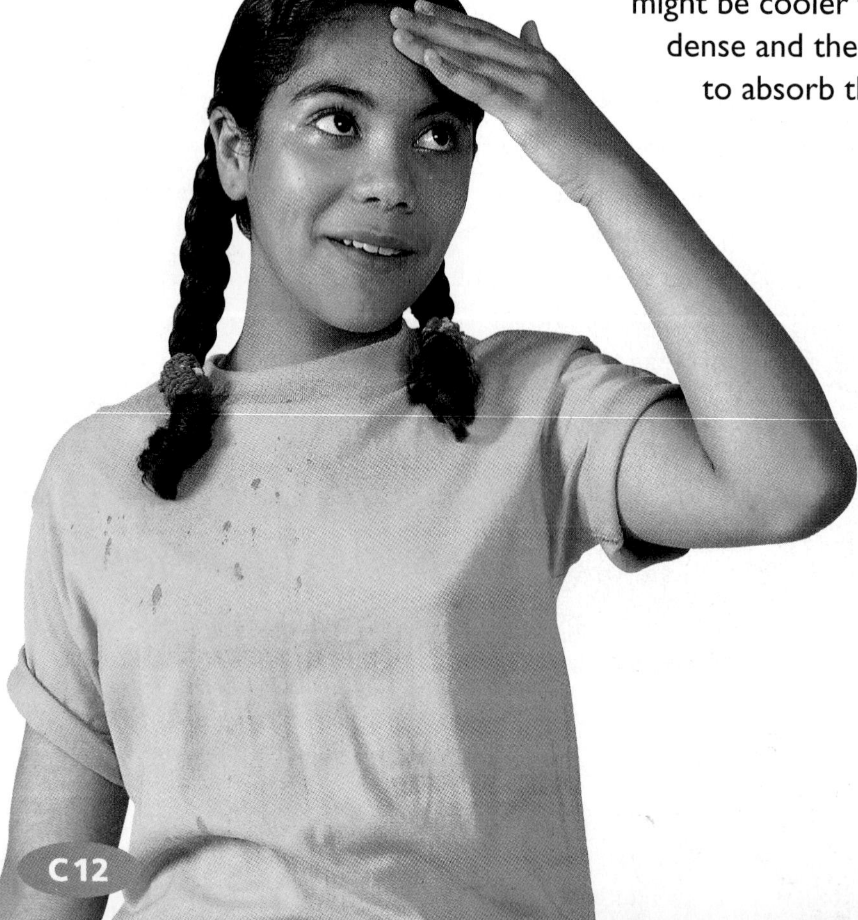

Humidity is moisture in the air in the form of a gas called water vapor. This water vapor comes from oceans, lakes, rainfall, and other sources from which water evaporates into the air.

Sometimes the air has more water vapor than at other times. The amount of water vapor that air can hold depends largely on the air temperature. Imagine you have a container like the one to the right. Notice that the warmer the temperature, the more water vapor the container can hold. Lower the temperature, and you lower the amount of water vapor the air can hold.

Meteorologists refer to relative humidity when reporting how much water vapor is in the air. **Relative humidity** is a ratio that compares the amount of water vapor in the air to the largest amount of moisture the air can hold at that temperature. A 65 percent relative humidity means the air is holding 65 percent of the water vapor it can hold at that temperature. If the temperature increases, would the relative humidity increase, decrease, or stay the same? Why?

Once air has reached 100 percent relative humidity, it can't hold any more water vapor. At this point, water vapor condenses, or returns to its liquid form. The temperature at which water vapor condenses is called a **dew point.** The water droplets on the plant in the picture formed when the cooler night air reached its dew point.

Have you noticed that grass and flowers are often wet in the early morning, even if it has not rained? Drops of dew form when water vapor condenses out of the cool night air. ▼

Glossary

humidity (hyü mid′ə tē), water vapor in the air

relative humidity (rel′ə tiv hyü mid′ə tē), measurement that compares the amount of water vapor in air with the amount the air can hold at a certain temperature

dew point (dü point), the temperature at which a volume of air cannot hold any more water vapor

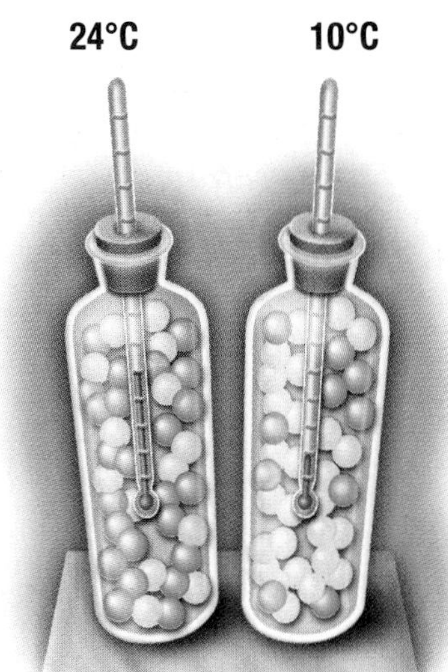

▲ *Warmer air can hold more water vapor than the same volume of cooler air.*

Clouds and Precipitation

Have you seen any water in the air today? If there are clouds in the sky, you could answer "yes." That's mostly what clouds are—water.

To understand how clouds form, remember how changes in temperature affect humidity. Then think of this example. It is a clear spring day. Throughout the day, the sun warms the ground, which in turn warms the air. This warm air holds a certain amount of water vapor. The warm air rises and cools, as in the first drawing to the left. At the cooler temperature, the air can no longer hold that much water vapor. The "extra" water vapor condenses onto microscopic particles of salt and dust in the air. Tiny water droplets form. They are so small and light that they float in the air. Collections of millions of these droplets form clouds. Because the temperature in clouds can be below freezing, even in the summer, some of the water vapor turns into tiny ice crystals.

Did you ever try to find different shapes in clouds? As clouds move in the wind and evaporate, they may take on the shape of anything you can imagine. However, clouds can be classified into a few basic kinds with a few basic shapes. The names of clouds give a clue to their appearance. For example, the term *strato* means "sheetlike," *cirro* means "curl," *nimbo* means "rain," and *cumulo* means "pile or heap." The types of clouds are grouped according to their height above the ground. You can see the four basic types of clouds on the next page.

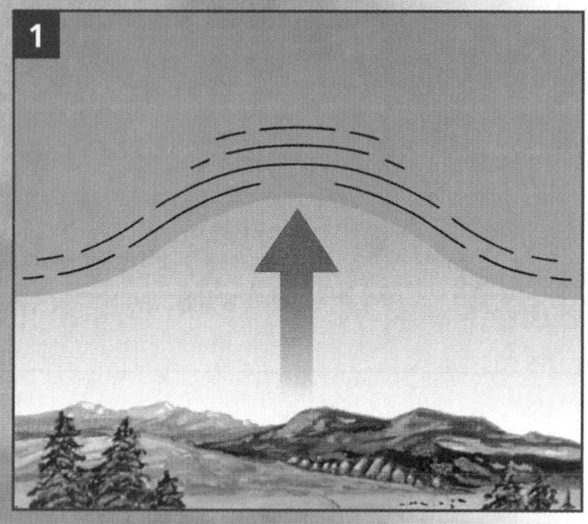

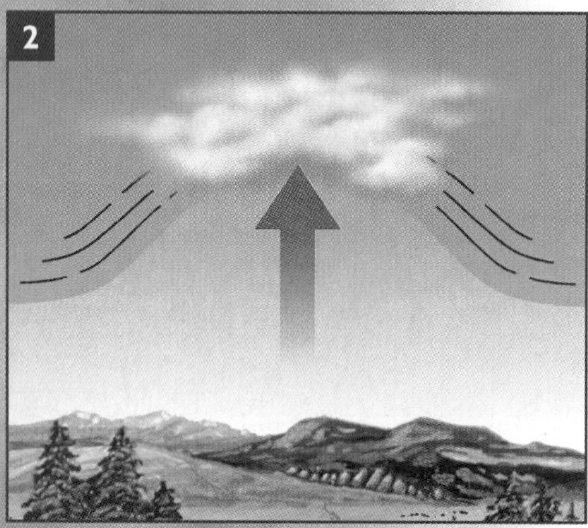

Forming Clouds

◀ *(1) The sun heats the ground, sending up columns of air where the ground is warmest. (2) If the air is moist enough, clouds form when the rising air cools to its dew point. (3) The clouds grow as rising moist air continues to condense into millions of tiny water droplets and ice crystals.*

Classification of Clouds

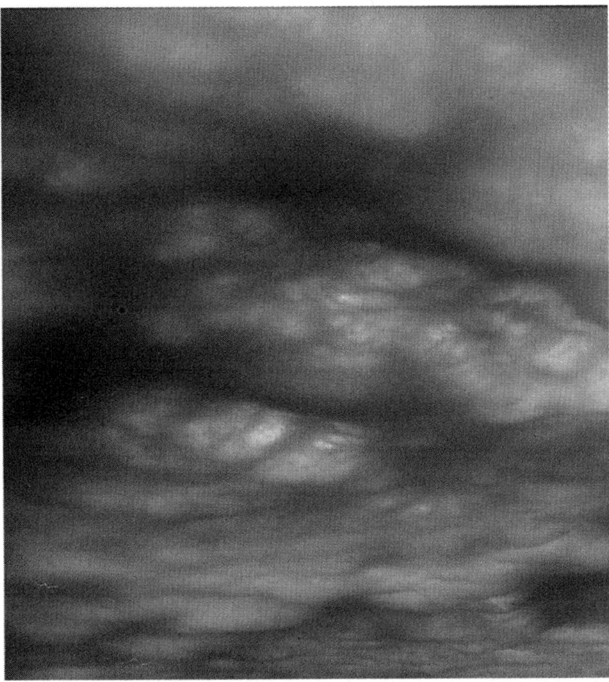

Low Clouds

Low clouds such as stratus clouds are usually seen as smooth, even sheets. They may appear as a thick, gray blanket that can bring drizzle, rain, or snow.

Middle Clouds

Middle clouds include altocumulus clouds, which can appear as small patches arranged in bands across the sky or in irregular groups.

High Clouds

High clouds like these cirrus clouds are the delicate, wispy clouds with curled edges that appear in the sky at high altitudes. Cirrus clouds are so high and cold that they are made completely of ice crystals.

Vertical Clouds

Vertical clouds appear at more than one height. An example is the cumulonimbus cloud that rises to great heights while its base is near the ground. These clouds often produce thunderstorms.

It is probably no surprise to you that clouds are associated with precipitation such as rain and snow. However, it may surprise you to learn that most rain that falls in the United States begins as snow. Ice crystals that are high in the clouds grow when more and more water vapor condenses on them. Eventually, they become so heavy that they start to fall. As the ice crystals fall through a cloud, they may collide and combine with other ice crystals or water droplets. When the crystals become too heavy to float in the air, they fall as precipitation.

The pictures below, and on the next page, show what happens to ice crystals when they fall through bands of air at different temperatures. If the air remains cold, the crystals reach the ground as snow. If the ice crystals fall far enough through air that is warm, the crystals melt and reach the ground as rain.

Sometimes rain briefly passes through a band of colder air just before reaching the ground. The water droplets freeze the moment they hit something. This precipitation is called freezing rain. It can be dangerous because it glazes roads and sidewalks with ice.

Types of Precipitation

Most precipitation in the United States starts as ice crystals. The kind of precipitation that reaches the ground depends on the temperature of the air through which it falls. ▼

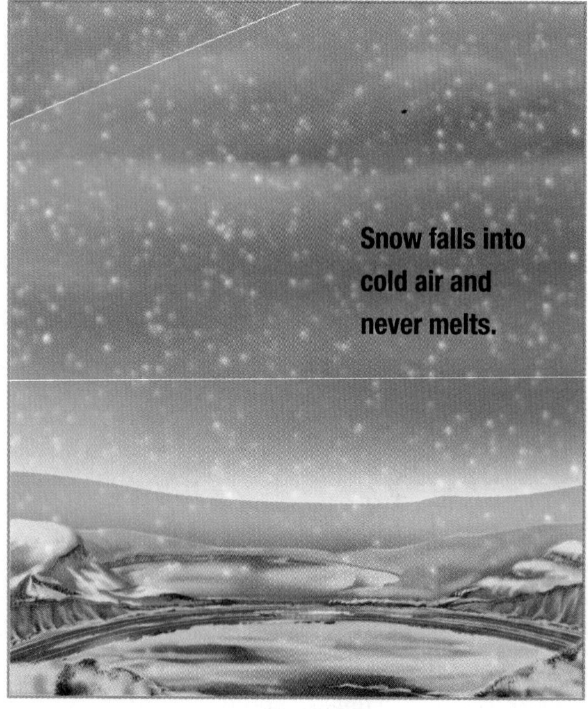

Snow falls into
cold air and
never melts.

Snow

Snow falls from
clouds and melts
into rain in the
warm air.

Rain

Sleet forms when the ice crystals melt into raindrops but refreeze during a long journey through cold air. The frozen raindrops of sleet can sting when they hit your uncovered skin. The photo shows an unusual kind of precipitation—hail. These pellets of ice form as air currents toss ice crystals up and down within a cumulonimbus cloud. Water collects on the crystal as it falls through the cloud and freezes on the crystal as it rises higher in the cloud. The hailstone grows in this way until it becomes too heavy for the air to hold up and falls to the ground. Which kind of precipitation has most recently fallen where you live?

Lesson 2 Review

1. What causes wind?
2. How is temperature related to humidity?
3. How do different types of precipitation form?
4. **Percent**
   The relative humidity at a particular location on Day 1 is 60 percent. On Day 2 it is 75 percent. On which day does the air hold more water vapor?

▲ *Hail sometimes falls during a powerful thunderstorm. Hailstones may be as small as a sand grain or as large as a baseball.*

Snow melts in
warm air, . . .
. . . and refreezes
into sleet in
. . . cools before
freezing in cold
air, and becomes
ice when it hits
the ground.

Freezing Rain

Sleet

You will learn:

- how forecasting technologies have changed over time.
- what tools are currently used to collect weather data.
- how scientists collect data about the upper atmosphere.

Lesson 3

How Is Technology Used to Collect Weather Data?

"Sea gull, sea gull, sit on the sand. It's a sign of a rain when you are at hand." What does that mean?! This rhyme is one of the many rules of thumb people once used to help predict the weather. Is there any truth to it? How did forecasting get from rhymes to where we are today?

History of Forecasting

History of Science

The ancient Babylonians were among the first people who tried to forecast weather. They observed nature and recorded on clay tablets thousands of omens, or signs, about the weather. Two of these tablets are shown in the picture.

One of the earliest-known weather instruments was a wind vane used in ancient Rome. This type of instrument is still a useful tool for determining wind direction.

The ancient Greeks were also involved in early forecasting. In fact, the word *meteorology* comes from a Greek term, *meteora,* which means "things in the air." Aristotle, a philosopher of ancient Greece, wrote a book about weather in 340 B.C. His ideas were based on his observations of the sky.

People sometimes created weather sayings, or proverbs, based on observations they made. Farmers and sailors especially used these proverbs and passed them down through the ages. Look at a small sampling of such proverbs on the next page. Some of them were fairly reliable, especially those that refer to conditions of the air such as clouds, winds, or the sky.

People's desire and need to understand the weather is as old as civilization itself. Ancient Babylonians recorded weather data on these clay tablets. ▼

In the 1500s and 1600s, many instruments were invented to measure weather conditions. For example, an Italian scientist named Galileo Galilei invented a thermometer in 1593. About 50 years later, a student of Galileo's named Evangelista Torricelli invented a **barometer.** This instrument measures air pressure. As the picture shows, Torricelli's barometer consisted of a dish of mercury and a glass tube. Air pushing down on the mercury in the dish holds the column of mercury in the tube at a certain height. As the pressure on the mercury in the dish changes, the height of the column changes. Scientists used these new instruments along with their knowledge about matter and motion to speculate about the weather.

The development of weather technology continued. In 1837, an American inventor, Samuel F. B. Morse, perfected the telegraph. This technology enabled meteorologists to quickly share their weather observations from one place to another, and warn people of approaching storms. Eventually, weather information was being shared among weather services of different countries. The United States established its own Weather Bureau in 1890.

◀ *Torricelli proved Galileo's finding that air had weight when he built this simple barometer in 1643.*

Glossary

barometer
(bə rom′ə tər), an instrument used to measure air pressure

Proverbs

Sea gull, sea gull, sit on the sand. It's a sign of a rain when you are at hand.

Red sky at night, sailor's delight, red sky in morning, sailors take warning.

Frogs croak before a rain, but in the sun stay quiet again.

The higher the clouds, the better the weather.

▲ *Do you think any of these proverbs have scientific truth? Write some of your own weather proverbs.*

Glossary

anemometer
(an′ə mom′ə tər), an instrument used to measure wind speed

psychrometer
(sī krom′ə tər), an instrument used to measure relative humidity

Collecting Weather Data

Watching the weather can be anything but dull! To keep track of all the factors that make up the weather, you need to measure changes in conditions such as temperature, wind speed, humidity, and air pressure. What tools can you use to do this?

Anemometer

◀ *This hand-held, high-tech* ***anemometer*** *measures wind speed. It's a modern version of the instrument that Leonardo da Vinci invented more than 500 years ago. The cups catch the wind and spin, turning a dial that measures wind speed. You can estimate wind speed too. Just look out the window and compare what you see with this chart.*

Wind Speed	
km/h	**Evidence of Speed**
Less than 1	Calm; smoke rises straight up
2–5	Smoke moves in direction of wind
6–12	Wind felt on face; leaves rustle
13–20	Leaves and small twigs move
21–29	Dust and loose paper move
30–39	Small trees move
40–50	Large branches move
51–60	Large trees move

Psychrometer

A **psychrometer** is an instrument that uses two thermometers to measure relative humidity. Notice that a wet cloth covers the bulb on one of the thermometers. Water evaporates from this cloth, lowering the temperature on that thermometer. Relative humidity is found by comparing the two different temperatures on a special chart. ▶

Aneroid Barometer

This instrument is more sensitive to changes in air pressure than Torricelli's mercury barometer. The word aneroid *means "non-liquid." This barometer is made of a metal box from which most of the air has been removed. Changes in air pressure outside the box cause it to expand or contract, moving a needle on a dial. The numbers on the dial show what height a column of mercury would be at that air pressure.* ▼

Thermometer

Thermometers can measure air temperature because matter expands when heated. Most thermometers are closed glass tubes containing liquids such as alcohol. The liquid expands and rises when it is heated by the air around it. Numbers on a Fahrenheit or Celsius scale next to the tube tell you the temperature in degrees. ▶

▲ *Weather data is transmitted by radio waves to a monitor, where it can be read easily.*

During the 1900s, great advances were made in developing equipment for observing and reporting the weather. Also, mathematicians and scientists developed mathematical equations that used weather data to forecast the weather. Once solved, the equations would provide predicted data—a forecast. The complex calculations took too much time to be practical until computers were developed in the 1940s. Meteorologists now use computers to quickly solve mathematical equations and make weather forecasts.

Today, weather data collection is highly computerized and automated. Electronic measuring devices and monitors, such as the one to the above left, have largely replaced traditional instruments. For example, a thermal sensor is often used in place of a thermometer. Tiny wires in the sensor expand in response to the temperature. Data from the sensors can be fed automatically into computers to make forecasts.

Upper Atmosphere Data

As early as the 1890s, meteorologists knew that weather near Earth's surface related to winds high in the atmosphere. In the 1930s, the Weather Bureau paid pilots bonuses to fly above 5,500 meters to observe high-altitude weather. Unfortunately, the pilots suffered from lack of oxygen at this altitude and many passed out. A safer way to gather high-altitude data was to launch balloons that carried instruments.

Today, around the world, hundreds of small instrument packages—each containing special sensors and a radio transmitter—are still lifted aloft twice daily. They measure temperature, wind direction, wind speed, and moisture as each balloon drifts into the upper air. The data is radioed to computers and transmitted around the world.

◀ *People at hundreds of weather stations around the world—including this one in Antarctica—release weather balloons at exactly the same time, twice a day. The data collected by weather balloons is extremely important in making forecasts.*

In an airport control tower, radar tracks flying airplanes. Radar uses radio waves, which bounce off objects like an echo. By measuring the time the signal takes to return, the distance to the object can be calculated. What flying objects are meteorologists looking for? They are looking for precipitation that can be found when radar bounces off rain or snow.

Doppler radar is an advanced type of radar that not only locates the presence of a storm but also tracks the direction the storm is moving. As shown below, precipitation moving toward the radar reflects radio waves at a higher frequency than does precipitation moving away from the radar. Doppler radar detects these differences. You can see on the Doppler radar screen below that these different frequencies appear as different colors. By watching the movement of precipitation and winds within a storm, meteorologists can better predict violent weather.

Glossary

Doppler radar
(dop′lər rā′där), a type of radar that calculates distance and shows direction of movement

What difference can you see in the reflected radio waves from these two clouds? ▼

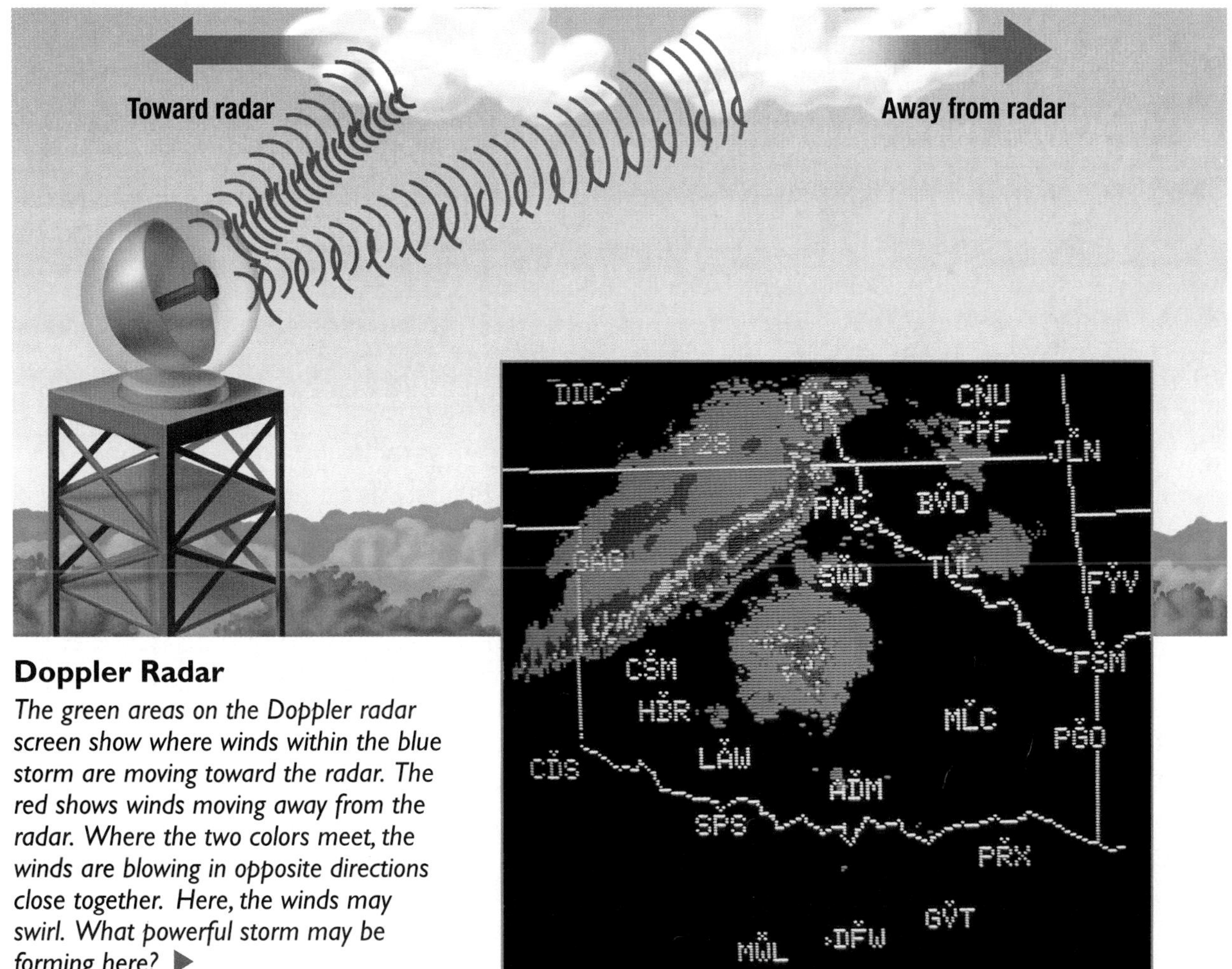

Doppler Radar

The green areas on the Doppler radar screen show where winds within the blue storm are moving toward the radar. The red shows winds moving away from the radar. Where the two colors meet, the winds are blowing in opposite directions close together. Here, the winds may swirl. What powerful storm may be forming here? ▶

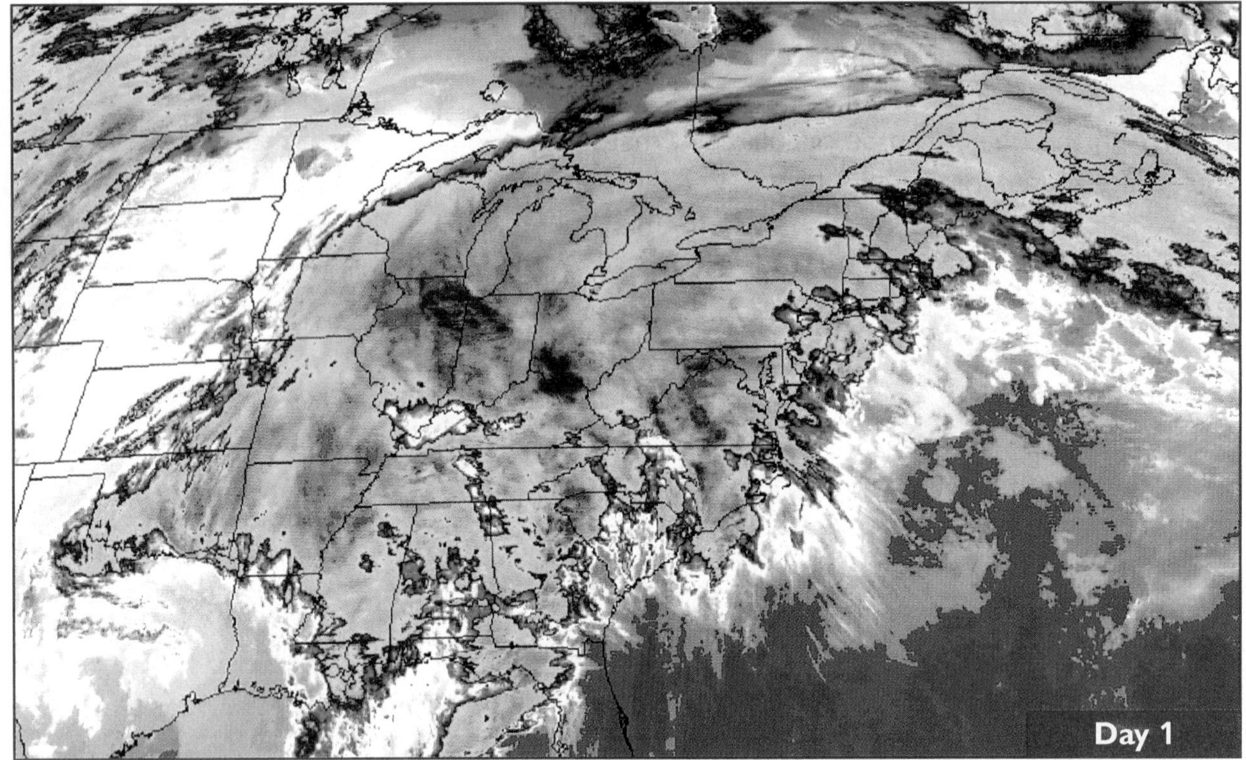

▲ *The satellite views on these two pages have been color-enhanced. Red represents the most precipitation and blue represents the least. These images were taken one day apart.*

Winds blow around the globe. Warm, moist air near the equator rises and moves toward the poles. Cold, dry air from the polar regions drifts toward the equator. What do all these movements tell you? One thing they tell you is that your local weather is influenced by weather patterns all around the world. Therefore, in order to make accurate forecasts, meteorologists need a view like the one at the top of the page. They need a tool that gives them the "big picture." The photo below to the left shows one such tool—a weather satellite.

The first weather satellite was launched in 1960. It carried television cameras and stored the pictures on tape for later broadcast on Earth. Since then, many weather satellites have been launched. Some orbit Earth quickly, sending data about an entire path around Earth every 110 minutes. Other satellites, called geostationary

Weather Satellites

◀ *Weather satellites not only detect large weather systems across the globe but also monitor worldwide vegetation and determine damage to the environment. Almost anyone with a computer can access satellite information.*

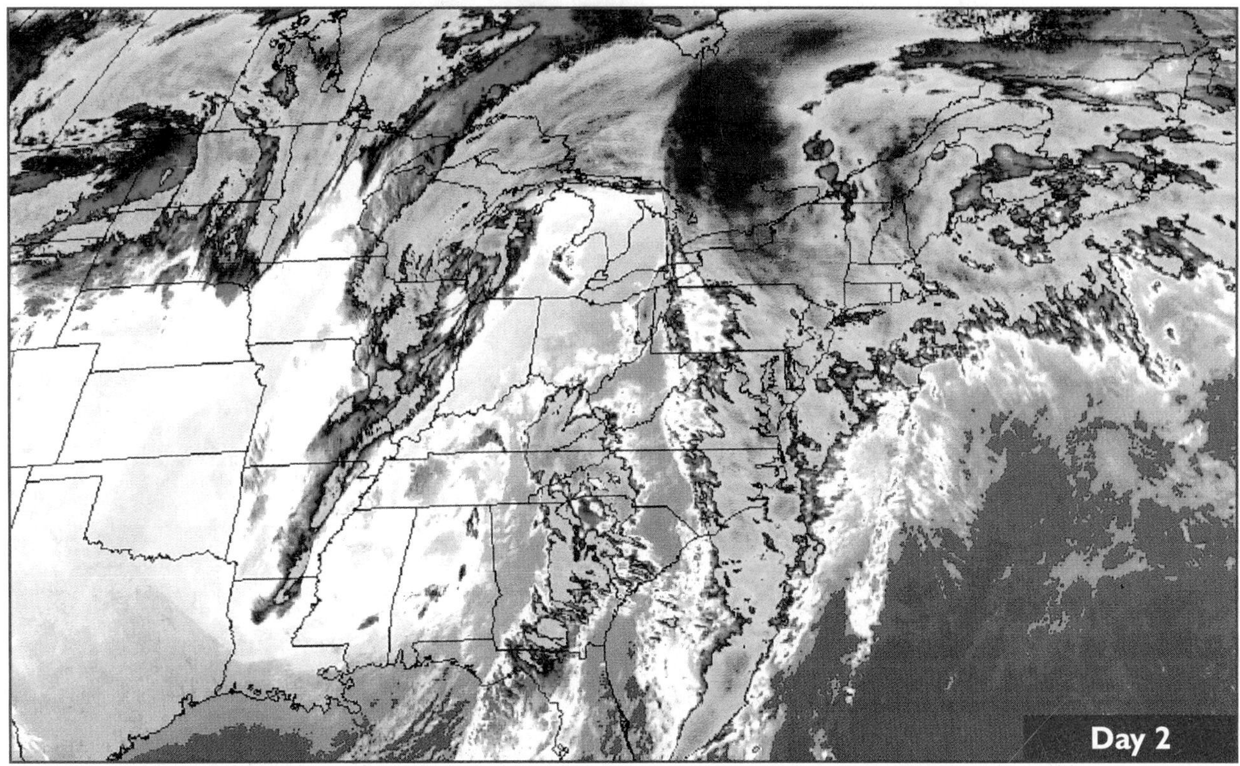

satellites, are fixed over certain areas of the earth. They move at the same speed as Earth rotates. Therefore, these satellites send data only about the areas over which they are fixed.

Today, a network of satellites uses radio signals to beam images back to weather stations on Earth. They show movements of water vapor or provide a color analysis of the world's ocean temperatures. Compare the satellite photos on these two pages. They were taken one day apart. What kind of movement do they show? What are some advantages to using satellite images such as these?

Lesson 3 Review

1. How have forecasting techniques changed over time?
2. What tools are currently used to collect weather data?
3. How do scientists collect data about the upper atmosphere?
4. **Context Clues**
   Write a definition of *geostationary satellite*. Tell what context clues you used to figure out the definition.

Measuring Relative Humidity

Process Skills

Process Skills

- estimating and measuring
- observing
- collecting and interpreting data
- inferring

Materials

- safety goggles
- cheesecloth
- 2 thermometers
- 2 rubber bands
- milk carton with hole
- water

Getting Ready

In this activity, you will make a psychrometer, an instrument that is used to determine relative humidity. Review the information about humidity on pages C12 and C13 before you begin this activity.

Follow This Procedure

1. Make a chart like the one shown. Use your chart to record your observations.

Wet bulb (°C)	Dry bulb (°C)	Difference (°C)	Relative humidity (%)

2. Put on your safety goggles. Tie a piece of cheesecloth around the bulb end of a thermometer. The thermometer will have two "tails" of cheesecloth hanging from it. Position these tails at the back of the thermometer. This is your wet-bulb thermometer (Photo A).

Self-Monitoring

Does the cheesecloth tightly cover the bulb of the thermometer?

3. Slide two rubber bands onto the milk carton.

4. Locate the side of the milk carton with a hole cut into it. Slip the wet-bulb thermometer under the rubber bands, just above the hole. Push the cheesecloth "tails" of the wet-bulb thermometer through the hole in the carton (Photo B).

5. Slip another thermometer under the rubber bands on the milk carton as shown in Photo B. This is your dry-bulb thermometer. You will use it to **measure** air temperature.

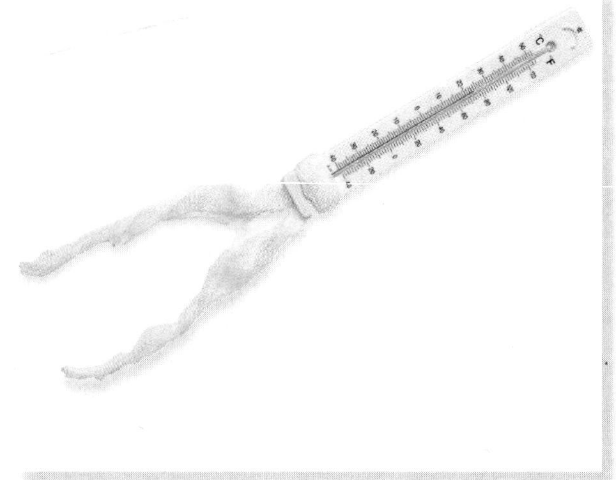

Photo A

6 Add water to the milk carton to a point just below the hole in its side. Make certain the cheesecloth tails from the thermometer extend into the water. Set the milk carton in a place where it will not be disturbed.

7 After a few minutes, the cheesecloth around the thermometer bulb will feel wet. **Observe** the change in the temperature of the wet bulb as water evaporates from the cheesecloth.

8 When the temperature reading of the wet-bulb thermometer stops changing, **collect data** from the two thermometers by recording the temperature readings in your chart. Then calculate the difference between the two temperature readings and record it in your chart.

9 Use the Relative Humidity table to determine relative humidity. Record the relative humidity in your chart.

Interpret Your Results

1. Explain why the wet-bulb thermometer reading is lower than the dry-bulb thermometer reading.

2. Make an **inference.** If the difference between the wet-bulb reading and the dry bulb reading is large, is the air relatively dry or relatively humid?

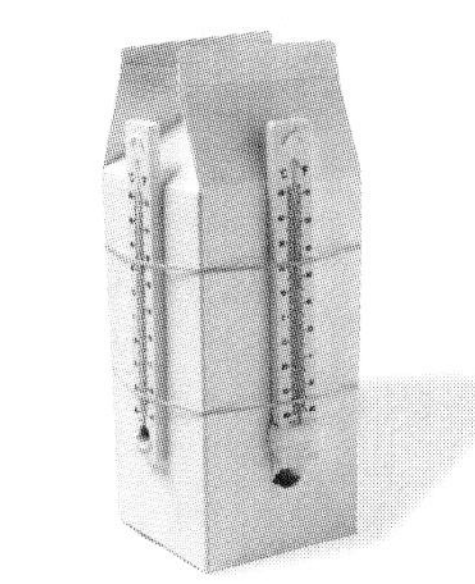

Photo B

Relative Humidity (percent)

Dry bulb (°C)	Difference between wet and dry bulb readings (°C)									
	1	**2**	**3**	**4**	**5**	**6**	**7**	**8**	**9**	**10**
18	91	82	73	65	57	49	41	34	27	20
19	91	82	74	65	58	50	43	36	29	22
20	91	83	74	67	59	53	46	39	32	26
21	91	83	75	67	60	53	46	39	32	26
22	92	83	76	68	61	54	47	40	34	28
23	92	84	76	69	62	55	48	42	36	30
24	92	84	77	69	62	56	49	43	37	31
25	92	84	77	70	63	57	50	44	39	33

Inquire Further

What would the difference be between wet-bulb and dry-bulb thermometer readings if the relative humidity were 100 percent? Develop a plan to answer this or other questions you may have.

Self-Assessment

- I followed the directions to make a psychrometer for measuring relative humidity.
- I **observed** the change in the wet-bulb thermometer.
- I **measured** and recorded the temperatures of the two thermometers.
- I used my **data** and the table to determine the relative humidity.
- I **inferred** the relationship between relative humidity and a large change in the wet-bulb temperature reading.

You will learn:

- how fronts and pressure systems affect weather.
- how technology is used to forecast weather.
- how to use weather maps to forecast weather.

Lesson 4

How Are Weather Forecasts Made?

OH NO! It was supposed to be sunny today! You know only too well that weather forecasts aren't correct all of the time. Even with today's technology, forecasters can't know every weather condition that affects a prediction—but forecasts are getting better!

Glossary

Glossary

air mass (er mas), a large body of air having similar properties or weather conditions

Fronts and Pressure Systems

Sometimes you may have been outside on a warm day and felt the temperature drop many degrees in a matter of minutes. What happened? The warm air didn't change—it moved out! Cooler air moved in.

At this moment, the air that surrounds your school and home is part of an air mass. An **air mass** is a very large body of air that has similar properties or weather conditions throughout. Air masses are huge—two or three of them can cover an entire country. Meteorologists track the movement of air masses to help predict the temperature, humidity, and air pressure of the area into which they are moving.

Weather typically moves from west to east across the United States. ▼

When a warm air mass meets a cold air mass, the air in the different masses usually doesn't mix. The reason is because the properties of the two air masses are different. A boundary, or **front**, forms between the two different air masses. The dramatic drop in temperature described at the beginning of this lesson resulted as a cold front moved across the area. A cold front forms where a cold air mass moves into a warm air mass. A warm front forms where a warm air mass moves into a cold air mass.

How do fronts and air masses explain the weather you see at different places in the picture? Let's start with Los Angeles. Yesterday, a cold front passed through, causing thunderstorms. Today, Los Angeles is enjoying clear skies and cooler temperatures. Now the cold front is passing through Phoenix. The denser, cooler air wedges itself under the warmer air and lifts it. If the warm air is moist enough, cumulonimbus clouds may form and produce thunderstorms. That's what is happening in Phoenix. The storms may be violent but last less than an hour. About 400 kilometers to the east, a warm front has just passed through Dallas. The warm air mass glides up over the cold air mass. The rise is gradual and extends for many kilometers. Stratus clouds and precipitation extend almost all the way to New Orleans.

Weather generally moves across the United States from west to east. This movement is caused by the wind patterns across the earth. Use what you know about weather to predict the weather tomorrow for all the places in the picture.

Glossary

front (frunt), the boundary between warm and cold air masses

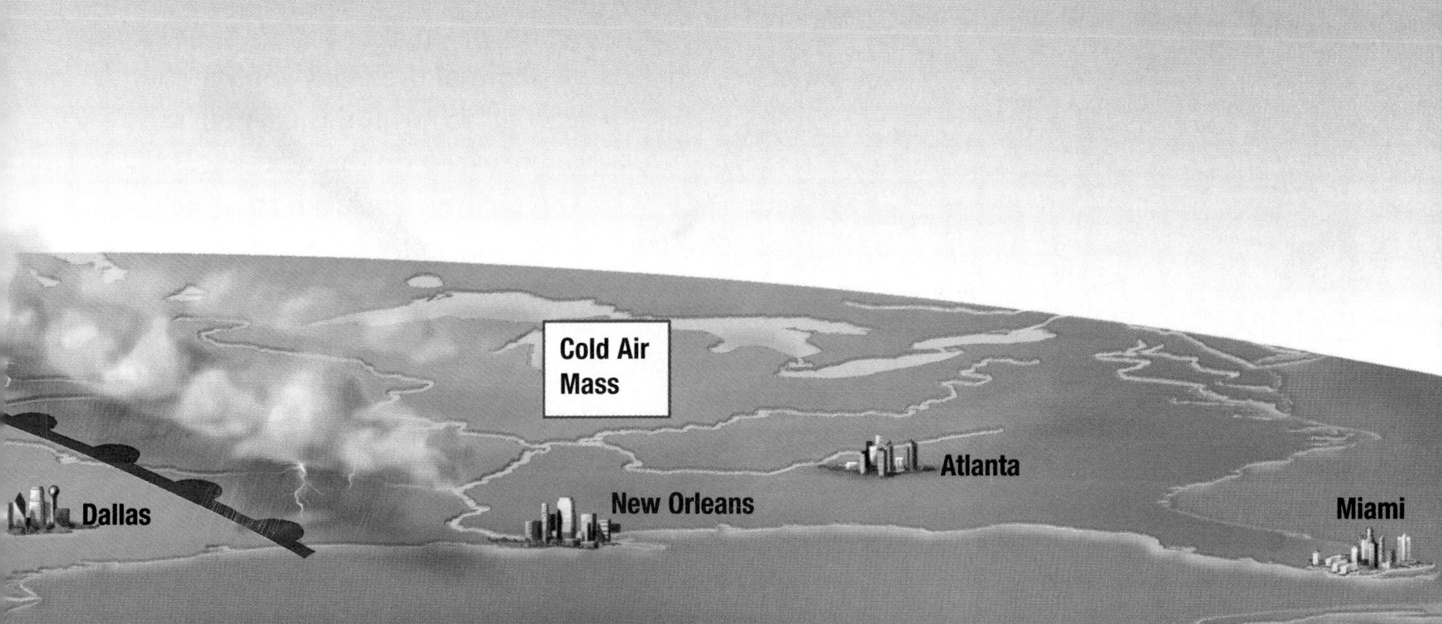

Air masses and fronts are major clues that you, as well as meteorologists, can use to forecast the weather. A third major clue has to do with air pressure systems. Certain weather is associated with lows and highs. For example, as winds blow into a low, warm air is rising. This upward flow of air often creates clouds and precipitation. On the other hand, a high usually brings fair weather. The heavier air of a high pushes downward and is usually colder and drier.

Technology and Weather Forecasts

To predict the weather, a forecaster relies on technology available through the National Weather Service (NWS). The picture below represents some of the newest technology from the NWS. The group of sensors is one of about 900 Automated Surface Observing Systems (ASOS) installed at airports nationwide to gather, process, and distribute weather data. ASOS equipment gathers information on cloud cover, visibility, temperature, humidity, air pressure, wind speed and direction, and precipitation.

Automated Surface Observing Systems consist of sensors that transmit weather data directly to the National Weather Service. ▼

ASOS data are recorded automatically each minute and reported directly to NWS offices. At the offices, the data are fed into the Advanced Weather Interactive Processing System (AWIPS). What's so special about AWIPS? This system allows forecasters to have access to and efficiently use all the weather data collected around the world to predict local weather conditions.

Some of the ideas you've learned so far in this chapter are summarized on the next page. The pictures illustrate the role technology plays in gathering weather data, processing it, analyzing it to make forecasts, and sharing all this information with others.

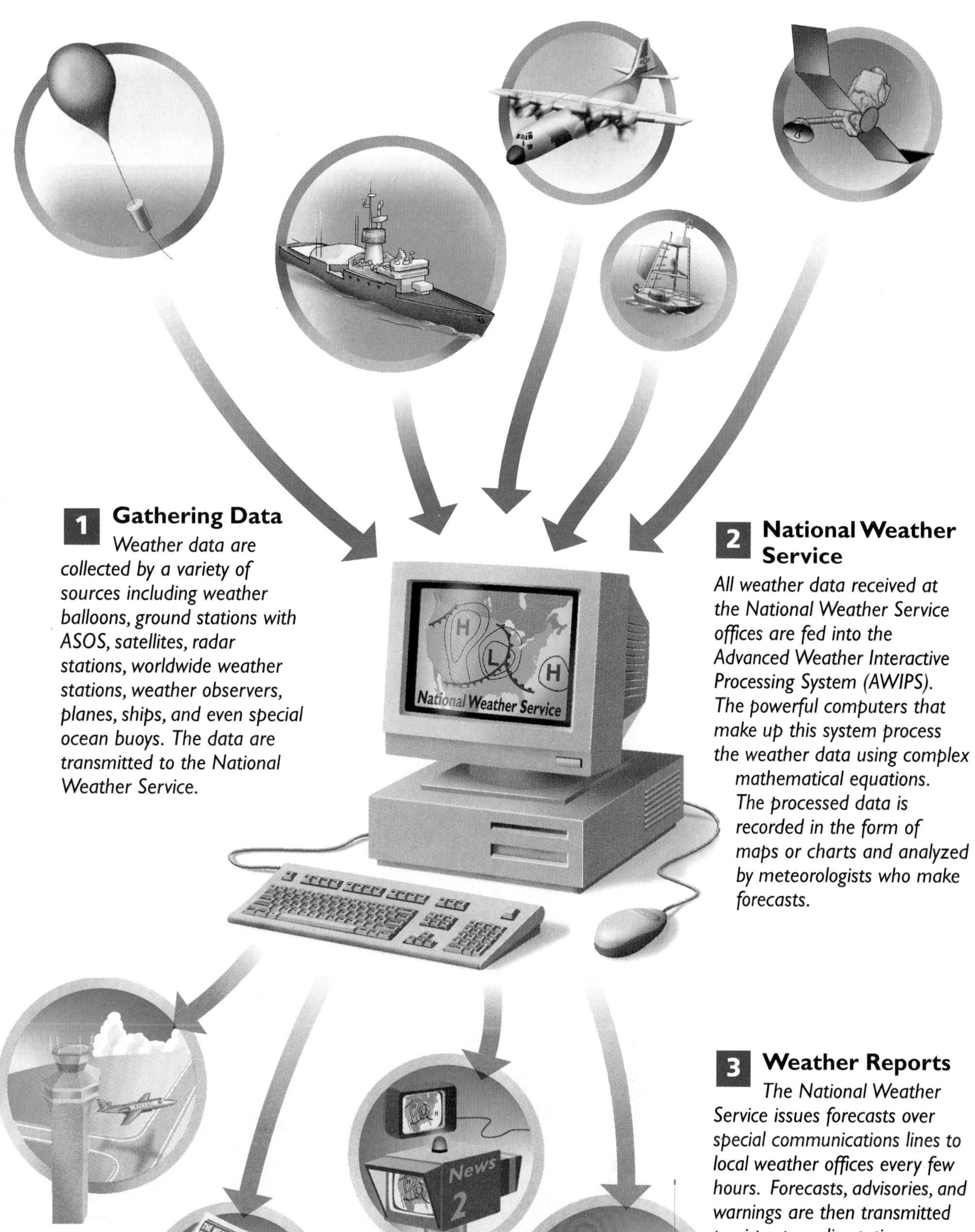

1 Gathering Data

Weather data are collected by a variety of sources including weather balloons, ground stations with ASOS, satellites, radar stations, worldwide weather stations, weather observers, planes, ships, and even special ocean buoys. The data are transmitted to the National Weather Service.

2 National Weather Service

All weather data received at the National Weather Service offices are fed into the Advanced Weather Interactive Processing System (AWIPS). The powerful computers that make up this system process the weather data using complex mathematical equations. The processed data is recorded in the form of maps or charts and analyzed by meteorologists who make forecasts.

3 Weather Reports

The National Weather Service issues forecasts over special communications lines to local weather offices every few hours. Forecasts, advisories, and warnings are then transmitted to airports, radio stations, television stations, newspapers, military bases, and other nations.

Using Weather Maps

The picture on pages C28–29 is a useful tool for understanding what fronts are and how they affect weather. However, it doesn't give much information for any places except the few cities on the drawing. A better way to represent the weather over a large area is with a weather map. You probably have seen many kinds of weather maps in newspapers and on TV. Different maps may use slightly different symbols, but they likely all use symbols similar to those on the map on the next page. What weather information is included on this map? Use the key to find out.

Notice on the map that fronts extend from lows. Find a cold front and a warm front. What kind of weather is occurring along the fronts? Is this what you would expect? The map also shows a stationary front. Such a front occurs when an air mass stops moving. Precipitation may occur for several days along a stationary front. Where do you think the weather shown in the photo below is occurring?

This storm is most likely occurring along a cold front or in a low-pressure area. ▼

Weather Map

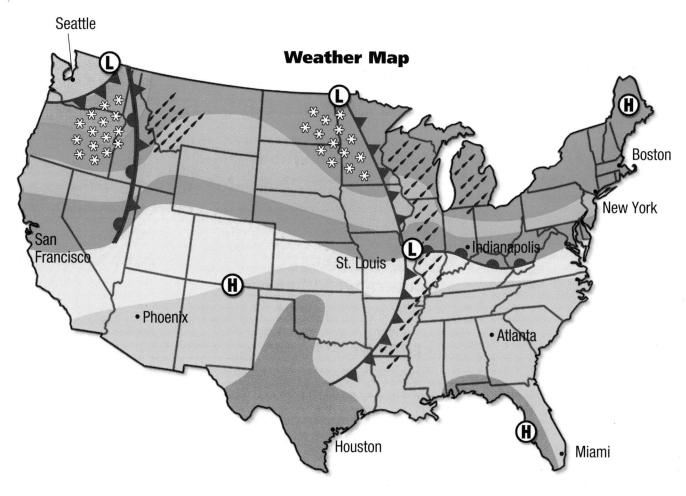

Seattle
San Francisco
Phoenix
Houston
St. Louis
Indianapolis
Atlanta
Boston
New York
Miami

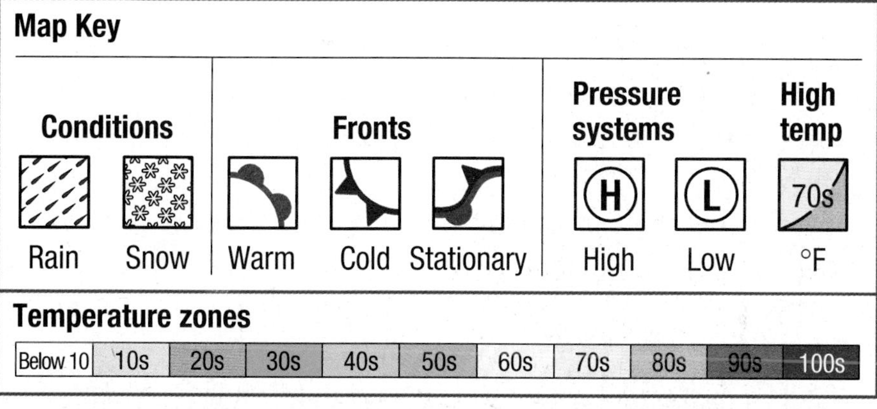

Lesson 4 Review

1. How do fronts and pressure systems affect weather?
2. How is technology used to forecast weather?
3. How can you use weather maps to forecast weather?
4. **Percent**
   What percentage of the states in the map above have temperatures in the 90s?

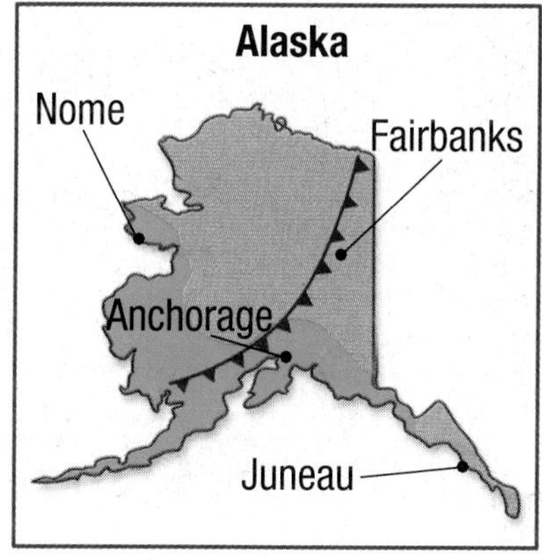

You will learn:

- how different types of storms develop.
- how to be safe in severe weather.

Lesson 5

What Happens During Severe Weather?

Huge cumulonimbus clouds had been building all day. Now they are overhead. The sky darkens and takes on strange hues of gray and green. A distant siren adds to the eerie scene. virrrRRR What's happening? What will you do?

Types of Storms

As you learned in the last lesson, storms often accompany fronts and low-pressure systems. Thunderstorms, for example, form either along a cold front or within a warm air mass, as warm, moist air rises quickly. The rapid, continuous condensation of water vapor produces tall cumulus clouds, like the one in the picture to the left. The tops of the clouds may be more than 15,000 meters high. Here, the clouds are made of ice crystals, while the lower portions of the clouds are made of water droplets. The ice crystals and water droplets grow as they collide with other crystals and droplets. Eventually, they become large enough and heavy enough to fall. The ice melts when it falls through warmer air in the lower portion of the cloud. The melted ice joins the other drops as rain.

The falling rain pulls cold air with it, producing downward air currents called downdrafts. Meanwhile, warm air continues to rise, producing updrafts. If you've ever been in an airplane flying through a storm cloud, these rising and falling air currents likely produced a bumpy ride.

Updrafts and downdrafts are responsible for another characteristic of thunderstorms—lightning. The moving air causes electrical charges to build in the cloud. Notice in the picture how negative and positive charges are distributed throughout the cloud. When the difference

Lightning results when positive and negative electrical charges flow between a cloud and the ground, between different clouds, or within the same cloud. ▼

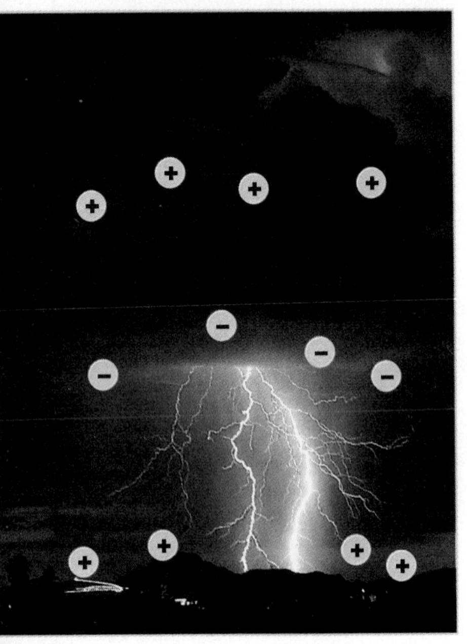

▲ *The dark appearance of a funnel cloud is caused by the density of cloud particles and by soil and debris being swept up by the winds.*

between the negative and positive charges is great enough, electrons flow between them. This momentary flow of electrons is an electric current called lightning. The streak of lightning heats the air along its path tremendously, causing the air to expand explosively. This expansion of air produces a sound wave you hear as thunder.

Storms can contain layers of air that move at different speeds. When this happens, air between the layers can start rolling like a pencil across a table. It is believed that a tornado forms when a strong updraft lifts one end of the rolling air. A **tornado** is a violent, funnel-shaped cloud with extremely strong winds.

A tornado might last only a few minutes, but the destruction it causes can be devastating. Although the tornado itself moves an average of only about 60 kilometers per hour, the swirling winds within the tornado can reach 500 kilometers per hour. These winds can lift a roof off a building. Flying debris breaks windows, which allows the wind inside. The wind can push out on the walls and push up on the roof. Only the foundation may be left.

Meteorologists have much to learn about tornadoes. Researchers, such as T. Theodore Fujita, shown here, are working to predict when and where these storms will occur. Some progress has been made. As you learned in Lesson 3, Doppler radar is a helpful tool for seeing where tornadoes are likely to form.

Glossary

tornado (tôr nā′dō), a violent, funnel-shaped cloud with extremely strong winds

Glossary

▲ *T. Theodore Fujita uses dry ice and fans to generate model tornadoes. These models provide clues about how real tornadoes form.*

Glossary

hurricane (hėr′ə kān), a large tropical storm that forms over warm oceans and whose winds have a velocity of at least 110 kilometers per hour

Tornadoes are the most destructive storms, but hurricanes are the most powerful. A **hurricane** is a large tropical storm that forms over warm oceans and whose winds reach at least 110 kilometers per hour. Hurricanes are more powerful than tornadoes because of their huge size—usually at least 200 kilometers across.

Like other severe storms, hurricanes form around very low-pressure areas. The warm, moist ocean air spirals upward around the low and forms the cloud pattern you see in the satellite picture below. These circulating clouds bring high winds and heavy rain. The strong, steady winds over the ocean produce large waves that add to the destruction along the coast, as you can see below.

When the hurricane moves over land, it is no longer fed by warm, moist ocean air. The condensation of water vapor that gave the hurricane much of its energy stops occurring. After a couple of days, the storm loses power and the spiraling pattern of winds breaks up.

Much of a hurricane's damage is caused by huge waves that sweep over the shoreline, bulldozing everything in its way. ▶

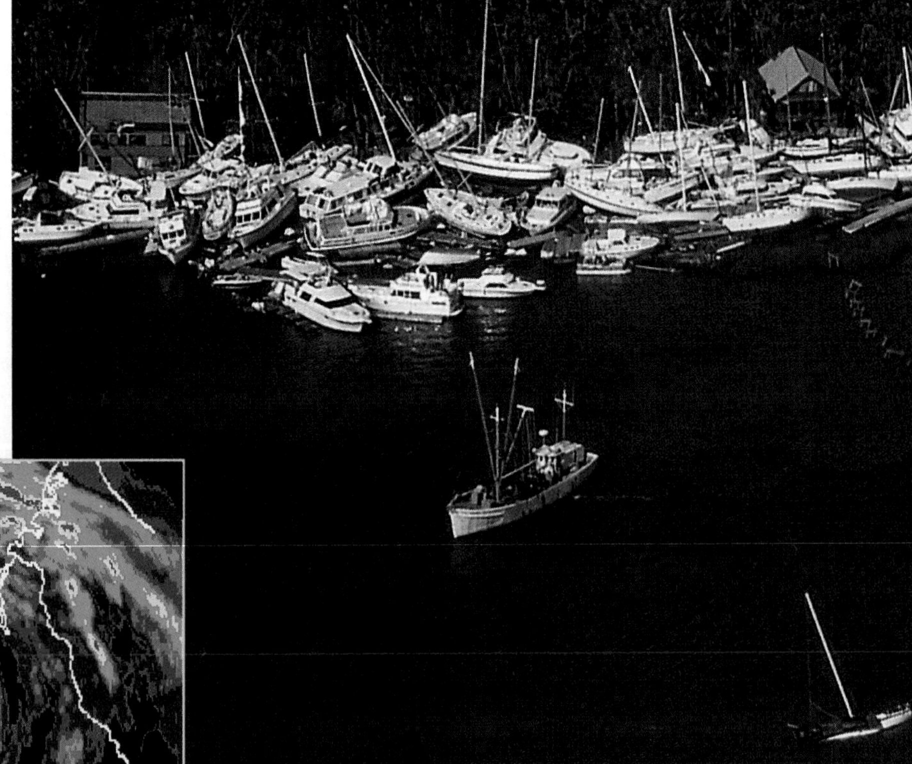

◀ *In this photo, you can see that few clouds form in the center, or eye, of a hurricane. The eye is an area of relative calm while the storm rages all around.*

Safety in Severe Weather

Storms may be interesting to watch, but they are dangerous. Safety precautions should be taken seriously. The greatest danger of thunderstorms comes from lightning. So get indoors away from open windows and doors whenever a thunderstorm approaches. Avoid touching telephones, appliances, or metal plumbing—lightning can travel easily through these objects. If you're outside and unable to get indoors, do not seek shelter under a tree. Lightning tends to strike the highest objects in an area. If you're in the open, you may be the highest object. So lie down on the ground or crouch in a low area, such as a ditch. If you are swimming or in a boat, leave the water immediately—water conducts electricity.

Meteorologists keep a careful watch on developing weather conditions. If conditions are favorable for a tornado to form, the National Weather Service issues a tornado watch. A watch means you should be alert to rapid weather changes and plan for your safety. When a tornado has been sighted, the NWS issues a tornado warning. This is a time to take action. Read the safety tips to the right to find out what you should do.

Unlike tornadoes, people usually have several days to prepare for a hurricane. The NWS tracks a hurricane to predict where it will hit land. Mobile homes, vehicles, or boats are not safe places to be during a hurricane. Get into a sturdy building that can withstand strong winds and high, crashing waves. If you live in a low-lying area, you may need to leave your home until after the storm.

Tornado Safety Tips

- **Seek shelter indoors in a basement or an interior room, such as a bathroom or closet, at the lowest level.**
- **Stay away from windows and get under anything that can protect you from flying objects.**
- **Avoid wide-span roofs when in public buildings.**
- **Abandon vehicles and mobile homes.**
- **Huddle in a ditch, under an overpass, or near something solid if there is no shelter nearby.**

Lesson 5 Review

1. How do thunderstorms, tornadoes, and hurricanes develop?
2. List two safety precautions each for a thunderstorm, a tornado, and a hurricane.
3. **Cause and Effect**
   Moving air in updrafts and down drafts causes electrical charges to build up in clouds. What effect does this buildup of charge cause?

Chapter 1 Review

Chapter Main Ideas

Lesson 1

• Extreme weather can create hazards and affect leisure and work activities.

• People can plan for their safety when weather extremes are predicted.

Lesson 2

• Wind is air moving from a region of high pressure to a region of low pressure.

• Warmer air can hold more humidity than cooler air.

• Most precipitation begins as snow. The temperature of air through which the precipitation falls determines the type.

Lesson 3

• Simple observations of nature evolved into forecasting, with the help of instruments such as the barometer.

• Currently, sophisticated computers and electronic measuring devices are used along with traditional weather tools.

• Data about the upper atmosphere is collected by balloon-carried weather instruments, by Doppler radar, and by weather satellites.

Lesson 4

• Fronts move from west to east, carrying weather changes.

• Weather data is widely collected and transmitted to the National Weather Service (NWS). There computers analyze the information to predict weather.

• The weather information shown as symbols on weather maps can be used to determine fronts and pressure systems.

Lesson 5

• When warm, moist air rises quickly along cold fronts, thunderstorms and tornadoes develop on land and hurricanes develop over the ocean.

• When severe weather threatens, seek appropriate shelter and heed advice from the National Weather Service.

Reviewing Science Words and Concepts

Write the letter of the word or phrase that best completes each sentence.

a. air mass
b. air pressure
c. anemometer
d. barometer
e. dew point
f. Doppler radar
g. forecast
h. front
i. humidity
j. hurricane
k. meteorologist
l. psychrometer
m. relative humidity
n. tornado

1. An instrument that measures wind speed is the ___.
2. An instrument for determining relative humidity is the ___.
3. A(n) ___ measures air pressure.
4. A person who studies the weather is called a(n) ___.
5. The boundary between warm and cold air masses is a(n) ___.
6. A large body of air having similar properties is a(n) ___.
7. A type of radio transmission that tracks precipitation is called ___.

8. The temperature at which a volume of air cannot hold any more water vapor is called the ___.

9. A(n) ___ is a tropical storm with high winds that forms over oceans.

10. A measurement that compares the amount of water vapor in air with the amount it can hold at a given temperature is called ___.

11. The amount of water vapor in the air is ___.

12. A prediction of what the weather will be like in the near future is a(n) ___.

13. As air cools, the ___ increases.

14. A violent, funnel-shaped cloud is a(n) ___.

Explaining Science

Write a paragraph or an outline that explains these questions.

1. How do forecasts help people?

2. What conditions affect weather?

3. How has weather technology evolved?

4. How do meteorologists forecast weather?

5. What characteristics and precautions are associated with thunderstorms, tornadoes, and hurricanes?

Using Skills

1. Observe local weather for one week. Determine the **percentage** of rainy days.

2. Communicate. Write a list of questions for an interview with a meteorologist about the history of forecasting.

3. Collect data on the latest weather developments in nearby cities to the west of where you live by listening to weather reports or interpreting a weather map. Then **predict** what kind of weather you can expect soon.

Critical Thinking

1. Evaluate the role of the telegraph in weather forecasting. Write a paragraph explaining whether or not the telegraph was an important development.

2. Imagine a hurricane has just been predicted for your area. **Make a decision** about what safety precautions you should take. List the precautions.

3. Imagine you are a meteorologist. Draw a flow chart showing the **sequence** of steps involved in making a forecast.

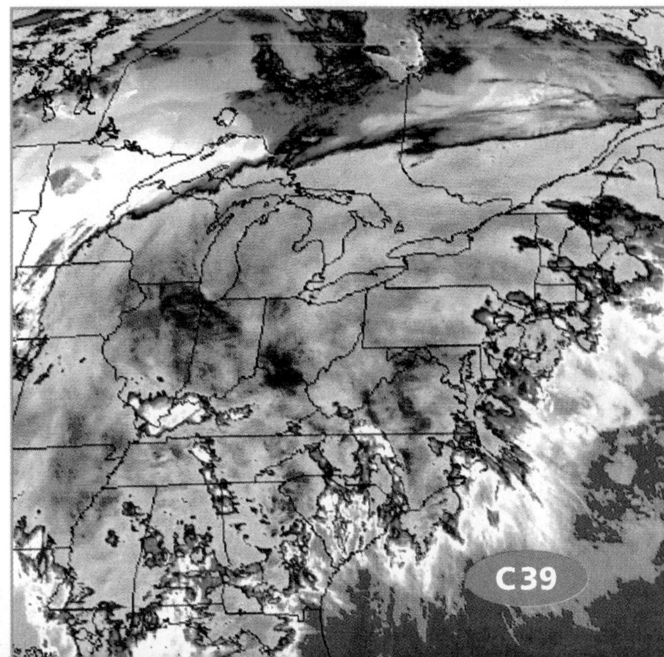

Shifting Sands

It's easy to see how these layers of sand are made. But what about the layers of sand, rocks, and other minerals in Earth's crust? How were those made? Which were laid down first?

Chapter 2

Earth Processes

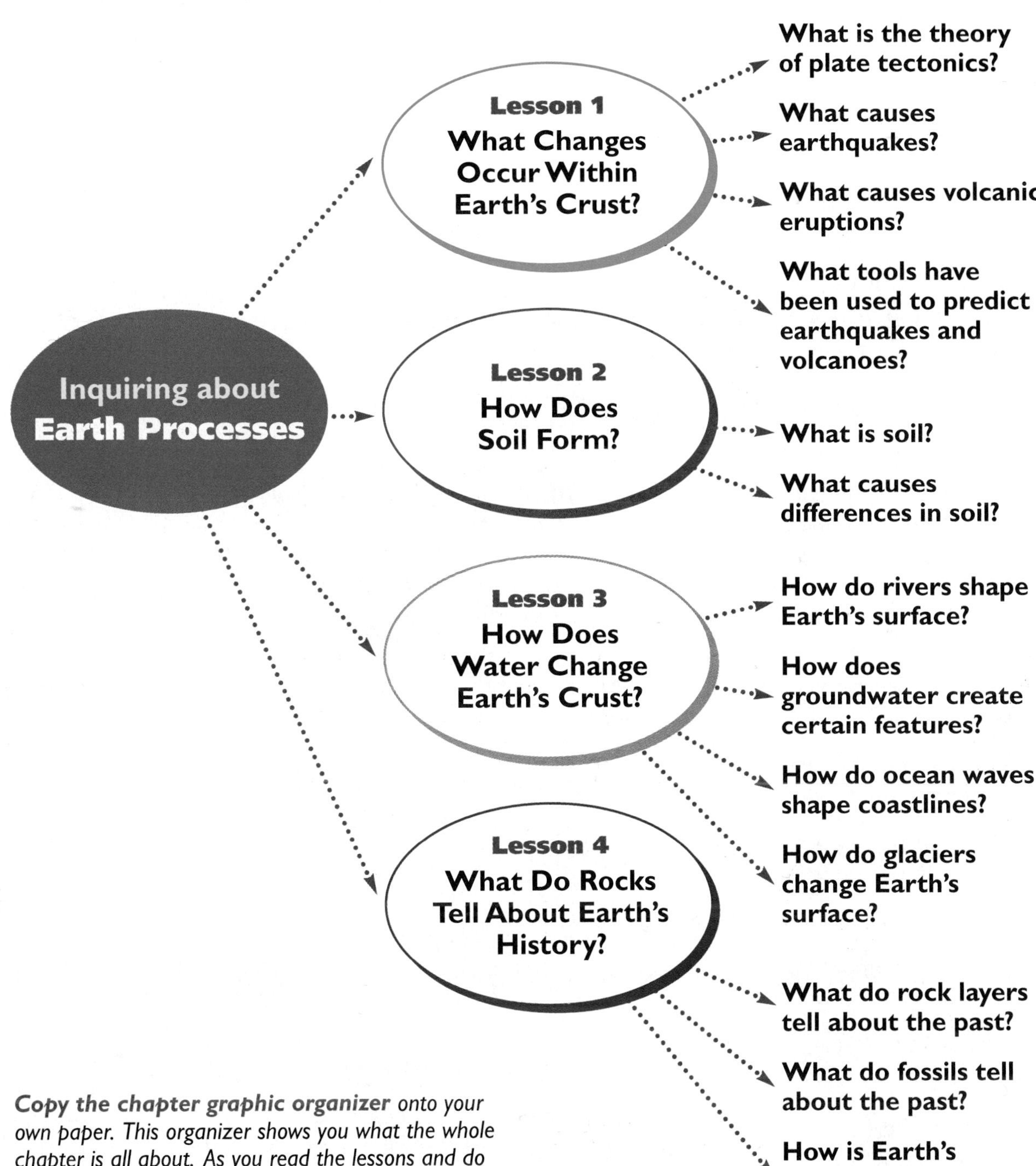

Copy the chapter graphic organizer *onto your own paper. This organizer shows you what the whole chapter is all about. As you read the lessons and do the activities, look for answers to the questions and write them on your organizer.*

Explore Activity

Exploring Properties of the Earth's Mantle

Process Skills

Process Skills

- estimating and measuring
- observing

Materials

- newspaper
- masking tape
- water
- plastic graduated cup
- spoon
- cornstarch
- wax paper

Explore

1. Cover your desk or lab table with several sheets of newspaper. Tape the newspaper in place.
2. **Measure** 25 mL of water into a plastic graduated cup.
3. Add 3 heaping spoonfuls of cornstarch to the water. Mix well with the spoon until no powder is visible, as shown in the photo.
4. Place a piece of wax paper on top of the newspaper on your desk. Place one spoonful of the substance in the cup on the wax paper. **Observe** what happens to the substance.
5. Pick up the substance, and roll it into a ball in your hands. Observe what happens as you touch it and as it sets in your hand.

Reflect

1. What characteristics did you find as you observed the substance?

2. Did the substance act like a liquid or a solid? Explain.

Inquire Further

What would happen if you made a large ball of the substance? How could you make the ball keep its shape? Develop a plan to answer these or other questions you may have.

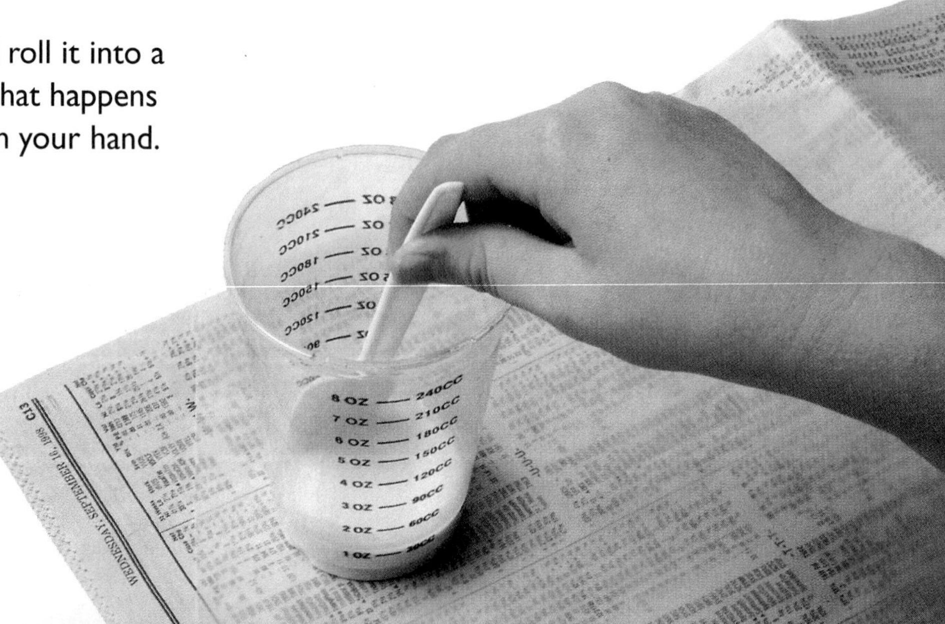

Using Graphic Sources

When reading science, it is important to know how to use graphic sources. A graphic source can be a picture, a diagram, or a chart that provides an example or explains an idea. As you read Lesson 1, *What Changes Occur Within Earth's Crust?,* be alert for key words such as *shows, look at, illustrates,* and *notice.* These words give you a purpose for using the graphics.

Example

Look at the picture below from page C45. Read the title and caption. Look for labels or callouts. Then pay attention to details in the graphic. Finally, ask yourself what main idea can be learned from studying the graphic.

Earth's Tectonic Plates

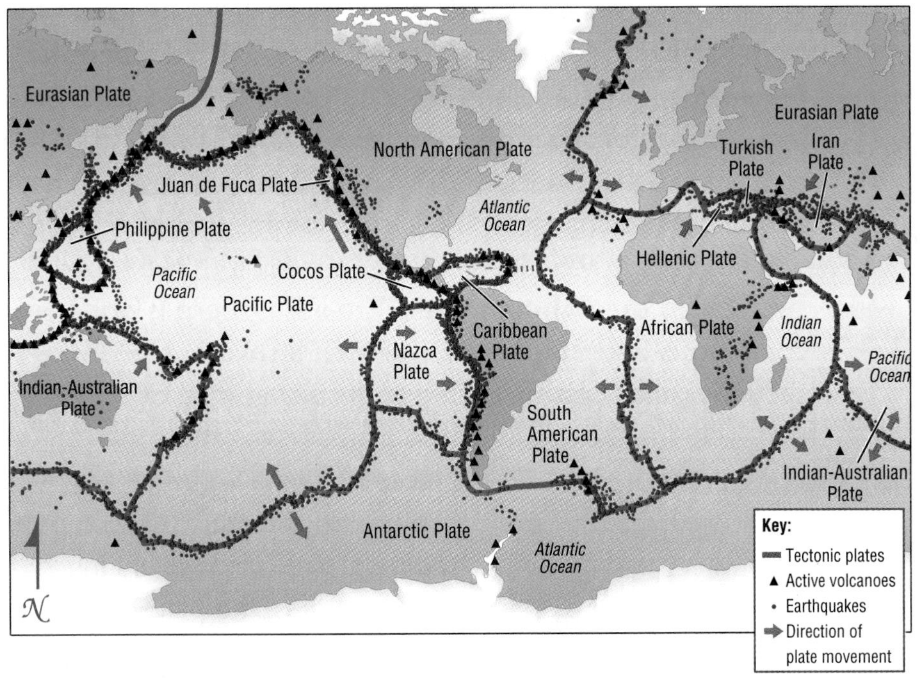

◀ *Earth's plates can move toward, away from, or past each other, as the arrows indicate.*

Talk About It!

1. How can graphics help you understand what you are reading?

2. What did you learn about plate movement from looking at the graphic?

You will learn:

- what the theory of plate tectonics is.
- what causes earthquakes.
- what causes volcanic eruptions.
- what tools have been used to predict earthquakes and volcanoes.

Lesson 1

What Changes Occur Within Earth's Crust?

Mmmm. . . Bite into a warm piece of French bread. CRUNCH! That's the crust—the thin outer layer of bread. Now think about a different kind of crust—not quite so tasty!

Plate Tectonics

Earth's crust is the outermost solid layer of the planet. It includes the features shown on the globe below—the continents and the floor of the oceans. Scientists think that 200 million years ago, Earth's crust was much different from what the globe below shows. Seas existed where mountains now stand, and the land consisted of one large mass instead of separate continents. Obviously, Earth's crust has changed a lot in the past 200 million years. What explains these changes? The answer begins with the crust.

The crust is actually the upper part of a thicker solid layer called the **lithosphere**. The lithosphere is not a continuous layer. Rather, it is broken into about 20 sections called plates. Each plate is a huge slab of rock that includes the crust. These plates fit together like pieces of a jigsaw puzzle, as you can see on the map at the top of the next page. However, unlike jigsaw puzzles, the plates don't stay put. The solid plates float on a layer of partly melted rock. This idea that the lithosphere is broken into moving plates is called the theory of **plate tectonics**. This theory explains much about how the earth looks.

Glossary

Glossary

lithosphere (lith′ə sfir), the solid rocky outer layer of the earth that includes the crust

plate tectonics (plāt tek ton′iks), theory that states that the lithosphere is broken into plates that move

This globe shows Earth as it appears today. Scientists have gathered evidence suggesting that Earth did not always look like this. ▶

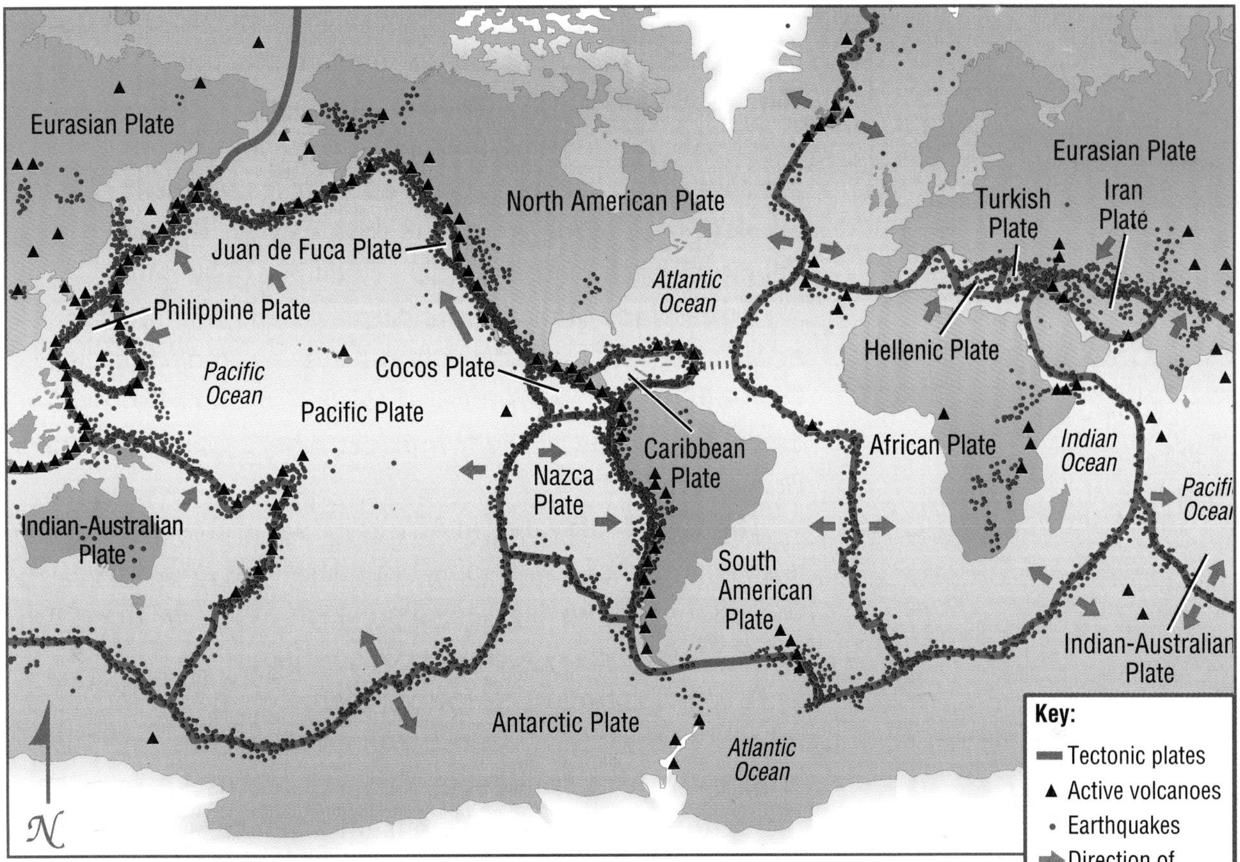

Earth's Tectonic Plates

▲ *Earth's plates can move toward, away from, or past each other, as the arrows indicate.*

Look again at the map. The arrows show that the plates move in different directions. Scientists have determined that some plates move at an average rate of about 2 centimeters per year. That's only about as fast as your fingernails grow! Others move as fast as 15 centimeters per year. You can see why it takes millions of years for continents to change positions very much.

What makes the plates move? The picture below shows one explanation—slow-moving convection currents beneath the plates. A convection current is a movement of matter. In a convection current, hot matter rises, while cooler matter sinks. The differences in temperature cause material to move in a circular pattern. This process occurs in the mantle when hot, partially melted rock rises up to the plates and spreads out sideways. The spreading carries the plates along. As the magma spreads, it cools. Then the material sinks back into the mantle, where it heats and rises again.

Convection Currents

Convection currents in the mantle cause hot, partially melted rock to move, dragging continents and ocean floors with it. ▼

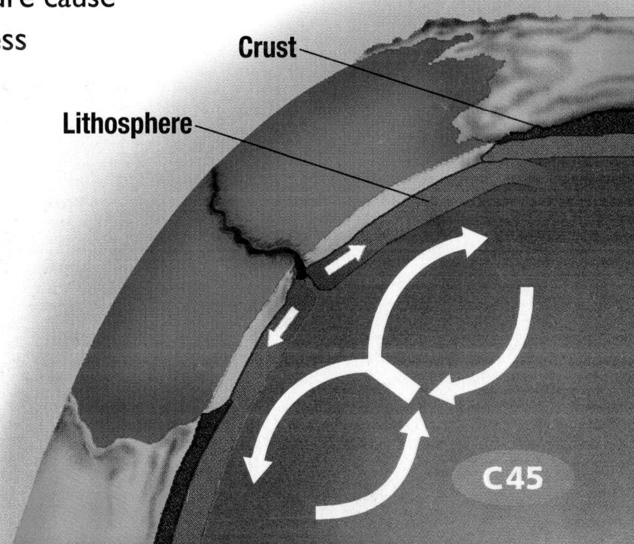

Glossary

Glossary

fault (fôlt), a crack in the earth's crust along which rock moves

Tremendous changes in Earth's crust occur at plate boundaries where two plates meet. Here, the plates may slide past each other, collide, or move away from each other. All this grinding, pushing, and pulling of rock produces many faults at plate boundaries. A **fault** is a break in rock along which the rock moves. By this definition, each plate boundary itself is a huge fault.

Three kinds of plate boundaries occur. A fault boundary is an area where two plates are moving past each other. The San Andreas Fault in California, shown below left, is one of the few places where a fault boundary occurs on land.

The Great Rift Valley in Africa, shown in the circle below is an example of a spreading boundary—an area where two plates are moving away from each other. As the plates move apart, a valley forms between them.

A colliding boundary forms where two plates move toward each other. Often, ocean crust collides with the crust that forms continents. The ocean crust sinks below the continental crust and melts into the mantle. The continental crust buckles into mountains. If two continental plates collide, they both buckle into tall mountains, such as the Himalayas shown below.

At the San Andreas Fault in California, two plates move past each other at a relatively fast rate of 5 centimeters per year. What events often occur near this boundary? ▼

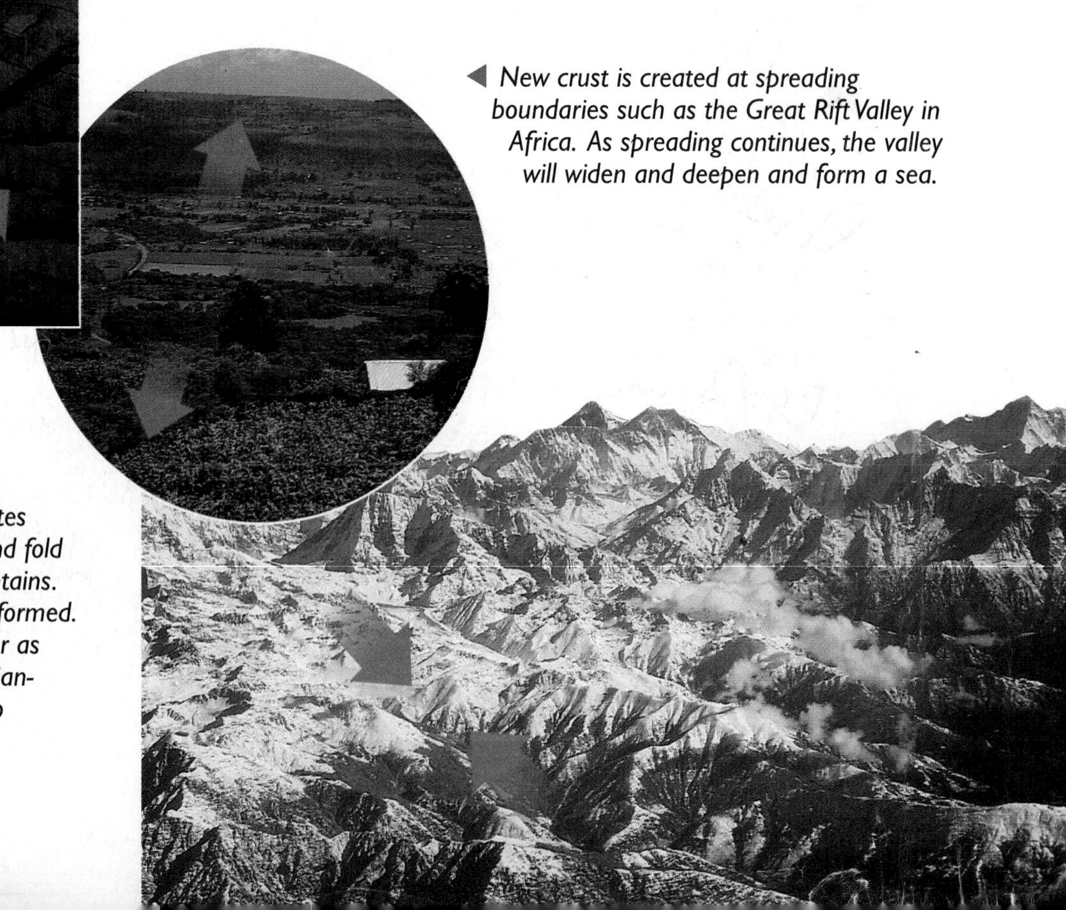

◀ *New crust is created at spreading boundaries such as the Great Rift Valley in Africa. As spreading continues, the valley will widen and deepen and form a sea.*

At colliding boundaries, plates push against each other and fold rock layers into huge mountains. That's how the Himalayas formed. They continue to grow taller as the Eurasian Plate and Indian-Australian Plate continue to collide. ▶

Earthquakes

You don't have to worry about a crustal plate zooming by—plates move very slowly. In fact, sometimes they don't move at all for many years. Parts of the plates may snag on each other. Then pressure builds until the rock breaks and lurches forward several centimeters all at once. This sudden movement makes the crust shake. The sudden shaking or vibrating of the earth's crust is an earthquake. Most earthquakes occur near plate boundaries, as you can see on the map on page C45. This outcome makes sense because earthquakes occur as rock moves suddenly along faults, and most faults are at plate boundaries.

How does an earthquake cause the kind of damage you see in the building below? When a huge slab of rock suddenly slips, the energy that has been building up is quickly released. The drawing shows how the released energy travels in waves away from the point where the rock first moves—the **focus**. The waves make the ground shake, just as waves in water make a small boat bob up and down.

Glossary

focus (fō′kəs), the point along a fault where rock first breaks or moves, causing an earthquake

▲ *When an earthquake occurs, waves of energy move outward from the focus in all directions.*

During an earthquake, waves can cause the ground to roll, shake, or suddenly lift. These movements can destroy roads and other structures, such as this building. ▶

Glossary

seismograph
(sīz′mə graf), instrument that records the strengths of the earth's movements, based on the amount of energy released

Richter scale
(rik′tər skāl), a scale used to compare the strengths of earthquakes

During an earthquake, as the energy waves move away from the focus, they lose energy. If you stood directly above the focus of a strong earthquake, you'd be the first person to feel the ground shake. A person standing many miles away from you wouldn't feel the earthquake as quickly or as strongly.

About 800,000 earthquakes occur around the world every year. Most of them are too weak to be felt by people. However, an instrument called a **seismograph** can measure and record even the slightest vibration from the weakest earthquake. A seismograph includes a revolving paper drum like the one shown in the picture on the left. When the ground shakes, a pen records these movements as a pattern of zigzag lines.

Zigzag lines on this seismograph provide a record of waves produced by an earthquake. ▼

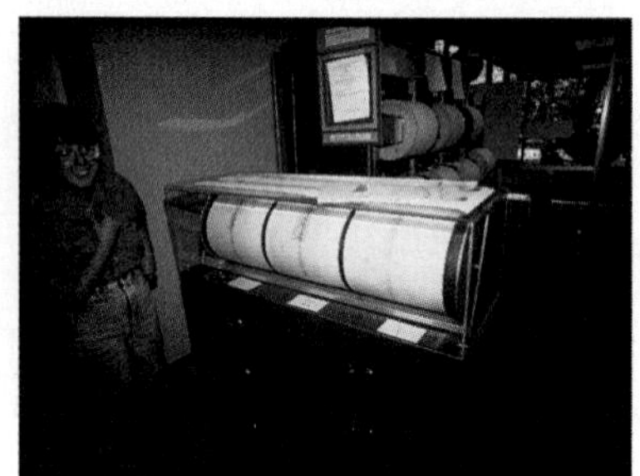

When you hear about an earthquake that occurred, the description usually includes a number on the Richter scale. The **Richter scale**, shown below, is a series of numbers used to describe the strength of an earthquake. The number is based on the total amount of energy released. The scale was developed in the 1930s by an American scientist named Charles Richter. Each whole number on the scale represents an earthquake ten times stronger than an earthquake with a number below it. For example, an earthquake that measures 6.0 on the Richter scale is ten times stronger than one that measures 5.0. The strength of the earthquake at any particular place depends on how close that place is to the focus of the earthquake—the closer to the focus, the stronger the waves and the more damage they can do.

Richter Scale

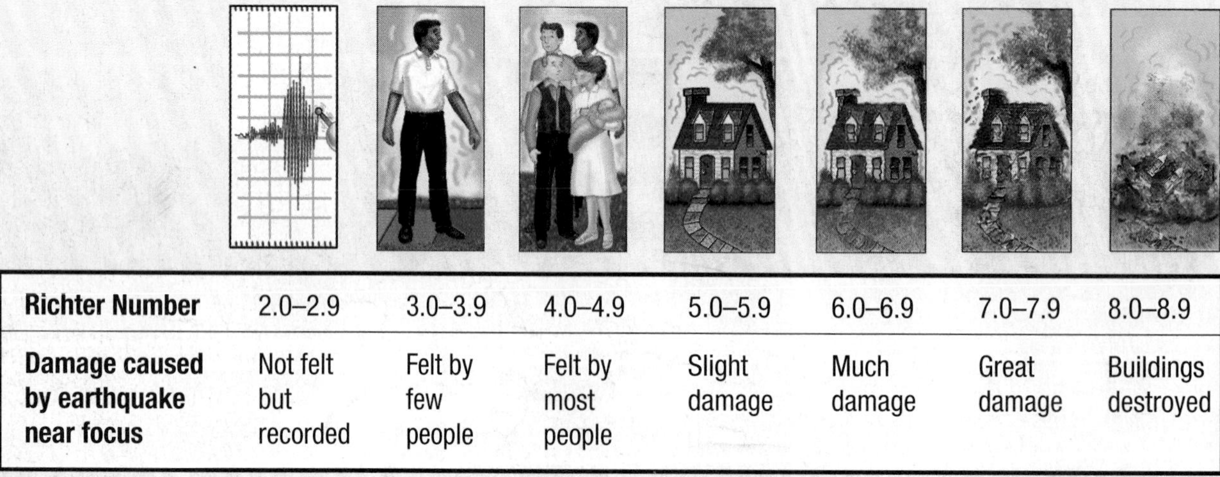

Richter Number	2.0–2.9	3.0–3.9	4.0–4.9	5.0–5.9	6.0–6.9	7.0–7.9	8.0–8.9
Damage caused by earthquake near focus	Not felt but recorded	Felt by few people	Felt by most people	Slight damage	Much damage	Great damage	Buildings destroyed

Volcanoes

A volcano is an opening on the surface of the earth through which magma rises. As the map on page C45 shows, volcanoes are closely related to plate movement. Like earthquakes, most of the world's volcanoes practically outline the plate boundaries, both on the continents and on the ocean floor.

What's the connection between volcanoes and plate tectonics? At colliding boundaries, one plate often sinks beneath the other plate. The sinking crust melts into magma as it enters the mantle. Since hot magma is less dense than solid rock, the magma rises through openings in the crust. Gases within the magma cause pressure to build, much the way pressure builds when you shake a can of carbonated beverage. Eventually the pressure is so great that magma breaks through the surface as lava, exploding like the drink spraying from an opened can.

Volcanic eruptions on land, such as Mt. Arenal in Costa Rica, shown below, are big news items. However, you never hear about most volcanic activity because it takes place at spreading boundaries on the ocean floor. These eruptions are gentle compared to those at colliding boundaries. Lava quietly flows out onto the surface of the plate, adding new crust to the ocean floor. The hot lava cools when it reaches the cold ocean water and hardens into rock.

A volcano can build as ash and lava gather around the opening. However, some eruptions are so explosive, they destroy part of the volcano. ▼

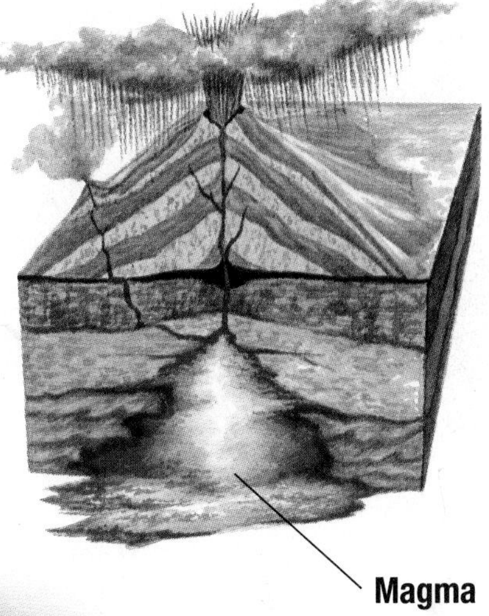

Predicting Earthquakes and Volcanoes

Earthquakes and volcanic eruptions have plagued civilizations throughout recorded history. People have long recognized that lives could be saved if these destructive events could be predicted. Today, scientists have many complex instruments to monitor earthquakes and volcanoes. Some instruments that are more than a thousand years old, however, seem just as ingenious.

The Ruins of Pompeii

One of the most destructive volcanic eruptions in history took place in Italy in the year A.D. 79, when Mount Vesuvius suddenly exploded. The towns of Pompeii and nearby Herculaneum were quickly buried beneath ash and mud. Plaster casts made of some of the victims provide an eerie reminder of Earth's awesome power. ▼

First Seismograph

In the year A.D. 132, a Chinese inventor named Chang Heng presented this earthquake detector to the Chinese court. When the ground shook even slightly, the dragon on the side closest to the focus would drop a ball into the open mouth of a toad below. From this action, people were able to identify the direction from which the earthquake came. A series of pins, levers, and pendulums inside the vase made this seismograph work. ▶

Tiltmeter

Another device to help scientists predict volcanic eruptions is a tiltmeter. It detects changes in the slope of a volcano. A change in the slope of a volcano might mean that magma is moving within the mountain. ▶

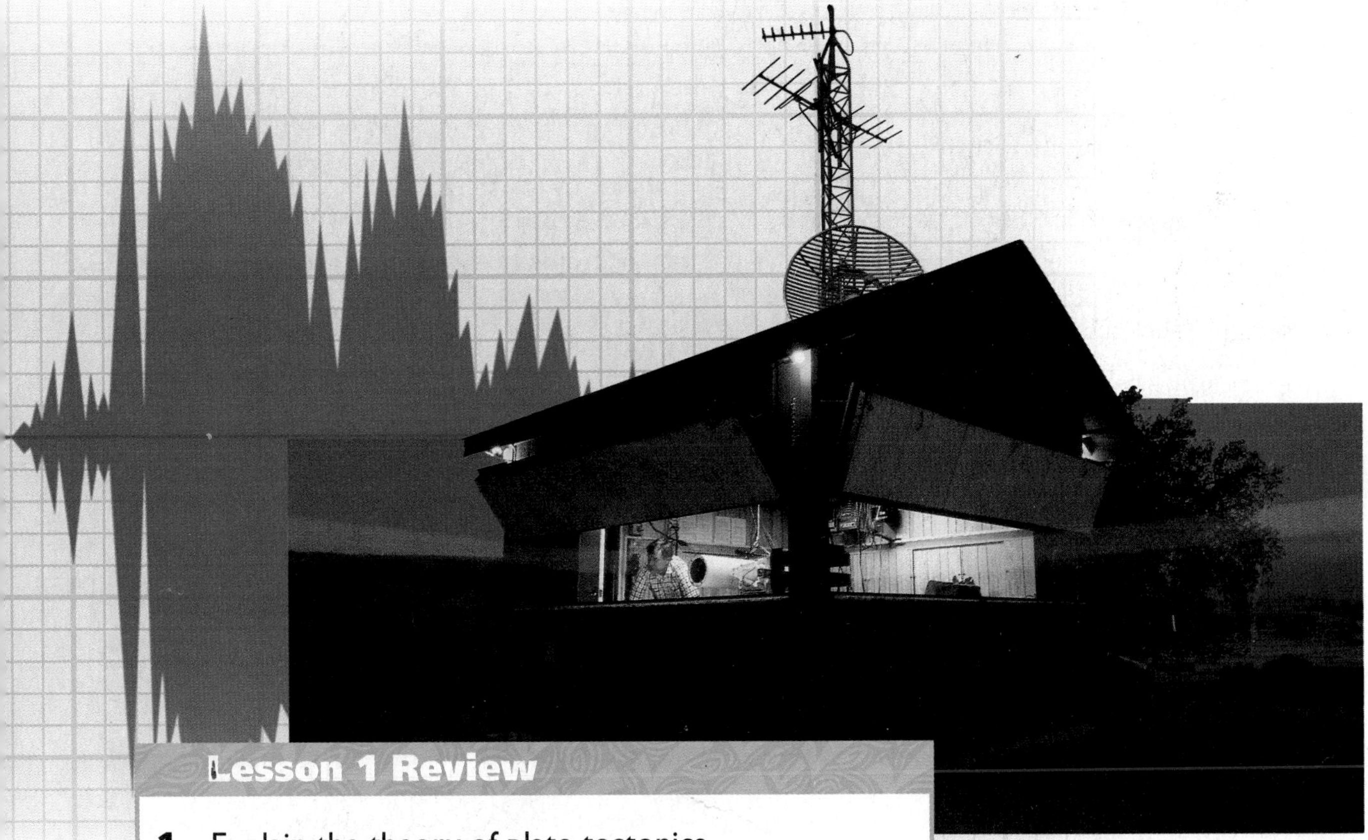

Laser Detector

▲ *Today, lasers are used to detect earth movement. A beam of laser light is aimed at a reflector on the other side of a plate boundary. Scientists record the time it takes for the light to travel this distance and back. Any change might mean that an earthquake is coming. Lasers are also used to detect bulges in a volcano—a sign that an eruption may occur soon.*

Lesson 1 Review

1. Explain the theory of plate tectonics.
2. What causes earthquakes?
3. What causes volcanic eruptions?
4. What are some tools that have been used to predict earthquakes and volcanoes?
5. **Graphic Sources**
   Find the map on page C45. On which plate is the United States? In which direction is that plate moving?

Making a Model Seismograph

Process Skills

- making and using models
- predicting
- observing
- inferring

Materials

- safety goggles
- shoe box
- cafeteria tray
- masking tape
- ruler
- rubber bands
- 2 washers
- clay
- felt tip pen

Getting Ready

In this activity, you will make a model seismograph.

Review the information about seismographs on page C48.

Follow This Procedure

1. Make several copies of the chart shown below. These will become seismograms that record the intensity of your "earthquakes."

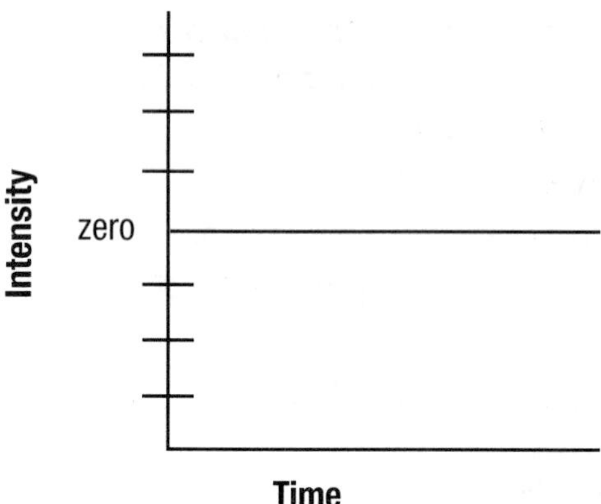

2. Put on your safety goggles. Make a **model** of a seismograph. Stand a shoe box on a cafeteria tray. Tape the shoe box to the tray.

3. Tape a ruler to the top of the shoe box.

4. Make a chain of rubber bands. Place one band through another. Thread the end of one rubber band through itself. Pull both bands tight to form a knot. Add 4 more rubber bands (Photo A). Add a washer to each end of the chain.

5. Wrap a small strip of clay around the top of a pen. Attach each washer to the strip of clay by pressing it into the clay. Hang the chain over the ruler.

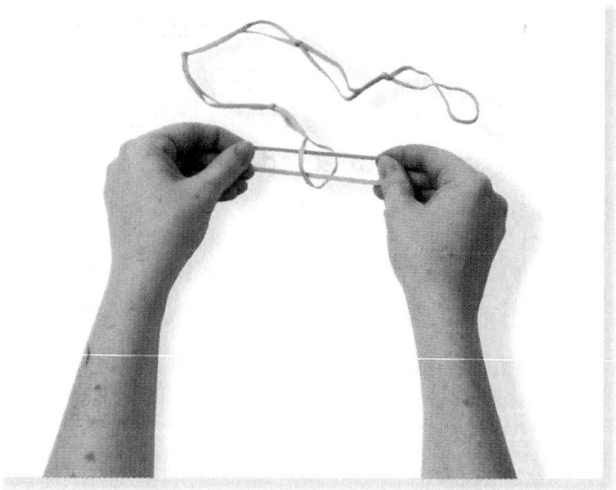

Photo A

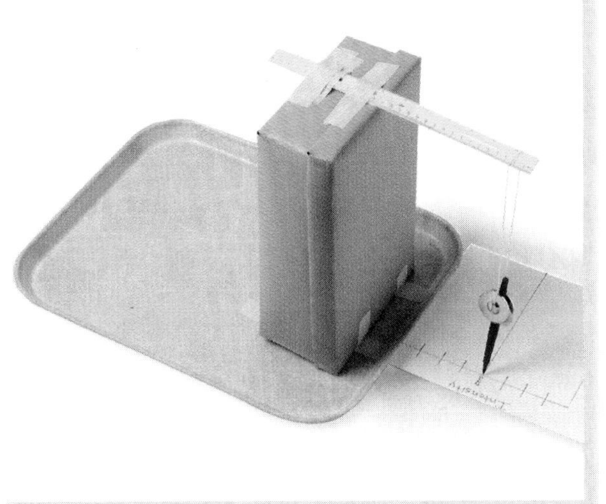

Photo B

6 Place your chart under the pen (Photo B). Adjust the clay and the washers so that the tip of the pen will just touch the paper. Tape the chain in place on the ruler. Remove the cap from the pen.

7 Allow each partner to practice pulling the sheet of paper across the table at an even speed. **Predict** what will happen if the tray is moved while someone pulls the paper.

8 Make a seismogram of a simulated earthquake. Have one student pull the paper. Have a partner gently shake the tray to produce an "earthquake." **Observe** how the seismograph and seismogram are affected by each earthquake.

9 Take turns producing earthquakes and recording their intensities on different seismograms. Compare the different seismograms you make.

Interpret Your Results

1. What did you observe as your seismograph recorded an earthquake? What do the lines on your chart represent?

2. Describe how you and your partners were able to produce different seismograms.

3. Make an **inference**. Tell how seismographs are used to measure the energy released during an earthquake.

Inquire Further

How could you use your seismograph to tell how many seconds or minutes an earthquake lasted? Develop a plan to answer this or other questions you may have.

Self-Assessment

- I followed the directions to make a **model** seismograph.
- I **predicted** what would happen if the table moved while a partner pulled the paper under the pen.
- I **observed** the effects of simulated earthquakes on the seismogram.
- I compared the seismograms of different earthquakes.
- I made an **inference** about how a seismograph can be used to indicate the energy released during an earthquake.

You will learn:

- what soil is.
- what causes differences in soil.

Lesson 2

How Does Soil Form?

Mix together tiny bits of weathered rocks and dust. Add some dried leaves and decayed animal parts. Sprinkle in some animal droppings and fragments of animal fur or bird feathers. Mix well. YUK! What IS this? It's a "recipe" for soil.

Soil

In Lesson 1, you learned about changes in Earth's crust that happen when processes occur deep within the Earth. Soil formation is a process too, but it occurs on Earth's surface. Soil forms when rocks, animal life, plant life, air, water, and chemicals interact. Like many earth processes, soil formation takes a long time. The interactions that formed the handful of soil in the picture occurred over thousands of years.

What do you see in this handful of soil? Look closely. Try to find some of the "ingredients" mentioned above. Perhaps all you see is something that gets your hands dirty. Actually, soil is as important to life as water, air, and sunlight. Most life on Earth depends on soil. Without soil, animals—and you—would have few plants to use for food or shelter. Think about it! What have you used today that depended on soil in one way or another? Did you think about the paper of this book?

Soil is a mixture of weathered rock and decayed plant and animal matter that formed over a long period of time. The diagram on the next page will help you understand why soil takes thousands of years to form.

Soil is a mixture of grains of rock and organic matter. How many different ingredients can you find in this handful of soil? ▼

Soil Formation

1 *Soil formation begins with the break up of rock.*

2 *At the surface, rock weathers into stones and grains of sand. This material mixes with moss and other organic matter to form a thin layer of soil. More plants take root in the developing soil, which attracts more animal life. Their decaying bodies and wastes make the soil thicker and richer.*

3 *As weathering continues and organic matter builds, the soil becomes fully developed and can support a greater variety of plants.*

As you see in the first picture, soil begins as rock. When rock is exposed at or near the surface, it begins to break apart. Water and gases in the air form a weak acid that eats away at rock. Also, water in the cracks of rock expands as it freezes and wedges the rock apart. This group of processes that break down rock is called **weathering.** The processes of weathering gradually break rock into smaller and smaller fragments. Mosses and a few other types of vegetation grow on these fragments. The rock weathers further into grains of sand, silt, and clay.

In the next stages, the soil becomes thicker and richer. As moss and other plants die, they decay and become part of the soil. Insects, worms, bacteria, and fungi start to live among the plant roots and rock particles. Seeds of grasses and shrubs blow into the area, take root, and grow. As organisms die, their decaying bodies form dark-colored organic matter called humus. Animal droppings add to the growing richness of the soil, which can now support a greater variety of plant life. As worms and insects burrow, they mix the humus with the fragments of weathered rock to form the rich fertile soil you see in the last drawing.

Glossary

weathering
(weᴛʜ′ər ing), group of processes that break rocks into smaller pieces

Differences in Soil

Have you ever seen different layers of soil where a hill was cut to form a road? Perhaps you noticed plants growing in a dark layer at the top. The layers below may have been lighter in color. These layers of soil make up a soil profile. Most soil profiles show three distinct layers.

Usually, the dark top layer, called topsoil, is rich in humus. When rain water filters through the topsoil, it often carries dissolved minerals down to the second layer. The third and lowest layer is partly weathered rock that is just beginning the long, slow process of changing into soil from the rock below.

Notice the different thicknesses and types of soil layers in the soil profiles shown below. The differences depend on the climate and type of rock from which the soil formed. Other factors that affect a soil profile include the shape of the land, the amount of humus available, and how long the soil has been forming.

Soil Profiles
Compare these two profiles. ▶

Topsoil
Subsoil
Bedrock

Lesson 2 Review

1. What is soil?
2. What causes differences in soil?
3. **Graphic Sources**
   According to the picture on page C55, how does soil formation affect plant life at the surface of the soil?

Lesson 3

How Does Water Change Earth's Crust?

Paddle in . . . paddle out . . . paddle in . . . paddle out . . . What a FANTASTIC day to be on the water! Be careful, though, the current is STRONG. Watch out for that boulder! A stream flows into the river up ahead. The waters will be choppy there.

You will learn:

- **how rivers shape Earth's surface.**
- **how groundwater creates certain features.**
- **how ocean waves shape coastlines.**
- **how glaciers change Earth's surface.**

Rivers

A river is always coming from one place and going someplace else. The river shown here begins as a trickle of melting snow high on a mountain many kilometers upstream. Gravity causes the water to flow downhill. Along the way, more rainwater and melting snow running off the land join it. The trickle grows into a stream. Smaller streams that started the same way join the main stream, bringing it more water and making it grow. The stream grows this way to become the river you see here. How do you think the river below will look 30 kilometers downstream?

Streams that join larger streams are called tributaries. The main river and all its tributaries make a river system. The satellite photo to the right shows that a river system looks like the branching of a tree. The river system ends where the main river flows into the ocean or a lake.

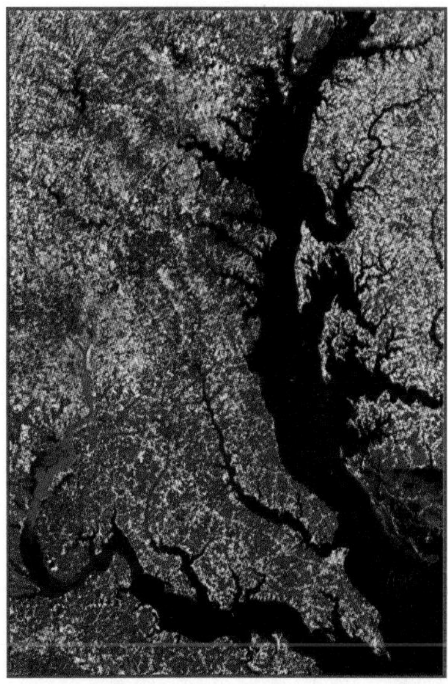

▲ *The people in the canoe below are on a mid-size tributary. Where might they be located on this satellite view of the river system?*

Glossary

drainage basin (drā′nij bā sin), the land area from which a river system gets its water

sediment (sed′ə mənt), rock and soil carried by water

The land area from which a river system gets its water is called a **drainage basin.** A drainage basin is like a sink. All water that falls into the sink eventually flows down toward the drain. Similarly, most water that flows over the land of a drainage basin eventually flows into the main river. The Mississippi River has the largest drainage basin in the United States. Its basin covers nearly two-thirds of the country!

If you were watering a garden with a hose, would you turn the hose on full blast? Most likely, you wouldn't because you know that the force of the water would dig up the soil and uproot the plants. Running water is a powerful sculptor. The running water of rivers wears away—or erodes—rock and soil. These materials, which are called **sediments,** flow with the river and make it an even better sculptor of the land. The pictures on these two pages show how a river changes the landscape along its route.

V-Shaped Valleys

The beginning, or headwaters, of a river is often in a mountainous or hilly area. The water flows fast because the slope is steep. The fast-moving water has much power to erode and cuts steep V-shaped valleys. The sediment is carried downstream. What other features are common in this part of the river? ▶

Floodplains

◀ *Further downstream, the slope of the river is gentler. The river is wider because by now many tributaries have joined it. The river forms looping bends called meanders, which erode the sides of the valley and make it wider. During floods, the stream overflows. A low-lying area called a floodplain forms.*

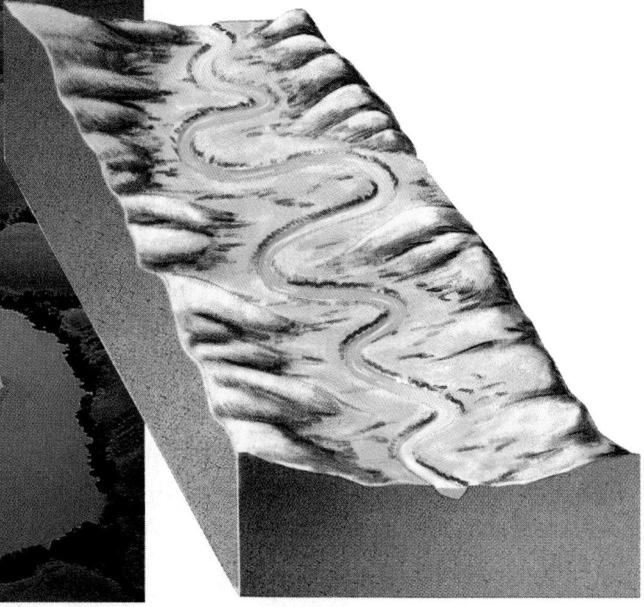

Meanders and Oxbows

◀ *The river moves much more slowly as it flows over flatter land toward the sea. Flooding is more common, and the floodwaters erode a wide floodplain. The river erodes mostly at its sides, causing well-developed meanders. Horseshoe-shaped oxbow lakes form when the river takes a straighter course, cutting off a meander.*

Glossary

Glossary

groundwater
(ground wȯ tər), water in the ground near Earth's surface

aquifer (ak′wə fər), a layer of rock in which ground water can accumulate and flow freely

water table
(wȯ′tər tā′bəl), the top of an aquifer

Ground Water

Not all of the water from rain and snow flows over the land into rivers. Some of the precipitation slowly sinks into the ground through the soil. It keeps seeping down through tiny cracks and spaces in the rock until it finally reaches a layer of rock that it can't pass through. This rock prevents the water from traveling down any farther. Now the water is part of an underground system of water called **groundwater**.

Notice in the drawing below how groundwater gathers in spaces in the rock layer above the impermeable rock. A layer of rock where groundwater can accumulate and flow freely is called an **aquifer**. You can see that groundwater accumulates to a certain level in an aquifer. The top of this water level is the **water table**.

The shape of the water table generally follows the shape of the land. It rises under hills and sinks under valleys. At times, the water table is visible at the surface. Groundwater near the surface may form swamps, marshes, and other wetlands, or it can flow out as a spring on hillsides.

Groundwater fills the air spaces in soil and in rock, like water in a sponge. ▼

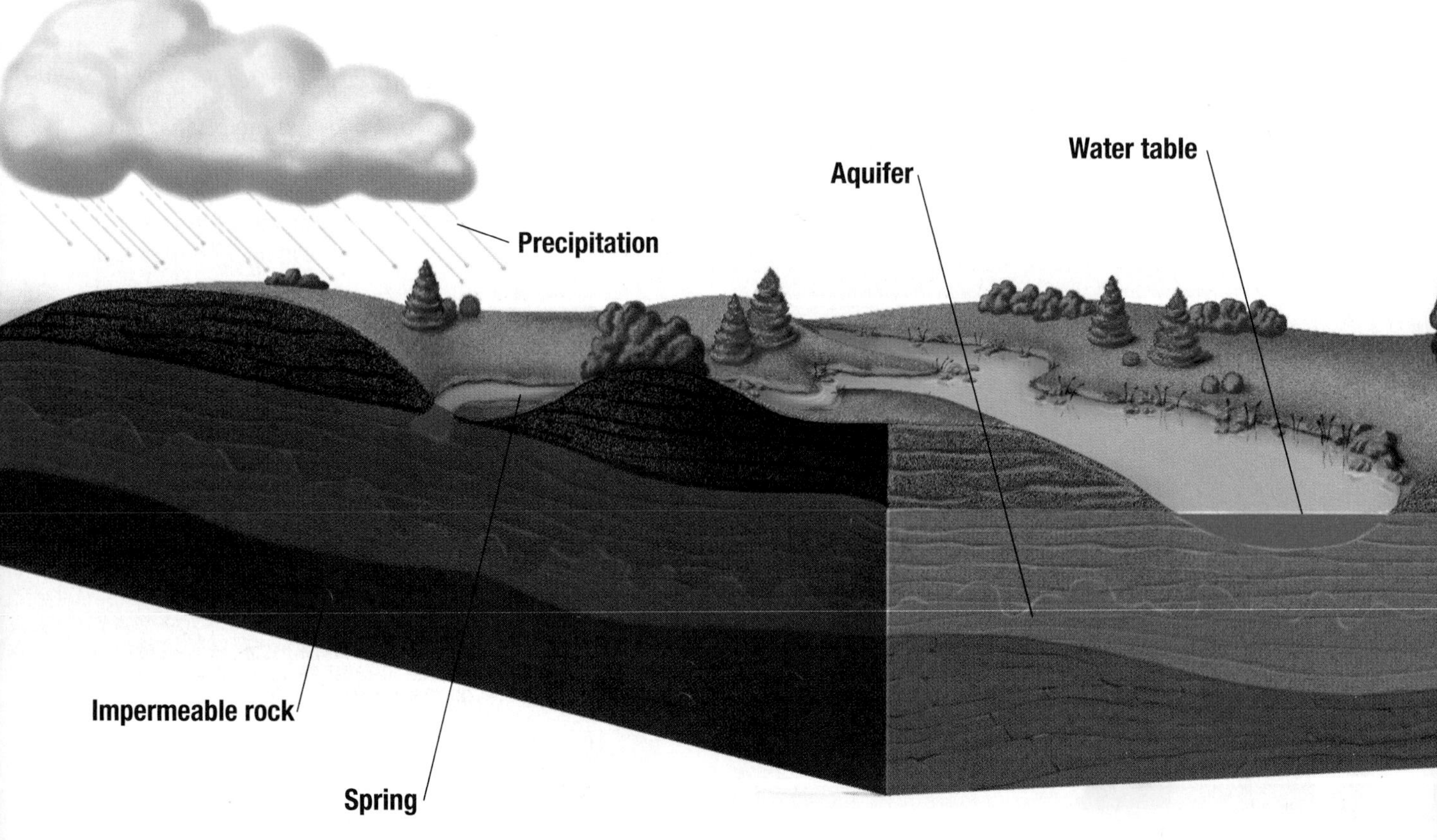

Half of the population of the United States depends on groundwater for its drinking water. People get this water by drilling wells into the aquifer. Groundwater flows into the well and is pumped to the surface. As you can see in the diagram, the bottom of a well must be placed below the water table. When too much water is used, or during dry seasons, the water table drops. Then the well goes dry until rain adds more water to the aquifer. Then the water table rises.

Groundwater produces some unusual features. The picture to the right shows one of them. If groundwater lies close to hot volcanic rock or magma, the water gets heated. The heated water rises to the surface and erupts in a fountain of hot water and steam called a geyser. The 200 geysers in Yellowstone National Park are a sign of this area's magma beneath its surface.

You know that water on Earth's surface erodes surface rock. Groundwater erodes rock too. When rainwater seeps downward through limestone, it dissolves calcium and other minerals in the limestone. Over time, groundwater carves out huge caverns. How huge? One cavern in Carlsbad Caverns, New Mexico, can hold the Unites States Capitol Building!

▲ *Old Faithful in Yellowstone National Park, Wyoming, is a geyser that erupts regularly when groundwater seeps into spaces near hot rock. Geysers are also found in Iceland and New Zealand.*

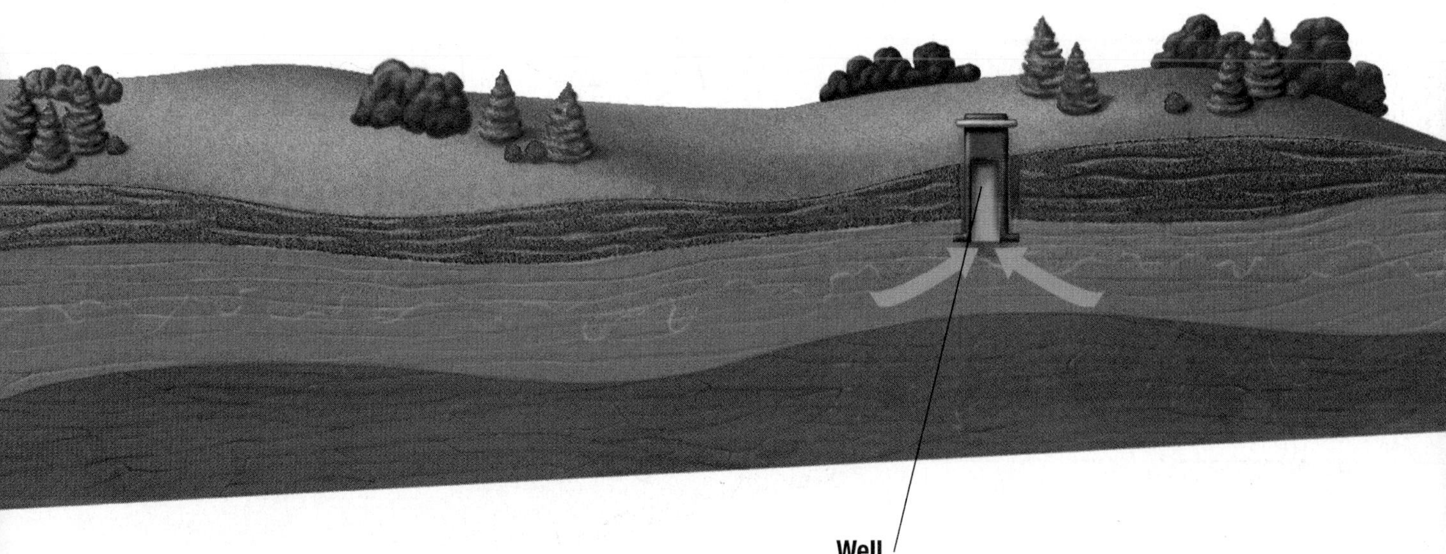

Ocean Waves

Rivers and some groundwater eventually flow to the ocean. The water that empties into the ocean brings sediments and a mixture of dissolved elements with it. Some of these dissolved elements combine to form new substances. Sea animals and plants use a dissolved element, calcium, to carry on their life processes, such as building shells or forming bones. Other elements form minerals on the ocean floor that are important resources for humans.

The waves shown here tell you something else about ocean water—it is powerful and in constant motion. Energy is needed to produce any kind of wave. If you hold the end of a rope and shake it, your arm provides the energy that makes the wave on the rope. Wind provides the energy that causes most ocean waves. The longer and stronger the wind blows, the larger the waves.

Ocean waves may travel thousands of kilometers before finally breaking on shore. ▼

A water particle moves up and down in a circle as a wave passes. Near shore, the circle flattens because of friction with the sea floor. ▼

Waves rolling toward the ocean shore may look as if they are moving forward. Actually, water is moving up and down in a wave. Remember the rope? As you shake the rope to make a wave, the wave moves forward, but the rope does not. The same thing happens in water waves. The diagram shows that water particles remain in about the same place, turning in a circle as the energy in each wave pushes forward.

▲ *Wave erosion formed the steep, jagged cliffs you see here. How will these features change as erosion continues?*

Notice that waves get taller as they approach the shoreline. That's because the water is getting shallower. Friction with the ocean bottom slows the bottom of the wave. The top of the wave moves slightly ahead and tumbles forward, breaking on shore. These waves are breakers. Water in a breaker no longer moves in circles; it actually moves forward onto the shore.

Waves constantly breaking against the shore created the rocky formations you see in the picture above. Waves also carry stones and sand that grind away at the rocky coast. While waves wear away the land in some places, they build it up in other places. For example, waves that strike the shore at an angle help move sand along the shoreline, forming sandy beaches.

Breaker

Glossary

glacier (glā′shər), a large mass of moving ice

moraine (mə rān′), a ridge formed when a glacier deposits its sediments

Glaciers

You've seen how Earth's crust is changed by rivers, groundwater, and ocean waves. Water as a flowing mass of ice can also change the crust.

In some cold areas, the amount of snow that falls each year is greater than the amount that melts. Over hundreds or thousands of years, the accumulating snow packs into ice. A large mass of slowly moving ice, called a **glacier,** forms. The picture below shows Mendenhall Glacier, which formed high in the mountains of Alaska. Gravity causes this river of ice to move slowly—several centimeters a day—downhill. A glacier also moves when pressure created by the heavy ice causes the bottom of the glacier to melt. The glacier then glides across the melted ice.

Glaciers shape the land in many ways. As glaciers move, they scrape away loose fragments of stone and soil. The loose materials are carried by the glacier. When the glacier melts, it deposits, or drops, its load of sediments in ridges along the sides and end of the glacier. This type of glacial deposit is called a **moraine.**

The Mendenhall Glacier near Juneau, Alaska, moves slowly down the mountain, carving and reshaping the valley as it goes. The dark stripes are rocks that have broken off the sides of the valley. The number of stripes tells you how many smaller glaciers have joined this one. ▼

◀ *The rounded, U-shape of this valley in Canada is a sign that a valley glacier once existed here. The glacier gouged out a valley that is deeper, wider, and rounder than the one that existed before.*

▲ *Jagged rocks trapped in the bottom of a glacier scraped grooves into this bedrock as a glacier slowly moved over it. The grooves indicate the direction the glacier was moving.*

Other changes in Earth's surface happen as melted water beneath the glacier seeps into cracks of rock and freezes. As the freezing water expands, chunks of rock break loose and become frozen into the bottom and sides of the glacier. The rocks, which have been plucked and frozen onto the glacier, scrape across the bedrock to form the scratches and grooves you see here to the right.

As glaciers gouge out the earth during their lifetime, they reshape narrow V-shaped river valleys into rounded, U-shaped valleys like the one shown above.

Lesson 3 Review

1. How do rivers change Earth's surface?
2. How does groundwater create certain features?
3. How do ocean waves shape coastlines?
4. How do glaciers change Earth's surface?
5. **Graphic Sources**
   Why do the arrows in the waves on the bottom of pages C62–C63 flatten as they move toward shore?

Making a Model Glacier

Process Skills

- making and using models
- predicting
- observing
- inferring
- communicating

Materials

- small milk carton opened at the top
- water
- metric ruler
- pebbles
- modeling clay
- safety goggles
- rectangular pan
- sand
- gravel
- plastic spoon

Getting Ready

In this activity, you will model how glaciers erode land.

Follow This Procedure

1. Make a chart like the one shown. Use your chart to record your observations.

Glacier on clay		
Action of glacier	Prediction	Observations
Moving		

Glacier on rocky mountain		
Action of glacier	Prediction	Observations
Moving		
Melting		
After melting		

2. Pour water into a small milk carton to a depth of about 5 cm. Add a single layer of pebbles to the water in the carton. Freeze this water-and-pebble mixture to make a **model** glacier.

3. Press some modeling clay on a flat surface. Carefully remove your glacier from the milk carton and place it pebble-side-down on the clay (Photo A).

4. **Predict** what will happen if you move the glacier along the surface of the clay. Record and then test your prediction. Record your **observations.**

Photo A

5 Put on your safety goggles. Make a "mountain" in a pan from moistened sand and gravel.

6 Use a plastic spoon to make a narrow groove down the side of the mountain. This groove represents a valley carved by a stream. Place your glacier in the valley at the top of the mountain (Photo B). Slide the glacier down the valley. Observe and record what happens.

7 Replace your glacier in the valley at the top of the mountain. Softly press the glacier into the mountain top so it stays in place. Predict what will happen as the glacier melts. Record and then test your prediction. Be sure to record what happens to the surface of the mountain as well as to the sediment deposited.

8 Leave your setup where it will not be disturbed. Check it again after all the ice has melted. Note the location of the pebbles that were once part of the glacier. Record your observations.

Photo B

Interpret Your Results

1. In step 4, what happened to the surface of the clay?

2. Make an **inference**. Based on your observations, describe how a glacier may transport rocks and soil from one place to another.

3. **Communicate**. Discuss how your observations in this activity compare to features made by real glaciers.

Inquire Further

How would a sudden change in average temperature—either an increase or a decrease—affect the erosion due to a glacier? Develop a plan to answer this or other questions you may have.

Self-Assessment

- I followed the directions to make **models** of two types of glaciers.
- I **predicted** the effects of glaciers on two types of landscapes.
- I recorded my **observations.**
- I made an **inference** about glaciers and the transport of materials from one place to another.
- I **communicated** my ideas about how the activity results compare with land features made by actual glaciers.

You will learn:

- how rock layers tell about the past.
- what fossils tell about the past.
- how Earth's history is interpreted and recorded.

Lesson 4

What Do Rocks Tell About Earth's History?

Want to read a good story? It's quite a mystery. It has some of the STRANGEST characters you'll ever run across. The book is loaded with clues that could be FUN to figure out. You won't be able to carry the book in your backpack, though. The pages are ROCKS!

Rocks Tell About the Past

What's one of the first things you notice about the rock formation below? You probably noticed the different colored stripes. Each stripe represents a different layer of sediment that formed into sedimentary rock. What can you tell about these rock layers? For one thing, you can be fairly certain that the bottom layer of rock is the oldest.

The rock in these sedimentary layers was once at the bottom of an ancient sea. Forces probably due to plate movement raised the rock above sea level. Erosion then exposed the formation as it appears now. ▼

Shale

If a series of sedimentary layers are not overturned, the oldest layer is always at the bottom and the youngest layer is always on top. It's like putting T-shirts one at a time in a drawer—the shirt you put in first will be on the bottom of the pile, and it will have been there the longest.

To fully understand how rocks tell a story about past earth processes, it's important to know how rocks are made. Sedimentary rock forms over long periods of time as sediments are deposited and then pressed and cemented together. Each sedimentary layer provides a record of a past event.

For example, one kind of sedimentary rock—limestone—forms from pieces of seashells and dissolved shells, bones, and other materials that collect on the bottom of shallow oceans. So the layer of limestone you see on these pages was formed under an ancient ocean. The fine grains that make up another kind of sedimentary rock—shale—settle out of water far from shore, indicating that this rock formed in deeper waters. Likewise, sandstone, another sedimentary rock, tells of past deserts or shallow sandy shores.

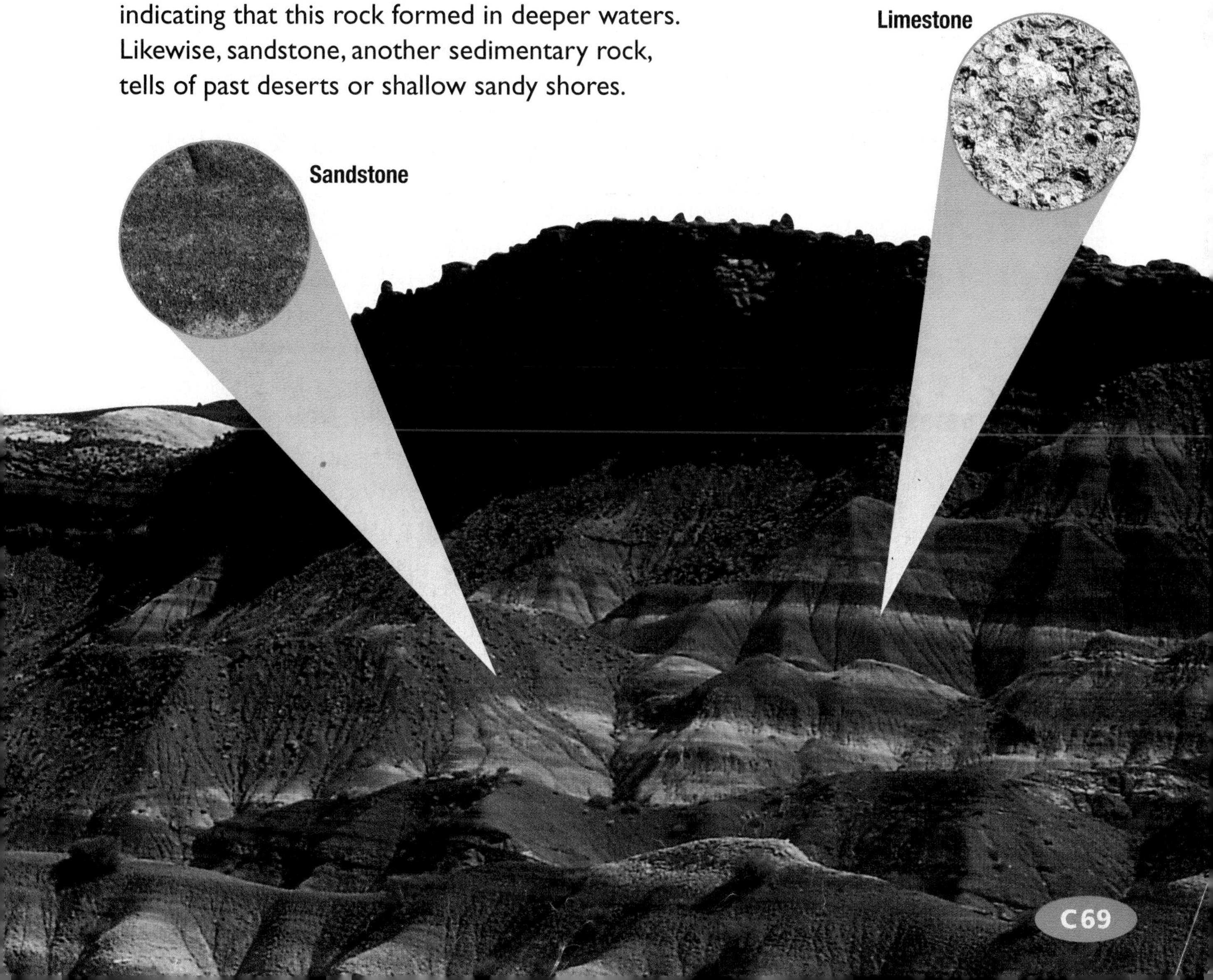

Limestone

Sandstone

Fossils Tell About the Past

One of the most important stories that rocks tell is about the kind of life that existed when the rocks were being formed. How can such a story be told? Dead organisms often get buried by sediments that later become sedimentary rock. Traces of the organisms sometimes become preserved in the rock as fossils. Sometimes, a fossil is a shell, a bone, or part of a plant that was gradually replaced by rock. It can even be a track or trail, or petrified animal droppings. Usually, the soft parts of an organism decay or get eaten by other creatures quickly. As a result, they don't last long enough to become fossilized. Hard parts, such as shells, bones, teeth, and wood, have a better chance of becoming fossils. To the left, you can see one way fossils form.

Fossils help paleontologists learn about Earth's past environments. For example, fossils of shellfish found high in the Alps, Rockies, Andes, and Himalayas are evidence that the rock of these mountains formed under water. How can paleontologists tell whether an underwater environment was a river, lake, swamp, or open sea? By comparing fossils with similar organisms that exist today, scientists can make inferences about the specific environment in the past.

Fossils also provide a history of past climates. For example, rocks in Antarctica near the South Pole contain fossils of tropical plants. This evidence suggests that Antarctica must have been much warmer in the past than it is today. How do you think plate tectonics supports this conclusion?

Every rock formation can tell a story, but it may be only a chapter. Paleontologists are often more interested in the larger story—how the evidence at one place relates to evidence found at other places around the world.

Forming Fossils

Some fossils form when dead organisms are covered with sediments, which harden into rock. The soft parts of the organism decay, leaving an impression in the rock. This impression can later be filled with other sediments that also harden, forming a fossil cast. As you can see below, the cast fossil resembles the actual organism. ▼

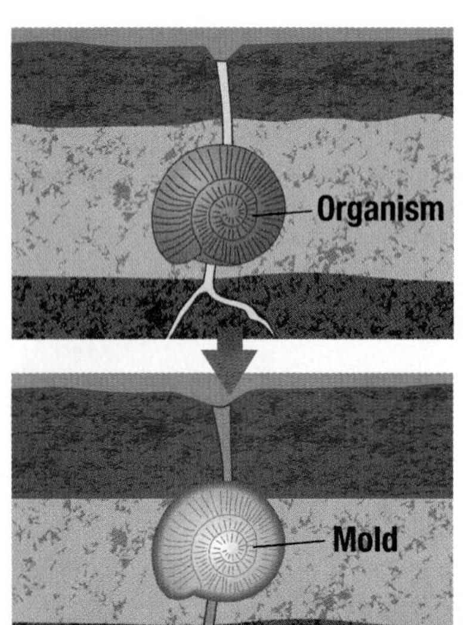

Therefore, they compare fossils in layers of rock from different areas, as shown below. Index fossils are especially helpful for comparison. An **index fossil** is a fossil of an organism that existed on Earth for a relatively short time and in many places. Therefore, an index fossil can be used to establish the age of any rock in which it is found. Index fossils can be used to match rock layers that appear in different places.

Glossary

index fossil
(in′deks fos′əl), a fossil of an organism that existed on Earth for a short time over a large geographic area

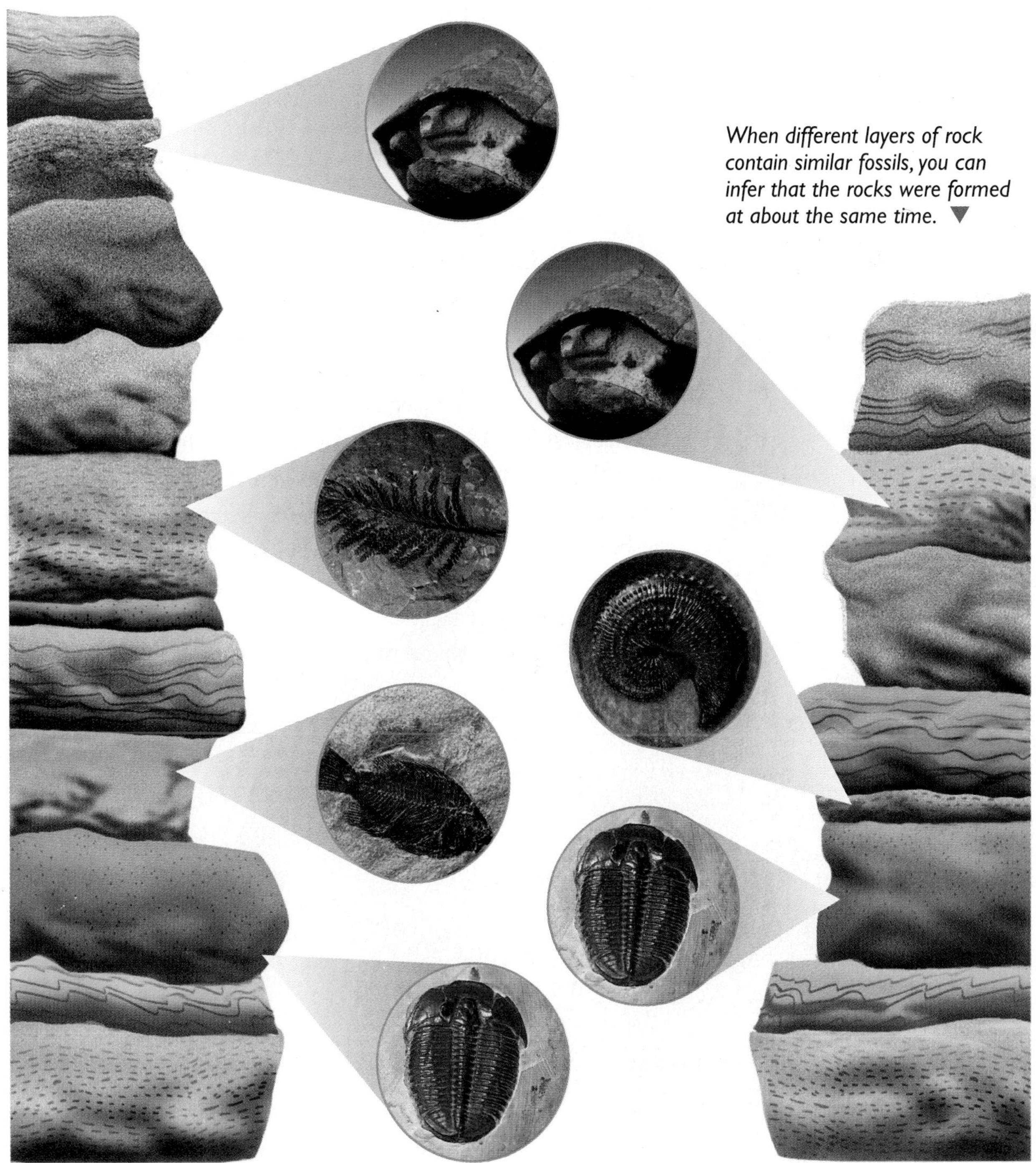

When different layers of rock contain similar fossils, you can infer that the rocks were formed at about the same time. ▼

Interpreting Earth's History

History of Science

While scientists figure out the order in which certain rock layers were formed, they also explain the fossil evidence the rocks contain. Fossils help scientists reconstruct an accurate picture of ancient life forms and their environments. These reconstructions are based on knowledge of life forms that live today.

For example, compare the three images shown below. The fossil, on the bottom left, is of a creature called *Archaeopteryx.* The fossil clearly shows that *Archaeopteryx* had characteristics of both a dinosaur and a bird. The limestone that contained this fossil suggests the animal lived about 150 million years ago on the shore of a shallow pond in Germany. From this fossil, scientists and an artist reconstructed how the animal might have looked at the time of its death. Another drawing shows how this birdlike dinosaur might have looked and acted in life. Both drawings are based on our knowledge of birds, reptiles, and other animals today.

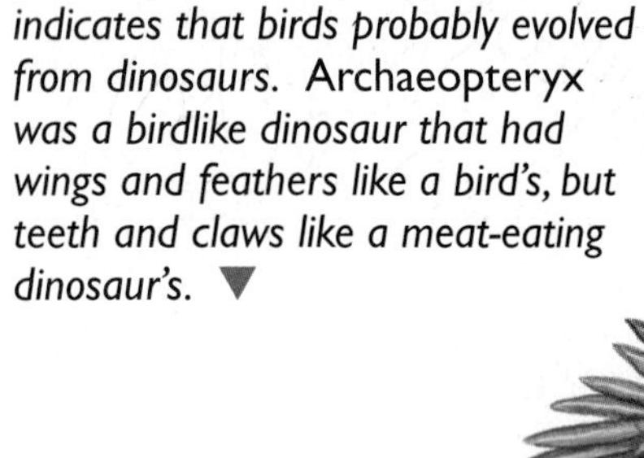

An interpretation of the fossil record indicates that birds probably evolved from dinosaurs. Archaeopteryx *was a birdlike dinosaur that had wings and feathers like a bird's, but teeth and claws like a meat-eating dinosaur's.* ▼

Artist rendering

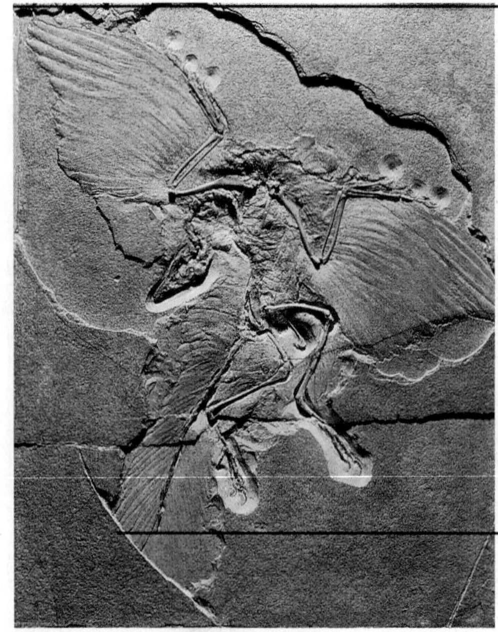

Fossil

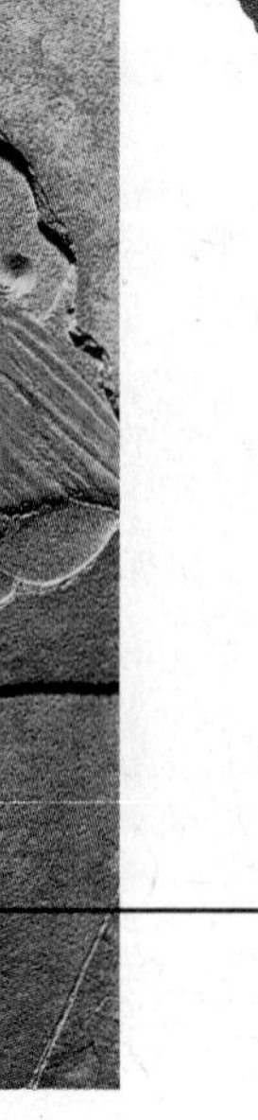

Artist reconstruction from fossil

Scientists also use fossils and the rocks that contain them to form theories about why certain life forms disappeared, or became extinct. For example, the trilobite fossil pictured to the right shows a hard-shelled sea creature that lived over 500 million years ago. Trilobites lived with other marine life when warm, shallow seas covered much of the earth's surface. The trilobites disappeared about 250 million years ago. Most paleontologists think they became extinct because shallow seas dried up when mountains were uplifted due to plate movement.

The trilobite, a multi-legged sea animal, became extinct about 250 million years ago, most likely because of mountain building that drained the seas. This fossil of the bottom surface of a trilobite shows much detail. ▼

Another interpretation of the rock and fossil records explains the extinction of the dinosaurs about 65 million years ago. Many scientists think that a huge asteroid or comet hit Earth and produced a giant cloud of dust that blocked the sun's light. Temperatures dropped, plants died, and many other forms of life, including the dinosaurs like the one below, either froze or starved to death. Among the evidence for this theory is that an unusual amount of the element iridium is found in rocks that are 65 million years old. Iridium is rare on Earth but it is much more common in the rock of asteroids and comets. Also, scientists think they have found the huge crater that such an impact would have made—in the Yucatan Peninsula and the Gulf of Mexico.

◀ *Dinosaurs like this Oreodontia, existed for 150 million years. They became extinct about 65 million years ago. Many scientists think they know why.*

Glossary

Glossary

geologic time scale
(jē ə loj′ik tīm skāl), a record of Earth's history based on events interpreted from the rock record and fossil evidence

History of Science

Scientists who attempt to interpret the rock and fossil evidence to determine Earth's history have a long period of time to account for. Earth has been around for about 4.6 billion years! No written records exist to tell when mountains were born or when seas covered continents. To record a history of such events, scientists have constructed a **geologic time scale.** The divisions of time on this scale are based on important events, such as the rise of new life forms and the formation of mountain ranges.

Geologic Time Scale

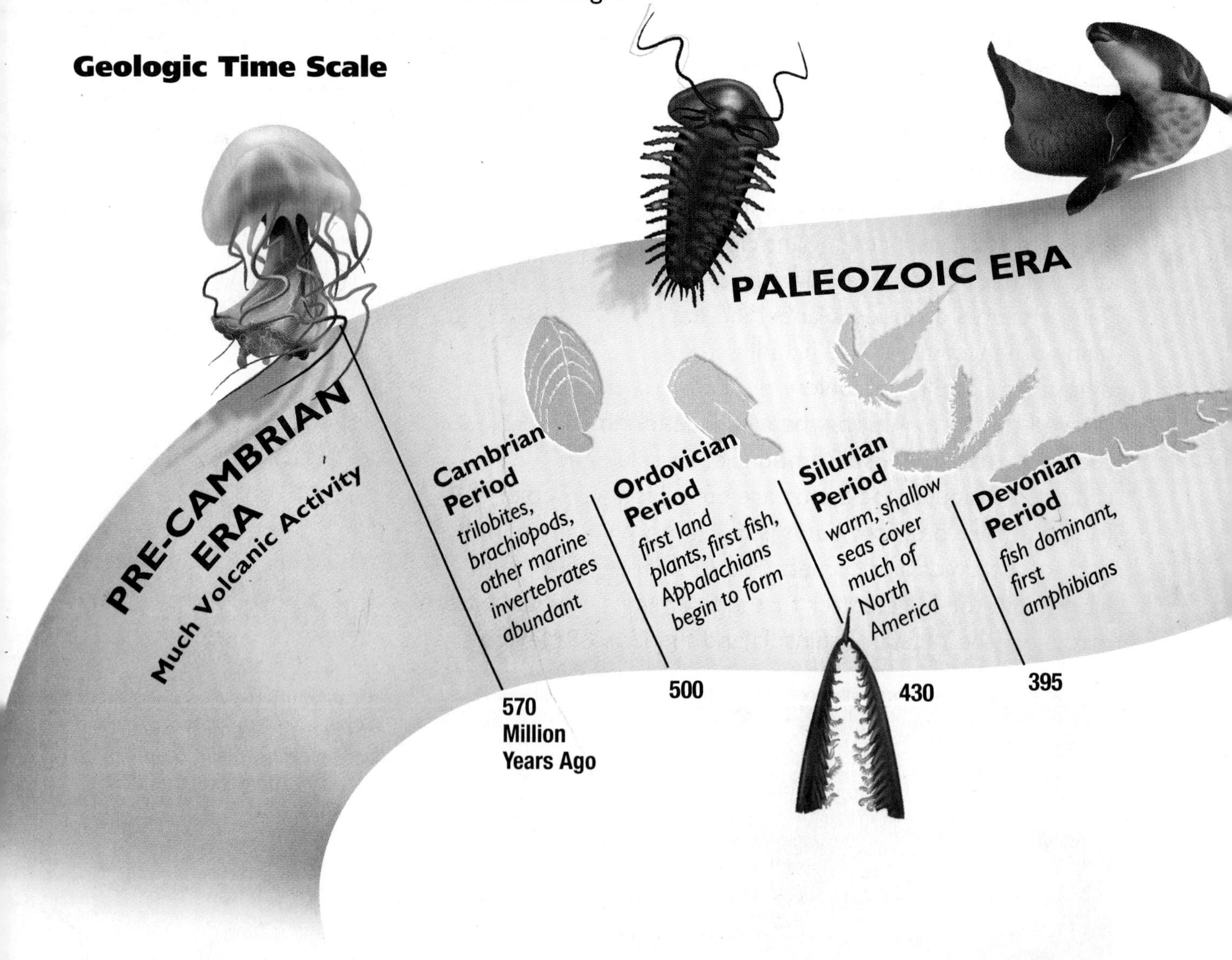

PALEOZOIC ERA

PRE-CAMBRIAN ERA
Much Volcanic Activity

Cambrian Period
trilobites, brachiopods, other marine invertebrates abundant

Ordovician Period
first land plants, first fish, Appalachians begin to form

Silurian Period
warm, shallow seas cover much of North America

Devonian Period
fish dominant, first amphibians

570 Million Years Ago

500

430

395

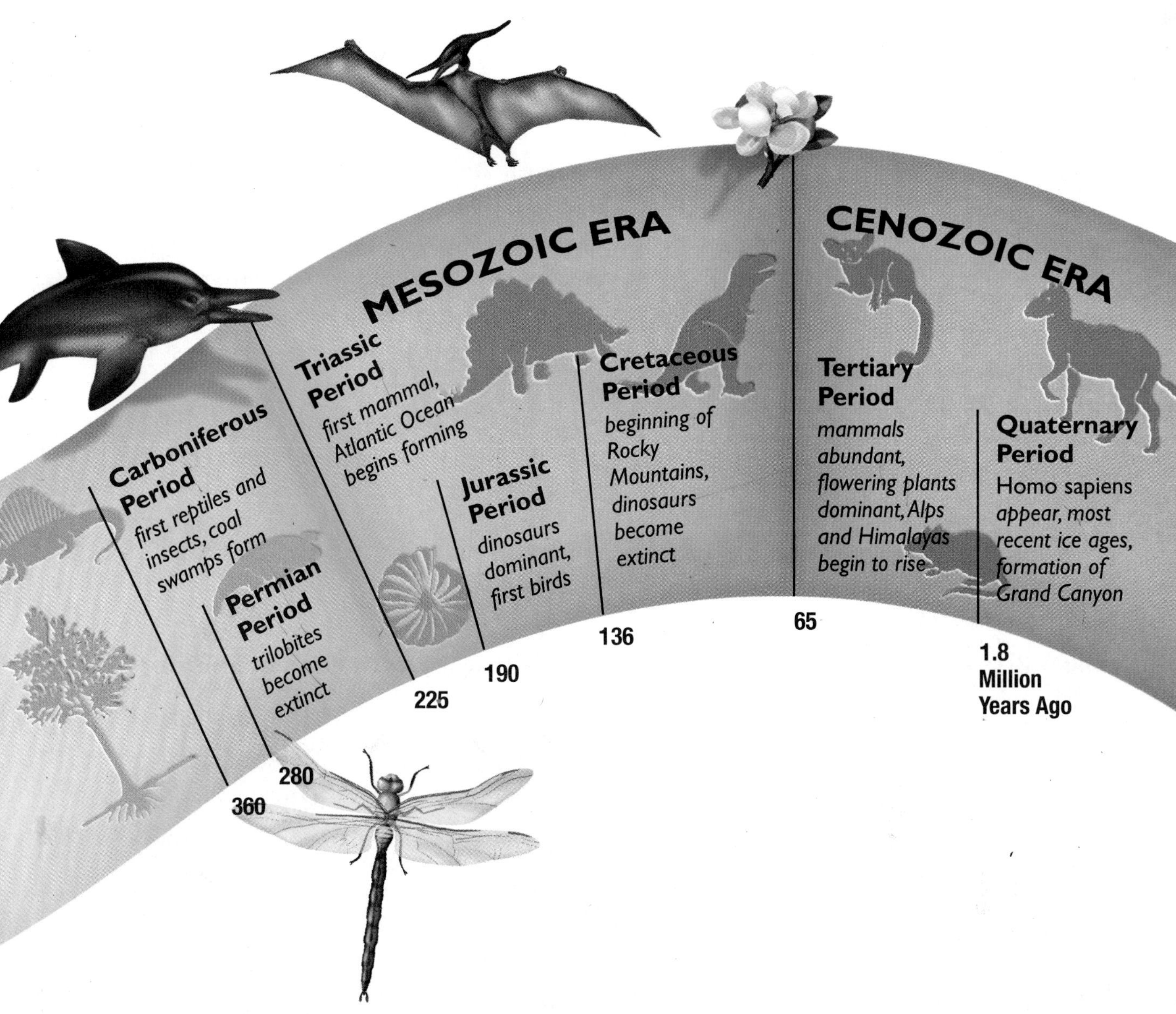

Lesson 4 Review

1. What do rock layers tell about Earth's past?
2. What do fossils tell about Earth's past?
3. How is Earth's history interpreted and recorded?
4. **Graphic Sources**
   According to the geologic time scale above, when did dinosaurs become extinct?

Chapter 2 Review

Chapter Main Ideas

Lesson 1

• Earth's moving plates build up or tear down the earth's crust as they float toward, away, or past one another on partly melted rock in the upper mantle.
• Earthquakes are the release of energy that occurs as plates slip past one another while moving in opposite directions.
• Volcanoes are caused by molten rock that rises at plate boundaries.
• Seismographs and lasers are used to monitor earth movement.

Lesson 2

• Soil is a mixture of weathered rock and decayed organic matter that formed over a very long time.
• Soils differ due to the type of bedrock and climate present when they were formed, the amount of humus available, and the time the soil has been forming.

Lesson 3

• River systems drain large areas of land, eroding the soil and depositing material along the way.
• Groundwater erupts as geysers when it is heated by magma and forms underground caverns when it dissolves minerals in limestone.
• Wave action can erode rock or deposit sand to create certain features along coastlines.
• Glaciers erode land or deposit sediments.

Lesson 4

• When layers of rock remain untouched, the types of rock and their arrangement provide a history of how and when the rocks were formed.
• Fossils tell about life forms, climates, and environments of the past.
• Scientists make inferences about the earth's history and record it on a geologic time scale.

Reviewing Science Words and Concepts

Write the letter of the word or words that go with each definition.

a. aquifer
b. drainage basin
c. fault
d. focus
e. geologic time scale
f. glacier
g. groundwater
h. index fossil
i. lithosphere
j. moraine
k. plate tectonics
l. relative dating
m. Richter scale
n. sediment
o. seismograph
p. water table
q. weathering

1. Two forms of water than can erode the earth are ___ and ___.

2. The layer of rock that forms the earth's crust is the ___.

3. The theory of ___ explains how plates move over the mantle.

4. A crack in the earth's crust along which rock layers move is a(n) ___.

5. The ___ is a scale for measuring the strength of earthquakes.

6. The ___ is a record of earth's history.
7. A ridge formed from glacial deposits is a(n) ___.
8. The land area drained by a river system is a(n) ___.
9. The point along a fault where rock first breaks is the ___.
10. Permeable rock where groundwater accumulates and flows freely is a(n) ___.
11. The remains of an organism that lived for a short time over a wide area is a(n) ___.
12. Scientists use a(n) ___ to record the strengths of earth movements.
13. Determining the age of rock by comparing it with other rock layers is ___.
14. The process in which rocks are broken down is ___.
15. Rock and mineral carried by water are ___.
16. The top of an aquifer is the ___.

Explaining Science

Use drawings or write a paragraph that explains these questions.

1. How does the theory of plate tectonics explain changes in the earth's crust?

2. How does rock turn into soil?

3. What land features are created by water?

4. How do rocks provide a history of the earth?

Using Skills

1. Prepare a time scale on a wide strip of paper that shows your life history. **Use graphics** to show eras and periods such as "Growing Up Era" or "Middle School Period."

2. Write a letter to the editor **communicating** why methods should be taken to protect soil from erosion.

3. Use the **model** of convection currents shown on page C45 to explain why the earth's plates move.

Critical Thinking

1. Imagine horizontal layers of sedimentary rock with a vertical strip of a different kind of rock—igneous rock—running through the layers. **Apply** what you know about how rock is formed to **infer** the relative age of the igneous rock.

2. You discover rock layers at the top of a mountain containing fossils of shells and other marine life. **Draw conclusions** about the geologic history of the area.

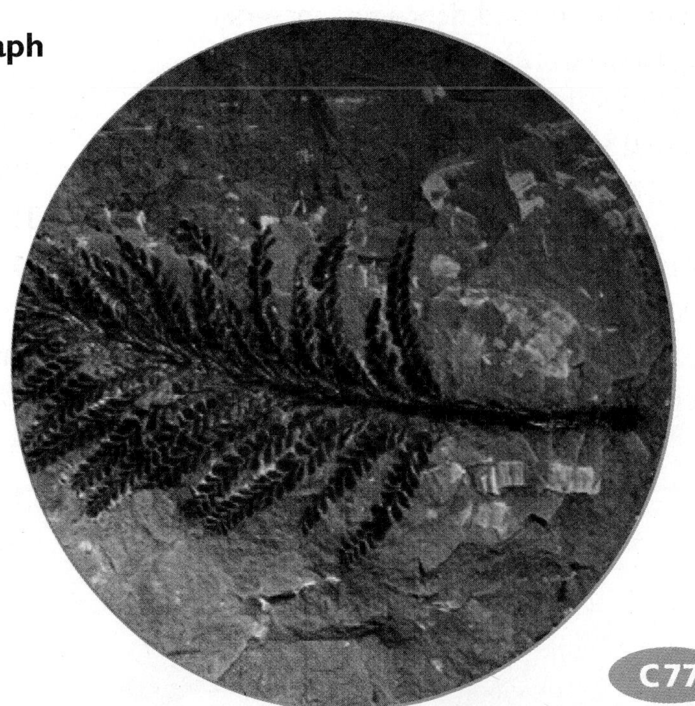

A Carnival Ride ?

What kind of ride is this boy on? Not an ordinary one! He's at the NASA Space Camp, learning about space travel. What can we learn from studying the universe? What do we already know?

Chapter 3

Exploring the Universe

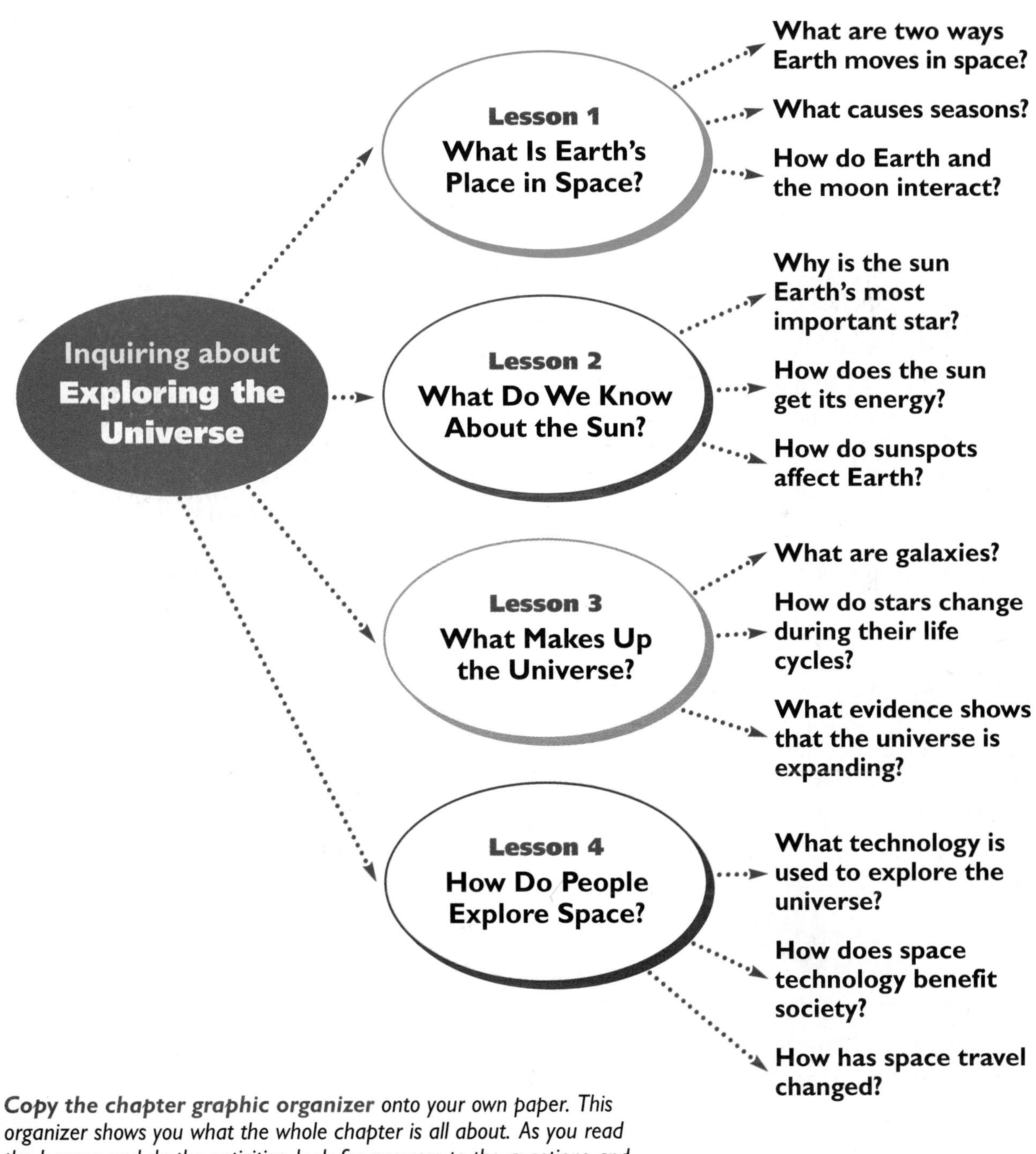

Inquiring about Exploring the Universe
Lesson 1
What Is Earth's Place in Space?
What are two ways Earth moves in space?
What causes seasons?
How do Earth and the moon interact?
Lesson 2
What Do We Know About the Sun?
Why is the sun Earth's most important star?
How does the sun get its energy?
How do sunspots affect Earth?
Lesson 3
What Makes Up the Universe?
What are galaxies?
How do stars change during their life cycles?
What evidence shows that the universe is expanding?
Lesson 4
How Do People Explore Space?
What technology is used to explore the universe?
How does space technology benefit society?
How has space travel changed?

Copy the chapter graphic organizer *onto your own paper. This organizer shows you what the whole chapter is all about. As you read the lessons and do the activities, look for answers to the questions and write them on your organizer.*

Exploring Lunar Eclipses

Process Skills

- making and using models
- observing

Materials

- compass
- cardboard
- marker
- scissors
- masking tape
- 2 plastic straws
- metric ruler
- flashlight

Explore

1. Make a **model** of a lunar eclipse. Use a compass to draw two circles on a piece of cardboard. One circle should be about 3 cm in diameter. Label this circle *Moon.* The other circle should be about 8 cm in diameter. Use a marker to label this circle *Earth.* Cut out the circles to make two discs.

2. Tape each cardboard disk to a straw.

3. Darken the room so that you can clearly see the lights and shadows in this demonstration.

4. One student should hold the Moon disk near the chalkboard or wall. A second student should stand about 1 m away and shine the flashlight directly at the Moon disk.

5. A third student should take the Earth disk and gradually move it across the beam of light illuminating the Moon. **Observe** the effect that the movement of the Earth disk has on the Moon disk.

Reflect

1. What part of the solar system does the flashlight represent in this activity?

2. What did you observe on the Moon disk when you passed the Earth disk between it and the light source?

Inquire Further

Suppose you moved the Moon disk between the light and the Earth disk. What would you observe happening to the light on the Earth? Develop a plan to answer this or other questions you may have.

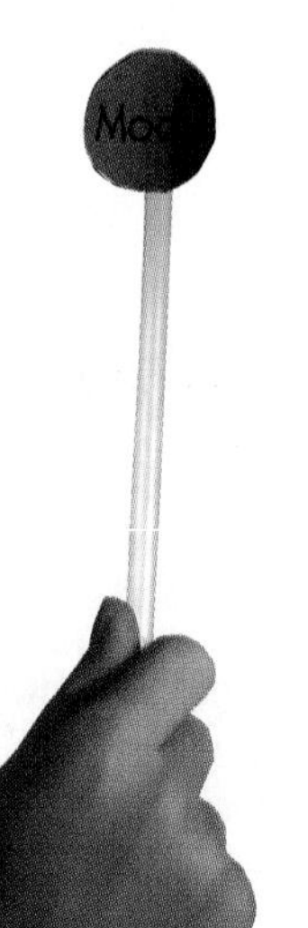

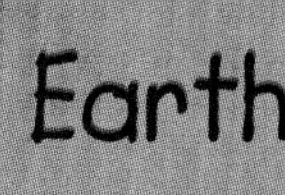

Large Numbers

Suppose you are the commander of a disabled spacecraft. Mission Control wants to know how far you are from Earth.

Your controls show that you are 45,000,000,000,000 km away. You report, "We are 45 trillion kilometers from Earth."

In order to use large numbers, you need to know the names of large **place values.** Look at the chart below. The digit 4 is in the ten-trillions place. It represents 4 ten-trillions, or 40,000,000,000,000. Where is the digit 5?

Math Vocabulary

place value, the multiple of ten telling how much a digit represents

Place Value

hundreds	tens	ones	hundreds	tens	ones	hundreds	tens	ones	hundreds	tens	ones	hundreds	tens	ones
	4	5	**0**	0	0	**0**	0	0	**0**	0	0	**0**	0	0
Trillions			Billions			Millions			Thousands			Ones		

Example

Find the place value of the *9* in Vega's diameter.

Diameters of Six Brightest Stars	
Name	**Diameter (mi)**
Sun	864,730
Sirius	1,556,500
Canopus	25,951,900
Alpha Centauri	1,037,700
Arcturus	19,888,800
Vega	2,594,200

Vega's diameter is 2,5<u>9</u>4,200 miles. The *9* is in the ten-thousands place. So, it represents 9 ten-thousands, or 90,000.

Talk About It!

1. Is there a name for every number, no matter how large? Explain.

You will learn:

- two ways Earth moves in space.
- what causes the seasons.
- how Earth and the moon interact.

Lesson 1

What Is Earth's Place in Space?

Hey! Stand still! What do you mean you can't do that? No matter how hard you try to stay in one place, Earth beneath you is moving. So, let's go for a spin! Spinning is just one way that Earth moves.

Earth's Motion

What do you know about the spheres shown below? You may already know that these spheres represent the nine planets that travel around the sun as part of our solar system. Perhaps you know that a band of small rocky objects called asteroids also moves around the sun. Of course, there's one place in the solar system you know quite a lot about—Earth! The third planet from the sun is the only planet scientists know of that supports life.

Earth and all objects in space are constantly rolling, tumbling, or moving in some way. All the planets spin, or rotate, on an imaginary line called an axis. As you can see on the next page, Earth's axis runs from the North Pole to the South Pole. Each planet rotates on its axis at a different speed. Earth takes 24 hours, or one day, to make one complete turn, or rotation.

Notice the relative position of each planet from the sun. If this drawing were made to scale, the sun would be the size of a beach ball. Earth and Venus would be about the size of a marble, and Pluto would be only as large as a pin head. The distances between the planets would be different too. ▼

As Earth is viewed from above the North Pole, it rotates on its tilted axis in a west-to-east direction. In other words, Earth rotates from west to east. While Earth rotates, half of the planet faces toward the sun. This half of the planet experiences day. At the same time, the other half of the planet faces away from the sun, creating night. You can't feel Earth's spinning motion, but you can see signs of it. For example, Earth's rotation makes the sun appear to move across the sky from east to west. Most of the other planets also rotate in the same counter-clockwise direction, but they do so at different speeds and at different angles, or tilts.

Earth moves in another way too. The planets and asteroids travel, or revolve, around the sun in paths called orbits. Earth takes about 365 days, or one year, to complete its orbit around the sun. This trip is one revolution.

The speed of other planets in their orbits may be faster or slower than Earth's, depending upon the planet's distance from the sun. For example, take a look at Mercury, the sun's nearest planet. Mercury takes only 88 Earth days to revolve around the sun because it has such a small orbit. The most distant planet, Pluto, has the largest orbit. Pluto takes 90,700 Earth days to complete one revolution. So how many Earth years is a year on Pluto?

It certainly seems that everything in space is on the move! While Earth revolves around the sun, the moon revolves around Earth, and other moons revolve around their planets. In fact, the sun and the entire solar system are moving. So, sit back and enjoy the ride as you learn what all this motion means and where everything is going!

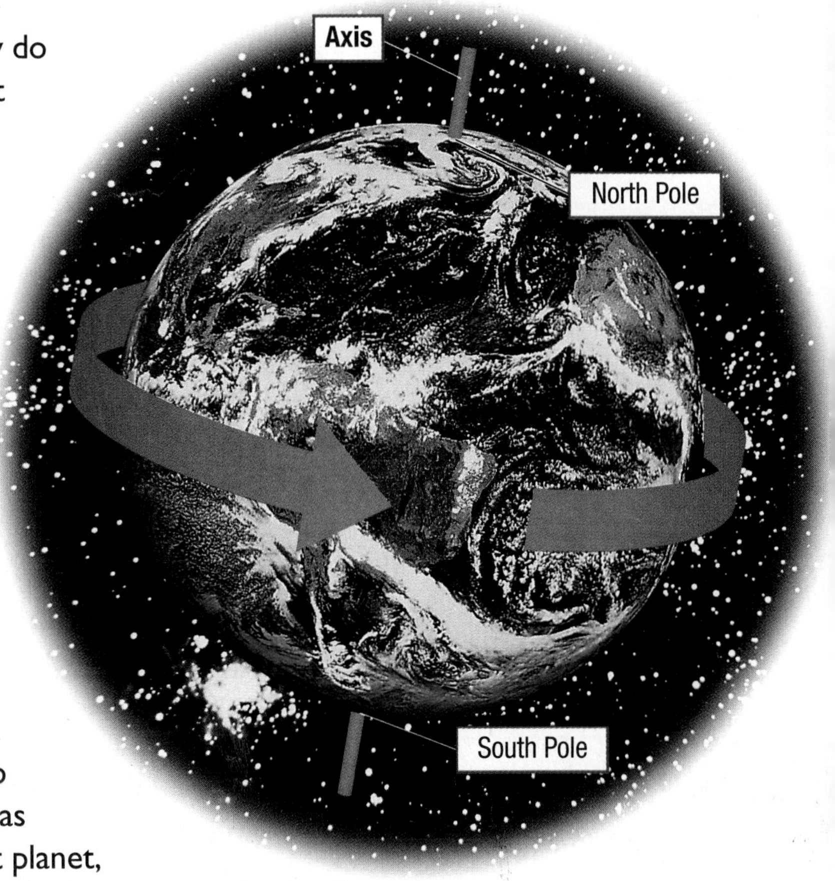

▲ *Even though you can't really see the North and South Poles of Earth, it helps to imagine them. Picture Earth rotating around a pole, or axis, that is tilted.*

Earth's Seasons

What do you notice in the picture below about the axis as Earth travels in its yearly orbit around the sun? Find a point where the North Pole leans toward the sun. At this point, the sun's rays strike areas north of the equator most directly, and the daylight hours are longer. The northern half of the world, or Northern Hemisphere, experiences summer. In the United States, you might be swimming, but in Argentina students will be putting on hats and gloves as they leave school. Why?

The seasons change as Earth tilts toward or away from the sun while making a revolution. A seasonal change occurs each time Earth moves one-fourth of the way around its yearly orbit. ▼

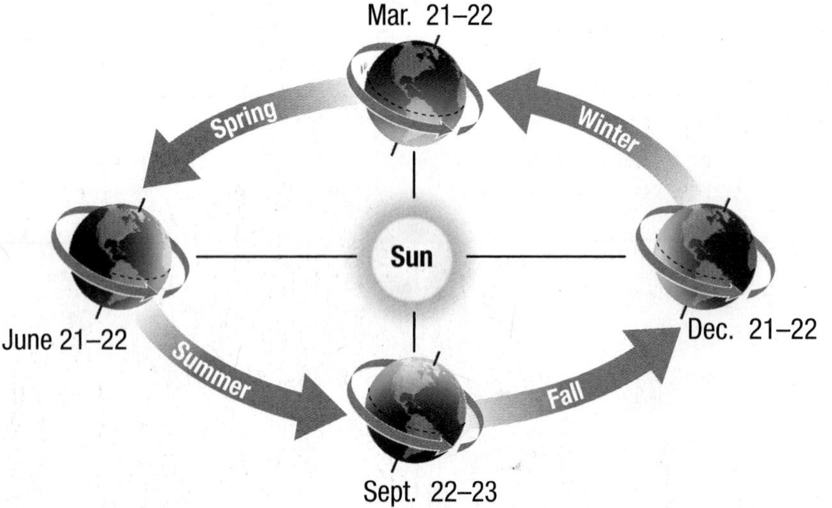

Notice in the picture that when the Northern Hemisphere experiences summer, the southern half of the world, or Southern Hemisphere, is tipped away from the sun. The sun's light strikes that part of Earth at an angle that is much less direct, and the daylight hours are shorter. At this time, the southern half of the world has winter.

The seasons change as Earth's axis either leans toward or away from the sun—or leans somewhere in between—at different times throughout its orbit. People at the equator do not experience this change in seasons because the effect of the tilt of that area of Earth doesn't change as much.

Have you noticed that the amount of sunlight also changes as season's change? When it's summer in your part of the world, the sun is high in the sky. Daylight lasts longer than at other times of the year. During summer, you can enjoy playing ball or other activities outside longer. If you live in the Northern Hemisphere, you'll experience the longest day of the year on June 21 or 22. This date is when the summer **solstice** takes place.

The shortest amount of daylight occurs in winter. At this time of the year, it might be nearly dark when you get home from school. Look at the picture. On what date does the winter solstice—the shortest day of the year—take place? The summer and winter solstices take place on opposite days of the year in the Southern Hemisphere.

Glossary

Glossary

solstice (sol′stis), a point in Earth's orbit around the sun where daylight is either the longest or the shortest amount possible

Twice a year, an **equinox** takes place when the sun is directly above the equator and the hours of daylight and night are equal. The first day of spring or fall begins on the equinox. You can expect 12 hours of daylight and 12 hours of night on these days.

Glossary

equinox (ē′kwə noks), a point in Earth's orbit around the sun where nights and days are the same length

Earth and the Moon Interact

On many nights when you look at the sky, the most noticeable thing you probably see is the moon. Did you know that the moon is Earth's nearest neighbor in space? Like any satellite, the moon orbits a larger body—in this case, Earth. The force of gravity between Earth and the moon keeps the moon in its orbit around Earth.

As it orbits Earth, the moon seems to change shape and disappear. Actually, your view of the part of the moon that is lit by the sun is what changes. Because the moon and Earth are always moving, the sunlit part of the moon that you can see from Earth depends on the moon's location in space. The shape of this lighted part of the moon that you see is called the moon's phase.

The diagrams show how only the side of the moon that faces the sun is lighted. Notice how at the new moon only the dark side of the moon faces us. As the moon continues around Earth, you start to see a sliver of the lighted moon called a crescent moon. About a week later, when the moon is a quarter of the way around its orbit, half of the lighted side is visible—a first-quarter moon. Next comes a gibbous moon. Halfway around its orbit, the entire side of the moon that faces us is lighted. You see it as a full moon. As the moon continues the second half of its orbit, you see another gibbous, quarter, and crescent phase before the next new moon.

Moon's Orbit

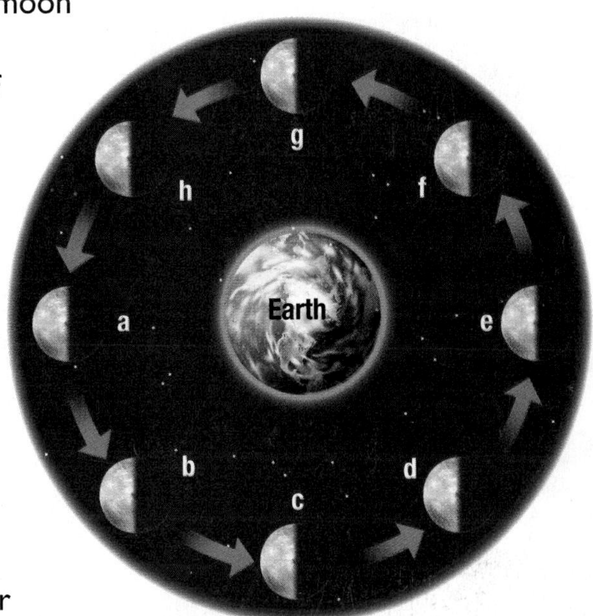

▲ *Compare the lighted part of the moon in each position of its orbit (above) to the phase you see from Earth (below). It takes the moon about one month to go through all of its different phases.* ▼

Phases of the Moon

Lunar Eclipse

An eclipse of the moon happens when the sun, Earth, and moon line up. During a lunar eclipse, the moon darkens for as much as an hour as it passes through Earth's shadow. Sometimes light passing through Earth's atmosphere makes the moon look red. ▶

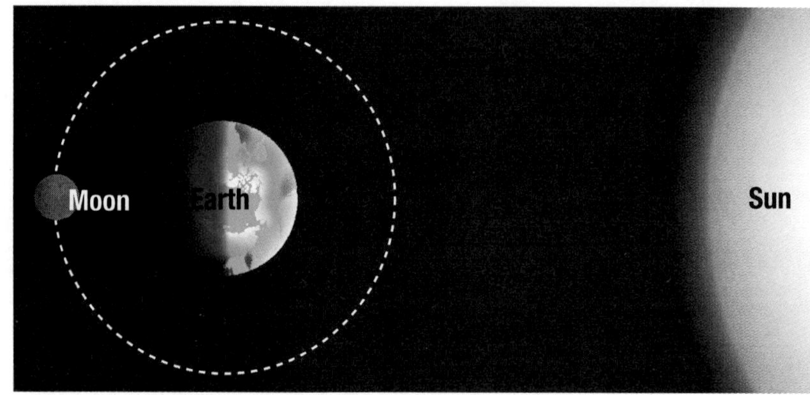

Glossary

Glossary

lunar eclipse
(lü′nər i klips′), a darkening of the moon when it passes through Earth's shadow

tides (tīdz), the rise and fall of water in the ocean and seas caused mainly by the gravitational pull of the moon on Earth

If you did the Explore Activity, you may have discovered how shadows form on spheres. Look at the picture above. Notice how Earth casts a huge shadow in space. Usually the moon passes above or below this shadow as it orbits Earth. Sometimes, however, it passes through the shadow, creating a **lunar eclipse.** During a lunar eclipse, the moon may be partially or totally shaded by Earth. A partial eclipse may happen several times in a year. A total lunar eclipse occurs less often.

The picture below shows another way that the moon and Earth interact. The pulling force of gravity exists among these objects. As the moon orbits Earth, the moon's gravity pulls on Earth's land and water. This gravitational pull slightly changes Earth's shape so that water rises or bulges in two places—the side facing the moon and the opposite side. This bulging causes high **tides**. Lower water levels form between the bulges, causing low tides. As Earth rotates on its axis, the two bulges move to stay in line with the moon.

Low tide

Earth

Pull of moon's gravity

High tide

Low tide

High tide

▲ *High and low tides are caused mainly by the moon's gravitational pull.*

Lesson 1 Review

1. What are two ways Earth moves in space?
2. What causes seasons?
3. How do Earth and the moon interact?
4. **Large Numbers**
   How many Earth days does Pluto take to complete one revolution? Write the number in its word form.

Lesson 2

What Do We Know About the Sun?

You will learn:

- **why the sun is Earth's most important star.**
- **how the sun gets its energy.**
- **how sunspots affect Earth.**

Ahh! The warm rays coming through the window on a chilly morning feel good when you stand in the sunlight. Other times . . . OUCH! They make your skin feel too hot. Whether or not you enjoy the sunshine on a given day, you always need it.

Earth's Most Important Star

About 150 million kilometers away from you, a star gives off light and other radiation that are necessary for life on Earth. Can you guess what that star is? If you said our sun, you're right! The sun is so far away that its light takes 8 minutes to reach Earth. Even so, it's a lot closer than the next nearest star, Alpha Centauri. Light from that star travels at a speed of almost 300,000 kilometers per second and takes almost 4 years to reach you!

Our sun gives us radiant energy. Some of this energy can be seen as the white light of sunlight. Other forms of solar energy, such as ultraviolet light, are invisible. Some of the sun's energy is stored in the form of fossil fuels, such as coal and oil, that are found beneath Earth's surface. We use this stored energy to heat our homes and power our cars.

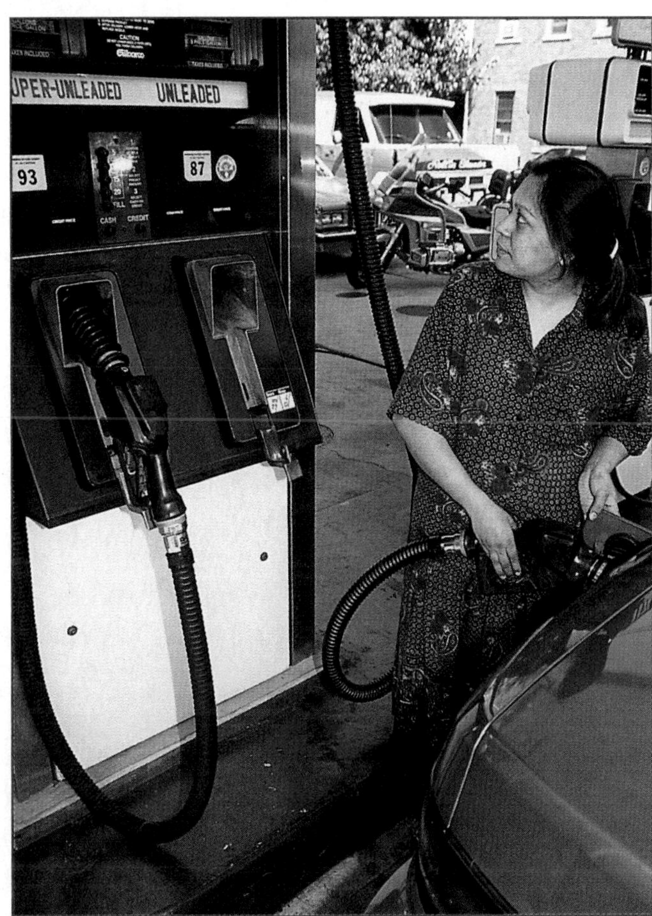

The sun supplies energy for fuel. How have you depended on the sun today? ▶

Glossary

fusion (fyü′zhən), the combining of less massive elements to form more massive elements

corona (kə rō′nə), a crown of glowing gases around the sun that can be seen during a total solar eclipse

The Sun's Energy

Compared with other stars, our sun is considered a medium-sized star. However, this medium-size star is big enough to fit over a million Earths inside it! Its yellow color tells us that the sun is somewhat cooler than hotter stars that glow blue or white. It is also warmer than stars that glow orange or red. Like any other star, however, the sun is made up of hot gases—mostly hydrogen and helium.

The sun started to shine nearly 5 billion years ago. It still shines today because its core—which you can see in the lower left picture—is about 15,000,000°C! At this super hot temperature, hydrogen atoms move at incredible speeds. Sometimes, particles in their nucleus, the central part of the atom, crash into one another. Because the atoms are moving so fast, the nuclear particles may fuse or stick together to form a single, larger nucleus, as shown below. During this process, called **fusion,** atoms of hydrogen combine to form a new element—helium.

During fusion, hydrogen nuclei combine to make a helium nucleus, some smaller particles, and a great amount of energy. ▶

Stars get all their energy from fusion. When the element hydrogen goes through fusion to create helium, a small amount of the mass is lost. This tiny bit of lost mass converts into a huge amount of energy. Small amounts of this energy reach Earth as sunlight and other forms of radiant energy. Scientists think that fusion will keep our sun shining for another 5 billion years.

Find the **corona,** the thin layer of gases that lies above its surface, in the picture to the left. The sun is so bright that ordinarily you can't see the corona. Gases in the corona are much hotter than the temperature at the sun's surface.

Currents of rising and sinking gases carry energy from the sun's core to its surface. ▼

Solar Eclipse

◀ *A solar eclipse takes place when the moon passes between Earth and the sun. (The sun is much farther away from the moon than shown in this picture.) Only people who live where the moon's narrow shadow falls on Earth can see a total solar eclipse—others may see a partial eclipse.*

Corona

▲ *The glowing gases that make up the sun's corona are normally not visible. They can be seen during a total solar eclipse through the use of cameras or special equipment that protect the eyes. The corona's gases expand into space.*

At certain times—such as during a solar eclipse—this outermost region of the sun is visible. You can see above that, during a **solar eclipse,** the moon moves exactly between Earth and the sun. Because the moon is so near to Earth, it appears about the same size as the sun and completely covers the sun's surface. The photo shows how easily the corona can be seen during the eclipse.

Sunspots

At one time or another, you might have experimented with a bar magnet. Did you notice how a magnetic field around the magnet pulled certain objects toward it? The sun has a magnetic field that is similar to that of a bar magnet. The **sunspots** shown below are places where the magnetic field is thousands of times stronger than at other places on the sun. Gases do not move very much in sunspots. These regions are much cooler than the rest of the surface. Since cooler gas shines less brightly than hotter gas, sunspots appear darker than the areas around them. The number of sunspots goes up and down about every 11 years in a period called the sunspot cycle.

Glossary

solar eclipse (sō′lər i klips′), an alignment of the sun, moon, and Earth where the moon blocks the sun from Earth's view

sunspot (sun′spot′), a region on the sun of very strong magnetic field

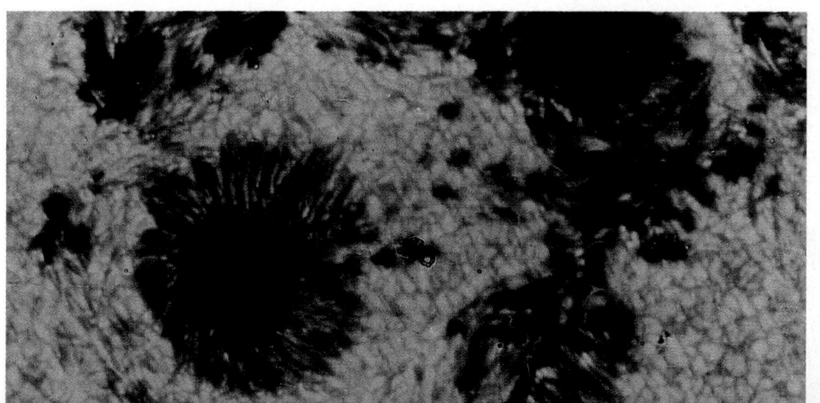

Sunspots

◀ *The dark areas you see in this photo of the sun are regions of cooler gas created from variations in the sun's magnetic field.*

Glossary

Glossary

solar flare
(sō′lər fler), powerful eruption on the sun

aurora (ô rôr′ə), the glow or display of lights in the skies near polar latitudes

Solar Flares

Temperatures in solar flares can reach 4,000,000°C! Earth's atmosphere usually blocks radiation that escapes from solar flares into space and keeps it from reaching Earth's surface. ▶

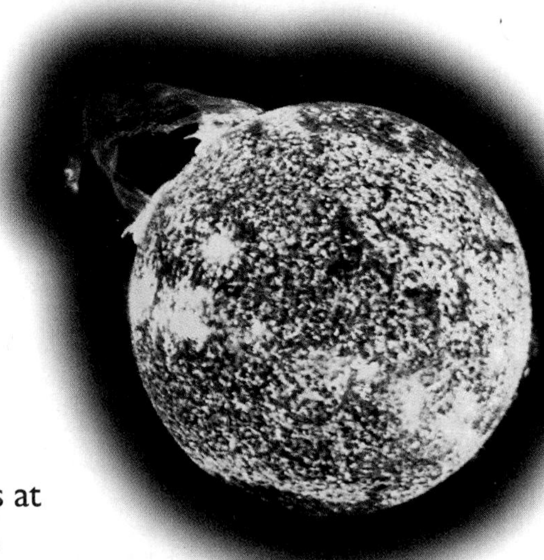

When the sunspot cycle is at its peak and there are a large number of sunspots, huge explosions occur on the sun. Notice in the picture how these **solar flares** which are many times the size of Earth erupt on the sun's surface. Particles and radiation from the solar flares escape into space and reach Earth's atmosphere. These particles can cause static interference on radios and power surges on electric lines. Blackouts sometimes result from these surges.

Auroras form in the sky over places far north, such as Alaska and Canada, or far south, such as Antarctica. ▼

Solar flares can cause colorful displays on Earth. The colorful bands or curtains of glowing light in this photo to the left are called **auroras**. The auroras form when particles given off by solar flares hit Earth's atmosphere over the magnetic north and south poles. When the particles hit the oxygen and nitrogen atoms in the upper atmosphere, the atoms sometimes give off a spectacular display of colored light.

Lesson 2 Review

1. Why is the sun Earth's most important star?
2. Explain how the sun gets its energy.
3. How do sunspots affect Earth?
4. **Large Numbers**
   The sun is 150 million kilometers away from Earth. What is the place value of the 5 in this measurement?

Lesson 3

What Makes Up the Universe?

Looking up at a clear night sky far from city lights can be AWESOME! You might see thousands of stars. With a telescope or binoculars, you'd see even more. Is that all there is? Not even close! Countless stars and other objects are just waiting to be seen.

You will learn:

- **what galaxies are.**
- **how stars change during their life cycles.**
- **what evidence shows that the universe is expanding.**

Galaxies

When you look at the night sky, you probably are seeing a lot more than you realize. For example, some of those points of light that you might think are individual stars are actually groups of stars called **galaxies**. All stars belong to a galaxy. Our sun and all the individual stars you can see from Earth belong to the Milky Way Galaxy. Just as planets travel around the sun in a solar system, stars travel around the center of their galaxy.

Scientists classify galaxies by their shapes. You can see the three main shapes below. Spiral galaxies are rotating disks with arms that spiral outward like a pinwheel. The Milky Way Galaxy is a spiral galaxy. Elliptical galaxies are shaped like an ellipse, or oval. Notice that their shape is similar to the center of a spiral galaxy. An irregular galaxy has no particular shape. The nearest galaxies to our own are two irregular galaxies called the Large and Small Magellanic Clouds. The Portuguese explorer Ferdinand Magellan recorded the presence of these galaxies during a voyage in the 1500s.

Glossary

galaxy (gal′ək sē), a system of billions of stars, gases, and dust

Types of Galaxies

Spiral galaxies probably formed from giant clouds of rapidly spinning hydrogen gas. Elliptical galaxies are the brightest and largest of the galaxies known. Most galaxies are elliptical. Irregular galaxies have more young stars than the other kinds of galaxies. ▼

Spiral galaxy

Elliptical galaxy

Irregular galaxy

Glossary

Glossary

quasars (kwā′ särz), brilliant objects in space that may be the powerhouses of developing galaxies

Our solar system is part of the Milky Way Galaxy. The diagram to the left shows that our solar system is located near the edge of one of the galaxy's spiraling arms. The sun is just one of billions of stars, along with gases and dust, that make up this galaxy.

Galaxies are huge. For example, our solar system is about 30,000 light years from the center of the Milky Way. That means that at the speed of light—300,000 kilometers per second—light takes about 30,000 years to travel from the center of the galaxy to our solar system. Most stars that you can see are at least hundreds of light years away.

Our galaxy is not alone. Galaxies exist in groups called clusters. A cluster can contain hundreds of galaxies. As the drawing below shows, the Milky Way is one of more than 30 other galaxies in a cluster known as the Local Group.

Beyond our Local Group are many distant clusters. Among these distant clusters are **quasars**—extremely bright objects that are thought to be the very active centers of young galaxies. Quasars shine as brightly as a trillion suns and are perhaps about 10 billion light years away. That means their brilliant light started traveling toward us 10 billion years ago!

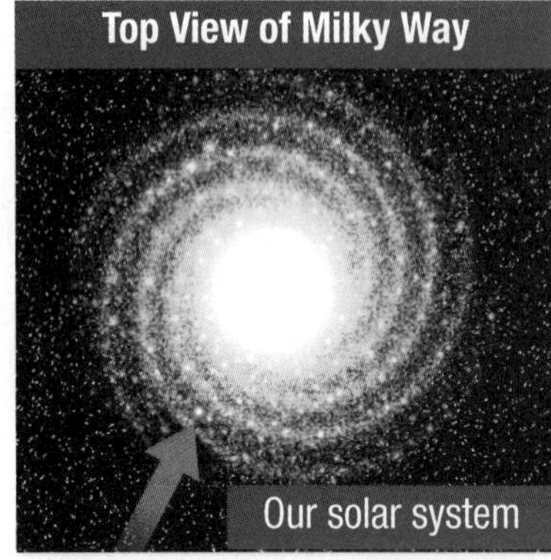

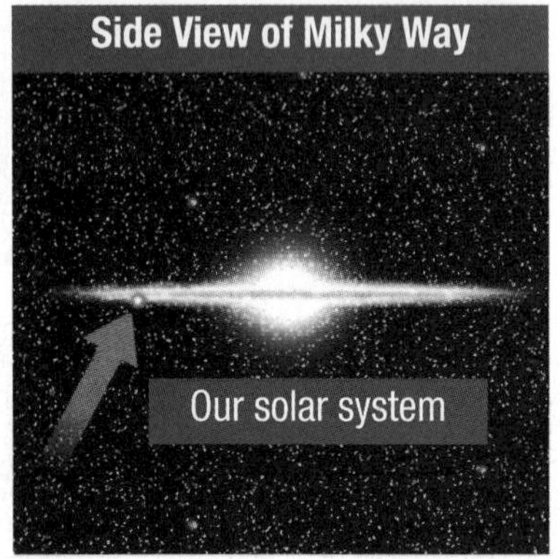

▲ *The diameter of the Milky Way Galaxy is about 100,000 light years.*

Our solar system is part of a much larger system of galaxies and space called the universe. ▼

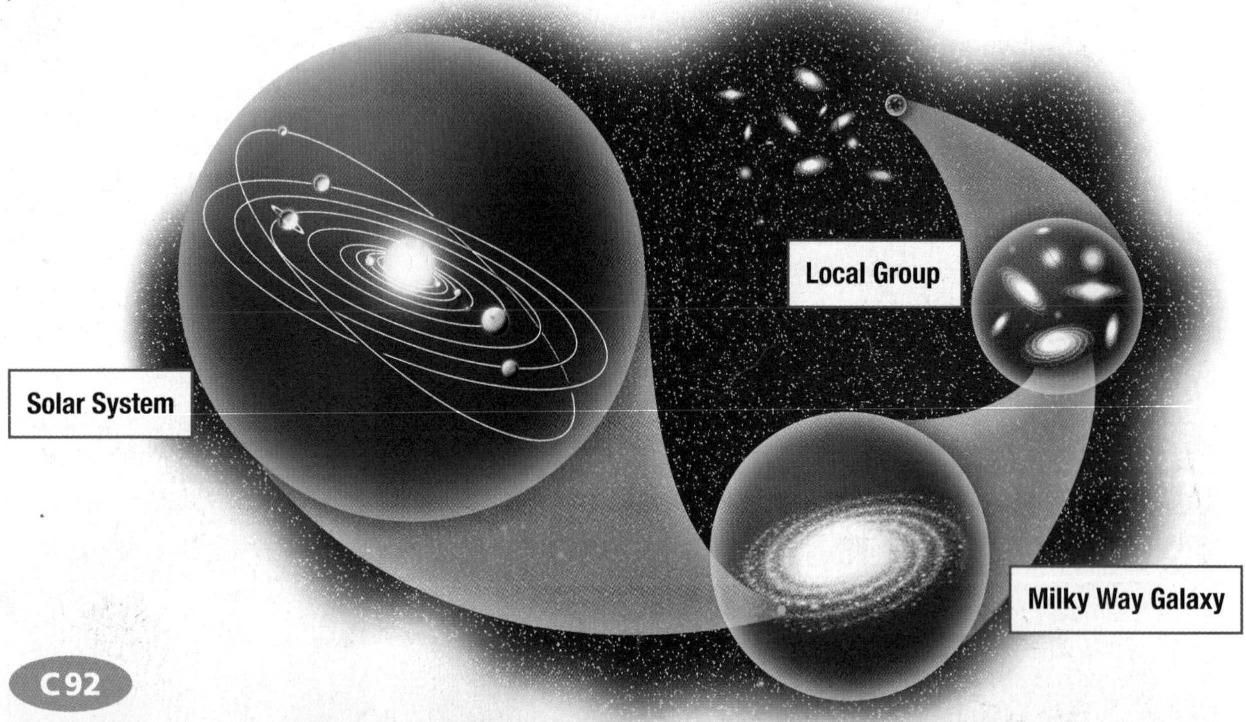

Star Life Cycles

Stars vary in their size, color, and brightness. Astronomers have determined that these differences happen as stars go through different stages during their lifetimes. During its life cycle, a star may appear either red, orange, yellow, white, or blue. A star's color depends on its surface temperature, which is related to the star's age and mass.

The region of gas and dust shown in the photo below is called a **nebula.** This first stage in the life cycle of a star begins when the gas and dust in the nebula are pulled together by the force of gravity. New stars form as pressure from these pulled materials causes the temperature to rise. Fusion begins in the star's core when the temperature reaches about 10,000,000°C. As hydrogen fuses to become helium, hot gases push outward and gravity pulls inward. When the outward push from fusion and the inward pull from gravity balance, a star is born. Energy from fusion reaches the star's surface and shines into space.

Glossary

nebula (neb′yə lə), cloud of gas and dust in space

Glossary

Nebula

Stars are born amid the dust and gas of a nebula. ▼

Glossary

Glossary

red giant (red jī′ənt), a star that has swelled and glows with a red color

Life and Death of a Star

How long a star lives depends on how long the star takes to use up the hydrogen in its core. Stars that are small or average in mass, such as the sun, shine for about 10 billion years. The most massive stars live for only about one million years because they use up their hydrogen more quickly.

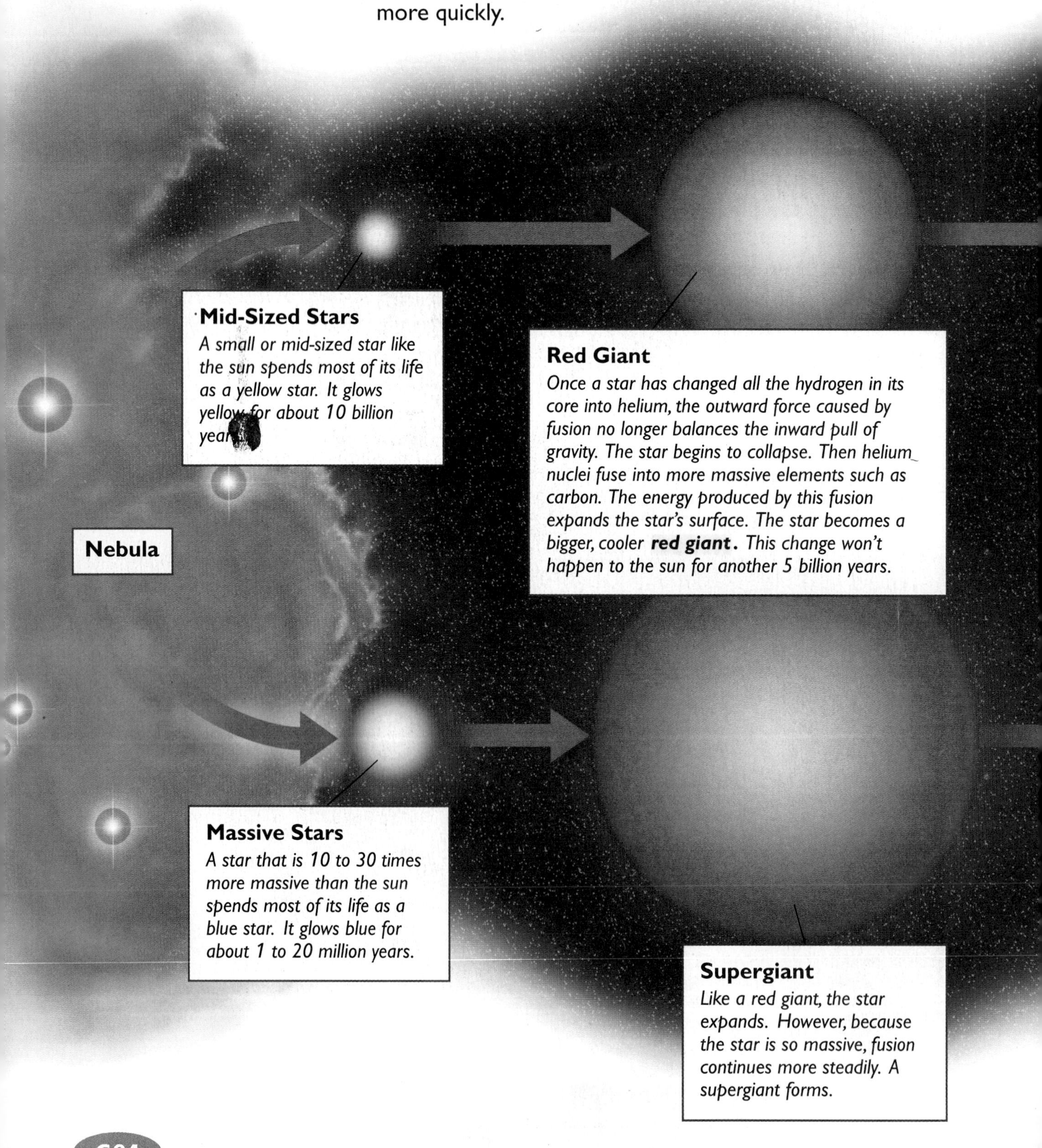

Mid-Sized Stars

A small or mid-sized star like the sun spends most of its life as a yellow star. It glows yellow for about 10 billion years.

Red Giant

Once a star has changed all the hydrogen in its core into helium, the outward force caused by fusion no longer balances the inward pull of gravity. The star begins to collapse. Then helium nuclei fuse into more massive elements such as carbon. The energy produced by this fusion expands the star's surface. The star becomes a bigger, cooler ***red giant.*** *This change won't happen to the sun for another 5 billion years.*

Nebula

Massive Stars

A star that is 10 to 30 times more massive than the sun spends most of its life as a blue star. It glows blue for about 1 to 20 million years.

Supergiant

Like a red giant, the star expands. However, because the star is so massive, fusion continues more steadily. A supergiant forms.

Glossary

supernova
(sü′ pər nō′ və), the explosion of a star, releasing huge amounts of light and other energy

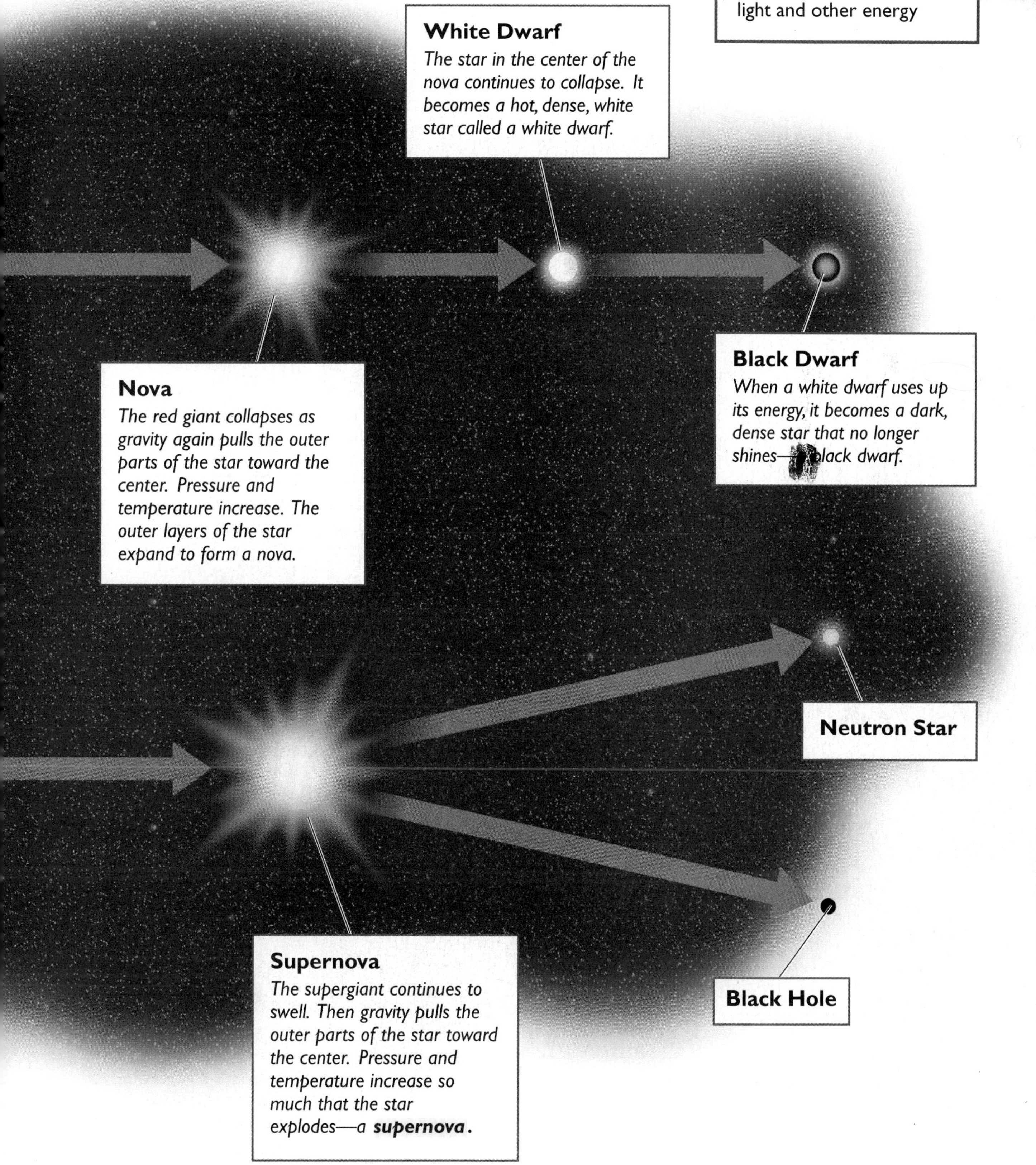

White Dwarf

The star in the center of the nova continues to collapse. It becomes a hot, dense, white star called a white dwarf.

Nova

The red giant collapses as gravity again pulls the outer parts of the star toward the center. Pressure and temperature increase. The outer layers of the star expand to form a nova.

Black Dwarf

When a white dwarf uses up its energy, it becomes a dark, dense star that no longer shines—a black dwarf.

Neutron Star

Supernova

The supergiant continues to swell. Then gravity pulls the outer parts of the star toward the center. Pressure and temperature increase so much that the star explodes—a ***supernova*.**

Black Hole

Glossary

Glossary

black hole (blak hōl), an invisible object in space whose mass and gravitational force is so great that not even light can escape

The explosion of a supernova may be the most powerful event that occurs in space. During a supernova, a star hurls its outer layers into space at one-tenth the speed of light. Its core crushes down to a compact ball that can't be packed any tighter. The resulting star is known as a neutron star. A neutron star may be only a few kilometers across. Its gases are so compressed that one teaspoonful of a neutron star has the mass of a billion metric tons!

Sometimes the supernova's remaining core is more compressed than usual. Some scientists think this happens when the explosion is so violent that the supernova hurls its material into space at nearly the speed of light. The resulting force of gravity among the gases that aren't hurled into space is so strong that they continue to collapse. Then an invisible object with great mass and gravitational pull, called a **black hole,** forms. The pull of gravity from a black hole is so great that it doesn't even allow light to escape or reflect back. The result is that the light can't be seen.

If no light escapes from a black hole, how do scientists know they exist? Scientists observe the behavior of visible stars that may be near a black hole. They think the black hole pulls gases from the visible star. This pulling away of the gases produces strong, continuous X rays, which astronomers can detect.

Find the black hole in the middle of the disk in this artist's drawing. The disk is made of matter that the black hole's gravity pulls from a nearby visible star. ▼

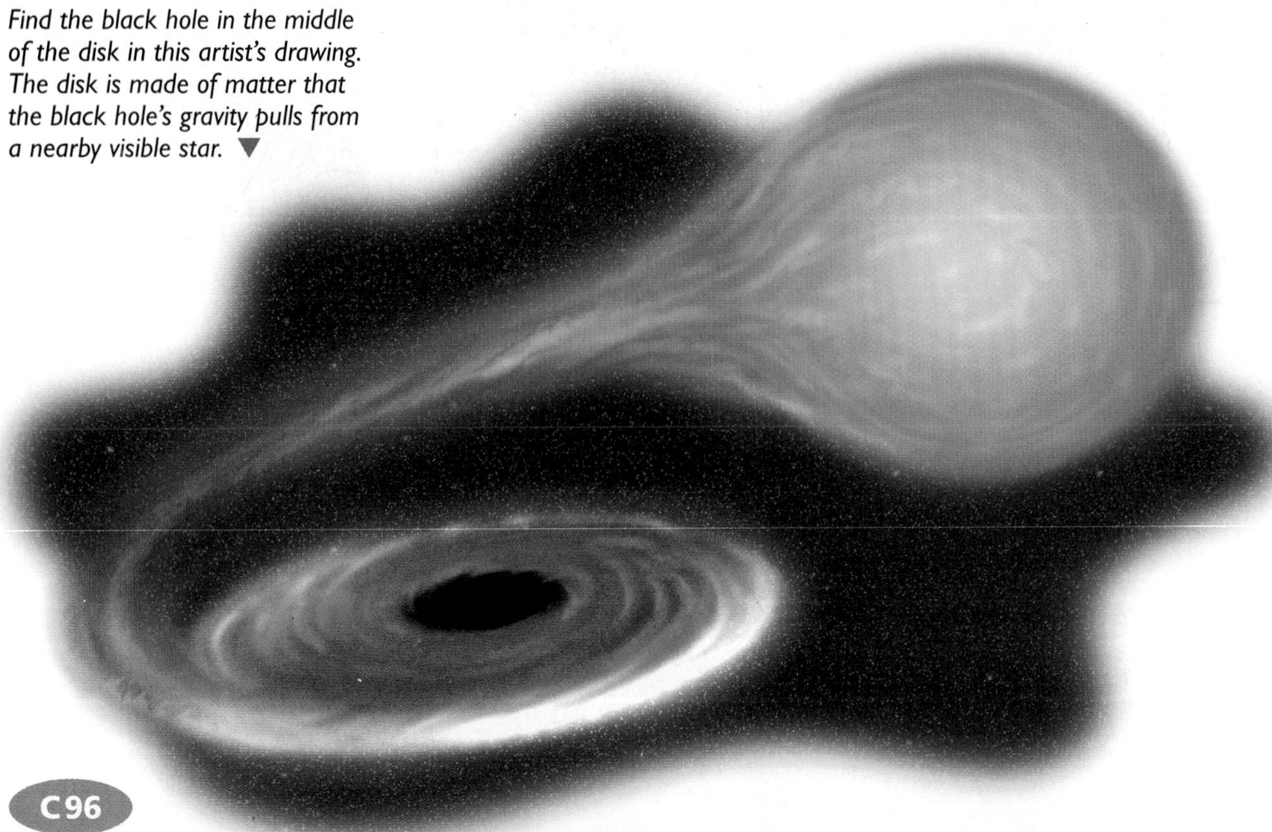

The Expanding Universe

Do you have photos of yourself when you were younger? How have you changed? Earth, too, has changed since it was born. How do scientists know this?

Scientists have developed many theories to explain the universe's history. Today, most scientists think the universe began as a huge explosion—or big bang—about 15 billion years ago. This explosion sent matter and energy traveling through space. The **big bang theory** states that the universe has been expanding ever since.

What proof do scientists have that the universe is expanding? Their proof is in the color of the light that stars give off. To help you understand this proof, think about the sound you would hear as a car passes blowing its horn. The sound has a higher pitch when the car moves toward you and a lower pitch when it moves away.

Just as sound from a moving object changes pitch, light from a moving object changes color. The color change depends on whether the object is moving toward or away. By observing light from distant objects, scientists can tell what direction the object is moving—toward or away from Earth.

Notice the visible light spectrum. When a distant object moves away from Earth, its color shifts toward the red end of the spectrum. Scientists have observed light waves from distant galaxies and found that light from all galaxies is shifted toward the red end of the spectrum. The greater this **red shift** is, the farther away the object is. This red shift tells scientists that galaxies are moving away from Earth and that the universe is expanding.

Lesson 3 Review

1. What are galaxies?
2. How do the stars change during their life cycles?
3. What evidence shows the universe is expanding?
4. **Context Clues**
   Use context clues to write a definition of the phrase *light year* on page C92.

Glossary

Glossary

big bang theory (big bang thē′ər ē), the idea that the universe started a huge explosion about 15 billion years ago

red shift (red shift), the change of light waves from retreating objects to the red end of the spectrum

▲ *Scientists use shifts in color toward the red end of the spectrum to tell that galaxies are moving away from Earth.*

Making a Model of the Expanding Universe

Process Skills

Process Skills

- making and using models
- estimating and measuring
- observing
- collecting and interpreting data
- inferring

Materials

- 2 pens of different colors
- large round balloon
- metric tape measure
- safety goggles
- string

Getting Ready

In this activity, you will make a model of the expanding universe.

Measuring will be easier if you keep all your dots on one side of the uninflated balloon.

Follow This Procedure

1. Make a chart like the one shown. Use your chart to record your observations.

Dot number	Distance between numbered dot and red dot (cm)		
	Empty balloon	Balloon half full	Balloon full
1			
2			
3			
4			

2. Make a **model** of the universe. With a pen, draw one red dot anywhere on an empty balloon.

3. Using a pen of a different color, draw 4 more dots on the balloon. Place the dots at different distances from the red dot. Number these dots *1, 2, 3,* and *4.*

Self-Monitoring

Did I make my dots dark enough?

4. **Measure** the distance from each numbered dot to the red dot. Record your measurements (Photo A).

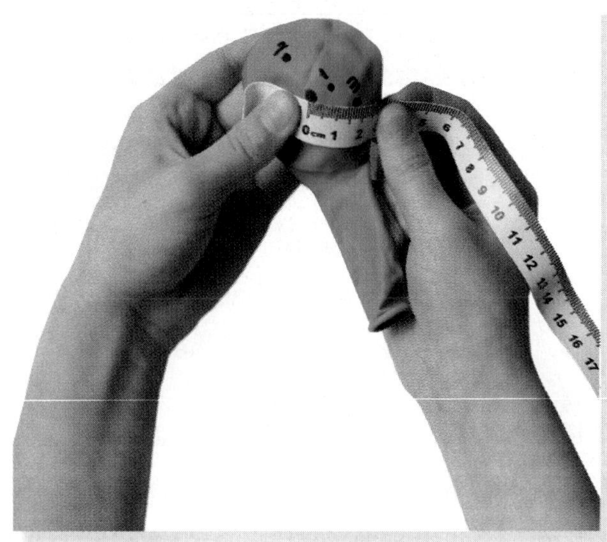

Photo A

5 Put on your safety goggles. Blow up the balloon halfway and hold it closed with your fingers. **Observe** the difference in the balloon and the positions of the dots.

6 Have a teammate measure the distances between the numbered dots and the red dot. Record your measurements (Photo B).

7 Blow up the balloon to its full size. Hold the opening closed while a teammate ties a string tightly around the neck of the balloon.

8 Repeat step 6.

Interpret Your Results

1. In this model, the red dot represents Earth and the balloon represents the boundaries of the universe. What do the numbered dots represent?

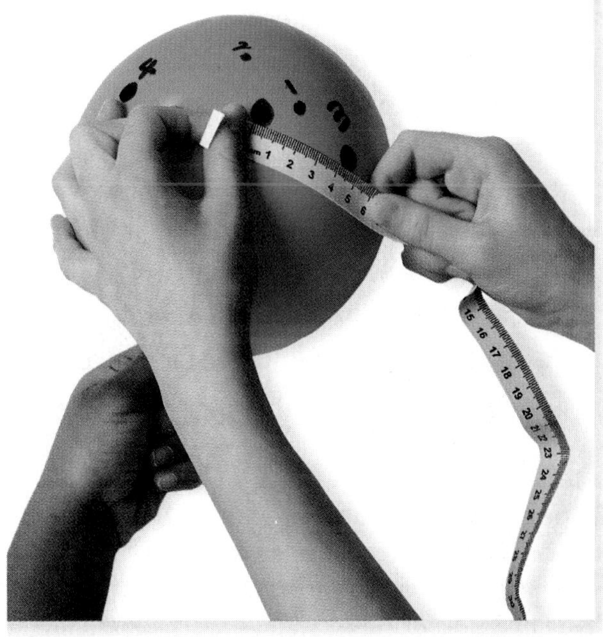

Photo B

2. Interpret the **data** you collected and recorded in your table. Which of the numbered dots moved the farthest from the red dot?

3. Make an **inference**. Which numbered dot moved the fastest?

Inquire Further

How could you prove which dot moved the fastest? Develop a plan to answer this or other questions you may have.

Self-Assessment

- I followed the directions to make a model of the expanding universe.
- I made **measurements** and recorded my **observations.**
- I described what each of the elements of the **model** represented.
- I **interpreted** my **data** to find out which dot moved farthest.
- I made an **inference** about which of the numbered dots on the balloon moved the fastest.

You will learn:
- what technology is used to explore the universe.
- how space technology benefits society.
- how space travel has changed.

Lesson 4

How Do People Explore Space?

Let's see . . . one, two, three, four . . . I count ten stars in this part of the sky. Then I look again with a telescope.  **WOW! Where did all those stars come from?! Patches of sky that looked completely black are suddenly filled with pinpoints of light. How did the telescope help?**

Exploring the Universe

What do your eyes and the optical telescope in the picture have in common? They both are used to collect light. Scientists all over the world use telescopes to help them learn about the universe. Many of these telescopes look a lot different from the one in the photo below.

The Keck telescope is located on top of Mauna Kea—a large volcanic mountain in Hawaii. This telescope has a total weight of 270 metric tons and is made up of 36 hexagonal mirrors, each about 2 meters wide. These mirrors fit together like tiles on a floor. Each mirror rests on a movable support that is adjusted by a computer twice each second. This constant adjustment enables the mirrors to work together as a single mirror. The Keck telescope is the world's largest light collector. With its great light-collecting power, it is used to look for distant galaxies.

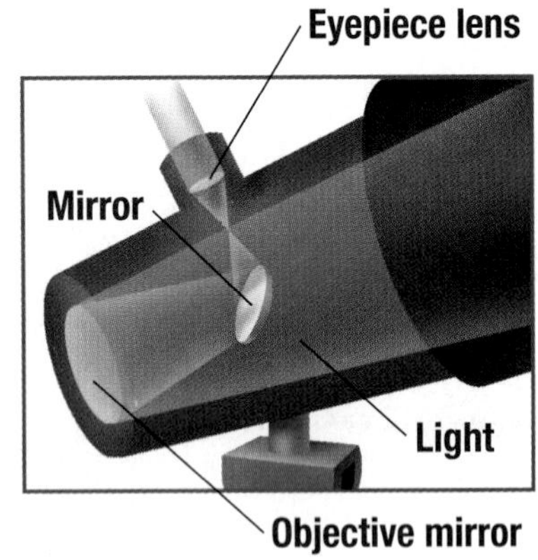

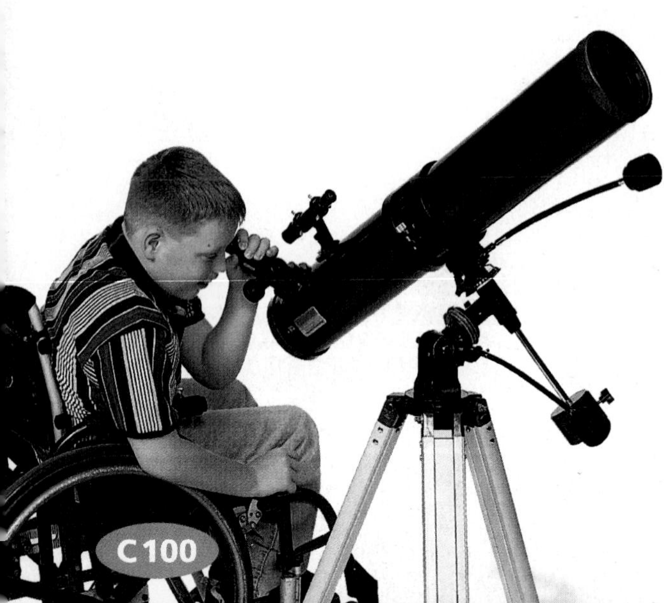

Reflecting Telescope

◀ A reflecting telescope uses a mirror to collect light. The mirrors of some large telescopes at observatories are 10 meters in diameter. These mirrors collect light from faint, distant objects and focus it in a small area. The larger the mirror, the more light it can collect.

Observatories are the homes of telescopes. These buildings are built high on mountaintops where the telescopes can get the very best views of space. At these high locations, the telescopes are away from city lights that interfere with the images they collect. The observatory in the photo to the right houses the Keck telescope.

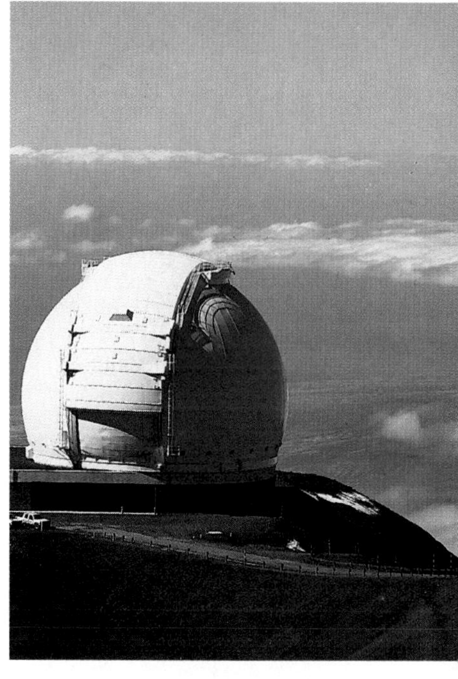

▲ *The Keck telescope, located in this observatory, can collect information about space much faster than other telescopes. It can see deeper into space than other telescopes too.*

Objects in space not only give off light waves, they also give off other electromagnetic radiation—gamma rays, X rays, ultraviolet waves, infrared waves, and radio waves. Sometimes, these electromagnetic waves coming from space can't easily pass through Earth's atmosphere. For example, light and radio waves can be distorted by the gases in the atmosphere. Some kinds of waves are best studied high above Earth's atmosphere.

Instruments in space can collect information about the universe without interference from Earth's atmosphere. Satellites carry instruments that collect and transmit information about energy in space. In the United States, the National Aeronautics and Space Administration (NASA) is the agency that launches satellites into orbit around Earth.

One of the most important satellites used for exploring space is the Hubble Space Telescope, shown to the lower right. The Hubble was put into Earth orbit in 1990. It has provided views of the universe no one had ever seen before and continues to serve as a useful observatory in space. One important use of this telescope is to help scientists determine the age of the universe.

In 1993, a flawed mirror in the Hubble Telescope was repaired in space. Since then, the Hubble has dazzled people with clear views of deep space, such as the distant galaxies shown here. ▼

In addition to satellites, scientists have launched space probes. A space probe is a spacecraft without people that leaves Earth orbit to explore space. It collects and sends data about the regions through which it passes. *Voyager, Pioneer, Mariner,* and *Galileo* are some of the earlier probes that have explored our solar system.

What are some advantages of using space probes such as Cassini *to explore the solar system rather than using astronauts?* ▼

A more recent space probe called *Cassini* is shown to the left. It should reach Saturn's moon, Titan, in November 2004. Once there, *Cassini* will drop another probe—*Huygens*—into Titan's atmosphere. *Cassini* will remain above Titan, recording data transmitted by the probe and transmitting the data back to Earth.

A major advancement in the exploration of space has come through NASA's Space Shuttle Program. Space shuttles are reusable vehicles that carry people and equipment into Earth orbit and back. Shuttle astronauts and mission specialists work and live in space for various amounts of time. They conduct experiments, release satellites, and make repairs in space, as shown below.

Longer stays in space are possible with space stations. Early space stations were built by the U.S. and the U.S.S.R. In 1986, the Russian space station *Mir* was launched. Both Russian and American astronauts have lived and conducted experiments in the space laboratory.

Several countries are working together on an international space station. When it is completed, scientists will continue to conduct new experiments in space.

Astronauts Kathryn Thornton and Thomas Akers practice skills that will be necessary for constructing a space station in orbit. ▶

Technology from Space Exploration

Is your home one of the millions that has its very own Earth station? It is if you receive your TV signals with a satellite dish. Satellites developed for space exploration have many other practical uses on Earth. For example, certain satellites keep track of changing weather conditions for the National Weather Service. Other satellites carry telephone signals around the world. These signals allow the girl in the photo below to use her cellular phone. Some satellites can even track small, special radios on the ground below to help find missing aircraft.

The pacemaker shown on the right is just one of many medical benefits provided by space technology. Portable medical equipment, monitoring devices, implantable heart pumps, and pacemakers all had their roots as equipment designed for use in space.

Chances are, every day you use something that resulted from the exploration of space. The silicon chip used in home computers and calculators is another useful product, or spinoff, that has resulted from space research and exploration.

It would be hard to escape all the space technology that has found its way into everyday life. Smoke detectors, microwave ovens, and computer bar codes are often taken for granted, but they are all space spinoffs. Some spinoffs came from technology developed to protect astronauts from temperature extremes in space. Some items, such as bullet-proof vests, came from technology developed to provide strong, lightweight fabrics for space use.

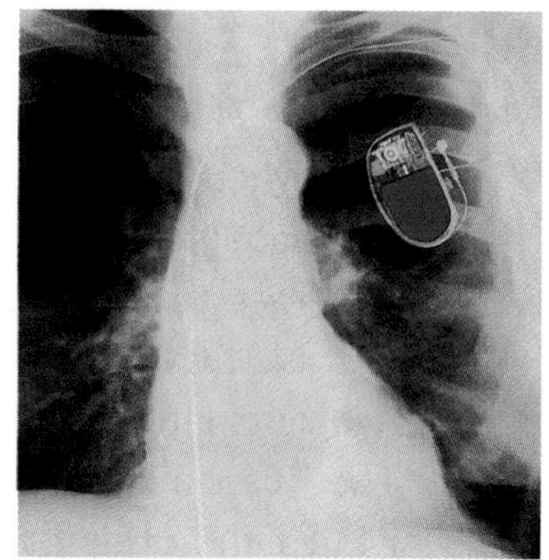

▲ *Technology developed for space programs has led to many medical benefits, including smaller and improved pacemakers that help the heart pump correctly.*

Space technology has led to the development of cellular phones. ▶

History of Space Travel

History of Science

The door opened to space travel in 1957 when the former Soviet Union launched the satellite *Sputnik*. A few years later, the great race to put a person on the moon was on! NASA used increasingly powerful rockets to place astronauts into orbits and eventually on the moon. The Russian space program concentrated on living in Earth's orbit for long periods. The space race eventually changed into cooperative international missions that continue today.

1957

The former Soviet Union launched Sputnik, *the first artificial satellite, into Earth orbit. This technological triumph challenged the United States to begin its own space program. On October 1, 1958, the National Aeronautics and Space Administration (NASA) officially began efforts to explore space.*

1965

Ed White became the first American to walk in space—an important task for making repairs in space.

1961

In his round capsule, Russian cosmonaut Yuri A. Gagarin became the first person in space. A Redstone rocket boosted the first American into space—Alan B. Shepard.

1969
Neil Armstrong and Edwin Aldrin, during the Apollo 11 *mission, became the first people to walk on the moon. Michael Collins orbited in the waiting spacecraft overhead.*

1981
The first launch and safe return of the space shuttle Columbia *in 1981 marked the beginning of a new space era. Space shuttles enable people to do a variety of research and to work in space.*

2000 and Beyond
Scientists, engineers, and astronauts from many countries are cooperating to plan the further exploration and use of space. Future international missions include a large space station that will orbit Earth and a possible mission to Mars.

Lesson 4 Review

1. What technology is used to explore the universe?
2. How does space technology benefit society?
3. How has space travel changed since the launch of *Sputnik?*
4. **Using Graphic Sources**
   Use the picture on page C100 to write a few sentences that explain how a telescope works.

Chapter 3 Review

Chapter Main Ideas

Lesson 1

• Earth rotates in a counterclockwise direction on its tilted axis as it revolves in an elliptical orbit around the sun.

• The seasons change as parts of the earth are tilted either toward or away from the sun at different times throughout its orbit.

• Earth, the moon, and the sun interact to cause tides, eclipses, and moon phases.

Lesson 2

• Our nearest star is the sun, which gives us radiant energy.

• The sun is made up of hot gases and gets its energy from fusion.

• Sunspot activity is accompanied by solar flares, which send radiation into space, causing radio static, power surges, and auroras on Earth.

Lesson 3

• A galaxy is a group of billions of stars with gas and dust.

• During its life cycle, a star changes in size, color, and brightness.

• Scientists have noticed that light from distant galaxies is shifting to the red end of the spectrum. This shift indicates that galaxies are moving away in an expanding universe.

Lesson 4

• Telescopes, artificial satellites, space probes, and space shuttles are used to explore the universe.

• Space technology has provided many useful products that we use every day.

• Space travel began with a race to the moon, followed by unmanned space probes, a space station, and space shuttles.

Reviewing Science Words and Concepts

Write the letter of the word or phrase that best completes each sentence.

a. auroras
b. big bang theory
c. black hole
d. corona
e. equinox
f. fusion
g. galaxy
h. lunar eclipse
i. nebula
j. quasars
k. red giant
l. red shift
m. solar eclipse
n. solar flares
o. solstice
p. sunspot
q. supernova
r. tides

1. The longest or shortest day of the year is the ___.

2. During a(n) ___, Earth's shadow is over the moon.

3. During the ___, there's an equal amount of night and day.

4. The powerhouses of developing galaxies are ___.

5. The gas and dust of a beginning star is a(n) ___.

6. A huge, red glowing star is a(n) ___.

7. The pull of the moon's gravity on Earth causes ___.

8. A dense, invisible object in space is a(n) ___.

9. Atoms combine to form new elements during ___.

10. An exploding star is a(n) ___.

11. The idea that explains how the universe started is the ___.

12. The change of a star's color to the red end of the spectrum is ___.

13. The light display in northern skies are ___.

14. Eruptions on the sun are ___.

15. The crown of glowing gases around the sun is the ___.

16. A region of strong magnetic field on the sun is a(n) ___.

17. When the moon's shadow falls on the earth, a(n) ___ occurs.

18. All stars belong to a(n) ___.

Explaining Science

Draw and label pictures or write sentences on a chart that explain these questions.

1. How does Earth move and interact with other bodies in space?

2. What characteristics of the sun affect Earth?

3. How are stars and galaxies related?

4. How is the universe explored from Earth and from space?

Using Skills

1. Earth is 149,598,000 kilometers from the sun. Write this **large number** in word form.

2. Review the information about seasons on page C84. Then write a procedure for an **experiment** to test whether direct light heats an object more than light hitting an object at an angle. Identify the **variables** you will control.

3. **Formulate questions** you would like investigated on a future space exploration mission.

Critical Thinking

1. Kim lives in Michigan, where winters can be quite harsh. Her brother, Chu, lives in Australia. **Apply** what you know about the seasons to help Kim decide whether to visit her brother during her summer vacation, or during her winter break in January instead.

2. Imagine you could travel to a black hole. **Hypothesize** what would happen as you came upon the black hole's strong gravitational pull.

Reduce! Re-Use! Recycle!

Who said backpacks can't be made from old tire rubber! Learning to conserve resources is one way of thinking about the things we use. What other things did this girl find new ways to use?

Chapter 4

Resources and Conservation

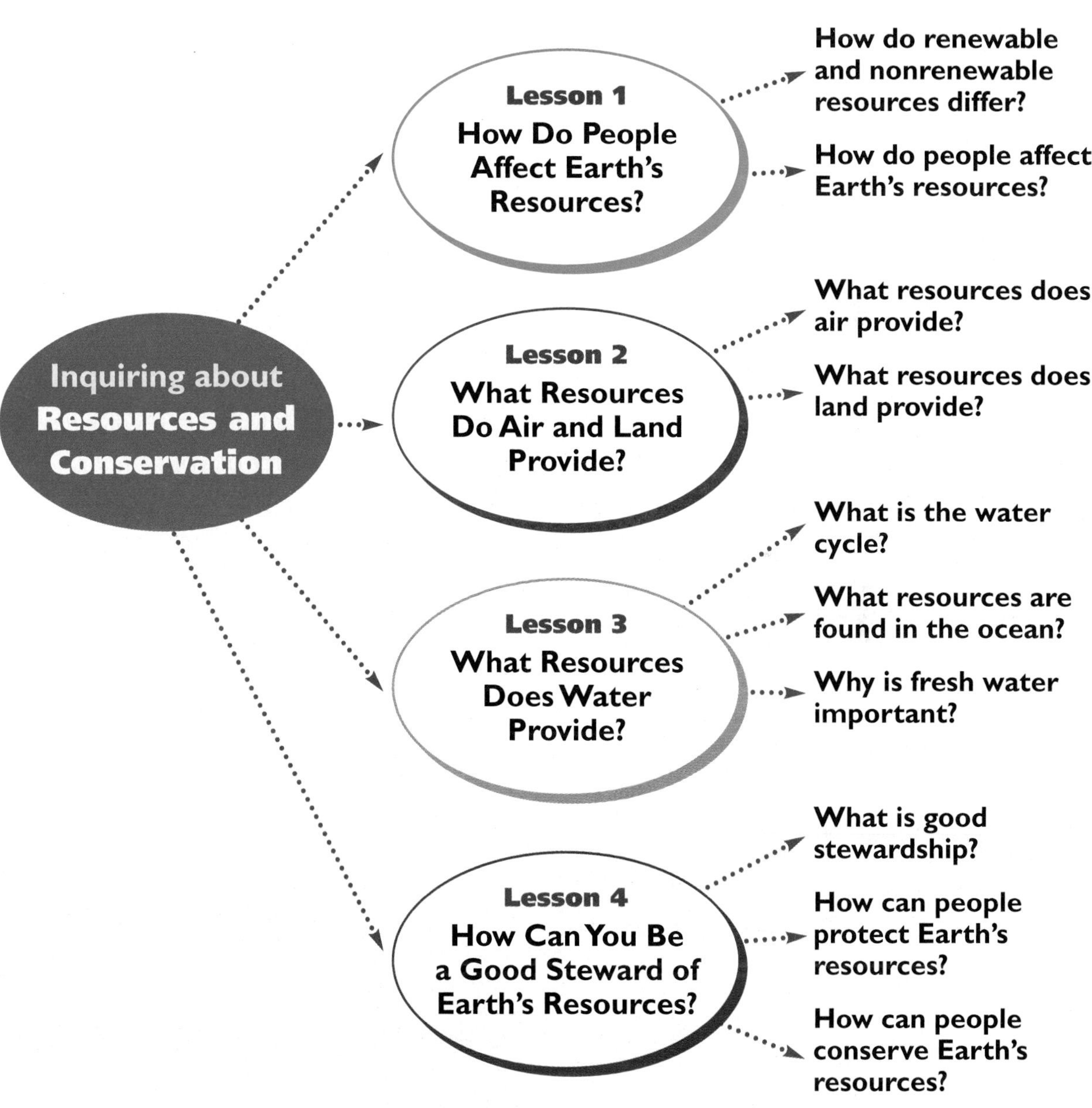

***Copy the chapter graphic organizer** onto your own paper. This organizer shows you what the whole chapter is all about. As you read the lessons and do the activities, look for answers to the questions and write them on your organizer.*

Explore Activity

Exploring Recycling

Process Skills

Process Skills

- observing
- communicating

Materials

- newspaper
- plastic cup
- paper pulp
- foil pan
- window screening
- wood board

Explore

1. Cover your desk with newspaper.

2. Place 2 cupfuls of paper pulp in a pan. Dip your screen into the paper pulp. Using your hands, spread a thin layer of the pulp on the screen, as shown in the photo.

Safety Note *Be careful not to scratch or cut yourself on the screen.*

3. Place the screen on the newspaper. The pulp should be facing up. Carefully cover the pulp with additional newspapers.

4. Turn the newspaper-screen-pulp sandwich over so that the screen is on top of the pulp.

5. Use the wood board to press your pulp, removing most of the water from between the fibers. Turn the screen over so that the pulp is on top.

6. Label your screen and place it in a place where it can dry. Let the mixture dry for 1–2 days. Then peel your recycled paper from the screen. **Observe** the recycled paper.

Reflect

1. Describe your recycled paper.

2. Communicate. Discuss the characteristics of your recycled paper with classmates. Make a list of the ways you could test the quality of your paper.

Inquire Further

Your recycled paper is made from shredded newspaper. How would using other materials change the characteristics of the recycled paper? Develop a plan to answer this or other questions you may have.

Comparing and Contrasting

An important part of science is comparing and contrasting events, ideas, or objects. To **compare** things, you identify how they are alike. When you **contrast** them, you identify how they differ. As you read Lesson 1, *How Do People Affect Earth's Resources?* compare and contrast Earth's resources.

Reading Vocabulary

compare, to find out how things are alike

contrast, to find out how things are different

Example

You can often use a diagram like the one below to compare and contrast things. Each circle represents a type of resource—renewable and nonrenewable. Fill in each circle with characteristics of the type of resource. When both types share a characteristic, write the characteristic in the area where the circles overlap. One characteristic has been done for you.

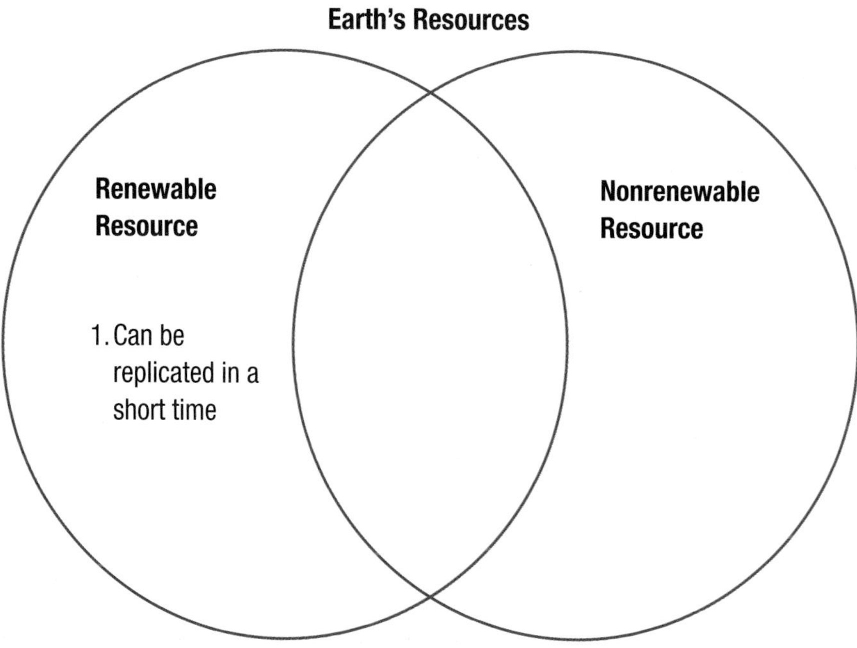

Talk About It!

1. How does comparing and contrasting help you understand what you read?

2. How could you use a similar diagram to compare and contrast three objects?

You will learn:

- how renewable and nonrenewable resources differ.
- how people affect Earth's resources.

Lesson 1

How Do People Affect Earth's Resources?

You wake up. AH! You take a deep breath of fresh air. ZAP! The electricity flows when you turn on the light. Then WHOOSH, clean water flows when you turn on the tap. All day and night, you depend on Earth's air, water, and land.

Glossary

Glossary

renewable resource (ri nü′ə bəl ri sôrs′), a resource that can be replaced within a reasonably short time

nonrenewable resource (non′ri nü′ə bəl ri sôrs′), a resource that cannot be replaced

Renewable and Nonrenewable Resources

As you go about your daily activities, what are some of the items you use? Food, beverages, clothes, paper, and pencils are just a few of the items you might mention. Any material that makes up the items you use is called a resource. Every item you use is made from one or more resources. Do you know what resources were used to make the items you used today?

The girl to the left is holding items from two groups of resources: renewable and nonrenewable. A **renewable resource** is a resource that can be replaced within a reasonably short time. For example, paper and wood products are made from trees that can be replanted once they have been cut. Food and cotton are also renewable resources because they can be grown or raised by farmers.

A **nonrenewable resource** is a resource that can't be replaced. Many fuels, such as gas and oil, are nonrenewable resources because they take millions of years to form.

What renewable resource is this girl holding? ▼

Because people use gas and oil much faster than they can be replaced, all the gas and oil on Earth will someday be used up. Why is the coal that the girl on the previous page is holding considered a nonrenewable resource?

When deciding whether a resource is renewable or nonrenewable, think about how fast it can be replaced. For example, how much fresh water is available in the area of the country where you live? Fresh water is abundant in the Great Lakes region of the United States. Frequent rainfalls easily replenish the water supply there. On the other hand, water is not so abundant in areas such as the southwest desert where people face serious water shortages. In places like Arizona, the low amount of rainfall can't replenish the amount of water people use.

People Affect Resources

Imagine the enormous hole that an earthmover as large as a 20 story building could dig! The machine shown to the right quickly removes huge amounts of soil and rock, one layer at a time, to expose and remove underlying coal or minerals. An entire hilltop can be removed by this method, which is called open-pit mining or strip-mining.

As people use Earth's resources, there are risks, benefits, and costs. How would you feel if an area near your home was going to be strip-mined? You might not like the big, bare hole that is created as soil, rocks, and plants are removed from a large area. In that case, this use of resources could be considered a cost.

Strip Mining

Gigantic earth moving equipment like the "Big John" strips away layers of soil and rock to remove coal or minerals from the land. In this method of mining, valuable topsoil is buried or washed away. ▼

Strip-mining can have benefits too. It costs less money and is less risky than underground mining. Underground mining can result in cave-ins, gas explosions, and water pollution. The United States government now requires companies to refill strip-mined areas and to plant vegetation. This process is called "reclaiming the land." Reclaiming may be an expensive process, but it is beneficial. Reclaimed land eventually can provide new wildlife habitats or be developed for recreation.

Now think about the risks, benefits, and costs associated with another use of Earth's resources. The photos to the left show some of the effects of building a dam to create a reservoir and provide hydroelectricity. What other impacts might the dammed water have on the area?

▲ *Dams, like the one at the top of the page, control the flow of water in flood-prone areas. Although some farmland and forested areas may be lost behind the dam, it provides a a supply of pure water and a place for recreation.*

Lesson 1 Review

1. What is the difference between renewable and nonrenewable resources?
2. How do people affect Earth's resources?
3. **Compare and Contrast**
   Compare and contrast the use of resources in your home and in a friend's.

Lesson 2

What Resources Do Air and Land Provide?

You will learn:

- **what resources air provides.**
- **what resources land provides.**

Have you ever tried to hold your breath for as long as you can? GASP! It's not very long before you start gasping for air. People and many animals can't live without air for more than a few minutes. Why is air so important?

Resources in Air

The atmosphere, or air, that you breathe is made up of a variety of gases that you can't see. Nitrogen and oxygen are the two main gases that make up the air. Air also contains smaller amounts of carbon dioxide and other gases. Organisms need these gases to live. Luckily these gases are renewable resources.

In Unit A, you read about the carbon dioxide–oxygen cycle. In this cycle, carbon dioxide and oxygen are continually renewed.

The carbon dioxide–oxygen cycle is part of a larger cycle called the carbon cycle, in which carbon is cycled throughout the environment. Plants take in carbon dioxide from the air to produce carbon-containing molecules. As animals, such as these bison, eat plants, they take in the carbon-containing molecules. When plants or animals die, stored carbon either remains in the ground, or it is released back into the atmosphere as carbon dioxide when matter decomposes.

Nature continually cycles carbon in the environment. ▼

Nitrogen is another renewable resource which all living things need in order to grow and repair cells. Nitrogen gas can't be taken directly from the air. In the nitrogen cycle, the air's nitrogen is changed into a usable form that organisms can use.

Plants of the legume family include alfalfa, peas, clover, and soybeans. The bacteria in swellings on the roots of these plants change the air's nitrogen into nitrogen compounds that plants use to make proteins. As nitrogen-containing plants and animal wastes decompose, a nitrogen compound is released in soil. Plants can take in this form of nitrogen through their roots. However, some of the nitrogen compound is changed by soil bacteria into nitrogen gas, which goes back into the atmosphere.

You can see another renewable resource that comes from air in the photos below. What do you think the resource is? Windmills such as these use wind to turn turbines that generate electricity.

The energy of the movement of air can be captured by windmills. The huge blades on the windmills to the right help to turn turbines that generate electricity. ▼

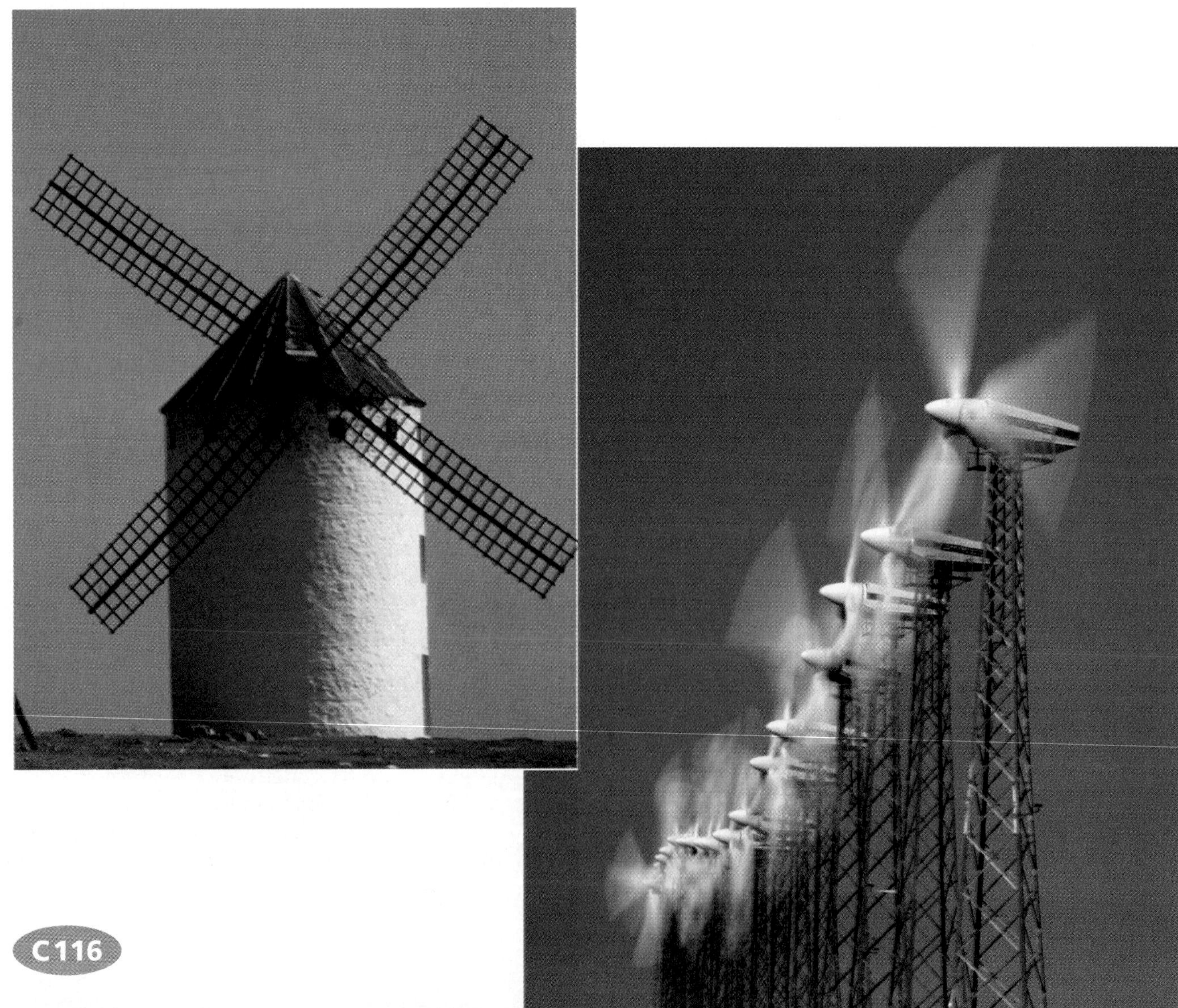

Resources on Land

When you hear the word *precious* what comes to mind? Did you think of precious stones or metals such as diamonds or gold? Both are types of minerals. Although not all minerals are precious, all minerals are nonrenewable resources that come from the earth. Generally, minerals are found in **ore,** a type of rock that contains enough of a mineral to be of value. The pictures below show some familiar items that are made from minerals.

Soil is one of the most precious resources of all. People use soil to grow the plants they need to live. As plants grow, they take in minerals from the soil. When the plants die and decay, these minerals are returned to the soil. In this way, soil can be used over and over again. Is soil a renewable or nonrenewable resource?

Another important resource is trees. What uses can you think of for the tree being cut down in the photo? You know from Lesson 1 that renewable resources are sometimes used up faster than they can be replaced. Trees are an example of a renewable resource that must be used wisely. People must care for land resources by preventing soil erosion and by replanting trees that have been cut down.

Glossary

ore (ôr), a rock that contains enough of a mineral to be of value

▲ *Trees are an important resource that provides many things we use.*

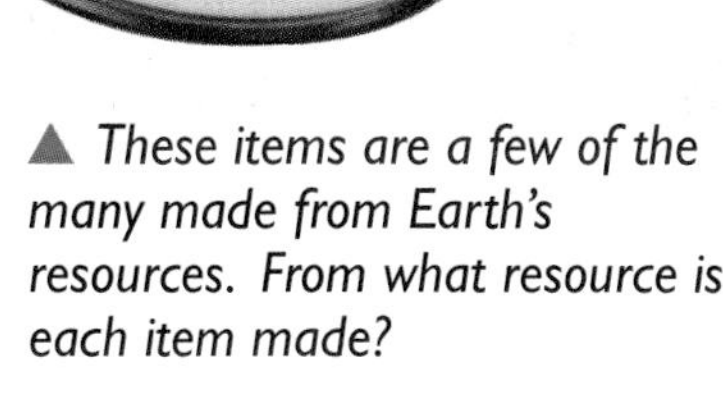

▲ *These items are a few of the many made from Earth's resources. From what resource is each item made?*

Glossary

Glossary

fossil fuels
(fos′əl fyü′əlz), fuels such as coal, natural gas, and oil that formed underground millions of years ago from decaying organic matter

Equally important resources are fossil fuels. **Fossil fuels** include coal, oil, and natural gas. These fuels were formed millions of years ago from the remains of buried plants or animals. Fossil fuels provide energy. Think about the many things you do that require energy. You use energy to cook food, to heat buildings, to drive from one place to another, and to power electrical appliances such as CD players. You can see on the graph that most of the energy that is used in the United States comes from fossil fuels. Smaller amounts of energy come from nuclear power and other sources.

Energy Production

Fossil fuels and the uranium used for nuclear power are nonrenewable resources that are found in the ground. Uranium and coal are obtained by mining. Wells are drilled to obtain underground gas and oil. At the current rate of use, scientists think all the fossil fuels in the world will be used up within a few hundred years. So remember that each time you turn off a light or ride your bike instead of riding in a car, you save fossil fuels.

Lesson 2 Review

1. What resources does air provide?
2. What resources does land provide?
3. **Compare and Contrast**
   Compare and contrast soil and air as resources.

Lesson 3

What Resources Does Water Provide?

You will learn:
- **what the water cycle is.**
- **what resources are found in the ocean.**
- **why fresh water is important.**

Rinse the dishes. Bathe the dog. Wash the car. Take a shower. Brush your teeth. Gee! Is washing things all that water is good for? No, in fact, the cells of all living things need water for life processes.

The Water Cycle

The water cycle provides organisms with a constant supply of the water they need. As you see below, water cycles from the atmosphere to the land and back into the atmosphere. That's why water is a renewable resource.

Evaporation
Water evaporates from the land, from bodies of water, and from organisms.

Precipitation
In the air, evaporated water condenses to form clouds. The water eventually returns to the earth as rain, snow, sleet, or hail.

Transportation
The water that falls to earth as precipitation is carried by river systems to lakes and oceans. Some of it soaks into the ground and is stored as underground water.

▲ *These nodules on the floor of the Atlantic Ocean are made of manganese.*

Ocean Resources

To the left, you see an interesting source of minerals that came from the ocean floor. Each rounded lump of minerals is called a nodule. Minerals such as manganese, iron, and cobalt are found in the nodules. No one knows for sure how nodules formed. The minerals in the ocean water might have collected around a small object, such as a shark's tooth.

Right now, minerals are easier to get from the land than from the ocean floor. However, as minerals on land become more scarce, more will be taken from the oceans. Some people are looking ahead to this time. One machine, a tractorlike robot, has been designed to move across the ocean floor. It scoops up nodules, crushes them, and transports the minerals to the ocean's surface.

Salt is another ocean resource that is found in large amounts. Different types of salts can be obtained from ocean water by evaporating the water. The picture below shows beds of salt that were left by pools of ocean water on the beach. Where pools of ocean water evaporate, the salt remains. Most of the salt in the oceans is sodium chloride, better known as table salt.

Table salt can be removed easily from the ocean by evaporating the ocean water. ▶

In the photo to the right, you see what looks like a miniature chimney on the ocean floor. This opening on the ocean floor is called a **vent**. The black smoke you see escaping from the vent is actually hot water that is rich in sulfur minerals oozing from Earth's crust. If you recall what you know about heat and plate movement, it shouldn't surprise you that vents are commonly found in areas where plate boundaries occur.

When the fountains of hot water rich in sulfur minerals hit the cold seawater, they form crystals that build up around the vent. Many minerals are deposited on the ocean floor around vent openings in this manner. Lead, copper, iron, and zinc are minerals that are found in large amounts near vents on the ocean floor.

Mining these mineral resources from the ocean floor is still too difficult and expensive. Meanwhile, bacteria deep in the ocean use the sulfur minerals that comes from the vents as an energy source. Animals living around the vents then feed on these bacteria.

You might know that oil and natural gas deposits are located under the land. Did you know some of these fuel deposits occur under the oceans as well? Most geologists think that oil deposits formed from carbon in the remains of tiny organisms that once lived in the ocean millions of years ago. These oil deposits are called petroleum or crude oil. Natural gas was produced by a similar process.

To obtain the valuable oil and natural gas resources from beneath the ocean floor, oil wells are drilled into the bottom of the ocean. As you probably can imagine, it is more difficult to drill an oil well under water than on land. Most offshore wells are located somewhat close to shorelines. A diagram of an offshore drilling operation appears on the next page.

Glossary

vent (vent), opening on the ocean floor

Glossary

▲ *Vents on the ocean floor provide a source of minerals that may be able to be mined in the future.*

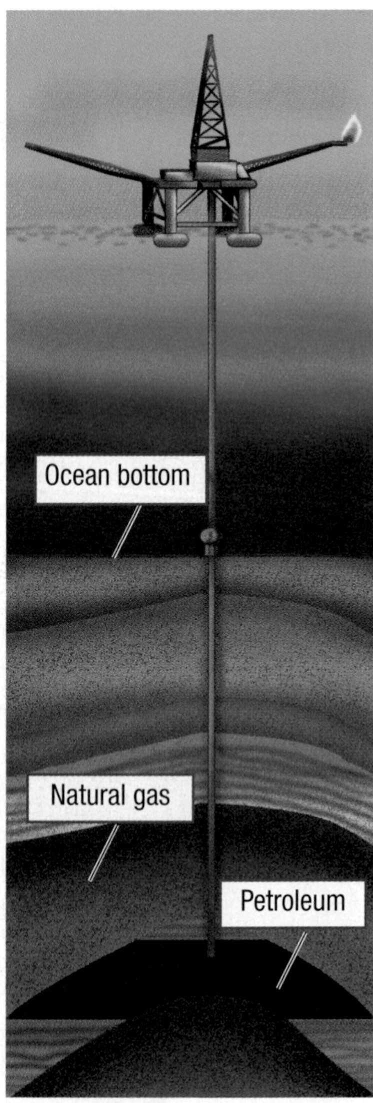

Oil Rig

▲ *Offshore drilling in deep water can be done by drilling ships or floating rigs, like the one above. In shallow water, fixed platforms can be used.*

The diagram to the left shows a huge platform that is constructed to support offshore oil drilling equipment. Workers and equipment must be transported by boat or helicopter to these structures, called rigs. In waters such as the Arctic Ocean or the North Sea, storms or floating icebergs can damage rigs, making offshore drilling dangerous for the workers.

Once the oil has been pumped to the surface, it is loaded onto large ships, called tankers. Tankers have huge compartments for carrying the oil to a refinery for processing. Since some tankers can hold as many as one million barrels of petroleum, care must be taken to prevent oil from spilling into the ocean. Oil spills in water can have disastrous effects on plants, animals, and other organisms that live in or near the water.

Oil and natural gas are not the only sources of energy from the oceans. Remember that ocean water moves in regular patterns called tides. The water that moves during tides has much energy. The photo below shows the Annapolis Tidal Generating Station in Nova Scotia, Canada, which is one of several plants that use tidal energy to produce electricity. This plant provides electricity to cities in Canada and the United States. Other tidal power stations can be found in France, China, and the Soviet Union.

Some of the resources from the ocean come from living organisms. Did you use toothpaste, creams, or lotions today? Maybe you enjoyed a dish of ice cream or pudding. All of these items contain a substance that comes from kelp, a type of seaweed that grows in the ocean. The pictures on the next page show many other living resources that come from the oceans.

Tidal Power

This tidal generating station uses tidal movement to turn turbines that generate electricity. ▶

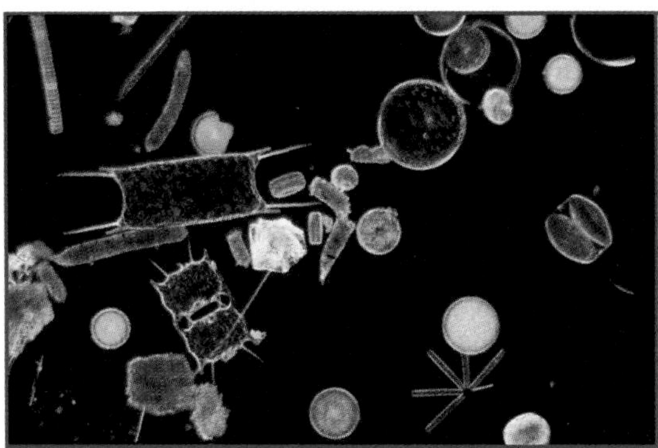

Plankton

◀ *Another resource that comes from the ocean are tiny, free-floating organisms called plankton. Plankton includes microscopic organisms such as algae. Algae are a major source of Earth's oxygen as they make food using photosynthesis. They account for up to half of all the photosynthesis that occurs on Earth. Algae are also a major source of food for organisms at the bottom of the ocean's food chain.*

Seaweed

Many kinds of seaweed can be eaten. The seaweed in this picture, called kelp, can grow to be 60 meters long. A product extracted from seaweed is used as an additive in cosmetics, toothpastes, medicines, and foods such as jellies or salad dressings. Another product, called agar, from red algae is used to grow bacteria in laboratories. ▶

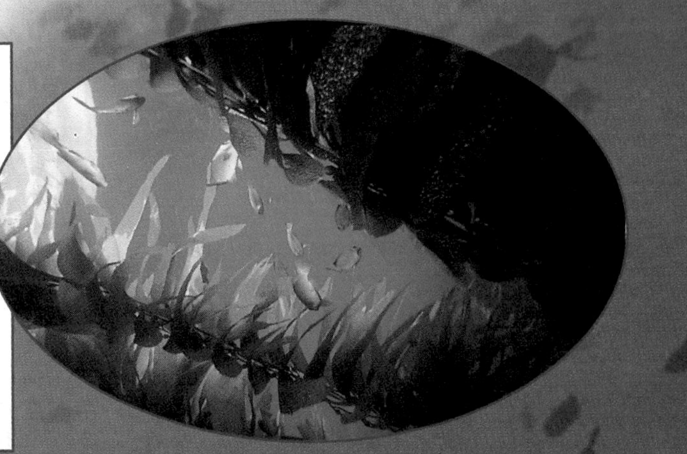

Food Supply

Oceans are a major source of food, including clams, oysters, shrimp, lobster, and many types of fish. Much of the world's population, especially in Asia, depends on fish as the major source of protein. Some of the ocean's fish are processed into fish meal and fed to livestock. ▼

Farm-Raised Seafood

▲ *To keep up with the world's demand for seafood, some ocean resources such as oysters and mussels are raised in special containers near shore. Protected from predators, large numbers of sea organisms can grow in small areas and be easily harvested.*

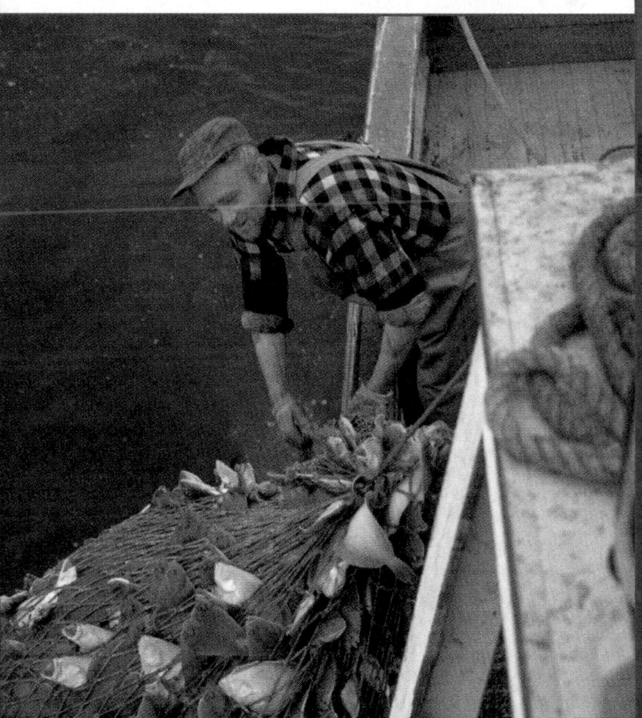

Glossary

reservoir (rez′ ər vwär), artificial lake used to collect and store water

Fresh Water Resources

Just think about all the water your family uses each day. Each flush of the toilet uses between 13 and 26 liters of water. Taking a 2 to 3 minute shower with the water on full force can use around 75 liters of water. A large load of laundry may use up to 185 liters!

Besides using water for cleaning purposes, you need fresh water—water that contains little or no salt—for your cells to carry out life processes. You might survive weeks without food, but you could not last more than a few days without water.

Fresh water is used to manufacture many types of products. Companies use water as an ingredient in many products or to cool down equipment that becomes hot in the manufacturing process. To make enough steel for a bicycle almost 250 liters of water is used.

Don't forget that animals and plants use water too. For example, cows need more than 10 liters of water to make about 4 liters of milk. It takes as much as 98 liters of water to produce an ear of corn!

Fresh water can be found in lakes, rivers, and groundwater. It is constantly renewed by precipitation that comes from the water cycle. Although some places seem to have plenty of fresh water, the world's available supply of fresh water is less than three percent of all of Earth's water, and it is not evenly distributed. In some places, dams are built to harness a large supply of fresh water in an artificial lake, called a **reservoir**. As you can see in the picture of the irrigated field, in some areas, water is pumped from one location to water crops at another location.

Not only do you need an adequate supply of fresh water, you also need that water to be clean and safe to drink. Places like New York City must provide water for as many as 8 million residents each day. The pictures on the next page show how this might be done. As you study how water comes to you, think about ways you can preserve this valuable resource.

Water is an essential ingredient in food crops. In dry areas farmers may have to water their crops by using irrigation methods, such as the one in this picture. ▼

Supplying Water

Water from distant sources, such as a mountain stream in upstate New York, can be carried by underground pipelines to a location where it is needed. ▶

Large artificial lakes, such as this reservoir in New York City's Central Park, collect and store large supplies of fresh water. The reservoirs are sometimes used for recreation purposes. ▼

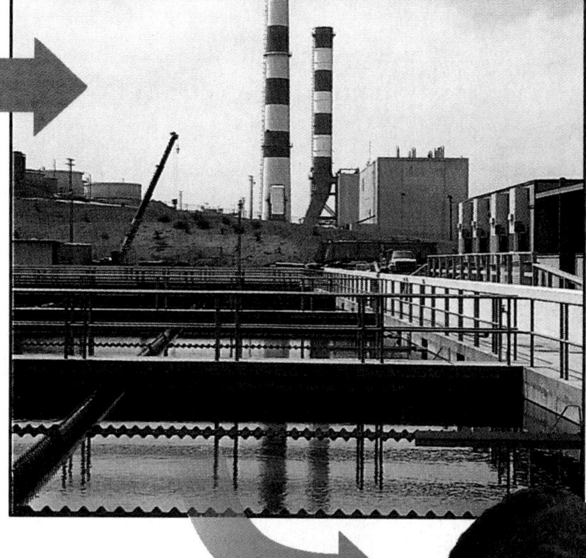

Water purification plants process the supply of fresh water to remove many of the impurities. Chemicals such as chlorine are then added to the water to kill harmful bacteria. Special equipment is used to constantly monitor the quality and supply of water. ▶

Purified water is pumped from the water treatment plant to homes, schools, businesses, and playgrounds through a network of underground pipes. The water flowing from the fountain you see pictured here, may eventually find its way back to the reservoir to be recycled. ▶

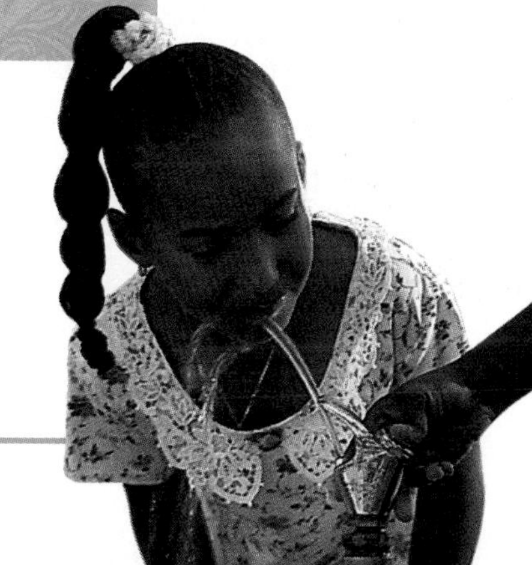

Lesson 3 Review

1. What is the water cycle?
2. What resources are found in the ocean?
3. Why is fresh water important?
4. **Compare and Contrast**
   How is the ocean similar to a farm field?

Investigate Activity

Purifying Water

Process Skills

- predicting
- observing
- communicating

Materials

- water
- 3 plastic graduated cups
- food coloring
- spoon
- pepper
- cotton balls
- funnel
- coffee filter

Getting Ready

In this activity, you will pollute water and then try to remove the pollutants from the water.

Follow This Procedure

1 Make a chart like the one shown. Use your chart to record your observations.

Type of filter	Pollutants filter removed	
	Pepper	Food coloring
Cotton ball		
Coffee filter		

2 Pour 60 mL of clean water into a plastic graduated cup.

3 Add a drop of food coloring to the water in the cup. Add a spoonful of pepper to the colored water. These materials are your pollutants. Set the polluted water aside.

4 Place a coffee filter into a funnel. Set the funnel on top of a clean plastic cup (Photo A). **Predict** what will happen if the polluted water is poured through the filter. Will the pollutants be filtered out of the water?

5 Have one partner hold the funnel in place over the clean cup. Have another partner use the spoon to carefully stir the polluted water in the cup to distribute the pepper and then quickly pour about 10 mL of it into the funnel.

Safety Note *Stir and pour the water carefully so as not to spill it. Food coloring will stain clothes and skin.*

6 **Observe** what happens as the water passes through the coffee filter. Record your observations of the filtered water in your chart. Compare a sample of the polluted water with the filtered water.

Photo A

Photo B

7 Remove the coffee filter from the funnel. Stuff a cotton ball into the thin neck of the funnel (Photo B). If the diameter of the neck of the funnel is not completely filled with cotton, add another cotton ball. Repeat steps 5–6.

Interpret Your Results

1. What did you observe as your polluted water passed through the filter? Was the water slowed down by the filter?

2. Compare the water before and after it was filtered. Were your filters able to remove all of the pollutants?

3. Communicate. Discuss with your group how the results of this activity can be used to explain why chlorine is added to drinking water even after it has been filtered.

Inquire Further

What other materials could you use to filter water? Develop a plan to answer this or other questions you may have.

Self-Assessment

- I followed the directions to filter water.
- I **predicted** what would happen when the water was poured through the filter.
- I **observed** the water being filtered.
- I compared the water before and after it was filtered by two different filters.
- I **communicated** ideas about why chlorine is added to water after it has been filtered.

You will learn:
- what good stewardship is.
- how people can protect Earth's resources.
- how people can conserve Earth's resources.

Lesson 4

How Can You Be a Good Steward of Earth's Resources?

Crash! Sort the glass. Clank! Recycle that soda can. Clunk! Drop those old phone books into the recycling bin. A community cleanup is just one of the things you can do to help take care of our planet and the resources it provides.

Stewardship

Throughout this chapter, you have seen that people—and all living organisms—can't live without Earth's resources. As in the past, living organisms of the future will also need Earth's resources to live—enough clean air, water, and food. As citizens of planet Earth, it is important to be good stewards of Earth's resources. A steward is a person who is put in charge of property for another.

Using Earth's Resources

Pre European | **1800s**

Native Americans found a use for every part of the animals they killed. They didn't waste resources. Instead, they took from nature only what they could use or needed to survive.

Many pioneers who settled the West in the 1800s had little regard for the future needs of others. They littered the land and killed buffalo nearly to the point of extinction.

Think about the last time you borrowed a library book. The librarian entrusted you with its care. For a short while, you were the steward of the book. You kept it in good condition so it could be used by others later.

You've also been entrusted with the care of Earth's resources. Just like you, the people born after you will want to live on a planet that is clean, safe, and beautiful. It is your duty as a steward to protect Earth's resources and make sure they will be available in sufficient amounts for future generations. Good **stewardship** means doing what you can to ensure the quality and quantity of Earth's resources for others who will follow you.

As resources are used, good stewards weigh the benefits of their use against the risks involved and make wise judgments. History has shown that people haven't always used Earth's resources wisely. Some people had great respect for nature's gifts. Others mistakenly thought that the supply of resources would last forever. The timeline on these pages shows the way people have used Earth's resources. It shows some events that are leading toward better stewardship. In the sections that follow, you will learn about simple things you can do to be a good steward.

Glossary

stewardship
(stü′ərd ship), the taking care of Earth's resources to ensure their quality and quantity for future generations

Glossary

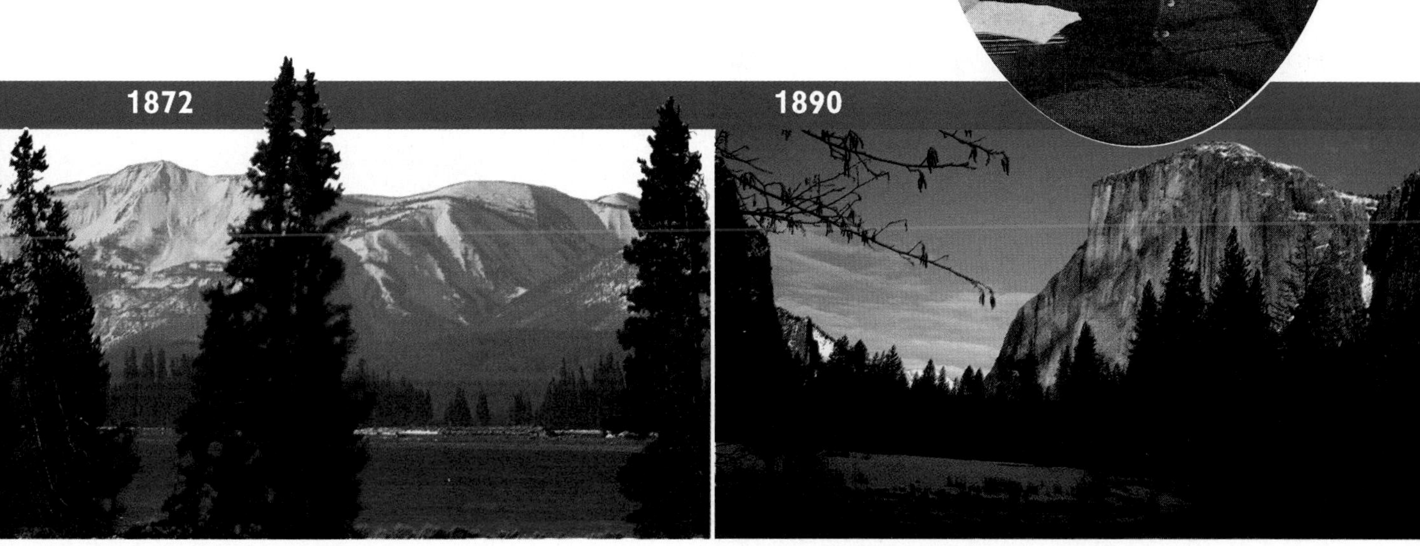

1872

The federal government recognized the need to preserve its natural wonders when in 1872 it established the country's first national park—Yellowstone. The National Park Service was established to manage and protect the park's wildlife.

1890

John Muir was an explorer, naturalist, and writer who campaigned for forest conservation in the U.S. His influence led to the establishment of Yosemite and Sequoia National Parks.

Glossary

Glossary

pollutant (pə lüt′ nt), harmful substance in the environment

Protecting Earth's Resources

At one time, most people lived as farmers or worked as craftspeople who made goods by hand. Then power-driven machines were developed and society changed. The population increased and people flocked to cities to work in factories. Farmland and forests gave way to large urban areas. Chemical fertilizers were used on remaining farmland to produce larger crops to feed the growing population. Exhaust and smoke from cars and factories became common.

As more fuel was burned, air pollution resulted from increased amounts of carbon dioxide and dirty particles being released into the air. Also, waste products were dumped into streams and onto the land. By the 1960s, groups of people began taking steps to fight the harmful substances, or **pollutants**, that were making air, water, and land resources unsafe to use. Pressure from these groups caused the government to pass laws to protect the environment. Since then, companies have also taken voluntary steps to reduce pollution.

Today automobiles have pollution control devices. Treatment plants operated by cities and factories remove human or chemical wastes from water before they are dumped into rivers or lakes. Factories and power plants use devices called scrubbers on their smokestacks to cut down on pollutants being released into the air.

1901

To discourage the waste of natural resources, President Theodore Roosevelt set aside land for national wildlife refuges and forest preserves.

1930

The Civilian Conservation Corps was set up to hire unemployed young men in the 1930s. The CCC planted trees, developed recreation areas, and did other conservation work.

1934

The Migratory Bird Hunting Stamp Act imposed a fee for hunting waterfowl. These and other hunting taxes have been used to buy land for habitat preservation.

It is important for both the nation and individuals to weigh the benefits and risks of actions that affect pollution. Some people are now saying that government environmental standards carry a high price tag. They worry that jobs are being lost to save the environment.

Another environmental debate is going on. More than 20 years ago, some scientists predicted that extra carbon dioxide building up in our atmosphere from human activity would trap more of the sun's heat on our planet. Some scientists have feared that this global warming would result in hot summers, warmer winters, and rising ocean levels. Now some scientists think that the knowledge about global warming is seriously incomplete. They argue that the predicted global warming is not occurring and think that government steps to reduce fuel emissions are not needed at this time.

Regardless of current debates, you can reduce pollution that comes from chemicals you use. Paints, cleaners, glues, and even products like hair spray can cause pollution. You can use biodegradable products that slowly disappear into the soil instead. People can also avoid polluting the environment by disposing of oil and hazardous chemicals properly at special collection sites.

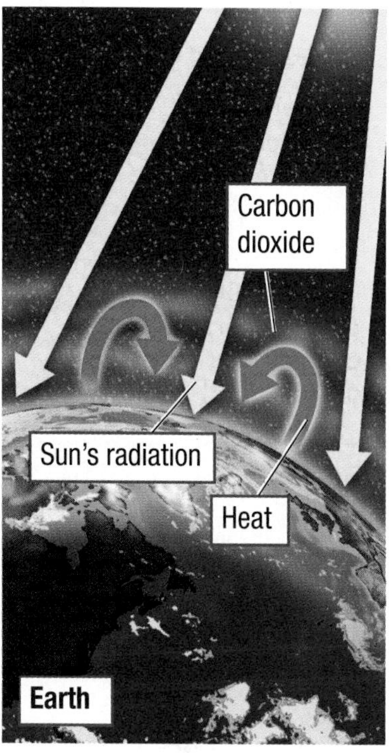

Global Warming

▲ *Some scientists think the huge amounts of carbon dioxide released into the atmosphere by human activity is trapping the sun's heat and causing global warming.*

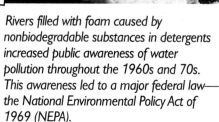

Twenty people were killed and 6,000 became ill from air pollution at a steel mill in Donora, Pennsylvania in 1948. As a result, people began to question the acceptance of air pollution for the sake of economic progress.

Rachel Carson's book Silent Spring *began the environmental movement. The book described pollution from pesticides and other chemicals.*

Rivers filled with foam caused by nonbiodegradable substances in detergents increased public awareness of water pollution throughout the 1960s and 70s. This awareness led to a major federal law—the National Environmental Policy Act of 1969 (NEPA).

Glossary

Glossary

conservation (kon′sər vā′shən), careful use of resources so they will last longer

alternative energy source (ôl tėr′nə tiv en ər jē sôrs), source of energy other than fossil fuels

Conserving Earth's Resources

Not only can resources be polluted, they can also be wasted. If a resource is nonrenewable, it will someday be used up. If a renewable resource is used more quickly than it is being replaced, it too can be used up. When resources are wasted, they disappear even more quickly. **Conservation** is the careful use of resources so that they will last longer.

Fossil fuels are used to make electricity. Therefore, one method of conserving fossil fuels is to reduce the use of energy in your home. Think about all the times you leave the television on when no one is watching. Lights are also left on when they are not needed. What are some other ways you could save energy in your home?

Gasoline can be conserved by riding a bicycle or public transportation instead of using a car. Carpooling is another way of saving gasoline. In carpooling, several people ride together instead of riding in separate cars.

You can also conserve fossil fuels by using other kinds of energy sources, called **alternative energy sources**, to generate electricity. As you learned earlier, in some areas wind energy and moving water can generate electricity. Geothermal energy, energy that comes from hot rock inside Earth, can be used to heat water to steam. The steam can then be used to turn generators.

1970

1970s

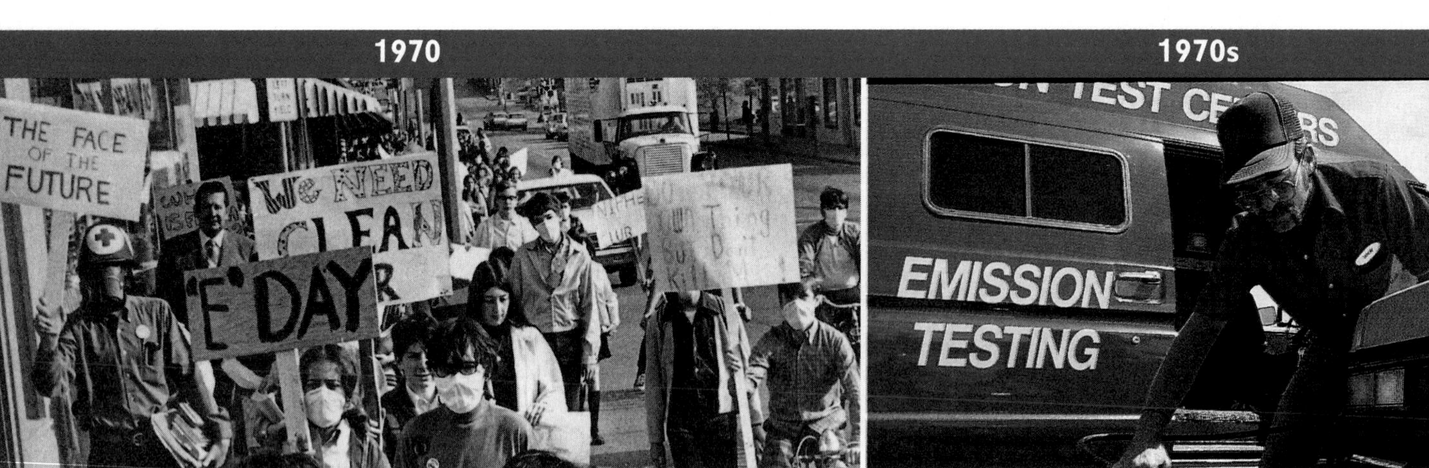

The celebration of the first Earth Day in 1970 helped spread public awareness of the need to save the Earth.

The state of the environment began to improve after passage of many environmental laws throughout the 1970s.

Solar energy is another alternative energy source that can be used to heat buildings in some places. Some homes are built so the sun shines in large windows during the winter. These windows are shaded during the summer. Other buildings have solar energy collectors like those on the building to the right that absorb and transfer heat to liquid flowing through pipes in the collectors. The liquid circulates through the building, releasing the heat. Also, solar cells can convert solar energy into electricity. You may have seen solar energy at work if you have ever used a solar-cell calculator.

Use of alternative energy sources may save fossil fuels, but they have limitations. Solar energy or wind power work only when the weather cooperates. Geothermal energy and tidal power work only in places where geothermal or tidal activity are present.

Another alternative energy source is nuclear power. Nuclear power uses the energy that comes when atoms of uranium or plutonium are split in a reactor. Nuclear reactors create electricity without the use of coal or oil. They do not pollute the air as fossil fuels do. However, the water that is used to cool nuclear power systems can cause thermal pollution in lakes or streams. Also, the dangerous, radioactive wastes produced by the reactors must be eventually dispersed into the environment.

Glossary

solar energy
(sō′lər en ər jē), radiant energy that comes from the sun

The sun heats water in coils beneath solar panels on the roof of this home. The heated water provides radiant heating as it circulates through the house and returns to the roof to be warmed again by the sun. ▼

Glossary

1980

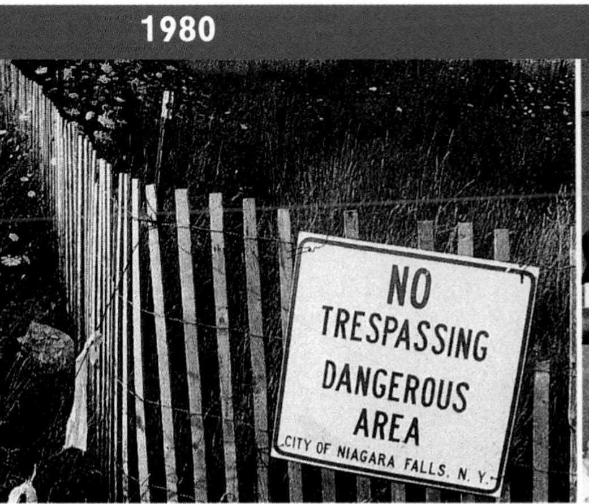

The pollution of a residential community built on top of the contaminated Love Canal near Niagara Falls, New York led to an increase of money for cleaning hazardous waste sites.

1997

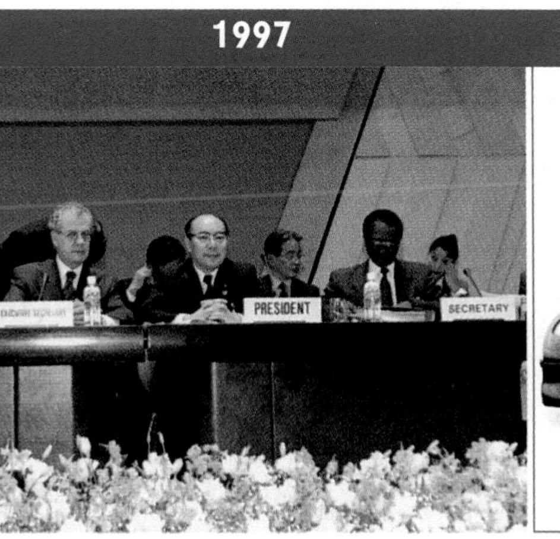

Representatives from different nations gathered in Kyoto, Japan to discuss global warming.

2000+

High-mileage electric cars that are virtually pollution-free may be developed as early as 2005. Fuel cells are being developed that use oxygen from the air and hydrogen to produce electricity.

Another method of conserving resources is to recycle them. Newspapers, aluminum, glass, and plastics are some resources being recycled. Some cities provide special recycling bins to homeowners. Trucks pick up the recyclable materials weekly and take them to recycling centers where materials are sorted. Other places have collection sites where people can take recyclable materials sorted at home. If your school doesn't have a recycling plan, you might develop one, like the students to the left.

These students are helping to conserve resources. ▼

Conservation also involves reusing or reducing solid wastes. For instance, instead of throwing away items you no longer use, they can be donated to thrift shops for others to use. You might also want to reduce land pollution by taking part in a community cleanup. Like the students to the left, you can set aside recyclables and take them to community recycling centers. Other trash can be taken to solid waste disposal sites.

Soil is another renewable resource that must be conserved. Wind or water erosion can remove soil that takes hundreds of years to form. To conserve soil, farmers plant crops in ways that prevent water from washing the soil away. They also plant trees along fields to prevent wind erosion.

People can conserve resources in many ways. You can do many things that will make a difference in resources now and in the future.

Lesson 4 Review

1. What is good stewardship?
2. How can people protect Earth's resources?
3. How can people conserve Earth's resources?
4. **Compare and Contrast**
   How has the use of Earth's resources changed in the last century?

Experimenting with Erosion Control

Materials

- 1 qt paper milk carton with one side cut away
- foil pan
- soil
- cup of water
- plastic spoon
- clock or timer
- 2 books
- 2 graduated cups
- newspaper

Process Skills

- formulating questions and hypotheses
- identifying and controlling variables
- experimenting
- observing
- estimating and measuring
- collecting and interpreting data
- communicating

State the Problem

Farmers try to reduce soil erosion and water runoff by plowing the soil in certain ways. Does the method of plowing affect the amount of water runoff from the soil?

Formulate Your Hypotheses

Look at Photos B and C to see two methods of plowing. If you use contour plowing on a hillside, will erosion be less, more, or the same as with terraced plowing? Write your **hypothesis.**

Identify and Control the Variables

The type of contouring is the **variable.** Two plowing methods will be used. Some groups will use contour plowing and other groups will use terraced plowing. Be sure to control all other variables.

Test Your Hypothesis

Follow these steps to perform an **experiment.**

1. Make a chart like the one on the next page. Use your chart to record your data.
2. Place a milk carton on its side, spout down and open, in a foil pan. Add 2½ cupfuls of soil to the milk carton. Slightly moisten the soil with water so that it sticks together and can be molded.
3. Use your hands to pack the soil so that the surface slopes from the back end of the milk carton toward the spout (Photo A).

Photo A

Continued →

Photo B

Photo C

4 Using a plastic spoon, carve indentations into the soil across the width of the milk carton according to your teacher's directions. Some groups will carve terraces (Photo B) and other groups will carve furrows (Photo C).

5 Allow the soil to dry for about 30 minutes.

6 Use several books to prop up a foil pan. Place the milk carton in the foil pan with the spout facing the lower end.

7 Measure 240 mL of water into a graduated cup. When the surface of the soil is firm to the touch, slowly pour the 240 mL of water down the slope of soil in the milk carton. **Observe** the setup while allowing it to remain undisturbed for 3 minutes. Record your observations in your chart.

8 Carefully remove the milk carton from the pan and place the milk carton on sheets of newspaper. Pour the water that has collected in the pan into a graduated cup. **Measure** the volume of the water. Record your data in your chart.

9 Observe the water's degree of cloudiness. The cloudiness of the water is an indication of the amount of erosion. Rate the water as slightly cloudy, moderately cloudy, or very cloudy. Record your data in your chart.

Collect Your Data

Type of plowing	Volume of runoff	Cloudiness of runoff

Interpret Your Data

1. Combine your data with that of other groups to make a data table. To interpret the data from all the groups, label two sheets of grid paper as shown. Use the data from the group chart to make two bar graphs that show the amount of erosion observed and the amount of runoff measured.

2. Study your bar graphs. Describe what happened in the "fields" with contour plowing compared with fields with terraced plowing. Which method of plowing resulted in less erosion? Which method resulted in less runoff?

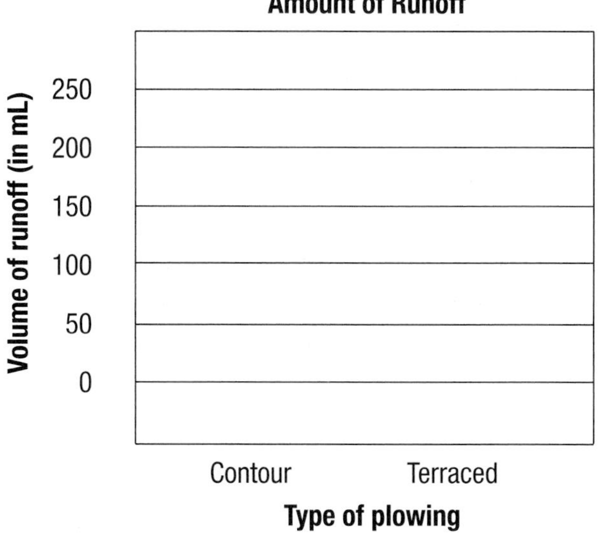

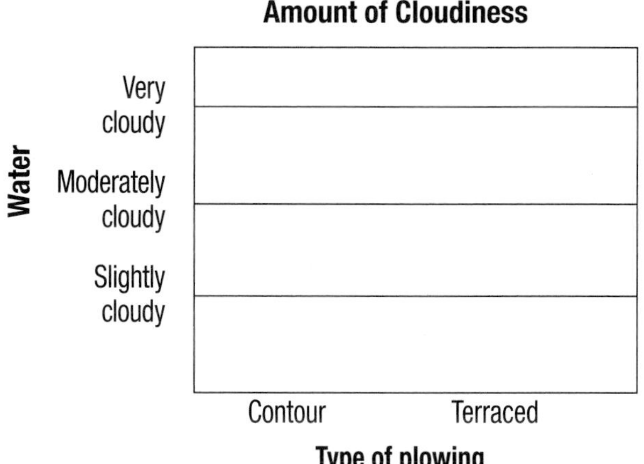

State Your Conclusion

Communicate your results. Was your hypothesis supported by the data? Explain how the plowing pattern in a sloping field might affect the amount of erosion and water runoff by the soil. Is one method of plowing superior to the other?

Inquire Further

If you added plants to the soil in the experiment, would the amounts of erosion and runoff increase, decrease, or remain the same? Develop a plan to answer this or other questions you may have.

Self-Assessment

- I made a **hypothesis** about how the pattern of plowing can affect the amount of soil erosion and water runoff in a sloping field.
- I identified and controlled **variables.**
- I followed instructions to perform an **experiment** to test methods of erosion control.
- I **observed** the degree of erosion and **measured** the amount of water runoff.
- I constructed bar graphs to help me interpret my **data.**

Chapter 4 Review

Chapter Main Ideas

Lesson 1

• Renewable resources can be replaced within a short time. Nonrenewable resources can't be replaced or are used up faster than their rate of replacement.

• Human use of resources can have positive and negative effects.

Lesson 2

• Air provides wind energy, as well as oxygen, carbon dioxide, and nitrogen, which living organisms need for their survival.

• The land provides minerals, fossil fuels, soil, and trees.

Lesson 3

• Water cycles through the land to the atmosphere and back again through the water cycle.

• Ocean resources include minerals, fossil fuels, and tidal energy, as well as living resources used for food and cosmetics.

• Fresh water is used for consumption, cleaning, manufacturing, and agriculture.

Lesson 4

• Good stewardship means doing what you can to ensure the quantity and quality of the earth's resources for others who will follow you.

• Individuals can protect the earth's resources by making wise judgments about resource use and pollution.

• People can conserve the earth's resources by reducing energy use, by using alternative energy sources, by reducing or reusing waste, and by preventing soil erosion.

Reviewing Science Words and Concepts

Write the letter of the word or phrase that best completes each sentence.

a. alternative energy source
b. conservation
c. fossil fuel
d. nodule
e. nonrenewable resource
f. ore
g. pollutant
h. renewable resource
i. reservoir
j. solar energy
k. stewardship
l. vent

1. A tree is an example of a(n) ___.
2. A resource that takes millions of years to form is a(n) ___.
3. Most minerals are found in ___.
4. A fuel that formed from the remains of buried plants and animals is a(n) ___.
5. A source of minerals from the ocean floor is a(n) ___.
6. Water rich in sulfur minerals escapes from an opening, called a(n) ___, in the ocean floor.
7. A large artificial lake that holds a supply of fresh water is a(n) ___.
8. Making sure that future generations have sufficient resources is good ___.
9. A harmful substance that is dumped into a lake is a ___.
10. Using resources in a way that makes them last longer is ___.

11. Geothermal energy is an example of a(n) ____.

12. The radiant energy that comes from the sun is ____.

Explaining Science

Create a poster or write a paragraph that answers each question.

1. How do humans hurt and help the earth's resources?

2. How do people depend on the earth's air and land?

3. Why is water considered a resource?

4. What can individuals do to save and protect the earth's resources?

Using Skills

1. Make a poster that **compares** and **contrasts** the effects of good and poor stewardship of the earth's resources.

2. **Formulate questions** you might ask a candidate for office to determine if he or she supports stewardship.

3. **Collect and interpret data** on the use of resources in your classroom or school to determine whether people at your school are good stewards of the environment.

Critical Thinking

1. Suppose a construction company wanted to build a new shopping center across the street from your home. What information would you like to know before you could **evaluate** how you feel about the construction?

2. List three things you can do to be a good steward of the earth's resources. Practice these ideas for one week. Then identify and **solve any problems** you may have had.

3. **Sequence** the events in the carbon cycle by writing them in numbered steps.

Unit C Review

Reviewing Words and Concepts

Choose at least three words from the Chapter 1 list below. Use the words to write a paragraph about how these concepts are related. Do the same for each of the other chapters.

Chapter 1
air mass
air pressure
barometer
Doppler radar
forecast
meteorologist

Chapter 2
aquifer
fault
focus
groundwater
lithosphere
water table

Chapter 3
auroras
equinox
fusion
solar flares
solstice
sunspots

Chapter 4
fossil fuel
nonrenewable resources
ore
pollutants
stewardship
vents

Reviewing Main Ideas

Each of the statements below is false. Change the underlined word or words to make each statement true.

1. Relative humidity is the point at which the air contains as much water vapor as it can hold.
2. Psychrometers are instruments used to measure wind speed.
3. A tornado is a large tropical storm over warm water.
4. Mountain ranges may be produced at a fault boundary.
5. A moraine is a large mass of slowly moving ice carrying sediment.
6. The earth takes a year to rotate around the sun.
7. During a solar eclipse, the earth lies between the sun and the moon.
8. A solar flare is a region on the sun with a strong magnetic field.
9. Ores containing precious metals are a renewable resource.
10. Conservation means taking care of Earth's resources for future generations.

Interpreting Data

The relative humidity is obtained by using the difference between temperatures shown on a dry thermometer and one whose bulb is covered by a damp cloth. The table shows the relative humidity at several temperatures.

Relative Humidity Table (shown in %)

Dry bulb	Difference between wet and dry bulb readings (°C)				
°C	1	2	3	4	5
10	88	77	66	55	44
11	89	78	67	56	46
12	89	78	68	58	48
13	89	79	69	59	50
14	90	79	70	60	51

1. If the dry bulb reads 13°C and the wet bulb reads 9°C, what is the relative humidity?

2. If the relative humidity is 55%, what are the wet and dry bulb readings?

3. How do you know that the wet bulb temperature is always lower than the dry bulb temperature?

Communicating Science

1. Write a paragraph explaining the relationships among air pressure, air temperature, and relative humidity.

2. Draw a diagram and write a paragraph that explains how and why the soil profile in various parts of the country may be different.

3. Draw and label a diagram showing how it can be summer at one location on the earth while it is winter at another location.

4. Make a table that gives examples of renewable and non-renewable resources from air, water, and land.

Applying Science

1. Write a paragraph describing the major weather conditions shown on the weather map below.

2. Write a diary entry about what it would be like to live on a space station. Try to include activities that you do in everyday life. Describe how these activities are different on the space station.

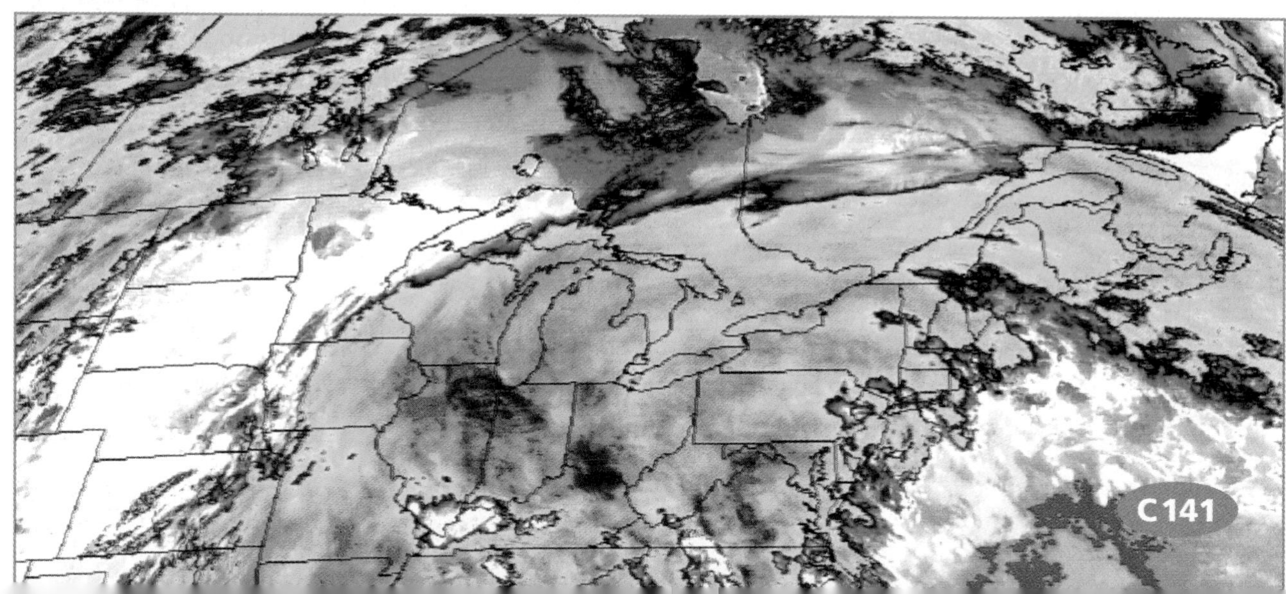

Unit C Performance Review

Planetarium

Using what you learned in this unit, help prepare exhibits and presentations for an Earth in the Universe Day to be held in your school. Complete one or more of the following activities. You may work by yourself or in a group.

Role-Playing

Working with other students, perform a demonstration showing how the phases of the moon are produced and observed. Have a student with a flashlight play the sun, another the earth, and another the moon. Plan how you will move so that an observer will understand why we see different moon phases during the month. Have a student narrate the demonstration.

Art

Make and label clay models showing the similarities and differences among fault boundaries, spreading boundaries, and colliding boundaries. Display your models with pictures of locations on Earth where such boundaries exist. Be prepared to explain your models.

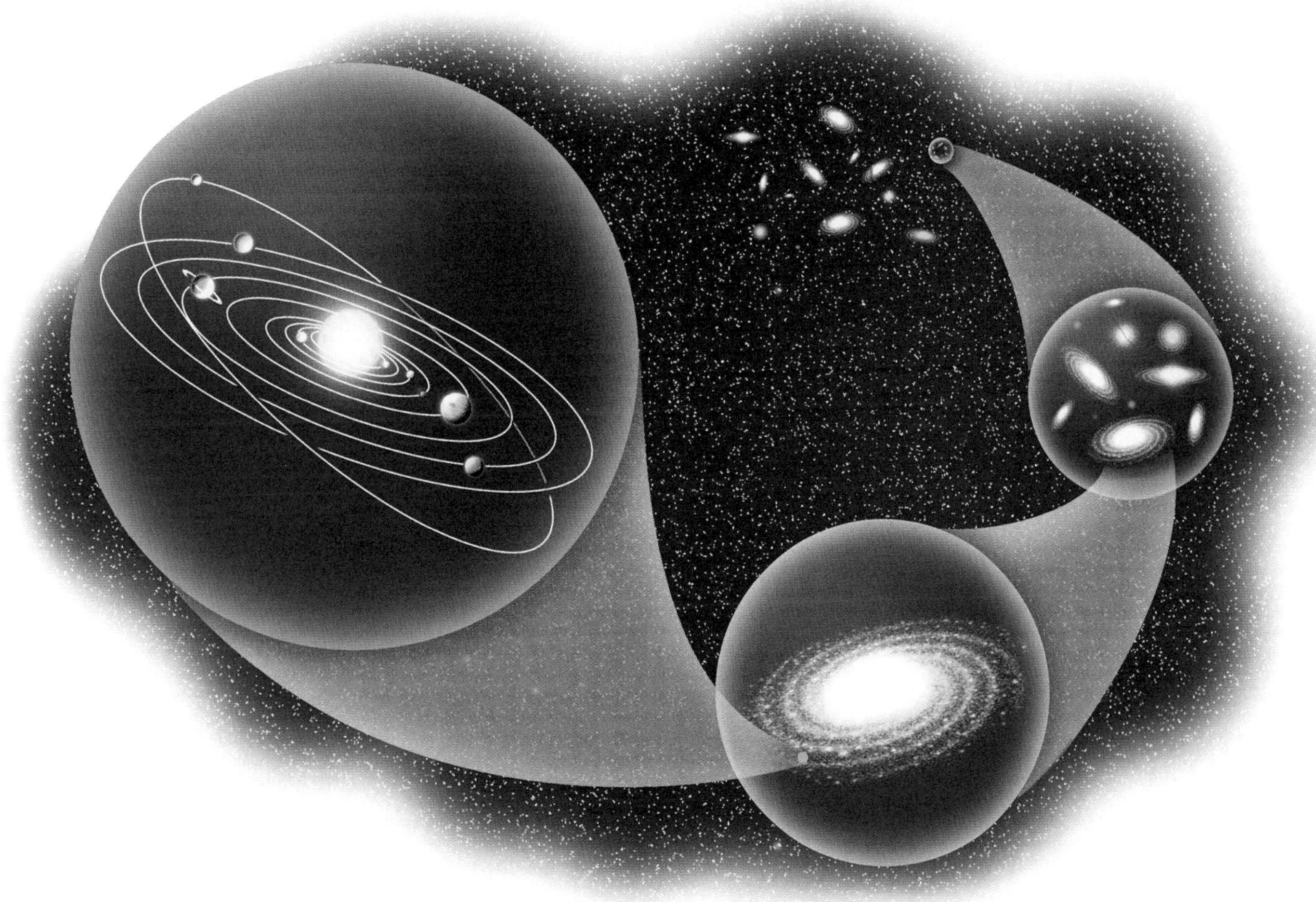

Mathematics

Prepare a scale model of the solar system. You will need to know the distances between the planets and the sun. Draw the planets in a way as to indicate their relative sizes.

Stewardship

Find out what stewardship efforts are being made in your community. Include efforts by government, industry, agriculture, or groups of concerned citizens. Organize a group of students to participate in one or more of the existing activities or develop one of your own.

Music

Research music, both classical and popular, written about stars and planets. For example, in a suite of music by Gustav Holst called *The Planets,* each of the seven movements is related to one of the planets. Find a number of songs about the sun, moon, stars, and planets. Plan a narration that ties the music together and prepare a presentation.

Using Reference Sources

You can use many different kinds of reference sources to do research. For example, to find the meaning of a word you may look in a dictionary. If you want to learn more about something you studied in school, you may read a book, an encyclopedia entry, or a newspaper or magazine article.

A great deal of information can be found on the World Wide Web. The National Aeronautics and Space Administration (NASA) has a popular Web site that provides a great deal of information about the exploration of space.

Go On-Line

In Chapter 3, you learned about some of the ways people explore space. To learn more about the history of the American space program, use a computer to contact the NASA Web site at the following address: http://www.nasa.gov.

As you surf through the site, list the names and dates of five space missions in which NASA has participated. Include details about the type of spacecraft used for each mission and a brief description of each mission's goals. If you need more information about a mission that interests you, try contacting NASA by e-mail to find what you need.

Write a Summary

Review the information you found on-line. Use this information to write a summary about two space missions you found particularly interesting. Be sure to include a main idea sentence and supporting details in each paragraph of your summary.

Remember to:

1. **Prewrite** Organize your thoughts before you write.
2. **Draft** Make an outline and write your summary.
3. **Revise** Share your work and then make changes.
4. **Edit** Proofread for mistakes and fix them.
5. **Publish** Share your summary with your class.

Unit D

Human Body

Your Science Handbook

Science and Technology

In Your World!

Robots that Sense Temperature

Today's body part replacements, called prostheses, use advances from robotics and electronics to make them feel and work as naturally as possible. For example, sensors can pick up information about temperature or texture and transfer it to the skin. Learn how information travels through the body in **Chapter 1 Your Body's Control Systems.**

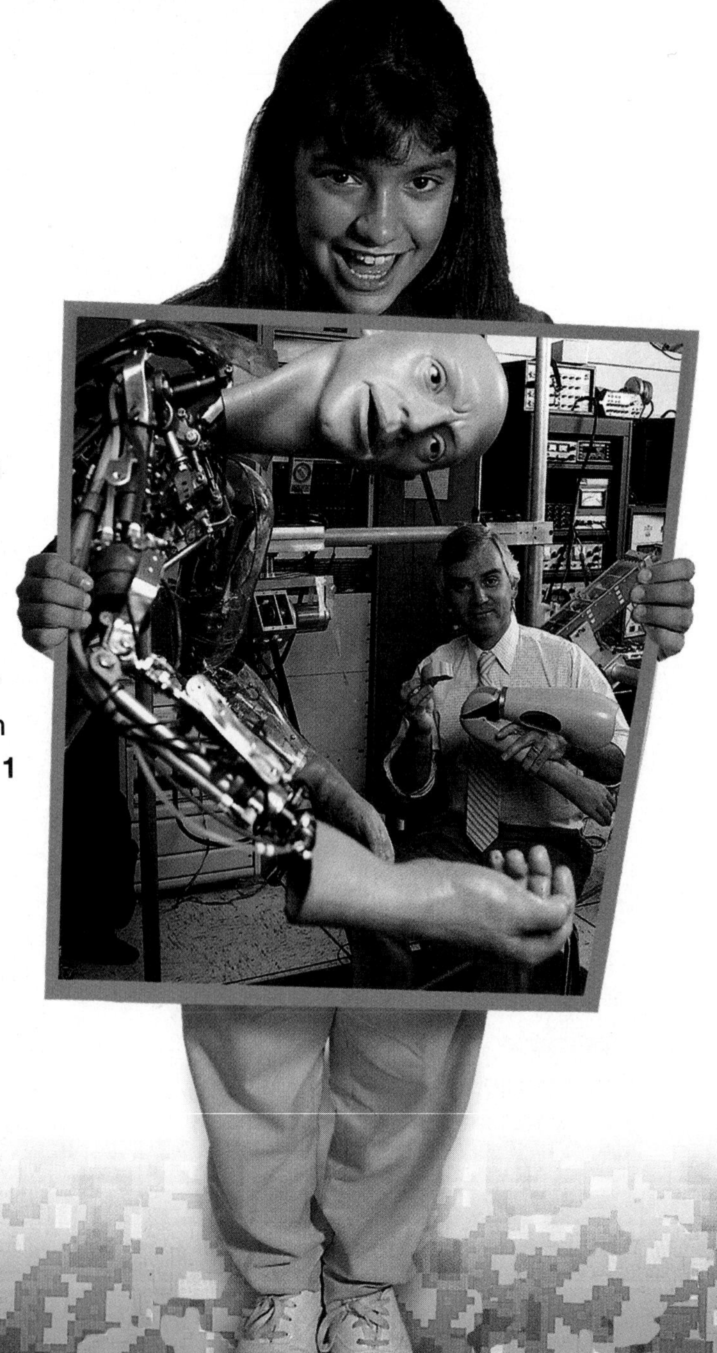

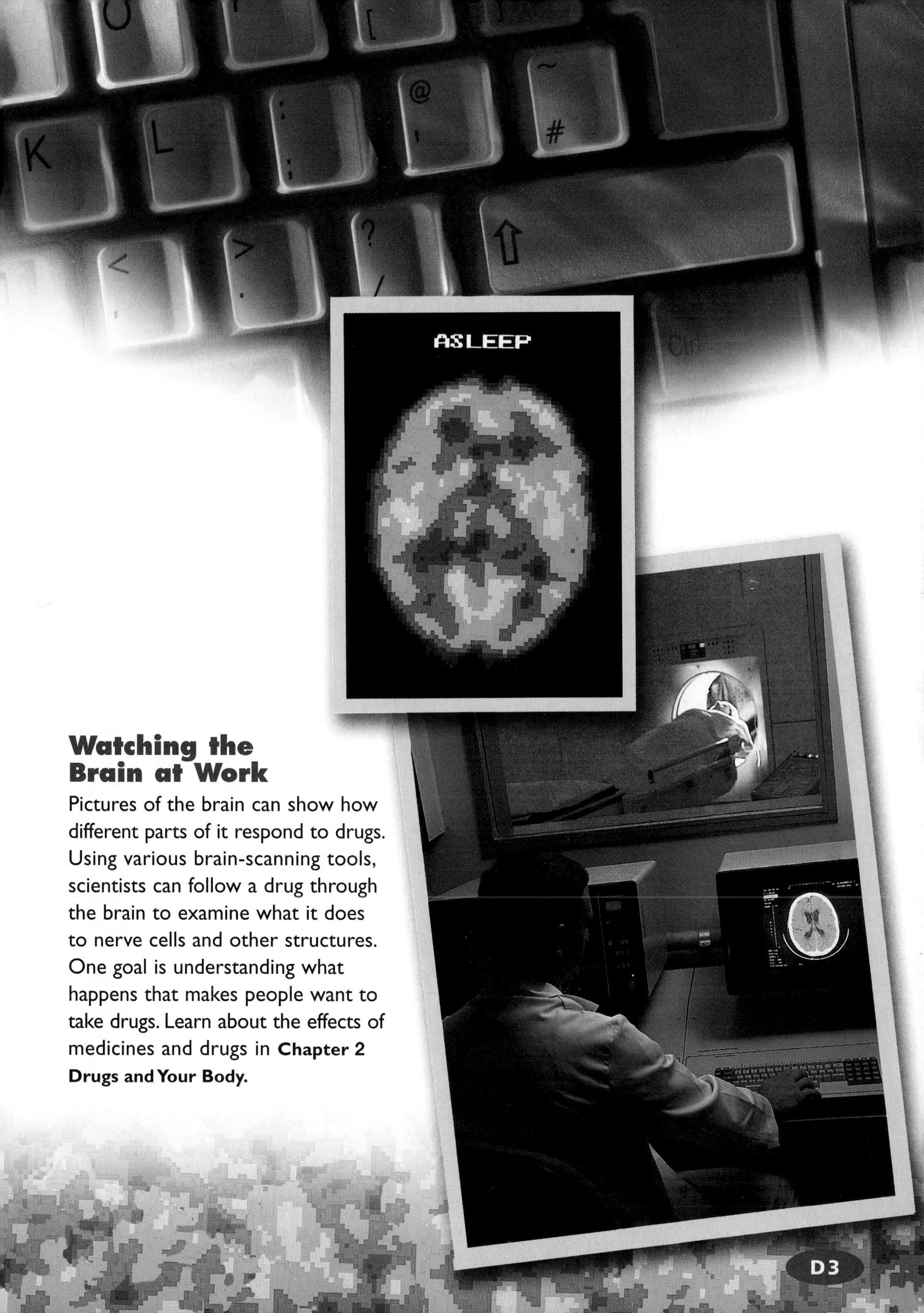

Watching the Brain at Work

Pictures of the brain can show how different parts of it respond to drugs. Using various brain-scanning tools, scientists can follow a drug through the brain to examine what it does to nerve cells and other structures. One goal is understanding what happens that makes people want to take drugs. Learn about the effects of medicines and drugs in **Chapter 2 Drugs and Your Body.**

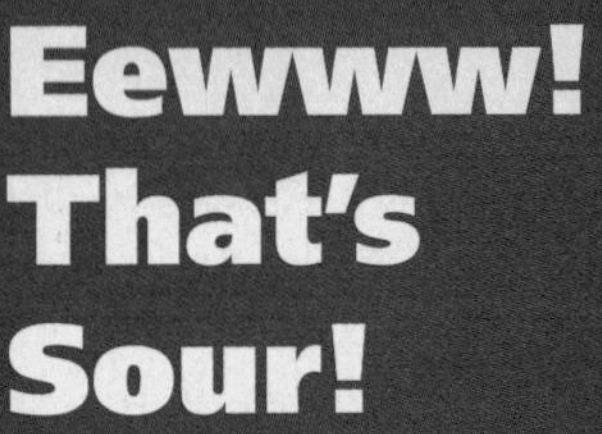

Eewww! That's Sour!

Just the thought of a lemon's sour taste can be enough to make your face pucker! It's amazing how fast your body responds to the world around it.

Chapter 1

Your Body's Control Systems

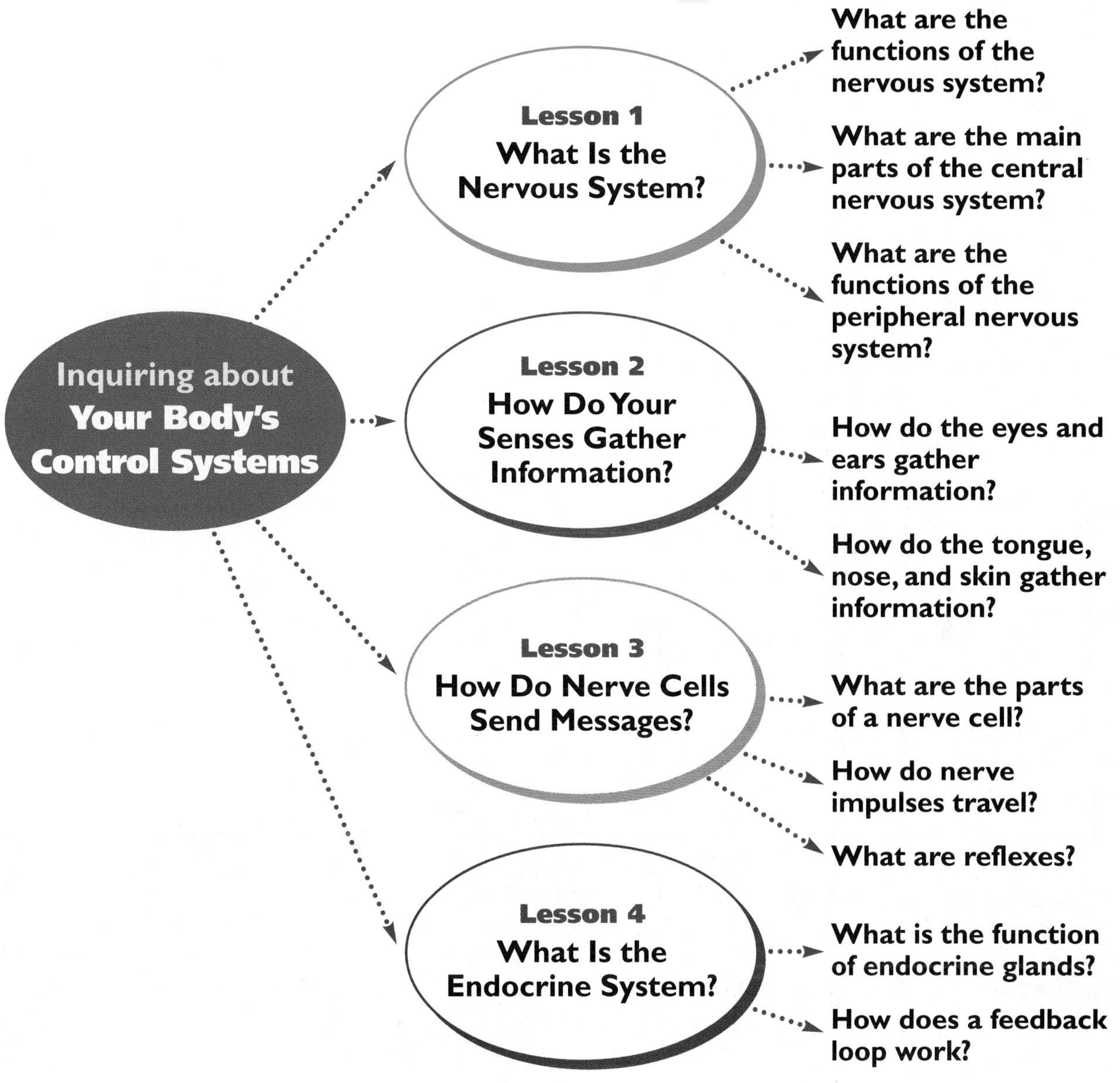

Inquiring about Your Body's Control Systems
Lesson 1
What Is the Nervous System?
What are the functions of the nervous system?
What are the main parts of the central nervous system?
What are the functions of the peripheral nervous system?
Lesson 2
How Do Your Senses Gather Information?
How do the eyes and ears gather information?
How do the tongue, nose, and skin gather information?
Lesson 3
How Do Nerve Cells Send Messages?
What are the parts of a nerve cell?
How do nerve impulses travel?
What are reflexes?
Lesson 4
What Is the Endocrine System?
What is the function of endocrine glands?
How does a feedback loop work?

***Copy the chapter graphic organizer** onto your own paper. This organizer shows you what the whole chapter is all about. As you read the lessons and do the activities, look for answers to the questions and write them on your organizer.*

Exploring Reaction Time

Process Skills

Process Skills

- observing
- predicting
- inferring
- communicating

Materials

- half-meter stick

Explore

1. Hold your hand open as shown in the photo. Ask your partner to suspend the half-meter stick above your hand. The 0-cm mark should be even with your hand, as shown in the photo.

2. Closely **observe** the half-meter stick. When your partner lets go of the half-meter stick, try to catch it in your hand.

3. Read the number closest to the top of your thumb. Record that number.

4. What will happen if you repeat the activity for nine more trials? Record your **prediction.**

5. Repeat steps 2–4 for nine more trials. Each time, record the number on the half-meter stick.

6. Repeat steps 2–5 until each group member has tested his or her reaction time.

Reflect

1. Make an **inference.** What does your data show about reaction time and the number of trials?

2. Communicate. Compare your data to those of other members of the group. Decide if others' data support your inference.

Inquire Further

Suppose you continued the activity for 50 trials. How do you think your reaction time would change? Develop a plan to answer this or other questions you may have.

Rate

The brain, the control center of the body, begins to develop before birth. In an unborn child, it adds 1,250,000 nerve cells—also called neurons—every 5 minutes. The **rate** 1,250,000 neurons/5 minutes compares the number of neurons to the number of minutes. This rate can be read "1,250,000 neurons *per* 5 minutes."

If the comparison is to 1 unit (1 minute instead of 5 minutes), the rate is called a **unit rate**.

$$\frac{1{,}250{,}000}{5 \text{ minutes}} = \frac{250{,}000}{1 \text{ minutes}}$$

The unit rate is 250,000 neurons per minute.

Math Vocabulary

rate, a ratio in which two quantities with different units of measure are compared

unit rate, a rate in which the second number in the comparison is one unit

Example

The ears send sensory impulses to the brain. One of the highest frequencies the human ear can detect is from the violin. It produces 100,000 vibrations in 5 seconds. What is the rate of vibrations per second?

The rate that compares 100,000 vibrations with 5 seconds is 100,000 vibrations/ 5 seconds.

If you divide both numbers by 5, you get the unit rate of 20,000 vibrations/ 1 second.

Talk About It!

How can you tell if a rate is a unit rate?

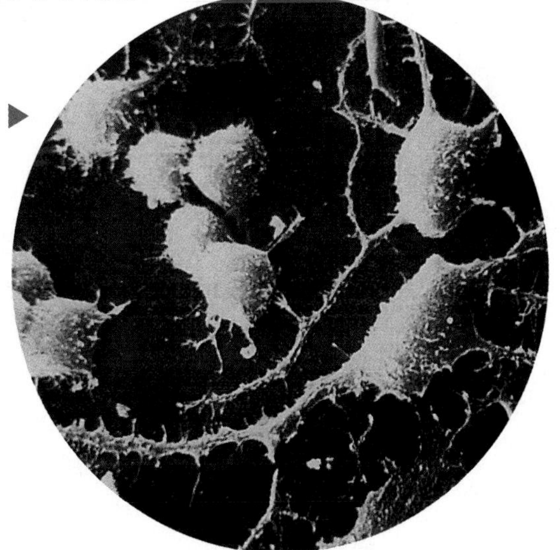
Nerve cells ▶

Did you know?

At birth, the human brain has the most nerve cells it will have during a person's life—20 billion to 200 billion.

You will learn:

- what the functions of the nervous system are.
- what the main parts of the central nervous system are.
- what the functions of the peripheral nervous system are.

Lesson 1

What Is the Nervous System?

"Hey! You've got your nerve!" Let's hope so! Nerves inside your body are like telephone lines that carry information back and forth between you and the outside world. How do they do it?

Functions of the Nervous System

During a typical school day, you look, read, listen, think, speak, write, breathe, eat, and play. Different parts of your body take part in each of these actions. For example, your eyes, arms, hands, and fingers work together to help you write. Your eyes, ears, arms, hands, legs, and feet help you play baseball. It's the job of your nervous system to make sure all these body parts work together correctly.

To do this job, your nervous system continuously collects information from inside and outside your body. It acts as your body's control center as it processes the information. The nervous system sends signals to your muscles to act, and it stores some information as memories. The nervous system also exchanges messages with your internal organs, which keeps them working properly.

Information travels to and from the nervous system at the same time, like a two-lane highway. For example, in the picture, the boy gathered information through his eyes about the flying disk. That information traveled to his brain. His brain immediately sent messages to his arms and hands, allowing him to catch the disk before it hit the ground. Just think how fast those signals had to travel. Some nerve signals travel as fast as 100 meters per second!

This boy's nervous system analyzes information about the disk and enables him to act to catch it. ▼

Your nervous system is made up of nerve cells called **neurons**. The nerves in your body are bundles of neurons. Neurons are similar to other cells in the body, but neurons also contain parts that allow them to communicate with one another. Neurons differ in size, shape, and function, depending on where they are located in your body.

Your nervous system has two main parts: the **central nervous system** (CNS) and the **peripheral nervous system** (PNS). The central nervous system is made up of the brain and the spinal cord. The peripheral nervous system is made up of neurons and other structures that connect the central nervous system with all other parts of the body.

As the girl shown below plays volleyball, the PNS gathers and sends information to her spinal cord and brain about what she sees and feels. The CNS processes the information that comes from the player's body parts and sends back information about what to do next. The PNS receives this information and signals the player's body to move properly.

The peripheral nervous system also connects internal organs, such as the stomach and the heart, to the central nervous system. Remember that the nervous system controls what goes on inside your body as well as how you respond to your environment.

Glossary

neuron (nür′on), a nerve cell

central nervous system (sen′trəl nėr′vəs sis′təm), part of the nervous system that consists of the brain and the spinal cord

peripheral nervous system (pə rif′ər əl nėr′vəs sis′təm), part of the nervous system that connects the central nervous system with all other parts of the body

Nervous System

◀ *You might think of the central nervous system as "the boss" and the peripheral nervous system as "the workers." The workers tell the boss what is happening, and the boss directs the workers what to do next.*

Glossary

Glossary

cerebrum (sə rē′brəm), the part of the brain that controls thinking and voluntary movements and receives information from the senses

cerebellum (ser′ə bel′əm), the part of the brain that coordinates movements and helps maintain balance

Central Nervous System

The boy in the picture is playing the flute. However, at the exact same time, he might also be smelling popcorn, tapping his foot, and thinking about his soccer game. All of these actions are controlled by the body's "boss," the brain. The brain is made up of about 100 billion neurons and trillions of other supporting cells. Although the brain makes up only 2 percent of your body's weight, it uses about 20 percent of your body's energy.

Look at the parts of the brain shown in the picture on the next page. Find the largest part of the brain, the **cerebrum** . It looks like the wrinkled halves of a walnut. The cerebrum is the part of the brain that allows you to think. It lets you play computer games, remember phone numbers, solve problems, and imagine stories. The cerebrum also interprets information from your senses. It lets you know what a bird looks like and what a flower smells like.

Part of the cerebrum controls voluntary, or conscious, movements of your body, such as lifting a book or combing your hair. The left half of the cerebrum controls movement of the right side of your body, and the right half of the cerebrum controls movement of the left side.

At the back of the brain, below the cerebrum, is the **cerebellum**, which means "little brain." The cerebellum is the part of the brain that coordinates your movements and helps you keep your balance. Some scientists think that the cerebellum also helps you do some things automatically, such as speaking or riding your bike, so you can think about other things at the same time.

This boy's cerebellum coordinates the movements of his hands, fingers, and eyes. ▶

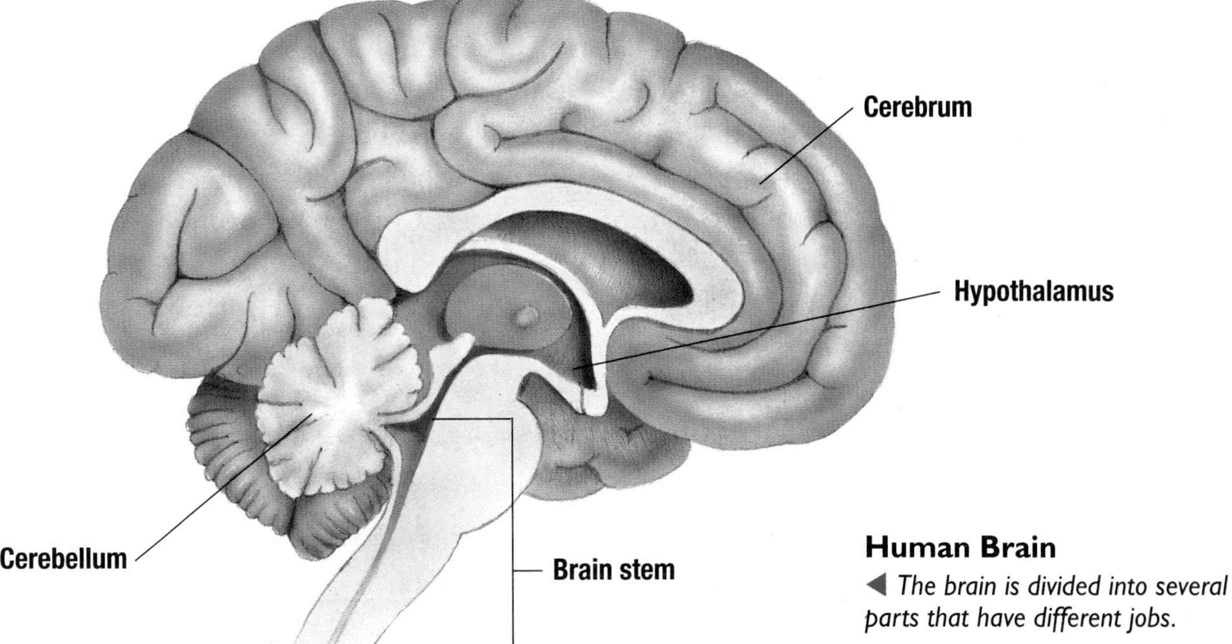

Human Brain

◀ *The brain is divided into several parts that have different jobs.*

Another small but important part of the brain is the **brain stem,** which lies below the cerebrum and in front of the cerebellum. The brain stem controls involuntary actions—functions such as breathing that must be performed to keep you alive. Wouldn't it be confusing if you had to remind your heart to pump blood or your stomach to digest a meal while you did other things? The brain stem takes care of all that. In addition, it connects the brain to the spinal cord.

About the size of a pea, the **hypothalamus** functions as the body's inner thermostat. It keeps your body temperature within the correct range by controlling such responses as shivering and sweating. The hypothalamus wakes you up in the morning and controls hunger and thirst. It also sends messages back and forth to the body system that controls molecules that make you feel emotions, such as excitement, anger, or happiness.

Feel the hard bones of your spinal column. These hard bones protect your **spinal cord.** The spinal cord is a long bundle of neurons that carries messages between the brain and different parts of the body. The spinal cord has over 13 million neurons. It runs about two-thirds of the way down your back through the spinal column. Neurons branch off the spinal cord to your arms, legs, and other parts of the body.

Glossary

brain stem (brān stem), part of the brain that controls involuntary actions, such as breathing; connects the brain to the spinal cord

hypothalamus (hī′pō thal′ə məs), part of the brain that controls body temperature, hunger, thirst, and emotions

spinal cord (spī′nl kord), bundle of neurons that carries messages back and forth between the brain and the rest of the body

Glossary

sensory receptor
(sen′sər ē ri sep′tər), cell within the peripheral nervous system that gathers information from the environment and from inside the body

Because it is so important to your health and well-being, the soft, gelatinlike brain must be protected from injury. Three materials surround the brain to protect it. Do you know what these materials are? You probably guessed that the bones of your skull are one. The others are a fluid in which the brain floats and a thick tissue surrounding the fluid. The spinal cord is protected by the fluid, tissue, and bones of the spine.

Even with all this protection, a hard blow to the head can cause the brain to bounce against the skull and be injured. This kind of injury might make a person stop breathing, lose consciousness, become blind, or suffer memory loss. Damage to the spinal cord can leave a person unable to feel or move certain body parts—to become paralyzed—or to have problems with internal organs.

Fortunately, you can do things to help protect yourself from brain and spinal cord injury. For example, remember to wear safety equipment, such as the helmet worn by Sammy Sosa in the picture, when participating in sports or working in unsafe areas. Wear seat belts when riding in a car. Never dive into a shallow pool or lake head first.

Peripheral Nervous System

Think about all the things you are sensing right now. While your eyes are seeing these words, can you hear papers rustling or the sound of your own breathing? How do your clothes feel against your body? What smells or tastes are you aware of? All these sensations are possible because of **sensory receptors** within your peripheral nervous system. Sensory receptors are cells that gather information from the environment and from inside your body. Millions of sensory receptors in your skin, eyes, muscles, tendons, and internal organs are sensitive to different conditions, such as temperature, pressure changes, pain, light, chemicals, vibrations, and larger body movements.

Sammy Sosa's helmet helps protect his brain from injury. Sammy Sosa was the 1997 Most Valuable Player for the National League. ▼

Information gathered by sensory receptors is picked up by **sensory neurons**—nerve cells of the peripheral nervous system that carry information from sensory receptors to the brain and spinal cord. The neurons don't actually move. They send information by passing it from one sensory neuron to another until it reaches the central nervous system.

Once the brain knows what's out there, what happens next? The brain processes the signals from the sensory neurons. It decides what needs to be done, and sends back a message telling the body what action to take. These messages travel through cells called **motor neurons**. Motor neurons carry messages from the brain and spinal cord to skeletal muscles and to organs, such as the heart and stomach. Motor neurons tell the body to produce many different kinds of movement. For example, they can cause an eye to blink and the heart to pump blood faster.

Look at the picture of the girl. What kinds of information do you think are being carried by her sensory neurons? What messages might be carried by her motor neurons?

Glossary

sensory neuron
(sen′sər ē nür′on), nerve cell in the peripheral nervous system that carries information from sensory receptors to the CNS

motor neuron
(mō′tər nür on), nerve cell in the peripheral nervous system that carries information from the CNS to muscles and organs

Messages carried by sensory and motor neurons enable this girl to eat and enjoy her food. ▶

Lesson 1 Review

1. What are the functions of the nervous system?
2. What are the main parts of the central nervous system?
3. What are the functions of the peripheral nervous system?
4. **Compare and Contrast**
   Compare and contrast the central nervous system and the peripheral nervous system.

You will learn:

- how the eyes and ears gather information.
- how the tongue, nose, and skin gather information.

Lesson 2

How Do Your Senses Gather Information?

"I see what you're saying." Huh? We can't "see" a sound. Yet when we communicate, we often use words describing our senses. What are senses?

Eyes and Ears

When a number of sensory receptors work together to collect a certain kind of information such as light, odor, taste, touch, or sound, they form a sense organ. Messages from each of these organs travel to a particular part of the brain that can process those messages.

You've probably looked into a mirror often and seen your eyes. What you see is actually only a small part of these sense organs. As you can see in the picture, the **retina** is a layer of light receptors at the back of the eye. The retina has four types of receptors. Three of the receptor types are cones. Each type of cone is sensitive to one of the three primary colors of light—red, blue, or green.

Rods are the fourth type of light receptor. Rods are sensitive to light and dark, shape, and movement. They can work in much lower levels of light than cones can. "Rod vision" occurs when light is dim, such as in the evening. Rods allow you to see objects clearly, but with little color.

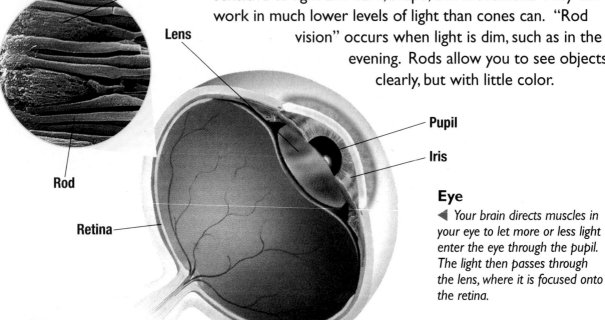

Glossary

Glossary

retina (ret′nə), an area at the back of the eye that contains sensory receptors for light

Rods and Cones

There are more cones near the center of the retina and more rods around the edges. Thus, you can see better at night if you look at things out of the "corner" of your eye. ▼

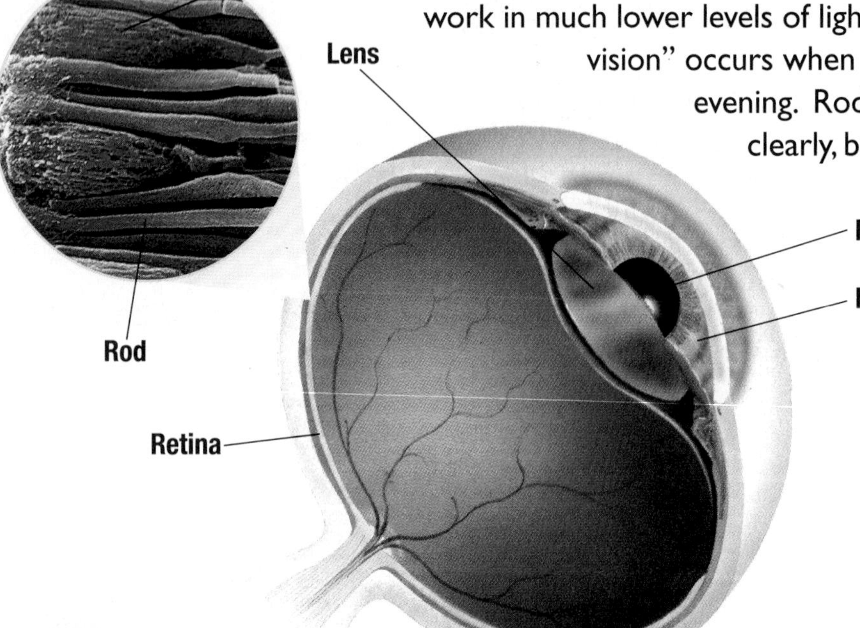

Eye

◀ *Your brain directs muscles in your eye to let more or less light enter the eye through the pupil. The light then passes through the lens, where it is focused onto the retina.*

Recall that sound travels as waves. Sensory receptors in your ears are sensitive to these sound waves. You can see the parts of the ear in the picture below. Sound waves in the air enter the outer ear and make the eardrum vibrate. Three tiny bones in the middle ear pass the vibrations along to the inner ear, where they enter a snail-shaped structure. This structure contains tiny hair cells of different lengths. As these hairs vibrate, the hair cells send a message by way of the auditory nerve to the hearing, or auditory, part of the brain. This part of the brain identifies the sound.

In addition to helping the girl to the right hear, the inner ear helps the girl keep her balance. It contains fluid-filled tubes with hair cells that sense the position of her head. The cells send messages to her brain, which then controls her body movements to keep her balanced.

Hair cells in this girl's inner ear help her stay balanced. ▼

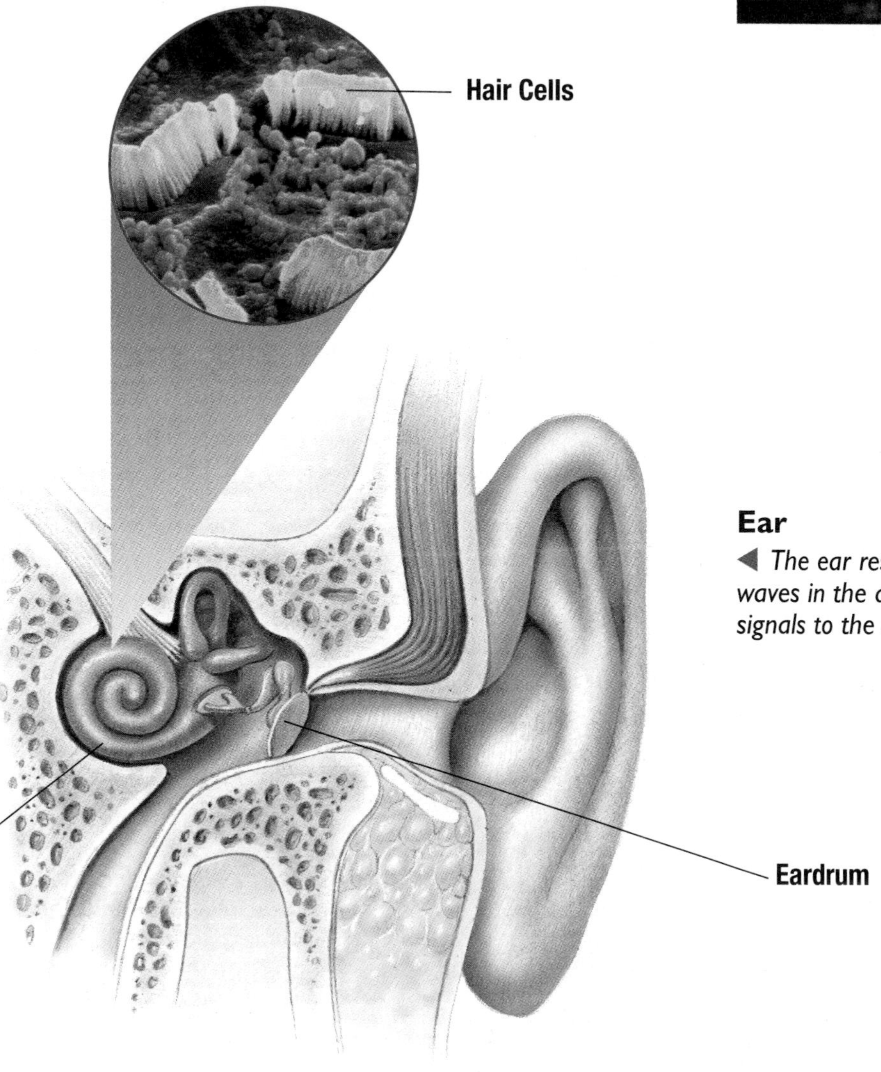

Hair Cells

Inner ear

Eardrum

Ear

◀ *The ear responds to sound waves in the air and sends nerve signals to the brain.*

The Tongue, Nose, and Skin

▲ *Molecules from this orange travel through the air. When these molecules come in contact with sense organs in your nose, you smell the orange's fragrance.*

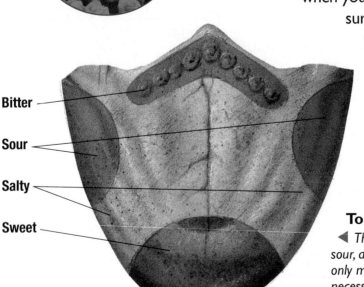

Believe it or not, tiny hair cells in your nose are the sensory receptors for smell. Scientists think that when molecules from your favorite food drift through the air and into your nose, the hair cells respond to either the shape or the electric charge of the molecules. When the brain receives signals from the nose, it identifies the smell so that you can recognize it.

The sense of taste is closely linked with the sense of smell. To experience this yourself, try holding your nose while you taste an orange. Chances are that the orange will taste sour, but it won't have the flavor of an orange. Taste buds on your tongue are sensitive only to four main tastes—sweet, sour, salty, and bitter. Find the location of each of these taste areas in the picture of the tongue below. Your brain combines the sour taste of the orange with its odor, and you can identify the flavor of the fruit.

What's tough, washable, stretchy, waterproof, covers your whole body, and keeps your insides in? Skin—the largest organ in your body. Skin contains different kinds of sensory receptors that are sensitive to temperature changes, pressure changes, pain, and vibrations.

Some skin receptors send their messages slowly, such as ones that react to an ongoing situation—your clothes touching your body, for example. Other skin receptors send messages quickly, such as when you touch your finger to a hot surface. These messages allow you to react immediately, pulling your finger away before it is badly burned.

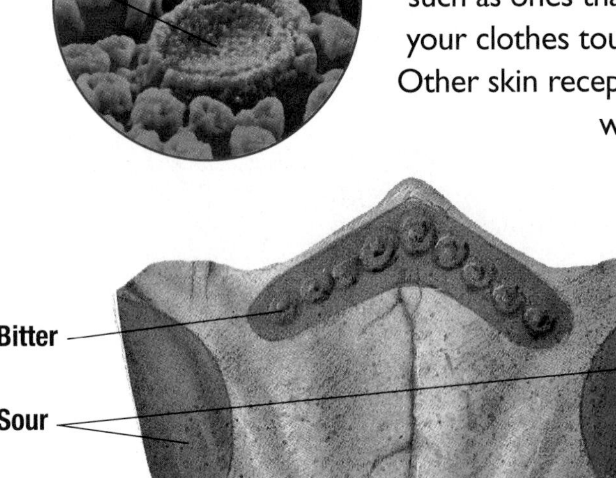

Tongue

◀ *The tongue is sensitive to sweet, salty, sour, and bitter tastes. The sense of taste not only makes eating more interesting, it also is necessary for survival. It warns you against what is not good to eat.*

Hearing

Humans hear sounds between 20 and 20,000 cycles per second, or hertz. The higher the number of hertz, the higher is the pitch of the sound. As people get older, their range of hearing may get smaller.

Vision

The human eye is sensitive to a very small part of the electromagnetic spectrum. About 6,000,000 cone cells and 120,000,000 rod cells in each eye respond to the visible light part of the spectrum.

Smell

Humans have about 40 million smell receptors. Humans can distinguish between 3,000 and 10,000 different odors. People can identify some smells when just one molecule is present in a trillion.

Touch

A human adult's skin weighs from six to ten pounds and covers about 2 square meters. Some parts of the skin, such as the fingertips, contain many more receptors than do other parts, such as the back of the neck.

Taste

The human tongue has about 9,000 taste buds. Bitter tastes register 10,000 times more strongly than sweet ones.

Lesson 2 Review

1. How do the eyes and ears gather information?
2. How do the tongue, nose, and skin gather information?
3. **Rate**
   Which sound would have a higher pitch—one with 300 cycles per second or one with 10,000 per second?

Investigating Vision

Process Skills

- predicting
- inferring
- identifying and controlling variables

Materials

- plastic cup
- 15 beans
- metric ruler

Getting Ready

In this activity, you will investigate the differences in what you see when using only one eye and when using two eyes.

When one eye is supposed to be covered, don't peek or you'll ruin your results.

Follow This Procedure

1. Make a chart like the one shown. Use the chart to record your test results.

Trial	One eye	Two eyes
1		
2		
3		
4		
5		
6		
7		
8		
9		
10		
11		
12		
13		
14		
15		
Total Points		

2. Sit at the corner of a desk or table, perpendicular to a partner, as shown in Photo A. Place an empty cup between you and the partner. The cup should be an arm's length from each of you (Photo A).

Photo A

3 Cover one eye with your hand. Have your partner take a bean, and hold it about 20 cm over the table near the cup. As your partner slowly moves the bean around, decide at what position the bean will fall into the cup. At that position, say "Now." Your partner should drop the bean from that position (Photo B).

4 Record the result. Enter 1 in the data table if the bean fell into the cup. Enter 0 if the bean hits the table.

5 Repeat steps 3 and 4 for a total of 15 trials.

6 Will the bean fall into the cup more often if you repeat steps 3–5 using both eyes? Record your **prediction.**

7 Repeat steps 3–5 using both eyes.

Photo B

Interpret Your Results

1. Tally your scores. Were you able to make the target more often using one eye or both eyes?

2. Vision in which a person uses two eyes is called stereo vision. Use the results of this activity to **infer** why stereo vision might be an advantage over monovision, vision using only one eye.

3. What is the **variable** you tested in this activity? What other variables did you control?

Inquire Further

How does the speed at which your partner moves the bean affect the results of this activity? Develop a plan to answer this or other questions you may have.

Self-Assessment

- I followed the directions to test stereo vision.
- I recorded the results of each trial in a chart.
- I **predicted** what would happen when I repeated the activity using both eyes.
- I made an **inference** why using two eyes might be an advantage over using one eye.
- I identified the **variables** in the activity.

You will learn:

- what the parts of a nerve cell are.
- how nerve impulses travel.
- what reflexes are.

Lesson 3

How Do Nerve Cells Send Messages?

Sniff! The smell reminds you of camping in the woods last summer. Every sensation, movement, memory, and feeling that you have is the result of messages passing through and between neurons.

Nerve Cells

Most neurons, or nerve cells, are thinner than the period at the end of this sentence, yet they are the longest cells in the body. Some neurons are more than a meter long! Neurons are similar to other cells, but they have parts that allow them to receive and send messages.

The picture on these pages shows the parts of a neuron. Find the cell body in the diagram. The cell body of a neuron contains the nucleus. Molecules that the neuron needs to function and survive are made in the cell body. Dendrites, like branches and twigs on a tree, extend out from the cell body. **Dendrites** collect information from other neurons. How does the structure of the dendrites help them collect information?

As the dendrites collect information, they form messages called **nerve impulses.** The nerve impulses travel from the dendrites, through the cell body, and along the **axon.** Find the axon in the picture. Describe its shape.

Glossary

dendrite (den′drīt), part of a neuron that collects information from other neurons

nerve impulse (nėrv im′puls), message that travels from the dendrites of a neuron to the axon

axon (ak′son), part of a neuron that carries messages away from the cell body

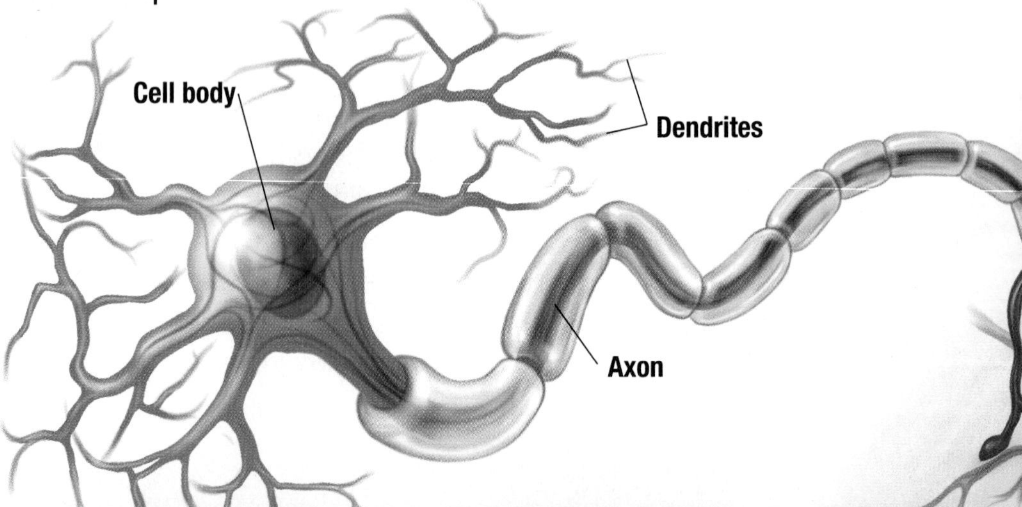

The neurons you have now are the ones you were born with. Some neurons have many dendrites, but others have only a few. ▶

How Nerve Impulses Travel

How does your brain instruct your legs to move or your heart to beat? How does information about something you see, hear, or feel travel through your body? All these things happen because of the movement of nerve impulses through the nervous system. Each dendrite of a neuron receives messages from another neuron. When enough information is received, a small electrical charge forms within the dendrite. This electrical charge is a nerve impulse, which travels through the neuron. It carries messages from the dendrite, to the cell body, and then through the axon to the opposite end of the neuron.

Between the axon of one neuron and a dendrite of another neuron, there is a gap called a **synapse.** When a nerve impulse reaches the end of an axon, chemical messengers are released from the axon into the synapse. The chemicals cross the synapse and attach themselves to a dendrite on the next neuron. When enough of the chemicals become attached, the dendrite forms a nerve impulse. The nerve impulse then travels through the cell body and along the axon to the end of the neuron. The process continues as the nerve impulse passes from neuron to neuron.

When nerve impulses pass through sensory neurons, the impulses move toward the spinal cord and brain, where they are processed and interpreted. When nerve impulses travel through motor neurons, they eventually reach organs and muscles, causing them to move and function properly.

Glossary

synapse (si naps′), the gap between the axon of one neuron and the dendrite of a second neuron

The branching pattern of the nerve cell enables it to receive nerve impulses with many other nerve cells. ▼

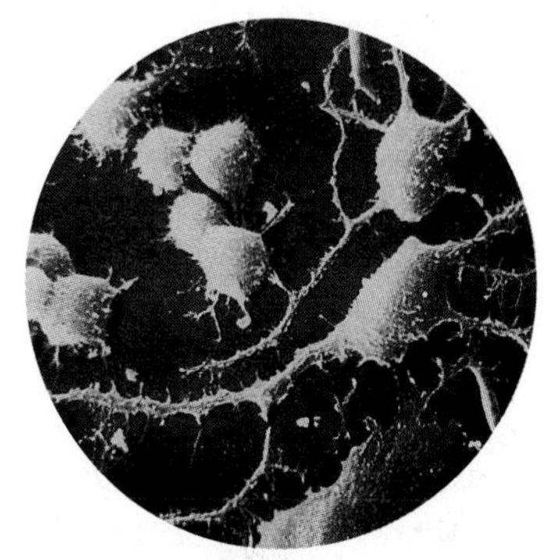

Certain diseases can damage the nervous system. For example, Lou Gehrig's disease—named for a baseball player who suffered from the disease—causes motor neurons to shrink and die. As a result, the muscles in the body weaken through lack of use.

Multiple sclerosis is another disease that causes muscles to weaken by damaging neurons. Multiple sclerosis destroys a protective coating that is found around the axons of neurons.

Parkinson's disease damages brain cells that produce a chemical needed to control movement. People suffering from this disease may tremble or otherwise have trouble controlling their movements.

Researchers are working to find cures for these diseases, as well as learning more about how the nervous system works. For example, in recent years, scientists have discovered that the more you use your brain, the more dendrites its neurons develop. More dendrites mean that the neurons can gather more information, which helps the brain make decisions and take action.

Reflexes

Reflexes protect us in many ways. For example, this baseball player didn't have to think about moving in order to avoid being hit by the ball. ▼

Suppose, like the baseball player in the picture, you're standing at bat when a pitched ball comes too close to your head. Before you even have time to think about it, you jump to the side to protect yourself. By the time your brain figures out what you saw, the rest of your nervous system has already reacted. Any quick, unplanned response that occurs without your brain "thinking about it" is a reflex. Reflexes are basic responses that can protect your body from danger and help you adjust to your surroundings. Some common reflexes include sneezing, coughing, and blinking. When you hear a loud, unexpected sound, you might often look toward the sound and jerk your body. In what way might this reflex protect you?

To understand how reflexes work, follow what happens as the girl in the picture on the next page pricks her finger on a cactus. First, sensory receptors in the girl's finger sense pain. Nerve impulses from these receptors travel through sensory neurons to the spinal cord. One

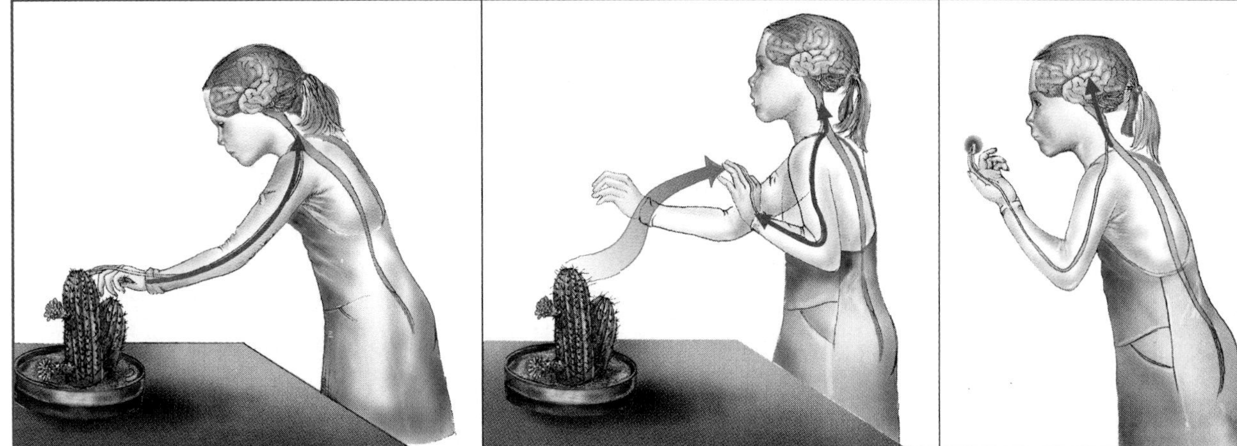

▲ *Study these pictures to see the pathway that impulses take during a reflex. Notice that the girl reacts before the message that her finger has been pricked reaches her brain.*

or more neurons in the spinal cord transfer the nerve impulses directly to motor neurons, which carry the impulses to the girl's arm. The arm muscles move, pulling the girl's finger away from the cactus quickly—without the girl having to think about it.

Meanwhile, the spinal cord transfers nerve impulses from the sensory neurons to the girl's brain. When the impulses arrive there, the brain interprets what just happened and gives the girl the message: "OUCH! *Pain.*" Luckily for the girl, her finger was already out of danger.

Compare how nerve impulses travel in responses that involve reflexes with those that don't. In a response that doesn't involve a reflex—for example, when you scratch an itch—nerve impulses travel along sensory neurons, through the spinal cord, and to the brain where the information is processed before any action is taken. In a reflex response, nerve impulses set the action in motion right away, without waiting for the brain to decide what to do.

Lesson 3 Review

1. What are the parts of a nerve cell?
2. How do nerve impulses travel?
3. What are reflexes?
4. **Rate**
   A nerve impulse takes about 3 seconds to travel 300 meters—the length of 3 football fields. What is its unit rate?

You will learn:

- what the function of endocrine glands is.
- how a feedback loop works.

Lesson 4

What Is the Endocrine System?

"Wow! Is she tall for her age!" You may have noticed differences in height among your classmates. Everyone grows at a different rate. Growth is only one of the many body functions controlled by your endocrine glands.

Glossary

Glossary

endocrine gland (en′dō krən gland), a tissue or organ that releases chemical substances into the bloodstream

hormone (hôr′mōn), chemical released by glands that causes target cells to perform specific activities

Endocrine Glands

An **endocrine gland** is a tissue or organ that releases chemical substances called **hormones** into the bloodstream. Hormones stimulate target cells in specific body parts to perform different activities. Hormones control activities that make bones grow, store sugar, or cause the development of male or female characteristics.

Endocrine glands produce hormones that control body activities. The word hormone *comes from the Greek* hormao *which means "I excite."* ▼

Endocrine Gland	Function
pituitary	controls development and body growth controls the thyroid, ovaries, testes, and others
thyroid	controls how cells release energy
parathyroids	controls the amount of calcium and phosphorous in the blood
adrenals	controls the body's reaction to anger, fright, or fear
pancreas	controls amount of glucose in blood
ovaries	controls female characteristics and the menstrual cycle
testes	controls male characteristics

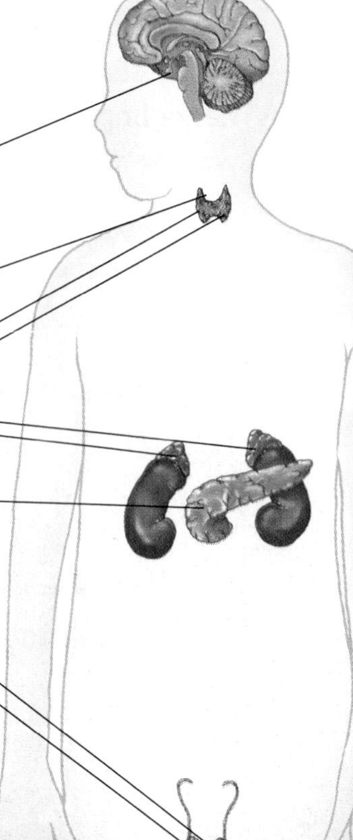

The glands, hormones, and target cells make up the **endocrine system**, which you can see on the previous page. This system constantly checks your body's condition, causing hormones to be released whenever necessary. The whole process may work in seconds. Consider the people fleeing the fire below. The hypothalamus in the brain of each person reacts to signals from sensory neurons that warn about the dangerous fire. The hypothalamus then sends messages to the adrenal gland found on top of each kidney to produce adrenalin, a hormone that helps the person "fight or take flight"—that is, the person either fights the source of danger or runs away from it. In this case, the person flees. The hormones make the heart beat faster. The faster heart rate causes the lungs to take in more oxygen and increases the amount of blood flowing to muscles.

Glossary

endocrine system (en′dō krən sis′təm), body system consisting of glands, hormones, and target cells that work together to control various functions in the body

Feedback Loop

Think about how the temperature inside your home is kept at an even level. A thermostat, which contains a thermometer, turns the furnace off when the temperature inside your home becomes too high and turns it on when the temperature becomes too low. This action-reaction cycle is called a feedback loop. Most body activities that are controlled by hormones include feedback loops. The feedback loops keep the activities at an even level by telling the endocrine glands when to release more or fewer hormones.

How does the endocrine system help these people flee the dangerous fire? ▼

Think about what happens when you eat. First, your digestive system breaks the food down into simpler substances that your body cells can use. One of these substances is glucose, a sugar. Glucose is one of the main sources of energy for the body. When food is digested, glucose enters the bloodstream. Then the body's biofeedback loop takes control.

Your pancreas—an endocrine gland—continuously detects the amount of glucose in your blood. If the level of glucose in the blood becomes too high, the pancreas releases more of the hormone insulin. Insulin decreases the blood's glucose level by signaling body cells to take in more glucose and causing the liver to store any extra glucose that the cells can't use. When the level of glucose in the blood decreases, the pancreas detects the change and releases less insulin. This feedback process ensures that the pancreas releases the right amount of insulin, keeping the glucose in the blood at a normal level. The diagram below summarizes this process.

Biofeedback Loop

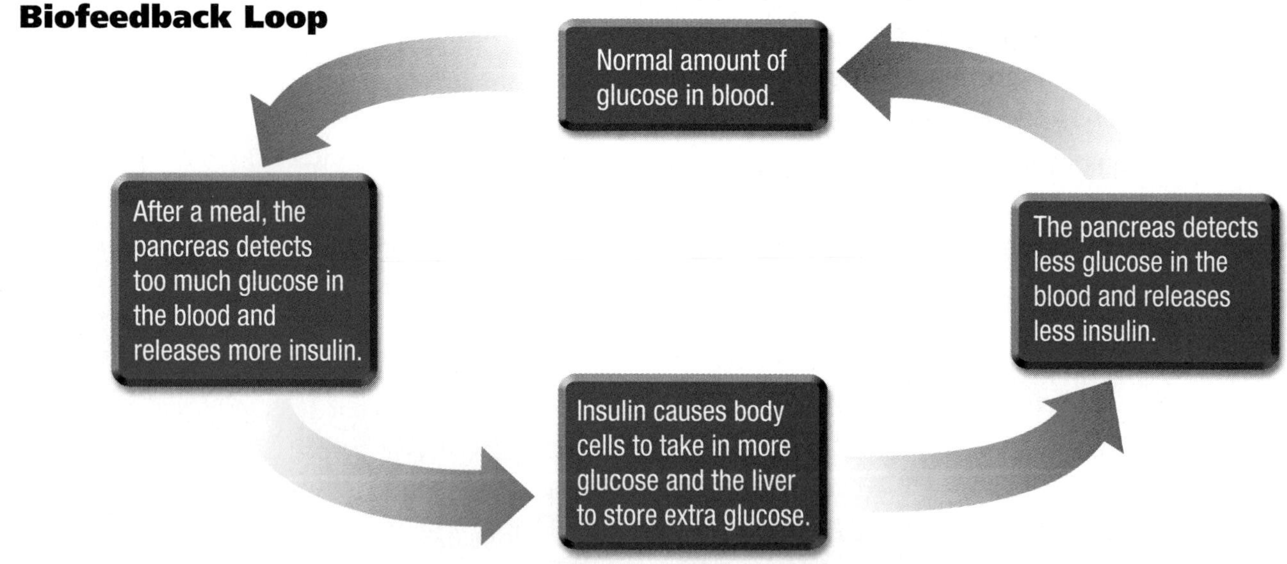

Normal amount of glucose in blood.
After a meal, the pancreas detects too much glucose in the blood and releases more insulin.
Insulin causes body cells to take in more glucose and the liver to store extra glucose.
The pancreas detects less glucose in the blood and releases less insulin.

Lesson 4 Review

1. What is the function of endocrine glands?
2. How does a feedback loop work?
3. **Graphic Sources**
   Use a diagram to describe what events would take place in the body of a person in the picture on page D25.

Testing Temperature Sensors

Materials

- 3 plastic graduated cups
- masking tape
- marker
- ice water
- room-temperature water
- warm water
- clock or watch with second hand
- paper towels

Process Skills

- formulating questions and hypotheses
- identifying and controlling variables
- experimenting
- observing
- collecting and interpreting data
- communicating

State the Problem

You have nerve cells throughout your body that work as "thermometers," telling you when you touch something hot or something cold. Do the body's sensors for heat and cold detect true temperature like a thermometer does, or can they be "tricked" by adjusting variables in their environment?

Formulate Your Hypothesis

If you test the temperature sensors of your hands under different conditions, will they give the same information each time? Or will the same temperature applied to the skin feel different under different conditions? Write your **hypothesis.**

Identify and Control the Variables

The temperature of the water is the **variable.** You will use water with three different temperatures—warm, cold, and room temperature. Be sure to keep all other variables the same.

Test Your Hypothesis

Follow these steps to perform an **experiment.**

1. Make a chart like the one on the next page. Use your chart to record your observations.

2. Use masking tape and a marker to label 3 cups *Room temperature, Warm,* and *Cold.* Fill each cup with 210 mL of water as indicated on the cup's label (Photo A).

Photo A

Continued →

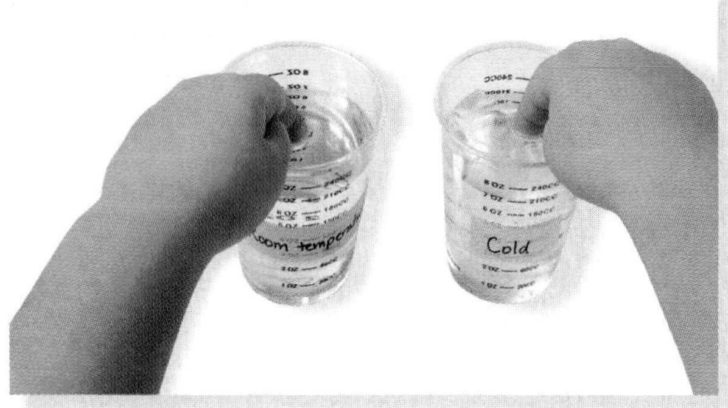

Photo B

3 Wash your hands with soap and warm water.

4 Dip the fingers of the left hand into the cup of room-temperature water. Dip the fingers of the right hand into the cup of ice water (Photo B). Wait 30 seconds.

Safety Note *Do not participate in this activity if you have an open sore or broken skin on your hands, or if you have other medical conditions that affect your hands.*

5 Dip both hands into the room-temperature water. How does the water feel to each hand—cold, cool, room temperature, warm, or hot? Wipe your hands with a paper towel. Record your **observations** in the chart.

6 Dip the fingers of the left hand into the cup of room-temperature water. Dip the fingers of the right hand into the cup of warm water. Wait 30 seconds. Then dip both hands into the room-temperature water. Observe how the water feels. Wipe your hands with the paper towel. Record your **data** in the chart.

7 Dip the fingers of the left hand in ice water and the fingers of the right hand in warm water. Wait 30 seconds. Then dip the fingers of both hands into the room-temperature water at the same time. How does the water temperature feel to each hand? Wipe your hands with the paper towel. Record your observations in your chart.

Collect Your Data

	How room-temperature water feels	
	Left hand	**Right hand**
Step 5		
Step 6		
Step 7		

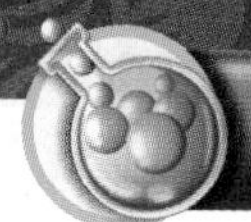

Interpret Your Data

1. Label a sheet of grid paper as shown. Use the data from your chart to make a bar graph on your grid paper.

2. Study your graph. Are temperature sensors in your hands affected by variables in their environment? Is your hypothesis supported by the experimental data?

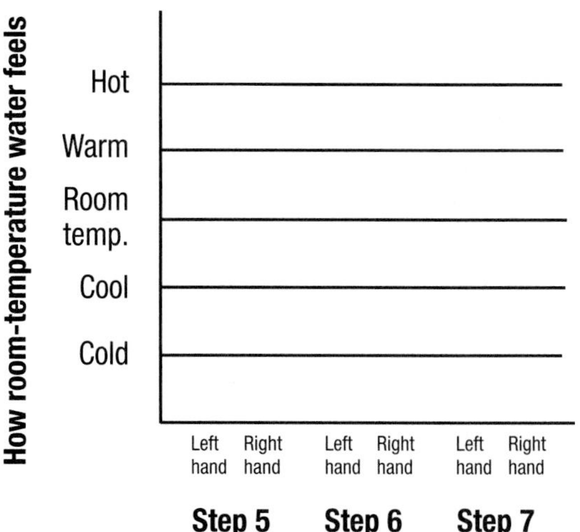

State Your Conclusion

Communicate your results. Describe how the temperature sensors in your hand are similar to thermometers. How are they different? State whether the sensation of heat and cold can be changed by prior exposure to heat and cold.

Inquire Further

If you tested other types of sensors, such as for pressure, would you get similar results? Develop a plan to answer this or other questions you may have.

Self-Assessment

- I made a **hypothesis** about how temperature sensors in the hands respond to different conditions.
- I **identified** and **controlled variables.**
- I **experimented** to test my hypothesis.
- I constructed a bar graph to help me interpret my **data.**
- I compared my experimental results and my hypothesis.

Chapter 1 Review

Chapter Main Ideas

Lesson 1

- The nervous system is the body's control center.
- The main parts of the central nervous system are the brain and the spinal cord.
- The peripheral nervous system gathers information from the environment.

Lesson 2

- Sensory receptors in the eye and ear collect information about the environment.
- The tongue, nose, and skin are organs that contain sensory neurons.

Lesson 3

- A nerve cell is composed of dendrites, a cell body, and an axon.
- Nerve impulses carry information as electrical signals between neurons.
- In a reflex, information from sensory neurons signals the spinal cord to trigger motor neurons for fast action.

Lesson 4

- Endocrine glands release chemicals into the blood to control the body's condition.
- Feedback loops keep the body's activities at an even level by controlling the endocrine glands.

Reviewing Science Words and Concepts

Write the letter of the word or phrase that best completes each sentence.

a. axon
b. brain stem
c. central nervous system
d. cerebellum
e. cerebrum
f. dendrite
g. endocrine gland
h. endocrine system
i. hormones
j. hypothalamus
k. motor neurons
l. neuron
m. nerve impulse
n. peripheral nervous system
o. retina
p. sensory neurons
q. sensory receptors
r. spinal cord
s. synapse

1. The part of the brain that helps you keep your balance is the ___.
2. Cells that are sensitive to light, pressure, and pain are called ___.
3. An electrical signal that carries information through a neuron is a(n) ___.
4. Branching out from the cell body, a(n) ___ receives information from other neurons.
5. The part of the eye that contains sensory receptors for light is the ___.
6. The ___ controls such actions as heartbeat, blood flow to organs, and the development of male and female characteristics.

7. Nerve impulses travel through the ____ before they reach the synapse.
8. Temperature, hunger, thirst, and some emotions are controlled by the ___.
9. The ____ consists of the brain and spinal cord.
10. The part of the CNS that passes through the spine is the ___.
11. The thinking part of the brain is the ___.
12. The general name for a cell in the nervous system is ___.
13. An ___ releases chemicals into the bloodstream to encourage bone growth, the storage of sugar, or other actions the body requires.
14. Nerve cells that carry information from the sensory receptors to the spinal cord and brain are ___.
15. Breathing and digesting food are controlled by the ___.
16. The gap where chemicals carry messages between neurons is the ___.
17. The ___ connects the central nervous system to the rest of the body.
18. Chemicals that "excite" target cells into performing certain functions are ___.
19. Nerve cells that carry information to muscles are ___.

Explaining Science

Write a paragraph or draw a graphic organizer to explain these questions.

1. How do the central nervous system and peripheral nervous system work together to control the body?

2. How do sensory receptors for light work?

3. How is a reflex different from the regular operation of sensory and motor neurons?

4. How does a feedback loop work?

Using Skills

1. In the captions on page D17, which of the numbers represents a **rate**?

2. **Observe** a classmate for 3 minutes. List any actions of the classmate that you observe. **Classify** the actions as voluntary or involuntary.

3. What **variables** can you **identify** that might be part of the feedback loop on page D26?

Critical Thinking

1. Suppose that your friend calls your name and then tosses a ball to you. **Sequence** the parts of your nervous system involved in catching the ball.

2. People who have practiced an action, such as typing, can generally do it more quickly and easily than someone who does it for the first time. What would you **infer** produces this change?

3. Which part of your hand is more sensitive—the palm or the back? Describe an **experiment** you might do to answer this question. Identify the **variables**.

At Your Service!

What is always working for you, without you even having to ask? [Hint: You couldn't skate, paint, read, or do anything without it.] It's your body!

Chapter 2

Drugs and Your Body

Inquiring about
Drugs and
Your Body
Lesson 1
What Should
You Know About
Drugs?
How can you use medicines safely?
How do drugs affect the body?
How can you avoid drug abuse?
Lesson 2
How Does Tobacco
Affect Your Body?
How does smoking tobacco affect the body?
How does using smokeless tobacco affect the body?
Why do some people choose to be tobacco free?
Lesson 3
What Are
the Dangers of
Marijuana Use?
What are the immediate effects of using marijuana?
What are the long-term effects of using marijuana?
Lesson 4
How Does Alcohol
Harm Your Body?
What are the effects of using alcohol?
Why is alcohol abuse dangerous?
How can you avoid using alcohol?

***Copy the chapter graphic organizer** onto your own paper. This organizer shows you what the whole chapter is all about. As you read the lessons and do the activities, look for answers to the questions and write them on your organizer.*

Exploring Healthful Habits

Process Skills

Process Skills

- observing
- communicating
- classifying

Materials

- magazines and newspapers
- scissors

Explore

1 Look through newspapers and magazines. **Observe** the different kinds of activities shown. Search for images of people involved in healthful activities.

2 Find as many different types of activities as you can. Cut out at least 10 images of healthful activities.

3 **Communicate.** With your group, discuss how the activities are alike and different. **Classify** the images you find into categories.

Reflect

1. What characteristics did your group use to classify the activities?

2. How does your group's classification system compare to those of other groups?

3. What kinds of activities are part of a healthful lifestyle? Discuss your ideas with your group.

Inquire Further

Are there images in newspapers and periodicals showing unhealthful activities and habits? Are healthful or unhealthful images more common? Develop a plan to answer these or other questions you may have.

Supporting Facts and Details

As you read any information, including science, it is important to recognize supporting facts and details that describe or explain a main idea. Facts and details contain important and useful information about a topic.

Example

One way to identify the supporting facts and details as you read Lesson 1, *What Should You Know About Drugs?,* is to take notes in an outline form. Use a Roman numeral for main ideas. Use capital letters for supporting facts. Read the following paragraph and compare it to the student's outline.

> Although a medicine may help in treating a certain problem or preventing disease, it can also create other problems. For example, some medicines cause sleepiness or an upset stomach. Other unwanted effects include dry eyes or mouth. These unwanted effects are called side effects.

I. Medicines
- A. Benefits
  1. Treat problem
  2. Prevent disease
- B. Side Effects
  1. Sleepiness
  2. Upset stomach
  3. Dry eyes
  4. Dry mouth

▲ *Some medicines can cause a person to feel tired and sleepy.*

Talk About It!

1. What is the difference between a supporting fact and a detail?

2. What facts and details in the paragraph support the idea that medicine can cause side effects?

You will learn:

- how you can use medicines safely.
- how drugs affect the body.
- how you can avoid drug abuse.

Lesson 1

What Should You Know About Drugs?

You have brains in your head.
You have feet in your shoes.
You can steer yourself
any direction you choose.
by Dr. Seuss

Glossary

Glossary

drug (drug), a substance that acts on the body to change the way it works

Using Medicines Safely

When you get sick, your body's internal balance is upset. Sometimes drugs can help restore your natural balance. A **drug** is a substance that acts on the body to change the way it works in some way. Drugs are given to people to treat or prevent disease, to relieve pain, or to improve or control some other condition in the body or mind that is not normal. When a drug is used in this way, it is called a *medicine*.

Medicine Bottle
The label on a medicine container should include the information shown. ▶

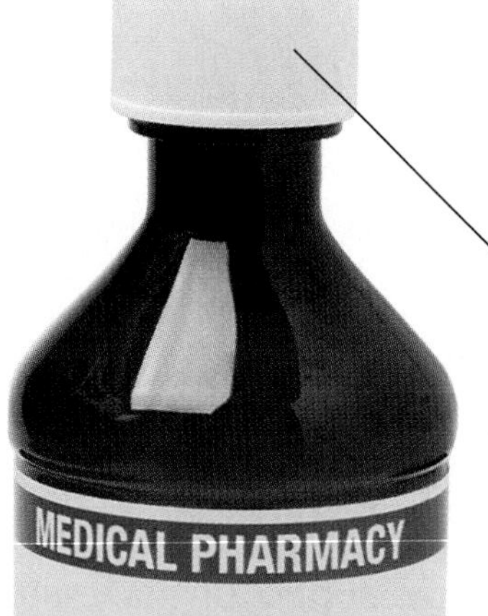

MEDICAL PHARMACY
Rx NO.6655599 Dr. Homer
Stansel, Margaret
Take one tablespoon by
at bedtime.
For > Marax
Ranitidine 150MG Syrup
Refill - 2 Discard after
CAUTION: FEDERAL LAW PROHIBITS
THE TRANSFER OF THIS DRUG TO ANY
OTHER THAN THE PATIENT FOR WHOM

To protect small children from medicines that might harm them, the cap on some medicine containers is made so that it is difficult to remove. Medicines bought without a prescription should have a seal around the cap to ensure that the container hasn't been opened.

Name of the person for whom the medicine is prepared.

Name of the doctor who prescribed the medicine.

Directions given by the doctor for how often and in what way the medicine should be taken.

Name of the medicine and its strength.

History of Science

People have used medicines for centuries. Ancient Greek, Roman, and Egyptian doctors used drugs made from plants. The drugs were helpful in treating many physical problems. Arabs in the 12th century used ground sponge—a sea animal whose body contains a substance called iodine—to cure a common problem caused by too little iodine in the body. Today, iodine is added to table salt to help keep people healthy.

Today many different kinds of medicines are available. Some of them, such as aspirin, antacids, or cough and cold medicines, can be found in grocery or drug stores. These types of drugs are called over-the-counter medicines. To purchase other medicines, you need an order from a doctor called a prescription. Examples of prescription medicines include antibiotics and some allergy medicines.

Doctors have the training to know how the many available medicines work in the body and what physical or mental problems they might help. Doctors also know what amount, or dosage, of a medicine is best for a certain patient. This amount may depend on the age or size of the person or on what other medicines the person is using.

Although a medicine may help in treating a certain problem, it can also create other problems. For example, some medicines cause sleepiness, dry eyes or mouth, or an upset stomach. These unwanted effects of medicines are called **side effects**. Not everyone who takes a medicine will suffer from side effects, but some people may experience such serious side effects that they must stop taking the medicine. The pharmacist who prepares the prescription can tell you what side effects the medicine might produce.

Although medicines can help people who are ill, any medicine or drug can be harmful or dangerous if taken in the wrong way or by the wrong person. Medicine that is safe for one person may be harmful for another. For this reason, you should never take another person's prescription medicine. Safety rules, such as those shown to the right, are reminders of what people should or shouldn't do with medicines.

Glossary

side effect (sīd ə fekt′), unwanted effect of a medicine or drug

Glossary

Medicine Safety Rules

- **Always check with an adult before taking any medicine.**
- **Never use a prescription medicine unless your doctor ordered it for you.**
- **Read directions and warnings on the drug label.**
- **Always take the proper dose as instructed on the label.**
- **Don't take two or more medicines at the same time without instructions from your doctor.**
- **Never take any medicine if you are unsure of what it is.**
- **Throw out unlabeled and outdated medicines.**
- **Keep all medicines out of the reach of children.**

Glossary

drug abuse
(drug ə byus′), using legal or illegal drugs for purposes other than mental or physical illness

addiction (ə dik′shən), an illness affecting both the mind and body that makes people unable to go without something, such as a drug

stimulant
(stim′ yōō lənt), a drug that speeds up the nervous system

caffeine (kaf′ēn′), a mild stimulant found in coffee, tea, colas, and chocolate

Drugs and the Body

As you just learned, when drugs are used properly, they can help you. Sometimes, people use drugs for purposes other than health. Using any drug when no health need exists is **drug abuse.** The abuse of drugs can have many harmful effects on the body. Some of the effects happen right away. Other harmful effects occur after a person abuses the drug over a period of time. One harmful effect is addiction.

Addiction is an illness that affects both the mind and the body. People who are addicted to a drug have a physical and mental need to take the drug again and again. The need is called dependence.

Addicted drug users spend a lot of time thinking about the drug. They are never sure what will happen when they use it. They continue to use the drug even when it causes problems in their life. Because an addicted person's brain may no longer be able to make healthy choices, people who are dependent on a drug may take too much of it—an overdose. An overdose can result in a scene like the one in the picture. Addiction is very difficult to cure.

Addiction is only one effect a drug can have. Other effects vary with the type of drug. A **stimulant** is a drug that speeds up the nervous system. All stimulants raise the heart rate, breathing rate, and blood pressure. The result is that the heart and blood vessels work harder than normal. How do you think this might affect the body over time?

Look at the drinks in the picture to the right. What do they have in common? They all contain **caffeine**, a mild stimulant. At first, caffeine may make a person feel more awake and active. As the body uses up the caffeine, these effects wear off. After this burst of energy, people often feel more tired than normal.

Because drugs change the way a person thinks, drug abusers may not realize that they are taking a dangerous amount of the drug. Mixing drugs can also cause a drug overdose. When this happens, emergency medical attention is needed. ▼

If you drink too many colas or other high-caffeine beverages to keep yourself going when you get tired, you're forcing your body to work overtime when it needs rest. As a result, you may begin to feel nervous or depressed, suffer a loss of appetite, or your thinking may slow down.

Some powerful stimulants are found in prescription medicines. When they are used properly, these stimulants can be helpful and safe. Stimulants are not part of the body's normal chemistry. Therefore, when they aren't used properly, they can produce harmful changes in the body. For example, improper use of stimulants may cause mental disorders, tissue damage, or even heart failure. Cocaine, one powerful stimulant, is a prescription drug that has a few medical uses. When it's used legally, the drug can be helpful. Most often, cocaine is used illegally, usually without a prescription. When used illegally, cocaine can have dangerous effects, including death. One especially strong form of cocaine, called crack, is always illegal.

A **depressant** is a drug, such as alcohol, that slows down the rate at which nerve impulses travel through the nervous system. Breathing, heart rate, and reaction time are all slowed by depressants. Doctors may prescribe some depressants, such as tranquilizers or barbiturates, to calm people and help them sleep.

If your nervous system is working normally, taking depressants can make you slur your words or move awkwardly. Large doses of depressants can cause memory loss or may make a person's breathing and heart stop.

Glossary

depressant (di pres′nt), a drug that slows down the nervous system

Glossary

▲ *Many colas are made with kola nuts, which contain caffeine. Lemon-lime drinks and some root beers contain no caffeine.*

Cocoa and chocolate are made from cacao seeds. A cup of cocoa contains only about one-tenth of the caffeine found in a cup of coffee. Tea also contains caffeine. ▼

Glossary

inhalants (in hā′lənt), drugs that enter your body with the air you breathe

hallucinogen (hə lü′sn ə jen), drugs that affect brain activity, changing the way a person senses the world

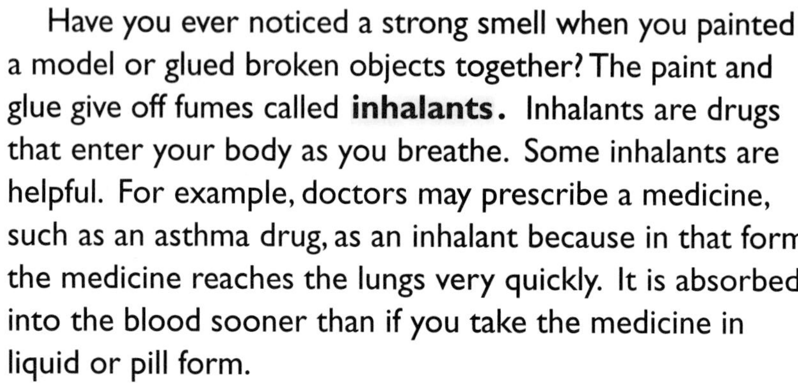

Have you ever noticed a strong smell when you painted a model or glued broken objects together? The paint and glue give off fumes called **inhalants.** Inhalants are drugs that enter your body as you breathe. Some inhalants are helpful. For example, doctors may prescribe a medicine, such as an asthma drug, as an inhalant because in that form the medicine reaches the lungs very quickly. It is absorbed into the blood sooner than if you take the medicine in liquid or pill form.

Fumes from certain products that people use every day can also be inhalants. The products include those in the picture, as well as glues, paints, nail-polish remover, cleaning fluids, and gasoline. The fumes in these products have a depressant effect on the body and can cause dizziness, nausea, headaches, nosebleeds, and death. They can also cause damage to the lungs, nose, brain, and internal organs. People who work with inhalants wear filtering masks to keep from breathing the fumes.

Another kind of drug, **hallucinogens**, affect brain activity, changing the way a person senses the world. The person may see, hear, or feel things that don't really exist. These experiences are called hallucinations. LSD, PCP, and mescaline are hallucinogens, and they are illegal.

People abusing hallucinogens may not be able to recognize where they are. This confusion can cause serious accidents, such as falls, drownings, burns, or auto crashes. They may not be able to sense pain, so that if they are injured, they may not realize it. One frightening side effect of hallucinogens is called a flashback. Years after a person has stopped taking hallucinogens, he or she can have hallucinations just like the ones experienced when the drugs were taken. That is because hallucinogens stay in a person's body for years and may create permanent changes to the nervous system.

Many young people think that it won't hurt to try something "just once." Unfortunately, you can never be sure how your body will react to a certain drug. You can suffer serious or permanent damage after only one use.

Effects of Inhalants

- **vomiting**
- **nosebleeds**
- **loss of coordination**
- **loss of thinking ability**
- **damage to liver, kidneys, heart, bones, blood cells**
- **permanent damage to nervous system**
- **death caused by suffocation or heart failure**

These inhalants are common household products. ▼

Avoiding Drug Abuse

Young people sometimes think that they have no control over their lives or that adults make all the decisions for them. One area in which you always have some choices is in maintaining the health of your body. You may choose to play sports or exercise to keep your muscles strong. You may watch what you eat to provide good fuel for your growing body. "Saying NO" to harmful drugs is another way to keep your body and mind healthy and to choose to avoid the disease of addiction.

Sometimes, friends may try to talk you into doing something you really don't want to do. "Everyone's doing it," they may tell you, even though it's not true. This is called peer pressure. What kind of friend would ask you to do something that could threaten your health or even your life? If you give in to peer pressure because you're afraid of what those so-called friends will think of you, you are giving away your choice to someone else. With friends like that, you don't need enemies!

One way to avoid this kind of peer pressure is to make friends with people who are participating in interesting activities you enjoy. Most people choose not to abuse drugs. Choose to join them! Play sports, join clubs, or volunteer in your community. It's your choice!

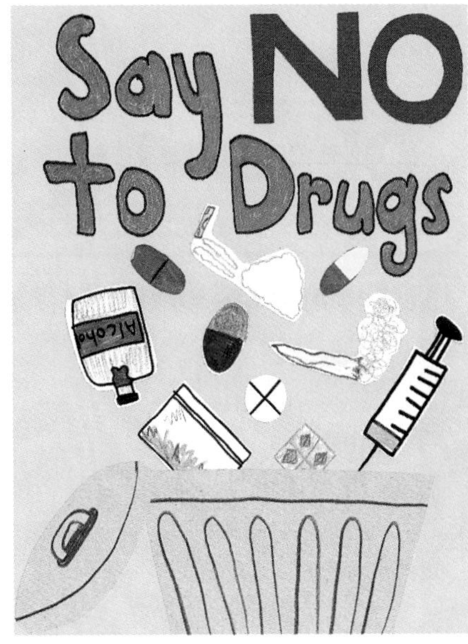

▲ *The poster was drawn by a young person who has chosen to "say NO to drugs."*

Lesson 1 Review

1. How can you use medicines safely?
2. How do drugs affect the body?
3. How can you avoid drug abuse?
4. **Supporting Facts and Details**
   Find four facts from this lesson to support the statement that drug abuse is dangerous.

Investigate Activity

Observing Particle Distribution

Process Skills

Process Skills

- observing
- making and using models
- inferring
- communicating

Materials

- newspaper
- shoebox with lid and hole in the bottom
- black construction paper
- scissors
- safety goggles
- masking tape
- plastic dispensing bottle
- funnel
- cornstarch
- spoon
- stirrer

Getting Ready

In this activity, you will investigate how particles of matter travel through the air.

Follow This Procedure

1. Make a chart like the one shown. Use your chart to record your observations.

	Observations
Box with lid	
Box without lid	

2. Cover the table with newspaper. Line a shoebox with black construction paper by cutting and taping pieces of the paper inside the box (Photo A).

3. Put on your safety goggles. Remove the top of the bottle. Place the funnel in the bottle.

4. Fill the bottle almost full with cornstarch, one spoonful at a time. Use the stirrer to help push the cornstarch through the funnel. Put the lid back on the bottle.

Photo A

5. Gently push the pointed end of the bottle lid through the hole in the box (Photo B).

6. Place the lid on the box. Have a partner hold the box while you gently squeeze the bottle.

 ***Safety Note*** *Be careful not to inhale the powder.*

7. Remove the lid and **observe** the pattern of the cornstarch inside the box. Record your observations.

8. Empty the cornstarch from the box by gently tapping it upside down on the newspaper covering the table.

9. Repeat steps 5–7 without placing the lid on the box.

Interpret Your Results

1. How does the pattern of cornstarch compare in the box with and without the lid?

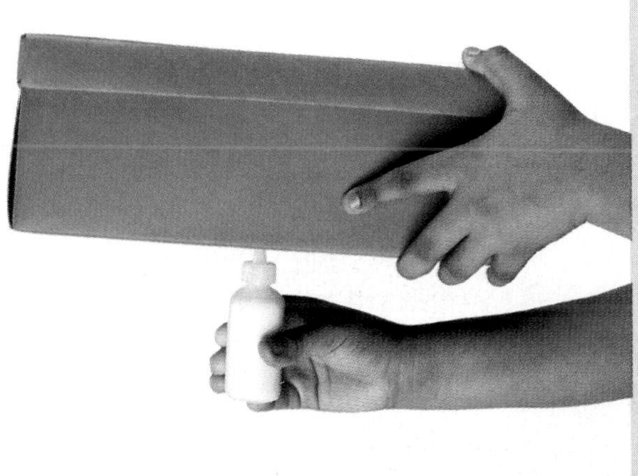

Photo B

2. Explain how this activity can be used as a **model** for explaining the behavior of cigarette smoke.

3. Make an **inference.** Use what you learned in this activity to determine good characteristics of nonsmoking areas in public places. **Communicate** your ideas to your classmates.

 Inquire Further

How would holes in the box affect the distribution of the cornstarch? Develop a plan to answer this or other questions you may have.

Self-Assessment

- I followed instructions to test the distribution of cornstarch and recorded my **observations.**
- I compared the distribution of the cornstarch in the two tests.
- I explained how this activity can be used as a **model** to explain the behavior of cigarette smoke.
- I **inferred** what good characteristics of a nonsmoking area would be.
- I **communicated** my ideas to my classmates.

You will learn:

- how smoking tobacco affects the body.
- how using smokeless tobacco affects the body.
- why some people choose to be tobacco free.

Lesson 2

How Does Tobacco Affect Your Body?

Hey! Is someone burning something in here? Actually, they're burning shredded, dried leaves—tobacco leaves. Someone is smoking tobacco.

Effects of Smoking Tobacco

You probably know that tobacco is found in cigarettes and other products. But what is tobacco and where does it come from? Tobacco comes from the leaves of the tobacco plant. When it's growing in the field, tobacco looks much like overgrown spinach. In the photo below, you can see leaves from the plant being harvested. After harvesting, they are tied together in pairs on sticks or strings and allowed to dry.

After tobacco leaves have dried and aged for more than a year, some are rolled into cigars or shredded for use in cigarettes and pipes. Some are processed as snuff or chewing tobacco. Snuff and chewing tobacco are called **smokeless tobacco** because they are used without being burned.

All tobacco products contain a stimulant drug called **nicotine**. Nicotine is one of several chemicals that plants make to discourage animals from eating them. Animals dislike the bitter taste of nicotine. Nicotine is only one of about 4,000 chemicals that are released as tobacco burns. Many of these chemicals have been linked to diseases, such as cancer. The picture on the next page explains what happens as smoke travels through a person's respiratory system.

Glossary

Glossary

smokeless tobacco
tobacco, such as chewing tobacco or snuff, that is not smoked when it is used

nicotine (nik′ə tēn), a stimulant drug found in tobacco

There are many different varieties of tobacco plants. The taste and chemical content of each variety is different. ▼

The information on this page describes how smoke affects a person's respiratory system. Because this girl chose not to smoke, her respiratory system will not be affected by tobacco.

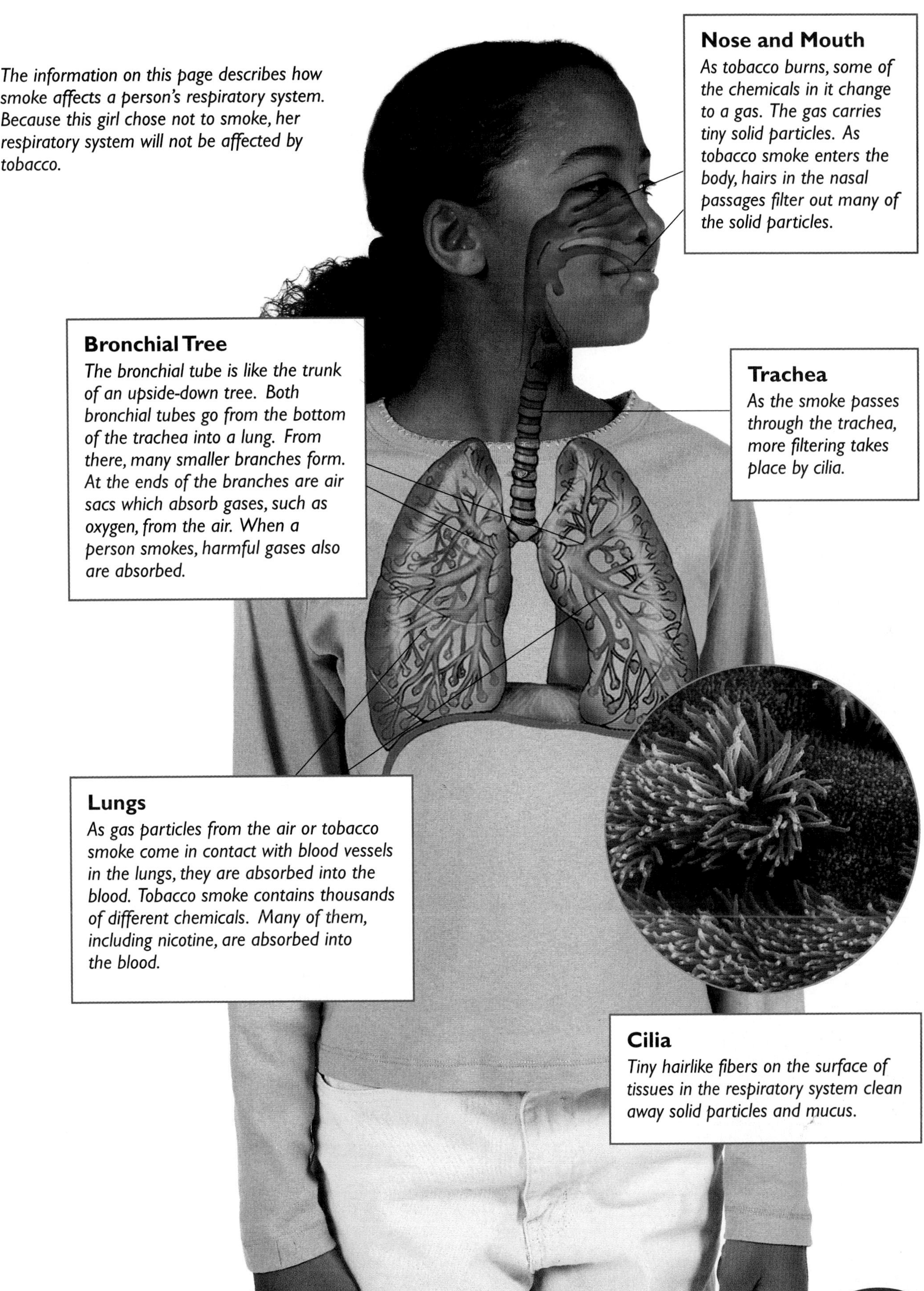

Nose and Mouth

As tobacco burns, some of the chemicals in it change to a gas. The gas carries tiny solid particles. As tobacco smoke enters the body, hairs in the nasal passages filter out many of the solid particles.

Bronchial Tree

The bronchial tube is like the trunk of an upside-down tree. Both bronchial tubes go from the bottom of the trachea into a lung. From there, many smaller branches form. At the ends of the branches are air sacs which absorb gases, such as oxygen, from the air. When a person smokes, harmful gases also are absorbed.

Trachea

As the smoke passes through the trachea, more filtering takes place by cilia.

Lungs

As gas particles from the air or tobacco smoke come in contact with blood vessels in the lungs, they are absorbed into the blood. Tobacco smoke contains thousands of different chemicals. Many of them, including nicotine, are absorbed into the blood.

Cilia

Tiny hairlike fibers on the surface of tissues in the respiratory system clean away solid particles and mucus.

Glossary

Glossary

carbon monoxide (kär′bən mo nok′sīd), a gas found in cigarette smoke that replaces some of the blood's oxygen when inhaled

tar (tär), a sticky, gluelike substance found in cigarette smoke

Today over a billion people worldwide use tobacco. If tobacco is a drug, why do so many people smoke? When a person first starts smoking, nicotine stimulates the central nervous system and the endocrine glands. This stimulation causes a release of glucose for energy. At first, smoking makes people feel good. However, that good feeling doesn't last. Although your body makes chemicals that make you feel good naturally, nicotine and other addicting drugs make you use up all those chemicals very quickly. Until your body can make more, you can't feel good unless you have another cigarette—which starts the whole cycle over again. Before long, your body wants the cigarette just to feel normal. Then you're hooked! Nicotine is addictive.

In addition to nicotine, cigarette smoke contains a gas called **carbon monoxide**. When it is inhaled, carbon monoxide takes the place of some of the blood's oxygen. This decrease in the amount of oxygen makes a person feel weak and dizzy. Carbon monoxide can also increase the chance of getting heart disease.

Healthy Lungs

A healthy person's lungs are pink and smooth. ▼

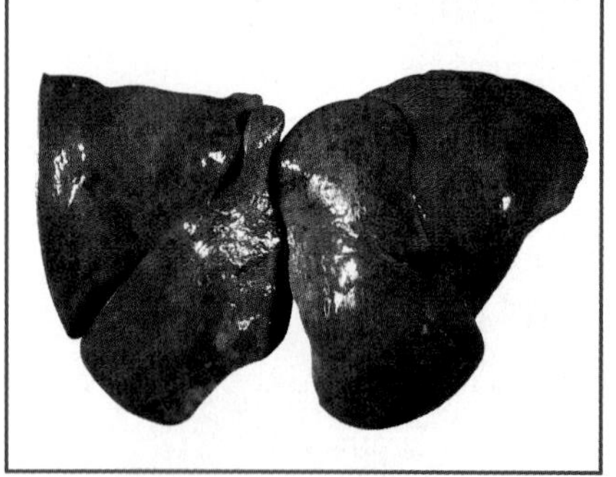

Tar is a sticky substance that also is found in cigarette smoke. Tar is like dark-brown glue. People who smoke fill their lungs with tiny particles of tar. Over time, the lungs begin to look like the smoker's lungs in the bottom picture to the left instead of the healthy lungs shown in the top photo.

Tar coats the cilia in the lungs and prevents them from filtering the air that a smoker breathes. Tar gets into the bronchial tubes and can cause the tubes to swell. If this happens, the smoker coughs a lot to get rid of the mucus.

Damaged Lungs

After inhaling tar and other chemicals from cigarette smoke, the lungs become darker and darker as tar builds up on the tissue. ▼

When the tar builds up in the lungs, it damages the walls of the air sacs. As a result, oxygen is less able to pass into the bloodstream. The person feels short of breath all the time. This problem, called emphysema, can lead to death if the smoker doesn't stop smoking.

People who smoke often complain that their hands or feet feel cold or numb. That's because every puff of smoke tightens the body's blood vessels, reducing the amount of blood that reaches parts of the body. The heart must work much harder to pump the blood through the tiny vessels. In the pictures on the next page, you can see how smoking changes the body's blood flow.

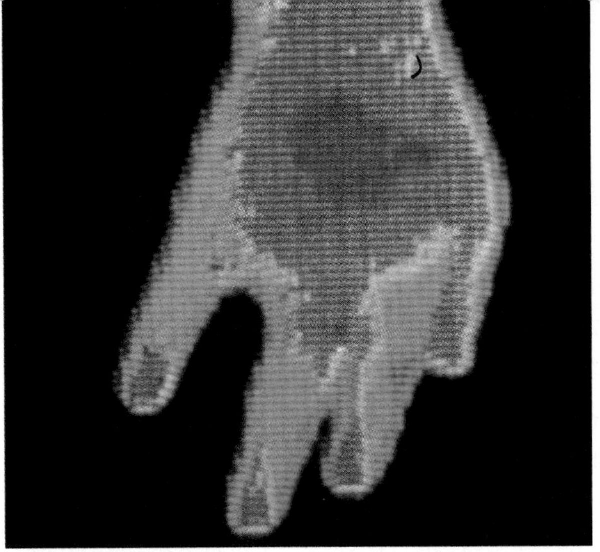

Before Smoking

▲ *This picture is a thermogram of a person's hand prior to smoking. The blue parts are cool areas and the red parts are warm.*

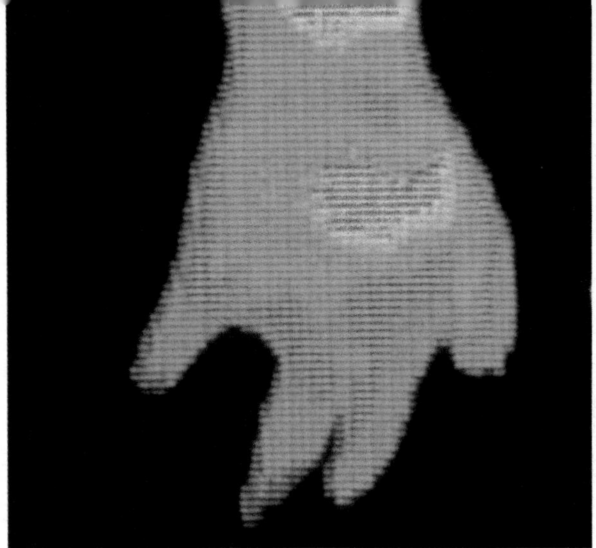

After Smoking

▲ *Notice how more of the hand is blue compared with the hand to the left. After smoking, this person's blood vessels tighten and blood doesn't reach the hands as easily.*

The most serious effect of cigarette smoke is that it causes certain types of cancer. Cancer means that abnormal cells grow uncontrollably, damaging healthy tissue and endangering life. The ingredients in cigarettes damage a part of the body's control system that is responsible for stopping uncontrolled cell growth.

One type of cancer linked to smoking is lung cancer. Lung cancer develops very quickly and has few warning signs. Therefore, it's difficult to treat lung cancer before it is too late. Cigarette smoking is also associated with cancers of the esophagus, mouth, lips, and larynx. The larynx is a part of the throat that allows you to speak. Other effects of smoking tobacco are shown in the chart.

Whether you smoke or not, if you're in the same room with a person who is smoking, you breathe the same chemicals. This is called secondhand smoke. A smoke-filled room can have six times the air pollution as a busy highway. That's why many restaurants and public buildings don't allow smoking.

Secondhand smoke is especially harmful to babies and small children because their bodies are just beginning to develop. Children who are exposed to secondhand smoke have more colds and breathing problems. To keep babies healthy, people should never smoke around them.

Effects of Smoking Tobacco

- **bad breath**
- **wrinkles**
- **nausea and vomiting**
- **loss of thinking ability**
- **stains on teeth and fingers**
- **chronic bronchitis**
- **emphysema**
- **heart disease**
- **lung and other cancers**

Smokeless Tobacco

Effects of Smokeless Tobacco

- **bad breath**
- **brown stains on teeth**
- **gum disease**
- **loss of teeth**
- **heart disease**
- **cancer of mouth, throat, and esophagus**

Some people use smokeless forms of tobacco, such as the chewing tobacco or snuff in the picture. When these products are used, the nicotine in them dissolves in the person's saliva. In fact, they release more nicotine than two cigarettes. The dissolved nicotine is absorbed into the bloodstream through cells in the mouth.

Smokeless tobacco is as dangerous as, and even more addictive than, smoking. As you can see in the chart to the left, the appearance of people who use smokeless tobacco suffers. The sweeteners, tars, and other chemicals in smokeless tobacco can cause tooth decay. They wear away gum tissue, which can result in tooth loss. People who use smokeless tobacco have a greatly increased chance of getting cancers in the mouth. Smokeless tobacco is NOT a safe way to use tobacco.

Choosing to Be Tobacco Free

Some young people decide to smoke cigarettes or use tobacco for the first time because they believe it will help them "look cool" or feel grown up. That first cigarette is a choice. However, after smoking as few as three cigarettes, those same young people may find that a cigarette is no longer a choice—it's a necessity. They have already become addicted. Nicotine is so addictive that even when people have had heart surgery or lost a lung to cancer because of smoking, many still can't quit.

The younger people are when they start smoking, the more likely they are to become strongly addicted to nicotine, because their bodies are still developing. Seventy percent of young smokers admitted that they were addicted and that they smoked more than 100 cigarettes a month.

Smokeless Tobacco

Because snuff and chewing tobacco come in direct contact with mouth tissue, they offer a greater risk of cancer of the mouth and lips. These forms of tobacco also loosen teeth. ▼

Seventy-five percent of young smokers say that they want to quit smoking, but they can't break the habit. They say that if they had the choice again, they wouldn't start smoking in the first place.

Besides being unhealthy, smoking is a very expensive habit, as you can see below. Smokers who stop smoking feel healthier. They find that food tastes better and that they are better able to play sports without becoming short of breath. The smartest and healthiest thing you can do is to never start using tobacco in any form.

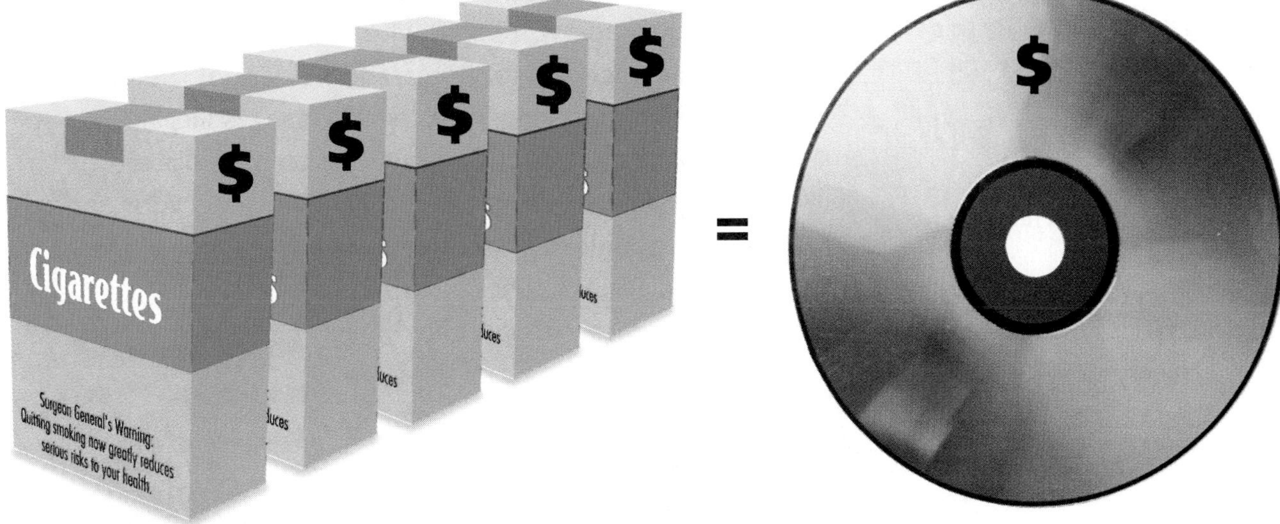

How much does a pack of cigarettes cost? If a person smoked a pack a day, how much would he or she have to spend in one week? What else could you buy for that amount—things that you'd really like to have? ▼

Lesson 2 Review

1. How does smoking tobacco affect the body?
2. How does using smokeless tobacco affect the body?
3. Why do some people choose to be tobacco free?
4. **Supporting Facts and Details**
   What facts would you give someone to persuade him or her not to use tobacco?

You will learn:

- what the immediate effects of using marijuana are.
- what the long-term effects of using marijuana are.

Effects of Marijuana

- Loss of coordination and timing
- Poor sense of balance
- Reduced ability to concentrate, learn, and remember
- Difficulty in judging distances
- Slower reaction time
- Eyes cannot follow moving objects
- Sleepiness after a few hours

Lesson 3

What Are the Dangers of Marijuana Use?

Grass. Pot. Reefer. Weed. What in the world are you talking about? All of these are other words for marijuana. Marijuana is an illegal drug.

Marijuana and Its Immediate Effects

Marijuana is the world's most commonly used hallucinogenic drug. It comes from a plant called *Cannabis sativa*, shown below. People who abuse this drug usually smoke the dried leaves, stems, and flowers of the plant. Buying, selling, growing, or using this drug is illegal.

Marijuana can produce a number of immediate, damaging effects. Users may become very nervous and think that people are trying to harm them. For some people, marijuana causes hallucinations, raises blood pressure, and can double the normal heart rate. It can even cause young people to suffer heart attacks. The chart lists some other effects of marijuana.

People who use marijuana often appear "spaced out" to others. Their eyes may look red and sleepy, and their movements seem awkward. While using marijuana, people often don't realize that their reaction time is slower than normal or that their judgment may be impaired.

Marijuana is sometimes called pot, grass, and weed. ▶

Long-Term Effects of Marijuana

Because marijuana contains large amounts of tar and other chemicals, the effects of smoking marijuana are similar to those of smoking tobacco. For example, the lungs get a big dose of chemicals that increase the chances of lung problems, such as bronchitis and emphysema, later in life.

Although some people think that smoking marijuana is no more dangerous than smoking tobacco, recent studies show that marijuana can do much more damage to the lungs. Many chemicals in marijuana smoke become stored in body fat and are released slowly over time. These chemicals can result in cancers of the head and neck and can bring on mental problems.

In addition to the harm it does by itself, marijuana is sometimes called a "gateway drug." This means that, while marijuana may not cause physical addiction, people become mentally dependent on it. They take more and more of the drug to get the same feeling that a small amount used to give them. From there, the user may go on to use other drugs that are addictive.

Some studies have shown that babies born to marijuana users were shorter, weighed less, and had smaller heads than those born to mothers who didn't use the drug. Smaller babies are more likely to develop health problems.

One of the biggest problems for many marijuana users is that dependence on the drug can affect relationships with family and friends. It can also decrease the ability to do well in school or at work. Using marijuana can result in loss of energy and interest in activities.

Lesson 3 Review

1. What are the immediate effects of using marijuana?
2. What are the long-term effects of using marijuana?
3. **Supporting Facts and Details**
   Give details to explain why participating in sports is better than using drugs.

You will learn:
- what the effects of using alcohol are.
- why alcohol abuse is dangerous.
- how you can avoid using alcohol.

Lesson 4

How Does Alcohol Harm Your Body?

If you are ever offered a drink, STOP! Think about what alcohol can do to your body and to your mind. Alcohol is a drug and illegal for you to use. Drinking it can have serious consequences.

Alcohol and Its Effects

Alcohol is the name commonly used to describe drinks such as beer, wine, and liquor. The common name comes from the depressant drug found in these drinks. Alcohol is produced when certain grains or fruits ferment, or chemically change over time.

Alcohol may be the world's oldest known drug. People probably first discovered the effects of alcohol by eating old fruit. Later, people figured out how to separate the alcohol from the fruit and use the alcohol in various ways. In many cultures, alcohol has been used for thousands of years with meals, in religious ceremonies, and at social events. However, when alcohol is abused, it can be a dangerous drug, changing the way people think, act, and feel. The effects of alcohol become more dangerous as more alcohol is consumed.

When a person drinks, alcohol enters the stomach and is absorbed into the bloodstream quickly. Alcohol travels through the entire body as the circulatory system carries the blood through the body, as shown in the picture on the next page. The alcohol in an average drink, such as a can of beer, remains in the bloodstream for about an hour.

Some people believe that drinking beer has less effect on the body than drinking liquor because beer contains less alcohol. However, drinking beer instead of liquor doesn't necessarily mean that a person is consuming less alcohol.

Glossary

Glossary

alcohol (al′kə hôl), depressant drug found in beer, wine, and liquor

Short-Term Effects of Alcohol

- slowed responses
- reduced coordination
- decreased ability to think clearly
- memory loss
- vomiting
- blurred vision
- inability to stand or walk
- loss of concentration
- coma
- death

Beverage	Amount of Alcohol
12 oz. beer	15 mL
6 oz. wine	15 mL
1 oz. liquor	15 mL

◀ *Although the percentage of alcohol in beer, wine, and liquor varies, a typical serving size of each kind of drink contains about the same amount of alcohol.*

Although wine, beer, and liquor contain different percentages of alcohol, as you can see in the chart above, the typical serving size of each is different. Therefore, one typical serving of each type of drink may contain the same amount of alcohol.

Because alcohol is a depressant, it slows the nervous system, breathing, and heart rate, and it lowers blood pressure. As more alcohol enters the blood, its effects on the body become stronger. Drinkers may lose the ability to focus their eyes or control their muscles. This causes staggering and slurred speech. Drinkers may also lose the ability to think clearly. When this happens, they can no longer make wise decisions. When a drinker experiences some of these symptoms, he or she is **intoxicated**.

Intoxicated people who continue drinking may reach a stage in which they are unable to walk or stand. They may feel sick. Eventually, they "pass out" or lose consciousness because their nervous system has slowed down so much.

An intoxicated person who has become completely unconscious is suffering from alcohol poisoning. This condition carries a risk of death because the intoxicated person may not be able to breathe. Like any poisoning, alcohol poisoning requires emergency medical treatment.

Glossary

intoxicated
(in tok′sə ka′tid), experiencing the symptoms of alcohol consumption

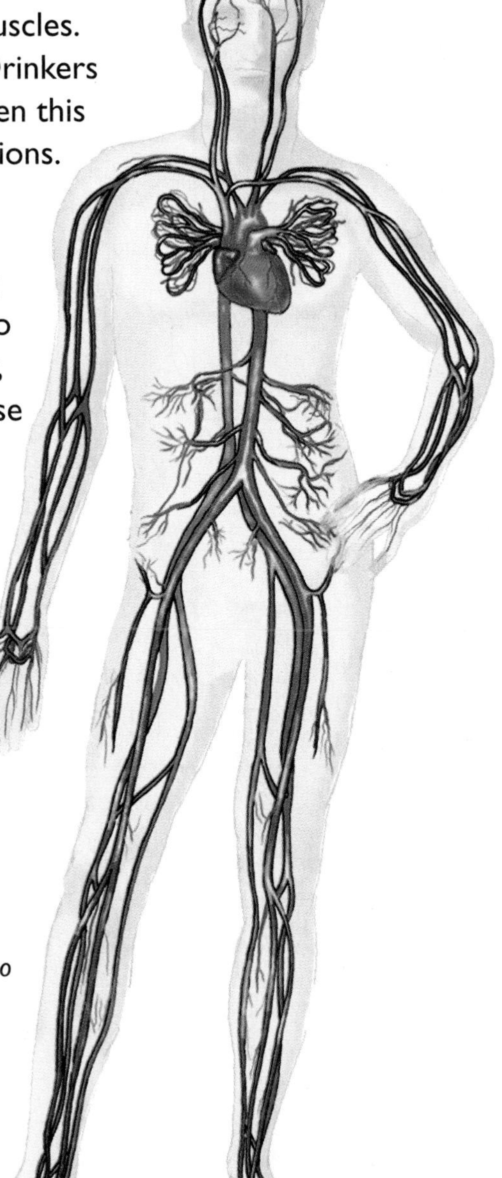

Circulatory System

The circulatory system moves blood through the body. When a person drinks alcohol, the alcohol also is carried to many sites in the body, including the brain, and other parts of the nervous system. ▶

Not everyone is affected by alcohol to the same degree. How alcohol affects a particular person can be influenced by various factors, such as the person's size, physical condition, the amount of food he or she has eaten, and other drugs or medicines the person may also be taking. Most young people have smaller bodies and weigh less than adults do, so they are usually affected more quickly by the same amount of alcohol. The effects of alcohol also depend on the maturity of the person who is drinking and on the development of his or her nervous system. Recent research has shown that the effect of alcohol on a young brain is much greater than on an adult brain. A young brain may react to alcohol more quickly, and it may increase the risk of addiction to alcohol. For these reasons, alcohol use is illegal for people under a certain age.

The pictures show a healthy liver and one affected by cirrhosis. Cirrhosis is a condition where liver cells die and the walls of the liver thicken. Because the liver's job is to filter out harmful chemicals from the body, it is especially affected by alcohol. Cirrhosis also destroys the ability of the liver to store and release food for the body. ▼

Diseased Liver

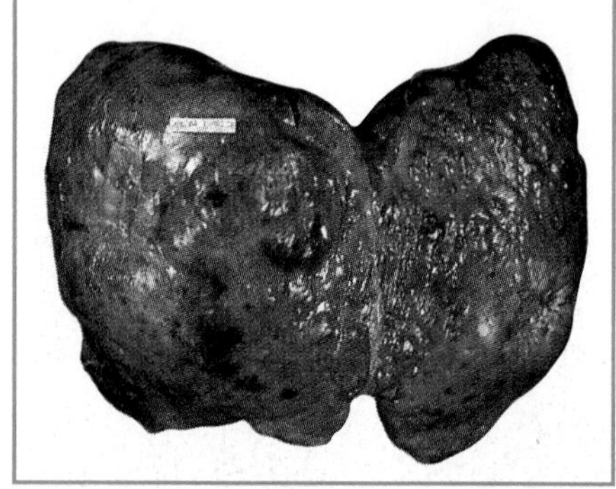

Healthy Liver

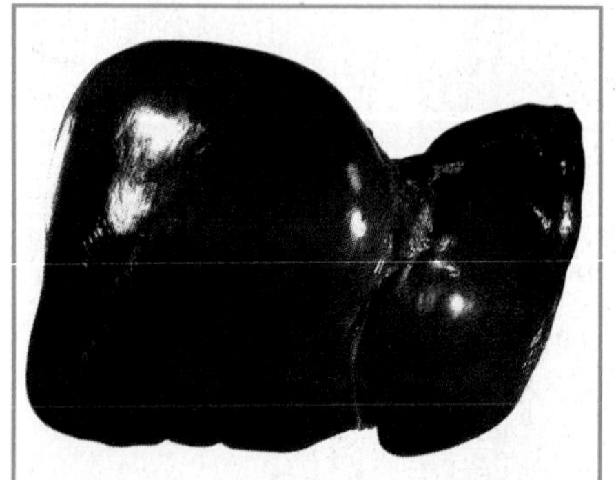

Alcohol Abuse

Any drinking of alcohol that harms or endangers the drinker or other people is called alcohol abuse. Alcohol abuse generally happens any time a person drinks to the point of being intoxicated. Also, whenever an underaged person drinks alcohol, it is considered alcohol abuse.

Drinking a lot of alcohol at one time or drinking over a long period of time harms important body systems. Alcohol increases or decreases the production of brain chemicals and can actually destroy brain cells and nerves. This can result in mental confusion and uncontrollable shaking.

Alcohol also causes damage to the heart, stomach, and endocrine glands. One of the most seriously affected organs is the liver, which filters impurities from the blood. Alcohol collects in the liver and causes diseases such as cirrhosis. The pictures show what happens to a liver affected by cirrhosis. Liver failure can be fatal.

Alcohol abuse can have harmful effects other than physical ones. For example, drinking may cause people to act in inappropriate ways at home and when they are on the job or to be absent from work. These kinds of behaviors can cause them to lose their jobs. This problem hurts not only the drinkers but also their families.

When people who have been drinking alcohol get behind the wheel of a car, they put not only themselves in danger but other people as well. Currently, there is about one alcohol-related death every 30 minutes in the United States. If police stop an intoxicated driver, that driver could lose his or her license and the privilege of driving or go to jail.

Long-Term Effects of Alcohol

- alcoholism
- blackouts
- cirrhosis of liver
- damage to brain and nervous system
- heart disease
- cancer
- malnutrition
- shortened life
- death from alcohol-related accidents or health problems

When a driver has been drinking, family members or innocent people in other vehicles may be injured or killed. ▼

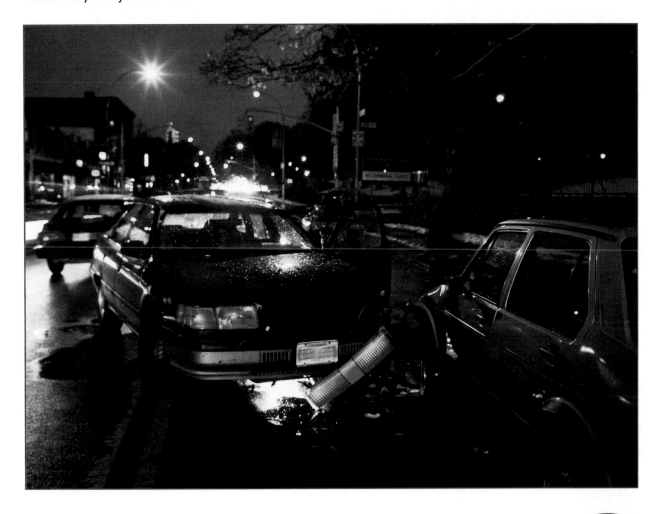

Glossary

Glossary

alcoholic, a person who does not have control over his or her drinking

alcoholism, a disease in which a person is unable to stop abusing alcohol

Many adults who choose to drink do so safely and with control. Others, however, may not be able to drink at all because of the way their body works. Statistics show that one in nine people who drink alcohol become addicted. They are called **alcoholics**. Alcoholics have little or no control over their drinking. Just as other drug addicts feel they must take more of the drug they are addicted to, alcoholics feel the need to drink. The inability to stop drinking is called **alcoholism**.

Alcoholism prevents people from leading normal lives. Because alcoholics often feel sick, they are sometimes unable to work, study, or even play. Many alcoholics are lonely because they know that they have hurt many people. They find that people don't want to be around them because of the way they behave.

Young alcoholics may have to drop out of school. Older people may lose their jobs because their employers can no longer depend on them.

Alcoholics may need to go through a hospital stay to stop drinking. They are often very sick while they're trying to stop, but when they succeed, they feel much better than they did when they were drinking. Often, alcoholics need to get help and talk about other problems in their lives. By working out those problems, they may no longer feel they have to drink.

There are many organizations that help alcoholics. The picture at left shows a group of people meeting to talk about their addiction to alcohol. By doing so, they work to help one another stop drinking.

◀ *Groups such as Alcoholics Anonymous and Rational Recovery help alcoholics stop drinking and not start again. Another group, called Al-Anon, works with families and friends of alcoholics to help them understand this disease and how to deal with those who have it.*

Choosing to Avoid Alcohol

Millions of adults in the United States choose not to drink alcohol. Some cultures don't approve of drinking. Many people simply don't like the way alcohol affects their behavior. Others don't drink alcohol because they are concerned with their health. Some simply don't like alcohol, just as you may not like a certain food or other beverage. You don't have to drink just because you believe that "everyone does it." They don't!

If you are concerned with having a healthy body and mind, that should be enough to make you avoid alcohol and other drugs. Think about your plans for the future. How will they be affected if you drink? Will you hurt your family or lose some of the friends you enjoy being with? Will you have to give up activities you enjoy because you feel sick or are afraid someone will find out you're drinking? The choice to drink or not to drink is a decision that only you should make for yourself—don't let peer pressure make it for you.

Many of the activities mentioned in Lesson 1 can help you make a healthy choice about alcohol. Having a plan about how you can say "No" will also help. If you are in a situation where you need to make a decision about using alcohol, follow the steps to the right for making decisions. As you can see from the photo, there are many other beverages from which you can choose.

Making Decisions

1. *Realize that a decision is needed.*
2. *List the possible choices.*
3. *List the possible results of each choice.*
4. *Decide which choice is best.*
5. *Judge the decision.*

Lesson 4 Review

1. What are the effects of using alcohol?
2. Why is alcohol abuse dangerous?
3. How can you avoid using alcohol?
4. **Supporting Facts and Details** Give facts to support the idea that a person should not drink and drive.

These students are making a fruit drink–just one of many beverages you can use in place of alcohol. ▼

Chapter 2 Review

Chapter Main Ideas

Lesson 1

• Medicines can be taken safely by following safety rules and label directions.
• Drugs affect the body and mind in many different ways.
• Developing healthy activities can help people avoid drug abuse.

Lesson 2

• Tobacco contains the stimulant drug nicotine, which is linked to many diseases such as heart disease, cancer, and emphysema.
• Smokeless tobacco is as dangerous and more addictive than smoking.
• Many people choose not to use tobacco because it is harmful to health and also is expensive.

Lesson 3

• Immediate effects of marijuana may include hallucinations, raised blood pressure, and increased heart rate.
• Long-term effects of marijuana include many of the same effects as tobacco.

Lesson 4

• Alcohol slows the nervous system, breathing, and heart rate and damages the ability to make good decisions.
• Alcohol abuse can destroy brain cells and nerves and seriously affect body organs.
• Making healthy choices about your friends and activities can help you avoid alcohol.

Reviewing Science Words and Concepts

Write the letter of the word or phrase that best completes each sentence.

a. addiction
b. alcohol
c. alcoholic
d. alcoholism
e. caffeine
f. carbon monoxide
g. depressant
h. drug
i. drug abuse
j. hallucinogen
k. inhalant
l. intoxicated
m. nicotine
n. side effect
o. smokeless tobacco
p. stimulant
q. tar

1. A person who has become addicted to alcohol is a(n) ___.

2. A(n) ___ is a drug that enters the body through the lungs as you breathe.

3. A bitter-tasting chemical produced by a plant to prevent animals from eating it is ___.

4. The gas ___ , which is found in cigarette smoke, replaces some of the blood's oxygen.

5. A person who is unable to avoid doing or using a drug is suffering from a(n) ___.

6. A substance that changes the way the body works is a(n) ___.

7. The disease of ___ prevents people from stopping the abuse of alcohol.

8. Seeing things that aren't really there is a result of using a(n) ___.

9. A(n) ___ increases the rate at which the nervous system works.

10. Found in cigarette smoke, ___ is a sticky substance that can block your lungs.

11. Even legal medicines may produce an unexpected and unwanted ___.

12. People who are ___ may do things that they later regret.

13. Using a drug for a purpose other than health is ___.

14. A(n) ___ is a drug that slows down the actions of the nervous system and organs.

15. Some beverages that people use to feel more awake contain ___, a mild stimulant.

16. Because more nicotine enters the system during its use, ___ can be more addictive than smoking.

17. The drug found in beer and wine is ___.

Explaining Science

Write a paragraph to answer these questions, or discuss them with a classmate.

1. Compare and contrast the terms *medicine* and *drug*.

2. What is the most convincing reason for not beginning to smoke?

3. What is a "gateway drug"?

4. List three ways that alcohol harms the body.

Using Skills

1. In each lesson of the chapter, locate at least one example of **a supporting fact or detail** based on studies or statistics.

2. Oxygen in the blood is needed to release energy from food. Use what you know about the effects of tobacco smoke to **infer** how smoking affects a person's ability to participate in sports.

3. How can you help people learn about the dangers of drugs? **Communicate** your ideas by describing a plan.

Critical Thinking

1. A classmate tells you that you are "out of it" because you don't choose to smoke or drink. In **making a decision** about how you react, what ideas would you consider?

2. Draw a conclusion about the effects of drinking too many colas while doing your homework.

3. Create a chart that **compares and contrasts** the effects of stimulants and depressants on the body. Include the names of stimulant and depressant drugs on your chart.

Unit D Review

Reviewing Words and Concepts

Choose at least three words from the Chapter 1 list below. Use the words to write a paragraph about how these concepts are related. Do the same for Chapter 2.

Chapter 1
axon
dendrite
endocrine gland
hormones
neuron
synapse

Chapter 2
addiction
alcohol
drugs
stimulant
smokeless tobacco

Reviewing Main Ideas

Each of the statements below is false. Change the underlined word or words to make each statement true.

1. The main parts of the central nervous system are the brain and brain stem.
2. The central nervous system gathers information from the environment.
3. Motor neurons carry information from the senses to the CNS.
4. Neurons are composed of hormones, a cell body, and an axon.
5. Feedback loops regulate the body by controlling the nerve impulses.
6. Two common depressants are caffeine and cocaine.
7. The most addictive drug in tobacco is carbon monoxide.
8. Hallucinations, raised blood pressure, and increased heart rate are some long-term effects of marijuana.
9. Alcohol is a stimulant drug found in beer, wine, and liquor.
10. Smokeless tobacco can be as dangerous for people who don't smoke as those who do.

Interpreting Data

The following table shows the range of sound heard and produced by several different animals.

Frequencies Heard and Produced by People and Animals

Animal	Frequency Heard (Hz)	Frequency Produced (Hz)
Human	30–20,000	85–1,100
Dog	15–50,000	452–1,800
Cat	60–65,000	760–1,500
Bat	1,100–120,000	10,000–120,000
Porpoise	150–150,000	7,000–120,000
Frog	50–10,000	50–8,000
Robin	250–21,000	2,000–13,000

1. Which animal listed produces the lowest pitched sound?

2. Which animal produces most of the pitches that it can also hear?

3. Could a bat hear human speech? Explain.

Communicating Science

1. Draw and label a diagram showing how a nerve impulse gets from a sensory neuron to the brain.

2. Write a paragraph explaining how a nerve impulse passes from one neuron to another.

3. Draw a diagram and write an explanation of how a feedback loop works.

4. Make a chart or table contrasting drug abuse, drug dependence, and drug addiction.

Applying Science

1. Write a paragraph which explains how the body might react in a feedback loop when a person is exercising and then when the person stops.

2. Write and illustrate an article for a student newspaper explaining how tobacco affects the body.

Unit D Performance Review

Brain Awareness Day

Using what you learned in this unit, help prepare exhibits for a brain awareness day. Wherever possible, make your exhibits interactive, so that visitors may participate. You may work by yourself or in a group.

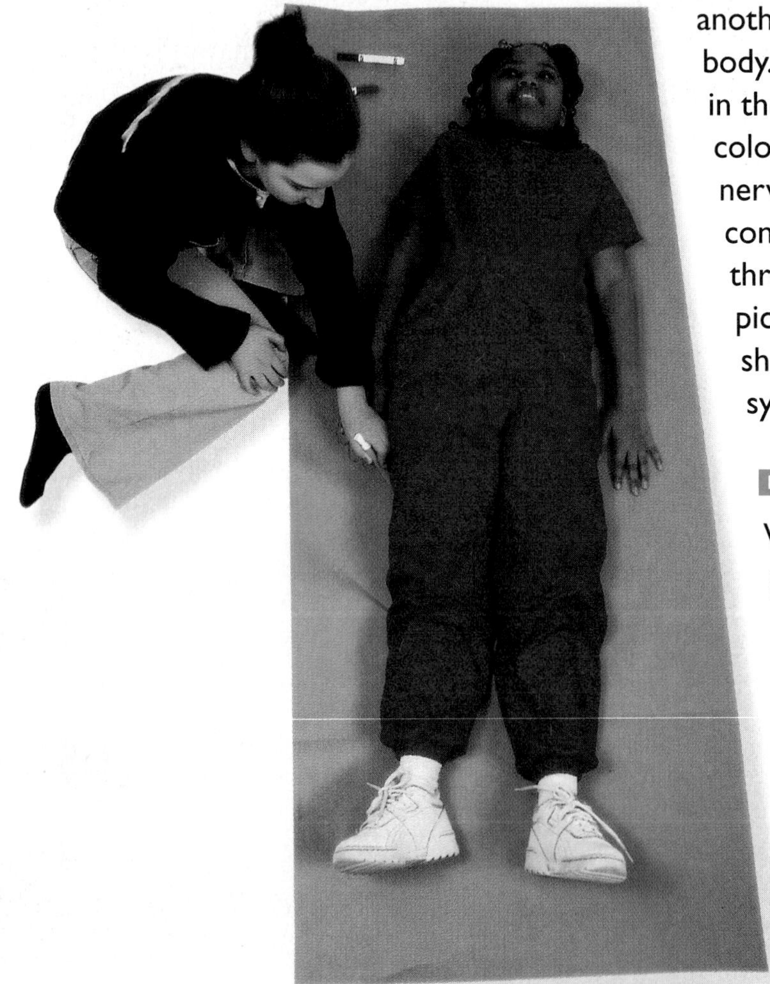

Art

Prepare an exhibit showing how information travels through the body. Lie down on a large sheet of paper and have another student draw an outline of your body. Use crayons or markers to draw in the brain and spinal cord and colored yarn to show how sensory nerve cells, motor nerve cells, and connecting nerve cells carry messages throughout the body. Mount the picture on a wall and use a pointer to show visitors how the nervous system operates.

Drama

Write a skit showing how various parts of the endocrine system work to regulate the body. Have characters representing the different glands, the blood stream, and control systems in the brain. Be sure your play explains how information and chemicals get from one place to another, and how this keeps the body working properly. Present the skit to the class.

Music

Write a song or rap lyrics about the safe use of medicines. You may wish to use a familiar melody for your lyrics or write your own music. Perform your song for the class or get friends to help you sing it. Teach the song to the class.

Journalism

Create and publish a newspaper, complete with headlines and stories about a day in the life of your brain. Write stories that include "interviews" of various brain parts or the sense organs. Illustrate your articles with cartoons or other pictures.

Senses

Organize a scavenger hunt in the classroom or around the school. Give students a list of ten items to locate, two for each of the senses, such as a rough surface, a bright object, a loud sound, a bad smell, or something sour. You may wish to have a teacher locate safe items to taste somewhere in the search area. Students may write the name of the objects they find on their lists rather than bringing them back with them.

Reading a Table

You can use a table to organize ideas before you write. A table lists related ideas about a topic in columns and rows. Headings at the top of the columns which are read from top to bottom, tell you what information is in the table. Each row which is read left to right, lists the information described in the columns for only one topic. The table below lists information about the control systems of the body that you learned about in Chapter 1.

The Body's Control Systems

System	What It Does	What It Includes
Nervous System	collects information from inside and outside the body, sends signals to muscles to act	brain, spinal cord, nerves, sense organs
Endocrine System	releases hormones to control various functions in the body	endocrine glands, hormones

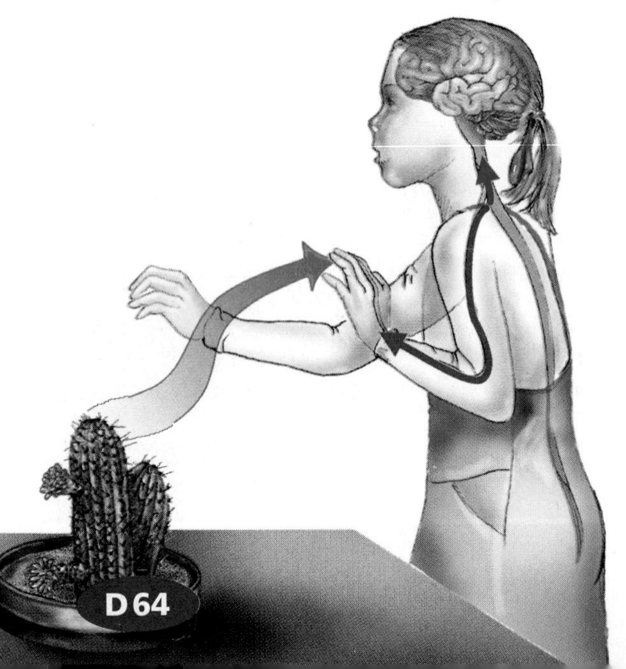

Make a Table

In Chapter 2, you learned about how some drugs can harm the body. Use the information in Chapter 2 to make a table. In the first column, identify the three types of drugs you read about. In the second column, include information about how each kind of drug can harm the body.

Write a Poem

Use the information in your table to write a poem that will convince other students in your school not to use drugs. You might want to divide your poem into sections, or stanzas, and give each stanza its own main idea. Though your poem doesn't have to rhyme, it should include imagery that helps express your feelings.

Remember to:

1. **Prewrite** Organize your thoughts before you write.
2. **Draft** Write your poem.
3. **Revise** Share your work and then make changes.
4. **Edit** Proofread for mistakes and fix them.
5. **Publish** Share your poem with your class.

Your Science Handbook

 Safety in Science

Scientists know they must work safely when doing experiments. You need to be careful when doing experiments too. Here are some safety tips to remember.

Safety Tips

- Read each experiment carefully.
- Wear safety goggles when needed.
- Clean up spills right away.
- Never taste or smell substances unless directed to do so by your teacher.
- Handle sharp items carefully.
- Tape sharp edges of materials.
- Handle thermometers carefully.
- Use chemicals carefully.
- Dispose of chemicals properly.
- Put materials away when you finish an experiment.
- Wash your hands after each experiment.

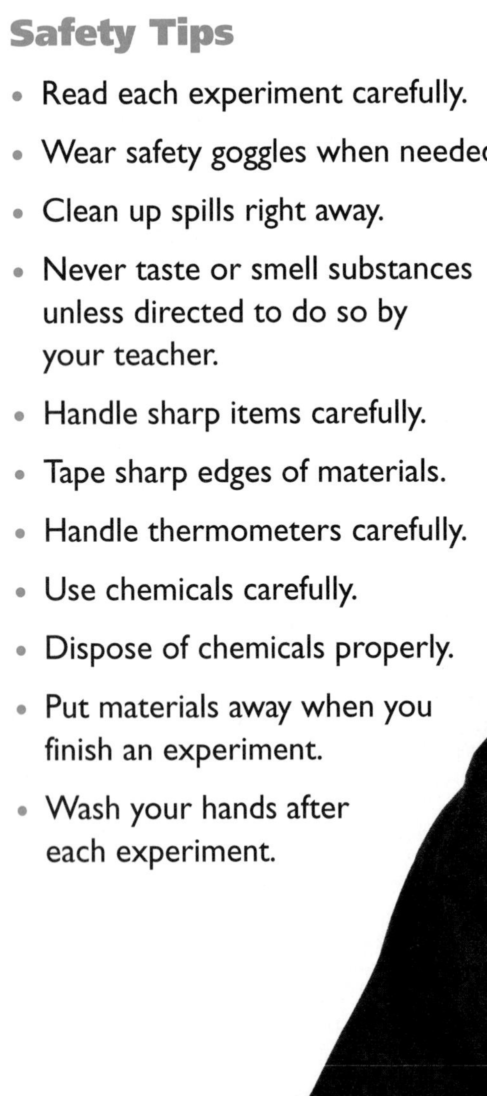

Using the Metric System

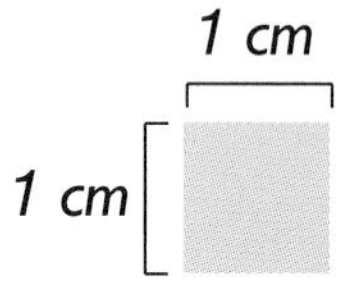

1 cm

1 cm

1 square centimeter

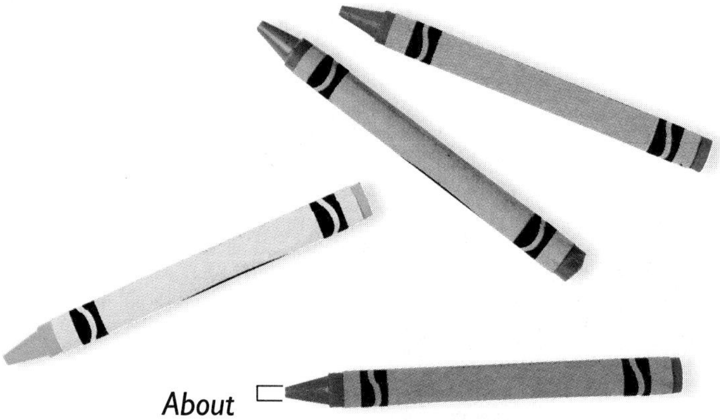

About 2 millimeters

1 cm

1 cm

1 cm

1 cubic centimeter

1 liter of water

11 football fields end to end is about 1 kilometer

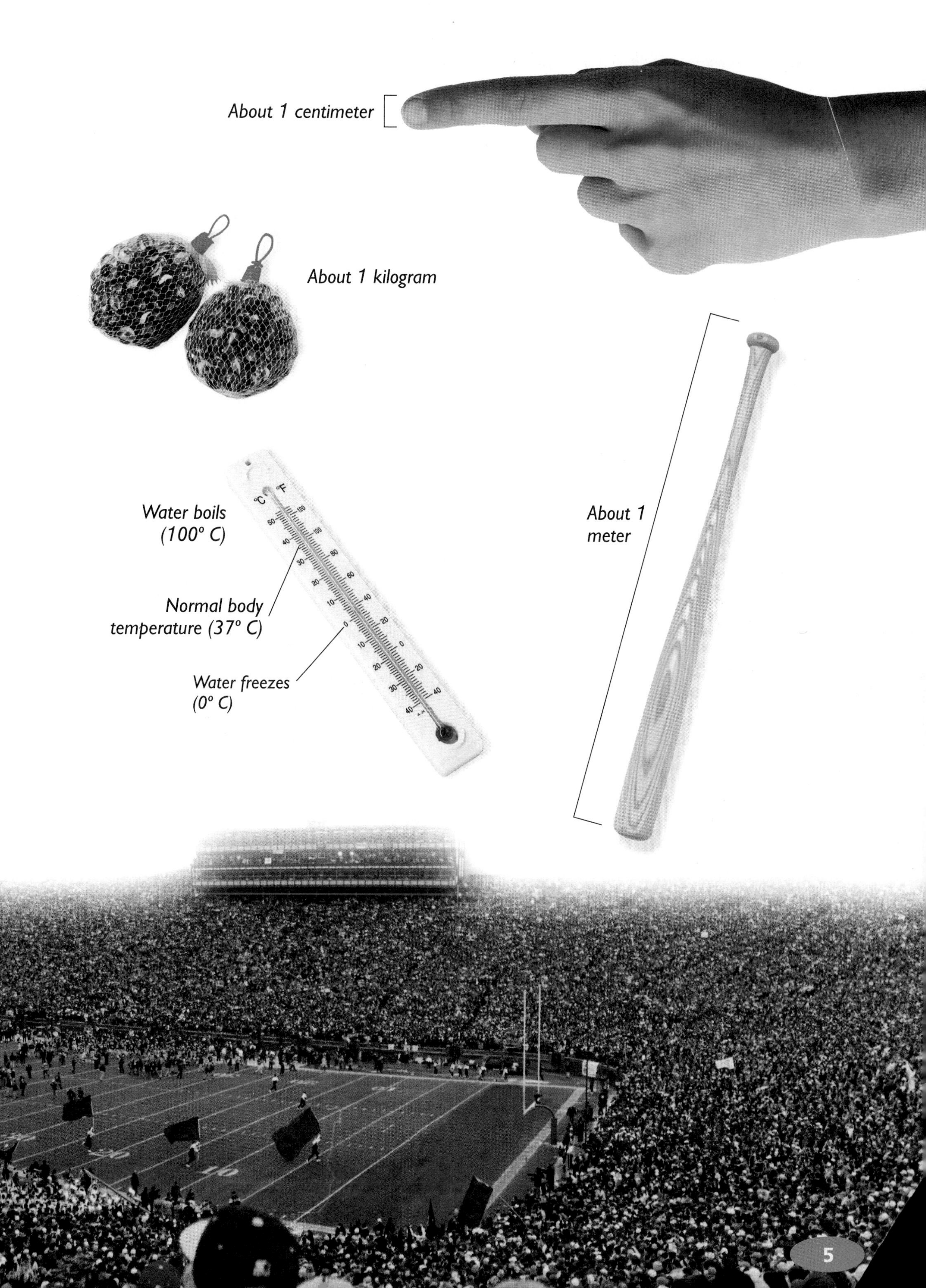
About 1 centimeter
About 1 kilogram
Water boils
(100° C)
Normal body
temperature (37° C)
Water freezes
(0° C)
About 1
meter

Observing

How can you increase your powers of observation?

Using your senses helps you understand and learn about the world around you. For example, imagine picking up a ball. Think about the texture. Is it soft, hard, or a combination of both of these things? Does smelling the ball tell you if it is made of plastic or rubber? Imagine shaking it. Is it solid or hollow? Can you tell if something is inside the ball? Are there any characteristics about the ball that can help you determine whether or not the ball can bounce?

As a result of careful observations, you will understand how things and events change. This understanding allows you to make accurate comparisons. Every observation you make is an important one.

Practice Observing

Materials

- box of unshelled peanuts
- marker
- index card
- metric ruler
- hand lens

Follow This Procedure:

1. Choose a peanut from the box.
2. Use a marker to place a small identifying mark on the peanut. Do not share your mark with other students.
3. Observe your peanut carefully. Record as many observations about your peanut as you can on an index card. Be specific.
4. When you've finished observing your peanut, place it back into the box.
5. Exchange your observation card with a classmate. Use the observations on the cards to identify each other's peanuts.

Thinking About Your Thinking

What senses did you use to observe your peanut? Did your partner use observations similar to those you used? What additional observations could you have recorded to better describe your peanut?

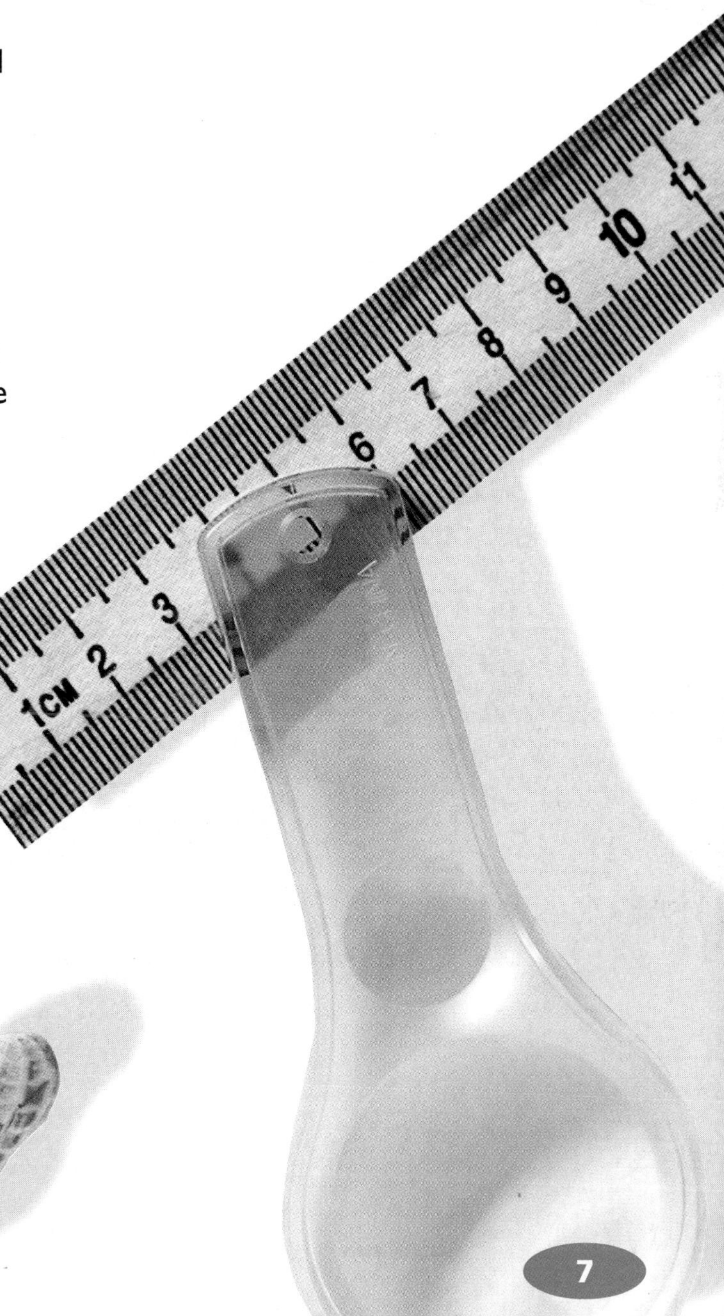

Communicating

How can you communicate in an effective and easily understood way?

Good scientific communication uses words, pictures, charts, and graphs to give information that it is easily understood by people all around the world.

When you make and record observations, it is important to use exact words and to give as much information as possible. Compare the following observations that two students wrote after they observed the same experiment.

> The liquid changed color and bubbles formed.
>
> The liquid changed from pale yellow to bright red. Bubbles began forming almost immediately. The liquid bubbled rapidly for 27 seconds and then stopped.

The second student's observations are more exact and complete. Anyone reading these observations can get a fairly good idea of what the student observed. This is not true of the first student's description. The second student communicated in a more meaningful way.

Practice Communicating

Materials

- box of cards with pictures on them
- colored pencils
- 2 sheets of drawing paper

Follow This Procedure

1. Work with a partner. Choose a picture card from the box. Don't show the card to your partner.
2. Look at the picture on your card. Think how you would describe the picture to another person. Where would you start? What words would you use?

3. Slowly and carefully describe the picture on your card to your partner. As you describe the picture, your partner should draw what you describe.
4. When you've completed your description, compare your partner's drawing to the picture on the card. How well did you communicate what you saw?
5. Reverse roles and repeat steps 1–4.

Thinking About Your Thinking

What process did you use to describe your picture? What part did you describe first? Why did you decide to start with that part of the picture? How could you have communicated your information more clearly?

Classifying

How can you classify objects?

Classifying is the process of organizing or arranging objects into groups according to characteristics they share. You classify objects in order to organize your thoughts and knowledge about a subject. This organization of information helps you better understand the objects and events you observe.

What characteristics do the birds on this page share? Based on these similarities, the canary and the duck are both classified as birds. With this information, you can make generalizations about these animals based on your knowledge of the bird group. For example, you can conclude that the canary and the duck lay eggs because egg laying is a characteristic shared by all birds.

In order to classify objects, you must be able to recognize the characteristics that are similar or different among a group of objects. Then you can group the objects according to one or more of their similar characteristics.

Practice Classifying

Materials

- paper
- pencil
- buttons

Follow This Procedure:

1. Observe a group of buttons. Notice how the buttons are similar and how they are different. Record your observations on a sheet of paper.
2. Choose one characteristic. You might choose size, shape, color, or any other characteristic. Based on this characteristic, classify the buttons into two different groups. Record the characteristics each group shares.
3. Now classify each group into various smaller groups based on other similar characteristics. How are the buttons in each group similar? How are they different? Record the characteristics of each group.
4. Report your group's classification to the class. Discuss how the classifications differed among the groups.

Thinking About Your Thinking

The same objects can be classified differently by different people. Why do you think this might occur? Support your answer with some examples.

Estimating and Measuring

How can you accurately estimate and measure?

An estimate is an intelligent guess about an object or an event. One common characteristic that people estimate is measurement. As you get more practice measuring objects, you should find that making estimates that are very close to actual measurements becomes easier.

Being able to estimate volume is often helpful as you do science experiments. Estimating volume can be difficult if an object is irregularly shaped, such as the pebbles below. However, by finding the volume of one pebble, you can better estimate the volume of the other three.

Practice Estimating and Measuring

Materials

- 50-mL plastic graduated cylinder
- water
- 4 irregularly-shaped pebbles of varying sizes

Follow This Procedure

1. Copy the chart onto a sheet of paper. Use your chart to record your observations.
2. Fill a graduated cylinder with water to the 25-mL mark.
3. Choose the pebble that you think has the smallest volume.
4. Estimate the level to which you think the water will rise if you place the pebble into the cylinder. Record your estimate.
5. Gently place the pebble in the water. Record the level of the water in the cylinder.
6. Compare your estimate of the water level to the actual measurement. Are you surprised by the new water level?
7. Find the volume of the pebble by subtracting 25 mL from the actual level of water. Record this volume.
8. Repeat steps 4–7 until you have estimated and measured the volume of all four rocks.

Thinking About Your Thinking

Do you think it will be easier to predict the volume of a regularly-shaped object such as a marble than it is to predict the volume of an irregularly-shaped object? Why or why not?

Pebble	Estimated level of water	Actual level of water	Volume of pebble
1			
2			
3			
4			

Inferring

How can you make a valid inference?

When you make an inference, you make a reasonable guess about information that is not obvious. An inference is based on observations and past experience. In order to make an inference, you must make good observations and consider all the information you have about a situation. Think about how what you've observed relates to situations you are familiar with.

Inferring is an important first step toward predicting outcomes of experiments and forming testable hypotheses. Although an inference must be based on observations or facts, it doesn't always have to be true. After further investigation and experimentation, you might discover that your original inference missed the mark. If necessary, you can make another inference based on the new information you gathered.

Practice Inferring

Materials

- safety goggles
- spoon
- baking soda
- 3 small plastic cups
- hand lens
- dropper
- 3 unknown substances marked A, B, and C
- vinegar

Follow This Procedure

1. Copy the chart onto a sheet of paper. Use your chart to record your observations.
2. Put on your safety goggles. Place a half spoonful of baking soda in a plastic cup. Observe the baking soda with a hand lens. Record your observations.
3. Repeat step 2 with the unknown substances.
4. Make an inference. Based on your observations, which substances are baking soda? Record your inference on your paper.
5. Use the dropper to add three drops of vinegar to the cup with the baking soda. Observe what happens. Record your observations in your chart.
6. Repeat step 5 with Unknowns A–C.
7. Review your inferences from step 4. If necessary, make new inferences based on your observations.

Substance	Observations	
	Without Vinegar	With Vinegar
Baking soda		
Unknown A		
Unknown B		
Unknown C		

Thinking About Your Thinking

What information from this activity did you use to make your inferences? What information from past experiences did you use? How did making additional observations affect your inferences?

Predicting

How can you improve your predicting skills?

When you make a prediction, you guess what will happen in a particular situation. Your prediction is based on knowing what has happened in similar situations. The more information you have and the better your observations, the more likely you are to make accurate predictions.

Look at the cars and ramps below. What amount of force is needed to pull the car up the ramp in the first two pictures? How does this force relate to the height of the ramp?

Now, use the information from the first two photos to predict the amount of force needed to pull the car up the third ramp. Based on your observations of the first two pictures, you can predict that the force needed is three times that in the first picture, or 75N.

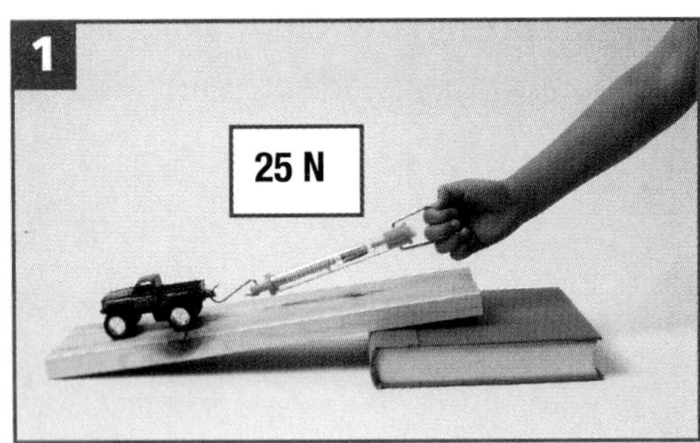

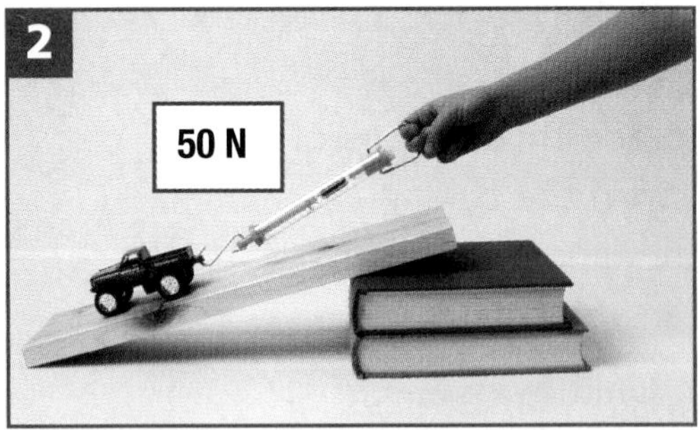

Practice Predicting

Materials

- feather
- book

Follow This Procedure:

1. Copy the chart onto a sheet of paper. Use your chart to record your predictions and observations.
2. Hold a book in one hand and a feather in the other. If you drop both at the same time, which will reach the ground first? Record your prediction in your chart.
3. Drop the two items. Record your results.
4. Place the feather on top of the book. If you drop the book with the feather lying on top, which will reach the ground first, the feather or the book? Record your prediction.
5. Drop the book with the feather on top of it. Record your results.

	Prediction	Observation
Feather and book dropped separately		
Book dropped with feather on top		

Thinking About Your Thinking

What information did you use to make your prediction in step 2? in step 4? What additional information would have helped you make better predictions?

Making Operational Definitions

How can you make an operational definition?

An operational definition is a definition or description of an object or an event based on the way you experience it.

An operational definition can describe many different qualities of an object or an event. It can explain what something does, what purpose something serves, or how an event takes place.

For example, look at the pictures below which show a strip of litmus paper that has been dipped into some vinegar. The pictures show that when the blue litmus paper is dipped into vinegar, which is an acid, it turns red. Based on this test, an operational definition for an acid might be "a substance that turns blue litmus paper red."

Practice Making Operational Definitions

Materials

- slice of potato
- paper towel
- dropper
- iodine solution
- slice of carrot
- small cup of water
- saltine
- piece of cooked egg white

Follow This Procedure

1. Copy the chart onto a sheet of paper. Use your chart to record your observations.
2. Place a slice of potato on a paper towel.
3. With the dropper, place a small drop of iodine solution on the potato. Observe what happens to the potato. Record your observations in your chart.
4. Repeat steps 2 and 3 with the remaining food items.
5. Look up the definition for the word *starch* in a dictionary. Write the definition on your paper below your chart.
6. Look in the chart to see which items contain starch. Use that information and the results of this activity to write an operational definition of a starch.

Food Item	Starch?	Color when iodine is added
Potato	yes	
Carrot	yes	
Water	no	
Saltine	yes	
Egg white	no	

Thinking About Your Thinking

How is your operational definition different from the definition of a starch in the dictionary? When might your operational definition be more useful than the dictionary definition?

Making and Using Models

How do scientific models help you understand science?

A scientific model can be an object or an idea that shows how something that you can't observe directly looks or works. Using models allows you to better understand objects, events, or ideas. Good models can be used to explain what you know and to predict what will happen.

The picture shows a model of one kind of object that is too tiny to see—a methane molecule. Scientists use models of molecules to explain why atoms act as they do and to predict how substances will react chemically with each other.

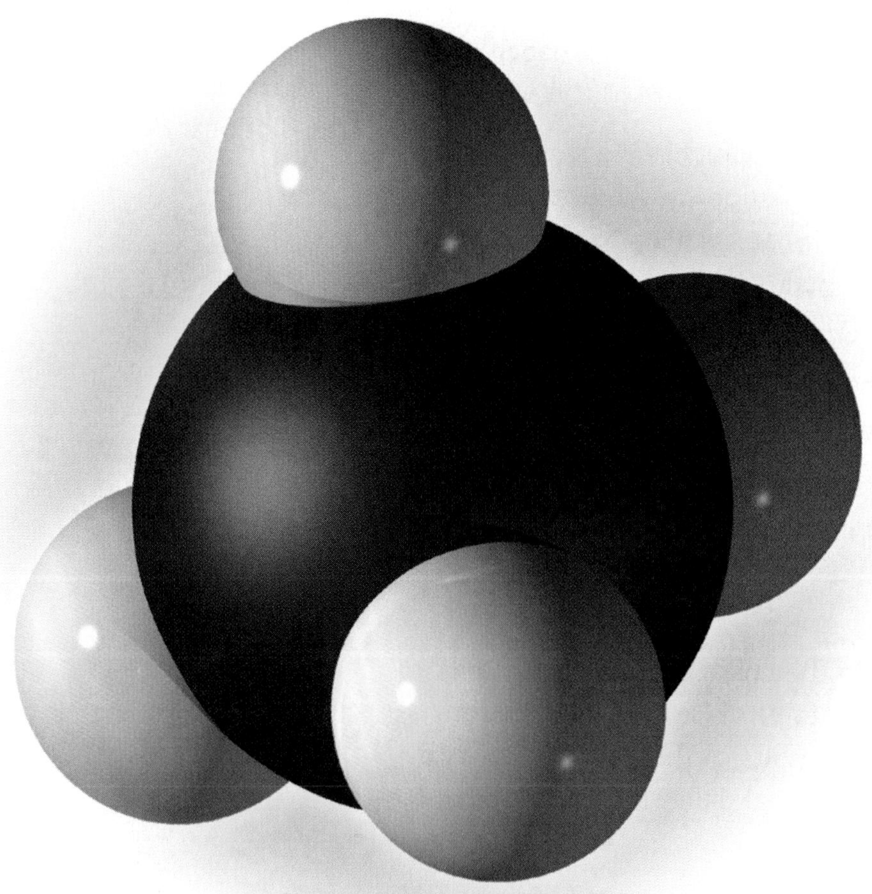

Methane Molecule

Practice Making and Using Models

Materials

- 2 different colors of clay
- toothpicks, broken in half

Follow This Procedure

1. Make a chart like the one shown. Use your chart to draw your molecules.
2. You will make clay models of molecules that contain hydrogen and oxygen atoms. Use one color of clay to make oxygen atoms for your model molecules. Use another color for hydrogen atoms.
3. Use the clay "atoms" to construct molecules of water, hydrogen peroxide, and hydrogen gas. The table shows how many atoms to include in each molecule and how the atoms are connected.
4. Complete the chart by making a drawing of your model.

Name	Atoms in one molecule	Arrangement	Drawing of molecule model
Water	2 hydrogen 1 oxygen	H\O/H	
Hydrogen peroxide	2 hydrogen 2 oxygen	H—O—O—H	
Hydrogen gas	2 hydrogen	H—H	

Thinking About Your Thinking

How does having a physical model help you understand these molecules? Use your models to explain how the molecules of different substances vary.

Formulating Questions and Hypotheses

Asking questions is an important part of the scientific process. Questions may come from a problem you have, from something you observe, or from things that interest you.

After you've identified a question, the next step is to formulate a hypothesis. Your hypothesis should be a clear statement that answers your question. A good hypothesis should also be testable. You should be able to design an experiment that would prove that your hypothesis is true or false.

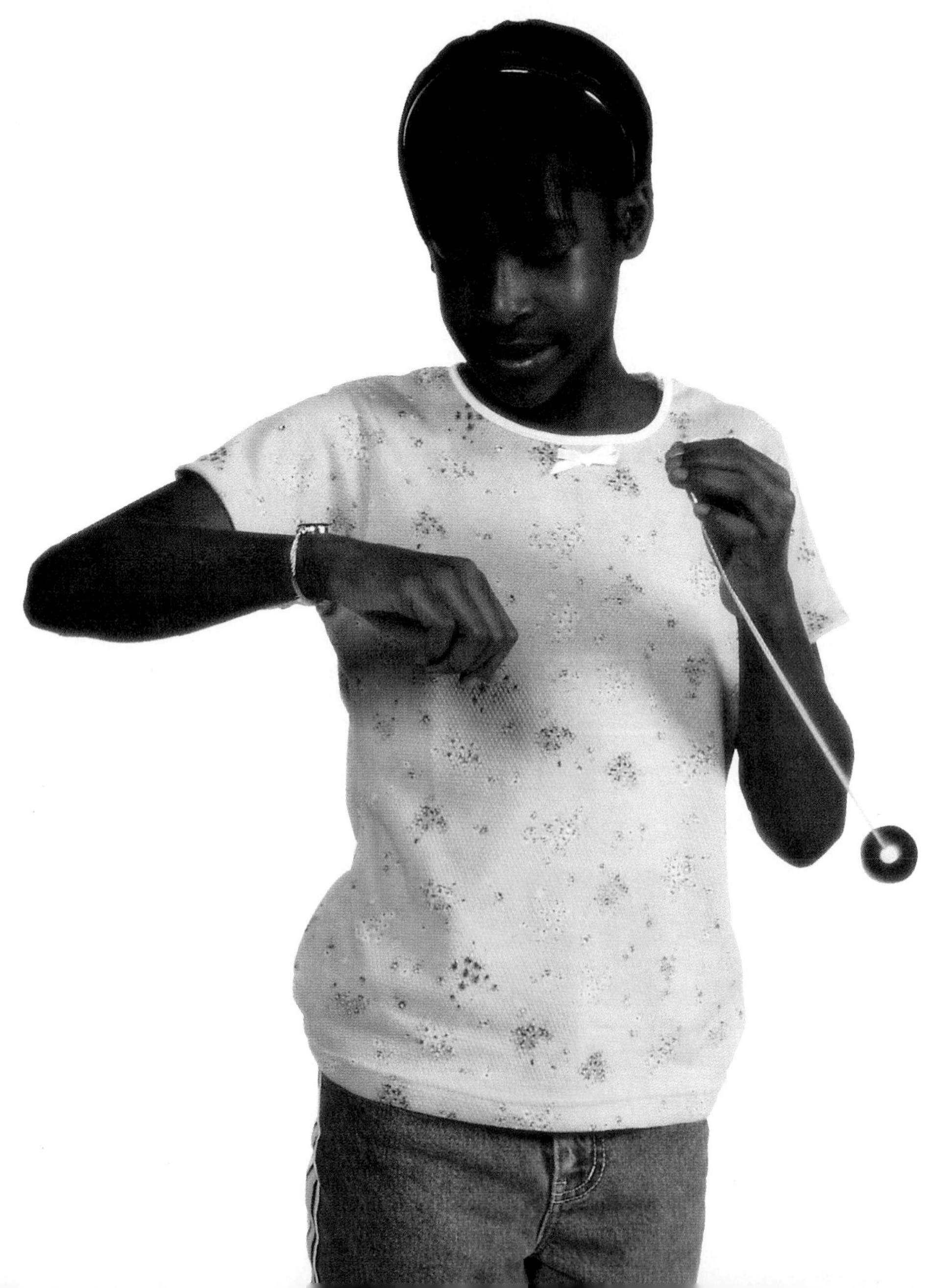

Practice Formulating Questions and Hypotheses

Materials

- scissors
- metric ruler
- string
- metal washer
- clock with a second hand

Follow This Procedure:

1. Make a chart like the one shown. Use your chart to record your data.
2. Cut and measure the length of a piece of string. Your string should be between 25 cm and 45 cm long. Record the length in your chart.
3. Tie a washer to one end of the string to make a pendulum.
4. Hold the washer out at about a 45° angle. This position is the start point for timing the period of the pendulum.
5. Release the washer. When the washer has swung back to the start point, one period has passed. Time how long it takes for 5 periods of the pendulum to occur. Record the time in your chart.
6. How do you think the length of the string affects the time it takes for one period? Write a hypothesis.
7. Test your hypothesis. Repeat steps 3–5 four more times, using a different length of string each time.

String length	Time for one period

Thinking About Your Thinking

On what information did you base your hypothesis? Did your data support your hypothesis? What other questions do you have as a result of this activity?

Collecting and Interpreting Data

How can you organize and interpret information that you collect?

When you make observations, you collect and interpret data. Arranging your data in graphs, tables, charts, or diagrams can make it easier to solve problems or answer questions. The best method of arranging your data depends on the type of data you collect and the way you plan to use it.

The graphics below display the same data in two different ways. Which graphic would you use to compare the growth of the two plants?

Plant Growth					
	Day 1	**Day 2**	**Day 3**	**Day 4**	**Day 5**
Plant in soil	3.0 cm	4.0 cm	4.5 cm	5.3 cm	6.0 cm
Plant in sand	3.0 cm	3.2 cm	3.6 cm	4.0 cm	4.1 cm

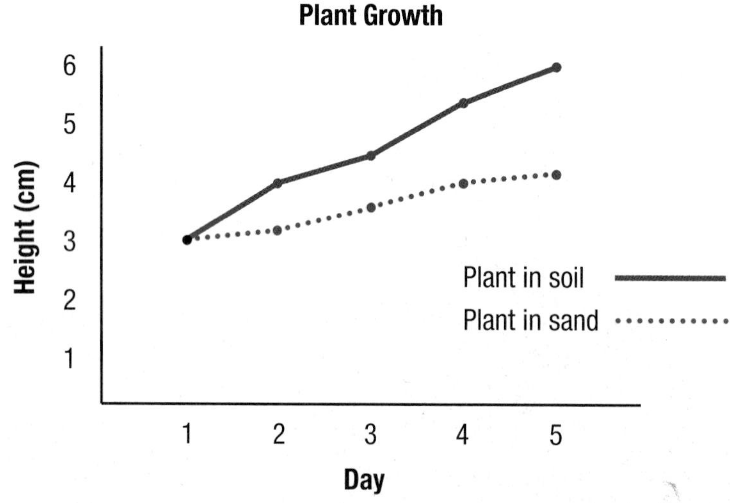

Practice Collecting and Interpreting Data

Follow This Procedure:

1. Work with a group. Collect the following data from each group member:
   - How many people are in the person's family?
   - What is the person's height?
   - What color is the person's hair?
   - What is the person's eye color
   - How many years has the person lived in your city?
2. Decide with your group how to organize and display the data.
3. Discuss with your group how you would interpret these data. What might these data help you say about your group as a whole?

Thinking About Your Thinking

Why did you organize the data in the manner you chose? Could you present it in another way to emphasize a different view of your group? What other information would you add to your data to give a better picture of your group?

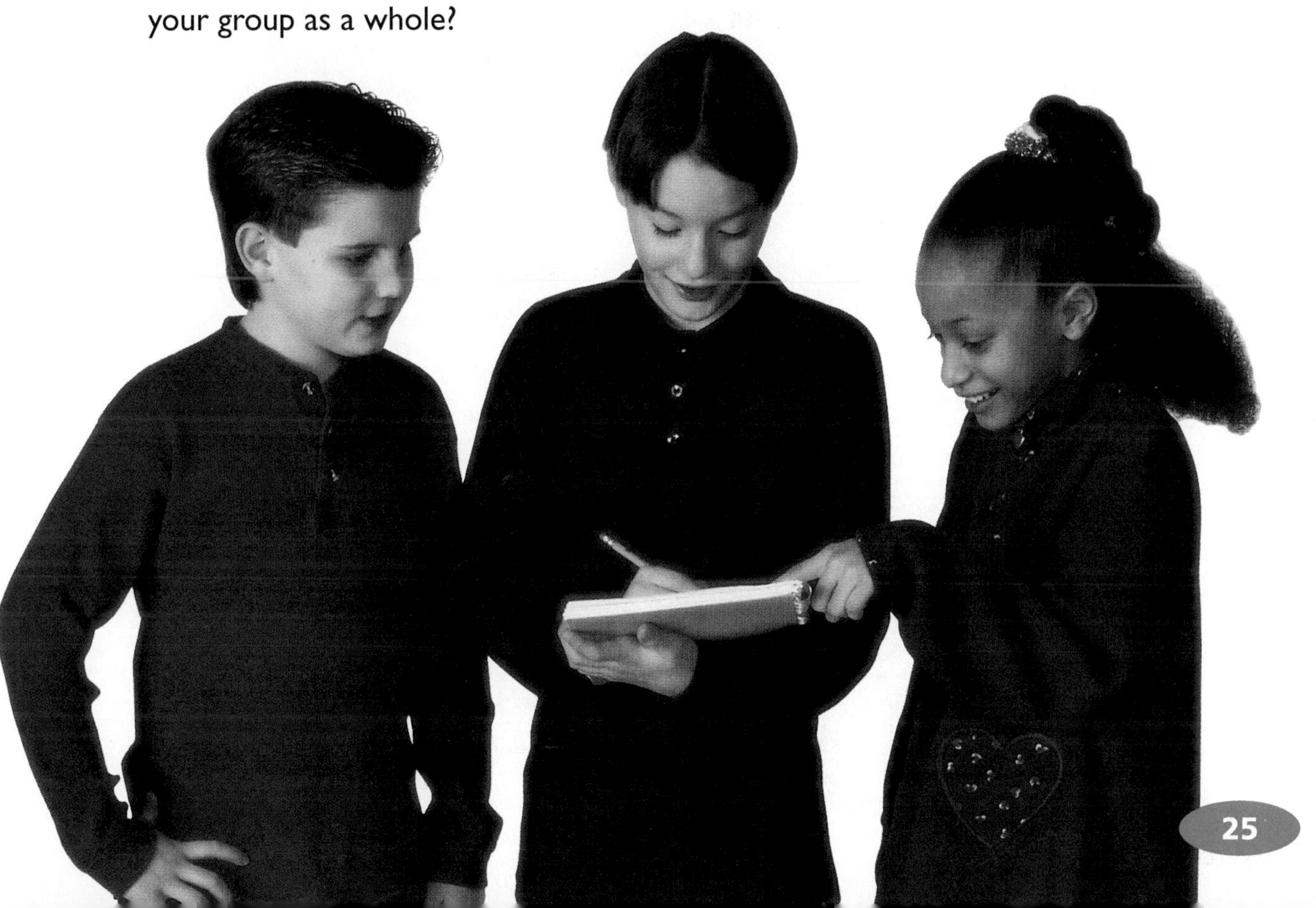

Identifying and Controlling Variables

How can you identify and control variables?

A variable is any factor that can change the outcome of an experiment. When you do experiments, it is important to identify and control variables. You do this by finding out which conditions make a difference in an experiment. To find how a particular variable affects the outcome of an experiment, you must control all other variables.

For example, suppose you wanted to find out whether more sugar dissolves in cold water or warm water. What variables would you control? What variable would change?

Practice Identifying and Controlling Variables

Materials

- measuring cup
- cold water
- 2 plastic cups
- 2 plastic spoons
- sugar
- very warm water

Follow This Procedure

1. Place 250 mL of cold water into a plastic cup.
2. Slowly add a half spoonful of sugar. Stir until all the sugar dissolves.
3. Keep adding sugar until no more will dissolve. Stir after each addition. Record the total amount of sugar you added to the cold water.
4. How much sugar will dissolve in very warm water? Decide how to test the warm water so that you can accurately compare it to the cold water. Decide on the following with your group as you develop a procedure to test the warm water.
   - How much water should you use?
   - How much sugar should you add at one time?
   - Should you stir or not stir? If you stir, how long should you stir?
5. Use your procedure to test the warm water. Compare your results to those from the cold water.

Thinking About Your Thinking

How much warm water did you use? Why did you choose that amount? What variables did you control? Why?

Experimenting

How can you perform valuable experiments?

Scientific experiments test a hypothesis or attempt to solve a problem. The results of the investigation can be used to form a conclusion about the hypothesis or to state an answer to the problem.

First, state the problem you are investigating as a clear question and write a hypothesis. Then identify the variables that might affect the results of your investigation. Identify the variable you will change. Keep all other variables the same.

Next, design your experiment. Write down the steps that you will use.

When you do the experiment, record your data clearly so that other people can understand what you did and how you did it. Your results should always be reported honestly, even if they were different from what you expected.

Finally, interpret your data and state your conclusions.

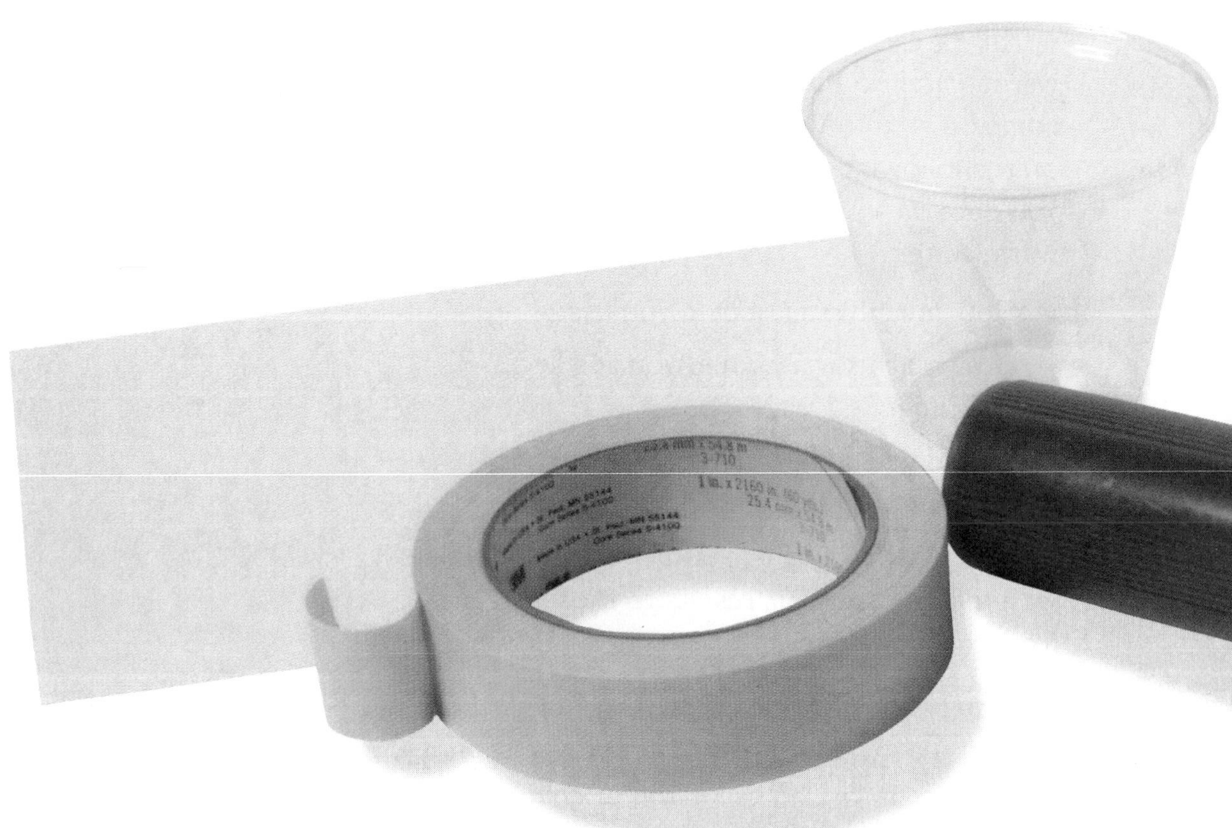

Practice Experimenting

Materials

- tape
- cup
- flashlight
- metric ruler

Follow This Procedure

1. Think about what you know about shadows. How does the distance between an object and a source of light affect the size of the object's shadow?
2. On a sheet of paper write a hypothesis to answer this question.
3. Design an experiment to test your hypotheses. Write a procedure. Use the materials in the materials list to do your experiment. Remember to identify and control the variables.
4. Make a chart to record your data.
5. Perform your experiment, following the steps in your procedure. Be sure to record your data.
6. Interpret your data and state your conclusion.

Thinking About Your Thinking

What is the difference between a hypothesis, as in step 2, and a conclusion, as in step 6? What information is your hypothesis based on? What information is your conclusion based on?

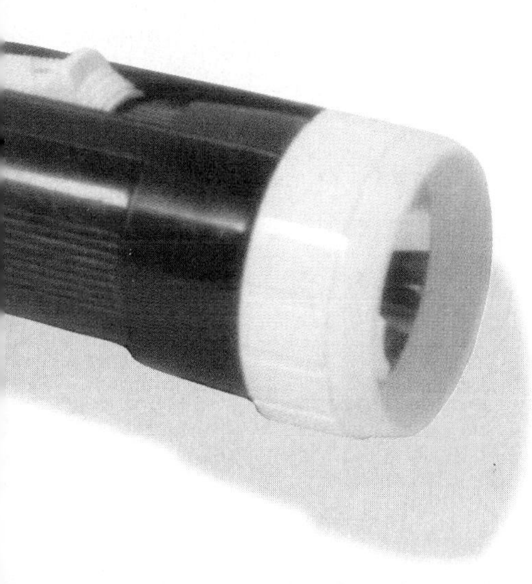

Classification of Living Things

Scientists classify different species of organisms into the five kingdoms you see below. All organisms that are now living or once lived can be placed into one of these kingdoms. Organisms within each kingdom share certain traits. Grouping organisms in this manner helps scientists learn more about them.

Kingdom	Monera	Protist	Fungi	Plant	Animal
Type of Cells	Prokaryotic	Eukaryotic	Eukaryotic	Eukaryotic	Eukaryotic
One-celled or Many-celled	One-celled	One-and many-celled	One-and many-celled	One-and many-celled	Many-celled
Movement	Some move	Some move	None move	None move	All move
Nutrition	Some make their own food. Others get it from other organisms.	Some make their own food. Others get it from other organisms.	All get food from other organisms.	All make their own food.	Eat plants or other animals.

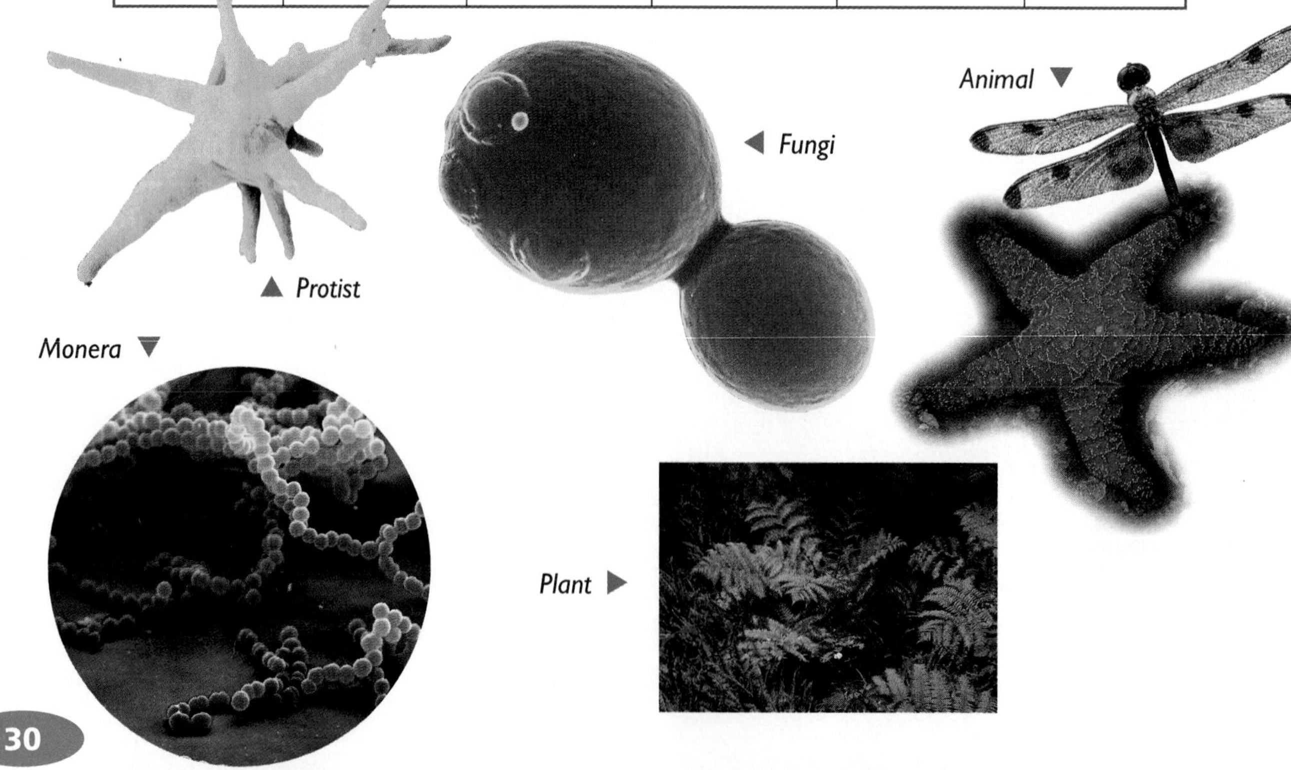
Protist
Fungi
Animal
Monera
Plant

Circuits

Electric current can flow only when it can follow a complete circuit. In series circuits, the current has only one path it can follow. Current can travel in more than one path in a parallel circuit.

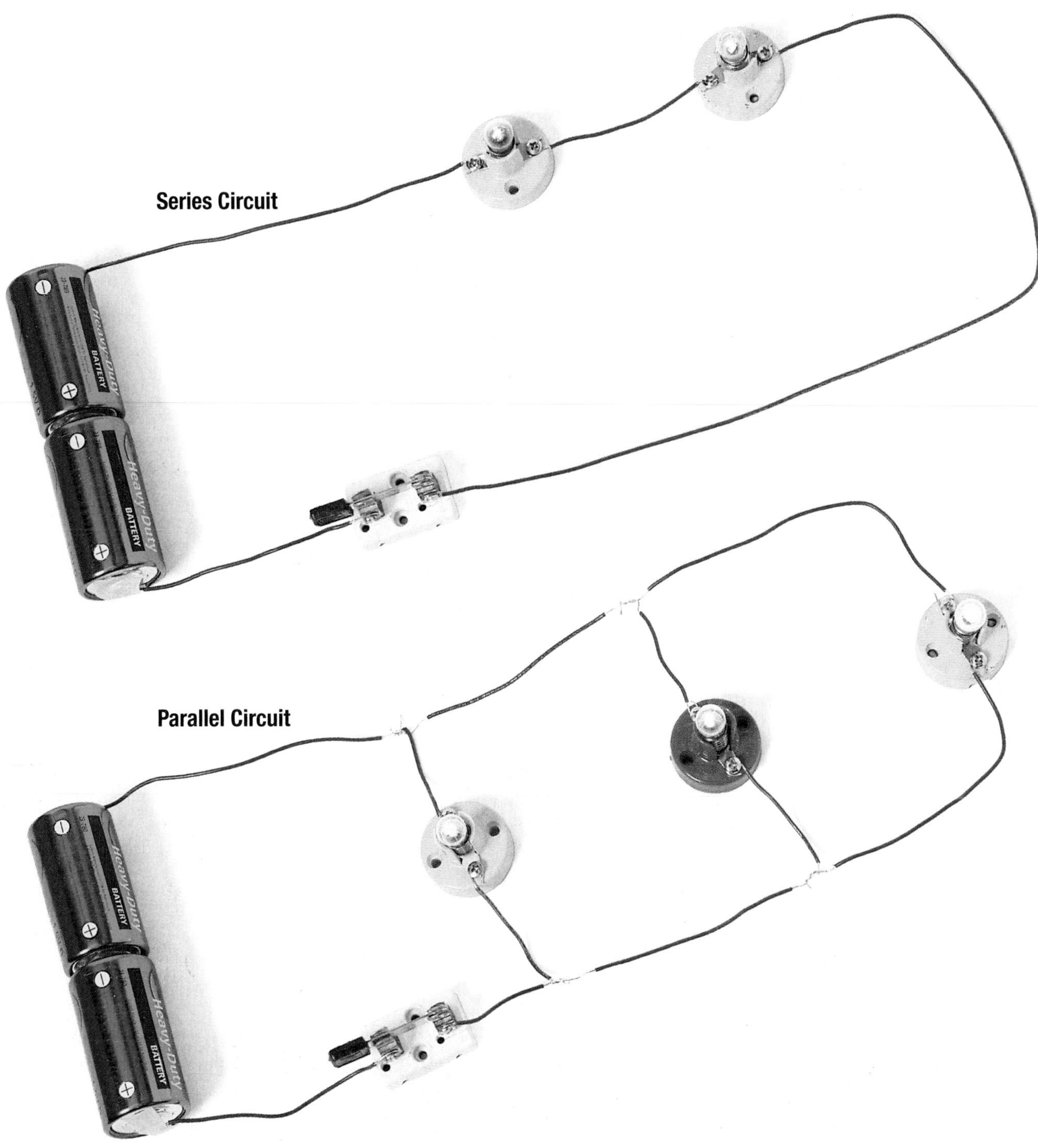

Energy in our World

The sun is the source of all energy on the earth. In fact, electromagnetic radiation of about 100 thousand million million joules reaches the earth from the sun each second. This energy is converted to different forms. You can follow some of these energy conversions in the pictures below.

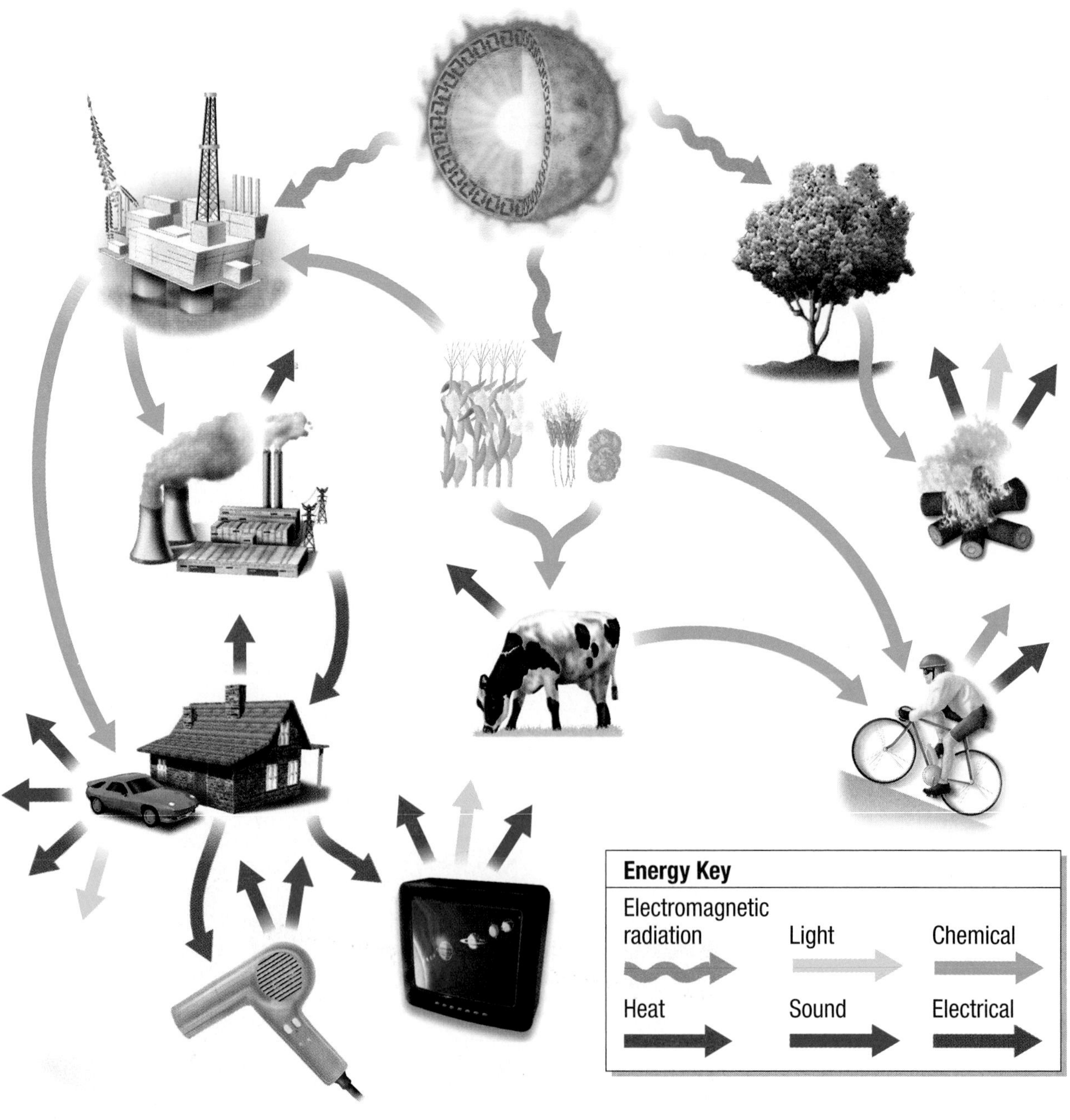

Simple Machines

Machines make work easier. Machines can be very simple, like the four simple machines shown on this page, or they can be complicated machines, such as automobiles.

Rock Cycle

Scientists classify rocks into three main types—igneous, metamorphic, and sedimentary. Each type of rock forms at least partly from other rocks. All rocks undergo continuous changes, which are brought about by heat, pressure, chemical reactions, or other forces that wear away or deposit materials. This change of rock from one type to another in a sequence is called the rock cycle.

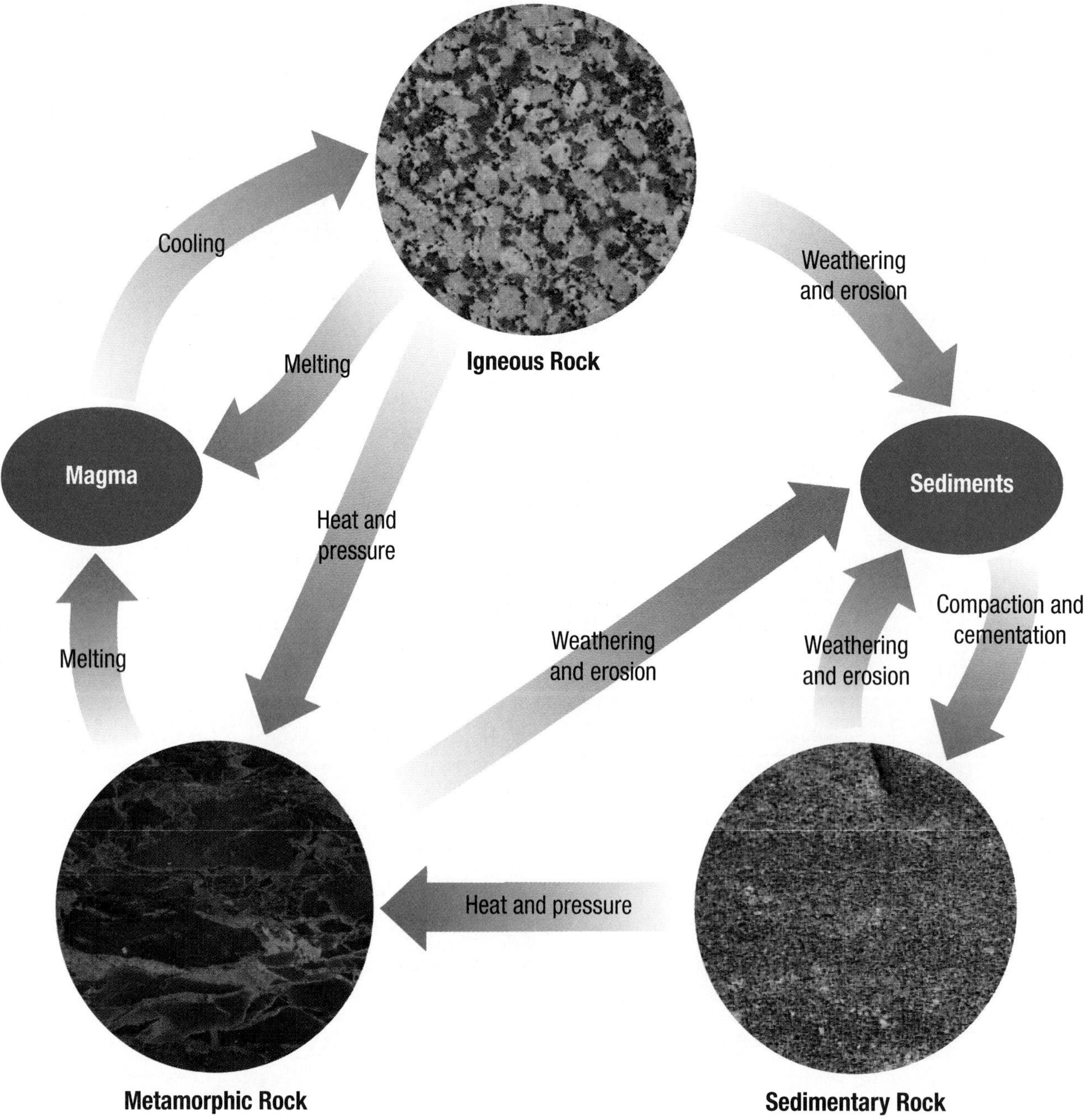

Characteristics of Planets

Planet	Mercury	Venus	Earth	Mars	Jupiter	Saturn	Uranus	Neptune	Pluto
Average distance to sun (AU)	0.387	0.723	1.000	1.524	5.203	9.529	19.191	30.061	39.529
Period of rotation days hours minutes	58 15 28	243 00 14	00 23 56	00 24 37	00 09 55	00 10 39	00 17 14	00 16 03	06 09 17
Period of revolution	87.97 days	224.70 days	365.26 days	686.98 days	11.86 years	29.46 years	84.04 years	164.79 years	248.53 years
Diameter	4,878	12,104	12,756	6,794	142,796	120,660	51,118	49,528	2,290
Mass (Earth=1)	0.06	0.82	1.00	0.11	317.83	95.15	14.54	17.23	0.002
Density (g/cm^3)	5.42	5.24	5.50	3.94	1.31	0.70	1.30	1.66	2.03
Surface gravity (Earth=1)	0.38	0.90	1.00	0.38	2.53	1.07	0.92	1.12	0.06
Number of known satellites	0	0	1	2	16	18	15	8	1
Known rings	0	0	0	0	4	thousands	11	4	0

Layers of the Atmosphere

Earth's atmosphere extends thousands of kilometers above Earth's surface. The higher you go, the thinner the atmosphere becomes. You can see the four layers of the atmosphere below. The ionosphere is an area of the atmosphere that is made up of ions that reflect radio waves.

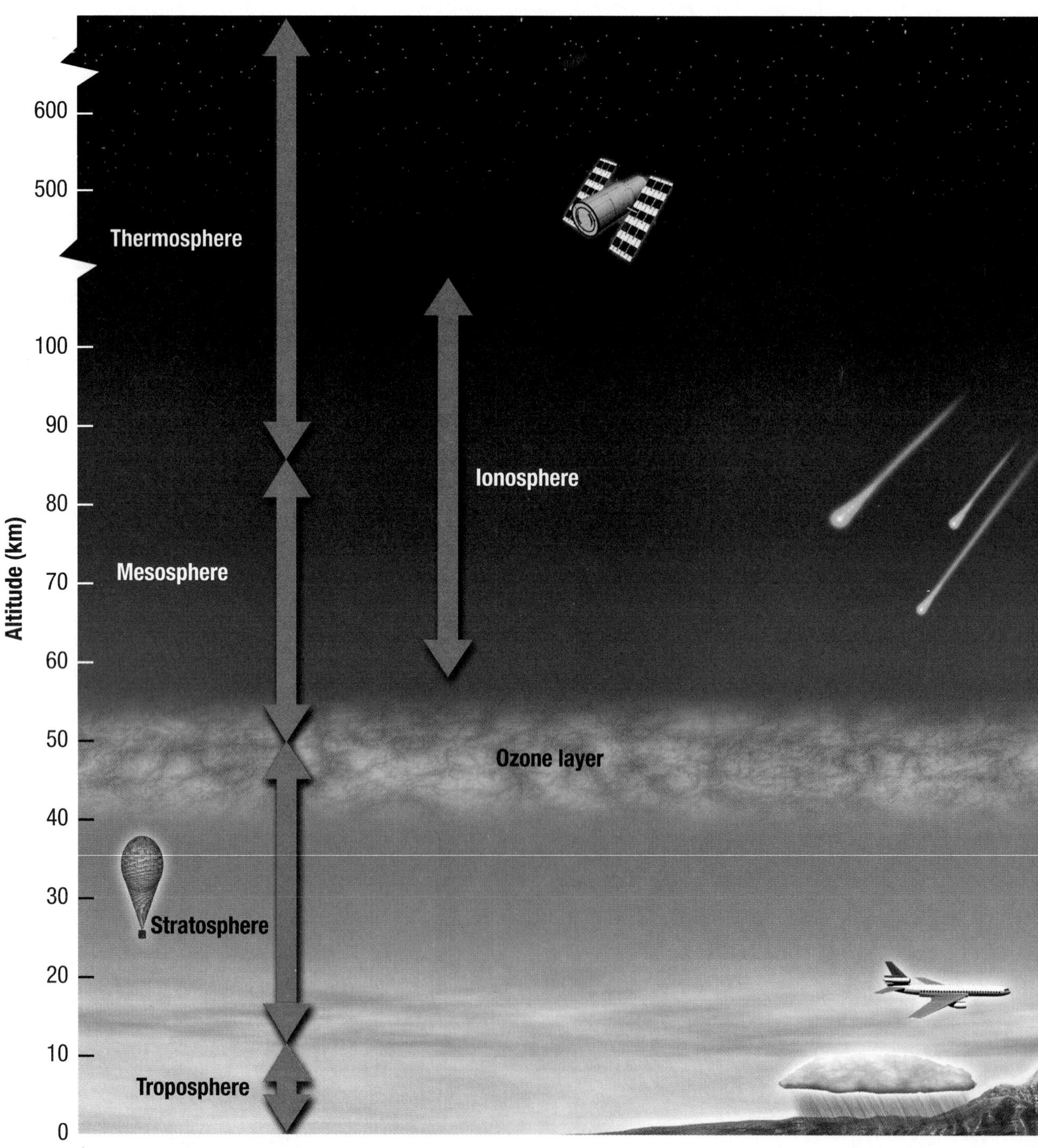

Atoms and Molecules

All matter is made of atoms, which are made of protons, neutrons, and electrons. Neutrons and protons form the nucleus of the atom. Electrons constantly change their positions as they travel around the nucleus. Atoms chemically combine to form a molecule.

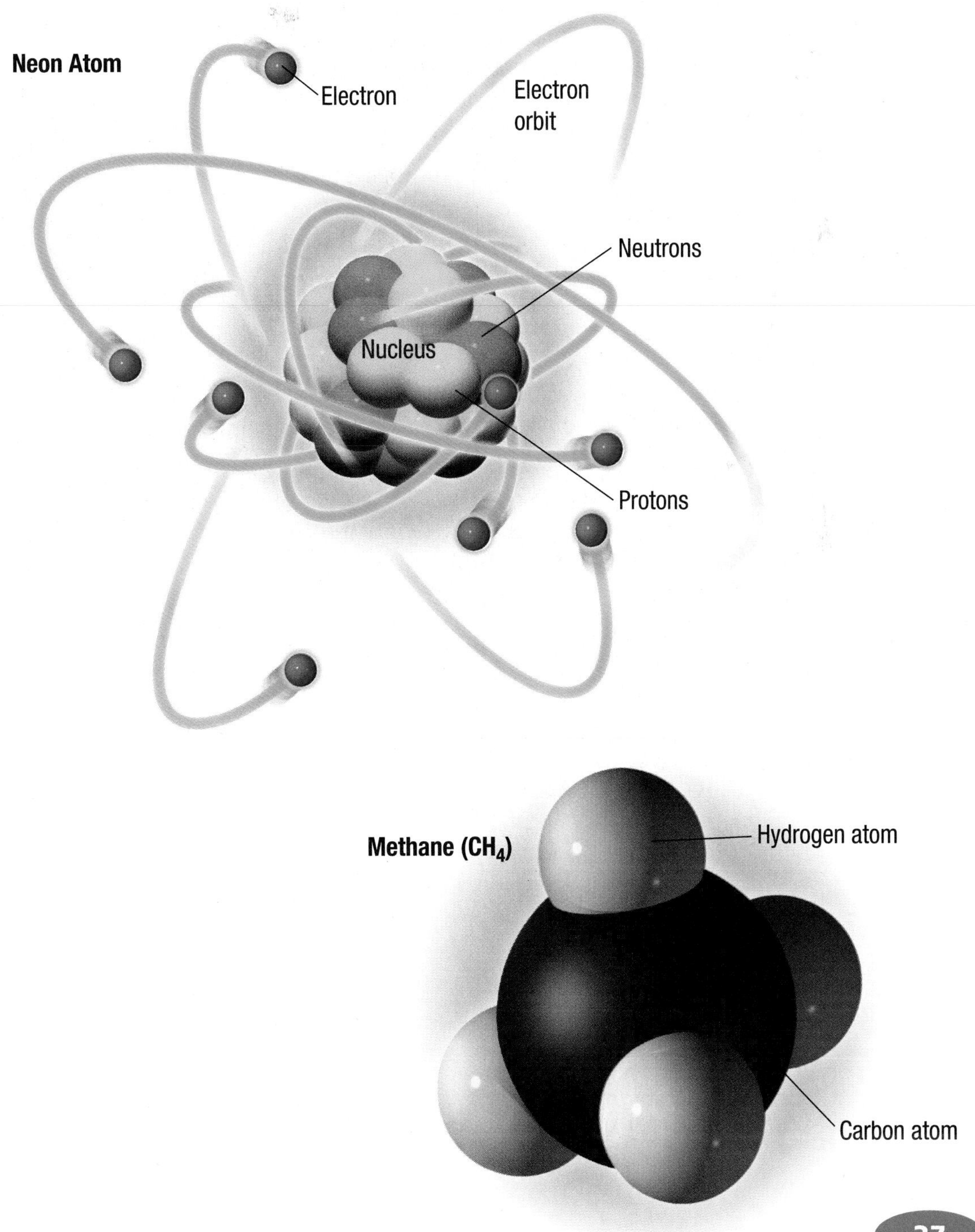

The Human Body

The different organs in your body make up organ systems. The parts of a simple system work together to perform a function. In a similar way, the organs in a system in your body work together to perform a function. All the systems work together to make your body work.

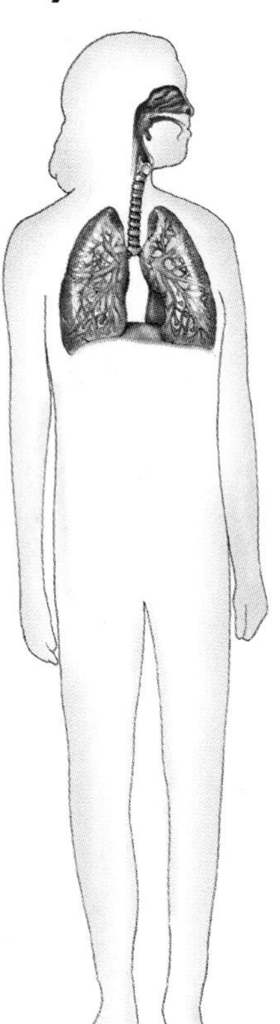

Respiratory System

◀ *Your respiratory system helps bring oxygen to the cells of your body and carries carbon dioxide and other wastes from cells. Air you breathe enters your lungs and passes into blood vessels that take it to all your cells.*

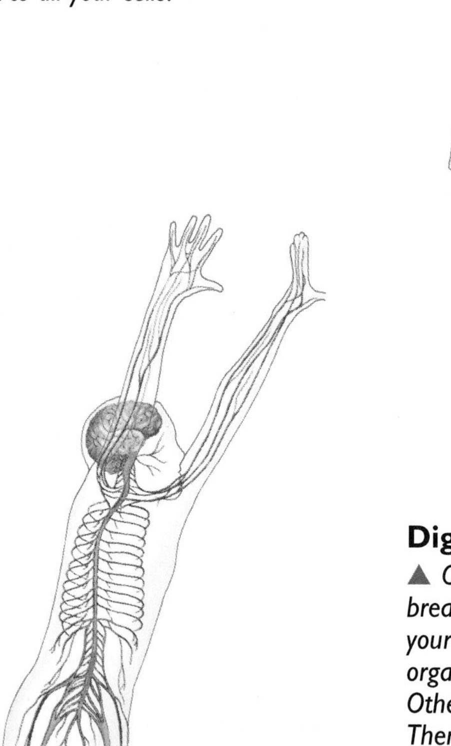

Digestive System

▲ *Organs in your digestive system break down food into nutrients that your cells can use. Some of the organs grind and mash the food. Others produce digestive fluids. Then blood vessels carry digested foods to all the cells of your body.*

Nervous System

◀ *Your nervous system includes your brain, spinal cord, and nerves. It gathers information from your environment, passes information to different parts of your body, and helps you interpret and use the information. Your brain sends signals to your muscles to let you move. Nerves send messages to and from other organs so they function properly.*

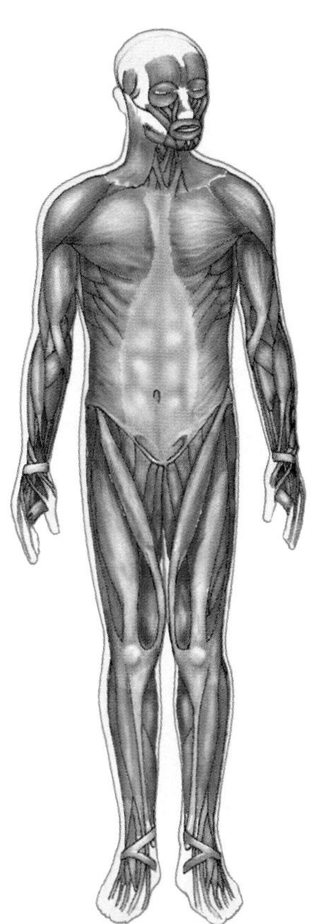

Circulatory System

Your heart, blood, and blood vessels make up your circulatory system. This system carries nutrients from your digestive system, oxygen brought in by your respiratory system, and wastes from both systems. These substances are transported to and from your body cells. ▶

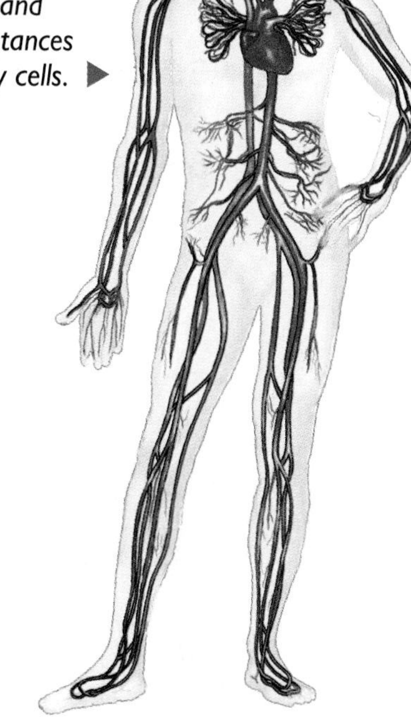

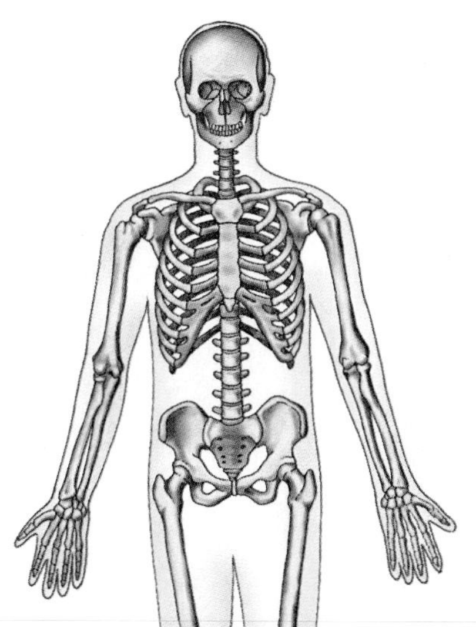

Muscular System

▲ *Many of the muscles in your body make up the muscular system. These muscles work with your bones to move the parts of your body. Nerves control the muscles. Blood vessels bring them the nutrients and oxygen they need to work.*

Skeletal System

◀ *All the bones in your body make up the skeletal system. They work together to protect and support your body and to help it move.*

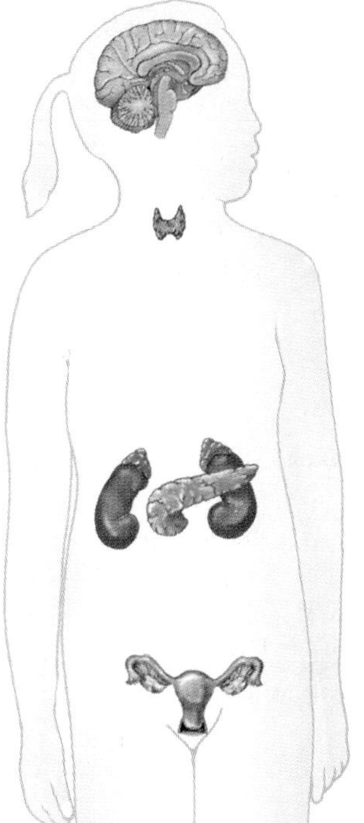

Endocrine System

◀ *The endocrine system is made up of glands that secrete hormones directly into the blood. These hormones control certain functions in your body.* ▶

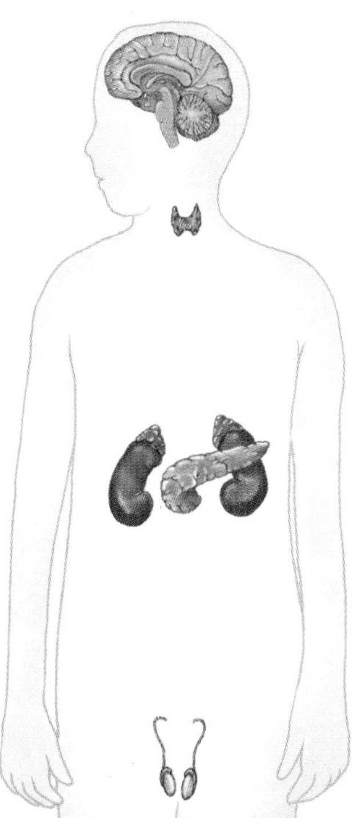

Tools of Science

Scientists use a variety of tools. You too will use tools as you do science activities. Some of those tools are shown on these two pages.

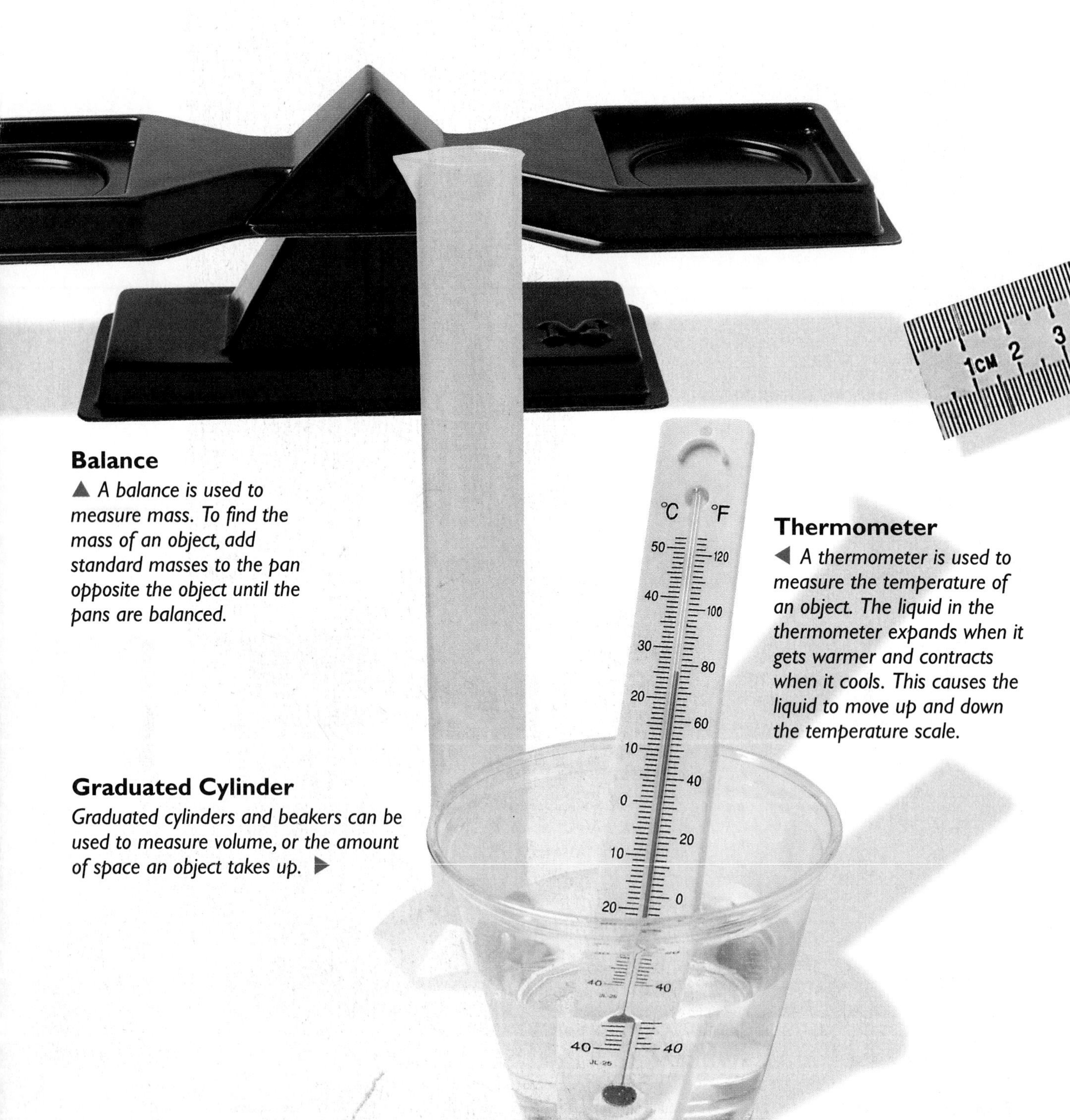

Balance

▲ *A balance is used to measure mass. To find the mass of an object, add standard masses to the pan opposite the object until the pans are balanced.*

Graduated Cylinder

Graduated cylinders and beakers can be used to measure volume, or the amount of space an object takes up. ▶

Thermometer

◀ *A thermometer is used to measure the temperature of an object. The liquid in the thermometer expands when it gets warmer and contracts when it cools. This causes the liquid to move up and down the temperature scale.*

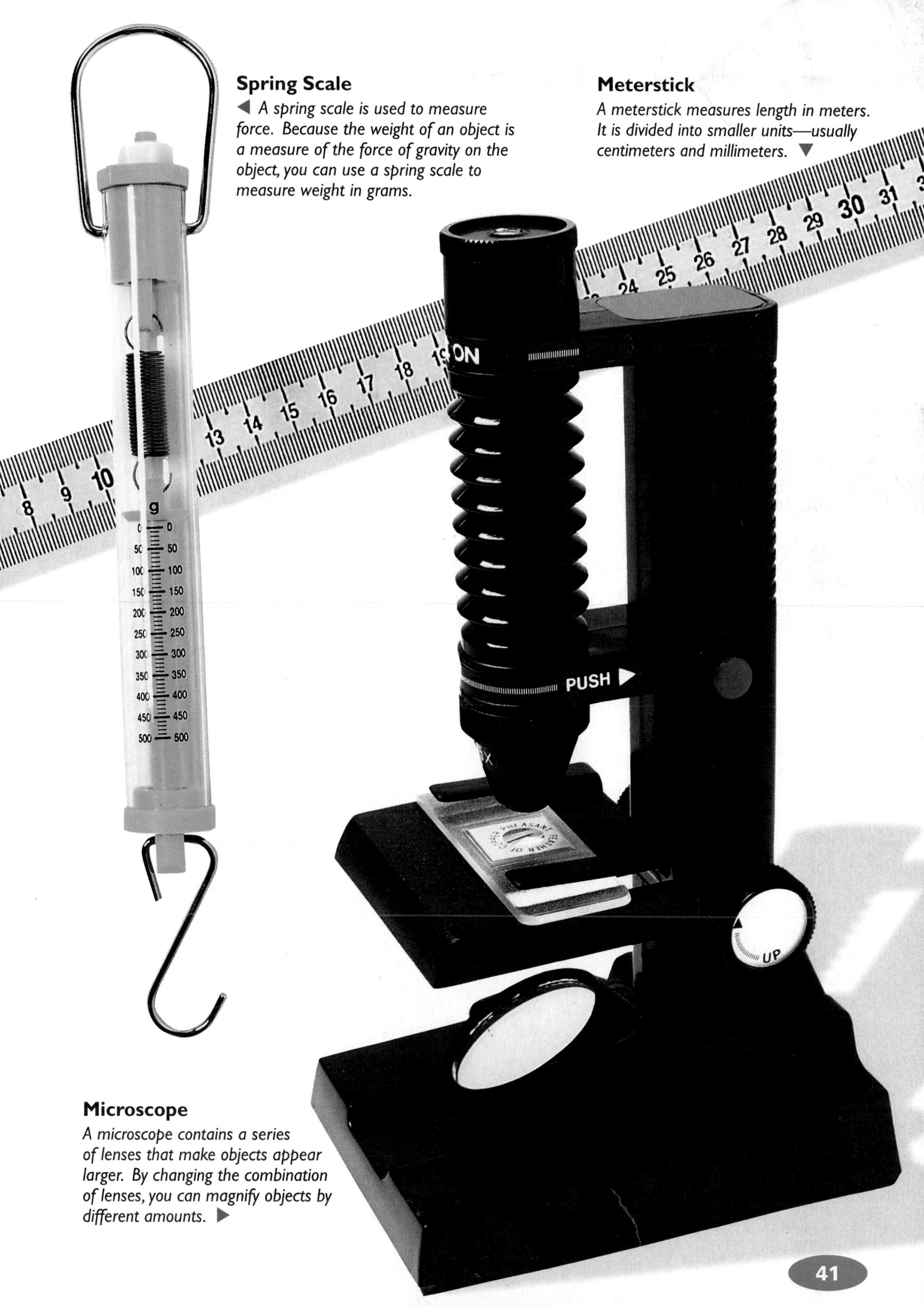

Spring Scale

◀ *A spring scale is used to measure force. Because the weight of an object is a measure of the force of gravity on the object, you can use a spring scale to measure weight in grams.*

Meterstick

A meterstick measures length in meters. It is divided into smaller units—usually centimeters and millimeters. ▼

Microscope

A microscope contains a series of lenses that make objects appear larger. By changing the combination of lenses, you can magnify objects by different amounts. ▶

Periodic Table of the Elements

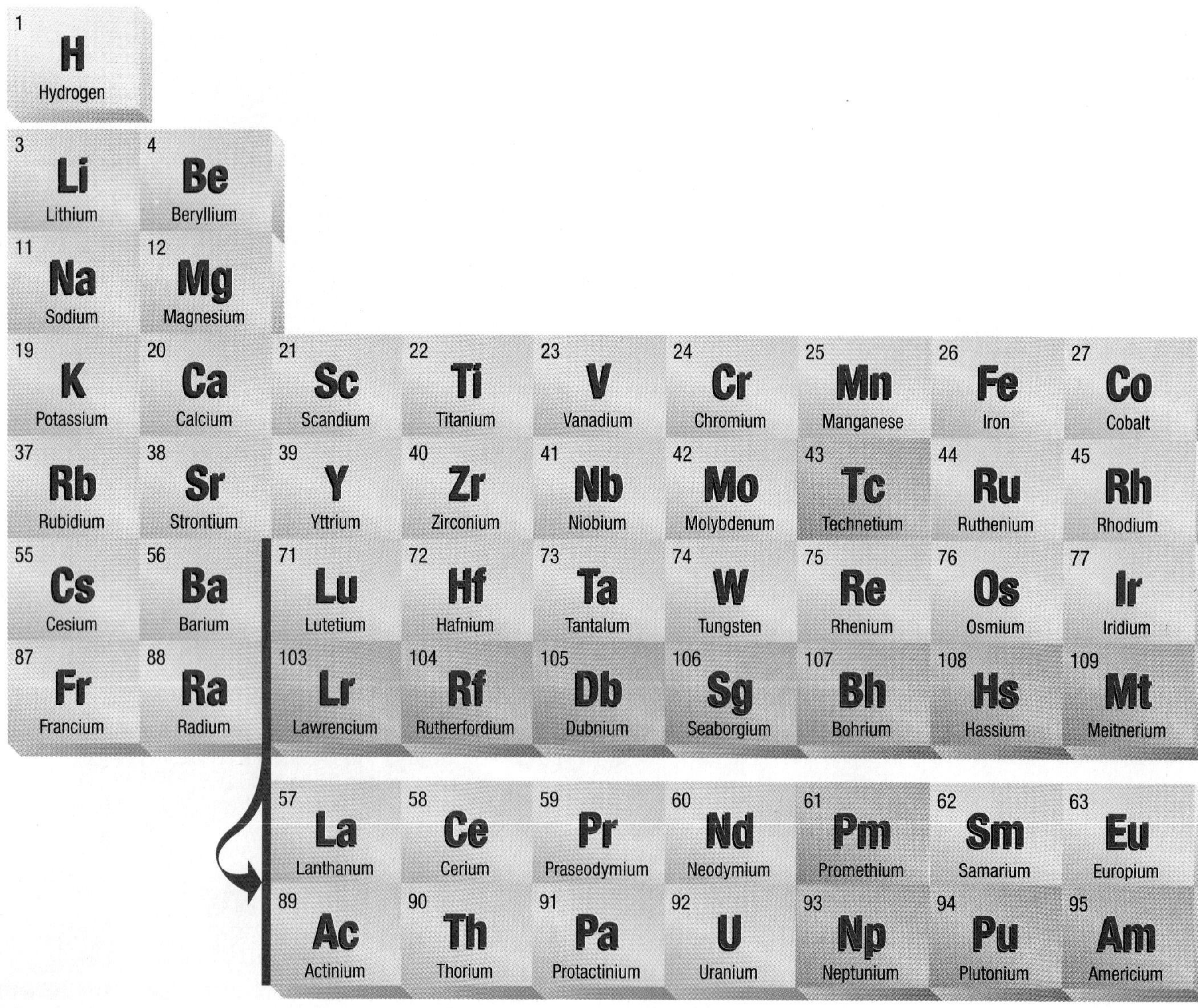

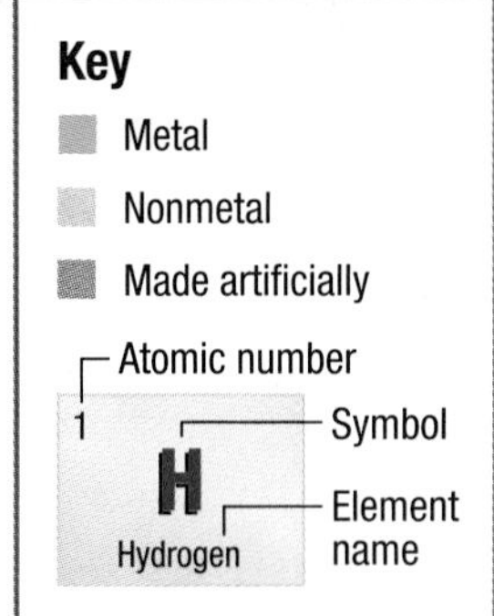

								2 He Helium
			5 B Boron	6 C Carbon	7 N Nitrogen	8 O Oxygen	9 F Fluorine	10 Ne Neon
			13 Al Aluminum	14 Si Silicon	15 P Phosphorous	16 S Sulfur	17 Cl Chlorine	18 Ar Argon
28 Ni Nickel	29 Cu Copper	30 Zn Zinc	31 Ga Gallium	32 Ge Germanium	33 As Arsenic	34 Se Selenium	35 Br Bromine	36 Kr Krypton
46 Pd Palladium	47 Ag Silver	48 Cd Cadmium	49 In Indium	50 Sn Tin	51 Sb Antimony	52 Te Tellurium	53 I Iodine	54 Xe Xenon
78 Pt Platinum	79 Au Gold	80 Hg Mercury	81 Tl Thallium	82 Pb Lead	83 Bi Bismuth	84 Po Polonium	85 At Astatine	86 Rn Radon
110 Uun Ununnilium	111 Uuu Unununium	112 Uub Ununbium						

64 Gd Gadolinium	65 Tb Terbium	66 Dy Dysprosium	67 Ho Holmium	68 Er Erbium	69 Tm Thulium	70 Yb Ytterbium
96 Cm Curium	97 Bk Berkelium	98 Cf Californium	99 Es Einsteinium	100 Fm Fermium	101 Md Mendelevium	102 No Nobelium

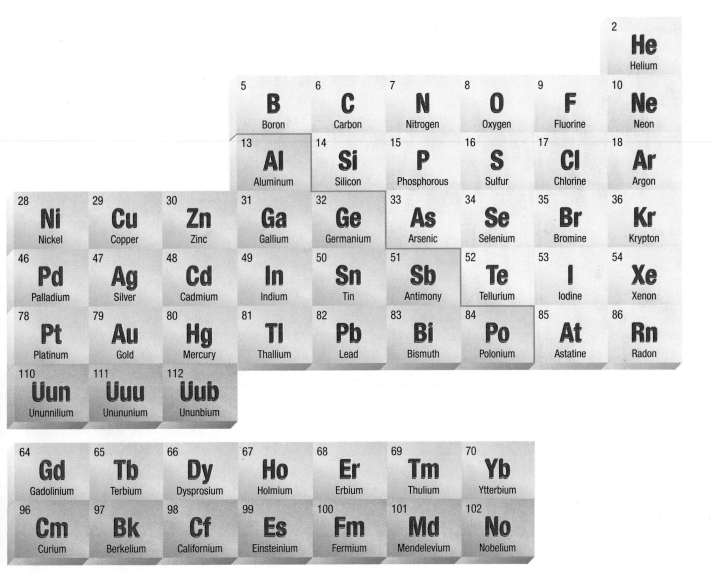

History of Science

	8000 B.C.	6000 B.C.	4000 B.C	2000 B.C.

Life Science

Physical Science

3000 B.C.
The Egyptians develop geometry. They use it to re-measure their farmlands after floods of the Nile River.

Earth Science

8000 B.C. Farming communities start as people use the plow for farming.

Human Body

500 B.C. | **400 B.C.** | **300 B.C.** | **200 B.C.** | **100 B.C.**

4th century B.C. Aristotle classifies plants and animals.

3rd century B.C. Aristarchus proposes that the earth revolves around the sun.

4th century B.C. Aristotle describes the motions of falling bodies. He believes that heavier things fall faster than lighter things.

260 B.C. Archimedes discovers the principles of buoyancy and the lever.

4th century B.C. Aristotle describes the motions of the planets.

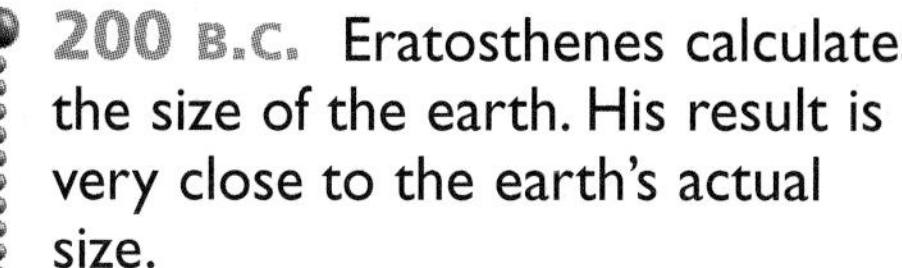

200 B.C. Eratosthenes calculates the size of the earth. His result is very close to the earth's actual size.

87 B.C. Chinese report observing an object in the sky that later became known as Halley's comet.

5th and 4th centuries B.C. Hippocrates and other Greek doctors record the symptoms of many diseases. They also urge people to eat a well-balanced diet.

110 AD	235	360	485	610	735

Life Science

Physical Science

83 A.D. Chinese travelers use the compass for navigation.

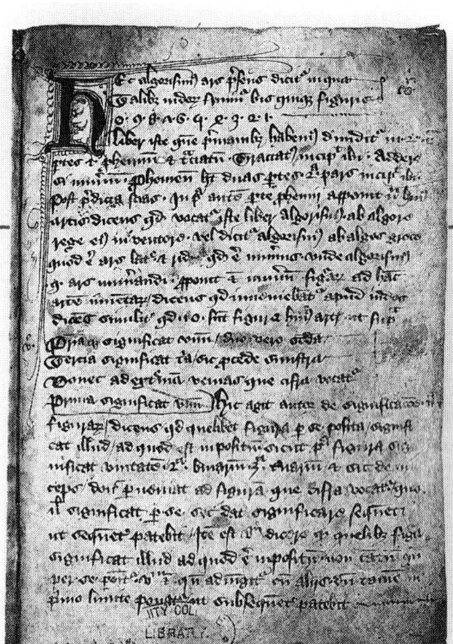

About 750–1250 Islamic scholars get scientific books from Europe. They translate them into Arabic and add more information.

Earth Science

140 Claudius Ptolemy draws a complete picture of an earth-centered universe.

132 The Chinese make the first seismograph, a device that measures the strength of earthquakes.

Human Body

2nd century Galen writes about anatomy and the causes of diseases.

860 985 1110 1225 1250 1475

1100s
Animal guide books begin to appear. They describe what animals look like and give facts about them.

1250
Albert the Great describes plants and animals in his book *On Vegetables and On Animals*.

1555
Pierre Belon finds similarities between the skeletons of humans and birds.

9th century
The Chinese invent block printing. By the 11th century, they had movable type.

1019
Abu Arrayhan Muhammad ibn Ahmad al'Biruni observed both a solar and lunar eclipse within a few months of each other.

1543
Nikolaus Copernicus publishes his book *On The Revolutions of the Celestial Orbs*. It says that the sun remains still and the earth moves in a circle around it.

1265
Nasir al-Din al-Tusi gets his own observatory. His ideas about how the planets move will influence Nikolaus Copernicus.

About 1000
Ibn Sina writes an encyclopedia of medical knowledge. For many years, doctors will use this as their main source of medical knowledge. Arab scientist Ibn Al-Haytham gives the first detailed explanation of how we see and how light forms images in our eyes.

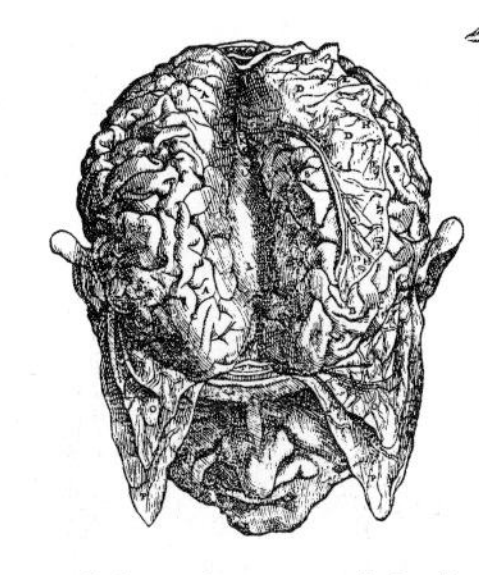

1543
Andreas Vesalius publishes *On the Makeup of the Human Body*. In this book he gives very detailed pictures of human anatomy.

1600	1620	1640	1660	1680

Life Science

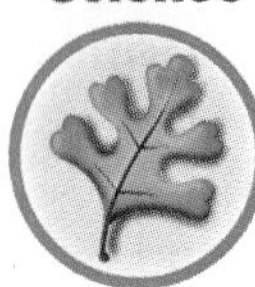

1663 Robert Hooke first sees the cells of living organisms through a microscope. Antoni van Leeuwenhoek discovers bacteria with the microscope in 1674.

1679 Maria Sibylla Merian paints the first detailed pictures of a caterpillar turning into a butterfly. She also develops new techniques for printing pictures.

Physical Science

1600 William Gilbert describes the behavior of magnets. He also shows that the attraction of a compass needle toward North is due to the earth's magnetic pole.

1632 Galileo Galilei shows that all objects fall at the same speed. Galileo also shows that all matter has inertia.

1687 Isaac Newton introduces his three laws of motion.

Earth Science

1609–1619 Johannes Kepler introduces the three laws of planetary motion.

1610 Galileo uses a telescope to see the rings around the planet Saturn and the moons of Jupiter.

1650 Maria Cunitz publishes a new set of tables to help astronomers find the positions of the planets and stars.

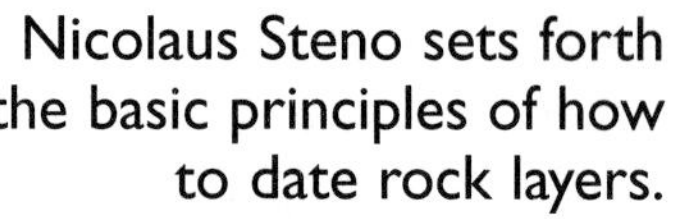

1669 Nicolaus Steno sets forth the basic principles of how to date rock layers.

1693–1698 Maria Eimmart draws 250 pictures depicting the phases of the moon. She also paints flowers and insects.

1687 Isaac Newton introduces the concept of gravity.

Human Body

1628 William Harvey shows how the heart circulates blood through the blood vessels.

1700 1720 1740 1760 1780 1800

1735 Carolus Linnaeus devises the modern system of naming living things.

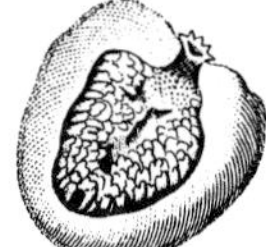

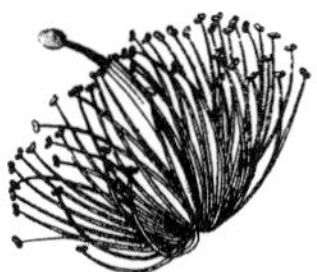

1704 Isaac Newton publishes his views on optics. He shows that white light contains many colors.

1759 Emile du Châtelet translates Isaac Newton's work into French. Her work still remains the only French translation.

1789 Antoine-Laurent Lavoisier claims that certain substances, such as oxygen, hydrogen, and nitrogen, cannot be broken down into anything simpler. He calls these substances "elements."

1729 Stephen Gray shows that electricity flows in a straight path from one place to another.

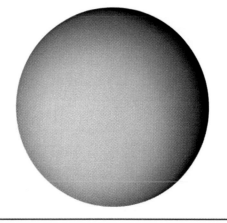

1781 Caroline and William Herschel (sister and brother) discover the planet Uranus.

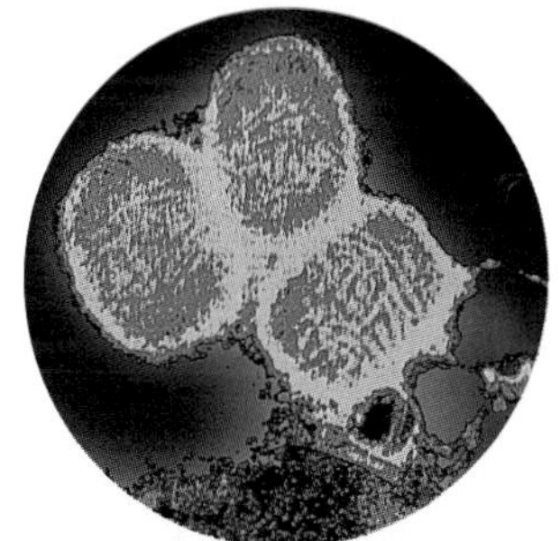

1784 French chemist Antoine-Laurent Lavoisier does the first extensive study of respiration.

1798 Edward Jenner reports the first successful vaccination for smallpox.

1721 Onesimus introduces to America the African method for inoculation against smallpox.

1805 1810 1815 1820 1825 1830 1835

Life Science

1808 French naturalist Georges Cuvier describes some fossilized bones as belonging to a giant, extinct marine lizard.

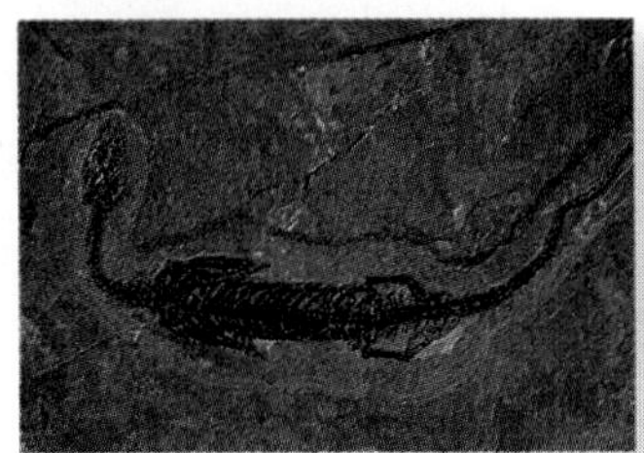

1838–1839 Matthias Schleiden and Theodor Schwann describe the cell as the basic unit of a living organism.

Physical Science

1800 Alessandro Volta makes the first dry cell (battery).

1808 John Dalton proposes that all matter is made of atoms.

1820 H.C. Oersted discovers that a wire with electric current running through it will deflect a compass needle. This showed that electricity and magnetism were related.

Earth Science

1803 Luke Howard assigns to clouds the basic names that we still use today—cumulus, stratus, and cirrus.

1830 Charles Lyell writes *Principles of Geology*. This is the first modern geology textbook.

Human Body

1840 1845 1850 1855 1860 1865 1870 1875

1842 Richard Owen gives the name "dinosaurs" to the extinct giant lizards.

1859 Charles Darwin proposes the theory of evolution by natural selection.

1863 Gregor Mendel shows that certain traits in peas are passed to succeeding generations in a regular fashion. He outlines the methods of heredity.

1847 Hermann Helmholtz states the law of conservation of energy. This law holds that energy cannot be created or destroyed. Energy only can be changed from one form to another.

1842 Christian Doppler explains why a car, train, plane, or any quickly moving object sounds higher pitched as it approaches and lower pitched as it moves away.

1866 Ernst Haeckel proposes the term "ecology" for the study of the environment.

Early 1860s Louis Pasteur realizes that tiny organisms cause wine and milk to turn sour. He shows that heating the liquids kills these germs. This process is called pasteurization.

1840s Doctors use anesthetic drugs to put their patients to sleep.

1850s and 1860s Ignaz P. Semmelweis and Sir Joseph Lister pioneer the use of antiseptics in medicine.

1875	1885	1895	1905

Life Science

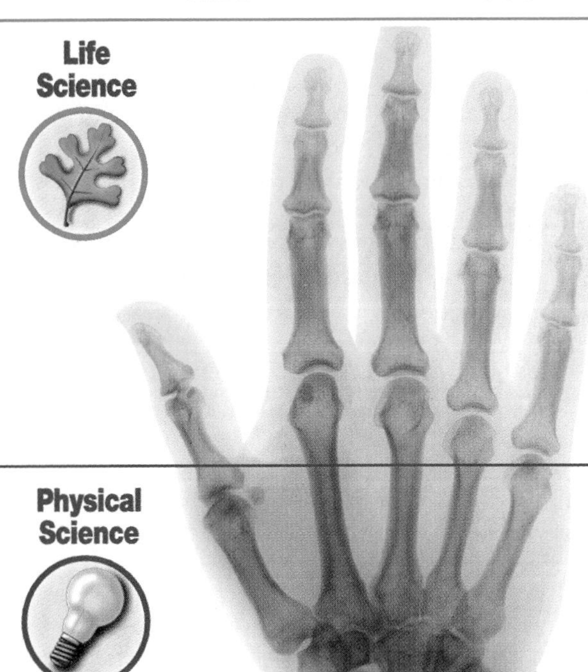

1900–1910 George Washington Carver, the son of slave parents, develops many new uses for old crops. He finds a way to make soybeans into rubber, cotton into road-paving material, and peanuts into paper.

Physical Science

1895 Wilhelm Roentgen discovers X rays.

1896 Henri Becquerel discovers radioactivity.

1897 J. J. Thomson discovers the electron.

1905 Albert Einstein introduces the theory of relativity.

Earth Science

1907 Bertram Boltwood introduces the idea of "radioactive" dating. This allows geologists to accurately measure the age of a fossil.

1912 Alfred Wegener proposes the theory of continental drift. This theory says that all land on the earth was once a single mass. It eventually broke apart and the continents slowly drifted away from each other.

Human Body

1885 Louis Pasteur gives the first vaccination for rabies. Pasteur thought that tiny organisms caused most diseases.

1915 1925 1935 1945

1920s Ernest Everett Just performs important research into how cells metabolize food.

1947 Archaeologist Mary Leakey unearths the skull of a *Proconsul africanus*, an example of a fossilized ape.

1913 Danish physicist Niels Bohr presents the modern theory of the atom.

1911 Ernst Rutherford discovers that atoms have a nucleus, or center.

1911 Marie Curie wins the Nobel Prize for chemistry. This makes her the first person ever to win two Nobel Prizes, the highest award a scientist can receive.

1938 Otto Hahn and Fritz Straussman split the uranium atom. This marks the beginning of the nuclear age.

1942 Enrico Fermi and Leo Szilard produce the first nuclear chain reaction.

1945 The first atomic bomb is exploded in the desert at Alamogordo, New Mexico.

1938 Lise Meitner and Otto Frisch explain how an atom can split in two.

1933 Meteorologist Tor Bergeron explains how raindrops form in clouds.

1946 Vincent Schaefer and Irving Langmuir use dry ice to produce the first artificial rain.

1917 Florence Sabin becomes the first woman professor at an American medical college.

1928 Alexander Fleming notices that the molds in his petri dish produced a substance, later called an antibiotic, that killed bacteria. He calls this substance penicillin.

1935 Chemist Percy Julian develops physostigmine, a drug used to fight the eye disease glaucoma.

1922 Doctors inject the first diabetes patient with insulin.

1950 1955 1960 1965 1970

Life Science

1951 Barbara McClintock discovers that genes can move to different places on a chromosome.

1953 The collective work of James D. Watson, Francis Crick, Maurice Wilkins, and Rosalind Franklin leads to the discovery of the structure of the DNA molecule.

1972 Researchers find human DNA to be 99% similar to that of chimpanzees.

Physical Science

1969 UCLA is host to the first computer node of ARPANET, the forerunner of the internet.

1974 Opening of TRIUMF, the world's largest particle accelerator, at the University of British Columbia.

Earth Science

1957 The first human-made object goes into orbit when the Soviet Union launches *Sputnik I*.

1972 Cygnus X-1 is first identified as a blackhole.

1969 Neil Armstrong is the first person to walk on the moon.

1967 Geophysicists introduce the theory of plate tectonics.

1962 John Glenn is the first American to orbit the earth.

Human Body

1954–1962 In 1954, Jonas Salk introduced the first vaccine for polio. In 1962, most doctors and hospitals substituted Albert Sabin's orally administered vaccine.

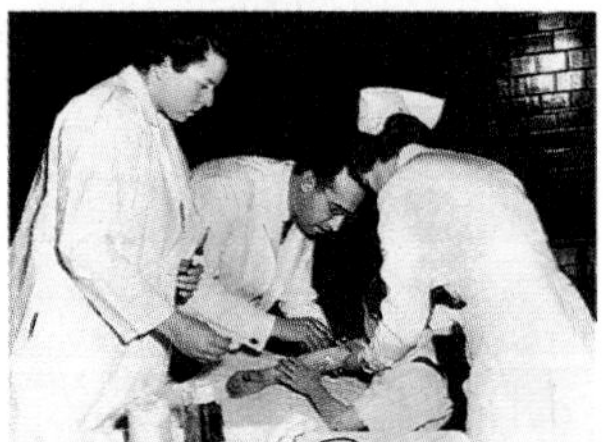

1967 Dr. Christiaan Barnard performs the first successful human heart transplant operation.

1964 The surgeon general's report on the hazards of smoking is released.

1975	1980	1985	1990	1995	2000

1988 Congress approves funding for the Human Genome Project. This project will map and sequence the human genetic code.

1997 Scientists in Edinburgh, Scotland, successfully clone a sheep, Dolly.

1975 The first personal computer goes for sale: The Altair.

1996 Scientists make "element 112" in the laboratory. This is the heaviest element yet created.

1979 A near meltdown occurs at the Three Mile Island nuclear power plant in Pennsylvania. This alerts the nation to the dangers of nuclear power.

1976 National Academy of Sciences reports on the dangers of chlorofluorocarbons (CFCs) for the earth's ozone layer.

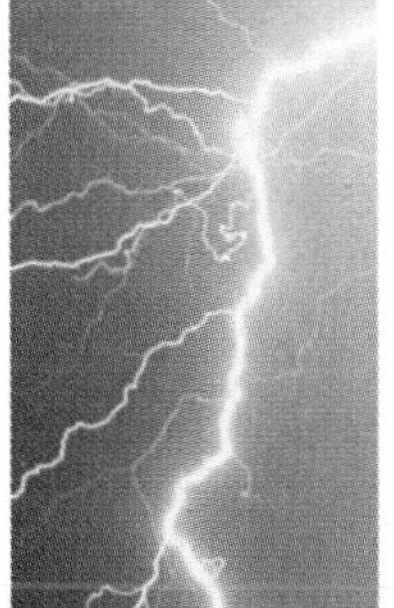

1995 The first "extra-solar" planet is discovered.

Early 1990s The National Severe Storms Laboratory develops NEXRAD, the national network of Doppler weather radar stations for early severe storm warnings.

1981 The first commercial Magnetic Resonance Imaging scanners are available. Doctors use MRI scanners to look at the non-bony parts of the body.

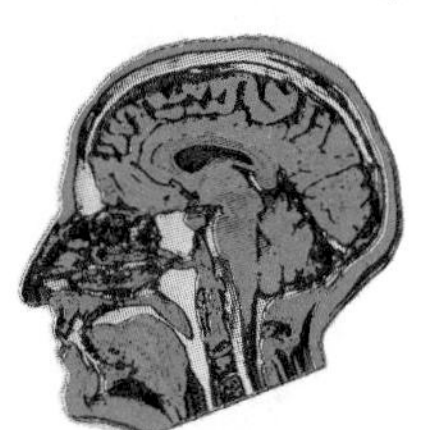

1982 Dr. Stanley Prusiner identifies a new kind of disease-causing agent—prions. Prions are responsible for many brain disorders.

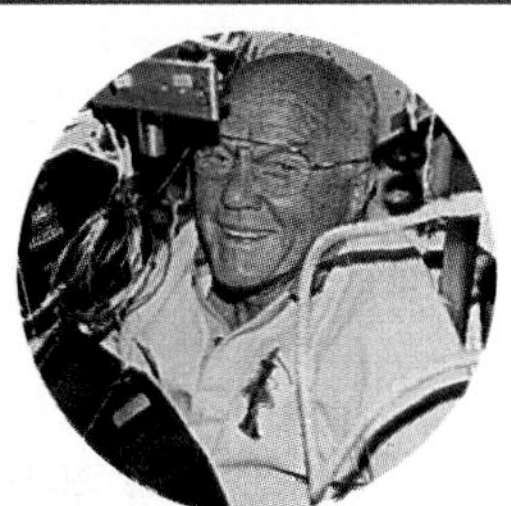

1998 John Glenn, age 77, orbits the earth aboard the space shuttle *Discovery*. Glenn is the oldest person to fly in space.

Glossary

Full Pronunciation Key

The pronunciation of each word is shown just after the word, in this way: **ab•bre•vi•ate** (ə brē′vē āt).

The letters and signs used are pronounced as in the words below.

The mark ′ is placed after a syllable with primary or heavy accent, as in the example above.

The mark ′ after a syllable shows a secondary or lighter accent, as in **ab•bre•vi•a•tion** (ə brē′vē ā′shən).

a	hat, cap	g	go, bag	ō	open, go	ŦH	then,	zh	measure,
ā	age, face	h	he, how	ȯ	all, caught		smooth		seizure
â	care, fair	i	it, pin	ô	order	u	cup, butter		
ä	father, far	ī	ice, five	oi	oil, voice	u̇	full, put	ə	represents:
b	bad, rob	j	jam, enjoy	ou	house, out	ü	rule, move		a in about
ch	child, much	k	kind, seek	p	paper, cup	v	very, save		e in taken
d	did, red	l	land, coal	r	run, try	w	will,		i in pencil
e	let, best	m	me, am	s	say, yes		woman		o in lemon
ē	equal, be	n	no, in	sh	she, rush	y	young, yet		u in circus
ėr	term, learn	ng	long, bring	t	tell, it	z	zero,		
f	fat, if	o	hot, rock	th	thin, both		breeze		

A

acceleration (ak sel′ə rā′shən), the change in velocity during a particular time period.

acid (a′sid), a compound that releases hydrogen ions in water.

adaptation (ad′ap tā′shən), an inherited trait that helps a species survive in its environment.

addiction (ə dik′shən), a disease affecting both the mind and body that makes people unable to go without something, such as a drug.

air mass (er mas), a large body of air having similar properties or weather conditions.

air pressure (er presh′ər), the force of air against Earth's surface.

air resistance (er ri zis′təns), the friction from air molecules hitting an object as the object moves through the air.

alcohol (al′kə hȯl), depressant drug found in beer, wine, and liquor.

alcoholic (al′kə hȯ lik), a person who does not have control over his or her drinking.

alcoholism (al′kə hȯ liz′əm), a disease in which a person is unable to stop abusing alcohol.

alternative energy sources (ôl tėr′nə tiv en ər jē sôrs), source of energy other than fossil fuels.

amplitude (am′plə tüd), the distance between a wave's midpoint and its crest or trough.

anemometer (an′ə mom′ə tər), an instrument used to measure wind speed.

aquifer (ak′wə fər), a layer of rock in which ground water can accumulate and flow freely.

asexual reproduction (ā sek′shü əl rē prə duk′shən), reproduction by one parent.

auroras (ô ror′əz), the glow or display of lights in the skies near polar latitudes.

axon (ak′son), part of a neuron that carries messages away from the cell body.

B

balanced forces (bal′enst fôrs′əs), equal forces acting in opposite directions.

barometer (bə rom′ə tər), an instrument used to measure air pressure.

base (bās), a compound that releases hydroxide ions when dissolved in water.

base (bās), one kind of molecule that makes up a DNA strand.

behavioral adaptation (bi hā′vyər əl ad′ap tā′shən), an action that aids survival.

big bang theory (big bang thē′ar ē), the idea that the universe started with a huge explosion about 15 billion years ago.

biome (bī′ōm), large geographic region with a particular kind of climate and community.

black hole (blak hōl), an invisible object in space whose mass and gravitational force is so great that not even light can escape.

brain stem (brān stem), part of the brain that controls involuntary actions, such as breathing; connects the brain to the spinal cord.

C

caffeine (kaf′ēn), a mild stimulant found in coffee, tea, colas, and chocolate.

carbon monoxide (kär′bən mo nok′sīd), a gas found in cigarette smoke that replaces some of the blood's oxygen when inhaled.

carnivore (kär′nə vôr), a consumer that eats only animals.

cell division (sel də vizh′ən), the dividing of a cell following mitosis.

cell membrane (sel mem′brān), thin outer covering that holds a cell together.

cell theory (sel thē′ər ē), theory stating that the cell is the basic unit of all living organisms, and only living cells can produce new living cells.

cell wall (sel wôl), tough, nonliving material that acts like an outside skeleton for each plant cell.

central nervous system (sen′trəl nėr′vəs sis′təm), part of the nervous system made up of the brain and spinal cord.

cerebellum (ser′ə bel′əm), part of the brain that coordinates movements and helps maintain balance.

cerebrum (sə rē′brəm), part of the brain that controls thinking and voluntary movements and receives information from the senses.

chemical equation (kem′ə kel i kwā′zhən), an arrangement of symbols and formulas used to show what happens during a chemical reaction.

chlorophyll (klôr′ə fil), green substance in chloroplasts that traps energy from sunlight.

chloroplast (klôr′ə plast), organelle that makes sugars, using carbon dioxide, water, and the energy from sunlight.

chromosome (kro′mə sōm), stringlike structure in a cell nucleus that carries information controlling all the cell's activities.

competition (kom′pə tish′ən), a situation in which two or more organisms attempt to use the same resource.

compound microscope (kom′pound mī′krə skōp), microscope having more than one lens.

compressional wave (kəm presh′ən əl wāv), wave in which matter vibrates in the same direction as the energy waves traveling through it.

concave mirror (kon kāv′ mir′ər), a mirror whose center curves away from an object.

concentrated (kon′sən trā′tid), describes a solution with a large amount of solute compared to the amount of solvent.

condensation (kon′den sā′shən), the change of state from a gas to a liquid.

conservation (kon′sər vā′shən), careful use of resources so they will last longer.

convex mirror (con veks′ mir′ər), a mirror whose center curves toward an object.

corona (kə rō′nə), a crown of glowing gases around the sun that can be seen during a total solar eclipse.

cytoplasm (sī′tə plaz′əm), clear, jellylike material that fills the space between the cell membrane and the nucleus.

D

dendrite (den′drīt), part of a neuron that collects information from other neurons.

depressant (di pres′nt), a drug that slows down the nervous system.

dew point (dü point), the temperature at which a volume of air cannot hold any more water vapor.

dilute (dī lüt′), describes a solution with a small amount of solute compared to the amount of solvent.

displacement (dis plās′mənt), the direction and shortest distance traveled during a change of position.

distance (dis′təns), the total length of the path between two points.

DNA (dē en ā), the molecule in each cell that directs the cell's activities.

dominant gene (dom′ə nənt jēn), a gene that prevents the expression of another gene.

Doppler radar (dop′lər rā′där), a type of radar that calculates distance and shows direction of movement.

drainage basin (drā′nij bā sin), the land area from which a river system gets its water.

drug (drug), a substance that acts on the body to change the way it works.

drug abuse (drug ə byüz), using drugs for purposes other than health.

E

endocrine gland (en′dō krən gland), a tissue or organ that releases chemical substances into the bloodstream.

endocrine system (en′dō krən sis′təm), body system consisting of glands, hormones, and target cells that work together to control various functions in the body.

endoplasmic reticulum (en′dō plaz′mik ri tik′yə ləm), organelle that transports materials inside the cell.

endothermic reaction (en′dō thėr′mik rē ak′shən), a chemical reaction in which more energy is taken in than given off.

energy pyramid (en′ər jē pir′ə mid), a model that shows how energy is used in a food chain or an ecosystem.

equinox (ē′kwə noks), a point in the Earth's orbit around the sun where nights and days are the same length.

estuary (es′chü er′ē), place where fresh water from rivers or streams mixes with saltwater from the ocean.

evaporation (i vap′ə rā′shən), the change of a state from liquid to gas at the surface of a liquid.

evolution (ev′ə lü shən), process that results in changes in the genetic makeup of a species over very long periods of time.

exothermic reaction (ek′sō thėr′mik rē ak′shən), a chemical reaction in which more energy is given off than is taken in.

F

fault (fôlt), a crack in the earth's crust along which rock moves.

fertilization (fër′tl ə zā′shən), the joining of an egg cell and a sperm cell during sexual reproduction.

focal point (fō′kəl point), the point at which light rays meet when reflected or refracted.

focus (fō′kəs), the point along a fault where rock first breaks or moves, causing an earthquake.

force (fôrs), a push or a pull.

forecast (fôr′kast′), a prediction of what the weather will be like in the near future.

formula (fôr′myə lə), arrangement of symbols that shows both the kinds and number of atoms in a compound.

fossil fuel (fos′əl fyü′əl), fuel such as coal, natural gas, and oil that formed underground millions of years ago from decaying organic matter.

frame of reference (frām ov ref′ər əns), the object an observer uses to detect motion.

frequency (frē′kwən sē), the number or waves (crests or troughs) that pass a point in a given amount of time.

freshwater biome (fresh′wō′tər bī′ōm), water biome that has a low salt content.

friction (frik′shən), a force between surfaces that resists the movement of one surface past the other surface.

front (frunt), the boundary between warm and cold air masses.

fusion (fyü′zhen), the combining of less massive elements to form more massive elements.

G

galaxy (gal′ək sē), a system of billions of stars, gases, and dust.

gene (jēn), a section of DNA on a chromosome that controls a trait.

geologic time scale (jē ə loj′ik tīm skāl), a record of Earth's history based on events interpreted from the rock record and fossil evidence.

glacier (glā′shər), a large mass of moving ice.

gravity (grav′ə tē), the force of attraction that exists between any two objects.

groundwater (ground wô′tər), water in the ground near the Earth's surface.

H

hallucinogen (hə lü′sn ə jen), drug that affects brain activity, changing the way a person senses the world.

herbivore (hėr′bə vôr), a consumer that eats plants or other producers.

heredity (hə red′ə tē), the process by which traits are passed from parents to offspring.

hormone (hôr′mōn), chemicals released by endocrine glands that cause target cells to perform specific activities.

humidity (hyü mid′ə tē), water vapor in the air.

hurricane (hėr′ə kān), a large tropical storm that forms over warm oceans and whose winds have a velocity of at least 110 kilometers per hour.

hybrid (hī′brid), an organism with one dominant and one recessive gene for a trait.

hypothalamus (hī′pō thal′ ə məs), part of the brain that controls body temperature, hunger, thirst, and emotions.

I

index fossil (in′deks fos′əl), a fossil of an organism that existed on Earth for a short time over a large geographic area.

indicator (in′də kā′tər), a substance that changes color at a certain range of pH values.

inertia (in ėr′shə), the resistance of an object to change in its state of motion.

inhalant (in hā′lənt), drug that enters your body with the air you breathe.

inherit (in her′it), to receive from one's mother or father.

instantaneous speed (in′stən tā′nē əs spēd), the speed at any given point.

instinct (in′stingkt), an inherited behavior.

intensity (in ten′sə tē), a measure of the amount of energy in a wave.

intoxicated (in tok′sə kā′tid), experiencing the symptoms of heavy alcohol consumption.

L

laser light (lā′zer līt), light of a single wavelength with all the waves lined up.

law (lȯ), a statement that describes events or relationships that exist in nature.

lithosphere (lith′ə sfir), the solid rocky outer layer of the earth that includes the crust.

lunar eclipse (lü′nər i klips′), a darkening of the moon when it passes through Earth's shadow.

M

mass (mas), the amount of matter in an object.

meiosis (mī ō′sis), the process by which sex cells form.

meteorologist (mē′tē ə rol′ə jist), scientist who studies the weather.

mitochondria (mī′tə kon′drē ə), organelles where food and oxygen react to release energy.

mitosis (mī tō′sis), the process by which a cell produces two new identical nuclei.

moraine (mə rān′), a ridge formed when a glacier deposits its sediments.

motor neuron (mō′tər nür′on), nerve cell in the peripheral nervous system that carries information from the central nervous system to muscles and organs.

music (myü′zik), pleasant sound with regular wave patterns.

mutation (myü tā′shən), a permanent change in DNA that occurs when DNA copies itself.

N

natural selection (nach′ər əl si lek′shən), the idea that those organisms best adapted to their environment will be the ones most likely to survive and reproduce.

nebula (neb′yə lə), cloud of dust and gas in space.

nerve impulse (nėrv im′puls), message that travels from the dendrites of a neuron to the axon.

net force (net fôrs), the combination of all the forces acting on an object.

neuron (nür′on), a nerve cell.

neutralization (nü′trə li zās′shən), a process in which an acid and a base react to produce a salt and water.

newton (nüt′n), in the metric system, the unit used to measure force or weight.

nicotine (nik′ə tēn), a stimulant drug found in tobacco.

noise (noiz), sound with no regular wave patterns.

nonrenewable resource (non′ri nü′ə bəl ri sôrs′), a resource that cannot be replaced.

nucleus (nü′klē əs), part of the cell that controls activities of other cell parts.

O

octave (ok′tiv), a musical sequence in which the top note has twice the frequency of the bottom note.

omnivore (om′ni vôr), a consumer that eats both producers and consumers.

opaque (ō pāk′), does not allow light to pass through.

ore (ôr), a rock that contains enough of a mineral to be of value.

organelle (or′gə nel′), tiny structure in the cytoplasm of a cell that performs a special job.

P

peripheral nervous system (pə rif′ər əl nėr′vəs sis′təm), part of the nervous system that connects the central nervous system with all other parts of the body.

permafrost (pėr′mə frôst′), ground that is permanently frozen.

pH scale (pē āch skāl), a set of numbers between 0 and 14 to measure the strength of acids and bases.

photon (fō′ton), a bundle of energy that is released when an atom loses some energy.

physiological adaptation (fiz′ē ə loj′ə kəl ad′ap tā′shən), adaptation that involves a body part's job of controlling a life process.

plankton (plangk′tən), microscopic, free-floating organisms that serve as food for larger organisms.

plate tectonics (plāt tek ton′iks), theory that states that the lithosphere is broken into plates that move.

pollutant (pə lüt′nt), harmful substance in the environment.

population (pop′yə lā′shən), all the organisms of one species that live in a certain place.

product (prod′əkt), a substance that is formed in a chemical reaction.

psychrometer (sī krom′ə tər), an instrument used to measure relative humidity.

purebred (pyür′bred′), an organism with two dominant or two recessive genes for a trait.

Q

quasar (kwā′sär), brilliant object in space that may be the powerhouses of developing galaxies.

R

reactant (rē ak′tənt), a substance that undergoes a chemical reaction, often by combining with another substance.

recessive gene (re ses′iv jēn), a gene whose expression is prevented by a dominant gene.

red giant (red jī′ənt), a star that has swelled and glows with a red color.

red shift (red shift), the change of light waves from retreating objects to the red end of the spectrum.

reflex (rē′fleks), quick, automatic response to a stimulus.

refraction (ri frak′shən), the bending of a light wave as it moves from one material to another.

relative humidity (rel′ə tiv hyü mid′ə tē), measurement that compares the amount of water vapor in the air with the amount air can hold at a certain temperature.

relative motion (rel′ə tiv mō′shən), the change in position of one object compared to the position of another.

renewable resource (ri nü′ə bəl ri sôrs′), a resource that can be replaced within a reasonably short time.

reservoir (rez′ər vwär), artificial lake used to collect and store water.

respiration (res′pə rā′shən), energy-producing process in which a cell combines oxygen with sugars and gives off carbon dioxide and water.

response (ri spons′), a reaction of an organism to a change in the environment.

retina (ret′nə), an area at the back of the eye that contains sensory receptors for light.

ribosome (ri′bə sōm), organelle that puts together proteins for the cell.

Richter scale (rik′tər skāl), a scale used to compare the strengths of earthquakes.

S

saltwater biome (sôlt′wô′tər bī′ōm) water biome that has high salt content.

sediment (sed′ə mənt), rock and soil carried by water.

seismograph (sīz′mə graf), instrument that records the strengths of the earth's movements, based on the amount of energy released.

sensory neuron (sen′sər ē nür′on), nerve cell in the peripheral nervous system that carries information from sensory receptors to the CNS.

sensory receptor (sen′sər ē ri sep′tər), cell within the peripheral nervous system that gathers information from the environment and from the inside of the body.

sex cell (seks sel), a type of cell produced only by an organism that reproduces sexually.

sexual reproduction (sek′shü əl rē prə duk′shən), reproduction by two parents.

side effect (sīd ə fekt′), unwanted effect of a medicine or drug.

smokeless tobacco (smōk′lis tə bak′ō), tobacco, such as chewing tobacco or snuff, that is not smoked when it is used.

soil profile (soil prō′fīl), layers of soil in an area.

solar eclipse (sō′lər i klips′), an alignment of the sun, moon, and Earth where the moon blocks the sun from Earth's view.

solar energy (sō′lər en ər jē), radiant energy that comes from the sun.

solar flare (sō′lər fler), powerful eruption of very hot gases from the sun.

solstice (sol′stis), a point in the Earth's orbit around the sun where daylight is either the longest or shortest amount possible.

solute (sol′yüt), a substance that is dissolved.

solvent (sol′vənt), a substance that dissolves other materials.

sonar (sō′när), a device that uses sound waves to measure distance.

species (spē′shēz), a group of organisms that have the same characteristics and are able to produce offspring that can reproduce.

speed (spēd), the distance an object moves in a certain period of time.

speedometer (spē dom′ə tər), a device that shows instantaneous speed.

spinal cord (spī′nl kord), bundle of neurons that carries messages back and forth between the brain and the rest of the body.

stewardship (stü′ərd ship), the taking care of Earth's resources to ensure their quality and quantity for future generations.

stimulant (stim′yōō lənt), a drug that speeds up the nervous system.

stimulus (stim′yə ləs), a change in the environment of an organism that causes a response.

structural adaptation (struk′cher əl ad′ap tā′shən), adaptation that involves body parts or color.

sunspot (sun′spot′), a region on the sun of very strong magnetic fields.

supernova (sü′pər nō′və), the explosion of a star, releasing huge amounts of light and other energy.

synapse (si naps′), the gap between the axon of one neuron and the dendrite of a second neuron.

T

taiga (tī′gə), forest biome just south of the tundra, characterized by conifers.

tar (tär), a sticky, gluelike substance found in cigarette smoke.

tides (tīdz), the rise and fall of water in the ocean and seas caused mainly by the gravitational pull of the moon on the earth.

tornado (tôr nā′dō), a violent, funnel-shaped cloud with extremely strong winds.

trait (trāt), a characteristic of an organism.

transparent (tran spər′ənt), allows light to pass through so that objects on the other side can be seen.

transverse wave (trans vėrs′ wāv), a wave in which the crests and troughs move at right angles to the direction of the wave's travel.

tundra (tun′drə), the northernmost and coldest biome.

V

vacuole (vak′yü ōl), saclike organelle used for storing materials.

velocity (və los′ə tē), a measure of both the speed and direction of a moving object.

vent (vent), opening on the ocean floor.

W

water table (wô′tər tā′bəl), the top of an aquifer.

weathering (weᴛʜ′ər ing), group of processes that break rocks into smaller pieces.

weight (wāt), a measure of the pull of gravity on an object's mass.

Z

zygote (zī′gōt), the first cell of an offspring, formed when an egg cell and sperm cell join.

Index

C

D

E

F

G

M

N

O

P

Retina, D14

T

U

V

W

Y

Z

Acknowledgments

Illustration
Borders Patti Green
Icons Precison Graphics

Unit A
8a John Zielinski
17 Carla Kiwior
19 Christine D. Young
21 Christine D. Young
22 Precision Graphics
41 Barbara Cousins
44 Vilma Ortiz-Dillon
47 Barbara Cousins
53 Barbara Cousins
54 Barbara Cousins
56 Barbara Cousins
58a Barbara Cousins
59 John Zielinski
63 Barbara Cousins
64 Richard Stergulz
65 Richard Stergulz
78 Barbara Harmon
82 Richard Stergulz
84 Precision Graphics
88 Carla Kiwior
90 Walter Stuart
91 Walter Stuart
114 Meryl Treatner
119 Carla Kiwior
120 Michael Digiorgio
121 Michael Digiorgio
124b Precision Graphics
126a Precision Graphics
128 Precision Graphics
130a Carla Kiwior
137a Precision Graphics
137b Michael Carroll
137c Michael Carroll
138 Precision Graphics
149 Carla Kiwior
150 Carla Kiwior
151 Carla Kiwior
152 Carla Kiwior
158 Barbara Cousins, Steven Edsey & Sons.

Unit B
12 Rob Schuster
15 J/B Woolsey
17 Michael Carroll
23 George Hamblin
34 J/B Woolsey
36 J/B Woolsey
38 J/B Woolsey
40 J/B Woolsey
44 J/B Woolsey
51 J/B Woolsey
58 Kenneth Batelman
65 Dave Merrill
86 John Massie
89 Kenneth Batelman
90 Walter Stuart
93 Precision Graphics
99 J/B Woolsey
107 Pedro Gonzalez
120 Kenneth Batelman
121 George Hamblin
122 J/B Woolsey
123 J/B Woolsey
124 J/B Woolsey
125 J/B Woolsey
127 J/B Woolsey
135 Kenneth Batelman
136 Kenneth Batelman
137 Michael Carroll
141 J/B Woolsey
142 J/B Woolsey
143 Michael Carroll
145 John Massie
147 Michael Carroll
150 Michael Carroll
151 Kenneth Batelman

Unit C
8 Kenneth Batelman
11 J/B Woolsey
12 Jared Schneidman
13 J/B Woolsey
14 Precision Graphics
16 Precision Graphics
21 John Zielinski
23 Michael Carroll
28 Precision Graphics
31 Precision Graphics
33 Precision Graphics
45a Precision Graphics
45b Nadine Sokol
47 Alan Cormack
48 George Hamblin
49 Alan Cormack
55 J/B Woolsey
58 J/B Woolsey
59 J/B Woolsey
60 Michael Carroll
62 Carla Kiwior
64 Precision Graphics
70 Nadine Sokol
71 Michael Digiorgio
72 Carla Kiwior
74 Precision Graphics
82 J/B Woolsey
84 J/B Woolsey
85 J/B Woolsey
86 J/B Woolsey
88 J/B Woolsey
89 J/B Woolsey
92 J/B Woolsey
94 J/B Woolsey
96 J/B Woolsey
100 John Zielinski
119 Precision Graphics
122 Michael Digiorgio
131 J/B Woolsey
133 Precision Graphics
143 J/B Woolsey

Unit D
9 Joel Ito
11 Rodd Ambroson
14 Rodd Ambroson
15 Rodd Ambroson
16 Rodd Ambroson
20 Christine D. Young
23 Joel Ito
24 Joel Ito
45 Joel Ito
52 Joel Ito

Photography
Unless otherwise credited, all photographs are the property of Scott Foresman, a division of Pearson Education. Page abbreviations are as follows: (T) top, (C) center, (B) bottom, (L) left, (R) right, (INS) inset.

Cover: Roda/Natural Selection Stock Photography, Inc.

iv BR M. Abbey/Visuals Unlimited
v TR Joe McDonald/Animals Animals/Earth Scenes
ix TR PhotoDisc, Inc

Unit A
1 Kenneth Edward/Photo Researchers
2 T Vincent O'Bryne/Panoramic Images
2 B-inset-2 Mark C. Burnett/Photo Researchers
2 C Dan McCoy/Rainbow
2 B Arie deZanger for Scott Foresman
2 B-inset 1 Photo Researchers
3 B J. F. Podevin/Image Bank
3 TCR NASA/SPL/Photo Researchers
3 BCR G. I. Bernard/Animals Animals/Earth Scenes
9 C Eddy Gray/SPL/SSC/Photo Researchers
9 BL Rod Planck/TOM STACK & ASSOCIATES
9 TR Steven David Miller/Animals Animals/Earth Scenes
9 BR Mike Bacon/TOM STACK & ASSOCIATES
9 TL Bruce Watkins/Animals Animals/Earth Scenes
10 B Cecil Fox/SS/Photo Researchers
10 T Science VU/Visuals Unlimited
12 T Jan Hinsch/SPL/SSC/Photo Researchers
12 B David Parker/SPL/SSC/Photo Researchers
12 C Andrew Syred/SPL/SSC/Photo Researchers
13 T Mike Abbey/Visuals Unlimited
13 B Anthony Bannister/Animals Animals/Earth Scenes
16 Profesors P. Motta & T. Naguro/SPL/SSC/Photo Researchers
18 Professor P. Motta/Dept. of Anatomy/University "La Sapienza", Rome/SPL/SSC/Photo Researchers
20 M. Eichelberger/Visuals Unlimited
23 T Superstock, Inc.
23 B S. Maslowski/Visuals Unlimited
26 B Ray Coleman/NASC/Photo Researchers
26 T John D. Cunningham/Visuals Unlimited
27 TL David M. Phillips/Visuals Unlimited
27 TR Superstock, Inc.
27 BL Oliver Meckes/Ottawa/SPL/SSC/Photo Researchers
27 BR Professors P. M. Andrews/K.R. Porter and J. Vial/SSC/Photo Researchers
28 CL M. Abbey/Visuals Unlimited
28 BL Stan Flegler/Visuals Unlimited
28 BR Cabisco/Visuals Unlimited
29 B Malcolm Boulton/Photo Researchers
29 T Gopal Murti/CNRI/Phototake
30 T Profesor P. Motta/Dept. of Anatomy/University "La Sapienza", Rome/SPL/SSC/Photo Researchers
30 B K. Aufderheide/Visuals Unlimited
35 S. Maslowski/Visuals Unlimited
40 David M. Phillips/Visuals Unlimited
42 T Scott Brenner/Ken IWagner/Visuals Unlimited
42 B PhotoDisc, Inc.
43 T Dr. E. R. Degginger/Color-Pic, Inc.
43 B David M. Phillips/Visuals Unlimited
44 BL J. Forsdyke/Gene Cox/SPL/Photo Researchers
44 BC Biophoto Associates/Photo Researchers
44 BR Biophoto Associates/Photo Researchers
44 T Oliver Meckes/Photo Researchers
45 R Biophoto Associates/Photo Researchers
45 L Biophoto Associates/Photo Researchers
46 David M. Phillips/Photo Researchers
48 BL VU/Cabisco/Visuals Unlimited
48 BR VU/Cabisco/Visuals Unlimited
49 T Chris Johns/Tony Stone Images
49 BL VU/Cabisco/Visuals Unlimited
49 BR VU/Cabisco/Visuals Unlimited
50 T PhotoDisc, Inc.
50 B G. Thomas Bishop/Custom Medical Stock Photo
52 M. P. Kahl/Photo Researchers
58 BR David Parker/SPL/Photo Researchers
62 Walter Hodges/Tony Stone Images
62 Background PhotoDisc, Inc.
67 T Joe McDonald/Visuals Unlimited
67 B Alex Kerstitch/Visuals Unlimited
71 Chris Johns/Tony Stone Images
75 L Lynn Stone/Animals Animals/Earth Scenes
75 C Leonard Lee Rue III/Photo Researchers
75 R Francois Gohier/Photo Researchers
76 Jeff Lepore/Photo Researchers
77 T Francois Gohier/Photo Researchers
77 B Michael Fogden/Animals Animals/Earth Scenes
77 C Anthony Bannister/Animals Animals/Earth Scenes
79 L Lynn Stone/Animals Animals/Earth Scenes
79 R Francois Gohier/Photo Researchers
79 C Leonard Lee Rue III/Photo Researchers
80 Don W. Fawcett/Visuals Unlimited
81 B J. Koivula/SS/Photo Researchers

81 C Joe McDonald/Animals Animals/Earth Scenes
81 T James L. Amos/Photo Researchers
85 T Ken Lucas/Visuals Unlimited
85 B Michael Dick/Animals Animals/Earth Scenes
86 The Granger Collection, New York
86 Background MetaPhotos
87 BR J.W. Verderber/Visuals Unlimited
87 TR Hal Beral/Visuals Unlimited
87 TL Alex Kerstitch/Visuals Unlimited
89 T Breck P. Kent/Animals Animals/Earth Scenes
92 L Jan L. Wassink/Visuals Unlimited
92 R David C. Fritts/Animals Animals/Earth Scenes
94 T James Watt/Animals Animals/Earth Scenes
94 B PhotoDisc, Inc.
95 T C. P. Hickman/Visuals Unlimited
95 C E. R. Degginger/Animals Animals/Earth Scenes
95 B Chris McLaughlin/Animals Animals/Earth Scenes
96 B Howard Hall/OSF/Animals Animals/Earth Scenes
96 T Andrew Syred/SPL/Photo Researchers
97 B Adrienne T. Gibson/Animals Animals/Earth Scenes
97 T M. Abbey/Visuals Unlimited
100 Fred Bruemmer
101 T Jonathan Blair/National Geographic Image Collection
101 B J. Alcock/Visuals Unlimited
101 C N. M. Collins/OSF/Animals Animals/Earth Scenes
102 L Lee F. Snyder/Photo Researchers
102 R Francis Lepine/Animals Animals/Earth Scenes
103 T J. A. L. Cooke/Animals Animals/Earth Scenes
104 Charles Gupton/Tony Stone Images
105 Alfred B. Thomas/Animals Animals/Earth Scenes
109 Lee F. Snyder/Photo Researchers
113 T PhotoDisc, Inc.
113 TC Rod Planck/Photo Researchers
113 BC J. H. Robinson/Photo Researchers
113 B Renee Lynn/Photo Researchers
116 E. R. Degginger/Color-Pic, Inc.
117 B WHOI/D.Foster/Visuals Unlimited
117 T Stanley Flegler/Visuals Unlimited
118 B Renee Lynn/Photo Researchers
118 BC J. H. Robinson/Photo Researchers
118 TC Rod Planck/Photo Researchers
118 T PhotoDisc, Inc.
126 Oliver Meckes/Photo Researchers
127 Cabisco/Visuals Unlimited
131 T Len Zell/OSF/Animals Animals/Earth Scenes
131 B F. Stuart Westmorland/Photo Researchers
132 T Stephen Dalton/Photo Researchers
132 B Mark Stouffer/Animals Animals/Earth Scenes
133 T Fritz Polking/Visuals Unlimited
134 T Charlie Ott/Photo Researchers
134 B Paul A. Grecian/Visuals Unlimited
134 B-Inset Andrew Martinez/Photo Researchers
135 C Pat Armstrong/Visuals Unlimited
135 T Courtesy General Motors Corporation/Wieck Photo DataBase
136 B PhotoDisc, Inc.
136 T PhotoDisc, Inc.
138 L Stephen J. Krasemann/Photo Researchers
138 R Robert W. Domm/Visuals Unlimited
138 C Doug Sokell/Visuals Unlimited
139 C Gary Braasch/Tony Stone Images
139 R David Matherly/Visuals Unlimited
139 L Ron Spomer/Visuals Unlimited
140 B-Inset Alan D. Carey/Photo Researchers
140 T Stephen J. Krasemann/Photo Researchers
140 B Jim Zipp/Photo Researchers
141 B E. R. Degginger/Color-Pic, Inc.
141 T Doug Sokell/Visuals Unlimited
142 CC Phil Degginger/Animals Animals/Earth Scenes
142 B North Wind Picture Archives
142 TC Patti Murray/Animals Animals/Earth Scenes
142 T Robert W. Domm/Visuals Unlimited
143 B Andy Sacks/Tony Stone Images
143 T Ron Spomer/Visuals Unlimited
144 T Gary Braasch/Tony Stone Images
144 B Superstock
144 B-INSET Cabisco/Visuals Unlimited
145 TL David Matherly/Visuals Unlimited
145 B E. R. Degginger/Color-Pic, Inc.
145 TR John Chard/Tony Stone Images
148 NASA
152 E. R. Degginger/Color-Pic, Inc.
153 PhotoDisc, Inc.
155 F. Stuart Westmorland/Photo Researchers
156 BL VU/Cabisco/Visuals Unlimited
156 BC VU/Cabisco/Visuals Unlimited
156 BR VU/Cabisco/Visuals Unlimited
157 Michael Fogden/Animals Animals/Earth Scenes
159 B J. Forsdyke/Gene Cox/SPL/Photo Researchers
159 T PhotoDisc, Inc.

Unit B

1 D. Boone/Corbis-Westlight
2 T Vincent O'Bryne/Panoramic Images
2 BL Arie deZanger for Scott Foresman
3 C Nicholas Pinturas/Tony Stone Images
11 T Arthur Tilley/FPG International Corp.
13 Dan McCoy/Rainbow
14 L Richard Megna/Fundamental Photographs
14 R Richard Megna/Fundamental Photographs
15 L Richard Megna/Fundamental Photographs
15 R Richard Megna/Fundamental Photographs
15 C Richard Megna/Fundamental Photographs
15 L Richard Megna/Fundamental Photographs
16 T Jill Birschbach
16 B William Wright/Fundamental Photographs
17 Dr. E. R. Degginger/Color-Pic, Inc.
21 R Randy Green/FPG International LLC
21 L Nancy Sheehan/PhotoEdit
24 James Schwabel/Panoramic Images
28 Randy Green/FPG International LLC
29 NASA/SS/Photo Researchers
33 Steve Satushek/Image Bank
35 Steve Kaufman/Corbis Media
36 NASA
37 Carr Clifton/Minden Pictures
38 David Young-Wolff/PhotoEdit
39 Steve Satushek/Image Bank
42 B Brooks/Brown/SSC/Photo Researchers
43 C Jeremy Burgess/Photo Researchers
50 L Boltin Picture Library
50 R Boltin Picture Library
50 BC Charles D. Winters/Photo Researchers
50 CC John Cancalosi/TOM STACK & ASSOCIATES
53 T Kal's Power Tools
54 T UPI/Corbis-Bettmann
55 B Lawrence Migdale/Photo Researchers
56 T E. R. Degginger/NASC/Photo Researchers
56 B Superstock, Inc.
59 PhotoDisc, Inc.
63 TR PhotoDisc, Inc.
63 CL PhotoDisc, Inc.
63 CR PhotoDisc, Inc.
65 T USDA Nature Source/Photo Researchers
66 T Gilbert S. Grant/NASC/Photo Researchers
66 C Michael Boys/Corbis Media
66 B Kevin R. Morris/Corbis Media
67 B Superstock, Inc.
67 T Peter Miller/NASC/Photo Researchers
68 Scott T. Smith/Corbis Media
78 Oxford Scientific Films/Animals Animals/Earth Scenes
79 T Mike Hewitt/Allsport
80 BL Akira Fujii
80 BR Craig J. Brown/Liaison Agency
80 T David Madison/Tony Stone Images
81 Tim Davis/Tony Stone Images
82 L NASA
82 R Akira Fujii
85 John Warden/Tony Stone Images
87 Jose Carrillo/PhotoEdit
88 Mark Wagner/Tony Stone Images
90 Laguna Photo/Liaison Agency
92 Tony Freeman/PhotoEdit
94 N. Pecnik/Visuals Unlimited
95 Jonathan Daniel/Allsport
96 L Don Smetzer/Tony Stone Images
96 R Joe Caputo/Liaison Agency
97 Novastock/PhotoEdit
105 Joseph McBride/Tony Stone Images
106 Jonathan Nourok/PhotoEdit
108 L Dan McCoy/Rainbow
108 R E. R. Degginger/Color-Pic, Inc.
109 T VCG/FPG International Corp.
109 B Jose Carrillo/PhotoEdit
118 Novastock/PhotoEdit
120 Vince Streano/Tony Stone Images
123 PhotoDisc, Inc.
124 Warren Stone/Visuals Unlimited
125 Spencer Grant/Photo Researchers
129 B Scott Camazine/Photo Researchers
129 T Rosenfeld Images LTD/SPL/Photo Researchers
132 David Parker/Photo Researchers
135 B Novastock/PhotoEdit
135 C Jerome Wexler/Photo Researchers
137 B Gregg Hadel/Tony Stone Images
138 R Paul Silverman/Fundamental Photographs
138 L Paul Silverman/Fundamental Photographs
139 T Jeff Greenberg/Visuals Unlimited
139 B Lawrence Migdale/Photo Researchers
143 T Breck P. Kent/Animals Animals/Earth Scenes
143 B Renee Lynn/Photo Researchers
145 Kim Westerskov/Tony Stone Images
146 Oliver Benn/Tony Stone Images
147 NASA/SS/Photo Researchers
148 Ulrike Welsch/Photo Researchers
149 B Sylvain Grandadam/Photo Researchers
150 Background PhotoDisc, Inc.
150 TC Phil McCarten/PhotoEdit
150 CR Corel
150 BL MetaTools
151 TL PhotoDisc, Inc.
151 TR David Young-Wolff/Tony Stone Images
155 Renee Lynn/Photo Researchers
157 UPI/Corbis-Bettmann
159 T PhotoDisc

Unit C

1 Merrilee Thomas/TOM STACK & ASSOCIATES
2 T Vincent O'Bryne/Panoramic Images
2 BL A. Gragera/Latin Stock/SPL/Photo Researchers
2 C Merrilee Thomas/TOM STACK & ASSOCIATES
3 C NASA
3 B Geoff Tompkinson/SPL/Photo Researchers
4 Inset NOAA/TOM STACK & ASSOCIATES
9 T Stephen Ferry/Liaison Agency
9 B NOAA/TOM STACK & ASSOCIATES
13 Gary W. Carter/Visuals Unlimited
15 BL Bayard H. Brattstrom/Visuals Unlimited
15 TR Robert Stahl/Tony Stone Images
15 TL A. J. Copley/Visuals Unlimited
15 BR Lincoln Nutting/Photo Researchers
17 Frank Oberle/Tony Stone Images
18 The Newberry Library/Stock Montage
19 Granger Collection
20 C Christian Grzimek/Okapia/Photo Researchers
20 Background PhotoDisc, Inc.
21 T Dr. E. R. Degginger/Color-Pic, Inc.
21 Background PhotoDisc
22 B Joyce Photographics/Photo Researchers
22 T Davis Instruments
23 Howard Bluestein/Photo Researchers
24 B David Parker/ESA/SPL/Photo Researchers
24 T TSADO/NCDC/NASA/TOM STACK & ASSOCIATES
25 T TSADO/NCDC/NASA/TOM STACK & ASSOCIATES"
30 Courtesy of NOAA Photo Library
32 Charles Doswell III/Tony Stone Images
34 Wetmore/Photo Researchers
35 T Alan R. Moller/Tony Stone Images
35 B Dan McCoy/Rainbow
36 L NASA/SPL/Photo Researchers
36 R R. Perron/Visuals Unlimited
37 Alan R. Moller/Tony Stone Images
39 TSADO/NCDC/NASA/TOM STACK & ASSOCIATES
46 L Francois Gohier/SSC/Photo Researchers

46 R Alison Wright/NASC/Photo Researchers
46 C Glenn Oliver/Visuals Unlimited
47 R Eye Ubiquitous/Corbis Media
48 U. S. Geological Survey
49 (c) Michael L. Smith
50 T Corbis/Ressmeyer
50 B Paulus Leeser
51 B David Parker/SPL/SSC/Photo Researchers
51 T U. S. Geological Survey
56 C William E. Ferguson
56 R William E. Ferguson
56 L Corel
57 B Superstock, Inc.
57 T U. S. Geological Survey/EROS Data Center
58 Carr Clifton/Minden Pictures
59 B Ray Fairbanks/NASC/Photo Researchers
59 T Frans Lanting/Minden Pictures
61 PhotoDisc, Inc.
62 Superstock, Inc.
63 PhotoDisc, Inc.
64 Superstock, Inc.
65 L Larry Blank/Visuals Unlimited
65 R Carr Clifton/Minden Pictures
68 Background Joe McDonald/Visuals Unlimited
68 Inset Ross Frid/Visuals Unlimited
69 BL A. J. Copley/Visuals Unlimited
69 BR John D. Cunningham/Visuals Unlimited
70 Tom Bean
71 BCR A. J. Copley/Visuals Unlimited
71 T Layne Kennedy/Corbis Media
71 CR James L. Amos/Corbis Media
71 TCL Wolfgang Kaehler/Corbis Media
71 TCR Layne Kennedy/Corbis Media
71 BCL Tom Bean/Corbis Media
71 B A. J. Copley/Visuals Unlimited
72 BL Copyright (c) Peabody Museum of Natural History, Yale University, New Haven, Connecticut. Painting by Shirley G. Hartman
73 T David M. Dennis/TOM STACK & ASSOCIATES
73 B Layne Kennedy/Corbis Media
77 Wolfgang Kaehler/Corbis Media
78 Photo courtesy of U. S. space Camp (c) U. S. Space & Rocket Center
83 Background Jay Pasachoff/Visuals Unlimited
83 Inset ESA/TSADO/TOM STACK & ASSOCIATES
87 Jeff Greenberg/MR/Visuals Unlimited
89 B SCIENCE VU/Visuals Unlimited
89 TR Tersch Enterprises
90 T NASA
90 B Johnny Johnson/Tony Stone Images
91 C USNO/TSADO/TOM STACK & ASSOCIATES
91 R United States Naval Observatory
91 L Science VU/Visuals Unlimited
93 The Association of Universities for Research III
101 T Simon Fraser/SPL/Photo Researchers
101 BL NASA
101 BR NASA
102 BR NASA
102 CL NASA
103 T Dept. of Clinical Radiology, Salisbury District Hospital/SPLPhoto Researchers
103 C Custom Medical Stock Photo
104 TL Sovfoto/Eastfoto
104 BC UPI/Corbis-Bettmann
104 CR NASA
104 BR PhotoDisc, Inc.
104 Background Ed Degginger/Color-Pic, Inc.
105 TL NASA
105 TR E. R. Degginger/Color-Pic, Inc.
105 BR NASA
107 NASA
113 BR Karl Gehring/Liaison Agency
114 T SuperStock, Inc.
114 BL SuperStock, Inc.
114 BR Jonathan Nourok/PhotoEdit
115 Tess Young/TOM STACK & ASSOCIATES
116 L PhotoDisc, Inc.
116 R PhotoDisc, Inc.
117 CL MetaPhotos
117 T SuperStock, Inc.
117 BL MetaPhotos
117 BR MetaPhotos
117 BC PhotoDisc, Inc.
118 PhotoDisc, Inc.
118 B-inset SuperStock, Inc.
120 T Institute of Oceanographic Sciences/NERC/SPL/Photo Researchers
120 BR John Moss/Photo Researchers
120 BL MetaTools
121 Dr. Ken MacDonald/SPL/Photo Researchers
122 BL Stephen J. Krasemann/Photo Researchers
123 Background PhotoDisc, Inc.
123 BL PhotoDisc, Inc.
123 BR Corel
123 TL D. P. Wilson/Photo Researchers
123 C Gregory Ochocki/Photo Researchers
124 PhotoDisc, Inc.
125 TR PhotoDisc, Inc.
125 CL Corel
125 CR Dana White/PhotoEdit
125 B Barbara Stitzer/PhotoEdit
128 L National Museum of American Art/Smithsonian Institution
128 R The Granger Collection, New York
129 BL Corel
129 C Library of Congress
129 BR PhotoDisc, Inc.
130 BL Library of Congress
130 BC UPI/Corbis-Bettmann
130 BR Federal Duck Stamp Program/U.S. Fish & Wildlife Service
131 BL UPI/Corbis-Bettmann
131 BC UPI/Corbis-Bettmann
132 BL UPI/Corbis-Bettmann
132 BR David R. Frazier/Tony Stone Images
133 BL Joe Traver/New York Times/Archive Photos
133 BC Kaku Kurita/Liaison Agency
133 BR Courtesy General Motors Corporation/Wieck Photo DataBase
134 Jeff Isaac Greenberg/Photo Researchers
139 SuperStock, Inc.
140 Alan R. Moller/Tony Stone Images
141 TSADO/NCDC/NASA/TOM STACK & ASSOCIATES
142 T PhotoDisc, Inc.
144 NASA

Unit D

1 Chris Trotman/Duomo Photography Inc.
2 T Vincent O'Bryne/Panoramic Images
2 C-Inset Dan McCoy/Rainbow
3 B Weinberg-Clark/Image Bank
3 C Hank Morgan/Photo Researchers
7 David M. Philips/Visuals Unlimited
12 Matthew Stockman/Allsport
13 Stephen McBrady/PhotoEdit
14 Ralph C. Eagle, Jr., MD/Photo Researchers
15 T Tony Duffy/Allsport
15 C Prof. P. Motta/Dept. of Anatomy/University "La Sapienza", Rome/SPL/Photo Researchers
16 C Omikron/Photo Researchers
16 T PhotoDisc, Inc.
17 Mary Kate Denny/PhotoEdit
21 David M. Philips/Visuals Unlimited
22 Brian Bahr/Allsport
25 Express/Archive Photos
30 Mary Kate Denny/PhotoEdit
37 PhotoDisc, Inc.
38 Hank Morgan/SS/Photo Researchers
39 T Charles O. Cecil/Visuals Unlimited
44 David Pollack/Stock Market
45 Inset Fred Hossler/Visuals Unlimited
46 B Martin Rotker/Phototake
46 T Martin Rotker/Phototake
47 L Barts Medical Library/Phototake
47 R Barts Medical Library/Phototake
49 PhotoDisc, Inc.
50 SPL/Photo Researchers
54 T Martin M. Rotker/Photo Researchers
54 b SIU/Photo Researchers
55 Rafael Macia/Photo Researchers
56 Larry Mulvehill/Photo Researchers
60 Brian Bahr/Allsport
61 David Pollack/Stock Market
63 T PhotoDisc, Inc.
63 B PhotoDisc, Inc.

End Matter

Illustration

20 J/B Woolsey
32 J/B Woolsey
33 Meryl Treatner
34 T Corel
34 BL Corel
34 BR A. J. Copley/Visuals Unlimited
35 J/B Woolsey
36 J/B Woolsey
37 J/B Woolsey
38 Joel Ito
39 Joel Ito
42 Ovresat Parades Design
43 Ovresat Parades Design

Photography

4 B Bob Kalmbach, University of Michigan Photo Services
10 L PhotoDisc, Inc.
10 R PhotoDisc, Inc.
30 BL Oliver Meckes/SPL/SSC/Photo Researchers
30 TL Stan Flegler/Visuals Unlimited
30 TC J. Forsdyke/Gene Cox/SPL/Photo Researchers
30 BR MetaTools
30 CR Bob and Clara Calhoun/Bruce Coleman Inc.
30 TR Joe McDonald/Animals Animals/Earth Scenes
34 T Corel
34 CR A. J. Copley/Visuals Unlimited
34 BL Corel
45 B NOAO/Lowell Observatory
45 T Alinari/Art Resource, NY
46 T Trinity College Library, Cambridge
46 B The Granger Collection, New York
47 R National Library of Medicine
47 L From "The Structure of the Human Body," 1543
48 B Metropolitan Museum of Art
48 T British Museum
48 TL National Museum of Women in the Arts, Washington, DC
48 TR From Robert Hooke, "Micrographia," 1665
48 C Public Domain
49 B London School of Hygiene & Tropical Medicine/SPL/Photo Researchers
49 TR Genera Plantarum, Leiden 1737/Public Domain
49 C JPL/NASA
49 TL Public Domain
50 TL James L. Amos/Photo Researchers
50 TR Hugh Spencer
50 c Mehau Kulyk/SPL/Photo Researchers
50 B David Frazier/Photo Researchers
51 T Courtesy Mr. G. P. Darwin, by permission of the Darwin Museum, Down House
51 C Courtesy Southern Pacific Railroad
51 B Harvard Medical Library, Francis A. Countway Library of Medicine
52 L PhotoDisc, Inc.
52 R UPI/Corbis-Bettmann
53 T Staatliches Museum fur Naturkunde, Stuttgart
53 C Charles D. Winters/Timeframe Photography Inc./Photo Researchers
53 B UPI/Corbis-Bettmann
54 T Tim Davis/Photo Researchers
54 C NASA
54 BL The Granger Collection, New York
55 T AP/Wide World
55 TC Computer Museum, Boston
55 CL Tim Shaffer/AP/Wide World
55 CR
55 BL Scott Camazine/Photo Researchers
55 BR NASA
57 B AP/Wide World